PRAISE FOR

GREEN WITH ENVY

"It's rare to encounter such honesty about the endless financial comparisons people make . . . Valiantly offers solutions to curb the temptation to believe our lives would be better with more stuff."
— *USA Today*

"Finally—an entertaining book about money."
— King Features Syndicate

"A fascinating morality play about what can happen to those trying to 'keep up.'"
— *Houston Chronicle*

"Not your typical book on personal finance. Boss's perfect mix of real-life stories and statistical facts offers a shocking, entirely new and life-altering perspective on how and why we are consistently living beyond our means—a book too fascinating to put down."
— *Armchair Interviews*

"Eye-opening stories."
— Yahoo! Finance

"Boss provides a much-needed reality check on how people are really making ends meet—or how they're not. The chapter debunking the myth of independently wealthy members of Congress is worth the price of the book. GREEN WITH ENVY is a must-read for those trying to achieve true wealth."
— *Black Enterprise*

more . . .

"If you've ever wondered how coworkers afford those vacations in exotic locales or your neighbors trade cars every two years, Shira Boss's new book has the answers."

—*San Antonio Express-News*

"Boss performs a real service by putting some of America's financial hang-ups on trial . . . Her case for candor is valuable."

—*Publishers Weekly*

"Voyeuristic . . . nicely backed up with a slew of eye-opening facts."

—*Charlotte Observer*

Green
with
Envy

A Whole New Way to Look at
Financial (Un)Happiness

SHIRA BOSS

WARNER
BUSINESS
BOOKS™

NEW YORK   BOSTON

Copyright © 2006 by Shira J. Boss
All rights reserved. Except as permitted under the U.S. Copyright Act of 1976,
no part of this publication may be reproduced, distributed, or transmitted in any form
or by any means, or stored in a database or retrieval system, without the prior
written permission of the publisher.

Warner Business Books
Hachette Book Group USA
237 Park Avenue
New York, NY 10169

Visit our Web site at www.HachetteBookGroupUSA.com

Printed in the United States of America

Originally published in hardcover by Warner Business Books,
an imprint of Warner Books, Inc.

First Trade Edition: May 2007
10 9 8 7 6 5 4 3 2 1

Warner Business Books is a trademark of Time Warner Inc.
or an affiliated company. Used under license by Hachette Book Group USA,
which is not affiliated with Time Warner Inc.

The Library of Congress has catalogued the hardcover edition as follows:
Boss, Shira.
Green with envy : why keeping up with the Joneses is keeping
us in debt / Shira Boss—1st. ed.
        p.   cm.
ISBN-13: 978-0-446-57835-6
ISBN-10: 0-446-57835-5
1. Money—Psychological aspects   2. Finance, Personal—Psychological aspects.
3. Wealth—Psychological aspects.   I. Title.
HG222.3.B67 2006
    332.024—dc22   2006002834

ISBN: 978-0-446-69598-5 (pbk.)

To Dad:
the best parent, teacher, supporter, and friend

Acknowledgments

Everyone loves the idea of finding out what's really going on with other people's finances, yet few of us feel ready to spill our own secrets. This book is possible because some people were brave and generous enough to let me interview them in detail about their personal lives—in all cases, in much more detail than I included here—and share their stories with you. Most of the characters requested anonymity, so I use their pseudonyms in expressing my thanks.

My husband was the first to recognize the good intentions of the project and patiently allowed me to expose our private life. Over the following two years he indulged my consuming interest in the lives of the other characters, gave advice and encouragement, and was the first to read and comment on each chapter. Thank you so much.

John and Tina not only frankly laid out the inside story of their finances and their relationship but never questioned my need to pry into these matters. If I'd known how cool you'd be about it, I would have asked sooner!

Dan and Tammy let me into a part of their lives that they couldn't share with even friends and family. I'm grateful you stepped forward with your time and patience in the interest of helping other families.

Acknowledgments

Jack Quinn and Sam Gejdenson without hesitation agreed to be interviewed, given the aim of the book. Jack Buechner took the time and interest to educate me candidly about the inner workings of Capitol Hill. They and other unnamed former members of Congress took off the veil and admitted what really went on financially and emotionally while they were in office. Your trust and honesty are heartening.

Tucker made himself available for hours of interviews on a short deadline, and he shared insights about his life with impressive candor. I am awed at how you materialized out of millions of potential boomer characters and dozens of declined requests for help with this chapter.

Middy and Citizen Q not only hosted me in their home and gave me a behind-the-scenes tour of their world but were early providers of curiosity, advice, and encouragement about the book. I admire you both in many ways, especially for your generosity of spirit.

Thank you to the experts who gave their insights and assistance: psychologist Scott Wetzler, the Reverend Stephen Bauman, attorney Jan Baran, advertising authority James Twitchell, Brad Sagarin in the psychology department at Northern Illinois University, Sarah Phillips in the history department at Columbia University, Jerry Climer at the Congressional Institute, credit counselors George Janus and Howard Dvorkin, financial adviser Dave Ramsey and his assistant Beth Tallent. Thanks also to my Financial Peace University hosts, Rob Davis and Brother John Cortes, and classmates at Christ Tabernacle.

Jennifer Carlson, my agent, is a true gem. She has guided me from the beginning, patiently and thoughtfully helped me develop this book from the idea stage, and promptly read every word as it was written. Sincere thanks to Jen, Henry, Betsy, Rolph, and Irene at Dunow, Carlson & Lerner Literary Agency for their support.

I am especially grateful to Beth de Guzman and Rick Wolff, my editors at Warner, who enthusiastically backed this project from the very beginning and helped shape it into an even better product.

Acknowledgments

Thank you to Sam Freedman for his rigorous book-writing seminar at Columbia's graduate journalism school, and to my colleagues from that alumni group, especially Lindsay Pollock, Ivor Hanson, Sarah Richards, Dave Lawrence, Mitra Kalita, Phyllis Vine, and Michael Bobelian.

Among the editors I work for, Alex Sachare, Erik Ipsen, and Brent Bowers have been especially supportive and inspiring.

I'm blessed with friends who have given me company and counsel, kept me entertained, helped me weather frustrations, and held my hand through the book birthing process, in some cases giving feedback on outlines and chapters. I wrap my heart around Roya Babanoury, Dina Cheney, Kendra Crook, Maria Ezpeleta, Adam and Kathleen Fifield, Chad Finley, Aina Lakis, John Madeira, and Mark Spellen. My friends and colleagues Lewis Taylor and Rebecca Nolan gave early contributions and inspirations. Liz Dribben has also been a persistent cheerleader.

The members of my family have believed in me wholeheartedly, given their support and encouragement in every way possible, and very patiently awaited this first book. My deepest love and gratitude to Dad, Mom, Murat, Debby, Erika, Jeff, Barbara, Julia, Anne, Baba, and Umut.

One final nugget, for readers who are book geeks like myself who peruse the acknowledgments as one way to learn more about book writing and publishing: If you want to develop a narrative nonfiction book, I highly recommend the book *Thinking Like Your Editor*, by Susan Rabiner and Alfred Fortunato. Then, to make sure the job gets done, turn to *The Clockwork Muse*, by Eviatar Zerubavel. Both have been indispensable to me.

Author's Note

The stories revealed in these pages are completely factual to the best of my knowledge. In order to protect personal identities, most of the characters' names have been omitted and pseudonymous first names used. The exception is Chapter 4, in which full, real names are used, or none at all.

Dialogue that was recollected appears in *italics*. If I heard it myself and wrote it down, it appears with quotation marks.

Contents

Green
with
Envy

CHAPTER ONE

◦◦

Green with Envy

It started even before the couple next door moved in. The comparison. The envy.

My husband and I live in a relatively small apartment building on the Upper West Side of Manhattan, where the gossip—the *news*, as it were—traffics in our cramped elevator or basement laundry room. Behind its thirty doors, our building houses a flutist, a filmmaker, lawyers (both corporate and public sector), interior designers, a nurse, an accountant, a grad student, an expatriate retiree who feeds the birds in Central Park, and the usual coterie of mystery inhabitants: They're around, even during the weekdays, they own cars (unusual in this area, where parking spaces start at $400 per month), they seem to be supporting themselves comfortably, but we're not sure how. The building has units from rectangular studios to penthouse two-bedrooms. Perhaps what sets the residents apart the most is how long each has lived here. Considering how real estate values have tumbled upward in recent years, the newcomers are consistently quite a bit better off than those of us already here. Five years after moving in, for example, our mortgage—the one we stretched our debt-to-income ratio to the absolute outside limit to get—is about equal to what the down payment would be now.

In this environment, the most prized fruit of the grapevine is which apartment is being sold, and for how much. So when our neighbors right next door to us put their place on the market, you can be sure we were interested in who was moving in, and at what price.

And then we heard. In the elevator. The seller told me that a young couple our age was buying it—for over the asking price—and that they were paying cash.

Cash?

Somebody's daddy has some money! our neighbor guessed.

Yeah, I guess so. We couldn't imagine living mortgage-free at our age in Manhattan. And most of our friends couldn't imagine owning any property here at all. We had been the envy of our friends for having scraped together a down payment and bargaining our way into a mortgage. But hearing about our new neighbors, who would have no mortgage at all, we were the ones who felt kind of behind. And certainly mystified. We couldn't help but wonder where that kind of money was coming from.

There were two possibilities as to how the buyers accomplished this very large cash purchase, and my husband and I speculated about them at length. Either, as the seller thought, Mommy and Daddy helped them out by writing an enormous check (and that's how we referred to them, "Mommy and Daddy," as opposed to when our parents helped us out, in which case they were referred to simply as "our parents"); or they belonged to that dreaded class of twentysomething dot-com millionaires. We weren't sure which was preferable. Both seemed frustratingly undeserved.

We met. We had been ready to be annoyed by them, for them to be privileged, East Egg people, or intolerable hipsters, but actually John and Tina were very nice, apparently normal people. They seemed like a quirkily mismatched couple: Tina, a petite, brunette

Italian, had a stylish haircut and wore chic clothes surely from a downtown boutique. John, a taller, blond, we-soon-learned Upper West Side Jewish native, seemed more like a kindred spirit to me. He had just gotten out of a PhD program for geography (we got that bit of info from looking them up on Google) and dressed simply in jeans and flannel shirts. They seemed to go to work in the morning like everyone else. I had visions of becoming good friends and living like the two couples on the 1950s sitcom *The Honeymooners*, always dropping in on each other. We put their finances out of our minds. *None of our business*, we told ourselves.

Then on a Friday afternoon I ran into Tina waiting in the lobby of our building with a small (new, chic) suitcase.

Going away for the weekend? I asked.

Yeah, I'm just waiting for John to bring the car around. We need so many things for the apartment—we're going antiquing Upstate.

Antiquing? Who uses *antique* as a verb? I wondered. Does it mean the same thing as hitting flea markets for neat old stuff? Because I would have been fine with hearing that, but the idea of our young neighbors going on an *antiquing* spree—when, years after moving in, we were still waiting to buy something to cover our windows—reminded me instantly of their wealth, and that they could afford to do things differently.

After making smalltalk about antiquing, I turned to the elevator and pushed the call button, but I was interrupted by a question:

Can you recommend a good cleaning lady?

I froze. We all have different definitions of financial success, and mine is being able to afford a cleaning lady. I had a boyfriend once who lived in his parents' six-bedroom place off Park Avenue, with a live-in cook and a cleaning lady who spent every other day scouring the apartment. It was like living in a 5-star hotel, or what I imagined that would be like. Thick white towels were always folded and fresh. When you threw anything into any wastebasket, it blinked back at you from the bottom. Clutter never had a chance. Nor dust, nor dirty dishes. The best part was that my boyfriend never had to give any of these chores a thought. To my mind he dwelled in house-keeping nirvana: total comfort, zero effort.

My husband and I have had the usual "discussions" about keep-ing our home clean, and not even *clean* clean, but just keeping it from sliding into squalor. We've often ended up with the solution that if we paid somebody else to do the dirty work even now and then, we wouldn't have this tension. I've heard that solution from married people and read it in women's magazines: "Hire a cleaner. It'll save you hundreds in therapy bills!" But it has always felt finan-cially impossible. Money that would go to a cleaner could be put toward a dozen more important things. Necessary things. *Later*, we end up saying, *when we have enough money.*

But our new neighbors, they evidently already had enough money, and they could afford a cleaning lady.

Rather than play along, I decided to confront the envy by just being frank.

No, I told her. *Actually, it's my dream to have a cleaning lady, though.*

Tina, being a nice person, tried to make me feel better by saying, *Yeah, it's been so long since we've had one.*

So what's changed recently? I wanted to know. Whence these cleaning lady funds?

I'm not proud to recount my conversation later with my hus-band. *Antiquing?* I mocked. *And who keeps a car in the city, any-way? That's ridiculous. It's cheaper to rent one whenever you need it. Insurance, parking, not to mention the cost of the car itself—what's the point of paying for all of that when you can hardly ever use a car here anyway?*

My husband's response was even more delicious. *Well, we know how they can afford it*, he said smugly. *Without a mortgage, we could afford a lot of extra things too.*

From then on, every expenditure we noticed—packages arriving seemingly daily from Bloomingdale's and Restoration Hardware, hiring someone to repaint their apartment, the installation of the antiques!—it was all dismissed as "mortgage money."

They are the Joneses, and we are not keeping up. However much we understand that we are not—*not*, under any circumstance—to covet our neighbor's anything or to attempt to keep up with the Joneses, we can't seem to help it. We are gripped by this involuntary urge, a drive to compare and compete that is ingrained, at least in Americans, if not all people.

We have been challenging ourselves to keep up with the Joneses for time eternal, even though it frays our nerves and is a quest without any destination. We know we shouldn't do it, we try not to, yet we find it irresistible.

It's not just that we want more for ourselves but that we specifically want more than, or at least as much as, what others have. That's how we know how much we deserve: It depends on what the other guy has. Since the days of Cain and Abel we have been bickering and jostling over who has the better lot. Wealth and well-being are largely a mindset, and how we're doing in relation to the company we keep is key to our contentment.

It would seem logical that the people we envy the most would be those at the top of the ladder, the rich and famous. It's true that we are fascinated by the wealthy and celebrities, and might fantasize about living their lives, but we are driven by just that, curiosity and fantasizing. We don't really expect that with enough hard work and some good luck we will end up with millions in the bank and our whereabouts splashed across the cover of *People* magazine. It might happen to some, but we don't count on it.

Who we truly envy are our closest peers. Psychologist Herbert

Hyman defined this phenomenon in 1942 in an article titled "The Psychology of Status." He said we compare ourselves within "reference groups" of those around us and who are similar to us. We look to our classmates, our co-workers, our siblings and our neighbors to see how we measure up and, secretly, who we must catch up with. The super rich and famous have too many variables for us to match, but those with similar backgrounds to ours, with similar advantages and opportunities, those are the people we believe we should be able to match. When one among us breaks away and does much better financially, we feel put down. We want some kind of explanation. Are they just smarter? Did they make better decisions? Why them and not us? Is this fair, after all?

Our visions of success are built on a scaffolding of comparison, and planked with envy. Envy is the only vice warned against in both the Ten Commandments and the Seven Deadly Sins. In Dante's purgatory, the closest rung to hell is pride, the second closest is envy. Manhattan therapist Anita Weinreb Katz describes envy like this: "You want what that person has, and you want to destroy the person who has it. It's a very primitive feeling."

It's not pretty. We're certainly not proud of it, and usually don't want to admit that we are in its jaws. That leads us straight into troublesome secrecy. The don't ask, don't tell policy of life that lets us live around other people. On the rare occasion that someone admits bald-faced envy, we nearly crumble with commiseration and relief. A treasured quote from writer Gore Vidal: "Whenever a friend succeeds, a little something in me dies." We can laugh that off as an artistic temperament, but when we're honest with ourselves we know that there is more there, that we suffer similarly, by letting our relative positions in our various groups affect our well-being, whether we mean to or not. So we can't help ourselves from quietly scoping others' situations, from private investigating to figure out what others have and, consequently, what we should have too.

Tina invited me over for a late-afternoon glass of wine, to get further acquainted. My *Honeymooners* plan was progressing. As we walked up the stairs to her living room, she asked me what I do and I told her I'm a journalist.

Really? she asked. She seemed excited by it, and I felt proud that my job impressed her. Then she announced, *I work for the* New York Times!

No way! I said, while I really did think to myself, NO WAY! A competitive mushroom popped out at me like an airbag. I might not care about her wearing better clothes, but when it comes to career I didn't need competition living next door, on staff at the *Times.* Forget the *Honeymooners*, that was two generations ago. Times were gentler. I wanted to go back down the stairs and ignore our new neighbors and their wealthy parents and paid-for apartment forevermore.

Instead, I kept up the conversation with a dry throat: *You're a reporter too? What do you cover?*

No, I work in Web development.

Oh, thank you, thank you, thank you. She is *not* a journalist! I do *not* have to read her articles in the paper, talk shop, or keep up in any way! What a relief. We can be friends again. Maybe I'll knock on the door to borrow half a cup of sugar one day. I even scoffed a little at Web development. *Boring*, I thought.

My relief was short-lived. By the time we reached the top of the stairs it came to me: Web development . . . the Internet . . . *dot-com millionaire.*

Everyone heard stories of twentysomething millionaires minted in the late 1990s. They couldn't be avoided. They were on television, they were on the covers of magazines, and there weren't just a few junior moguls, they seemed to be *everywhere*. The economy was shaken up like a snow globe, and money really did seem to grow on trees, there for the plucking. The idea of building up a career or business through years of hard work was actually mocked. People used to ask me what I was doing still writing for newspapers and magazines, those relics: Why didn't I get an Internet job?

Seeing our peers get enormously wealthy on stock options was, to say the least, irksome. We were just as smart and educated and ambitious—how was it fair that they were so much more successful financially? It shouldn't be any of our business how much money our cohorts make, or how they do it. Why *do* we chip away at clues, then, building a financial profile of our friends and figuring out where we fit on the scale?

In the United States, at least, where productivity is valued more highly than anything and is generally measured in dollars, this comparison and competition is inbred. It feeds the system. The drive to consume more, to have more and better things, and continually to raise our level of comfort, is stronger here than any other place on earth.

The American Dream itself—the novel system in which every one of us, regardless of background, is not only able but expected to move up, to do better and have more—is at its heart about competition. We're trained to gaze up one level from where we are and to aspire to get what those people have. Once we accomplish that much, we're looking up again. By cultural design, there is no end to it.

Setting our goals based on what others are doing goes even deeper than human nature. Fleas, for instance, do some keeping up with the Joneses of their own. They are the world's highest jumpers. When you put a population of fleas into a box and put the lid on, a few times they'll jump up and donk their heads on the ceiling. Pretty quickly, though, they learn to jump just as high as the ceiling without hitting it. Take the lid off and they still won't jump any higher— until a new flea moves into the box who doesn't know anything about the old lid. The new flea jumps to great heights. The others see it. Then they all start jumping higher again.

Climbing over the Joneses isn't only a social and financial phe-nomenon but an economic one. Moving up is our reward for hard work. Desire and envy are the engines that keep us going. Trade up. Earn more. Improve. This is what keeps our capitalist economy throbbing. So while we're told not to attempt to keep up with the Joneses, *tsk-tsk*, we're also shown that that is exactly what we should do. If we all minded our own business, if we were all content with our lot as it is, the economy would slow and our standard of living—which we measure, for the most part, in *things*—would tumble. "An economy primarily driven by growth must generate discontent," writes psychologist Paul Wachtel in *The Poverty of Affluence*. "We *cannot* be content or the entire economic machine would grind to a halt."

The trouble is that what's good for the whole is not necessarily healthy for us as individuals. As Wachtel describes it, "Our personal lives run aground on the perpetual generation of desire and dis-content." Americans are working longer hours and earning more money than ever before, but the reward in terms of greater satisfac-tion with our lives has failed to materialize. A survey asked who in America feels they have achieved the American Dream. Among those earning less than $15,000 per year, only 5 percent agreed. What about among those earning more than $50,000, which is the top half of the American public? A near tie, at 6 percent. In the Bible a teacher says, "And I saw that all labor and all achievement spring from man's envy of his neighbor. This too is meaningless, a chasing after the wind" (Ecclesiastes 4:4). Keeping up with the Joneses puts us on a never-ending, stomach-yanking roller coaster. And we bring it on ourselves.

As soon as John and Tina got back from their tropical honeymoon, she quit her job at the *Times*. The economy was in the midst of a major slump. Nobody who had a job was complaining, or at least nobody was quitting. But that's what dot-com millionairehood was all about: You did what you enjoyed, you worked while it was exciting, and then whenever you felt like it, you walked away. And so she did.

She was in the right industry at the right time, that's for sure, my husband said with a sigh.

Contrasting our situation with theirs was painful. Tina talked about how they would soon start "popping out the kids." The idea of us having children ourselves, while attractive in theory, seemed practically impossible. We figured John and Tina probably did argue, like everyone, but they probably didn't argue about money stress, like we did. It wasn't the material goodies we grew envious of, it was the ease with which they seemed to be able to live. From the clues we collected, John and Tina seemed able to afford a psychological lifestyle that, to our disappointment, far surpassed ours. While our lives felt suffocatingly on hold while we straightened out our financial issues, our next-door neighbors, at our age, were living carefree, apparently enjoying life and each other to the fullest.

As for us, after meeting each other in the Middle East, we spent two years in a very long-distance relationship. A lot of our funds went toward plane tickets and phone calls. After we got engaged, one of us had to move. He earned enough as an engineer to support us in his country, but I didn't speak the language at the time, and even though I had worked there for several months it had been quite stressful. English wasn't a problem for him, though, and we figured his European degree and engineering background were marketable anywhere. He would relocate and look for a job as a management consultant. At that time the economy was booming; there weren't enough workers to go around. As one of my friends assured me, *Your nail salon woman could get a job as a consultant.*

Except it didn't work out that way. He started job searching at what turned out to be the very beginning of the recession. Rather suddenly, everyone seemed to be cutting back rather than hiring. He looked for work for a full year before starting something entrepreneurial.

This was far from a fun time in our life. The first and most obvious challenge was that we hadn't planned on living on one income for very long. Certainly not one journalist's income. Even a successful writer's income is not designed to support two people in Manhattan. We considered moving, but it seemed a drastic measure for what we thought was surely a temporary problem. Instead we budgeted, itself a challenge when there is not a regular paycheck to allocate. As I have often joked about being freelance, living paycheck to paycheck is especially hard when you don't know when, exactly, the next paycheck is coming. We stopped going out, and since so few New Yorkers entertain at home, avoiding going out meant we didn't see friends very often. We spent a lot of time sulking.

That led into the second problem: keeping up appearances. One does not set out actually to lie about unemployment or financial stress, but they're not polite or comfortable subjects. And since my husband had started a company and was no longer actively job searching, people probably assumed he was doing fine. For my part, I didn't want to complain to friends about us not having enough money because they would guess it was due to my husband—since I was still working as I had—and that felt like an invasion of his privacy. It's not nice to complain, even worse to blame. We are taught that financial problems are personal, and they are especially personal when they involve a third party not participating in the conversation.

So when people did ask how my husband's work was going, I found myself replying *Good!* With my family we kept matters equally oblique. They surely picked up hints that we weren't doing great (like when we mentioned we might just skip going home for Thanksgiving), but we didn't go out of our way to explain the situation and they didn't ask. Even in the twenty-first century, it is expected that a man, if not the sole support of his family, should

11

contribute at least half of the household income. Even though there are alternative arrangements that are increasingly accepted, in general men who don't earn the socially prescribed amount have an element of shame to contend with that women do not experience. So I didn't feel entitled to disclose our details, especially since he had relocated halfway around the world specifically for our relationship. In the meantime, I endured some conversations like this one with my older sister. On the telephone, I complained vaguely about not being able to afford something, but she cut me off abruptly:

It must be nice to have two incomes, though!

I could have asked her what second income she was referring to, but instead I just sighed and hedged and hinted, common tactics when it comes to discussing money.

Well, I said, *it feels like supporting two people on one income.*

No kidding that's what it felt like, because that's what was going on. I just couldn't come out with the truth.

Privately, money was making our life miserable. I got itchy and irritable trying to work in a home office with someone else at home. He left when he could, but without being able to afford recreation, he resorted to wandering the streets or sitting alone in the park. It made matters worse that he had left his entire social circle behind to move here.

Determined to be responsible, we tracked our expenses in detail. But when we saw how much money we really needed to be making every month to cover our fixed and necessary expenses, we got depressed and stopped keeping track. Overwhelmed, my husband abandoned exercising and gained weight. I became a nagger. To keep pace financially, I took on more work than I could reasonably handle, and late at night, to get my mind off of the stress, I went to bed hiding behind the latest Harry Potter.

A couple of times I went trolling the Internet for some kind of support. Surely there had to be somebody talking about this kind of situation, about handling the social side of financial problems.

Wasn't there a money doctor out there who could make us feel better?

I had never before understood why money is the often-cited number-one reason for marital trouble and divorce. I had guessed it meant that couples, having two separate personalities, couldn't come to terms on how to handle the household money. Through experience, I realized that it is money itself, as a very real character in our lives—a companion that is as cranky, consuming, and irresistible as any lover—that causes the strife. It's the secrecy, the shame, the acting, the convoluted psychology of it all. We live in an ultra-open culture that freely shares our most intimate concerns— but rarely when they involve money. When it comes to the intersection of our personal finances and the orbit of the world outside our front doors, we are suddenly starved of the information that gushes on any other topic. I knew that other people were in our same shape, miserable because of their financial situations and even more so from the stress of covering them up, from leading a kind of double life. But how to communicate with those people? I couldn't even find them on the Internet, which meant that for all practical purposes we were indeed alone.

As for my friends, even though I was not direct with them about what was happening with us, I felt let down that they did not read between the lines and figure it out for themselves. I expected support and some kind of commiseration, even though their openly acknowledging the situation might have been embarrassing. In the meantime, their own endowments bothered me in a way they never had before: Every time a friend openly indulged herself, I was reminded that I couldn't afford to do so. I started wanting things I had never even wanted before, merely because I knew I couldn't have them.

The problem we grappled with that became the most damaging was the eventual rise of resentment. These were the first two years of our marriage. That we were being cheated out of what was supposed to be one of the most wonderful times in our lives frustrated me. *What did we do to deserve this?* I wondered. Through my gray-tinted glasses, every other couple on Broadway seemed to be having the time of their lives. I was sure that come Monday morning, each went off to their respective jobs, and when they got home they frolicked. I imagined their lives as cozy and romantic, not consumed by financial worries. *Everyone is enjoying life but us*, I convinced myself, even as I knew it wasn't really true. I laughed bitterly when I read an item in a women's magazine about how if a man earns less money than his partner does it often damages the couple's sex life.

In the midst of our angst, John and Tina, to our eyes, fit right into this carefree, honeymoon mold. So even though we had resolved to concentrate on minding our own business, Tina quitting her job to extract every second of joy out of life seemed to us like some sort of personal insult.

We were feeding our frustration with assumptions. If we had hunted down statistics and believed that they referred to just some of the people in our own circle, and if we could have heard them describe their own struggles, we wouldn't have felt so isolated.

In fact, we were far from the only ones living paycheck to paycheck. One survey reported that most households are doing so sometimes, most of the time, or always. The American Psychological Association recently reported a survey that showed money to be the number-one stress in our lives. The country as a whole owes $857 billion on its credit cards, making an average balance of more than $7,720 for each household if we divided up the debt among all of us. So some of that must belong to households right next to ours. Every year, the National Opinion Research Center asks people whether they are better or worse off financially than the previous year, and consistently, millions declare themselves worse off. In a recent survey, 78 percent of respondents said their debts were "making their home life unhappy."

We say we know that money doesn't buy happiness, but we don't seem to believe it. We want more, and the more we get the more we want. According to research presented in the book *The Overspent American*, "Among those making $30,000 or less, 81 percent said they would need less than 20 percent more income to be satisfied, while only 40 percent of those in the $75,000+ category would be satisfied with a 20 percent increase."

We certainly were not the only ones whose relationship was being strained by financial issues. We've all heard that money is the leading cause of problems in marriages. Some research on bankruptcy shows that couples who file for bankruptcy are at least twice as likely to file for divorce as the general population.

As for unemployment, the fallout it causes, ranging from temporary malaise to social and emotional implosion, is a shared experience but one that isn't discussed openly. "People who have lived through downward mobility," explains a book on the subject written by an anthropologist, "are often secretive and cloistered or so bewildered by their fate that they find it hard to explain to themselves, let alone to others, what has befallen them." Therefore most of us don't hear about it, don't understand it, and are never prepared for handling it.

My husband's and my problem, as it often happens, was larger than fretting over the personal side of our finances. We were equally, or perhaps more so, upset by contrasting ourselves to our better-off friends and neighbors. It doesn't make logical sense why we should concern ourselves with the financial situations of those around us. After all, they're not paying our bills and we're not paying theirs. Life is not a zero-sum game, with one person's gain having to be another person's loss. So we have no real reason *not* to be glad for another's success. Right? If only it worked that way. In fact, it does matter to us. And the more difficulties we are having, the more the success of others, frankly, aggravates us.

In our competitive, comparison-minded culture, relative success is what matters. So another person's gain really can feel like our loss. Economists refer to "positional goods," the things we buy that are meant to set us a notch higher than others who don't have them; and psychologists ponder "status anxiety," our worry that we are not keeping up with others. In measuring where we stand, relativity is everything.

Professors at Harvard and the University of Miami conducted a survey about income. They asked over 250 people whether they would prefer to earn $50,000 per year while those around them earned $25,000, or to earn $100,000 while those around them earned $200,000. More than half chose the first scenario, giving up having twice as much total money in order to have relatively more than others.

A more nuanced experiment showed even more strongly how important relative wealth is to us. Researchers in Britain set up a computer gambling game in which each player got 100 units of currency. The subjects played to increase their wealth, and as they played they could also see how well the other players were doing. Then a new level of the game was introduced: First some random players were given a 500 unit bonus, and then all players were given the ability to pay some of their own currency in order to "burn" other players and reduce the other players' wealth. In what came as a surprise to the researchers, the game became all about burning. The players who hadn't gotten the bonus immediately struck out against the newly rich. Although it hurt their own wealth, two-thirds of the players spent their own currency to bring the wealthier players down.

Another bit of Petri dish proof that we care all too much about how much money our peers have comes from a recent experiment conducted at Princeton. A series of two players were openly explained the terms of a game that would be played only once: One player was given ten dollars and had to make an offer of some amount of that money to the other player. If the other player accepted the offer, both players would get to keep their money. But if the other player refused the offer, then neither would get to keep any money. Rational behavior says that Player B would accept *any* offer, since doing so meant personal gain, while refusal of any amount meant getting nothing. But that's not what usually happened. When Player A's offer was seen as unfair (a piddling dollar, for instance), it was usually refused by Player B, leaving both players with zero. As one of the study's authors wrote, "Player B often gives up a smaller sum so Player A doesn't get a larger sum."

The awareness and concern over what other people have is an issue for us when we notice we have less, and also when we have more. When I lived in the Middle East I learned about the belief in the "evil eye." Everywhere you go in some regions, you are stared down by blue eyes, mostly flattened disks of colored glass. One hangs at the entrance to every home, from the rearview mirrors of taxis, and near a business' cash register. Cafe owners cement them into the sidewalks in front of their cafes, factory owners paint them on the sides of their factories. Small eyes are wired into the designs of jewelry, sewn on to the fringe of hand towels, glued to the tips of toothpicks. Recently they came up with a new way to get the eyes into their lives: melting them into the sides of tea glasses. *What*, visitors always ask, *is with the eyes everywhere?*

They are not the evil eye itself, they are warding off the evil eye. The evil eye is, essentially, envy. These people believe that if you enjoy good fortune, you'd better look out because others will envy you and you will attract negative energy. You'll be struck down. The thinking is similar to that of ancient Greece, when mortals were cautious about having too much fun or achieving too much success because the gods could get envious and bring them down. That is why modern-day business owners are especially careful to engage the talismanic services of the blue eyes. They want to do well, they certainly seek good fortune, but they don't want to *appear* to be doing well. The eyes help with that predicament.

At first I laughed this off as silly superstition. Now, however, having been through tough times and the emotional and social havoc they wreak, I am a believer in the evil eye. I don't know if blue charms help prevent it, but the evil eye itself—the destructive force of envy—seems very real. Maybe seeing the blue eyes everywhere helps people keep their own envy in check because they are constantly being reminded of it, that it is wrong and that they don't want it in their lives. As for myself I don't know if living among the eyes when we were under hardship would have helped me keep perspective, but, disconcertingly, what I saw happening during that time is this: When things were rolling along great for friends, I got glum. I didn't exactly wish them ill, but I didn't genuinely celebrate for them, either. And believing that life's cycle of ups and downs would spin around to everyone eventually did make me, very privately, almost shamefully, feel better.

Tina decided to launch a new career as an interior designer. *My mom has a really good decorator*, she explained, *and I've always been interested in it.*

She started taking classes at the same time my husband entered business school. The two of them commiserated about having homework; John and I commiserated about having to do the cooking while our spouses studied.

But on our side of the wall, our talk was not about how similar we were to our neighbors but about how aggravatingly different. When my husband was accepted to business school we nearly cried out of relief and happiness. We had decided that if he didn't get in, he would have to go back to his country and work there again for a while. Going back to school meant our taking on six figures of student loans and braving two more years on a single income, but it also meant we could stay together, and it meant—or we had to believe it meant—nearly being guaranteed a well-paying job after two years.

Tina, on the other hand, had voluntarily given up a well-paying job and was going back to school on a whim because she happened to be interested in it. To fill her idle time, apparently. To amuse herself.

Or so we figured. After a few months of classes, something shocking happened.

Okay, I was not deliberately eavesdropping, but our building has very thin walls. Really, everybody knows this. You don't have a conversation in the hallway or while waiting for the elevator if you don't want the neighbors in on it. Usually this is a drawback.

Yet Tina had, for some very odd reason, come up to her apartment talking on her cell phone, and rather than entering her apartment, she conversed in the hallway, right outside our doors.

And here's what I—inadvertently!—discovered: Things were not as they had seemed. As I heard what she told her friend, I was not only fascinated but guiltily thrilled.

We're paying $115 for cable. Say, $90 for our cell phones. Car insurance is, like, $120 a month. Electricity, a hundred bucks, about . . .

She gave the sympathetic listener (not meant to be me, mind you) a detailed inventory of their monthly bills and announced a grand total with alarm in her voice.

This kind of goody doesn't land at your doorstep every day—or, normally, ever. I quickly and shamelessly compared their tab to our own.

And that's before, you know, just living, she said with despair. She didn't know how they were making it, she reported.

The fact was, they *weren't* making it.

The worst part about comparisons is that we often make them based on misinformation. We try to keep up with the Joneses, then it turns out, as it did in our case, that the Joneses as we know them don't even exist. Even when someone does in fact have the money it looks like they have, which is often not the case, the funds do not add up to contentment. Among American households surveyed that earn more than $100,000 per year, 27 percent said that they did not have enough money to buy the things they "really need." That gives new meaning to the concept of *personal* finance. Our financial situations and what they mean to our personal lives really do depend on our individual circumstances, surroundings, and mindset. We cannot, even if we wanted to, step into somebody else's life and experience what appears to be so good about it. Whatever we thought we would enjoy of theirs—*if we only had what they have*—wouldn't be the magic bullet we envision.

We perplex ourselves over scenarios that are not even true. My husband and I had constructed the dossier of our next-door neighbors out of circumstantial evidence and what turned out to be misleading appearances. In the absence of hard information and honest explanations, we cobble together our own image of the lives of the people we know and to whom we compare ourselves. Even though we know, intellectually, that everyone has his or her own problems, truly believing that the couple next door, our co-worker, or better-off sibling doesn't really have it better than we do is another matter. Nothing, in my experience, gives greater comfort at these times of envy than recalling that *things are not as they seem*.

The day I overheard Tina's conversation, I couldn't wait for my husband to come home so that I could reveal the juicy gossip of The Real Situation Next Door. We had gone wrong somewhere in our analysis. Tina was apparently not a dot-com millionaire after all, not a lady of leisure. And, mortgage or no mortgage, they *did* have money worries like the rest of us. We had heard them complain briefly about various expenses before, but we hadn't taken them seriously. After all, the more money someone has, the more they seem to feel obligated to complain publicly about high costs. (I had seen this in my Park Avenue boyfriend. When we opened the menu at an expensive restaurant, he would announce, *Twenty-eight dollars for pasta—who are they kidding?!*)

On the surface it was gossip, but on a deeper level, learning of our neighbors' troubles was significant to us because we had come to feel so achingly alone in our bleak financial world. Just as we had read into their having a fully funded, joyful life together, now we could project that just as we sometimes lost sleep over money, so did they. We no longer felt singled out for suffering financial stress at the beginning of a marriage. We had some proof that a couple just like us could be in a somewhat similar situation, even though it didn't look like it from the outside.

However, rather than commiserating—how could we, given that we weren't supposed to know their problems anyway—I gleefully recounted the entire scene to several friends: *You know our next-door neighbors without the mortgage? Listen to this . . .*

S ome information and honesty go a long way toward curing the comparisons that ail us. If we would only talk to one another about money and status, about our desires and discontent. If only it were okay to reveal what really goes on in our financial lives, not just factually but emotionally, how much better off we would be. Truth is healing. Like having daylight return after a night spent worrying in the darkness, constructive confessions can banish our loneliness and soothe our financial fretting. How much damage we do ourselves by hiding our money misgivings, and how unnecessary this collective burden is. Our financial and emotional welfare depend not on

earning more or owing less but on opening up and coming to understand the reality of those around us. The Joneses lose their power
over us when we get to know them and understand what their own
lives are really like, behind what is usually a tightly closed door.

How much better could my husband and I have felt if we had
known the details of what was going on with the money next door,
let alone with a few other people? Much. I can say this because I
went investigating—prying, even—to figure out a few Joneses and
solve our compulsion to keep up. I started by knocking on our
neighbors' door and spending some time truly catching up with the
Joneses. From there I went deeper into America, from suburbia
to the nation's leaders and across generations. And just to make
absolutely sure that money doesn't solve our problems, I got to
know a billionaire and heard what most of us never know about that
world.

You are about to learn the intimate details of what has been
called America's last secret.

CHAPTER TWO

⌒

The Money Next Door

What was going on with the money next door was another version of the hiding and struggling that was going on behind our door. We just never knew it about each other.

I didn't get all of the details right away, of course. I had to ease into it. Even though I ask questions for a living, it is, shall we say, not normal or acceptable to knock on your neighbors' door and ask them what's been going on with their money. But I did it. For me and for you. Because I know you've been wondering about your neighbors too. And if I can show (which I will) that things are not as they seem, we might all stop paying envious attention to what other people have—or seem to.

I called Tina from my side of the wall and asked if I could come over for a chat.

"Yeah, the door's open!" she said.

I slinked over there.

She was a few months' pregnant and had quit her job—again. How smoothly their plan seemed to be progressing: starting to "pop out the kids," as she had said they would. She was reclining on the couch with a day-by-day pregnancy notebook. It seemed so luxurious to me, staying home with an entirely silent child and reading. And here I came, to ask about their finances.

Well, I didn't put it that way, exactly. Since we were neighbors and friendly, I used the excuse that I was researching an idea for a book about the social side of money and wanted to talk to people about it. All of that was true; I just didn't tell her yet that she and her husband held a special spot in the story. I told her how I had been inspired by hiding some of our own financial stresses.

I didn't have to say any more.

"Money is, by far, my number-one stress," she declared.

That first meeting I got a very general picture of their issues, but I didn't ask specifics. She said that she and John have very different attitudes toward money: She had been raised in the materialistic suburbs and described herself as "practically a compulsive spender." He, meanwhile, had been "raised by a Marxist and can live on practically nothing. That causes major problems." They couldn't live on her husband's salary, so her parents helped support them. (Even though her father, an accountant, thinks of her as a failure, she said, for not being able to manage money.) They couldn't afford the trip they were taking to Paris that weekend, but they were going anyway. As far as the luxury of not working went, she explained that now that she had quit her job, she realized how much our society defines everyone by what they do for a living, and she dreaded people asking her the question. She couldn't wait for the baby to be born so that she would have a legitimate occupation.

Soon after that conversation, Tina and I were walking into our building together and stopped to pick up our mail in the lobby. We both read the label on a box from Bloomingdale's before we saw that it was for her. She snatched it up, groaning, "Oh god, you're seeing what a spender I am."

She was right that I had a different perspective on the string of packages arriving for them after I learned that her spending was an issue between them. But still I did not pick up on her hints that the problem in their household went deeper than her just being a dedicated shopper.

The next discovery came over lunch. We were chatting about banks, and Tina mentioned that they use a certain bank because their mortgage is through that bank. *Mortgage?!* Our envy of these neighbors had been touched off years before when we heard that they had paid cash for their apartment. Now I found out that was incorrect information? (*Was it possible the rumor mill was . . . flawed?*) This whole time they were making mortgage payments after all? Two sentences later she mentioned having to keep their checking account at this bank because by doing so they had gotten some of the interest knocked off their home equity line of credit. *Home equity line of credit?!* I was too stunned to admit to her that we had heard they hadn't carried a mortgage and had been envious.

Tapping a home equity line of credit, I marveled to myself. Even my husband and I, with one income and graduate school tuition, had not resorted to that. I left my husband a message on his cell phone: "I just had lunch with Tina. You're not going to believe this! See you tonight."

At night we continued speculating. What was really going on over there? Had their parents helped them get the apartment by paying cash, but then John and Tina had to pay them back? Or, worse, had they accepted the gift of an apartment, only then to turn around and take a mortgage on it for extra cash?

Shame on us for caring. Yes, I know. I *know*! At least I'm being honest (here). And I know we're not the only ones who have conversations like this. The point is that for anybody who has ever had even an itch of wanting what their friends or associates have, it is most useful first to understand what it is they do have. Or, as the case may be, what they do not have.

After I received a contract for this book I asked John and Tina if

I could officially interview them about their personal financial life. Surprisingly, they agreed, and so I got to find out the real deal about next door.

Let's start where it all started for us: how they paid for their apartment. It was neither an Internet fortune nor purely a parental handout but, rather, something we never would have guessed: John paid for most of it himself, out of an inheritance he had received in college from his grandfather. *John, son of the Marxist, was the one with the money?* Of course we hadn't figured that one out. Neither have their close friends. "Our friends must wonder how we can afford to live here, knowing that I work at a nonprofit and Tina's not working," John said a little slyly. When money does come up in conversation with them, he said, "We don't tell the truth about it."

So John had some family money. (Even though the whole family looked very modest. His grandfather was a shopkeeper in Brooklyn who never spent a dime he didn't have to and quietly amassed a fortune through decades of making steady investments in the stock market.) John kept the nest egg in a brokerage account and only spent some of the income for travel. Having some financial security right out of school meant he could get a PhD and not have to chase a high-paying career.

When John and Tina decided to move from a rental into our building, their strategy was to convert the stocks to real estate by paying mostly cash for their apartment. That way they wouldn't have a mortgage and could live on a smaller income. Her parents did contribute, but not on the magnitude we had assumed. They gave them about 15 percent of the cost of the apartment. After they closed, John and Tina took out a mortgage for about 10 percent of the apartment's value in order to restore some of the nest egg and free up some cash.

The antiquing spree? Her parents "chipped in," as they put it, to pay for new furniture as a housewarming gift. Okay, that was nice of them. What about the kitchen and bathroom renovations? That was done economically, they insisted, with John's dad doing some of the installation, and the materials paid for out of a home equity line of credit. *The home equity line of credit!*

Through all of this questioning—a dream come true in terms of being able to get the facts for a change rather than speculating and surmising—there was one thing, personally, I was eager to hear about: *the cleaning lady.*

Tina: "Well, we both hate to clean."

John: "*You* hate to clean."

Tina (with an eye roll): "It wasn't getting cleaned."

So far, so normal. It sounded like they'd been having the same "Why isn't the house clean, and how are we going to get it clean?" talks on their side of the wall as we had on ours. But the *money.* If they somehow had been choking on their budget just as we had been, how did they justify paying for help?

When they first moved in—when Tina asked me for a cleaning lady recommendation—they were both working. With the apartment purchase, their monthly housing cost, including the minor mortgage and the maintenance payment, dropped to about half of what they had been paying in rent. They could, therefore, afford the services of a cleaning lady. "Financially we were doing great," Tina said. Then she added, "For a short time."

My interviews with John and Tina were juicy. Satisfying. Imagine what it would be like for you to walk up to anybody you have envied or secretly competed with or wondered about and outright ask them the bare truth. The details. To reconcile your impressions of them with the full-blown reality of their lives.

Now picture the other side. What if someone came up to *you,* and wanted you to open your books, to disclose not only every number of your household finances but to reveal what thoughts you have had, what comparisons you have made, to explain how any issue related to money has ever gnawed at you.

For most of us, finding out about others would be most exhilarating, while having to come clean ourselves would fall somewhere between distasteful and mortifying. That's because, as has been pointed out again and again without anyone being able to do much about it, money is—gasp, whisper—*taboo*. In psychology circles money is given even higher hush status as the Last Taboo.

It used to have more company. The list of topics generally deemed off-limits for public or even private consumption a generation or so ago included illness (cancer, in particular), death, and sex. Mental health used to be nobody's business but your own, but that has certainly changed in recent years, when comparing prescriptions for antidepressants has become an accepted topic of conversation. A friend of mine speared two former taboos at once when he complained to me—in the middle of a crowd of his co-workers—that taking Prozac was killing his sex drive.

The age when married couples on television sitcoms slept in separate beds has long since past. For that matter, thanks to the breeding of afternoon talk shows, the time when people who committed adultery with their friends' spouses kept that information off national television is apparently gone too. An editor I met for the first time, who was in agreement that money reigns over a final zone of secrecy, blurted out when we were discussing what's left *not* to be discussed: "I used to think sex with animals was the last taboo, but now that's out the window!" (*It is?* Well, anyway . . .)

A recent cover story in *Money* magazine, "Secrets, Lies and Money," showed the results of their survey of 1,001 adults with household incomes above $50,000. What scenario would they find most uncomfortable? one question asked. Their guests seeing their bottle of the impotency drug Viagra? Fifteen percent chose that as supremely embarrassing. Guests seeing their pay stub or tax return? More than twice as many respondents chose that, at 34 percent.

In introducing a week of articles focused on money, *Salon* called money "our totem and fetish object." The Reverend Stephen Bauman, a preacher in New York City, said in his Sunday sermon recently—after one mention of Christ, two mentions of Jesus, one mention of Viagra, and six mentions of sex—"There is one last taboo, one last holy of holies in our private lives, one secret arena that is too personal, considered too impolite for sharing: that's our financial situation." A psychologist who has researched money's effect on our relationships wrote in a professional journal, "The money taboo is a serious psychological problem because, though we do not talk freely about money, it is of major concern to almost everybody in America." Or, as a journalist friend of mine put it, "Everyone wants to know, but nobody wants to tell."

The same goes for having money, and being out about that. "There's a code of silence about wealth that you're not supposed to break," said Jamie Johnson, a young heir to the Band-Aid company fortune who made a documentary film about children of very wealthy families. Not only did he have a lot of trouble recruiting subjects for his film—most people wouldn't talk, and others who did later said they regretted it, while one even sued—but Johnson himself has been shunned by some of his wealthy peers for being a "traitor." Among the insults: no more invitations to debutante parties. "I guess I used to be considered an eligible bachelor," he said. "But not anymore." After all, who would want to welcome into their family someone so uncouth and slippery as to talk openly about money?

I wanted to deconstruct this taboo and try to figure out where this destructive nonsense came from. The most basic building block of the money taboo is plain manners. Social custom. We're taught from a young age, usually by example but sometimes outright instructed, that money talk is just not polite, so we shouldn't do it. I have on my reference shelf, I'll admit, the hefty sixteenth edition of *Emily Post's Etiquette*. When I went to see what it had to say on the topic of discussing money, I found that, like popular culture itself, the book had more to say about sex. In the chapter "Your Personal Life," readers are instructed: "Lovemaking is a personal matter that does not belong in public. Displays of affection or attraction are often embarrassing to others, are not appropriate in the presence of children, and belong in a private setting. In this country, holding hands, affectionate greetings accompanied by a kiss on the cheek, or a quick hug are perfectly acceptable in public. Passion is not."

When it comes to money, though, only two scant lines are listed in the index: "gifts of" and "as wedding gifts." But with some digging, I found *tsk-tsks* against discussing finances under other headings. In a section on "Good Neighborliness" it is pointed out that, "Just as you would be appalled to hear someone talking about your financial difficulties, another would be hurt to hear you gossiping about hers." (Oops.) But wait: When would we or our neighbor have learned about our respective financial difficulties? The only other mention of talking about money—and this book does actually cover how to have a conversation and what to write in friendly letters—is under the heading "Snoops" and addresses how to respond if someone asks how much something of yours cost. "Inquiries about money matters are usually in poor taste and should be given short shrift. You cannot say, 'None of your business,' but you can say, 'I'd rather not talk about that, if you don't mind. With the cost of living what it is, the whole subject is too depressing . . .' and change the subject."

Change the subject. That does sum up what has evolved as common sense on the matter. But why? Why are we so afraid of discussing money? Where does the money gag come from? And why can't we shake it, even in the reign of the Information Age?

I went looking further back, to the Bible. Scripture has plenty to say about money, wealth, poverty, making money, giving money away, what is virtuous about having money, and also how love of it can be our downfall. Jesus, by example, talked quite openly about finances, both his own and others'. "Interestingly, and tellingly, of all the words ascribed to Jesus in the Gospels, one-sixth of them pertain to money—the only subject he speaks about more is the King-dom of God," said the Reverend Bauman in his sermon on—*his* title, not mine—"The Last Taboo." Bauman confirmed for me that there's nothing in Scripture about keeping our financial lives to our-selves. Yet even in his position as a minister, he doesn't get congre-gants consulting with him on the issue of money, even when it comes to tithing or charitable contributions. "Almost never," Bau-man says. "They'd be much more prone to discuss *any* issue or problem than their finances."

In another sermon about money, similarly entitled "The Taboo," the minister of a church in Toronto gave this explanation about our inhibitions:

> Why is money so difficult to talk about? Because when we talk about money we are never talking just about money. Money we come to believe is a reflection of a person's value. You have it and you're good, you don't and you're not, or at least not as good as. On the other hand some people feel embarrassed by how much they have or, having it, are wary of being taken for what they have . . . "So please let's not talk about it so I don't have to deal with the feelings I have about money—wariness and fear, the anger, the embarrassment and shame."

Psychologists have come to similar conclusions. But not, I must say, as far back as Sigmund Freud. Not to gossip about a great thinker, but Freud was kind of the original sinner when it came to whitewashing money talk. Although he had a lot to do with breaking the sexual taboo, he actually contributed to building up the money taboo. In a 1903 essay, he described money's legacy of being dirty: "In the ancient civilizations, in myths, in fairy tales and supersti-tions, in unconscious thinking, in dreams and in neuroses—money is brought into the most intimate relationship with dirt." He points to "ancient Babylonian doctrine" as equating gold with shit and goes on to explain that a child's fascination with his own excrement can carry over into adulthood by becoming a fascination with money.

That much is about what we would expect from Freud. The really interesting part is when we turn the looking glass on Freud's own private life. In his personal correspondence he points to money as his biggest concern. When Emma Jung, the wife of Freud's fellow psychotherapist Carl Jung, asked Freud about his interpretation of his own children's dreams, Freud told her he hadn't done any analysis of them. Emma wrote to him, recalling their exchange, "You said that you didn't have time to analyze your children's dreams because you had to earn money so they could go on dreaming."

And he had other issues. As psychologist Richard Trachtman points out, "Referring to his father's financial setbacks, [Freud] admitted that he preferred to suppress rather than explore their impact on him. About the 'hard years' he wrote, 'I think nothing about them was worth remembering.' This is a striking statement for a man to whom exploration of traumatic childhood memories was a linchpin of early psychoanalysis."

Freud's turning his back on money—after portraying it as the lowest dirt—paved the way for about three generations of therapists who hardly looked into their patients' money issues. So even in a professional setting, an artificially safe environment designed for us to bring to the surface our problems and solve them, the money taboo has remained strong and counterproductive.

As I faced down the money taboo and interviewed John and Tina, the picture was somewhat coming together. And, frankly, it really did look pretty cushy. Not many people, certainly not many sons of leftists, can write a check for their first home, especially not in their twenties. That does seem certifiably enviable. But fine, some people do inherit a stack of money, and there's nothing the rest of us can do about it—except not assume that inheriting a nest egg means a care-free life.

With so much money flowing in from their families, one might naturally start to think, as we had, *It must be nice to be John and Tina!* But there was more to it, and when I learned the rest of the story, my envy pretty much evaporated.

More about our supposed lady of leisure, Tina: Her family gives her money, her husband has money. What is she *talking* about, money is her number-one stress?

She is an only child who has been spoiled her whole life. Yet she's not entirely thankful. "There's a reason it's called being 'spoiled,'" she said. Having everything she's ever wanted handed to her (albeit with strings attached) killed her ambition, as she tells it. Not that that's true of everyone whose parents are generous with them. Tina, for example, has always compared herself to and envied her cousin of the same age. Tina's uncle, a real estate tycoon, gave his daughter a lot, just as Tina had been given a lot by her father. But the uncle did it differently. He involved his daughter in his real estate business early on, taught her how the transactions worked, and eventually let her manage a small portfolio. Tina's father works more on the hand-out system, with doses of meddling. *You can have anything you want*, he tells her. *Just tell me what it is and I'll get it for you.* So things have materialized in her life, but she has never managed money. Tina has watched her cousin grow into a successful business owner, while Tina hasn't been able to settle into a career or build any wealth herself, which makes her feel incapable. "I never had to work for anything," she said. "My life ever since college has been a struggle about 'What am I going to do with my life?'"

Remember how it looked to us when Tina quit her job at the newspaper and went to interior design school? Here's what really happened:

Tina was miserable at her job. She found spending every day at a computer tedious and boring. It felt like drudgery. The upside was that she was making over $60,000 per year—nearly twice as much as

John—and for the first time in her life had managed to save money regularly, about $500 per month. Her dad for once trusted her enough to hand her some assets, and she had about $20,000 in a stock brokerage account.

They were feeling secure financially. John and Tina sat down to figure out whether they could afford for her to quit. John looked over the numbers—he was always the one handling the finances—and said that it would be very tight, but they could manage it. Of course the frugal one felt they could live on less. He didn't acknowledge how different his wife was.

Tina knew. In her gut she knew that tightening the financial belt was going to be a cinch that would only come undone.

She gave her notice to her boss anyway. She thought it would be a huge relief, to be free of her job. But it wasn't. *What am I going to do with my life?* she wondered. And then there were thoughts of the money. Tina didn't like the idea of cutting back their lifestyle, getting rid of cable and not being able to buy new clothes. Within a few days of quitting, while she was finishing up her last two weeks of work, she went back to her boss. She told him she had made a mistake and that she wanted her job back.

No.

It was too late to change her mind. Tina returned to her desk and sat there in a panic. *What about her career?* she wondered. What about making money? Then something hit her: *If I want to keep my job and my boss says no, then I was just fired.* She went to the human resources department and applied for unemployment. That income would help tide them over until she figured out what else to do, she thought. With the unemployment checks, and $500 per month given to them by her parents since she "lost her job," and with her parents paying her health insurance, John and Tina were getting by financially. But staying at home wasn't the luxury she had thought it would be. She was bored. She felt guilty. She wanted to be productive and find work she enjoyed, plus she still wanted to earn an income.

This was late in the summer before my husband started business school. That's when we heard that Tina was going back to school herself to learn interior design.

She was trying to make something of her life. She wanted to have a job she wasn't miserable at and to earn her own living. Having gone through many years of graduate school, John said he could hardly refuse to support her going back to school. And her father made them an offer: Finish the program, and he would pay back the tuition. In the meantime, they increased the home equity line of credit by $25,000 to pay for the classes.

She didn't finish. After the first semester, when she heard that her classmates were blasting résumés to all of the city's best interior designers, Tina did the same. After interviewing with one of the town's most talked-about designers, she was offered an entry-level job. It paid $30,000 per year, less than half her former salary, but the position was considered a great starting point in the industry, even had she graduated with a degree. "It was a dream come true," she said. Even if that's not how it turned out.

The designer worked for famous people and society ladies. His job was to decorate or redecorate their homes with the most extravagant furniture, fabrics, and finishes they could cull from the corners of the world. As Tina put it, "All of his clients had shitloads of money." For some reason—the combination of hearing "ladies" and lots of money, I guess—I pictured these clients as older women, divorcées or widows perhaps, with large-gem jewelry hugging sun-spotted skin. Not the case. Unfortunately for Tina, the clients were our age, in their thirties. They were not only young but beautiful. And stylish. *Stylish*!

Among the jobs taking place in Park Avenue residences and Greenwich Village townhouses, there was one client in particular. Not only close to Tina's age but exactly her age. A full-time socialite with a family fortune listed on the *Forbes* 400 list of wealthiest Americans. She ordered "Louis Quinze" chairs, as they called them, and for the color scheme of one room she told the designer she was determined to match the shade of cream a friend had used in his European residence.

Tina was sometimes alone at the client's home, to do things such as make sure the flooring guys laid down the carpet in the right room. She ventured into the woman's bedroom, through to the dressing area, and straight to her closet. Or closets, rather, as they lined the room. Inside, she encountered a section of perfectly hung jeans that stretched across four feet of a rack and other garments and shoes from top designers: Oscar de la Renta, Marc Jacobs, Manolo Blahnik. Not just ready-to-wear pieces but also the high-end collections. Couture. Outfits photographed on runways and featured in magazines. Tina could hardly fathom owning such a trove of fashion.

Then there was the storage room. In there, Tina saw racks and racks of similar clothing that the woman didn't wear anymore, that was to be gotten rid of somehow.

On the days Tina came face-to-face with the client, it was to drop off a package of fabric samples or hand her paint chips. "I was basically a gofer," she said. "I felt totally inferior."

She still made an effort to compete. "I did everything I could to be their equal in the presentation of myself," she said of the wealthy clients. She kept up with manicures and made sure she was creative with her hairstyles. But most of all she agonized over her outfits. She wanted to look *impeccable*.

Tina had always paid attention to fashion and was often shopping for new clothes and shoes, but now she ratcheted up her obsession. At Bloomingdale's she lost herself in the designer boutiques. She went to Barney's, New York's high-end department store. And she riffled through the chic shops of SoHo, near the office where she worked.

She was in search of the ultimate pair of jeans, unusual T-shirts, trendy handbags and classic coats. When she targeted an item, she didn't buy impulsively. She kept it in mind. She visited it again, tried it on. After three or four passes, if she was sure, she acquired it.

At first she dipped into the $7,000 savings she had built up when she was working at her last job. She used a credit card, which she wasn't supposed to have, and used her savings to pay off the bill.

She wasn't supposed to have the credit card because she had run up debt on it before. Repeatedly. In college she would buy clothes with the credit card and build balances of $5,000 or $6,000 that she couldn't pay off. As a Christmas or birthday present, her dad would pay off the balance. Then she would start over.

When John and Tina were looking to buy their apartment, John didn't want their credit reports showing any debt. When he found out Tina was carrying a $9,000 balance on her card, he clipped away some of his inheritance to pay it off. Then he ceremoniously cut up her card and made her agree not to use a credit card again. He thought that was the end of it.

Tina had planned for that to be the end of her charging, too. But just when she was burning through her savings shopping for clothes, a copy of the card, which she had forgotten she had, resurfaced. She furtively tucked it into her wallet.

For her job she was often running errands around New York, and she started stopping off to shop in between destinations. She developed a regular circuit and got to know all of the stores' inventories so that she could spot new arrivals in minutes. Within a twenty-four-hour period she would hit all three Barney's locations. On her lunch hour, instead of eating, Tina would go through SoHo shops, buy a couple of items, then pick up lunch on her way back to the office and eat it on the run or at her desk. When she got home, she would hide the packages in the back of their closet hoping John wouldn't figure out how much she was spending.

Her favorite shop became Marc Jacobs, the store of the designer whose creations lined the closets of the client she most envied. Tina was constantly in the store. She didn't invest in any exclusive Collection items but felt she could afford the ready-to-wear Marc by Marc line. The favorite price in that shop was $198. Or $298 for, say, a sweater. One by one, day by day, she collected much of the Marc Jacobs spring collection and then, over the summer, almost all of the fall collection: skirts, dresses, sweaters, and coats; $198, $198, $298 . . .

Not only were her $7,000 savings gone, but she had whittled away the money her dad had given her in the brokerage account. Every purchase was eventually going on The Card. It made her nervous, knowing she couldn't repay the balance. At home, before John got back from work, she would log on to her credit card account online and constantly check the balance. When a statement arrived in the mail she made sure to grab it before John saw it. *I'm done*, she would promise herself when she looked at the balance. *No more charging*. But then she would spot one more gorgeous item in a shop and say, *I have to have that*.

That was the summer my husband was still in school. All I saw was Tina looking fabulous. One morning we ran into each other in the hallway and walked to the subway together. She had her dark brown hair twisted into two short braids and wore a 1950s-style circle skirt with strappy sandals.

Wow! I told her. *You look so cute!*

Next to her I felt like a frump.

By August, Tina's shopping bills were ringing up at more than $1,000 per week, all on credit. She wore enough new clothes in front of John that he started to question what she was doing. *Is that new?* he was constantly asking her. She shrugged and kept telling him she was just getting a few things for her fall wardrobe.

Once John captured on TiVo a short segment on the local news about addictive shopping. He recognized some of the symptoms in Tina, such as when she found something she wanted she couldn't rest until she acquired it. He sat her down one evening and told her she needed to watch it. She was wiggling in her seat but insisted to John, *That's not me.*

They weren't spending much time together. John was busy training for the New York marathon, which meant getting to sleep in the evening and rising early to run. Tina was spiraling further into her funk and escaped into nights out late with her friends, getting drunk on rounds of rum-drenched, $8 mojitos.

In the thick of Tina's self-esteem crisis, a new woman was hired at the interior design firm: a six-foot-tall, blonde former model. A month later Tina was fired. She didn't even consider going back to any kind of work in interior design. She downplayed losing her job to her friends, explaining she had been preparing to quit anyway.

Nobody knew about her debt, even the girlfriends she was usually so close to. They saw her drinking heavily, though, and guessed she was down. One convinced Tina to go to the therapist the friend had been seeing. They set up back-to-back appointments on Wednesday nights, after which they would go to the friend's apartment, drink too much red wine, and gripe about their lives. Tina groaned that she "had debt and felt like shit." She didn't explain further. And her friend never asked.

At therapy, although Tina's secret credit card debt was weighing on her, along with her career crisis, session after session went by and she didn't bring it up. The therapist knew that money was an issue for Tina, because she had gotten a reduced rate due to financial hardship. Yet money as a topic wasn't directly addressed by the therapist or the patient. When Tina finally did come out with the problem, it took the whole hour for her to reveal the actual total of how much she owed. When the therapist heard it, she yelped, *Ti-na!*

That money is discussed at all in therapy is somewhat rare. The same taboo that stops the general public from addressing money openly often makes therapists themselves equally squeamish about it. "The social norm is so strong against discussing it. It just feels like financial voyeurism," says a therapist in Manhattan. I haven't heard of gynecologists or other doctors having invasion-of-privacy issues when it comes to treating their patients; how can the influence of money in someone's life be considered out of bounds for talk therapists?

Even when it comes to the doyen of therapy—the 12-step programs—the subject of money grinds confession to a halt. In a *New York Times Magazine* article, writer Carol Lloyd points out that while in other 12-step programs, participants are "expected to declare the worst about themselves—'I'm an alcoholic!' or 'I am a sex addict!'—Debtors Anonymous allows reticent members to introduce themselves, 'I'm Carol and I'm vague about money.' The question is, are we allowed to be anything else?" Lloyd describes her experiences further:

> Recently I was in a therapy group that put a premium on unexpurgated revelation. "Be specific," the psychologist urged us. "We don't want miscommunication." One day, a doctor in the group began worrying aloud about taxes. "How much money are we talking about here?" I burst out, unable to control myself. "What are the exact numbers?"
>
> The doctor glanced at the therapist, alarm engraved on his vast forehead. The other members of the group scowled at me: the woman who had shown us the scars from her cutting rites; the man who had recounted a graphic nightmare involving his mother and a boa constrictor; the woman who had given us a detailed account of her seduction of a married man. They were all appalled by my unseemly questions.
>
> "Carol, the issue here is feelings, not dollar signs," the therapist intoned. "Let's leave those details to the IRS."

Concern about money has been identified as the potential root of a host of personal problems including anxiety, depression, paranoia, impotence, impulse spending, gambling, social isolation, suicide, and murder. Yet there is something about money that has gagged us as well as the professional community of therapists. As the psychologist Trachtman writes, "It is perhaps the most ignored subject in the practice, literature and training of psychotherapy." Others in the field have pointed out the same void. Psychologist David Lansky described how during his fifteen years of clinical practice, financial issues rarely came up, because therapists don't bring them up. "They don't ask because they don't feel competent or culturally empowered to raise issues about money, about its meaning and impact on the lives of their clients," Lansky says. "It's a quandary then, isn't it? We know from common sense alone that concerns about money are ubiquitous in how we conduct our lives, and they have a central place in the problems that people in fact do bring to therapy . . . Yet, because of their unique set of blinders, therapists rarely hear the sound of money."

A handful of psychologists are building specialties in the financial psychology of money, and a larger group of financial planners are covering clients' personal relationships to money as a keystone of their practices. The problem is this: What little is being done by therapists and advisers concentrates on one's individual relationship with money, or the role of money in one's marriage or family. So those who are compulsive spenders, secret shoppers, money hoarders, or the like could, with some searching, find someone to help them unravel those issues in a therapeutic environment. Likewise, someone embroiled in family bickering over an estate plan, for example, could connect with a financial planner versed in psychological issues or working in tandem with such a therapist. Those fields and arrangements are relatively recent, but they exist for those knowledgeable and motivated enough to seek them out.

What is not being addressed—yet—is the social psychology of money. Social psychologists are not licensed as clinical practitioners and don't see patients. Psychologists and therapists who do take appointments still see our problems largely as our individual issues, and the connection hasn't formally been made that we are all stewing in a societal soup of discontent. The context of our financial issues hasn't been broadened to examine us in the context of our friendships, neighborhood, cohort group, larger community, and culture. These exert a tremendous influence over our *perception* of our well-being, and therefore over our actual well-being. If we are not consciously taking into account and confronting these influences, they are building and bending our reality for us without our even realizing it. And while we let the cause remain out of our hands, so too will effective recovery remain elusive, even for those proactive enough to get themselves into therapy.

When Tina revealed the hidden credit card debt to her therapist, she was told she had to confess to her husband, to break the destructive cycle of shopping and secrecy. What she wasn't told was how common her problem is, which could have been a helpful context in which to begin confronting her personal issues with secret debt. In the "Secrets, Lies and Money" survey by *Money* magazine, nearly half the spouses surveyed said they have lied to their partners about what they've bought or how much they've paid for a purchase. Credit counselors routinely work with only half of a married couple on managing debt. "I can't tell you how many notes I've made that say, 'Don't leave message! Husband doesn't know,'" says Howard Dvorkin, who founded Consolidated Credit Counseling Services. Suze Orman, on her weekly personal finance show, says that questions about hidden credit card debt are very common. When the issue comes up, she recommends that spouses check each other's credit reports, as often as quarterly if a partner has had a spending problem. That's the length to which Orman thinks we must go to force honesty about money—and that's with the person you sleep next to at night.

Before Tina mustered the courage to reveal the credit card balance to her husband, he brought it up himself. He got home one night and found Tina in another new outfit. *What's that?* he asked her. His tone was different from usual. He was agitated. Before Tina could answer, he asked, *And what's going on with your credit card? How much have you charged on it?*

He knew she had been charging again because he had come across a bill several weeks before. He had tried to put it in the back of his mind while he focused on training for the marathon. Now, a week before the race, he couldn't hold off. He thought back to having paid off the balance once, to having cut up the card, and he felt taken advantage of.

Even though Tina had planned to tell John about the debt, she cringed at being exposed. This was the scene she had been dreading for months: the public accounting of her problem, her husband's anger. She started crying. John stood in front of her, unaffected.

How much is it? he asked.

Tina kept mumbling through her tears about it being worse than he thought.

How much? he asked her sternly.

Twenty.

John paused to grasp the mountain of debt that had grown behind his back.

Twenty exactly? he asked.

Twenty-one.

That was the worst of it for both of them, having the $21,000 secret dragged between them. But having the truth come out also allowed Tina to stop the spiral. She stopped shopping and taking refuge in nights out on the town. John decided they would pay off the debt by increasing their home equity line of credit, and he made Tina handle the application, something he knew she would dread. He made sure the credit card account was closed down this time.

A month later they found out she was pregnant. That gave her a mission in life and solved her immediate career dilemma.

There was one last mystery about the money next door that I wanted to unsheathe: What, during that whole period, had John and Tina been thinking about our side of the wall? Did they wonder what money we had or didn't have? Had they realized we were stressed? Had they ever compared, as we had, Tina going back to design school with my husband going back to business school? As a denouement, I asked them these questions and waited expectantly.

They looked back at me blankly. I could tell they weren't being coy or just polite.

"Well, you're homeowners," John said flatly, as if that explained everything. "You had your place before we moved in, so you probably didn't pay that much for it. You always seemed to have work. And your husband worked. And when he went back to school, you probably took out loans."

A tidy package of noninterest.

Tina added that they wonder more about what their friends think of them. "For the most part we have more than our friends, and we always feel weird about that and feel uncomfortable."

"I always feel we're a mystery to people," John said. "You weren't a mystery."

Ah, but we were, as we all are. Even though we thought we had them figured out, John and Tina were a mystery to us. And although they hadn't given much thought to us, we were a mystery to them too. While I had built John and Tina into our mythical Joneses, Tina had made her wealthy clients into her personal Joneses. And no doubt the client she most envied feels the tug to keep up with a particular someone in her circle. We all have them, the Joneses are always there—even though they don't actually exist.

John and Tina had a safety net: They had family money to support them when their spending slid out of control. Most Americans don't have that luxury. And when they try to keep up with the Joneses, it can turn disastrous—all behind closed doors.

CHAPTER THREE

෧

Keeping Up with the Joneses

At first they were fortunate. And they knew it.

Dan and Tammy grew up in working-class families in the South and were married shortly after high school. He started out at minimum wage on the ground floor of a retail chain store, she worked as a secretary. They lived rent-free with family to save money, then moved into an apartment of their own. Dan wondered, at times, why Tammy was so cautious with their money. Often when he suggested they go out to Olive Garden for dinner, she turned him down and instead went to the Publix grocery store. Her father had worked in manufacturing and her mother was a homemaker skilled at stretching a dollar. For many years, Tammy drove the car her parents had given her when she turned sixteen. Not until Dan and Tammy made the five years of payments on Dan's car did they invest in a new one for her. Their frugality paid off: In their midtwenties, when most of their friends weren't even married yet, they bought a quarter-acre lot of land and had a house built.

They waited several years before starting a family. Both were working hard, both got promotions, and children seemed like too huge a responsibility. Eventually, though, everything seemed to come together at once. Dan was promoted to a manager position, Tammy was pregnant, and when they were relocated for Dan's job, she stopped working to be a stay-at-home mom.

They lived in a rental close to the beach while having a three-bedroom house built nearby, in a fast-growing coastal community in southern Florida. They spent a pleasantly anguish-filled year deciding on the property, the house's floor plan, then the fixtures and the finishes. They expected to be settled in there for a long time. When it neared completion, Dan considered it the nicest house on the block.

The community was friendly and relaxed, home to many retirees and middle-income families. Among their closest friends—who, like them, were all married with young children—one husband worked as a sales rep for a flooring store, another was a technician at a hospital, and a third was an aviation mechanic. Dan and Tammy had met them all through the local play group. Tammy's days revolved around meeting the other mothers for story hours at the local public library or for play dates at their homes, where the living-room floors were covered with toys.

They hadn't even finished unpacking in their new house when Dan got a call from work: *You're being transferred.* He was being moved to Orlando, to manage a bigger store. The couple had to sell their brand-new house, at a loss, and relocate.

The Realtor in Orlando showed them several houses, but one suburban neighborhood in particular captivated them. It was a fifteen-year-old planned community on the outskirts of the city, still expanding within its gates. Driving in was like entering another world. One turn from a busy street and they were enveloped by a shady, tree-lined entryway. Inside, the lawns were groomed like golf courses, with mounds of impatiens, blooming hibiscus trees, and bushes carved like giant dinner rolls. There were man-made lakes, majestic fountains, bricked lanes, and a low speed limit enforced by speed bumps. On their first drive through, Dan kept thinking, *This is so nice!* Tammy loved that there were so many families with children. Dan liked the idea that it was so safe, that when he was working late in the evenings he would know that hoodlums couldn't reach their house. When the Realtor talked up the barbecues and kids' activities held at the club, Dan had visions of lounging around the pool with his wife and kids on the weekends he didn't have to work.

It would be somewhat of a reach, buying a house in that neighborhood. But they could afford it—something Tammy had to convince Dan of—even though they would have to pay about 15 percent more than what they had planned on paying. They won a bid on a new four-bedroom house, one more bedroom than they had been looking for. It seemed like a lot of money, a *lot* of money. But Dan's salary would cover it. They had been married for nearly a decade and were often told what great credit they had. They didn't have a car payment or other loans. They used credit cards, but they kept the balances low and would pay them off every time Dan got a bonus payment of a few thousand dollars. Dan had also just started to receive some stock options from his employer. If the company did well, these would become more valuable over time. Their financial situation was only improving. The mortgage would slowly shrink, while Dan got raises and larger bonuses and more options.

Or at least that's how it could have gone.

The Joneses were a crowd Dan and Tammy had hardly encountered before: professionals, entrepreneurs, highly educated people with ambition bordering on aggression. At first the young couple was proud of their new nest. But suddenly, rather than having one of the nicest houses in the neighborhood, they were living on the low end. Surrounding them were people they looked up to, who had done better, gotten farther, had more. The couple they became best friends with owned their own business and lived in a house worth triple the value of Dan and Tammy's. Another friend sold his company and became a multimillionaire almost overnight. Tammy eventually became close with the wife of a pro sports player.

Dan and Tammy met many of these friends, as they had their old ones, through the local Mommy & Me group. But this group was different from the one in the old neighborhood. Instead of going to the library, they took morning day trips to Disney World, the Science Center or Universal Studios, where the families all had passes. Dan and Tammy bought passes too. When the mothers did meet in their homes, Tammy stepped into enormous properties, with inground pools and four-car garages. To maintain them and still have free time, the women hired an array of services: professional cleaners, gardeners, and nannies. Tammy painted the inside of their house herself, and she and Dan did their own yard work; but after a while she agreed with her friends that a housecleaner, at least, was worth the extra expense.

Their new friends seemed especially anxious about their children's development. They sent them to lessons and camps of all sorts, and they talked, even over diapers, of preparation for college. When Dan and Tammy were growing up, she joined sports teams through public school and a youth group through church, and he explored the local woods and canoed and fished with his brother. Now they learned about toys that tutored, birthday parties with petting zoos, and tennis camp for kindergartners that cost $200 per week. Within a year or so of moving to Orlando, they gave in to the peer pressure to join the local country club. At first they invested in a basic-level membership that had the lowest monthly fee and a two-figure monthly minimum on dining service. After their second child was born, they upgraded the membership to one that included the racquet courts and pool. Tammy followed her friends into the ladies' tennis league, a circle that required not only court fees and extensive coaching, but skirted white outfits and hours of child care.

Away from the club, a main social activity of Tammy's became shopping with her friends. They spent many afternoons at the mall constructing and reconstructing various wardrobes. Tammy upgraded her clothing, and she outfitted her children in many matching ensembles. At the checkout, she took advantage of the discount given to her when she opened credit accounts. As she returned to the circuit of stores and used the cards, the credit limits grew.

Their social life in the evenings was also transformed. Friends invited Dan and Tammy out to expensive restaurants. The crowd dressed stylishly and ordered bottles of vintage wine from the bottom of the list. To these couples, it was routine to spend on dinner what at first seemed to Dan and Tammy to be a small fortune. But they came to think, *This must be how people live.*

It wasn't how most people live.

When Dan and Tammy moved into their first apartment, they were making a household income within a few hundred dollars of the national median. So half of everyone else in the country was doing better than they were, and the other half not as well. When they built their first home two years later, they were ahead of most people their age: Only 38 percent of households headed by someone under age 35 owned their home.

The city they moved to in southern Florida, where they started their family, fell into the lower half of the country in terms of prosperity, measured by the income of its residents and home values. Within the town, Dan and Tammy firmly belonged to the upper echelon. Even with Tammy not working, their family brought in about twice the amount of money as those around them. Neither Dan nor Tammy had a college degree, but that didn't set them apart from the vast majority of their neighbors: Only 1 in 6 people in town had graduated from college. (Nationwide, the figure is 1 in 4.) In that environment, they were prospering.

Then came the call to relocate to Orlando. And the decision to move behind the gates.

The community inside the gates looked like a different world to Dan and Tammy, and it was. Dan felt proud that they had really moved up socially. In reality, relative to those around them, their status plummeted.

Most of the people living in their new neighborhood had graduated from college. Income-wise, Dan had far outpaced his peers nationwide who only had high school diplomas. By that time, he was making more money than most people in the country with a master's degree. But he was not, by a long shot, making more money than most of his neighbors. Families in the midrange of this community made more than double the national median income, and the median home was more than twice as expensive. Dan and Tammy fell into the lower half of the community's pay scale. And the house they bought, although expensive to them, was one of the cheapest inside the gates.

The year after Dan and Tammy moved into the new neighborhood, they bought a used SUV. Instead of financing it with an auto loan, they decided to pay for it by using the home equity line of credit that had been offered to them automatically when they signed their mortgage. Why not take advantage of the lower interest rate and the tax deductibility of the interest, they reasoned; then they would just pay it down like they would have paid an auto loan. They ended up not making as large a monthly payment as they would have on a term loan, however, so the car wasn't getting paid off as quickly.

They had always managed to save, but now, for life inside the gates, they started using all of their income. And a little more. Tammy had her hair colored every few weeks. She joined a top health club. It cost a premium over what a more basic gym charged, but she justified it because of how much better their child care was. The kids had a spacious playroom, and the staff kept them occupied with lots of games. Tammy could work out for two hours and take time to shower without ever worrying about them. After her workout, they would often have lunch together at the club's cafe, which was expensive but convenient.

Tammy's friends went one after another to the plastic surgeon for breast implants. Tammy, too, got the $5,000 operation, charged to a credit card.

Dan took up gourmet cooking, hunting down esoteric ingredients that would be used only for a single special recipe. On the weekends, they started accepting invitations to couples getaways to the beach. Instead of going for the day, they checked into oceanfront hotels for one or two nights. Once going on beach vacations became usual, they ventured farther away for annual vacations together. Following tips from their friends and sometimes traveling with them, they scheduled ski trips out West and stayed at trendy resorts. Then they took a different vacation every year with the kids.

No matter how much larger they lived, though, the people around them seemed to have more, be doing more, and generally enjoying a more exciting life. Their houses were more spacious, their cars more impressive, their parties always catered, their furniture made out of unheard-of species of woods. And these people were constantly traveling: to Las Vegas, to the Bahamas, to Latin America, to Europe. Dan and Tammy didn't see themselves as any different, and they felt they deserved the same as everyone else. *They're no smarter than I am*, Dan thought. *Their work ethic is no better than mine.* So why was everyone else's life more cushioned? Making matters worse was that the friends they met when they first moved in were all moving up, upgrading their lifestyles much more quickly than Dan and Tammy could keep pace. Tammy started to feel anxious about their life: Was she dressing well enough? Did the kids feel inferior when they went over to play at nicer houses? Shouldn't they themselves move into a larger house? Why wasn't Dan more ambitious?

For the first time in years, money got tight. More money than ever before was coming in, but even more was flowing out. Dan started getting larger bonuses, well into five figures. However, the amounts were unpredictable. Tammy, who had handled the household finances since the day they were married, let the balances on the credit cards creep up, always intending to pay everything off with the coming bonus. But once the bonus arrived, it wasn't enough. She asked Dan to cash in some of the stock options. That would make up for the shortfall. Her husband agreed and didn't ask questions.

To conserve the money coming in, Tammy started making minimum payments on the credit card accounts. The balances grew and multiplied. The more of their credit lines they used, the higher their interest rates were raised, from what had been a usual single-digit figure to as high as nearly 25 percent. That pushed the balances up higher and made even the minimum payments more expensive.

They didn't rein in their expenditures. They had a lot of money coming in, a lot of resources to fall back on, so Tammy didn't worry. It was just a matter of managing the cash flow, she thought. Dan consistently got raises, and there always seemed to be a bonus on the horizon. If things were tight, it was only temporary, she assured herself. In the meantime, the home equity line of credit, which had an interest rate now significantly lower than that of the cards, could easily be raised. With a phone call to the bank and a visit to sign the documents, they had several thousand more dollars at their disposal. When the checking account ran short, it was easy to transfer $1,000 or $2,000 from the equity line to the checking account just by tapping out the instruction at the ATM.

They still owned a lot of options, too, which was another easy way to flood the household accounts with cash, temporarily. Once they sold some the first time, they saw how easy it was to make a phone call and receive a check in the mail. Then their account balances ran high for a while, and they could shop or go out without worrying about not being able to afford it. They took on home improvement projects—putting in granite countertops and new appliances, replacing the light fixtures, taking up the carpet and replacing it with hardwood floors—that made their home look more like everyone else's around them. And they were continually in the market for the perfect sofa. *My husband has a good job*, Tammy told herself. *He gets stock and bonuses. We can afford it.*

Except one year the bonus was significantly smaller than what they had quickly grown used to. They needed it to pay down the debts that had accumulated, but it wouldn't cover a fraction of them. They needed money to keep up with their monthly expenses, so Tammy didn't put the bonus toward the balances on credit cards or the equity line and instead put the money toward financing their lifestyle. When they ran through the bonus money, she asked Dan to cash more options. A couple of months later, she had to ask again. Then again.

That's when Dan realized something was wrong. And getting worse. He knew they had been living large, and that they hadn't been able to rely on his regular paycheck income for some time. But since Tammy handled the money, he didn't know the details of how the credit balances had grown. *We should slow down,* he told his wife when she asked him to cash more options. She recoiled. *We can afford it*, she insisted. *You're about to get your bonus.*

She was right, the annual bonus was coming. And it was huge. By far the largest bonus they had ever gotten, it totaled nearly $100,000— much more than Dan's annual salary. Whatever problems they had gotten themselves into financially, this was going to resolve them. They would pay everything off and start over with a clean slate, the way they always used to.

Dan needed to make sure of it, though. Subconsciously he had known they were getting into trouble—otherwise they wouldn't have needed to supplement his income with stock sales—but he had trusted that Tammy was keeping everything under control. Now, with a Big Fix around the corner, he was ready to face up to the problem because he knew he could solve it. For the first time, Dan told his wife to give him all of their account statements. One night after work, he retreated with them into their home office.

He had never handled their personal finances before, and now he realized he needed to be methodical to get the detailed picture. Using the Internet, he figured out how to order a copy of each of their credit reports. He printed them out, not paying much attention to the card balances they listed because he knew those could be a couple of months out of date. What he used the credit reports for was to make sure he knew about each of their open accounts. Then he started going down the list. Using the stack of statements, he wrote down the current balance for each card. For the accounts he didn't have statements for, he called the companies for the up-to-date balances. Then he got out the calculator. As a store manager he was used to tallying up figures, but when he hit the total key he saw at a glance that he had been careless and made an entry error.

He started down the list again: American Express, MasterCard, Visa, another Visa, another MasterCard, Discover, Gap, Dillard's, Macy's, Ann Taylor . . . Again he hit the total key. This time he stared at it in disbelief. It showed the same figure he had seen a couple of minutes before. The one he had been certain was a mistake. A panicky feeling came over him. He felt sick. Overwhelmed. He had been deceived—not necessarily by his wife, but by himself—and uncovering the deception felt almost like finding out his spouse had had an affair. She hadn't shared with him how they had been falling farther and farther behind, and he had been looking the other way for too long. On credit cards alone, the couple owed nearly $100,000.

Tammy maps the slippery slope back to being given the home equity line of credit with their mortgage, and then using it. Dan traces their trouble to associating with people of higher means and attempting to match their lifestyle. The combination of having credit available and dipping into it to satisfy desires is a cocktail most of us have tasted. Living beyond our means is a habit easy to renounce yet difficult to resist.

Tapping home equity as a source of credit is a common tool that can become a financial death trap. Home equity becomes available to borrow against when a home is worth a certain amount more than the mortgage owed on it. That can happen by paying down the mortgage or—especially common in recent years with the real estate boom—the home's value rising with the market. A homeowner can take a home equity loan, which means borrowing a fixed amount of money to be paid back over a set number of years in monthly installments, which is why it is referred to as a second mortgage. An owner can also open a home equity line of credit, which is a pre-approved loan that doesn't have to be used at all, or it can be used all at once or in bites as needed, then paid back and reborrowed on a continual basis up to the credit limit, like a big credit card. The interest rates on home equity debt are lower than is typical on credit cards, and the interest is tax deductible within certain limits. Banks are usually quick to approve these loans backed by real estate.

The danger is that, unlike with credit card debt, which is unsecured, if borrowers have trouble making payments on home equity debt, they can lose their homes. So the arrangement is relatively low risk to the lender but relatively high risk to the borrower. "Lenders have continued to promote this product aggressively by waiving closing costs and other fees, offering low introductory interest rates, and increasing the acceptable limits on loan-to-value ratios," states a report by the Federal Reserve.

Historically, according to surveys by the Federal Reserve, home equity is borrowed against to pay for home improvements and to repay other debts. At the time Dan and Tammy were closing on their house in Orlando, the Fed reported a new development in home equity borrowing: "Credit lines were found to have additional uses not often found for most traditional loans, including vehicle purchases, education, and vacations." As Dan and Tammy were using their home equity line to pay for a car, 37 percent of borrowers used home equity lines for the same purpose. A third used their credit lines to borrow, for whatever purpose, as much money as Dan and Tammy did: $25,000 or more. Dan and Tammy and those around them in the gated community were typical customers for home equity borrowing. Most people with a home equity line had incomes above $50,000 per year, and a third were making at least $75,000.

As Dan and Tammy grew up and started their own family, the personal finances of the country as a whole were shifting negatively. More Americans bought houses, but on average they ended up owning less of their homes due to the rise in home equity borrowing. During the same time period, we stopped saving as much and started loading up on credit card debt. In 1981 families saved an average of 11 percent of their income and owed 4 percent of their income on credit cards. By 2000 the average savings had fallen below zero, which means we've gone into debt to spend more than we make. Credit card debt had risen to 12 percent of income.

The credit card industry mushroomed in the 1990s. Between 1993 and 2000, the countrywide credit card limit grew from $777 billion to $3 trillion. Only counting Visas and MasterCards, American households carry an average of five of these cards. How much do we owe on our credit cards? That's hard to say. Apparently a lot of us either don't know our balances or don't want to disclose them, even anonymously. When the Federal Reserve surveys consumers, the self-reported results show an average household balance on credit cards of $4,126. But when that figure is compared to how much the lending industry says we have borrowed from it on cards, the figure is about three times higher, at around $12,000. When we report our attitudes about the use of credit cards there is also a discrepancy between what we say and how much trouble, on the whole, we are in. A Federal Reserve report states, "Cardholders' opinions about their own experiences are almost the reverse of their views about consumers' experiences in general, suggesting considerable concern over the behavior of others and possibly a belief that 'I can handle credit cards, but other people cannot.'"

Lending practices have gotten more lenient, with more people being offered more and more credit, while terms of borrowing have gotten more onerous. So credit is easier to get but harder to manage. Grace periods during which a balance can be repaid without owing any interest, or a payment can be late without penalty, have been shortened or eliminated. Fees have jumped. And while introductory interest rate offers abound, they are canceled and often raised past 20 percent if a payment is late. Regular interest rates, too, are being raised for a greater variety of reasons, such as a card company deeming balances too high, or finding out a utility bill has been paid late. And while the interest charges have gone up with the higher rates, the minimum amount that must be repaid every month on the balance has gone down, from an old norm of 5 percent to about half that now. So customers paying the minimums take longer to pay off balances. If Dan and Tammy were to keep making minimum payments on their cards—which were costing them more than half of their take-home pay—it would take over fifty years to pay them off.

From the time he learned about their debts, Dan took over his family's finances. He put the big bonus toward their credit card accounts, despite the protests of Tammy, who thought the money needed to be saved. After taxes were taken out, the lump sum covered about 60 percent of the debt.

When he opened the card statements every month, though, he saw their spending hadn't slowed. Tammy would charge $2,000 or more in a month on a single store card for clothes. Dan surreptitiously made upgrades to his car, putting the charges on cards. They both lost the fear of debt that they had held for so long. Once they started relying on credit to support their lifestyle, it was difficult to stop. Nor did they acknowledge to themselves that they really did have to stop. They both relied on another big bonus coming, on selling stock options to cover the income gap.

Their debt was snowballing. With high interest rates and since they were still adding charges, the balances grew faster than they could be paid down. Some months it was hard to pay bills and make all of the minimum payments. They dipped into the home equity line of credit. When that was used up, they sometimes had to charge a utility bill. The "convenience checks" that periodically came in the mail from the credit card companies started being used to pay off other card accounts. When cash ran out before a payday, they took cash advances.

Dan didn't understand how anyone making such a decent income could be in such a disastrous financial situation. He talked with his wife about lowering their expenses, giving up some luxuries. Like the country club membership, he said. They were paying several hundred dollars every month so that she could play tennis and lunch with friends and the kids could go swimming. They could do without it, he argued. They *had* to do without it. *If we had a pool in our backyard*, she negotiated, *then we could cancel the membership*.

He worked out the math, comparing how much the monthly

payments would be on taking an additional loan from the home equity line of credit to pay for a pool, versus how much they were spending on the club membership. Seeing that it would indeed lower their monthly expenses, he agreed to the bargain. They applied for yet another increase in the home equity line and converted the whole credit line to a second mortgage that was nearly equal to the amount of their first mortgage. That paid for the pool to be put in. The only thing was, they never canceled the club membership.

Nor did they stop going out, both together and, increasingly, alone. For the first dozen years of their marriage it had been rare for either of them ever to go out in the evening without the other one. But slowly, at first imperceptibly, their interests diverged. Going out became increasingly important to Tammy—going out to the fashionable places, wearing the right outfit, making sure they were keeping up with the right crowd. When they went out to dinner, they moved on afterward with everyone else to a bar or a club. They stayed out until early morning before coming home to pay the babysitter for a six- or seven-hour shift. Tammy still found it fun and relaxing, while Dan started to find it stressful and exhausting. Some evenings he stayed home with the kids while his wife went out with friends.

How can she keep spending? Dan wondered, as he looked at account statements with charges for thousands of dollars. Later he would ask the same question about himself. What had *he* been thinking? Why couldn't he stand his ground, why didn't he insist on controlling themselves? The only answer he could come up with was that he was trying his hardest to keep his family happy. Being able to spend money, to shop and to go out with friends and to live the way they did, was the only thing that seemed to make his wife content anymore. He held hope that, by using the stock options and by receiving big bonuses, they would somehow be able to keep up. He dreaded saying no to her, disappointing her, seeing her miserable, causing arguments—especially if the children might overhear.

When they did argue, often when Dan had just opened a credit card statement and confronted her about it, Tammy had started to blame him outright, saying that their problem was that he didn't earn enough money. Why did the husbands among their friends do so much better? Dan couldn't figure out—yet he didn't try that hard to think it through—how they had gone so wrong, how they used to be happy on so little; and how now, with his earning several times what he used to when they were younger, he couldn't satisfy her.

The cash flow got tighter and tighter. Card accounts were hitting their ceilings. A couple of times cards were rejected at the cash register for being over their limits. They went to a furniture store and picked out a new bedroom set, which they tried to put on store credit. A few minutes after filling out the application, the saleswoman came back to them and said she was sorry, that the application had been denied. *No big deal*, Tammy said. *What?!* Dan asked. He told the saleswoman that they must have made a mistake. *Let me see the application*, he said, *you must have written down our Social Security numbers wrong*. He checked them, but they were correct. *Fine*, he said, handing over a credit card, *we'll pay for half of it now*. The charge went through, but later, at home, Dan knew that they didn't have any way to pay the other half of the bill and take delivery of the furniture. He called the store to cancel the order. A letter arrived in the mail explaining that their application for store credit had been denied because of their high credit balances. Dan was still in shock that they had been turned down, after so many years of stellar credit. He couldn't believe that they had hit some kind of limit.

Then one night he did believe it. He sat in his office to juggle the bills and figure out how to keep everything paid up, to get by until the next check. As he went over their accounts, he realized that they had maxed out everything. Except for a few store accounts, there was no credit left. There was no more going to the home equity line of credit, since the house was fully leveraged. All of the cards were at their limits. There wasn't any money at all in their checking account. He didn't know how he was going to pay for gas to get to work and make it through to payday. Then he remembered one limited resource: They kept two cans of fuel in the garage for the lawn mower. He would use that for his commute.

D an kept a close watch on the cards. If he paid $500 for a minimum payment and that freed up $100 of their credit line, he knew he could spend $100. If he didn't know off the top of his head which cards had a scrap of credit available, he would go online and look them up before they went out, to save the embarrassment of having a card declined in front of friends.

To his relief, they made it through to bonus time again. The payout was a fraction of the previous year's bonanza, but he was determined to make this one last. It would make up for the monthly shortfall and see them through the rest of the year. They could make their minimum payments and then some. It would last, he promised. This time, it really would last.

Except it didn't. It was like dropping a single planeful of water onto a forest in flames. The money evaporated within two months.

As Tammy had done, Dan turned to cashing stock options. With the extra liquidity, they could continue overspending. To celebrate their anniversary, they booked an extravagant vacation. There wasn't room to charge on any of the credit cards, so they withdrew cash they had gotten from selling stock. As they were checking out of an expensive resort, Dan watched two other couples who were traveling together checking in. After one of the men handed over his credit card, the desk clerk, attempting to preapprove charges on the card, told him that the card hadn't gone through. Dan watched the drama unfold. He saw panic in the guy's face and almost saw sweat start to bead on his forehead. The man didn't come up with another card. Instead, he leaned over the counter and said to the hotel clerk in a low voice, *See if you can put $720 on it.*

Dan understood exactly what was going on. The man had miscalculated how much credit was available on the card, and Dan could relate to it. The couple was as strapped as Dan and Tammy were, and yet they were both on vacation at a luxury resort. The man had to turn to his friend, who was standing at the other end of the counter, and tell him there was some problem with his card and ask if he minded putting their room on his friend's card. The friend looked confused, Dan thought, probably wondering why he was paying for the other guy's room, but he reluctantly handed over his card. *We'll settle up when we get back*, the guy with the maxed-out card said, acting as if it were no big deal. As if there were a lot of money back home, Dan commented to himself. He knew the situation so well. They were both going to return home to financial ruins.

The vacation would be the last possible break from reality. Dan started cashing options every few weeks to keep up with the bills, the mortgage, the second mortgage, the credit card payments, and their other expenses. The money was soaked up almost as quickly as it came in. When he got preapproved credit card offers in the mail, he called to accept them. As he was turned down by each one, he started to realize there really was going to be an end.

Dan and Tammy both knew the situation was grave, but they kept kidding themselves that more money coming in would fix it. They didn't talk about it. Dan still dreaded disappointing his wife by insisting that they could not, they clearly could *not*, live the lifestyle they had adopted. They had lived far beyond their means for more than three years, and even if they cut back at that point, the debt had already taken on a life of its own. They had been living on safety nets—the equity line, the options, the unpredictable bonuses—

and were finally falling through. Dan's regular income barely covered their first and second mortgage payments and the minimum payments on their nearly twenty credit cards. There was never any money in the checking account. Paychecks came in and went out immediately. So did the large checks from selling stock. They had already seen the Big Fix bonus happen once, and even that hadn't saved them.

Late one night, Dan sat alone in his home office. He had just cashed the very last stock options that they owned, for a take-home of a little more than $3,000. It wasn't even going to make a dent in what was owed that very month. They had been putting groceries and gas on credit cards, but they couldn't beat back the balances quickly enough to continue to do that. The bank wasn't going to let them borrow any more against their home. Dan didn't think the store had done well enough that year for him to earn much of a bonus, and if he got any at all, the payment wouldn't arrive for over six months. There was no more going to the well. They were heading for default.

Their life as they had somehow managed to keep it going for several years was over. Dan told himself that his family life as he knew it was about to change. His mind racing, he had visions of their becoming homeless. *What am I going to do?* he kept asking himself, sitting at his desk in tears. And he prayed for help.

There are two kinds of games we play with our image. The first is what psychologists call "impression management," which is when you fool other people about who you are or what's going on with you. The second is "self-deception," which is less of a game and more of a subconscious strategy. That's when you honestly fool yourself.

Dan and Tammy suffered from both. On the impression management side, they tried to look as if they fit in where they didn't really belong. On the self-deception side, a problem was growing, but they didn't admit it to themselves. I kept searching in their story for rational behavior, for confrontations with reality. I kept asking versions of the same unanswered question: How could you do this to yourself? Why didn't you make changes? But it wasn't like that, Dan tried to explain. They really didn't see the problem for what it was. There was concern, he said, but not enough to motivate them to alter their lifestyle. "We didn't see it coming until close to the end," he said. "It absolutely sneaks up on you. It's amazing how much of a dire situation you can be in and not change it."

Amazing, but real. Denial is a common phenomenon for people sinking deeper into the muck of debt. Thinking things are not that bad, or that they will surely get better very soon, is a common affliction for people in a financial crisis, and it makes matters worse. Everyone thinks that they are different, that meltdown can't and won't happen to them. "I see a lot of ostrich behavior," says Glenn, a bankruptcy attorney. "The husband brings home the check and the wife handles the finances." Just like Dan and Tammy. "The husband thinks, 'We must be okay.'" Or they keep spending today with a plan to pay shortly thereafter. When the paycheck arrives. When the bonus comes. "When the money comes in," Glenn says, "nobody wants to use that money to pay off balances. They want to spend it on something fun. That's truly the culture of America." When you're in the cycle, it seems okay to go on that way, even though keeping up means falling further behind.

People who owe a lot of money are often unsure how much it is that they owe. Credit counselors describe couples hiding debt not only from each other but from themselves, in the form of not looking at statements and not adding up the total. Even in the midst of financial catastrophe, when they have gotten themselves to a credit counselor or a bankruptcy court, many people, Dan and Tammy included, are eager to describe how they've always had such great credit.

The night Dan realized they were facing the end, he turned to the Internet and started researching what was out there to help people mired in debt. He hated admitting to himself that they had gotten themselves into a situation they couldn't get out of, that he couldn't get them out of. But he was also staring down a precipice. Unless they got help somehow, it was about to get worse. His whole life he had never been more than a month late with a payment, but now he didn't have any more resources to keep paying the bills, which far outpaced his income. Almost immediately they would fall behind. Then they would start getting the dreaded collection calls from creditors. Dan didn't know how they would be able to stop the downward spiral.

The first possibility he looked into was debt consolidation. He found organizations online that promised to help people cope with uncontrollable amounts of debt. Some trumpeted that they could reduce the amount clients owed. Dan read their claims and dismissed most of the organizations as shams. One national organization seemed legitimate. Dan called them and made an appointment. He took his statements with him, sat down in an office across from a credit counselor, and explained the situation. He never had to get out his statements. Sitting behind a fishbowl of cut-up credit cards, the counselor told Dan that they couldn't help him. Dan hadn't yet fallen behind, the counselor pointed out. No late fees had piled up. It looked to creditors as if he were still perfectly able to pay his bills, so this organization wouldn't have any bargaining power with them. The counselor gave him a budgeting worksheet. *This might help you figure out where you can reduce your expenses*, he advised. But Dan knew that trimming was no longer going to help. They were too far gone.

He searched more online, looking for another solution. As he searched the keywords "debt" and "help," one thing kept coming up: bankruptcy. He had been avoiding even looking into it. *We couldn't possibly have to go bankrupt*, he thought. Surely the problem was not *that* severe. Filing for bankruptcy would be so shameful. It would mean he was the ultimate failure.

Who had he heard of declaring bankruptcy? Famous people who had frittered away millions of dollars. Corrupt corporations. Nobody like them, certainly. Nobody that they would know. And for good reason, he thought. Honest people, middle-class families like theirs, people with means, had no excuse for not being able to pay their bills. Whenever he had seen people on TV blaming creditors for their problems, he had thought, *That's ridiculous!* He had always had disdain for people who declared bankruptcy. Once a customer at his store had run up several thousand dollars on credit and later declared bankruptcy. Dan had had to write it off the store's books, and it had disgusted him. He had seen the customer as taking advantage, as taking the easy way out. He didn't want to see himself like that.

Much as he hated going to his wife with the problem that they so steadfastly avoided, she was the only person he could turn to. He eased into it, mentioning that he was researching the options, one of which was bankruptcy. Tammy dismissed it. *That can't happen*, she told him. *Just do something! Keep researching. There must be something else that will help us.*

He got a book on bankruptcy from the bookstore and checked out another one from the library. He tried to show some sections of the books to his wife, but she didn't want to talk about it. *I don't want to deal with this*, she told him. *You handle it.*

Dan went by himself to meet with a bankruptcy lawyer. Like most people who end up in Glenn's office, Dan couldn't believe he was there. He asked the lawyer for some kind of reassurance: *Does this happen to anyone like me? Does anybody else who makes as much money as I do ever have to file for bankruptcy?*

As Dan learned before he met with the attorney, there are two kinds of bankruptcy for most people. The first, and by far the most common, option is filing under Chapter 7 of the federal bankruptcy code, which is often referred to as a "liquidation" or "straight" bankruptcy.

The process is fairly straightforward: You file forms with the court listing your income and expenses, anything of value that you own, recent transactions, and all of your debts. A bankruptcy trustee appointed to the case is responsible for selling your "non-exempt" assets and using the proceeds to pay off your creditors to the extent possible. Nonexempt assets are anything beyond what the law allows you to protect for basic living and working, so you can generally keep your clothing (not furs, though) and personal property including some jewelry, investments in most retirement plans, the cash value of insurance policies, and in some states a vehicle with a certain amount of equity in it. Florida is one of the states in which you don't have to sell your home to pay creditors as long as you can keep paying the mortgage.

About a month after filing, a debtor has to come to a "meeting of creditors" at the courthouse. The trustee asks basic questions about assets and so forth, and if any creditors want to come and ask the debtor questions, they can do so at this meeting. In practice, it's rare for any creditors to show up. In most cases, the trustee doesn't end up discovering assets to liquidate either. Therefore the meeting of creditors takes a minute or two, after which the debts owed are discharged by the court. Some debts are not eligible to be forgiven, such as child support or alimony payments, certain taxes, student loans, and criminal fines. Secured debts, like mortgages or car payments, need to be reaffirmed if the debtor wants to keep the collateral. A reaffirmation agreement signed by the debtor means that the debt remains owed after the bankruptcy.

In Orlando's bankruptcy court meeting room for Chapter 7 filers, a trustee sat behind a desk with a computer and tape recorder on it, a flag standing in the corner, and a small Department of Justice medallion on the wall. The rest of the small room was crammed with rows of chairs, where debtors and sometimes their attorneys waited to be called. After the routine list of questions and usually yes or no answers, an exchange that was typical went like this:

TRUSTEE: "Good luck to you."

DEBTOR: "What do I do now?"

"Go home and wait for a discharge" [a letter stating that the debts are officially gone].

"This is it?"

"Yes, this is it."

From the procedural standpoint, it does look easy. And if you get into trouble again, you can declare bankruptcy again after eight years. I've attended meetings of creditors at the bankruptcy courts in New York and Florida and, to be frank, both times had the same reaction: *This is bullcrap.* That's how a lot of laypersons view the bankruptcy system: *Why are some people let off so easy, while the rest of us are honest and keep struggling?*

There are a couple of things to point out. The first is that most people who go bankrupt are not doing it because they want to get away with something. According to the Consumer Bankruptcy Project, an ongoing research project conducted by several universities, the majority of people going bankrupt do so as a result of losing their jobs, getting divorced, or incurring medical bills.

That said, yes, some people can take advantage. They are probably not owning up to having an ability to pay some debts, and might not feel any guilt about having their debts wiped clean by court order. But that can't be a significant percentage of the people who seek the relief of the bankruptcy system, a claim that has been supported by research at the American Bankruptcy Institute. As with anything, the system has to not work sometimes in order to work most of the time for the people who truly need it. Where is the line in terms of what constitutes taking advantage of the system? Glenn, who has a reputation as one of the top consumer bankruptcy attorneys in the Orlando area, defines abusers as "people who have knowledge of the system before they file, and manipulate circumstances beforehand. People who say, 'I'm going to run up my credit cards and then file bankruptcy.' A few years ago, you could get away with that. Not now."

Glenn explains the difference as a civil enforcement initiative put in place by the U.S. Trustees office in 2001 to clamp down on bankruptcy abuse. The initiative called for local trustees to review every bankruptcy petition with renewed vigor, scrutinize the availability of assets and the reasonability of the expenses claimed, and, if they saw anything fishy, to file a motion indicating a bad faith filing. If trustees see any way a filer can afford to repay some of his or her debts, they'll argue that the debtor can't seek Chapter 7 and can only pursue a Chapter 13 bankruptcy with a repayment plan. In Dan and Tammy's case, if it weren't for their self-inflated lifestyle and consequently debilitating credit card payments, Dan was making more than enough money for the family to live on. Under those circumstances, filing a Chapter 7 case and asking for the credit card debts to be discharged might have triggered a claim of bad faith. Consequently, Dan and Tammy went into Chapter 13 bankruptcy.

The other point to make about the apparent ease of filing for bankruptcy is that the legal process of discharging debts is separate from the emotional turmoil that most debtors suffer, first from being in so much debt, and then from deciding to resort to bankruptcy. What the average observer sees in bankruptcy court is a slice of the formal part of the process; it doesn't reveal the meat of the action, what going bankrupt means in the personal lives of the debtors.

The second kind of bankruptcy, Chapter 13, is a little more involved. It is often called "reorganization bankruptcy" or a "wage-earner's plan." In this scenario, the debtor can't afford full payment of debts but can pay something. Unlike in Chapter 7, no property is sold to pay creditors (although, as in Chapter 7, if you fall behind on your mortgage payments, the house can still be foreclosed on). Instead, the debtor can take a certain allowance to live on, and the rest of his or her earnings is turned over every month to a bankruptcy trustee, who pays creditors according to a plan approved by the court. This goes on for three to five years, after which most remaining debts are discharged by the court. Debts that cannot be discharged under Chapter 13 include child support or alimony debts, certain taxes, student loans, and ongoing mortgage payments.

Bankruptcy reforms approved by Congress in the spring of 2005 that went into effect that October make it more difficult to file any bankruptcy, and they put stricter limits on who can go into Chapter 7 bankruptcy. The new rules compare debtors' incomes to the state median, applying additional standards for those earning above the median amount. Another major change is that instead of letting a judge decide if a debtor's living expenses are reasonable, the court calculates how much a debtor is allowed to live on based on IRS guidelines for family size and geographic location. A law firm in California explains the new law on its Web site like this: "The presumption that a debtor is entitled to relief from his debts is effectively replaced by presumptions that the debtor's filing is abusive until the debtor proves otherwise."

Glenn's office, in a high-rise building in downtown Orlando, very much resembles a doctor's office, with a receptionist sitting behind a sliding-glass window, shelves stuffed with tabbed manila folders, and end tables in the waiting room stacked with issues of magazines like *People* and *Baby Talk*, well-thumbed but probably unread. When a client comes in, Glenn always starts by asking them how they're doing, and many respond with some version of *Well, I'm not good, because I'm here*. The first appointment is usually punctuated by a lot of tears, admissions of shame, and anger—at themselves and at each other, if a husband and wife have come in together. A lot of people want to size themselves up even among the bankrupt population and want to know the same thing Dan did: *Am I the only one in this situation?* They say to Glenn, *Please say you've seen worse than this.*

The truth is that Glenn is seeing "worse" cases all the time. By "worse" he means people of higher and higher incomes, people one wouldn't expect to be overburdened by debts. When he started practicing bankruptcy law nearly a decade ago, the average client was a minority earning $8 or $9 an hour. Now more clients are in the middle class, earning $38,000, $60,000, even over $100,000. Some have lost jobs, some have been hit by medical expenses, but some are also like Dan and Tammy, caught in a whirlwind of living beyond their means.

"When I was a kid," Glenn says of growing up in the late 1960s and early '70s, "the BMWs and Mercedeses were driven by the doctors and the lawyers, not twenty-three-year-olds just out of college. There's been a societal shift to style over substance. And the amount and pervasiveness of advertising has increased. There are constant messages: *You need this. You need this. You need this. You need this.*"

Glenn's wife is also an attorney, in a different field. They don't see eye-to-eye on the use of credit. When she suggested using a home equity line of credit to pay for an extension on their house— after all, she said, she was about to get a distribution from her firm— Glenn said, *No way.* For him to be comfortable, first the money has to be in hand, then spent, and never the other way around. He carries one credit card, for use in case of an emergency. "I go home and see my wife use a credit card and I panic," he says. The people he sees in his office on a daily basis are too much like Glenn and his wife for him to feel safe from the slippery slope of indebtedness. He sees so clearly how it can happen, and how it does happen. "I go home and see twelve preapproved loans in the mail with pictures of homes and cruises, and part of me says, *I must be doing really well. These are the banks, they must know!* But then I know they are marketing gimmicks, because every day I see people in my office crying because they took advantage of these offers. I see it for what it is, but they don't. There has to be responsibility taken by the creditors. I think there really is this pusher out there."

From Glenn's perspective, most people taking on debt don't see the crisis building until it's too late. The balances rise, the interest rates are raised, the minimum payments get harder to pay, just as it happened with Dan and Tammy. They keep juggling and not really adding things up until, like Dan, they suddenly see a month when there is no way to pay. And there's not going to be any way to pay. Then they surface in Glenn's office, past the breaking point.

The hardest moment for Dan was realizing that they were actually going to go through with bankruptcy. *How could this have happened?* he wondered. How had he failed as a provider? Part of him wondered if his wife hadn't been right, if he couldn't have thrown himself into work more, worked longer hours, and been more aggressive about promotions.

Dan hadn't gone to college, but he had still made something of himself. He had built a successful career and made what he assured himself was more money than most people made who only had a high school education and started out at an hourly wage. He had two great children, and he constantly prayed that he would be as much of a role model for them as his father had been for him. Dan adored his father and his upbringing in a family of very modest means that had still provided him a wonderful childhood. Dan and his wife had started out so very happy, at a time when they had little money and few opportunities to travel or go out much. Now he looked back on the past few years and wondered: How had they lost sight of where they came from? And that they had actually been very fortunate to have gotten as far as they had?

Tammy had to go with Dan to the lawyer for the third meeting, the one when the bankruptcy documents had to be signed. When they sat down, the first question she asked the lawyer was, *Doesn't your job depress you?*

Depress me? Glenn said. *No, I love my job! I help people. I save people's homes, I save marriages.*

Tammy didn't feel saved. The deeper they got into the bankruptcy process, the more isolated she became. She was cut off from spending money they didn't have, from shopping or going out, and she went through what Dan saw as a sort of withdrawal. She worried about their children, about their lives changing. She didn't want them to have to give up their activities. She worried that the kids would see themselves as different from their friends, as not having as much as other families had. And she had similar concerns about her own social circle, about what their own friends and neighbors would think of them if they found out. She made Dan promise not to tell a soul about their bankruptcy.

The lawyer told them that a bankruptcy filing is public record and that their names might be printed in the local newspaper. Tammy was petrified of being exposed. She was an active parent volunteer at school and on a neighborhood committee, in addition to having a social life with friends. She worried about being seen as different, a failure, and her normal life essentially ending.

Dan started scouring the *Orlando Sentinel* to see the bankruptcy filing list. He wanted to see how easy it was to spot, what was the wording and how big was the font size. When he didn't find it for a couple of weeks, he called the paper to ask about it and was told they had recently stopped printing it. He researched other ways their bankruptcy might be publicized. What about their friends who worked in banking? Were they automatically notified of everyone in bankruptcy? Was there any way people they knew would see their names on some kind of blacklist? And what about the public record? Dan went to the bankruptcy court Web site and tried to look up cases but figured out that people at least have to go to the bother of getting a paid account and logging in to search anything. And his lawyer told him there wasn't any blacklist but that any time they applied for credit, a new job, or if they had to move or rent a home during the next decade, the bankruptcy was going to show up on their credit report.

To keep their secret as safe as possible—and also because they couldn't afford to go out much anymore—they started cloistering themselves. When they were invited out, they started making excuses:

They had other plans.

He would be working late.

They couldn't find a sitter.

They must be wondering what's become of us, why we never go out anymore, Tammy thought. She hated the lies. The coverups. But she thought telling anyone the truth would be worse for sure. She didn't want to be judged or criticized, and she expected that if anyone knew they were bankrupt, she and Dan would have to endure both judgment and criticism.

A common argument explaining the swelling of bankruptcy cases in recent years is that the stigma of bankruptcy is gone. *It's not shameful the way it used to be*, critics say. These claims are rarely accompanied by any real, live bankrupt individual or family describing their bankruptcy as a routine event. Bankruptcy attorneys, including Glenn, have described some clients who do see bankruptcy as a business decision, who don't seem ashamed and who don't talk about fearing any social consequences. These types do not make up a large percentage of the people going through bankruptcy, however. And the more they are described in public accounts, the more the rest of us misunderstand and even turn against bankruptcy and those seeking its protection.

The reality, as those who meet average bankrupt families discover, is that for most bankrupt people, the stigma, the shame, and the extreme anxiety of being found out are very much alive. In the bathroom outside of the bankruptcy courtrooms in Orlando, a box of tissues is permanently bolted to the counter. Not many people say they feel good about bankruptcy (although a feeling of relief is common), and few willingly disclose their experiences with it. This is especially true of people in Dan and Tammy's category, the overspenders. One reason is that they probably feel more culpable (*We did it to ourselves! We are failures!*) and another is that after going to extremes to keep up and fit in with a certain crowd, they don't want to be branded as different (*You don't belong here! You're not one of us!*).

That's why most of us don't think we know very many people who have been through bankruptcy. The reality is that most of us probably do know somebody in that situation, if not a friend or family member, then a neighbor, an acquaintance, or someone at work. But most of them are effectively in hiding. They are showing us one side of their lives while going through personal trauma behind closed doors.

Dan and Tammy learned that 1.6 million families per year are going bankrupt. That makes 45 percent more bankruptcies these days than there are divorces. So statistically, if you know two couples who've gotten divorced in the past year, you also know three families that have recently declared bankruptcy. Also, more people are going bankrupt now than are graduating from four-year colleges. Dan and Tammy's lawyer assured them that there are others like them. But they are invisible to Dan and Tammy, just as Dan and Tammy are invisible to them.

One researcher who studied bankrupt families reported that 61 percent of those she surveyed said they didn't want their closest friend to know about their bankruptcy. The most recent book based on the findings of the Consumer Bankruptcy Project reports that 84 percent of the bankrupt people surveyed said they would be "embarrassed" or "very embarrassed" if their families, friends, or neighbors learned of their bankruptcy. Many families contacted on behalf of my research didn't want to talk about what they have gone through, even anonymously. Other researchers have had the same difficulty. As explained in the book *The Two-Income Trap*, in a large anonymous survey conducted by the University of Michigan, "The families in the survey willingly share data about their incomes, their purchases, their debts, their investments, and scores of other financial data with the researchers. And yet, when asked about whether they had filed for bankruptcy, only about half of the predicted number confessed to a bankruptcy filing. Either the sample is badly skewed, which no researcher has claimed, or the families concealed their bankruptcy filings."

Unlike in cases of divorce, there is no support system people going bankrupt can turn to. The personal side of the event is not addressed. The common response to going bankrupt is to isolate oneself. Parents inadvertently extend the stress to their children by cutting them off from the usual support network too. As the authors explain in *The Two-Income Trap*:

> When a radical change occurs in a child's life—divorce, a move to a new city, or even the birth of a new sibling—parents typically alert other adults in the child's life, asking them to give additional support and to watch for signs of trouble. But middle-class parents don't tell the teachers, the pediatrician, the school counselor, or the babysitter that their youngster may be experiencing distress because mom and dad are on the brink of bankruptcy. This leaves children isolated, confused, and conscious that something shameful is going on. The code of silence makes it difficult for these chil-

76

dren to seek out friends who have lived through the same experience. Children become more isolated, cut off from their peers. Over time, this can evolve into keeping secrets and telling lies.

Deborah Thorne, in her dissertation on the stigma of bankruptcy, writes, "I would argue that the insolvent individual has long been a venerable lightning rod of contempt. The Old Testament taught us this lesson: 'Evil men borrow and cannot pay it back' (Psalms 37:21)." According to Thorne's research, bankrupt people specifically want to keep their secret from three groups: their friends, their employers or co-workers, and most of all their parents. They feel ashamed and do not want to be diminished in their parents' eyes. And the secrecy slices both ways. One mother described admonishing her son for filing bankruptcy, telling him that his grandmothers would "roll over in their graves." Then she said to the interviewer, "And of course I don't know if they know we did [file too] or not. But we never said anything."

The usual network we rely on to get us through personal crises is dismantled in the case of financial failure. Just when we need to turn to friends and family, when we need to make honest disclosures and hear reassurances, instead we draw up inside our shells. "When stress is encountered, other people serve as 'buffers,'" explains a social psychology textbook. "For example, if someone has lost a job, friends or relatives can provide a place to stay or food to eat, along with affection and encouragement. Support helps the person get through a bad experience." The social psychologists cite experiments showing that the relief provided by tapping into a network and having someone listen sympathetically extends to a positive physical effect, reducing physiological stress. The text concludes, "It seems that confession is good not only for the soul but for the body as well."

They also have a name for what happens when we take the opposite path, when we think one thing but say or act like something else is the case. Cognitive dissonance, they call it, when our private reality and public presentation don't match up. That makes most of us nervous, uncomfortable. In other words, it's stressful to live a lie.

Dan worried about Tammy's depression. He wanted to convince her that they were not horrible people. He thought that if she could just see that they weren't the only ones, that there were other people who were family-oriented and even made good money who were in the same position, she would feel better. He searched online for any kind of support group for people going through bankruptcy. To his shock, he couldn't find a single connection, anywhere to turn to for help. He asked his lawyer if he knew of anything, but he didn't. They were on their own.

Even more so, Dan was on his own. Tammy didn't want anything more to do with the bankruptcy than she absolutely had to.

Dan went to bankruptcy court alone. The thought of going through with it, and in a public forum no less, caused an anxiety attack. He thought about what it would be like to run into somebody they knew, even though anybody else would be there for the same reason and be just as surprised to be seen. He expected courtroom drama, to be personally on trial and to be questioned in an antagonistic way on every expense, every financial move he had made. He figured a judge earned about the same income he did, and he imagined the judge saying, *I make what you make, and I pay my bills. Why can't you pay yours?!* He expected to have to explain why they had been taking vacations, why they had made home improvements, how they could justify spending so much on credit. What made him most nervous was that he knew he didn't have good answers to those questions. The only thing he could say, and what he believed, was that he had honestly thought they could keep up. That the next big bonus would take care of the debts. That somehow he could handle it.

Court was nothing like he had feared. No creditors came to the meeting, the trustee was friendly, and the process all business. He responded to minimal questions, and his whole appointment was over in about one minute.

It still didn't make going bankrupt painless. As Dan got further along, he fretted more about the fallout from it. When he had checked his credit report the first night he tallied up their card debts, he had seen that his employer had run credit checks periodically. What would they think of him when the next time they looked, they found out he had declared bankruptcy? The lawyer had informed him that it is illegal for employers to discriminate against people for being bankrupt. But as a practical matter, Florida is an "at will" employment state, which means workers can be fired for any reason not expressly prohibited, so it can be difficult to argue a discrimination case. The legal protection also doesn't extend to being hired by a new employer, and employers usually do run credit checks on prospective hires.

Dan had a concrete reason to believe that he wouldn't be trusted anymore to manage a business. He had been given a preview of how his company might respond. A week before he had to be in court himself, he was sitting with his boss when they reviewed a confidential employee request for time off to attend court for a bankruptcy hearing. The boss had turned to Dan and warned him, *Keep a close eye on that one.*

Dan himself does look at people differently now. He wonders about some of their friends and the people they see: Can they afford their lifestyle, or are they too falling behind? Who else is in trouble? He thinks he recognizes the signs sometimes. He wants to say something, he wants to tell them what his family has been through, what a mistake the overspending was and how he wishes he could roll back five years of his life and do it over. He wants to grab them and look them straight in the eye and say, *You've got to stop! If from one year to the next your credit card debt has gone up, you're headed for disaster.*

Bankruptcy forced Dan and Tammy to break their cycle of overspending. According to the terms of their case, every month for five years they must pay a significant portion of their income to the court. They also must surrender any bonuses or extra payments they receive. They are living on a budget designed to cover necessities only. Dan says, "It makes you question putting money in a vending machine to buy a soda." But they are still living in the same gated community, are still mingling with the better-off Joneses, and their kids still want to go to the same summer camps as their friends.

Through church, Dan and Tammy joined a couples Bible study group. They meet once a week in their homes, rotating each week. The group's members profess support for one another, often saying how they know that if any of them needed anything at all, even in the middle of the night, they could call on anyone in the group and they would be there for one another. But Dan and Tammy won't reveal to the other couples what they are going through. "These are people we know," Tammy said. "We don't want to be viewed differently."

But they are different, and Tammy can't help but notice that. The other couples do live in much bigger houses. They drive better cars. When it's Dan and Tammy's turn to have the Bible study meeting at their home, she complains that they don't have enough space. Dan tells her to be proud of what they have, but she's embarrassed. She dreads hosting.

If only she understood how common their predicament is, how many of us are burdened by keeping up appearances when things are not as they seem.

CHAPTER FOUR

ॐ

Capitol Secrets

Everyone thinks you're rich!

It's a definite problem, especially when thousands of people think they know you personally. That's the position national politicians are in. Capitol Hill, when you dig down to the level of the politicians' personal lives, is in some ways a Potemkin Village: What we think we see going on is much rosier than what is actually happening.

As Jack Buechner, a former member of the House of Representatives from Missouri, put it: "The minute you're elected, you immediately become a Prince or a Princess." Everyone knows that those kinds of characters lead fairy-tale lives, that they don't have to contend with the financial problems of ordinary folk.

Jack Quinn thought his family life in western New York state was nothing extraordinary. His son came home from high school with news to the contrary.

Dad, he said, *the kids at school are saying, "Your dad's a congressman, your family must be rich!"*

Then the boy had to ask: *Are we?*

The congressman's reaction fell somewhere between amusement and frustration: *No. We're not rich. But . . . we're comfortable.*

The family was comfortable, yes, living in a four-bedroom colonial in a suburb of Buffalo. However, they were not as comfortable as some other politicians, the ones who get a lot of press for being independently wealthy. At the same time, the family was nowhere near as comfortable as people assumed they were because of Quinn's high-profile job. In that context, the family wasn't doing nearly as well as people expected.

Quinn's salary of over $130,000 per year would be considered a lot of money to most constituents in the district he represented in Congress until 2004. At first it seemed like a lot of money to Quinn too. When he was elected to the House of Representatives he was working as a town supervisor making half as much money. Not that he got into politics to make money, but he and his wife, a nurse who worked part-time, naturally thought that doubling his income would mean a respite from squeezing the budget so hard for their household of four.

That didn't quite turn out to be true. This is the inside story that even the insiders don't talk about.

It's easy to confuse fame with fortune. To their constituents, national politicians can look like they're living a fast-track life of paid-for travel, cushy benefits, elaborate dinners with other high-powered people, a stream of luxurious gifts and lucrative gigs on the side.

The media encourage this image, with headlines like "Congress's Millionaires—A Thriving Breed" (*U.S. News and World Report*) and "Lawmakers Don't Feel Your Pain" (*Houston Chronicle*). Al Gore's campaign consultant said average people view Capitol Hill as "the Gucci scene." Former Nebraska senator Bob Kerrey used to bristle when constituents would tell him "You don't live in the real world like I do." When Sam Gejdenson, a former representative from Connecticut, was in office and locals saw him pushing his shopping cart while buying groceries at the discount warehouse, he would be asked, *You do your own shopping?!*

As with many misperceptions, it starts with a kernel of truth. Some members of Congress *are* independently wealthy and, before a recent rule change, lobbyists really did treat lawmakers to lavish dinners on a regular basis. But for the most part, the public conception of what life is like for the legislators is off. Distressingly off. Not many members talk about the reality of their personal lives as it relates to money. The culture of Capitol Hill is so rife with gossip, paranoia, spin, and back-watching that even those on the inside sometimes don't get what it's really like on the inside.

A former five-term representative, finally away from public scrutiny, confessed, "I have *never* been so stressed about money as when I was serving in the U.S. Congress." He wasn't talking about managing his office budget or fundraising for campaigns. He was talking about the same red and black juggling act that plagues most households, with additional expenses piled on as part of the lifestyle and obligations of being a politician.

Former Speaker of the House Tom Foley held a focus group among constituents in Washington state and the group was asked what they thought dinner would be like at the home of a congressman. An ironworker "responded that he would be picked up by an enormous limousine, taken to a huge mansion in Georgetown, seated at a fancy table laid with silverware he didn't know how to use and served food he didn't know how to eat," Foley recounted in an interview later. "All I could think of," Foley said, "was the humble basement apartment I lived in while I was flying back and forth to my district every weekend."

The benefits that legislators receive are a common source of confusion. Retirement benefits have even been the subject of mass letters being forwarded on the Internet. These claim that members of

Congress don't pay anything into Social Security or any other retirement plan, but then even after they retire they make the same salary until death. These reports are totally untrue.

It's not just amateur e-mail reports that contribute to the myths. An article in the *Tampa Tribune* talked about "platinum parachutes" for politicians. "Unlike many Americans, public servants face few financial anxieties over retirement," the article states. "From President Bush to members of Congress, political retirees' financial security is guaranteed, courtesy of the taxpayer." Legislators do have the rare benefit of both a pension and a retirement savings plan like a 401(k) that they contribute to out of their income, but that doesn't mean the money spigots are opened full force for anyone who has served in the House or the Senate. The pension benefits build up slowly over many years of service, assuming the member keeps being reelected. Like anyone, the politicians still have to set aside precious nuggets from their paychecks to fund their retirement— and many of them, like many of us, don't quite get around to making the sacrifice. "Whenever we do radio shows, people always ask questions on retirement and healthcare benefits," says Steve Tomaszewski, the press secretary for Rep. John Shimkus of Illinois. "They think congressmen are in some sort of super-special program." Which, he points out, they're not. Jack Quinn turned down his federal healthcare benefits because his wife's employer offered a more generous plan, with vision and dental and longer coverage for their children, and he heard of colleagues doing the same.

Shimkus's office was thrown by his being portrayed as one of the wealthy members of Congress after he bought a half-million-dollar townhouse in the capital. The complete picture is that he also owes a hefty mortgage on it, and he affords the payments by sharing the space with three other lawmaker tenants. Shimkus has scrimped to support his wife, a part-time schoolteacher, and three children while commuting to work in Washington. While saving up the down payment for the property, Shimkus spent two years sleeping on an air mattress in his Capitol Hill office. He wasn't the first to come up with the arrangement. The halls of Congress might get quiet in the middle of the night, but they're not empty.

Members of Congress currently make $165,200 per year (which is taxed, yes). That's a lot of money to most people, and politicians must be careful not to complain about it. That only adds to the tension. But it's not even the relatively high salary that gives the public the misimpression of an elaborate lifestyle. It's their stockpiled wealth, whether it is real or imagined. When it's real, as with senators Edward Kennedy from Massachusetts ($10 million, family trusts), Jay Rockefeller from West Virginia (at least $200 million, Standard Oil fortune heir) or Jon Corzine from New Jersey ($262 million, former CEO of Goldman Sachs), those are the exceptions. The majority of members are not independently wealthy. People in Jack Quinn's home district would spot his picture in the newspaper with Jim Kelly, quarterback of the Buffalo Bills, or the president or other luminaries. "Because of some of the company you keep," Quinn said, "by association they think you're wealthy too."

An article in the *Houston Chronicle* describing how much better off financially members of Congress are than the average American states, "For the majority of the Senate and a growing percentage of the House, that base pay is just a drop in the buckets of assets they have that make them millionaires."

Another myth is how much these politicians rake in on the side, from giving speeches, writing books, accepting free vacations, and getting other gifts and perks. How much money legislators make and the gifts they can receive are prime subjects in the "Myth Buster" section of the Congressional Institute's Web site. It explains that members of Congress are allowed to earn from outside income only up to 15 percent of their regular salary, which means they can't sign million-dollar book deals while in office or profit in other ways. They cannot accept payments for making speeches at events (they can have up to $2,000 donated to a charity instead).

Since a rule change in the mid-'90s, they cannot accept gifts over $50—that means no free meals, either—or more than $100 total worth of gifts from any one individual or organization during a year. They can, granted, make money from investments like stocks and real estate, since those are not seen as potentially causing conflicts of interest.

However, not everyone elected to be a senator or representative has an investment portfolio working for them. Some have as few assets (sometimes none) and are just as deep (or deeper) in debt as many other Americans. Even for that, though, they find themselves criticized. Check out this account in a New York newspaper: "Imagine the kind of person who might accumulate $50,000 to $100,000 in credit card debt. That person might be out of work for a year or more. He might be sick and in the hospital. She might have a gambling problem. Or the person might be a member of the House of Representatives, earning about $158,000 a year plus full health benefits, plus travel expenses and a small stipend for housing." *For shame!* we readers are meant to hiss. *There's certainly no excuse for that!* So the politicians are portrayed as being sequestered from us, the Real People, whether they have a lot of money or are in a lot of debt.

And the article above, by the way, is wrong about the housing stipend: There isn't one. It's almost excusable that the journalist didn't know that—even some of the lawmakers themselves don't realize it at first.

When Quinn asked his wife if he could run for Congress, she said yes on two conditions: They weren't going to remortgage the house to help pay for the campaign, and they weren't going to move the family from Buffalo to Washington, D.C. That was their agreement. So he got through the campaign without tapping home equity, and when he won the election they knew he would be living in Washington alone during the weeks Congress was in session. Beyond that, they didn't talk much about how it would all work out financially. He would be making a lot more money than he had been, that much they knew, so they didn't worry. Nobody had told him about the extra expenses that would eat away at his government salary.

Quinn showed up on Capitol Hill at the orientation for new members, waiting to hear how much of their living expenses in Washington would be covered. He figured they would be getting a per diem allowance, just like a businessperson gets when traveling for a company, and like many states pay their legislators when they're working in the state capital. He was shocked to find out there was no such living allowance. Members must support their home-away-from-home completely out of their personal paychecks. And unlike other taxpayers, they cannot fully deduct the cost as a business expense. Their travel back and forth to their districts is covered by an office budget, but it never covers one's spouse or children. Quinn summed up the help he'd be getting settling into the new double life this way: *"You're here! Good luck!"*

Another representative from his state advised Quinn to call the landlord of Hill House, a boxy brick apartment building close to the Capitol building where a lot of politicians live, almost as if it's a dormitory. He was lucky to get a lease on a small, rectangular studio apartment there, but he had to pay more than $700 a month for it. The monthly rent was more than the family was paying for the mortgage and taxes on their four-bedroom house back home. The attraction was that he wouldn't have to keep a car in D.C. He borrowed furniture from everyone in the family—no allowance for that, either—and his dad helped him drive the mismatched pieces to Washington in a U-Haul.

Maintaining a double residence is the biggest challenge in the personal lives of most members of Congress. They live in one city and work in Washington, D.C., midweek, or else they move their family to Washington and commute back home to work part of the time in their districts. Either way, they have one foot each in two different places, which often strains their marriages, their families, and definitely their finances. "If most people have one mortgage and boiler to work with, you have two," says former representative Sam Gejdenson. While he was in office, he lived in a borrowed fourteen-foot trailer on his parents' dairy farm in Connecticut while building a house himself bit by bit as he put together the money. Some single politicians or couples move in with their parents or a sibling in their home district as a way to free up funds to support a primary household close to the capital.

Buying or renting real estate in or near Washington, D.C., is expensive and getting more so all the time. One-bedroom apartments currently rent for $900 to $1,600 per month. That can easily amount to more than legislators are paying for their housing back home. Rent in the suburbs is less, but living there requires having a car, so it's a tradeoff.

Those whose homes are conceivably close enough to the capital, even if beyond usual commuting distance, sometimes attempt a daily commute, via train or car, while Congress is in session. Others share apartments or rent rooms in boardinghouse-type arrangements. For his Washington residence, Speaker of the House Dennis Hastert from Illinois shares a townhouse with two aides. Many other members also share local apartments or townhouses, sometimes with several of them under one roof. That can bring one's share of the monthly rent, on the low end, down to the $500 range.

One of the longest-term communal living arrangements has gained a reputation among Washington insiders. The two-bedroom townhouse even has a nickname: Animal House. It's owned by Rep. George Miller of California. He and his wife bought it for their family nearly thirty years ago, but when they decided the children would go to school back home, Miller took in roommates to help cover the cost of the second home in Washington. Since the early 1980s, long-term roomies have come and gone as they are in and out of office. One thing they have all had in common is an unwillingness or inability to disgorge large sums of money on their local residences. The three roommates each pay Miller $550 per month. If he hadn't refinanced the house, he would nearly own it outright by now, but like many Americans he has borrowed against it to raise money. The property, according to his financial disclosure statement, is worth between $250,000 and $500,000. The refinanced mortgage stands between $100,000 and $250,000, and he has a home equity loan of between $15,000 and $50,000.

It isn't luxury, oh no. The house is known for its disarray. "Friends would come by the house and they were stunned," says Gejdenson, who lived in the house for eight years. "They had these visions of a brick mansion in colonial Williamsburg."

The furniture of Animal House comprises various secondhand pieces cobbled together over the years, the window air-conditioning unit is propped up by a hunk of construction wood, and the ceiling has had leaks, even holes. Miller and Sen. Dick Durbin of Illinois each have their own bedroom, while Sen. Chuck Schumer of New York and Rep. Bill Delahunt of Massachusetts crash in the living room. Schumer used to sleep on one battered couch and then another but eventually graduated to a twin bed. There's hardly ever any food in the refrigerator besides condiments, drinks, and the occasional leftover pizza. Over the years, various infestations have been an issue: ants, flies, crickets, mice, and worse. "The rats were enormous," Durbin described, "like little cocker spaniels."

The apartment chock full of politicians was the inspiration for a sitcom proposed to CBS by humorist Al Franken, who knew that most Americans have the wrong impression of how legislators live. "Four guys sitting around in their boxers watching TV and eating fast food," he said. "The wild lifestyle of the rich and famous." Marty Russo, who when he lived in Miller's house was a representative from Illinois, was the only tenant who kept a car in town. He used to drive the others around, and when he had his tires replaced for $200 he billed $50 to each of the roomies.

It gets worse. Some members don't have any residence in the capital to call home. Instead, they sleep rent-free in their offices. This has been going on at least since Rep. Dick Armey of Texas, who eventually became House Majority Leader, started camping on a cot in the modest House gym after he was elected in 1984. The Speaker, Tip O'Neill, kicked him out, saying it was against the rules. Armey only moved as far as his own office, where he slept for the next several years.

Many others have since followed. After working late, they creep on to couches, pump up inflatable mattresses, fold out futons, and cozy up in sleeping bags. Before their staffs arrive in the morning, they restore the office spaces to working conditions and shower and shave in the House gym, or nowadays at the Gold's gym down the street.

When stories surface about the dozens of members who have set up residence in their offices, they almost always explain how the member needed a place temporarily, spent a few nights in the office out of necessity, and ended up not leaving for some time. That's how it happened for Sam Gejdenson from Connecticut (three months on a couch), John Shimkus from Illinois (two years on an air mattress), Scott McInnis from Colorado (twelve years on a couch or in his desk chair), J.D. Hayworth from Arizona (on a couch with an air mattress since 1995), and Pete Hoekstra from Michigan (on a couch since 1993). One former member who spent some nights on his office couch pointed out that the furniture in most of the offices on Capitol Hill is well worn. (Members are not allowed to upgrade furniture out of their personal funds, only out of their office budgets.) He says of his own accommodations, "I could identify every spring in that sofa." Gejdenson says the discomfort went beyond the furniture. "It was very spooky," he says. "But it's one way to save dough."

Some articles featuring the surprising arrangements note that real estate in Washington is expensive and give a single mention of the practice as "saving money," but the financial mechanics of the job are never discussed in any detail. The members themselves, when they do grant interviews on the subject, don't speak frankly about the economics. They talk about the convenience of it, saving the time of a commute, about how they work so late and are up so early: *Why leave the office at all?* Another take on it is to claim that crashing on a couch saves the politicians from getting too enmeshed in Washington and the moral grime that some constituents associate with it. That could explain why some who do own heaps of assets, like Jack Kingston of Georgia, have also taken up residence in their offices.

For Christmas, Quinn's kids bought him a television for his apartment in Washington. He put it on top of a used dresser he had painted white, and he pivoted it to face wherever he was in the apartment: the kitchen, the couch, or the bed. When his brother-in-law came to visit he announced, *I'm going to tell everyone back home how Quinn has it made! He's got a TV in every room!* Joking aside, Quinn said, that's how the stories get started. The stories of the luxurious lives that national politicians lead.

After a couple of reelections, Quinn's son, also named Jack, was in college. Jack continued to hear from his friends about the lavish lifestyle his family must be leading. *Your dad gets a ton of money for living in D.C.*, they would comment to him. "Good friends of yours, without your even knowing it, think you're wealthy," Jack says. One of his friends saw the real deal. During two summers, Jack and his friend got summer internships in D.C. Rather than rent a place of their own, the two squeezed into the studio with Quinn. The congressman got the bed, one young man took the couch, and the other set up an air mattress on the floor. "It was surreal," Jack says.

Quinn stayed in the apartment for several years, until the rent ratcheted up past $1,000 per month. Then he relocated to an apartment in the suburbs, which meant he needed to get a car. He bought a used Ford Contour, which, since he is 6'5", he had to fold himself into.

The used compact car wasn't what people expected a congressman to be driving around the capital. Buffalo Night is a big celebration on Capitol Hill every year hosted by western New Yorkers. The guest of honor one year was Marv Levy, the former coach of the Buffalo Bills. At the reception, Quinn asked Levy where he was staying and how he was getting back there. Levy planned to take a taxi to his hotel.

Nonsense, Quinn said, *I'll drive you!*

Levy accepted and asked, *Who's your driver?*

My driver?! Quinn repeated with a belly laugh. *Me! I'm my driver!*

With the congressman and the football coach stuffed into the Contour, there wouldn't have been room for a chauffeur anyway.

There's more to the financial stress of serving as a politician in Washington than supporting a second residence.

Before they have even won an election, there is the voracious appetite of the campaign trail. For members of the House, who are elected for two-year terms, the campaigning is constant. And it costs— a lot. The average contested House campaign now costs $1 million, and vying for a Senate seat can cost more than $10 million. Headlines about these expenditures contribute to the stereotype that politicians are high rollers. "The whole thing seems suspect," Gejdenson says of the public's point of view. "You're paying $1 million for a job that pays $160,000 a year."

Fundraising is a must for those who are not independently wealthy. That means spending time with the people with the money. For politicians who come from working-class backgrounds, the fundraising aspect of campaigning can expose them to a new social scene, which revolves around having money—any kind of money. ("The nouveau riche are the *worst*," one former congressman said.) It might seem glamorous to attend parties in your honor, but it's actually stressful, even humiliating. The constant, uncloaked begging for others to help pay for your expenses is so distasteful to some politicians that they drop out of the field altogether.

A new candidate can't seriously campaign while working full time, so most of them quit their jobs. The families must get by without that paycheck for a year or more before they even know if they'll have a new job in Congress. The family budget often has to be supplemented by digging into personal savings. That is, if there are any savings. Otherwise it falls entirely on the spouse to keep supporting the family, and most also have to take on debt. Whether borrowed money is used to cover living expenses or campaign expenditures, debt is practically a necessity for middle-class politicians. It is typical for them to take second mortgages on the family home, get personal bank loans, and use credit cards.

Even in office, politicians, too, build up credit card balances. The most recent financial disclosures showed forty-three members of the House carrying credit card balances over $10,000. Rep. Tim Bishop from New York attributed his $25,000 to $60,000 credit card debt to the cost of campaigning after leaving his job in academia. "The story is that unless you are a millionaire it is awfully tough to run for Congress and be successful at it," he said. When representatives Jan Schakowsky and Melissa Bean from Illinois each revealed credit card balances of over $20,000, the Illinois Republican party issued a press release asking, "How can we trust Bean and Schakowsky to spend the taxpayer's money responsibly when their own fiscal house is in disarray?" Even if we don't think like that directly, most of the public as well as the media are completely ignorant about the reality of the personal finances of politicians.

If they do win their elections, and the whole family moves, that usually means the trailing spouse must give up his or her job back home. Employers in D.C. are often reluctant to hire politicians' spouses because they might be there for only two years, pending reelection, if the member serves in the House, or because of real or perceived conflicts of interest. That further contributes to loss of income.

Income that is earned is nipped at by myriad expenses that come with serving in Congress. It starts with getting to Washington, D.C., to start the job. Many new legislators are shocked to learn that not only is there no housing allowance for working in Washington, there's no allowance for moving expenses either. That's all paid for out of pocket. Some families drive their belongings themselves to minimize costs. Others relocate just as a squirrel stashes acorns, bit by bit with a lot of back and forth. On each trip from the home district, another suitcase of belongings is carried to D.C. One member was embarrassed at the D.C. airport's baggage claim when his suitcase popped open and pots and pans came tumbling out.

When senators and representatives are going back and forth between Washington and their home districts on business, the expenses are covered by their official office allowance. Everything else is out of pocket, including tickets for family members and any travel that is not strictly business, which includes trips for fundraising. Those add up quickly.

When you're a politician representing the people, the people need to be impressed, constantly. Appearances need to be kept up, which means wearing decent clothing and—no matter what's really going on with your finances—looking and acting like you're in complete control. There's not much fashion competition among the members themselves, but female spouses feel pressure to live up to an image. They're not so much keeping up with each other, although there is certainly some of that, as much as keeping up with expectations that they look and act the part of a celebrity. Going to receptions at embassies and being photographed at formal fundraising events, they often feel, requires a nice new outfit. Some wives cobble together their wardrobes by getting together for shopping excursions at outlets or going to consignment shops. Others are not as thrifty, even though they need to be. In either case, for those who are stretched to begin with, debt levels are quite likely to rise.

Although the perception is that politicians are constantly wined and dined, the reality is that although they can go to receptions and snack on hors d'oeuvres for as many hours and evenings as they want, sit-down meals are strictly limited by ethics rules. The $50 gift limit applies to dining too, and that is quickly exhausted at a nice restaurant. Yet lunch and dinner meetings are still part of the job— it's just that the member is often obligated to pick up the check, and sometimes not just for himself or herself. Thinking the legislators are on an expense account, dining companions frequently assume the member will take them out. When constituents visit Washington, D.C., sometimes their representative takes them to breakfast or lunch in the members' dining room and pays for it out of pocket. The rules limit what the congressional office budget can cover, and food or entertainment is never on the list. That also means that when staffs are working late or their boss wants to reward them with a pizza or sandwiches, that has to be paid for out of the lawmaker's personal money.

Contributions to charity become a big issue. Those come out of the family budget too, even though they become a professional as well as personal obligation. Seemingly every institution, club, and group in one's home district expects their elected official to support their cause. Adults think there is an expense account for it, one former representative pointed out, and kids think they're writing directly to the government for money. The requests roll in, hundreds of them every year, for donations of cash or something to be auctioned, to purchase raffle tickets or attend a fundraising event. Jack Buechner of Missouri says a standard giveaway of his was a personal tour of the Capitol building, which was economical except for the time involved, and a meal hosted by him in the members' dining room, which he tried to hold to under $50. Sometimes he gave American flags that have flown over the Capitol building—those are popular and cost a member only around $20.

Charities don't seem to fathom that a member of Congress could be battling personal budget problems. When they are turned down, which becomes an absolute necessity in many cases, "No matter what you say, people will be ticked off at you," Buechner says. "Either you feel blackmailed to give money you don't want to give, or you're viewed as a cheapskate and an ingrate. It has the potential to become a major expense, or a major public relations expense. Either way, you pay."

Even though everyone has an equal vote, Congress is in one way rather divided: those who are independently wealthy and those who are not. Among those living on their salaries alone, there are hints of envy of their peers who self-financed their campaigns and are able to live a higher lifestyle from investment income.

Besides the financial disclosures, the public documents detailing their assets, liabilities, and gifts that members have to file each year, they can tell (or they think they can tell) who's who by how everyone talks when they're hanging around the floor of the Senate or House. Quinn, for instance, often talked about his kids back home in Buffalo, about their group camping trips with other families. Others chatted in their circles about jetting off to ski weekends or to vacations in Paris.

While some of the members are sharing grungy apartments or bunking in their offices, others are living on virtual estates in Virginia and Maryland. The better-off members whose families are living back home can afford to fly them in for visits whenever they want to. Quinn and his wife, on the other hand, had to limit their time on the phone each night so they didn't run up their long-distance bill. When there was an argument or plenty to talk about and Quinn called back once or twice, his wife, whom he calls "the finance minister," had to cut him off: *Get off the phone! Save it for tomorrow!*

On the rare occasion Quinn's family came to visit in Washington, they went out for pizza or sometimes to an Irish pub. They couldn't afford to eat at the well-known Palm restaurant or Morton's of Chicago steak house where the wealthier politicians were known to dine.

A representative who had lost a previous bid for Congress was ecstatic to arrive with his wife in Washington. They felt totally ready for the go-go lifestyle: meeting people, attending events, entertaining. They rented half of a townhouse, two bedrooms and two baths, in a nice neighborhood, and stocked it with their special china and stemware from home. They brought their leased German luxury car to town. They bought some clothes that were finer than what they were used to wearing in their home state. The last thing on their minds was a budget. "We just sort of jumped in and were pretty optimistic," he says.

In a matter of weeks, they realized they were in too deep financially. Their cash flow was negative. After having spent their savings on the campaign, they didn't have reserves to support them. They could no longer afford to pay school tuition out of income and had to borrow for it. When a tax bill came due, the couple took a loan from Dad. They sold their three-bedroom house back home to get equity out of it and pay down debt. Within months they found someone else to take over the lease on the D.C. townhouse, while they downsized to the most spartan one-bedroom apartment they could find. The dishes for guests who weren't going to come—there turned out to be no time for dinner parties anyway—had to be shipped back. They felt as if they were living in student housing and jostled for time in the small bathroom. "It had a pedestal sink," the politician recalled glumly after reminiscing about the master bath in the house they had to sell back home. "There was no place to put anything."

They essentially went undercover with their new frugal lifestyle. When they had arrived in Washington, what the representative's new colleagues and staff saw were the townhouse and the luxury car. They must have figured he was one of the members who had plenty of money. "There was some bullshit that went on," the former representative admits. "People assumed I had money, and I didn't want to let them know I was struggling." He became friends with another representative who was apparently well off. "Maybe he didn't have money either," he says. "But we both talked to each other like we did."

Behind the scenes, the family's financial situation was adding significant pressure to an already high-tension way of life. He stressed over making the monthly $600 car payment. "We couldn't get out of it," he says of the multiyear lease. "It really saddled us. I wanted to get rid of that thing in the worst way." Be careful what you wish for: After they moved to the small apartment and had to jockey for parking on the street, the car was stolen.

"Nobody teaches you to be a member of Congress," the former representative says. "They don't talk about these issues. I guess because if you have enough moxie and talent to get elected to Congress, you should be able to work this out. If somebody had just said 'Take a deep breath. Talk to somebody about rentals and costs, and think it through.'"

Nobody in the know gives that advice, though. Everyone keeps the secret to themselves. It is of utmost importance to politicians that they present the right image to the outside world. "In Washington, appearances are four-fifths of the game," says Rep. Bill Pascrell from New Jersey. That means impressing the media, the public, and occasionally even one another. They're being watched. They're being judged. The walls of Washington are built with ears. At the office you're being observed by your mostly young, admiring staff. In the home district, you're being followed by constituents. In either place, you're likely to be trailed by reporters. Your every move, at almost any moment, is possibly being monitored, recorded, talked about. Your image and your reputation—and therefore your job— are at stake. "You live in a glass bowl," Buechner says, "and the sooner you learn that, the better."

Regarding their personal finances, most politicians adopt the unofficial policy of the less said the better. If you're independently wealthy, you'll want to work at playing the average Joe, because you don't want to seem out of touch with reality. Yet if you're pinched, if you're as stretched financially as most Americans, you can't exactly admit that, either. "You can't whine about making $125,000," says one former member. "You can't talk about it publicly, and you can hardly talk about it privately." The current salary of $162,100 is nearly four times the median household income in America. If you complain about financial problems, if you try to delineate how much your life is costing and why you're not quite managing to live within your means, you'll get accused of being out of touch.

"It's the bastard child at the family reunion," Buechner says of money. "When you're in the upper 1 percent of wage earners in the United States, and asking people to give you the job, you're reluctant to talk about something like how much it costs. That's a pretty nervous vein to strike."

The press can ask about it, but they won't get answered. Politicians don't want to be on the record unspooling a tale of financial woe. Even if confidentiality is promised, it's too delicate a topic to take the risk. *What if somebody figured out who was talking? Why start the rumor mill churning?* Besides, there are the facts to contend with: Members are making huge salaries compared with the majority of Americans. "If I were to explain this situation as I am now," says the former member who had to downsize out of the townhouse, "I'd probably get criticized for not managing my affairs well." Both the press and constituents are getting by (or not) on much less. So there's no question of sympathy from them, because there won't be any.

Sam Gejdenson recalls that after he voted for a pay raise in Congress, a television reporter spit out the sarcastic question, *Come on, Congressman, you didn't need that raise to feed your children, did you?!* Gejdenson, who was always short on money, was so offended by the question that years later he's still stewing about it. But he hadn't tried to set the reporter straight. "I bit my tongue," he says.

It's an art that politicians must perfect: the polished appearance. The front. We're all doing it to a degree—sanitizing our images—but they are the professionals. Even after they're out of office, the paranoia and defense mechanisms linger. When I was talking with Jack Quinn, even though he was trying to be completely open and honest, the politician in him frequently popped up, making disclaimers for the record. The battle between presenting the truth and presenting an image played out again and again:

When describing his surprise at there not being a living allowance: "Not to complain! I knew what the job paid," Quinn said. "Being a member of Congress is the greatest job in the United States."

After describing being surrounded in Washington by people with lots of money: "Since we didn't run for Congress to make money, it worked out fine. We never wanted for anything."

Talking about how, despite people thinking they were wealthy, the family didn't have much in savings, his wife shopped at Kmart, and family vacations were spent camping in state parks: "We never talked about it, because who can complain about making over $150,000 a year? We had everything we needed."

Discussing retiring from Congress to become a lobbyist making three times as much money: "Money didn't come up a lot in the discussions [with his wife] of whether to change [jobs]." Just as I was thinking *Nonsense!*, his next statement was, "Of course, we did talk about money."

Of course the couple talked about money—quite a bit, behind closed doors. Because everyone must manage their personal finances as well as figure out how much is necessary or safe to reveal to the outside world. It's a tradeoff. The more honest you are, the more you tell the naked truth, the more opportunity you will have to commiserate with others in similar situations. However, the more you reveal, the more vulnerable you make yourself to criticism. Better to suffer alone, behind the scenes, than to open yourself up to misinterpretation and possibly being portrayed as incapable, ungrateful, or even unfit for public office.

The accepted social wisdom is to avoid any semblance of squawking. That's even true on the inside, among members themselves. The culture of Capitol Hill revolves around the pressure of performing your job and holding on to your seat. Avoiding personal money as a topic starts before the politicians even get to town. More than one former member described how the financial strains came as a complete surprise to them and their families. "As a candidate, you think what everyone else thinks: that congressmen make a lot of money and it's a great life," says the spouse of a former representative. "When you talk to members and former members, you're talking about strategy and how to get there. You're not even thinking about how it'll be when you get there. You just want to get there."

On the Hill, when personal money does comes up, it's water

cooler talk, mentioning a child going off to college and that being expensive or whatnot. It's not about mechanics, not about the personal pressure. Just as they insulate themselves from outsiders, they also insulate themselves from one another. They don't know a lot about what's going on with one another's finances, beyond realizing who has outside money and who doesn't, and when they do hear of shortages there isn't much sympathy. They're all being paid the same, they reason, and they all have to make it work. Their personal finances are almost expected to be the last thing on their minds (which is one reason that day-to-day responsibility for managing them is usually outsourced to the spouse, when there is one). "There's as much talk of that as there would be among twenty middle-aged guys sitting around talking about impotency," Buechner says. "You just don't do it."

Besides, there is the natural tendency toward avoidance. You feel financial stress but don't want to deal with it, maybe not even admit it to yourself. "You have to have an ego to run for these jobs," Buechner says. "People tell you all the time how special you are. And while they're telling you how special you are, you don't want to change the subject and talk about how ordinary you are, and that *I can't afford to have this job.*"

Although nobody runs for Congress for the paycheck, some do decide to give it up because of financial pressure. "If you don't have family money and are honest, which most are," a former representative says, "you don't have the opportunity to build wealth while you're in office." Some leave Capitol Hill looking for high-paying positions in the private sector, which some can get and others can't. The stereotypical money-making route is to become a lobbyist. The field is competitive, and not as many former legislators go into lobbying as many people think. As before, it's the few super-high earners who get the headlines.

After twelve years in office, Jack Quinn had earned retirement benefits of $22,400 per year, to start at retirement age. Since his wife had been working part-time, she hadn't built up any retirement account. After his working as a politician and their raising a family and helping the kids through college, the couple, approaching their midfifties, hadn't squirreled away much savings.

He gave up his seat in the House by not running for reelection. From among several offers, he chose a job as a lobbyist for a salary of about $500,000. (That sounds high—until you find out that some of his peers who became lobbyists have cracked seven figures.) He's reluctant to say that financial considerations played much of a role in the decision, but he says his family's lifestyle still hasn't changed much. He does concede that he and his wife can go out to dinner more now ("Nothing fancy!" he insists), and that they are helping their children with student loans, paying off bills, and, for once, building up savings. "We believe we have another chapter to work. Now that I think about it," he says, "this phase of our life might be to help us prepare for retirement."

People might have assumed he was rich all along, but now, despite the high income, Quinn and his wife are in the same perilous position as so many Americans their age: piecing together their nest egg just a few years away from what would be retirement.

CHAPTER FIVE

∾

Baby Boomers Beware

There is something pretty big that they don't tell you in school. We don't talk about it among ourselves. Parents don't usually warn you about it either.

"Why would they?" Tucker asks. In his midfifties now, he has learned it on his own. "Who's going to tell you that when you're younger? If they did, you'd say 'That sounds too hard!'"

At some point it just scrapes against you. And you have to handle it, however you can. Privately. What they don't tell you is: *The money won't always be there.*

At first Tucker never really thought about money. Or what he was going to do with his life. Or how he would get by. That was the thinking as the baby boomers grew up: *There are so many opportunities. Things will just work out.* Nobody was nervous.

His parents had been nervous while Tucker was growing up. His father came back from World War II and bounced around a little, unsure of a career path. He ended up working for Tucker's grandfather, selling insurance. Tucker's mother was a columnist for the local newspaper until she couldn't afford it any longer. Raising three children in an industrial town in Michigan, the couple ended up needing two solid incomes. She stopped writing to earn her teaching certificate and got a job as a high-school teacher.

"That should have tipped me off," Tucker says. It should have tipped him off to the financial realities of life, to the tradeoffs. "It didn't."

On Tucker's block while he was growing up lived a manager at the local power company, a manufacturer of prefab houses, a writer. When his parents went to potluck dinners, the social set was higher end: a lawyer, a successful insurance salesman, the local shipbuilder. Some kids at school worked on their families' farms. They never had time for anything except their chores. When Tucker went to some of his friends' houses the woodwork was too dark, the wallpaper frayed. The houses hadn't been redone in years. Other friends of his parents took the back off of their house and converted the space to a work studio. Some sent their kids to music camp. Tucker didn't think through the differences among these groups.

His parents, who were college-educated, weren't strivers. They wanted the same things all the other families did in the boom after the war: a house, a car, a television. They saved for those things and paid mostly cash for them. The times they struggled with money, they never let the children see it. They knew all about anxiety and necessity from the war and the Depression, and they never wanted their children to feel at risk, to feel threatened the way they had. Tucker and his siblings were shielded. During their childhood in the 1950s and early 1960s, life seemed pretty comfortable, the world was stable, they were secure.

Tucker's parents told their children to go to college, to broaden their intellectual and cultural horizons. When Tucker got into an Ivy League school, his parents helped him pay some of the tuition. The rest of the bill he paid by working at factory jobs in the summers and by taking out student loans about equal to the price of a Ford

Pinto. His parents sent fifty dollars now and then, and it went far. He never worried a moment about the student loans he took out. He even thought, *Fuck it. If I default, what can they do to me?*

"I thought for about fifteen minutes about what I wanted to do with my life after graduation," Tucker says. "I just said, *That stuff will take care of itself.*"

It didn't.

Baby boomers have had high expectations from the beginning. It's not just their large numbers that make them different as a generation (about 76 million born between 1946 and 1964). Unlike their parents, who had been deprived during the Depression and war years, the boomers were born into the post–World War II euphoria. The economy roared, more women entered the workforce, and by the mid-1950s for the first time white-collar workers outnumbered blue-collar workers. The average American family prospered, many with two incomes, and embraced a new suburban, consumerist lifestyle.

Children were a focus of attention, even indulged. *Dr. Spock's Baby and Child Care* first came out in 1945 and deemphasized punishment. The architecture of houses featured more open, shared living spaces that allowed family togetherness. The boomer children were the first generation to grow up with television. As they came of age, housing became more affordable and higher education more inclusive and accessible. By the mid-1960s, nearly 40 percent of high-school graduates were going on to college, more than twice the amount that did so in their parents' generation.

"We were steeped in a mentality that you could do and be whatever the hell you wanted to be," says Scott Wetzler, a baby boomer who is now a psychologist. "We were the generation that was going to define things. The world revolved around us."

Beyond the usual adolescent pulling away from parents, the early boomers mastered rebellion. They were gregarious, competitive, and free-spirited, eager to make their own way in the world—and determined to have it their way. Known as the Now Generation and the Me Generation, they adopted in the '60s the mantra *Don't trust anyone over 30.*

When Tucker was in high school, *Time* magazine made the generation their "Man of the Year" for 1966. The cover story exalting everyone under twenty-five described them like this:

> That generation looms larger than all the exponential promises of science and technology . . . Never have the young been so assertive or so articulate, so well educated or so worldly . . . This is not just a new generation, but a new kind of generation . . . [The baby boomer] has a unique sense of control over his own destiny . . . Science and the knowledge explosion have armed him with more tools to choose his life pattern than he can always use: physical and intellectual mobility, personal and financial opportunity, a vista of change accelerating in every direction. Untold adventure awaits him. He is the man who will land on the moon, cure cancer and the common cold, lay out blight-proof, smog-free cities, enrich the underdeveloped world and, no doubt, write finis to poverty and war.

But no pressure.

Another catchphrase the boomers adopted in their youth: *Tell it like it is.*

As the boomers are today becoming the patriarchs of society, they're having more trouble than anyone with that dictum. Not every boomer, even the college-educated ones with the intellect and promise described by *Time*, has been able to live up to the expectations that both they and society had of their generation. As they turn fifty and square off to reality, especially when it comes to the shortfall in their personal finances, the letdown can be crushing. Not that many of them talk about it.

Even if Tucker didn't have high expectations of what he wanted to achieve with a career—he had vague notions of working with language in some way—others did have high hopes for him. In his senior year at college he won a Rhodes scholarship, perhaps the most prestigious award available to students in the United States. The highly competitive scholarship is awarded to a handful of students from each region of the country every year and covers all of their expenses for graduate school at Oxford in England. Rhodes scholars are expected to be the leaders of their time, in whatever their field of endeavor. Tucker studied English.

When he returned from England he got a job as an editor at a commercial publishing house. The higher ups were impressed by his background, especially that he was a Rhodes scholar, and he was told he was being groomed for great things. He liked the idea of working in publishing, and he saw the opportunities: to move up, to make much more money, and eventually to write his own books.

He was impatient, however. He had to play the game of climbing the corporate ladder, and he wasn't up for it. The Now Generation wasn't about making long-term plans and following them. Life was more about the liberty of the moment. That's what Tucker and his friends had talked about in college, and he wasn't giving up on it.

Not happy at work, and earning barely enough money on which to get by, Tucker decided to test the situation. He went in to see his boss.

I've been here for a year, he said. *Let's talk about compensation. I do a lot of things, I'm working hard, I think I deserve a raise.*

The boss saw the situation quite differently.

One, you're not happy here, he said. *And two, we publish books, and you haven't published any!*

Tucker explained why he had passed over every manuscript that had come to him: *I haven't seen anything good!*

He left the meeting without a raise, and without a job.

What he wanted to do, it was more clear than ever, was to write. Tucker went back to graduate school, in the Ivy League, with a fellowship and by taking on more student loans. Again the financial commitment didn't concern him. It would be doable. It would work out.

Grad school didn't go smoothly, though. The teachers didn't give him the kind of feedback he thought he had signed up for. His girlfriend kicked him out of their apartment. His brother was killed in an auto accident. All within a few months of being fired from the only real job he'd ever had.

It wasn't a time of mentors and encouragement. Nobody had answers for him about how to do what he wanted to do. He started to feel like an outsider. Classmates from college and Oxford seemed to be on straightforward, upward career paths. They went to graduate school and became academics, they went to law school and became lawyers, they entered the military and became officers. All around him, others his age were moving up, up, up.

It's not that everyone was really doing better than Tucker. The challenge, as usual, is the pond. Within the mass of baby boomers, as with every generation, were subgroups of lesser and greater expected potential. Those with college educations, then as now, are expected to be high achievers, the leaders, the most successful and stable in their careers and their finances.

Once you've graduated from college, your classmates make up a ready pool of comparison. Their achievements come in waves—and keep on coming and keep on coming. As a member of the Class of 1977 said of graduating from Harvard, "It's a tyranny. It hangs over you the rest of your life. Did you live up to it?"

Others in your class sure seem to be living up to it. They make sure you notice their every step up, because they are the ones who write in to the Class Notes column of the alumni magazine. If there were ever a forum predisposing us to share good news, Class Notes is it. "You hear from people who want to brag," says an Ivy League correspondent of the Class of 1978. "It's a fascinating issue: the bourgeois panic that goes on as people try to one-up." Writer Daphne Merkin, a 1975 graduate of Barnard College in New York, describes reading her class's alumni notes "with a mixture of rabid curiosity and an apprehension bordering on dread."

Tucker went to a reunion of Rhodes scholars a few years after returning from England and found it upsetting. He came dressed casually, the others wore suits. The lawyers in the group, even in their twenties, talked about cases and addressed each other as "counselor." He didn't have much to say about his own career. After that he didn't bother keeping in touch for many years. He preferred not to know.

We're supposed to get over that phase in life, the keeping track and keeping up. Graduates who have been out in the world for a couple of decades or more like to say they and their classmates have matured, that later in life it's less about accomplishment and competition and more about meaningful relationships. *Hmmm.* That sounds good, but unfortunately not everyone gets past the competition stage. Witness some evidence from these Ivy Leaguers past their twenty-fifth reunions:

Actual note: "I'm teaching Chaucer to undergraduates and Plato, Aristotle, Nietzsche, Derrida, et al. to the graduate students . . . I'm preparing to apply to graduate schools for a second PhD in computer science this fall." (Class of 1978)

Actual note: "My hobbies include culinary arts, sports and rare cars." (Class of 1979)

Actual note: "I have unfortunately not yet realized my lifelong ambition to open a water ski school, but instead I have acquired three advanced degrees and held a succession of high-powered information technology positions in government, insurance, publishing and banking." (Class of 1971)

Occasionally there's a tension-breaking reality check from inside the ranks, like this one:

Actual note: "After lo these many months of reading about classmates' successes and triumphs, I am aligning some recycled electrons to provide an update . . . Authored no books, wrote no papers, chaired no committees, received no awards. It's been a full life." (Class of 1971)

For those under the spell of a competitive spirit, nothing will stoke it like learning of the latest career milestone reached by a classmate, someone who by definition had very similar opportunities as you and the exact same amount of time to take advantage of them. College classmates, at least some of whom are going to do *very* well, can turn into a sickening comparison cohort. Merkin explains the keeping-up-with-classmates phenomenon this way: "It involves what I can only call a Machiavellian form of emotional accounting, the sort of bottom-line, three-o'clock-in-the-morning realizations that leave one inwardly gasping, *Is this my life?*"

Accomplishments of any sort can inspire envy, but our standard measure of success is still money. That is the missionary position of social comparison. At least it is for the men. "It's disproportionately weighted, regardless of the needs it's supposed to fulfill. It really is a way of keeping score," says Scott Wetzler, who in his psychology practice in New York sees male patients, even those with seven-figure incomes, wrestle with feeling financially inferior.

Since subsistence-level food, shelter, and clothing are pretty much givens for the majority in the United States, accumulating money has almost become a primal instinct. "Self-preservation anxieties from our caveman days have been transferred onto finances," Wetzler says. Fighting for our physical lives doesn't happen much anymore, but fighting for financial security does, daily. Even the baby boomers have succumbed to concern over money. "Financial security is what made the world a safe place for us," Wetzler says. "When our finances are bad, that's when we feel threatened."

But almost nobody is showing it. That has become part of the survival strategy.

Tucker dropped out of graduate school. He was sleeping on a friend's couch, with three people crowded into the apartment, dorm-style. Again he looked for a job, but this time around it was more difficult to get in the door. He had been fired from his latest job and walked out of a graduate program. Still, with an Ivy League degree and a Rhodes scholarship on his résumé, he heard the "you're overqualified" line a lot.

Months went by and he wasn't employed. His parents helped him scrape by. For the first time lack of money became a reality for him, but he still managed not to think about it. Finally he found a job in publishing. It was a major step down the totem pole from where he had been before. He worked as a copyeditor and, in his words, the job sucked.

He did, however, meet the woman whom he would marry. She was also working in publishing, and she also didn't love her job. He moved into her apartment. They commiserated about being stuck working for money. After a few months of talking about this problem, they looked at each other and said, *Fuck this! We're out of here!* They quit their jobs, and with a little money she got from her parents, they disappeared for two months to New England to write.

The time spent writing during their escape was like a honeymoon, blissful. She got a good start on a novel. He wrote drafts of various stories but didn't complete anything. They loved this writing life, except that all honeymoons eventually end. They returned to the city, and reality hit hard.

He was getting minimal help from his parents, who couldn't afford much. Her parents were well off and weren't going to let her starve, but they weren't going to support her, either. He freelanced for the publishing company he had worked for and wrote some low-paying book reviews.

It wasn't enough to pay the rent and get groceries. They counted pennies. They never ate at a restaurant. They didn't go to the movies. Tucker rode his bike everywhere to save bus or train fare. If he saw a book he wanted being sold used for less than a dollar, he still passed it up.

Their lives revolved around the issue of money, and not having it. "It became totally real," Tucker says. They needed money, and quickly. They talked about it all the time. They argued over it. Both wanted to be writers, but they had to ask each other, *How are two of us going to do this if neither is very successful at it?*

It became a Darwinian struggle, especially after they married. His wife insisted that she had a real project in gear with her novel, so he had to be the one to go out and get a steady job. He didn't exactly agree, but there was no denying that making money was an absolute necessity.

Again he was looking for work, and again his search had to slip into less and less desirable jobs. He ended up at an hourly job at a local college, as a tutor in a program for underprivileged students. He was making less than he'd been making in publishing. He worked a lot of hours, but it still wasn't enough to pay for the basics.

He kept that job and looked for a second one. He landed a year-long research fellowship at a library. The two incomes together finally brought in enough money to live on without constant worry. However, there was a tradeoff. "Now I was a working person," Tucker says. "What I wanted to do, which was to be a writer, was going to be very difficult." He and his wife diverged down two separate paths: She became the novelist, he became more of a worker bee.

He had opportunities for more stimulating jobs. Like one at a respected national institution. He got far in the interview process, the job was virtually given to him . . . but then he didn't get it. He was crestfallen, and mystified. Tucker didn't understand how the world was working, why it was so difficult for him to get what he wanted. "I had no idea things weren't always as they seemed. You don't get things you think are yours, things fall through. That's the way things go. But I was clueless. I took it personally."

The bits of writing he was squeezing in on the side weren't going well, either. Two or three longer pieces of literary criticism that he wrote, unpaid, were killed as the publications went to press. Tucker was disappointed enough to give up most of his attempts at writing anything for publication.

For their wedding, his fiancée's parents had bought them a house. So they were able to live without having to make a rent or mortgage payment. That became a permanent saving grace in their financial lives. The house was a fixer-upper, however, and the repairs were their own responsibility. It had plumbing problems. The electrical wiring was faulty. Doors didn't fit. For that matter, some of the walls didn't fit. Tucker and his wife got work done cheaply by doing it themselves and stretching it out over the years. For furniture they found usable stuff on the street. They'd pick an interesting chair frame off the curb and reupholster it themselves.

In addition to taking care of the needy property, the couple was expecting a baby. With that responsibility, Tucker needed a traditional, well-paying job. He looked in publishing again, but what he needed was an editor's job and he didn't have enough experience for that. What he found was a position working in communications for a company located in a downtown office tower. At last he was making what he considered decent money, about $24,000 in the early '80s. He was being paid a professional salary and receiving full benefits, including a retirement savings plan.

It felt good, for once, to have enough money. He had cash in his pocket, and he could spend it. One of the first things Tucker did was venture into a chichi boutique near his office. He spotted a leather Bottega Veneta purse. It was expensive, but he knew his wife would love it. She did.

For years they had been dragging around a small television passed down from his parents. It barely worked. They discussed getting a new one, nothing big, just enough to see the picture clearly. Tucker went to the electronics store and realized he could afford a full twenty-incher. He put down the money, hailed a cab, and took the big TV home.

For the first time in his life, he started shopping for clothes. After work he would wander through chic stores he never would have thought to enter before. He targeted beautiful items, waited for them to go on sale, then made the purchases.

Money made life *easier*. They had another baby and could afford to hire part-time help with childcare or support an au pair with room and board. Since Tucker had two and later three weeks of paid vacation, the family could travel. They had friends living in Europe and took them up on visiting. They even bought some new furniture.

However, the income came at a cost. Tucker had to hustle out the door for the morning commute. He worked from 9:30 in the morning until 6:30 or 7:00 at night. There was always more to do at the office than he had time to get done. It wasn't the stifling corporate environment he had always dreaded becoming a part of, but he was still too tired after work to get any writing done.

He had lawyer friends who were already making six figures. Although further behind them, Tucker was on the money-making trail. Very quickly, he was making more money than his father had ever made. After a few years he had moved up to vice president; he was making $50,000 and was poised to make much more if he stayed on as an executive. Every year he got bonuses. Earning more and more money felt great. He could see how people got hooked on it. The routine got its tentacles around him, and he worked for a salary for half a decade.

Each day he worked at the office, though, he had the same thought. It would come to him at some point during the day, often as he was packed into a train during rush hour: *What am I doing? Am I ever going to be a writer?*

Tucker had started life out with the notion that he could do what he wanted to do, and he refused to let go of that ideal because of needing money. There had to be a way to balance the two.

Years before, as an undergraduate student, he had been demonstrating and confronting the police and chanting '60s slogans about the country being corporate and corrupt and about people leading narrow, morally bankrupt lives. After a few years at an office job, he realized how true it all was. Some people were energized by their jobs, but not Tucker. The work didn't engage him, and he struggled with it. He still didn't know how to play the game. He couldn't put up a front for the sake of progressing in his career.

He felt suffocated. He realized, as he was supporting two children and a wife, how his parents' generation had fallen into the patterns he had criticized and rejected as a student: It was out of necessity. The idea of living free and things just working out? That just wasn't the reality. He felt the pressure to support a family and a lifestyle, and that pressure was never going to go away. Disappointment set in. "I had no inkling things were going to be like this," Tucker says. "It all relates to money."

He could still make a choice. He could give up the well-paying job with the benefits. He would be going back to financial insecurity, in exchange for a return to writing. That was still the tradeoff, and there wasn't any way around it. It was never going to *just work out*. He had to choose between security and freedom.

At thirty-seven years old, he chose freedom. He quit the job. His plan was to continue working on a freelance basis, and the boss went for it. The first year, his income dropped about 20 percent, and the family's expenses went up because he had to pay for things like their health insurance. When he left the job he took a check for the $4,000 that had accumulated in his retirement account. It melted into living expenses. He no longer set aside any of his income for retirement.

The money stress returned, and it would never go away again. Their account ran dry before the end of the month. They had to borrow money to pay taxes. The familiar arguments came back. His wife, who continued to write fiction and was taking care of the children, questioned whether he was making enough for his freelance work. They didn't have money for indulgences, not for clothes, sometimes not even for books. They opened a home equity line of credit to make up for frequent shortfalls. Their lifestyle consisted of robbing Peter to pay Paul.

But Tucker was writing again. In between the work he had to do to get paid, he got some things published, and it made him proud.

"All of this stuff is more complicated than I ever imagined," he says. "But you have to figure it out."

The baby boomers, generally, have not done a very good job of figuring it out. They themselves don't even know how to think about where they've ended up. We hear, from the media, about two sides of the generation: The first is that they're the most prosperous generation ever, controlling sacks of assets and about to inherit even more, and ready to spend lavishly on go-go retirement years. The second is that they're totally unprepared to support themselves in retirement and are headed for doom as Social Security buckles under their bulk and they haven't saved enough of their own to live on. Both sides are true of groups within the generation. What is interesting is that a boomer can fit into one group and still feel or act as if they fit into the other.

Tucker and his wife, as their property value appreciated and together they eventually reached a household income double the median amount for their state, entered society's upper echelon—at least statistically. They are in better shape than most others their age. However, psychologically they are almost as anxious about the future as the boomers who will likely have to rely on monthly Social Security checks.

The boomers, in their peak earning years, are making more than anyone. They also control a lot of assets. As with the country as a whole, however, the wealth is far from divvied up evenly. The boomer generation is the most bifurcate of all, with the money bunched up at the top. And the rich really do get richer: The generation is coming into at least a $1 trillion collective inheritance over the next decade, which will be staying with those at the top who have been well off all along. Despite headlines about the massive wealth transfer that make it sound as if boomers are about to win some kind of lottery, most inheritances in America are less than $25,000. And as *American Demographics* starkly announced, "The vast majority of boomers will never inherit a single dime."

The boomers are an affluent generation, but they're big spenders rather than savers. The early boomers spend more on new cars, entertainment, and household furnishings than any other group. *Time* magazine recently reported on boomers taking their families to Canyon Ranch or on extended Mexican cruises to celebrate the holidays instead of hosting at home. They are putting pools on their properties like there's no tomorrow.

Like there's no tomorrow. That's the only way the equation balances: The baby boomers can spend so much because many of them have been living at or beyond their means. Remember the environment that the first wave of boomers was born into: one of prosperity, security, plenty. As they got older, they didn't necessarily shed that Now Generation mentality. They have generally been able to indulge themselves by sacrificing savings and relying on debt. The boomers have higher credit card balances than any other age group.

A report written for those who sell pools characterized boomer customers like this: *"I've got money—sort of.* Baby boomers are indeed a huge economic prospect for anyone in sales-oriented fields. Yet, many boomers really aren't in the financial position to buy pricey durable goods but will do so anyway, according to demographers." They're not overspending to keep up with each other as much as to keep up with their own expectations of what they deserve, no matter what the reality of the circumstances.

The boomers have a completely different attitude toward debt than their parents had. Tucker describes what debt meant to his parents: "It meant you had to go to the bank and say 'It's not working. Can you help me?' It meant foreclosure. It meant failure." To his generation, on the other hand, it has become a tool. "We use debt to finance our operating expenses," Tucker says.

As the boomers age they are more likely to take on additional debt than to pay it off and increase their savings. It's not all because of an overly optimistic attitude about living for the day. Some of the trouble stems from a shift in demographics. More boomers had children later in life than did previous generations, either the first time around or as second families. A think tank recently noted that the timing "pushes high-cost expenditures like higher education, family housing, and dependent health care closer to retirement age. For each of these expenditures, there is a correlating form of debt on the rise: college debt, mortgage debt, credit card debt."

In addition to having children later, boomers are holding on to them longer. "Permaparenting," supporting children financially well into adulthood, has become a trend among baby boomer parents. Boomers themselves generally couldn't wait to separate from their own parents when they came of age, but their own kids are roosting in the family nest into adulthood. The most recent census found half of all single people between 18 and 24 years old living at home with their parents. That's more than 13 million "kids," known as *boomerangers*. Their parents often let them live rent-free, and they pay the kids' health and car insurance, cell phone bill, and other expenses. They'll even help with the down payment on a house.

Even though they are being generous, the boomers again are focusing on the here and now at the expense of their own future. "Permaparents suffer potential financial and emotional repercussions," reports *Psychology Today*. "The empty-nest years are a crucial time for adults to bone up for retirement, rather than pay off their child's credit cards or feed another mouth." The president of a national credit counseling agency says more boomer-age people are asking for help in managing debt, and one reason they have overextended themselves is that they have helped their children too much.

After an adulthood of living and spending to the max, the boomers have got to keep going into what could have been retirement. Their financial obligations—helping children pay college tuition, making payments on mortgages that have been refinanced rather than paid off, taming credit card debt, shouldering healthcare expenses—make it a practical impossibility for many to stop earning. Financial planners used to estimate we would need a fraction of our current income after we retire, because some expenses, like supporting children and paying the mortgage, would have gone away by then. With the boomer generation, the ideal estimate has commonly stretched not only to matching current income but to exceeding it. Expenses are higher, lifestyles are faster, and lives are longer.

Since many boomers have managed to keep their expectations high while not preparing to support themselves in retirement, the solution, mixed with denial or panic, is to keep working and keep earning, and to hope the opportunities don't run out. Just as Tucker plans to do.

Some of the boomer rhetoric is that the generation is unstoppably energetic, that they wouldn't *want* a golden years–style retirement on the golf course. That could be partly true, but more likely we're seeing a psychological phenomenon of retrofitting: Faced with a reality, we not only adjust to it but start seeing it as what we wanted all along. It's a coping mechanism that is well suited to boomers over age fifty.

Work used to be called the pension of the poor. Now it has become a widespread strategy for even the comparatively well-off boomers, like Tucker. Even though he and his wife make a fat salary compared to others, in the context of their lifestyle it doesn't consistently cover the expenses. They haven't been setting aside income to tap later, so they don't foresee the day when they will be able to live without earning a paycheck. Multiple surveys show that the majority of baby boomers plan to keep working past traditional retirement age. In one such survey, just under half of the younger boomers and well over a third of the older boomers said they plan to do so because they need the money.

Three out of four boomers in one survey said paying for health insurance is a top financial concern. And it should be: Medical costs are rising faster than income in the United States. The country spent $250 billion on medical care in 1980 and is now spending $1.4 trillion a year. The percentage of large companies offering health insurance to retirees has dropped to a third, and considering most Americans are employed by small businesses rather than big companies, and paying for employees' health insurance is an especially onerous expense for small businesses, the vast majority of us will be paying for our insurance on our own or relying solely on Medicare.

The median net worth for families with heads of household ages 45 to 54 is $145,000. Take out the home equity portion, and the assets ring up at a median of $72,000. These boomer-led families make more money than any other age group, a median of $61,100. Yet more than 4 in 10 of them don't have any retirement account, and the same number report they're not saving anything. Among those who do have retirement accounts, the median balance, for the family, is $55,500.

A recent survey by AARP of Americans over age 45 underscores the dynamic at work. "An astounding 50 percent of all midlife and older Americans go to sleep every night concerned about having enough money to pay for basic monthly costs such as telephone, groceries and utilities," the researchers report. "We found that despite serious financial concerns among 45+ consumers, a significant number of people say they will spend money on leisure activities in the next two years." Fifty-seven percent say they'll save for retirement, while 63 percent report they'll go on vacation.

Expectations and reality just don't match up. No wonder boomers don't want to talk about this topic.

Since giving up the office job, Tucker has lived irregular paycheck to irregular paycheck. Even when the income is high, the expenses are still hard to keep up with. If he had had to make a mortgage payment all these years, he would've had to have made further sacrifices. As it is, when he has needed money for home repairs or to get by during lean periods, he has borrowed against the house, taking as much as $50,000 cumulatively from the home equity line of credit. Having to pay that back on top of covering their regular expenses puts them in a palpable pinch.

That's not what people see, though. The family looks affluent. The three children all went to private school. The neighbors must have noticed that neither Tucker nor his wife go to a regular job. Some know that she is a novelist, but few know what he does for a living, and even fewer (like none) realize how he has to scramble to make it work. Nobody has ever asked.

The biggest green flag waving is their property. To buy it today would be prohibitively expensive for anybody not making at least $500,000. Over the years, others on their block have supported the expense by renting out part of their townhouses. Many have cashed out and moved to less expensive regions. It sure must seem to observers that Tucker and his wife don't have money stress.

Tucker knows this game, the game of figuring out how other

people are getting by. He plays it himself, by sizing up situations, making assumptions, and running his own calculations. "I look at my neighbors," he says, "and ask, *How does what they say square with how they live?*" Often it doesn't. Take the family down the street. Tucker and his wife have known them for years. In that household, he is a professor, she works sporadically. They have two kids in private colleges, without scholarship funding. The house is paid off, Tucker and his wife know, but how does this couple afford the traveling that they do? They disappear to New Orleans, Paris, India—for two or three weeks at a time! And then they complain of how expensive everything is. They tell Tucker and his wife that when their son came home from college, they made him pay rent because they couldn't afford to have another person living and eating there without paying for it.

"I add all those things up and say, *Who are we kidding here?!*" Tucker says. "I don't have patience for conversations like that." There's money oozing from the family tree and Tucker knows it. That *has* to be it. They're not genuinely strapped, Tucker thinks, because he has noticed that they never say things like, *We can't afford to do that this year.* They keep traveling, they keep getting work done on the house—it's all getting paid for somehow.

Then there's a longtime artist friend. Tucker can't figure out how this guy affords his lifestyle either. He is also a world traveler, he eats out all the time, and on top of it he has purchased investment properties. A few years back, the friend talked about a gallery wanting to raise the price of his artwork, and that gave Tucker the opening to find out just how much he sells the pieces for. Tucker took the number and started calculating, backward and forward. He figured out how much art the friend has to sell to finance what Tucker guesses are his expenses. *He has to be an assembly line!* he figures. It still doesn't quite make sense to him, though, because artists don't become artists to work like assembly lines.

Tucker frequently runs into this same hitch in the game: It just doesn't add up. There's a trace of mystery. He's not going to out-right *ask*, of course. That would be . . . simply forbidden. "I don't know how much any of my friends make. Not a single one. I'm curious. I'm *really* curious, in a couple of cases," he says. "But I can't ask. I want to avoid the topic so much in my own life, I don't want to raise it in anyone else's."

Yet he thinks he has found the key that fits the lockbox of all of these situations. When the money that must be coming in isn't cov-ering the money that must be going out, there's money behind the scenes.

They have family money.

They have trust funds.

They have rich wives.

He knows something is going on that he can't see. Money is being injected from somewhere.

One way he knows this is because that's the secret in his own household. In more ways than one.

The house, as explained, was given to them outright. His in-laws also paid the children's school tuition bills, including college. Other-wise, the kids would have gone to public school and taken student loans for college. Also, although they have never used any of it to live on, his wife has accumulated a nest egg from her parents. Except for the house, that's their only asset, and they don't dip into it. If things get desperate, they could use it. It will probably have to be used in their retirement, if that stage in their lives ever actually hap-pens, which to them seems doubtful. *How far would it go? I mean, just how large is this nest egg?*

Tucker pauses.

"That's a very good question," he says.

He actually doesn't know.

"It's really her business," he says. He *could* figure it out, roughly, from their taxes—except she does the taxes and he doesn't examine them. Or he could look at a statement. Or he could simply ask her, after more than twenty-five years of marriage, about their nest egg.

It's not that she doesn't want him to know. In fact, she wonders why he doesn't find out about the money. It comes out in arguments, when she says in exasperation, *You don't even know how much money I have in the bank!*

Like with the finances of his neighbors and friends, he speculates. He can roughly piece it together. He has a guesstimate.

I would have thought that as one gets older, the money taboo would fade. I thought that with maturity would come, well, maturity: that we would only grow more self-confident, that we would have a lower tolerance for bull, and that at last money would lose its grip on our psyche.

But not so. In fact, the taboo gets stronger.

Let's note first that money as a basis of comparison and a measure of self-worth is generally more important to men than to women, according to psychologists and financial advisers. So we'll address what is basically the male mentality.

Here's what is at work: We expect that once we're all grown up and have a career behind us, we'll finally be settled, financially and emotionally. The crossing-over point seems to be around age fifty. That's when the gentlemen start to come into the role of patriarch. Their parents are fading, and they're next in line to be in charge. They're not the kids anymore, and if they still need help, they're going to have to figure it out themselves. Scary.

The last thing anybody wants to face down is that they're not ready to be in charge, that they're financially unprepared, that they're not where they think they should be, and time is running out. Once you've reached full maturity, drawing that line at around fifty, having financial stress is personally and socially unacceptable. It feels shameful.

So the clam tightens.

Sociologist Erving Goffman noted that "embarrassment has to do with unfulfilled expectations." He was talking about personal encounters, but that's also true in a general social context. We become, consciously or subconsciously, skilled at deception. "Whatever his position in society," Goffman wrote, "the person insulates himself by blindness, half-truths, illusions and rationalizations." That pretty much covers what's going on at this stage with a large swath of the boomers. Because they are not financially secure, they feel threatened. They're anxious, and they're hiding it.

Hiding the anxiety only makes it worse, for the individual and for everyone else. The more we suffer alone, the more we suffer. "Anxiety is not obvious in the way depression is obvious," says psychologist Scott Wetzler. "It's more of a personal, internal experience. You can hide it, and most people *do*. Don't let that fool you into thinking others aren't also anxious."

That's what we do, though. We go by appearances: *Others seem to be doing fine, so they must be doing fine.* We, by comparison, then become self-diagnosed failures. "In this age of soaring expectations, life is inevitably full of personal failures," writes psychologist Martin Seligman. He is trying to explain why the baby boomers, even nearly twenty years ago, had higher rates of depression than any other age group. Although one might guess that the highest rate of suicide is among young people, actually the highest rate is among those age sixty-five and older. With their history of depression combined with real or perceived financial woes, the boomers, as they get old, seem poised to have an even bigger problem with that than others have had.

The better you feel you should have done, the more difficult the letdown. If you're a college graduate headed for your twenty-fifth reunion, the expectations are high. They're high at every reunion, but the twenty-fifth, after a goodly chunk of your career, marks a special point of dead reckoning: where are you expected to be versus where have you gotten. That's what the college-educated boomers are in the midst of right now: attending, or avoiding, their twenty-fifth reunions.

One response for self-defined underperformers is simply not to show up. As writer Daphne Merkin puts it, "The problem with college reunions—I know this without having attended any—is that they leave room for too much soul-scorching realism . . . When it comes to one's peers it's not hard to find oneself at either pole of envy or smugness." The first thing to realize about reunion gatherings is this: Those most susceptible to envy are more likely to stay home, while the smug can't wait to get there. It's Class Notes on cocktails.

Take the example of one of the toughest crowds out there: the twenty-fifth reunion of the Harvard Class of 1977. "There's the usual Harvardian raft of venture capitalists, retired boy wonder tech starter-uppers, chiefs of surgery and lawyers of every stripe," class member Bo Emerson, a journalist, describes it. According to a class survey, the median income for the men was $200,000. (Bill Gates would have pushed it up a notch—and exploded the average—but he dropped out before graduation.) "Everyone at the reunion had some anxiety and trepidation, and most of us had some sleepless nights over it," says psychologist Scott Wetzler, himself a member of the class. He led a group discussion at the reunion on "Aspirations, Then and Now." Once the discussion got rolling, classmates talked about how they had disappointed themselves, with a common complaint being that they hadn't made enough money. It didn't matter how well they had actually done—some had made millions and still felt let down; it was all about comparisons to others, and about what they expected of themselves. But they also realize it's not okay to discuss these hangups. "We'll never complain about this out loud, out in the real world," Emerson says. "It's like complaining about the lack of well-trained butlers. Nobody wants to know about the painful expectations weighing on overprivileged Harvard grads."

Except maybe we do want to know about it, because the rest of us, while we assume at least the Harvard gang must be doing fine, are also wrestling with living up to expectations. Getting through life has become as big a head game as getting through the night.

Payday is coming. And not in a good way.

The boomer fantasy—that anything is possible, that money is something tangential—for Tucker is pretty much gone. "Money is the thing that colors everything. It's the underlying reality of everything," he says. "I'd rather think about other things, but it's something that's not going to take care of itself."

For him that means forgetting a green vista of retirement. Possibly forgetting retirement altogether. Certainly forgetting what some others his age are starting to talk about: winding down, stopping the daily grind, maybe retreating to a second home half of the year.

"I can't even think in those terms," Tucker says. "I'm still trying to figure out what I'm doing next. There are realities that are now hitting home. I never lived my life for a pension—so I have to deal with that now."

He is facing the reality that after age fifty there are more working years behind him than ahead. Tucker sits down every day to work and asks himself consciously, *Is this how I should be spending my time?*

Every minute now has become precious. Tucker has had to let go of a key notion his generation was raised with: the sense of limitlessness. The feelings that he could do *this*, or *that*, or *write that novel!* have been replaced with cold assessments about what is really possible, and how deep the sacrifices can go.

At this age, Tucker feels the tug of three generations at once. He has himself and his wife to think about, and their security and comfort as they approach retirement age. That's why he went to work for a regular paycheck when they were first married, and that's why he's still taking on assignments in his midfifties.

He still worries if his three children, who are still students, will have everything they need. "It's an issue," he says. "What if they try to live like me? I don't have anything to help out and make their lives easier."

And there are his parents. They're in their mideighties now and getting frail. They haven't planned for the expense of long-term care, should they need it. "It's not a pretty thing," Tucker says. "I can't help them. It's going to be rough. I've got my fingers crossed." Depending on what happens and what the expenses are, Tucker has thought about having to dive back into the proper working world. After all this time of somehow juggling to make his life work, he could end up in a job he doesn't want so that he can support his parents. "We have to come to grips with the practical realities," he says of the boomers. "The only way around it is to have *serious* money. That's something I never expected, and others didn't either."

As with many of the baby boomers, Tucker's major asset is his house. He and his wife could live off the money from selling it—assuming the real estate market holds until they would sell it, which is a risky assumption—but they would have to downsize and live in a far less expensive area. Preferably someplace that provides health-care beyond Medicare. Tucker has visited these places, he has heard about their advantages: incentives for retirees, tax-free zones, discounted medical care, and cheap property, with views. Others like him have already gone: to Mexico, Costa Rica, Panama, Belize. These places have marketed to American retirees. With a sort of Statue-of-Liberty style pitch, they say, *Come* here, *even with a modest income. You'll live well, we'll take care of you. We want you.*

It could be a final tradeoff: leave the country altogether and move to Central or South America.

"Is it time to cash out and do things differently?" Tucker wonders. "I'm thinking hard about cutting and running."

CHAPTER SIX

～

Behind the Hedges

When I told my sister I was going to Palm Beach for an interview, she advised me to drive around the nice neighborhood by the ocean.

"That's where the gorgeous homes are," she told me, then added with disappointment, "not that you can see much, since they all have high hedges."

I didn't tell her that I expected to see plenty, that my interview was going to be *behind* the hedges.

I was, to be honest, slightly nervous. When I had arranged the interview with an assistant, I had been invited to stay. I wasn't sure what to expect. Would I be dealing with staff? Would my sources appear for the interview and then disappear for the rest of the day? What would I do the rest of the time? Or were they just like any family? Maybe we would curl up in the family room and watch a video after dinner?

My flight was delayed and I had to call the residence to tell them. I thought about calling the assistant instead—they seemed to like everything filtered through the assistant—but then thought, *That's silly. Just call.* The wife, Middy, answered the phone herself, even though it took me a while to realize it was her. She thanked me profusely for letting her know about the delayed flight and said she would be picking me up herself. She described her car for me: a blue *something*. Oh no, I thought, I'm terrible at recognizing cars. Since we live in New York City, I drive once or twice a year at most and my sisters laugh at me when I describe a rental car as "um, an SUV?"

"What kind of car is it again?" I asked Middy, hoping to understand the general shape of the thing.

"A big blue convertible."

Ah-ha! Now she was speaking my language.

I recognized her, all right. No problem. As I gazed along a line of cars creeping along the airport's pickup lane, an enormous convertible came whipping over from the fast lane. I would have described it as some sort of supersized Mercedes—I didn't know they even made them that big. Middy had one hand loosely on the reins of the car and was vigorously waving the other one overhead, bursting with enthusiasm at the sight of a visitor, even though I was almost a complete stranger to her. Her little white dog was hopping around on her lap. I tossed my bag in the backseat and we sped off toward the ocean.

When the gates opened to their property, we drove in beneath the palms, took a turn, and Middy announced, "We'll drop you at your house first, so you can get settled."

"Wow," I said as we pulled up alongside gardens and a golf-green–clipped lawn, leading to a large villa. "This is beautiful!"

As we got out of the car, knowing I would be impressed with the property, Middy said outright, "You want to write about money? Now you can see money." The car, which she had to point out to me was a Bentley, was meant as an appetizer.

"Yeah," I said, "but you're supposed to be telling me about the downside."

She froze for a full second, then recovered her congeniality. "I'll tell you that too," she promised.

And she kept her word.

There's something about Middy. At baseline, she's a free spirit. She can kind of suck you in with her energy and openheartedness. She has a definite irreverence for formality or even convention. Even when she barely knows you, she's interested in you. She's a hugger and a toucher, much like her terrier, who can't tell the famous guests from the plebeians, and wouldn't care anyway, so leaps up to lick both in the face.

She's in her fifties and doesn't try to disguise a day of it. She wears her gray and white hair naturally, no fussing. She gets ready to go out in a few minutes, whether it's for a walk on the beach or a black-tie dinner. Her body is strong—not molded-by-a-personal-trainer strong, but morning yoga and lots-of-time-in-nature strong.

Middy is no actor. When you say something she thinks is incorrect or incomprehensible, she won't smile politely or just give a hint of disagreement. "What?!" she'll say suddenly, and furrow her brow, and you almost want to apologize right then rather than explain yourself.

Her husband explained, "She doesn't care who anyone is!" in a way that said that he himself does care, quite a bit, who's who. Yet he meant it, I think, with both some embarrassment and some pride. Once they were at an international party and she danced a lot with an older gentleman. After the event, Middy's husband asked what she'd thought of the prince.

Who? she asked him. *I didn't meet any prince.*

When she was told she'd been dancing with him half the night, she snuffed, *He's a prince? I just saw some old fart sitting there and thought he could use some dancing!*

When Middy and her husband were sitting around at the weekend residence of the American president, the president was excitedly explaining the painting that hung over the mantel and described how much it changed when one looked at it close up. He told Middy to go look more closely and see what he meant. To the distress of her husband, she didn't budge from her seat and flatly told the president, *No. I'm comfortable right here.*

At first it all seems to fit: When you're one of the wealthiest people on the planet, you don't have to impress anyone. *Of course you're carefree!* I thought. *What a feeling it would be to have all of that money, to be able to go anywhere you want to and do anything and meet anyone and have anything you desire.*

Except it's not like that. That became clear even after two days in Palm Beach. Despite our fantasies, money cannot change your life that much—it can't change who you are, and it certainly can't take away your problems.

Middy sometimes seems like a sunflower that sprouted up in the middle of a formal garden. And it's the sunflower that makes the cultivated roses look like they are the ones out of place. But then, when you know her better, you find out that it's a struggle for the sunflower, just like for the roses and for everyone else.

A year before she met her husband—I call him Citizen Q—Middy had prayed for his arrival. She was on a retreat with Native Americans. It was July, and she and her boyfriend—a monk with no worldly possessions except his frock—had come out west on a hiking trip and were taking part in the Sun Dance ceremony. The men in the group spend three days in a ritual circle, fasting, chanting, dancing and drumming. Staying outside the circle, the women support them with prayers.

Middy was supposed to distance herself from the rest of the community because she had her period. Native Americans think of the "moon cycle" as a time of reflection and renewal for a woman.

So she carried her tent—in that case it's called a "moon hut"—away from the main camp and set it up along the river where she could be alone with nature. Listening to the drumming in the distance, Middy stripped off her clothes and slipped into the river. She floated on her back and felt the warm air and the cold water, which cleared her mind. When she climbed out of the water, she sat on a soft patch of green moss along the edge of the river and, as the Natives had taught her, let the blood flow back into the earth. She felt completely serene and connected with the world. She looked up into the sky, and at that moment she made some decisions, and some requests.

First, she'd had it with the monk. She had thought that money and material comforts made no difference to her. She had grown up in a well-off family, but money had been used to manipulate: Gifts were given with conditions or sometimes retracted, promises were made and often broken, she was alternately spoiled and denied. So sometimes she had money, sometimes she didn't, and she trained herself not to care, not to desire a material lifestyle. She didn't depend on it for her happiness. Middy is generous and a caretaker by nature, but on the moss she realized she didn't want always to be the one to support everyone else. It was tough enough being a single mother and responsible for making all of the decisions about her daughter's upbringing—she didn't want to be financially responsible for another adult too.

She was ready, she decided, for another man to come into her life. She wanted to find a partner, in all senses. And she asked, quite specifically, for him: *Let it be somebody who accepts me for who I am. Somebody older. And let it be somebody with money.*

After the hiking trip, Middy broke up with the monk and waited for her accepting, older man of means. Months passed. In the meantime, she kept busy with her work.

One day the next summer, someone handed Middy a tape at

work and asked her to play it. When she put it on, to her surprise she was surrounded by a familiar sound: Native American drumming. Her mind went straight back to the moments by the river out west the previous summer. *Ah-ha*, she thought with a smile.

Native Americans believe that prayers are answered one year later. She had recently met someone, and now she realized he was the one she had wished for.

She had to laugh, as she hiked through woods one afternoon thinking about her good fortune. All of her requests had been granted. The man she started dating was sensitive and accepting of her, just as she had wanted. He was indeed more mature. And as for the money . . .

I never meant to ask for someone with that *much money!* Middy told the trees as she hiked. *I just wanted someone with an income, maybe $100,000 a year. You can live quite well on that.*

Citizen Q was high on the list of the wealthiest people in the country. A billionaire.

At first it was pretty neat, of course. Middy and her daughter flew to New York City for the daughter's birthday, and Citizen Q had them over to his Fifth Avenue apartment for dinner. When they were driven back to their hotel in a limousine, they giggled at the fun of it.

For a change, rather than her always taking care of everyone else, someone was taking care of Middy. Citizen Q was an old-fashioned suitor who gave little gifts and called her every day. When she went to his farmhouse for dinner dates, she was wowed by the romance of a table brimming with fresh flowers and glowing with candlelight.

And yet, something was just slightly amiss. The romantic dinners for two were a little . . . crowded. As they talked and ate, the dining-room door flip-flapped, and other faces kept appearing. Their conversations wound into many different ears.

Citizen Q was used to it, and it didn't bother him at all that as they leaned in to each other, someone else was there filling their water glasses. Some of the time Middy thought it was a treat to be waited on. Other times, she couldn't wait to escape to the garden so they could walk hand in hand and sit together on a bench with some privacy.

One solution, a way to get away from the formal staff for an evening, was for Middy to have Citizen Q over to her place for dinner. It was more cozy there, and she would cook for him.

On the first attempt, Citizen Q came rolling up to the house in an unusual, brushed-metal sports car. When Middy came out to greet him, however, she saw that he hadn't come alone. He wasn't driving the sports car but riding in it. Middy tried to ignore this anomaly.

On the second such date, Citizen Q was chauffeured to her door on the wrong side of a sleek black Corvette. He was trying to show off his fleet of exotic cars, but she wasn't impressed. This time Middy told him how silly it was. The next time he came over, he managed to pilot a Land Rover on his own.

Just as she was more comfortable hosting him in her own quarters, he was more comfortable being waited on by hired help. He didn't want Middy to have to trouble herself with tasks like cooking. He had worked very hard amassing his fortune, and he enjoyed being able to delegate. He wanted to give that to Middy too, for her to be waited on in style.

They were back at his house for dinner. Middy wanted to make him as comfortable as he was trying to make her. But then . . .

Ding-ding! ding-ding!

Citizen Q was calling the help by ringing his little silver bell. Middy found it ridiculous.

You live like a king! she announced to him. *This is like royalty!*

She meant it as an observation more than a criticism, but to her surprise he took great offense.

What do you mean?! he erupted. *I do not!*

Citizen Q might have been as rich as a king, but he didn't think of himself that way. Perhaps because a few other people in the world really do live in palaces with official entourages. It's not about where we are but how we see ourselves.

Let's try to figure out the specifics of wealth. How much is enough? How much is "rich"?

The pitfall: The second you set out striving to get to a number and thinking that much will bring security and contentment, you've just put yourself in orbit to nowheresville. There's no there there. It's like trying to get to a parking spot at the horizon.

When I was in journalism school I talked to an alum who had written a lot of freelance articles for what was my favorite newspaper. He told me he wasn't writing for them much anymore, though, despite the prestige of the publication, because they didn't pay well enough. When I asked how much they paid, he said around $250.

Two hundred and fifty dollars?! I thought to myself. *Great!*

Before grad school I had been writing articles for a free weekly newspaper for $35 (and bartending on the side). So $250—half a month's rent at the time—seemed generous. You know what's coming, though. Soon I was writing articles for $400, $750, and then over $1,000, and I, too, had to cut back on my favorite publication because I felt I couldn't afford it anymore.

Did I just need to earn enough to live on? Yes and no. How much do any of us really need to live on? That's the Great Moving Target.

When I was at dinner with Middy and Citizen Q, he was talking about the high cost of living in New York City—a topic I am intimately familiar with. Except his version of you-can't-scrape-by-even-on-this-amount was quite different than mine.

"Apartments are so expensive. School tuition, child care, parking . . . even the groceries cost a lot," he lamented while I nodded in agreement. Then he announced, "Even on $500,000 a year, you're nowhere." I stopped midnod.

Nowhere?

The fact is, there are 8 million people living in New York City. Of those, an estimated 30,000 make more than $500,000. The rest of us, I'd say, are not *nowhere*, but right here.

But okay, we're off to the races with The Number.

For many years, the common notion of big-time income success was breaking six figures: $100,000. The *New York Times* recently ran an article formally announcing that $100,000 didn't mean much anymore, and that $200,000 is the new $100,000.

Yet, even going back to the late 1980s, the same newspaper trumpeted that "investment bankers under 30 with staggering $600,000-a-year incomes are not rich and may never be." That was two decades ago, which means that, at least in the bubble of New York, we're at a $1 million income threshold to be, as Citizen Q might put it, somewhere. A recent magazine cover story confirmed that figure (it's unclear with what degree of sarcasm) as the minimum needed for living well these days.

I interviewed the young owner of an advertising business once who thought he hadn't been making nearly enough money. His business was grossing $2 million with few employees and was very profitable, so much of that money was going into his pocket. The trouble, as he put it, was that his friends whom he met through the Young Entrepreneurs Organization were already buying summer houses and taking Fridays off. Even though he made an extraordinary amount of money compared to the vast majority of people, in the small subset of peers he compared himself to, he wasn't keeping up. At best, he was irked. At worst, he felt like a failure.

Maybe assets are what matter, not how much you make but how much you have in the storehouse. Not long ago, $1 million was viewed as more money than one could possibly need over a lifetime. Does $1 million now make a person wealthy, let alone set for life? It should, since only about 1 in 100 Americans ever accumulates that kind of money. We live on misperceptions, however. Ask those who do have $1 million just how much it is, and for many it doesn't seem like a whole lot, either because they're planning to get much more, or because they've settled on a lifestyle that even $1 million in assets cannot support.

Who's really wealthy, then? Who's not worrying? Who has *arrived*? The figure of $10 million has been floated in recent years as a solid target. Owning $10 million in assets (*liquid* assets) will get you into the private banking category at some banks and brokerage houses. It will not, however, mean you are entitled to their top-tier service. There are still plenty of wealthier people above you. The ultrahigh net worth categories start at $20 million or even $100 million.

One hundred million dollars. Enough? Not enough to get on the *Forbes* 400 list of wealthiest Americans. You currently need $750 million to dangle from the lowest rung there. And don't you think, once you were in that club, that you would gun for the big time, for $1 billion? (I mean, not *you*, of course. You yourself would never think $750 million wasn't plenty. It's the other people with the problem. It's always the other people.) And for the about 300 billionaires in the country who have made it there, is *that* enough? *Forbes* ran an article accompanying the annual list titled "Billionaire Blues," which led off with the statement, "Contrary to the popular myth, if you suddenly woke up and found that you had inherited $1 billion, you could not simply live off the interest on your fortune." They were referring to the pressure to live like other billionaires do, which means having at least a couple of well-placed residences, a private jet, a "proper" art collection, and certainly a yacht, with a year-round crew. Even billionaires must, after all, keep up with their Joneses.

The wealthy do still keep up with the Joneses. Oh yes. Like anyone, they are constantly confronted by people who have more. Not every one of them is materialistic and craves attention; as with the rest of the population, some are like that and some are not. For fun, let's look at the ones who are.

A story in the *Wall Street Journal* recently described turmoil in the world of yachts. Owning a yacht, and maintaining it and its staff all year round for the handful of times you'll actually use it, has for a number of years served as a status symbol that you're rich enough, for practical purposes, not to be counting your money anymore. The vessels can cost tens of millions of dollars to build and easily over $1 million a year to maintain. In that circle, a 100-foot yacht used to be quite impressive. A businessman who owns one that size said he used to consider it "a good-sized boat." Then a 130-footer pulled up next to him at a boat show in Florida, and his pride shriveled. Compared to the other boats, he complained, "Now it's like a dinghy."

You're not special now if your boat doesn't stretch a solid 200 feet. A few years ago, the CEO of Limited built a 315-footer that he named, optimistically, Limitless. It wasn't. Microsoft co-founder Paul Allen acquired a 354-footer. He then put in an order for what was to be the world's largest yacht, the *Octopus*, at 414 feet. At that time, the CEO of Oracle had his own craft under construction, named *Rising Sun*, that was initially to run 393 feet. As the *Octopus* stretched, however, so did *Rising Sun*. Measuring in at a final 452 feet, *Rising Sun* reigned as the world's biggest bath toy. For a moment. In the world's yacht battle, it's high noon again. In the spring of 2005 a prince in the United Arab Emirates floated a 525-footer.

Even at amounts of wealth that only the slimmest sliver of the world's population ever achieve, a pecking order emerges. Just as on any school playground, in any suburban neighborhood, comparisons are made. Inferiority is felt.

A journalist went on a mission in Manhattan to figure out who those people are who hang out in ritzy cafes on workday afternoons. At a chic cafe in SoHo, she talked to an expensively dressed twenty-four-year-old artist. He had dropped out of college after studying photography and now wasn't employed, to the chagrin of his family. He was spending the afternoon drinking multiple lemonades with two friends. Still, the young man professed, he isn't rich. Not like some people he knows. "Like the *Born Rich* movie," he said. "That's an entirely different ballgame. I'm the poorest kid of the rich kids."

What about the *Born Rich* kids, then? Those are the wealthy friends of Jamie Johnson whom he interviewed for his documentary about growing up with extreme wealth. Is it, indeed, a different game? Maybe their families do have more money, but the comparison and ranking continue. Although the sense of competition and keeping up is not discussed in the film, Johnson talks about it on the side, in interviews and in the director's commentary. He confesses that the day he was filming Donald Trump's daughter Ivanka in her girlhood bedroom on the 68th floor of Trump Tower, he was distracted by the view out the window, because he'd "never been to an apartment like that in New York until that day." Although to the unknowing eye, all of the characters in the film seem like they're in the same category—ultrawealthy—and their family fortunes are indeed among the biggest in the world, Johnson makes it clear that there are, to them, noticeable differences.

In the 1940s, anthropologist Margaret Mead distinguished the "upper upper" class member in America as "someone whose only possible social movement is downward." Even in Johnson's league, there's still room for upward mobility. So by Mead's standard, Johnson isn't a member of the upper upper class, even though it sure seems like it to the rest of us.

Citizen Q and Middy's first outing as a couple was a high-society fundraiser at the Waldorf in New York. They got dressed in black tie and evening gown and were driven to the hotel. Going to society events was a big part of Citizen Q's life, and when they walked in, Middy saw why. People crowded around and fell over him. Lots of photos were taken.

Nobody recognized her, and Citizen Q didn't introduce her. She got brushed aside. It was the school lunchroom dynamic all over again. Middy, even though she has a genuinely amiable, outgoing personality, retreated to a corner of the room and sat there alone. It was the first of many such evenings when that would happen. Citizen Q would get swept up in a tide of guests and hosts, and Middy would drift off by herself. She even learned to bring a book with her. "Sitting in the corner isn't so bad," she says. "You observe."

What she observed was that the room was full of two hundred or more guests, but they weren't mingling. Everyone there was wealthy, or they wouldn't have been invited. But Middy saw the guests stratify right before her. What mattered was *how* wealthy you were, how important, how famous. A pecking order emerged within what was already a top layer of society's pecking order. Middy was an unknown. An outsider. "People never knew I had a wealthy background," she says. "There I was, this poor little rich girl."

As soon as they got into the car at the end of that first evening, Middy turned to Citizen Q with annoyance.

You should have gone alone! she told him.

He didn't know what she was talking about. He thought they had both had a grand time.

It certainly hadn't been her scene. She not only didn't fit in, she didn't want to. People did have a lot of reasons to like Citizen Q for himself—he's a fun and giving person—but there wasn't much excuse for the fawning over him, except that he was fabulously wealthy. She saw the black-tie world as an illusion. "The life goal is money, and you have money, so they come to you," Middy explains. "You're treated differently before they know who you are. They aren't at all interested in you."

When they got home from the event, Middy showed her repulsion for the world of illusion by bowing down to Citizen Q and saying, *You're god, you're god.*

They had some negotiating to do. For Citizen Q, the reward for having been so successful financially was to indulge in high style and luxury. He bought a string of Bentleys and gave one to Middy. She liked the comfort and ease of having wealth, and she appreciated things like being able to buy beautiful art. She enjoyed the access to the interesting people who congregate around the wealthy.

"Most people think this lifestyle is very desirable," she says. And yet that's part of the pressure of it—that it is *supposed* to be so desirable, so wonderful, but there is a side to it that can be confining and uncomfortable. When she was dating Citizen Q, a friend asked her earnestly, *How is it making love with a billionaire?* She had to report, *It's the same as with anyone else.* Then she commented later, "Isn't it funny how we imagine there's something different?"

There are, of course, differences in the trappings of life, if not the life functions themselves. Citizen Q ran the household like a business, and scores of people were on the payroll. Gardeners alone numbered in the dozens. There was always somebody hovering. Yes, they were doing their jobs and trying to please Citizen Q and Middy—but there was also the constant lack of privacy that had initially bothered Middy. And there was intrigue. They found out that one servant used to listen at the door to their conversations and had been writing everything down in a little black book. (They had to burn it.)

Middy wasn't in favor of large household staffs and multiple residences. She didn't find it necessary or comfortable, and she explained this to Q. Wouldn't one house and three or four people to help out be more than enough? At first he agreed, and the staff was trimmed back dramatically. But soon Citizen Q acquired one European residence for them, then another, then another. He couldn't do it, he told her. He loved luxury. This was how people with copious

amounts of wealth could live, this is how the rest of his class *did*
live—and he wanted to, too.

Citizen Q bought an extensive set of fine china from an auction
house. It arrived in crates, and as the butler was unpacking and
unwrapping the plates, he kept *ooh*-ing and *ahh*-ing over them,
telling Middy how impressive they were. When she didn't show
much interest in the stack of new dishes, he asked with some
incredulity, *Aren't you excited?*

No, she explained flatly. *I'm not excited. These are just dishes. I
wouldn't know anything more precious than a child and a relationship.*

Sometimes, over the years of being with Citizen Q, Middy felt like
she was losing her own identity. The fakeness of the society circles
still got to her. People so clearly treated her differently because she
was Mrs. Q. Sometimes when she was entertaining at their home,
guests who didn't know who she was wouldn't reciprocate any
interest in talking to her. Then she watched their embarrassed reac-
tions when they realized she was the hostess. To her it shouldn't
have mattered, but to them it did.

Then there was the yacht incident. Citizen Q owned a yacht that
rivaled the best of them. Specially built for him in Europe, it came
with its own crew and a large staff that, as Middy described it, just
like at home would take care of everything for you except going to
the bathroom (although, of course, they would run the bathwater).
On one vacation, Middy's young daughter brought along her closest
friend from school. The friend, Lucy, lived in a mobile home. The
couple and the girls flew in a private plane down to the Caribbean.
From the boat they scuba-dived, and on board they were cooked for
and waited on. One morning, Citizen Q announced irritably to
Middy, *Lucy can't come with us on the boat again.*

Why? Middy asked, not able to imagine why Q would say that,
as Lucy was a sweet girl and a great friend to Middy's daughter.

She's rude, Citizen Q explained with exasperation. *She never says "good morning" to me!*

Middy exploded. She banged her hand down hard on the table and yelled at Q. *Do you have any idea what it's like for her?* she asked him. *Do you have any idea how intimidating all of this is to her? How intimidating you are? What if, just once, the Great Mr. Q would go over to Lucy and say "good morning" to her?!*

He looked at her silently, then tears came to his eyes. One overflowed down his cheek.

I never thought about it like that, he said.

Perceptions and misperceptions are a big problem in the world of the wealthy. Having an abundance of money can cause as many problems as having little of it. It's easy for us to cluck at that notion: *Oh, like what?!* Yet that reaction is a big part of the problem. While we say we know that money doesn't bring happiness, not so deep down we still believe it does.

Why, after all, are we so fascinated by the wealthy? We watch guided tours of their houses on TV, gawk at photos of their designer dresses, read about what they ate at a restaurant only they and theirs could get into, and want to see the hotel suite they stayed in on vacation. We imagine ourselves, for a moment, in their lives. With so much money, with so many toys, so many options, so much attention and assistance, so much luxury and glamour, their lives must be so exciting, so comfortable, so . . . happy! And when we discover any fault, see them caught frowning, hear of an argument, read of their troubles of any kind, we don't have the same sympathy we would normally have for anyone else, anyone more like us. We eat it up. We *want* them to have problems, we want to scoff. After all, they're just being petty and childish, we think. Their problems aren't *real*, like ours. The rest of us are genuinely struggling here, whereas they bring their nonsense on themselves. Don't they? They have no right to complain.

The rich, those with millions of dollars, let's say, are on to this. They can guess how we think of them, and they know we're not going to understand how they can have genuine problems. They've very well picked up on the idea that if you've got lots of money to spend and are living in a big house with lots of very expensive accoutrements, your life must be *fabulous!* Just like VH1 says it is.

The message is so strong that the rich are to be envied, that the wealthy themselves start to believe the myth. They themselves believe that their lives really should be better because they have so much wealth. When, as a wealthy person, your life does not seem so fabulous—because it is true that money *doesn't* buy happiness—it's that much more confusing, disappointing, and lonely.

To whom do you turn, then? With whom can you come clean, when you're rich but unhappy? Not very many people.

In all classes, money has been shepherded into its own special chamber of preoccupation and mystery. The taboo against discussing money, and any troubles it sprouts, is especially strong within the upper class. Children who grow up in wealthy families often either hear nothing on the subject, or they are given stern instructions not to discuss it. Either scenario leads them to see money as a secret, and having lots of it as something bad, something shameful. The grown-up version is to treat money, and especially its effects, as an intensely private matter. Even painfully private.

There's a big disconnect there to contend with: Society says you should be very happy if you have a lot of money. So when you do have a lot of money and are still not happy, you along with everyone else can start to wonder why. But you don't want to reveal the problems you're inevitably having, despite being wealthy, because then you'll feel the sting of criticism. You end up feeling pressured to live up to the societal expectations. Jessie O'Neill, granddaughter of a president of General Motors who inherited a fortune in her twenties, said, "Let's face it, we are seldom all that we appear to be, and the more glittering and attractive the external package, the greater the inner sense of dishonesty a person might feel for not living up to a larger-than-life image."

The wealthy are often even prevented from getting professional help from a therapist or an adviser. The first reason is a concern that nobody will sympathize. Therapists, even though they're trained to be professional, are still human, and most of them are not multimillionaires, which puts wealthy patients in the uncomfortable position of discussing money problems with someone who has much less than they do. And they're right that thoughts of ridicule do sometimes go through a therapist's mind. A therapist in Manhattan had a man come in depressed over losing $34 million in the stock market. He was in despair because he was poor now, he told the therapist. She got right down to work with him. Then it came out that he wasn't exactly *poor*, that he still had *some* money left, he said.

How much? the therapist asked him outright.

After some reluctance, he told her: *Fifteen million.*

When the therapist told me this story, she paused after the revelation of the $15 million and raised her eyebrows in silence. Her message was clear.

Another woman explained to the therapist that she could not afford to pay the full fee. Sympathetic, the therapist accepted a reduced rate, and their sessions went on for several months. Then one day the woman revealed that her income was $400,000. It wasn't that she couldn't afford the therapist's bill, she just felt like she didn't have enough. At times like that it becomes clear to both patient and therapist that they have different perspectives on the world.

A handful of super-wealthy people have themselves become therapists and set up practices designed specifically for clients like themselves. They start off with a personal understanding of the dynamics of wealth and can therefore set their patients more at ease from the beginning. The patients know they are less likely to be judged and more likely to find some sympathy when they are dealing with someone from their world. Because of the strong demand, some of these therapists have developed a booming niche business.

The second reason that members of the upper class can be reluctant to seek counseling is concern for privacy. Many of us are not comfortable with the idea of a stranger hearing our deepest problems and secrets, and that feeling is compounded when the therapist is likely to recognize your name and "who you are" when you come from a very wealthy family.

When Middy became increasingly confounded by her relationship with Citizen Q—they even bickered about money, like most couples—she tried to solve the problems by herself for maybe too long. On a couple of occasions she "left him" by packing her books and moving out—to the guest house. ("I realized I didn't have to move *out* to move out!" she says with some glee.) Friends eventually told her she should get help from a therapist. But the usual question arose: *Who?* She knew the therapists in town, did she want them hearing about their personal issues? And what would Citizen Q think of that?

The less that is revealed, the more dizzying the vicious circle of myth and secrecy about wealth becomes. The following poem is a powerful reminder that much goes on behind the scenes, even in the lives of those we envy, and that things are never as they seem:

Richard Cory

Whenever Richard Cory went down town,
We people on the pavement looked at him:
He was a gentleman from sole to crown,
Clean favored, and imperially slim.

He was always quietly arrayed,
And he was always human when he talked;
But still he fluttered pulses when he said,
"Good Morning," and he glittered when he walked.

And he was rich—yes, richer than a king—
And admirably schooled in every grace:
In fine, we thought that he was everything
To make us wish that we were in his place.

So on we worked, and waited for the light,
And went without the meat, and cursed the bread;
And Richard Cory, one calm summer night,
Went home and put a bullet through his head.

—Edwin A. Robinson (1869–1935)

In an anthology of best poems, the editors included this eerie footnote: "You can probably read an obituary for a Richard Cory in a local newspaper within the next twelve-month." In fact the poem, which later inspired the Simon and Garfunkel song of the same name, was derived from a newspaper story about a society man who committed suicide.

To my surprise, a couple of people I've shown the poem to said they didn't get it. *Why did the guy kill himself?* they asked. *What did I miss?*

That's exactly the point. How much we miss, and that we don't know what is really going on. Many readers of this poem are like the people on the pavement, seeing rich man Richard and maybe even feeling the envy. As the Simon and Garfunkel version goes, "He had everything a man could want: power, grace, style." What went wrong was that *we* were wrong. Richard was more miserable than any of us, yet all we saw were the "good things" in his life, and we wanted to be him without understanding him.

A wealthy woman, while growing up on the West Coast, watched the Richard Cory scenario unfold in her own life. Her father founded what is today an enormous corporation, and she and her siblings were raised amid great wealth, in what she calls "a beautiful, sheltered neighborhood." Even with the outward advantage of money, she had difficulty settling into a career, and she rushed into

149

marriages that failed. Some among her peers were having an even harder time. One fatally overdosed on drugs. Another shot himself. By the time the woman was in her midthirties, there had been five suicides in that "sheltered" neighborhood. She realized, at last, that she hadn't been the only one struggling with such privilege. She went back to school for a degree in social work and started a psychotherapy practice centered on helping inheritors work through the emotional issues that, she says, are "kept under greater societal lock and key than in other populations."

One issue that Middy and Citizen Q wrestled with was how much to indulge their children. A self-made man, Citizen Q was eager for the children to make their own way in the world, just as he had. *I don't want them to get a free ride*, he would tell Middy. The problem was that not everyone else in their position was thinking that way. Some of the Joneses took delight in indulging their own children. Then the adult children of different families ended up comparing themselves: Who had more help? Who was living more luxuriously?

One of their children in particular, Katie, as a young adult had an issue with how much support she was receiving from her family. Her friend's parents had given her friend a house: How come Katie wasn't given a house too? She watched Citizen Q giving millions away to nonprofits, and she accused him of taking care of everyone else before he took care of his own children. "There's a societal expectation," Middy says. "You can give your kids cars and a house, et cetera, and it's done by some, so there's an expectation for you to do it too."

Eventually they gave in and gave Katie a property. She sold it. Then she asked them for more money. They gave her another property. The more they gave her, the more kept . . . *disappearing*.

"We knew something was going on," Middy says.

They figured out what it was when one of their younger children came back from one of Katie's parties and talked about the guests having white powder on their noses.

Then it was time for sure to call in professional help. But again the important question was, *Who?* Normally they would rely on their financial adviser or lawyer for advice on how to handle money matters. But that wasn't personal enough for this kind of issue. They needed, as my husband and I had needed, someone knowledgeable about money issues who was also part psychologist, part confessor, and part fixer. Just as I had done when I had been bewildered, Middy turned to the Internet in search of some sort of money doctor.

She had better luck finding one than I had. Working with the superwealthy is a closet niche but a profitable one. So Middy was able to tap into the small, semi-underground group of experts trained to handle the touchy issues that surround having lots of money.

Some of the problems could be solved outside of the money doctors' offices if the wealthy were talking with one another. The taboo is real, though, so just like the rest of us, wealthy people too often wrestle with thinking it's only them. "There is generally great family pressure in the upper class to maintain that external appearance of perfection, never admitting that there is a problem in paradise," writes Jessie O'Neill in her book *The Golden Ghetto: The Psychology of Affluence.*

One issue that lurks—on a more basic level than problems like substance addiction, which we do hear something about—is guilt over good fortune. Despite what the rest of us think it would be like to have enormous wealth, it comes with carryons—too many for the overhead bin. Wealth guilt can strike anyone who realizes they are more fortunate than most people and can't quite account for why. That means it's a special concern for those who didn't make their money on their own but rather inherited it. Just as those who endure misfortune wonder what they have done to deserve their lot, so too do those who have come into good fortune wonder the same thing. For them, the *Why me?* question can be especially perplexing. If we had to have one problem or the other, most of us would choose to do our wondering in luxurious surroundings. If wealth were weighing on our conscience, we figure we would just give some of our money away to prove ourselves worthy of the stewardship. However, that doesn't always lift the burden of guilt.

Psychologists have identified the discomfort we feel when we have much more or less than someone else and can't figure out why. They refer to it as equity theory. It means we value fairness and believe we should pretty much get what we deserve and deserve what we get, in comparison to others. We're upset if we perceive someone else is getting more than their share, but *we can also get upset if we perceive that we ourselves are getting more than we deserve.*

There was an experiment done in which a simulated company hired three sets of male secretaries for two weeks. One group was told they were getting paid more than the others, the second group was told they were getting paid less, and the third group was told that everyone was earning the same pay. In actuality, all of the workers were paid the same. However, the overpaid workers ended up being more productive and the underpaid workers were less productive. The workers naturally tried to even the score by living up to their wages. Most interesting, however, is that both the overpaid and the underpaid groups reported being less satisfied with their jobs than the group of workers who thought everyone was being paid the same.

The reason inheritors struggle with the unfairness issue more often than self-made millionaires is that the self-made people have an explanation for their good fortune: They earned it. The inheritors, on the other hand, were just born into it. Just as any of us can look at a wealthier person and think to ourselves, or have a gut reaction, that *that's not fair, something is not right here*, the person we're looking at can have a similar reaction. They sometimes *also* have the thought that *something is not right here*.

Fueling that notion are certain passages from the Bible that are often misconstrued to come across as a message that wealth is wrong. Ever hear that "money is the root of all evil"? The Scripture actually reads that "the love of money is a root of all kinds of evil" (1 Timothy 6:10). Big difference there. The same difference applies to the distinction between money and *mammon*, which one scholar defines as "money personified and deified." It's not having money that is against Jesus' teachings but rather the devotion to it, the worship of it.

What about it being "easier for a camel to pass through the eye of a needle, than for a rich man to enter the kingdom of God" (Matthew 19:24; Luke 18:25)? That's surely not a favorite biblical quotation for a lot of wealthy Christians. But again, it has been truncated so that its true meaning is often lost: Jesus added that "with God all things are possible."

In the parable that contains the camel and the eye of the needle passage, Jesus was talking to a wealthy man who was keeping the commandments and asked how he could do even better. When Jesus suggested he should sell all he owned and give it to the poor, the man couldn't bring himself to do it. "The man was a fool because he was a self-centered materialist who had forgotten God; he was not a fool because he had been a successful businessman," explains theology professor Ronald Nash. "Claims that the Bible condemns wealth or that God hates all the rich are clearly incompatible with the teachings of Jesus, who saw nothing inherently evil in money, wealth, or private ownership. While Jesus certainly condemned materialism and the compulsive quest for wealth, He never condemned wealth per se." In fact the Bible encourages both the creation and enjoyment of wealth.

Even though it would seem that being wealthy would make one feel very secure, many end up battling insecurity. Again, this is mostly an issue for inheritors versus those who are self-made. The self-made are generally not worried about losing their fortunes because they figure they did it once, they can do it all again. Inheritors, though, are unlikely to experience another windfall, and they often feel incapable of amassing wealth on their own. One inheritor summed up this mistaken philosophy of scarcity by saying "There's only so much, and when it's gone, it's gone." Another inheritor, who became a social worker in Massachusetts, pointed out, "Welfare people and inheritors have a lot in common. They both know they can't survive on their own."

Something else the wealthy wrestle with: Do people love me for *me*? It's what Middy encountered, being treated differently with extreme wealth on her side, and it made her feel distrustful of new "friends." She tells her friends who've known her a long time, *I'm so glad I knew you before I had money!* When one grows up with wealth, there can be little escaping its influence. People recognize your name, they know "who your family is," and under those circumstances the world works a little differently, which isn't always welcome. "It is not uncommon for a young inheritor to develop an intense desire to find out what life would be like without recognition as a 'rich person,'" writes Thayer Willis, an inheritor and therapist, in her book about coping with wealth's pitfalls.

Some inheritors go to great lengths to get away from the pressures of the upper class. Specifically, Willis describes a minimigration of the children of prominent East Coast families to the more relaxed Northwest, where they can live "normally." There, people don't know their names, and in some cases the inheritors change their names. They get jobs they know they got on their own merit, and they build a social circle of people who only know them for *them.* "No doubt it's scary, but it can also be thrilling to leave a world of security and privilege to enter a life of anonymity and challenge, where everything you receive is *earned* by you, not simply placed in your lap," Willis says. "There are two sides, you see, to a life of privilege."

In parts of the Northwest, to generalize, keeping up with the Joneses hinges more on who can live further *beneath* their means. Just as some people in more materialistic communities of the country are stretching beyond their means to keep up appearances of affluence, some people living in the Northwest who really *are* very wealthy are "slumming it," obscuring their money and striving to be on the same (lower) level as those around them. A friend of mine in Oregon was dating a guy for a while; they both worked for a living, and nothing seemed at all out of the ordinary. Then as they got more serious, he revealed he was sitting on a fortune. Again, things are not as they seem, and figuring out who people really are and what their lives are like becomes an expedition to the center of the onion.

M iddy didn't stop working after she married Citizen Q. To be productive and to continue helping people was important to her, regardless of the income from it. "Even though I was making $30 an hour and he could make $30 million in a day," she says, "I thought it was the same impact."

Not that everyone without any need for earned income feels the same way. Middy was called to work with a client once, and when they came face-to-face, they recognized each other as fellow billionairesses. Middy went straight to work, but her peer was uncomfortable.

What are you doing here? the other billionairess asked, almost testily. *You don't need to work, why are you working?!*

Middy explained that she loved her work, so why give it up? In response, she got a lecture from the client, who was increasingly distraught.

I'll still do some work now and then, the billionairess client said, *but never for money!*

155

Middy was steadfast. She would do things her own way.

At the end of their session together, the client was still disconcerted over doing business with Middy.

Normally I would tip you, of course, she said. *But I know who you are . . .*

Middy herself wasn't troubled by the situation.

That's okay, she said. *You can go ahead and give me a tip.*

She didn't get one.

Despite the emphasis Americans put on work, our culture has a well-established fantasy of not having to work. The first thing that comes to mind when somebody hits the lottery, maybe after *shopping spree*, is *I don't have to work anymore*.

Yet a lot of lottery winners not only still work, but work at the same job they had before. A friend of mine had to call road service one night and got to talking with the serviceman who came out. He and his wife, a schoolteacher, had won the lottery. They quit their jobs, hung out for a while . . . and then decided they wanted their old lives back. She went back to teaching school, he went back to road service. There are lots of stories like that among lottery winners. Sudden wealth is just not what we think it's going to be.

What those people have discovered is that, despite what most of us might think, we don't work primarily for money. Yes, we usually do need the income (and feel like we need a little more than we're getting), but we probably need an occupation itself more than the paycheck. Raising children, for instance, although unpaid, is considered a legitimate occupation; but someone else who stays at home and inexplicably never works tends to raise suspicions. In some other cultures it is considered rude to ask a stranger "What do you do?" and it's not standard to have one's job be in the leading line in obituaries. Americans are conditioned—maybe from the Puritan work ethic and the fact that the country was built on individual enterprise rather than inherited fortunes—to value hard work, and then to reward ourselves for being productive. We don't enjoy the playtime unless we feel we've first earned it. That causes specific problems for those who have inherited or otherwise come into enough money not to have to work.

The first problem is identification. The question "What do you do?" is dreaded by people who don't have to *do* much of anything, not for money. A magazine for inheritors devoted an issue to work—or not working—and included a list of ways inheritors could answer the inevitable question:

Lie: (In the heat of summer) "I'm a ski instructor." (In January) "I'm a roofer."

Fudge: "I got some money from my family, and I'm taking time off to write children's books." (They don't need to know it's $2 million or that your "time off" has been five years and you've never been published.)

Tell a partial truth: "I coordinate volunteers at the shelter." So what if it's unpaid and only five hours a week?

The independently wealthy can feel the same embarrassment and social dismay that the unintentionally unemployed do when having to reveal that they are not working. On the one hand we fantasize about not having to work, but when it comes down to it, work is prized.

Some of us can get a taste of how some inheritors feel by noticing what happens when we are on vacation or during other downtimes. We think it'll be so great to laze around, and it is for a few days or weeks. Then we often get itchy. We need to *do* something, other than relax or indulge in hobbies. We have a natural urge to be productive, and to function as part of the great societal machine. Retirees often have this same problem: After years of making an important contribution, when they stop working they feel useless.

Since moving here from the Mediterranean, my husband has often lamented, "People here don't know how to relax." When Americans stop for too long, we fear the onset of sloth. How we triumph over it is by working and achieving. And we most often measure our success and achievement by how much money we have earned from our efforts.

Inheritors have a lot of money, so, by American logic, they must have achieved a lot, right? There's the problem. They haven't done diddly for their money, and they know it. They've gotten the reward without having done the work. And yet there is pressure to go about building a career like everyone else. Not to take advantage of the "land of opportunity" in America starts to feel shameful. Here it's about working your way up, and if you're no longer doing that—even if it's because you're a product of one or more generations who *did* work their way up and amassed a fortune doing it—your status is slipping.

Yet when you don't have an economic incentive to develop a career, another hurdle arises: lack of motivation. Most of us prepare for and pursue a life of work because we know we need to support ourselves. When you start out with enough money to live on comfortably, where does the drive come from to work hard at a job? Not that being an inheritor means one is lazy, but lack of motivation and persistence in developing a meaningful and productive career—something most of us take pride in—is a common problem for those who don't need the money. In her book, Thayer Willis describes an inheritor in his late thirties who hadn't been able to launch a career, even though he said he really wanted one: "He realized with a heavy heart that he could only admire—yes, he went through a period of envy—the motivation for earning money that drives most people and which they take entirely for granted. Great careers, he came to understand, have been built on the foundation of necessary income."

As anthropologist Margaret Mead said, "Those American families which settle back to maintain a position of having reached the top in most cases molder there for lack of occupation, ladder-climbers gone stale from sitting too long on the top step."

At the same time, those inheritors who are industrious and set out to build a career can find themselves paralyzed by an over-whelming array of options. In *Born Rich*, Jamie Johnson tries to figure out what to do with his life and asks his father, a recreational painter, for advice. The father, himself an inheritor who never pursued a paying career, seems baffled by his son's question and suggests maybe he could become a collector of documents and such. "Certainly nobody my age would consider collecting maps and documents as a realistic career," the young man says in his commentary. Yet, to indulge his father's advice, Johnson finds an antique-map dealer and sits down with him to discuss the business. When Johnson asks the dealer outright for advice—what would *he* do if he didn't have to work?—the man breaks into incredulous laughter. "Then don't work!" he chortles. "Why would anybody work, if you don't have to?!"

Even a social psychology textbook, which goes on to explain the inherent rewards we get from being part of the working world, reinforces the belief that somebody with enough money to afford full-time leisure wouldn't bother working. It states, "Unless they are fortunate enough to be born with or to acquire vast wealth, most people spend a majority of their waking hours performing some type of job." *But those who are fortunate enough to have wealth*, it is saying, *do not have a job*.

As usual, we are being plagued by a "grass is always greener on the other side of the fence" scenario. While the rest of us glorify the luxury of not having to work, those in that position are mystified by the prospect of full-time leisure. Jessie O'Neill described how miserable her inheritance made her: "I didn't have to work. I didn't have to get up in the morning. I didn't have to do anything. For an average person, that sounds great, but it's only great for a couple of days. Then it's terrifying."

What many of us haven't realized is that the "pursuit of happiness," declared as our inalienable right by Thomas Jefferson and so cherished in our national psyche, is not about the happiness but about the pursuit. The happiness *is* the pursuit.

When I asked Middy how she responds to people who envy her position, she told me quickly, "And I envy my friend who can go off to an island on retreat."

I was confused.

"But you can do that too," I told her. "You can do anything you want to."

"No, I can't. Because I have a husband and I want to be with him, and I have a daughter and I want to spend time with her . . ."

And there are her clients and students whom she wants to be available to help, and at one point during our interviews she was wearing herself out taking a friend back and forth to see doctors. Again she is caretaking, trying to be there for everyone else. Moments that she captures for herself are to spend in nature, or in meditation.

Meditation, or "mindfulness," as a Western version of the practice is called, is something Middy fell in love with years ago. Mindfulness trains you to focus on the present moment with all that it brings to you—pleasure, pain, confusion, anger, bliss—and to accept that moment, and a string of those moments, without any struggle, to indulge them completely.

I took a class in this, so I understand one way in which the practice is so useful to Middy, and to the rest of us, regardless of our life circumstances: It is an equalizer. Meditation breaks you down to the level of a breathing body . . . a heartbeat . . . a combination of particles . . . and then just vibrating energy, a part of the crust and ether of the cosmos. In that state, money makes entirely no difference. Status makes no difference. Possibilities, what you can or can't do, anybody waiting on you or not paying any attention to you at all—none of it makes any meaningful difference. You're throbbing or you're not. (And of course we all are.) When you learn to get into that state, when you're regularly reducing yourself to nothing and everything all at once, you feel a whole new perspective on life and how we experience it. And all of the material surroundings and opportunities that money can buy become mere accessories.

"Life is full of tiny detail," Middy says with appreciation. She still gets as conflicted as the rest of us. She has her moods, and she sometimes becomes overwhelmed and even bottomlessly blue. No amount of wealth can take those conditions away, and sometimes it exacerbates them. But Middy is also at peace. Like when she was floating in the river out west the summer before she met Citizen Q, when the air was heavy and hot and the water was tingly and cold but the combination was somehow perfect: Life offers the pleasantries and the pains in different packages but somehow proportions them equally to each of us.

Middy has been through heart-deflating experiences—some things I haven't told you about—and still she is buoyant, accepting, whole. And not at all because of living in gorgeous properties or having lunch with famous people or driving one of the world's most expensive cars.

"Don't you feel that God has these little feet everywhere?" Middy asked me. "Even the meanest thing, or the most manipulative thing," she said. "It's all out there to give you support. Everyone is there to help you as you need."

CHAPTER SEVEN

❦

Conclusion

I wish I had known then what I know now. We could have avoided so much angst.

The preoccupation we have with money, and the security and comfort it represents to us, is pretty deeply ingrained, and still baffling. We don't have to pretend that money doesn't matter. It does, to a degree. It can, of course, provide some comfort, some opportunities, some entertainment, some mental and physical respite. We shouldn't be shunning it by any means, nor giving up our striving for more material success, as long as we take pleasure being on that path.

What we need to do is tame money. We need to tame our preoccupation with what other people seem to have, and consciously to dull our fixation on how much better our lives would be if we had more. That is not easily accomplished, however, and I say that from my own experience. How easy it is to slip into feeling some vexation at what someone else has, a touch of greed for what we want for ourselves, and—the worst—the preoccupying belief that getting it will make us, finally, content. It won't.

You can tap into a way of thinking and managing your life that will change your mindset and put you in control of your well-being, no matter what is going on with your finances. Wisdom is out there that is enormously valuable—and right there for the plucking. When I learned about these tools, and started using them in my own life, I became less anxious, more comfortable, happier—all without my financial situation changing. Here's a taste of some of the strategies we can all use to feel better.

What Happened to Us

My recovery started rather strangely, with a book about how to run a marathon. My husband and I are not runners, but at some point in our funk period, my husband brought home a book called *The Non-Runner's Marathon Trainer.* He read the introduction and told me how the authors have taught a marathon class at the University of Northern Iowa, and they promise that anyone—whether they've ever jogged before or not—can complete a marathon by using their four-month training program. It was intriguing, but it sounded farfetched.

Written by a psychology professor and an exercise physiology professor, the book describes a study that they conducted on their students showing how the runners' moods improved over the course of the training and how they became "less tense, angry, depressed, confused and tired and more vigorous and energetic." In conclusion, "Such training seems to increase people's feelings of being in control of their own lives and, from a psychological point of view, we know that feeling that one can influence the events in one's life is part of being psychologically 'hardy' and being able to handle life's stresses and challenges."

I hadn't yet figured out that techniques from sports psychology could be applied to personal finance, but I knew that I had to do *something* that would put me in control of my own well-being. I started the training.

What's powerful about this program is that it trains the mind even more than the body. The average person, the authors explain, even with training, simply cannot access in their bodies the amount of fuel needed to go through the 26.2 miles of a marathon. Then they tell you, however, that you *will* get through it, not because of your body, but because of your mind. Your body can't do it, but your mind can. With the right mental tools and by shaping your mindset through practice, the body will do what the brain says it can. Pretty wild. And, I found out, *very* useful in everyday life.

Sports Psychology

Some of the ways runners and other athletes use psychological training can easily be used in life in general, specifically to conquer, on our own, anxiety over our financial situation.

An incredibly useful sports psychology technique taught through this marathon program is that we need to "create our own reality." That's the key to controlling our environment through our mindset. The idea is to take charge, to develop an "internal locus of control." It means deciding that things are not just happening to you without your having any say in them—you're making them happen.

Sometimes what you're controlling is your reaction to the situation. The marathon folks teach the technique of using the phrase "but it doesn't matter" after every negative thought or disappointment. As the authors suggest, I tried out this technique in other parts of life, at first for little things like when the line at the grocery store was taking forever (*But it doesn't matter!*), and then for more seemingly significant things, like the neighbors jetting to Tahoe for the weekend (*But it definitely doesn't matter!*). In this way, you start training and shaping your mindset so that you can start making life what you want it to be. You can concentrate more on action rather than wasting mental energy on constant reaction, such as the needless anxiety and sulking that come from concerning yourself with the Joneses.

Taking it one step further, the program teaches us to start acting "as if." In marathon terms, that means if you *want* to finish a marathon, start off by believing that you are already a marathoner. That's the reality because you decide on it. The actual reality comes later, and it comes a lot more easily and naturally because you've accepted it as true a long time before. You do that by actually seeing the future reality, in detail, using your mind's eye. This is what athletes are doing when they run through their routines mentally before the actual event.

This kind of mental shaping is worth trying out in your financial life. Start with what you have control over right now, and that's your thoughts, your psychological well-being. As Abraham Lincoln pointed out, "Most folks are about as happy as they make their minds up to be."

As I went through the marathon training program, blindly following all of the sports psychology lessons, my whole life started to change, because I was learning to change my perspective. I realized how the mind could be put to work on our personal finances. Yes, the budget stress was real—but how real? It wasn't that we didn't have a home or couldn't afford groceries or were facing debtor's prison. It's not that our friends and family had shunned us. We were bringing our misery on ourselves, by comparing our situation to a select few people around us; by comparing where we were to where we thought we should be and where we knew we were capable of being; by isolating ourselves and not admitting to others what we were going through; and by imagining others didn't share our stress. We had been creating our own reality, all right, but it was the wrong reality.

Brain Training

The wonderful thing about taking charge of your well-being is that when you do, help comes out of nowhere.

Money matters were still stressing out my husband and me

while he was in school and we were living on one income and taking on tens of thousands of dollars in loans. But once I decided to break out of the holding pattern of just waiting for our life to be "normal" (as if there's any such thing!), things started to come together rather miraculously. It had nothing to do with our finances improving.

I read an article in the *New York Times Magazine* about how Western doctors are studying the physical effects of Buddhist monks' meditating. Intrigued, I searched the Internet for Jon Kabat-Zinn, one of the doctors leading the research. I found out that he has developed a 12-week training program to introduce laypeople to the practice of "mindfulness meditation." One of these courses was being taught at a college within a mile of my home, starting in a few weeks. I signed up.

In the following weeks, the class learned various meditation exercises, different ways of using and being conscious of our minds, and how to make ourselves slow down and take notice of the little things in life. As Thoreau put it in *Walden*, "Why should we live with such hurry and waste of life? We are determined to be starved before we are hungry." Instead, we can change our environment by changing how we're looking at it and responding to it. But it takes practice.

Our meditation teacher talked about using a stress-reduction strategy of confronting problems only when they actually need to be dealt with, rather than wrestling with them repeatedly through imagined scenarios and inside-the-skull sparring. It started to make sense: The mind developed by the marathon program is so powerful when we train it to our advantage, but it can also, off its leash, go to battle against us. That's how we frustrate ourselves when it comes to our finances. We preoccupy ourselves with other people's situations even though they should be irrelevant to us. We construct imaginary worlds of bliss and then pine to belong to them (or sometimes go into debt trying to belong to them). We convince ourselves that contentment is just around the corner, where some other people seem to be already, *and we could join them if we could just get a little further along ourselves.*

What we need is to get a conscious grip on ourselves. And that takes some doing, because real-world forces are working against us.

The Wizard behind the Curtain

We are constantly being manipulated. I won't go into this deeply because this is not news to us; it's just that we could use constant reminders to stay aware of the ways we are being influenced. When we're looking with awareness, we see through it.

To start with, there's marketing. Inspiring us to keep up with the Joneses is an oldie but a goodie in the advertising industry. Actually, they take it a step further: Don't just keep up with others, try to one-up them (*and here's how!*). A recent print ad for a car stated simply, "Ditch the Joneses." This advertising genre extends back at least to the 1910s. The granddaddy was a 1915 Cadillac ad, which ran in the *Saturday Evening Post* and is still hailed today as a piece of advertising genius. It was a block of text titled "The Penalty of Leadership." The car wasn't pictured or even mentioned. Only the Cadillac logo appeared above the text. The essay spoke about how the downside of accomplishing great things is that people will envy you. Here's part of it:

> When a man's work becomes a standard for the whole world, it also becomes a target for the shafts of the envious few. If his work be merely mediocre, he will be left severely alone—if he achieves a masterpiece, it will set a million tongues a-wagging. Jealousy does not protrude its forked tongue at the artist who produces a commonplace painting . . . There is nothing new in this. It is as old as the world and as old as the human passions—envy, fear, greed, ambition, and the desire to surpass. And it all avails nothing.

The ad copy bemoans "the little world" and "spiteful little voices." It *appears* to be ridiculing envy. But what it really inspires is wanting to be one of those leaders, wanting to leave the little people in your wake and have their envy unleashed—at you. Advertising professor James Twitchell explains this legendary ad like this: "If you buy this, you'll change, you'll be special. People will look at you differently. You'll be despised." It appeals to our inner goblin. We'd certainly rather provoke envy in others than suffer from it ourselves.

When we're not worrying about and trying to control how other people will think about us, advertisers play on our concern about our own self-image. *Where should we be in life? How do we know we're successful?* They encourage us to find the answer in buying certain things. A Rolex watch, for example. A radio commercial for Rolex was extremely successful by linking the product to our sense of accomplishment. After a vivid description of you standing on the peak of Mount Everest, the announcer says, "In every life, there is a Mount Everest to be conquered. When you have conquered yours, you'll find your Rolex watch waiting patiently for you to come and pick it up." We are constantly being conditioned to associate achieving success with attaining material goods. Even though I came across this ad in a book about advertising that dissected why it worked so well—and therefore it shouldn't have been able to cast its spell on me—I still find myself, years later, wondering sometimes, *When do I get my Rolex?*

Need I mention credit card offers? How *special* the companies want us to feel for being so responsible that they will give us the privilege of charging on their "exclusive" cards? A pitch I got recently from a card company opened with the line "There's something we don't share with everyone," and closed with the same idea: "This is a feature we offer only to our most highly regarded Cardmembers." *Yeeeah, like those who are not bankrupt?* Oh wait a second, the newly bankrupt are being pitched the same way. A few months after declaring Chapter 13, Dan and Tammy in Florida received a credit card offer that told them, "We think you deserve more credit."

Then there's television and the movies. Are those real lives the people on screen are living? Do the characters live in houses with realistic mortgages and have wardrobes that are appropriate to their occupation and inferred income level? Often not. While it's justifiable because that is part of the entertainment—a make-believe world that looks shinier and more carefree than the reality we ourselves must contend with on a daily basis—it also contributes to building up our dream world, the one we find ourselves trying to live up to even though it doesn't exist.

As for what the media concentrates on, individuals' success stories are featured more often than failures. Americans are optimists. The American Dream is about the upward journey, and we want to be inspired. When we trip or feel we're not measuring up, we withdraw into solitude and silence. So travails and hardship are not detailed nearly as often as accomplishments, especially when it comes to the psychological pressures and social impact of not keeping up, of not getting ahead. It's just not really talked about. Therefore when trouble does come, it can seem like we have been left behind, while all the others have surged ahead. Not true. It helps to keep in mind that what we're hearing and seeing about those around us is a selective slice. Even if we can't see the others or meet them, we do all have plenty of company.

Reality Checks

We must struggle to keep a sense of reality. Just like the marathon program's mantra of *But it doesn't matter*, when the sting of envy hits us, in the midst of our comparisons and surmising, we need to remind ourselves: *Things are not as they seem*. Yank yourself back to reality.

There are some other specific ways to give yourself that yank. One is by using relativity to your advantage. Expose yourself to those who are worse off. As a social psychology textbook explains,

"Downward comparisons can increase self-esteem and reduce stress." When I find myself feeling blue (*still!*) about not being far enough ahead financially, I put myself in the place of someone living in the housing projects a few blocks from us. To them, our income is *more than* more than enough, our apartment is luxurious, our lifestyle enviable. They, in turn, are fortunate in the eyes of others. They have their own apartments, they have food in the refrigerator, the tap water is sanitary, they have free access to the Internet and to books at the library—more than many others have. Except for pockets of extreme poverty even in the United States, the standard of living here, traditionally measured, is far above most of the rest of the world's population.

Now is a good time to point out something the poor have that most of us don't. Because the poor are so stretched for resources, they tend to do less comparing and contrasting and more sharing and supporting. A book about unemployment points to urban anthropologists who explain how poor communities have developed "complex networks of exchange partners," including siblings, cousins, neighbors, and family friends, to share child care, clothing, food, money, and furniture among themselves as needed. Everyone needs the help, and it's obvious, so they help one another rather than compete. Even though they have fewer material resources, they apparently don't work themselves into a psychological pretzel over getting ahead of the Joneses. This brings to mind something I found in the thesaurus under *crisis*. It's a quote describing crisis as "God's call to us to reach a new level of humanity."

Another way to reach out to reality is by giving. You're well off. You are. You have more than others do, and you have more than you need to get by. So contribute some of what you have. Share your time, talents, and resources with an individual or organization that needs you. Make yourself useful to society, even if you are just one droplet on the windowpane. And don't be a martyr about it— do it your way, so you get personal pleasure out of it too. Don't volunteer at the soup kitchen if that doesn't genuinely appeal to you, and don't write a check to just any charity. Make it something you believe in and are truly motivated to help, something that makes you feel good.

Don't just help others, but help yourself. That's right, indulge yourself. It's not only okay, it's essential to your well-being. Some of us have to fight a tendency toward extravagance and greed, true, but others have to fight behaving like sacrificial lambs. Our culture sometimes praises too highly giving to others while frowning on taking for ourselves. Go ahead and take some for yourself. You know the biblical instruction to "love thy neighbor as thyself"? A rabbi pointed out that while we hear that and put the emphasis on loving others, the equally important part is loving yourself. You can't love your neighbor as you do yourself, he said, if you don't first love yourself.

Our yoga teacher spoke about the importance of taking care of *yourself*. "You have to cheer for yourself," she said, "because sometimes you're going to be the only one. And if you don't do it, who will?" Make some time for yourself, and give to yourself. Deliberately seek out even brief moments of joy—no matter what the external circumstances—and bring beauty and excitement into your life however you can. We each have to customize our buffet. Just follow your version of the instruction that "when all you have left in the world is two loaves of bread, sell one and buy hyacinths for the soul."

Now, I know that sometimes you're in no mood to cheer yourself up, especially if you are burdened by money problems. One thing that might help, even when you're in what you see as dire straits (which is relative, of course), is again to widen your perspective. In his book detailing the Debtors Anonymous program, Jerrold Mundis tells those feeling crushed by debts, "Right now, at this very moment, you have: 1. A roof over your head, 2. Clothes to wear, 3. Food to eat. So right now, today, you are perfectly all right—you have everything you need, you don't lack for anything essential." When you focus on the gloom and doom of the situation, you magnify it. You let your thoughts and imagination beat you down, even though you don't have to. Instead, you can use your mindset to make yourself feel better, to improve your situation just by how you look at it. As the self-help folks say, you can't always control or change the situation, but you can control and change how you respond to the situation. Master the part you do have control over, and let the rest of it fall into place. (Granted, when you take that too far, you end up in denial. You have to find the helpful mid-point between ignoring a financial issue you really need to attend to and letting the problem mentally mushroom.)

You have to search for new ways of looking at your situation. When it comes to the Joneses, another weapon you can use against envy is, selectively, to embrace it. Yes, it's a sin and it's supposed to feel awful when it strikes. But there is, as always, another way to look at it, another way to conquer it rather than trying to smother it. It goes like this: When you envy, you want something someone else has. You are filled by desire. Desire is actually one of the finer things in life. You need it to experience passion. It can inspire you to move toward what you want, it can energize you, it can lead to progress. Desire is the fuel for the pursuit of happiness. You try to get what you want, that's how you have fun. A grandson of Cornelius Vanderbilt complained of his inherited fortune, "It has left me with nothing to hope for, with nothing definite to seek or strive for." Fortunately most of us don't have that problem. What we are blessed with is the full thrill of the hunt, the thrill of the pursuit.

Thankfulness

In the midst of our pursuit, however, another reality check comes in super handy: gratitude. This is really an all-purpose fixer. It has been argued that cultivating gratitude is the only way truly to adjust your happiness barometer. It's a version of looking on the bright side, but it calls specifically for feeling thankful. This is something we should all be doing on at least a daily basis: enumerating some of the things that are going right. Many of us hear early on in life to "count our blessings," but maybe we forget. Even when things truly do seem to suck from all sides, for that is when we are very tempted to dismiss exercises like this, you can start by coming up with one thing to be grateful for. Or maybe . . . two? Get the gratitude rolling, and you'll find a better mood brewing. The more you do it, the more you'll notice your perspective shifting toward the positive. The Joneses, and whatever image we are struggling to live up to, start to fade when we recognize on a consistent basis how far we've come and what we already have, right now. To have some fun with it, take a tiptoe over to the Joneses' side of the fence and try to look at your life as others see it: What do you have, what *are* you, that they could (and maybe do) envy? Be grateful for that. Envy your own life for a change.

Abundance

Not to keep coming back to the doldrums, but I keep thinking about the worst-case scenario, about the times we feel not just the self-induced tug of inferiority but the heat of fiscal meltdown. After all, what works under those circumstances has to be good for pretty much all occasions, right? So here's something else I learned during the tough times my husband and I experienced, and from the wisdom that started coming into our lives as soon as we opened our minds to it: The universe will provide. You'll get what you really need as you need it.

That might sound a little farfetched, but it's real. There's not a logical explanation as to how it works, but when you have faith in the concept it does work. In his book *Creating Affluence*, Deepak Chopra tells how, when planning a world peace project, somebody asked this yogi, "Where is all the money going to come from?" And the yogi replied, "From wherever it is at the moment."

When you think about your own life, you can probably find examples of how this has already happened. Just what you needed shows up, inexplicably. Specifically, when you need it, and are open to it, money flows to you. I was explaining this belief to my sister one day at lunch, and since she is very straightforward and practical, I expected her to give me a raised eyebrow. Instead she said, "That's so true!" She described how when our other sister moved across the country, she wondered how she would afford to buy plane tickets to visit her all the time. Just then, she was offered a part-time job for a few hours per week, which gave her just the extra money she needed for the travel. (This lasted for two years, until our sister moved back. Mysteriously, the part-time job dried up a month later.)

A friend who makes less money than most people do was telling me that she gives 10 percent of her gross income to the church. She said that she could not afford to do it, especially when she had first decided to tithe. At that time she was making, as she described it, "pennies." She had a student loan payment to make every month, she helped out her younger sister, at lunch she couldn't pay for a sandwich from the deli. But she was determined to give to the church before anything else was paid, and so she did. What happened after that is something a lot of other people have described too: The money or thing she needed just showed up, every time. A check she wasn't expecting came in the mail, a friend gave her something she was going to have to buy, work went into overtime so she earned extra income. Somehow, each month, everything always worked out. The universe provided.

Part of the universe providing, however, requires that we recognize and accept the help when it comes. Middy enjoyed telling me a story she had heard from the Native Americans: A village is flooding and a man is in his house. Another villager comes by and says to the man in the house, *You can't stay here! Come with me!*

No, the man says. *God will save us.*

The villager walks on. The water rises past the first floor, and the man climbs to the second floor of his house. Other villagers come by the man's window in a boat.

Come on, they say, *this is the end! Come with us!*

No, I believe in God, and he will help me, the man insists.

The villagers must paddle on. The water rises, and now the man is on his roof. A helicopter arrives and hovers above.

Come on, you have to come with us! You'll drown!

No, God will save me.

But the water rises past the man's roof and he drowns. Then he complains to God, *God, I trusted you and you let me down!*

Give me a break! God responds. *I sent you a man, I sent you a boat, I sent you a helicopter!*

Sometimes the seed of just what you need is planted in the misfortune itself. During trying times, about the last thing you feel up to is wondering what good is coming of it. But developing some faith in this concept will help you get through crises and funks.

After I met Dan and Tammy and had been interviewing them about their bankruptcy, one evening a friend and I went out to a Japanese tea ceremony demonstration and talk. I had known about this class for years and had always wanted to go but had never made the reservation. Despite feeling like I didn't have any time to spare, suddenly I signed up and we went.

Then, as the world works, in the middle of the tea class it hit me why I was meant to be there. When I got home I was excited to call Dan and Tammy and tell them what had happened in the tea temple. I felt like it might, in some way, help them put their bankruptcy in perspective.

What happened is this: The elderly Japanese man who teaches the tea ceremony class explained to us that tea bowls in Japan are very expensive, routinely $1,000. The best ones are considered art. Once a tea bowl sold at an auction for $1 million, our teacher said, and more impressive was that the man who bought it wasn't just looking at it but was using it to drink tea! "Can you imagine," the teacher said gently as he cupped his hands and rocked the imaginary tea bowl in front of him, "a million dollars moving back and forth, back and forth?" Then he started to giggle. "Can you imagine the moment the bowl dropped and broke?" He paused. We felt the pain of the million-dollar bowl shattering. Then the teacher said through his smile, "Can you imagine the *freedom* of that moment?"

Making the First Move

So those are some things we can work at on our own to take charge of our well-being, no matter how much money we have or owe or want. We can also work toward cracking the money taboo. We can ease out of the closet, be more honest, ask more questions, share our concerns.

This is, as you know, easier said than done. But it's well worth working toward, bit by bit, because this secrecy and mystery, these fibs and fronts about our money, are making us all worse off.

Couples counselors talk about the importance of *someone* making the first move. I think it's the same with talk about money. Take a step toward being honest: Next time you're about to let a half-truth slip out, just don't. Tell it how it really is. Or admit how uncomfortable it is to talk about it, and ask if the other person feels the same. (They do.) Then step back and see how people respond. When I told people I was writing about keeping up with the Joneses, some of them scrambled right out of the rabbit hole. With the subject in the open, they admitted that they couldn't figure out how their best friends could afford their lifestyle, how they felt inferior to their siblings who made more money, how in one case my friend lied to his parents about his job because he was ashamed of not earning more and needing to moonlight. Even the really *nice* people, the ones you'd swear wish for the Joneses' good fortune even before their own, given the opportunity, they too sniped. *Oh my*, the things that tumble out when people consider it safe to talk! We need to hear it, because we need to understand how alike we all are, and to see how things are never as they seem.

So we can curb our own propaganda that we put out into the world, and we can nudge others in the same direction. However, some people, as you can guess, will not be nudged. The taboo is strong, and we are so used to defining ourselves by our financial status that we are afraid to expose any weaknesses related to money. Still, try never to be discouraged by . . . how to put it . . . *the jerk factor*. That will always be there. An editor of mine said it best when I complained about an uncooperative source: "The world is full of jerks, ranging from the merely annoying to the bloodthirsty." Braggers, those who savor the thought of igniting our envy, the ones who would rush to buy a Cadillac after reading that ad, fall roughly into this category. Just ignore them. You're too busy for their nonsense.

Getting Out There

There are some places you can go where money is being discussed. One of them is Debtors Anonymous, which isn't only for people in debt but for anyone who feels out of control over his or her financial life and wants to be more at peace with it. I was amazed how many meetings this organization has. In Manhattan there are around ten meetings a day, seven days a week, as early as seven in the morning and as late as eight at night. *Who are all these people?* I had to wonder. Like those in Alcoholics Anonymous, there is no typical profile. The best way to describe whom you're likely to come face-to-face with in a DA meeting is: someone like yourself. We keep our money issues so hidden, you can't tell who is troubled. It's the same story credit counselors and bankruptcy attorneys tell, that they have successful doctors and high-earning business owners coming in for help alongside those with more modest incomes.

I would like to have gotten inside DA and talked with some members, but when I got in touch with them in New York and asked if I could come to a meeting or at least talk with someone involved, the response was an identity-masked e-mail telling me to stay away. Whoever it was behind the mask—whom I reached via their e-mail address for press inquiries!—wrote to me that they take the anonymous part very seriously. It is certainly testament to the strength of the money taboo in our society that an organization designed to help people deal openly with money issues wouldn't put forward a single person willing to speak about it. Granted, the second time they turned me down, they noted, "Remember, we're here for you if you or anyone you know ever really needs us." So I'll pass that much along. Any group in which people are encouraged to speak frankly about their financial lives makes progress toward facing up to the taboo. In lieu of personal observation, I can recommend Jerrold Mundis's inspiring book, *How to Get Out of Debt, Stay Out of Debt & Live Prosperously*, which is based on his own experiences with DA.

It might not be any easier for you to show up at one of those meetings, though, than it was for me to get in the door. The social stigma we imagine attached to a group for debtors is enough to keep many people far away, no matter how much they need it. When I suggested to Dan in Florida that he and Tammy might check out DA, he quickly dismissed the idea: "I really can't see myself standing up at a meeting and saying, 'I'm Dan and I'm a debtor.'" First, that's not how you introduce yourself at DA, and second, so what? The last place you would expect to be judged and criticized, as Tammy feared their friends might do, is at a meeting where other intrepid souls have come for support. This is a sort of reverse keeping up with the Joneses phenomenon at work: Instead of thinking others have it better than we do, we insist we can't possibly be as bad off as *them*. We need to get over those comparisons on both sides. If money problems are making you miserable, it very well might help to meet others and talk, or at least hear their experiences.

If overabundance is your issue—and it is for some—there's a group for that too. More than Money, based in Massachusetts, organizes discussion groups in certain cities where members can talk about the concerns of having plenty of money. Past topics, inspired by their quarterly magazine, include How much to give? Does money make people happy? and Who knows you're rich?

Another place money talk is going on, to a degree, is at Financial Peace University, a three-month class and discussion group held regularly around the country. The program is Christian-based (meaning there is an occasional quotation from the Bible), so the meetings are often held in churches, but it is open and relevant to people of any faith. The class was developed by Dave Ramsey, someone who went from having no money to being a millionaire to going bankrupt to becoming a (multi)millionaire again. The format of the class is to learn in a larger group about financial topics such as cash flow management, insurance, and investing, then to break into smaller sections for guided discussion.

I attended the course at a church in Queens, and my experience was that in terms of unburdening yourself and finding personal support, the class is as helpful as you make it. When I stood up and told a group of strangers about struggling to get by on one income, I saw a lot of nods, and that alone was a huge relief. Early on, another young woman stood up and declared that she had $40,000 worth of credit card debt, mostly from catalog shopping, but she was determined to tackle it. We clapped to encourage her. An older man admitted to blowing $1,500 that he couldn't afford on gambling in Atlantic City. Who among us hasn't done some version of that, and it was helpful to hear the confession.

At other times, what happened in the class was what happens in life: People jumped up to share success stories more readily than setbacks. That's supposed to be inspirational, and sometimes it was, but not always. One woman stood up and shared the good news that she had put the first step of the program into action three weeks before and had saved $500 in her emergency fund. That weekend her pipes had frozen and the emergency repair bill came to $480. "It worked!" she told us happily. Except it didn't make the woman sitting in front of me very happy. She turned to her friend and whispered exasperatedly, "Five hundred dollars? *In three weeks?!*" She sighed and her shoulders drooped. If you do take one of these courses or something similar, get the most out of it by letting the others know what your issues are, what's making you nervous, and what you're working toward. Others will be in the same boat, and being honest helps both you and them. Be brave and get it out there.

Not that the Financial Peace class is meant as group therapy, but generally speaking, confession is good for us. Numerous studies have shown that writing or talking about stressful or disturbing events in our lives has both psychological and physical benefits. Keeping everything to ourselves, alternatively, can be damaging. "Not disclosing thoughts and feelings over time, then, is correlated with disease and mortality," summarizes one journal article, titled "The Psychophysiology of Confession." The studies that have been done often look at disclosing traumas like abuse, and they correlate higher rates of disease, elevated blood pressure, and other illnesses to not confiding. Money is such a big part of our lives that I would guess that keeping financial stress and trauma secret eats away at us in a similar way.

Another place to turn to commiserate with others is the intimate anonymity of the Internet. It's no coincidence that this is where I turned when I needed support, and it's where Dan turned and it's where Middy turned. We expect the Internet, and the community we know is out there, to solve our problems when nobody nearer to us can. If you want to discuss the personal and social side of finances, rather than the usual investment strategies or tips on saving, meet online at www.greenwithenvythebook.com.

In stepping forward to make changes in how you think about your personal financial situation and how we talk to one another about it, in confronting the taboo, keep in mind something the anthropologist Margaret Mead said: "We *are* our culture." The taboo lives because we are keeping it alive by following it. When we act boldly, when we make our own decisions about what we'll talk about and how we'll view things, we improve our own culture.

About Next Door . . .

You know how I mentioned it's easy to slip back into noticing and caring when we see others around us looking better off financially? The couple next door to us moved out, just when we had come really to know and understand them and be comfortable with them as our next-door partners. The nice thing was, we had another shot at digesting someone new moving in and never wondering about their business.

However. It turned into déjà vu, except with a higher price tag on the apartment. A young couple our age was buying the place. They were paying cash. We heard it was family money. Forget how we heard, but we *heard*. We even heard how much the family fortune was—or, correction, was *said to be*.

We were amazed by how similar the situation was. The wife even got pregnant shortly after moving in. *Am I being tested?* I wondered. You're not going to believe this, but they even got a ton of packages delivered. (*Does* everyone *do so much shopping by mail, or is it only whoever happens to move in next door to us?*)

We ordered in for dinner one night. When my husband went to the door and took the food from the delivery man, he noticed something in the hallway. He turned to me, gave a nod toward the new neighbors' apartment, and asked sort of covertly, *Have you seen this?*

I thought I had, but I joined him at our door to look out anyway. Ah yes, I'd seen it, but it had grown since the afternoon. We stood together peeking around the corner at the neighbors' door, which looked like a Christmas tree for all of the packages stacked up in front of it. (Away on vacation, *and* getting deliveries. *Hmph.*) Then my husband ushered us back inside and closed the door. We started laughing.

It didn't matter.

Endnotes

Chapter One: Green with Envy

Quote from anthropologist Margaret Mead: Margaret Mead, *And Keep Your Powder Dry: An Anthropologist Looks at America* (New York: W. Morrow and Co., 1942).

Quote from psychologist Anita Weinreb Katz: Alex Williams, "To Have and Have More," *New York Magazine* (June 14, 1999).

Flea research cited in class "Launching New Ventures" taught by Clifford Schorer, Columbia Business School, New York.

The American capitalist economy being driven by the creation of desire and discontent outlined in Paul Wachtel's *The Poverty of Affluence: A Psychological Portrait of the American Way of Life* (New York: Free Press, 1983); and in John Kenneth Galbraith's *The Affluent Society* (Boston: Houghton Mifflin, 1958).

Survey on achieving the American Dream: "Harper's Index," *Harper's Magazine* 277, no. 1661 (1988): 15.

Statistic on living paycheck to paycheck: "America Saves," survey by Princeton Survey Research Associates for the Consumer Federation of America (December 20, 2000).

American Psychological Association survey on money: "As Tax Deadline Approaches Americans Say Money Is Number One Cause of Stress," APA press release (March 31, 2004).

Statistic on credit card debt: Federal Reserve Statistical Release G.19, "Consumer Credit," (November 7, 2006).

Survey on debts making home life unhappy: Consolidated Credit Counseling Service 2004 Survey.

Quote from research in *The Overspent American*: Juliet B. Schor, *The Overspent American: Why We Want What We Don't Need* (New York: HarperPerennial, 1999), 215. (Research results are from Schor's own survey.)

Research showing couples in bankruptcy more likely to file for divorce: Elizabeth Warren and Amelia Warren Tyagi, *The Two-Income Trap: Why Middle-Class Mothers and Fathers Are Going Broke* (New York: Basic Books, 2003).

Quote from book by anthropologist on downward mobility: Katherine Newman, *Falling from Grace: The Experience of Downward Mobility in the American Middle Class* (New York: Vintage Books, 1989).

Harvard and University of Miami survey about income: Sara J. Solnick and David Hemenway, "Is More Always Better?: A Survey of Positional Concerns," *Journal of Economic Behavior and Organization* 37, no. 3 (1998): 373–383.

British experiment on relative wealth using computer gambling game: Daniel John Zizzo and Andrew Oswald, "Are People Willing to Pay to Reduce Others' Incomes?" The Warwick Economics Research Paper Series, Department of Economics, University of Warwick (July 2, 2001).

Princeton experiment with two players and accepting payoffs: Alan G. Sanfey, James K. Rilling, Jessica A. Aronson, et al., "The Neural Basis of Economic Decision-Making in the Ultimatum Game," *Science* 300, no. 5626 (2003): 1755–1758.

Survey of Americans earning more than $100,000 per year: Schor, *Overspent American*, 6.

Chapter Two: The Money Next Door

Money magazine survey results reported in Scott Medintz, "Secrets, Lies and Money," *Money* (April 2005): 121–128.

Quote from *Salon*: Scott Rosenberg, "Introducing Salon Money Week," *Salon.com* (October 27, 1997).

Quote from New York City sermon on money as taboo: Stephen P. Bauman, "The Last Taboo," Christ Church (October 12, 2003).

Quote from psychologist on money as taboo: Richard Trachtman, "The Money Taboo: Its Effects in Everyday Life and in the Practice of Psychotherapy," *Clinical Social Work Journal* 27, no. 3 (1999): 275–288.

Quotes from Jamie Johnson about code of silence among the wealthy and about being a traitor: from Julia Chaplin, "Biting the Silver Spoon That Feeds Him, on Film," *New York Times* (October 12, 2003).

Explanations of etiquette from Peggy Post, *Emily Post's Etiquette*, 16th edition (New York: HarperCollins, 1997).

Quote on discussion of money in the Bible from the Reverend Bauman's sermon "The Last Taboo," cited above. Other quote, on congrega[n]t[s] not discussing their finances, from personal interview.

Quote from sermon on why we don't discuss money: Mark D. Morri[son-]Reed, "The Taboo," First Unitarian Congregation of Toronto ([Octo]ber 21, 2001).

Freud's discussion of money's legacy of being dirty: Sigmun[d Freud,] "Character and Anal Erotism," *The Freud Reader* (New Y[ork: W. W.] Norton & Company, 1989), 296–297.

Quote from Emma Jung's letter to Freud: Sigmund Freud an[d C. G. Jung,] *The Freud/Jung Letters* (Princeton University Press, 199[4]).

Psychologist Richard Trachtman's quote about Freud: Tr[achtman, "The] Money Taboo," cited above.

Quote from Manhattan therapist: personal interview.

New York Times Magazine article on Debtors Anon[ymous:] Carol Lloyd, "Cents and Sensibility," *New Y[ork Times Magazine]* (December 28, 1997): 50.

List of problems that money has been identified as [a cause of:] Trachtman, "The Money Taboo," cited abo[ve. Also,] money being an ignored subject.

Quotes from psychologist David Lansky fro[m "Making] Meaning: 'Psychologically Informed' Pl[anning,"] *Estate Planning* (February/March 2003)[.]

Quote from Howard Dvorkin about sp[ending:] personal interview.

Chapter Three: Keeping Up with[...]

In reconstructing Dan and Tammy's f[inances, I used] court documents in addition to [...]

Comparisons to national and ne[ighborhood educational] attainment: Census Bureau d[ata...]

Comparison to national media[n...] of Education data of the re[...]

...otes from Federal Reserve and statistics on home equity lending and
...rrowing: Glenn Canner, Thomas Durkin, and Charles Luckett,
...nt Developments in Home Equity Lending," *Federal Reserve*
...(April 1998).

...buying homes but owning less of them: Javier Silva, "A
...s: Refinancing the American Dream," briefing paper
...os: A Network for Ideas & Action (January 9,

...it card debt as percentages of income: "The
...Forecasts, Causes and Risk Control,"
...94. Calculated with income figures
...e and debt figures from the Federal

...: Tamara Draut and Javier
...Growth of Credit Card
...mos: A Network for

...ousehold: *The*
...566 million
...seholds.
...stry-
..."

...son-
...Octo-

...Freud,
...ork: W.W.

...d C.G. Jung,
...4), 203. "The
...achtman,

...ymous experience:
...*rk Times Magazine*

...potential root of: from
...e. Also his quote about
...m his article "Money and
...nning," *Journal of Practical*

...uses hiding credit card debt:

...the Joneses
...nancial downfall, I used bankruptcy
...personal interviews.
...ghborhood medians and educational
...ta of the relevant years.
...incomes by education level: Department
...evant year.

Information from Consumer Bankruptcy Project: Elizabeth Warren, Jay Lawrence Westbrook, and Teresa A. Sullivan, *The Fragile Middle Class: Americans in Debt* (New Haven, CT: Yale University Press, 2000); and Elizabeth Warren and Amelia Warren Tyagi, *The Two-Income Trap: Why Middle-Class Mothers and Fathers Are Going Broke* (New York: Basic Books, 2003).

An insignificant percentage of people take advantage of the bankruptcy system: A resident scholar at the American Bankruptcy Institute estimated that fewer than 3 percent of filers could repay their debts but still filed bankruptcy.

Discussion of change in bankruptcy court policies: attorney Glenn; and Department of Justice, Executive Office for United States Trustees, "U.S. Trustee Program Launches Bankruptcy Civil Enforcement Initiative," press release (October 30, 2001).

Discussion of 2005 bankruptcy reform: Nolo (www.nolo.com), American Bankruptcy Institute (www.abiworld.org), and attorney Glenn.

Quote on new bankruptcy law by California law firm's Web site: Moran Law Group (www.moranlaw.net).

Statistics comparing numbers of bankruptcies to divorces and college graduates: U.S. Bankruptcy Courts (1.6 million personal bankruptcies in 2003 and 2004); Centers for Disease Control, National Vital Statistics Reports (1.1 million divorces in 2003 and 2004); Department of Education, National Center for Educational Statistics (1.3 million bachelor degrees earned in 2003).

Researcher who studied bankrupt families: Deborah K. Thorne, *Personal Bankruptcy through the Eyes of the Stigmatized: Insight into Issues of Shame, Gender and Marital Discord* (doctoral dissertation, Washington State University, 2001).

Book based on the findings of the Consumer Bankruptcy Project: Warren and Tyagi, *The Two-Income Trap*. The quotes that follow are taken from this book, pps. 212, 177.

Quotes from Deborah Thorne are from her dissertation, cited above.

Quote from social psychology textbook and discussion of cognitive dissonance: Baron and Byrne, *Social Psychology*.

Chapter Four: Capitol Secrets

All quotes from unnamed sources are from personal interviews with former members of Congress.

Quotes and information from Jack Buechner: personal interview.

Quinn's story and quotes: personal interviews with Jack Quinn and Jack Quinn III.

Newspaper article headline "Congress's Millionaires—A Thriving Breed": Jeffery L. Sheler with Robert Barr, *U.S. News and World Report* (June 3, 1985).

Newspaper article headline "Lawmakers Don't Feel Your Pain": Shannon Buggs, *Houston Chronicle* (May 16, 2005).

Quotes from Al Gore's campaign consultant (Bill Knapp) and Bob Kerrey: Sally Quinn, "It's Full of Corruption, Partisanship and Elitism. At Least, It's That Way Until People Move Here," *Washington Post* (April 12, 2001).

Quotes from Sam Gejdenson: personal interview.

Anecdote and quote from Tom Foley: Quinn, "Full of Corruption."

Myths about congressional retirement benefits: see urban legend debunking site www.snopes.com.

Quote from *Tampa Tribune* article about platinum parachutes: Keith Epstein, "When Career's Over, Politicians Spared Retirees' Usual Worries," *Tampa Tribune* (December 19, 2004).

Quote from Steve Tomaszewski: personal interview.

Congressional salary figure is as of 2006.

Net worths of Edward Kennedy, Jay Rockefeller, and Jon Corzine: Matthew Murray, "The 50 Richest Members of Congress," *Roll Call* (September 12, 2005).

Quote from *Houston Chronicle* on members being millionaires: Buggs, "Lawmakers Don't Feel Your Pain."

For more about the pay, benefits, and regulations of congressional compensation, see the Congressional Institute's Web site, www.conginst.org.

Characterizations of members' finances taken from review of publicly available financial disclosure documents, available from the Center for Responsive Politics, www.opensecrets.org.

Quote from New York newspaper article about credit card debt: Paul Vitello, "Bankruptcy Bill Could Be Debt of Us," *Newsday* (March 13, 2005).

Recent accounts of the Animal House owned by George Miller: Johanna Neuman, "At This 'Animal House,' the Party Is Democratic," *Los Angeles Times* (July 25, 2005); Katherine Marsh, "Chuck's Place," *New York Times* (March 3, 2002).

Quote from Dick Durbin about the size of the rats: Marsh, "Chuck's Place."

Quote from Al Franken: Andrea Estes, "Delahunt, Roommates Are Sitcom Fodder," *Boston Globe* (December 2, 2001).

Anecdote about Marty Russo billing for new tires: Marsh, "Chuck's Place."

Information about members sleeping in their offices: personal interviews with members or their press secretaries.

Cost of congressional races: Center for Responsive Politics.

For further discussion on the logistics and costs of members' families relocating to Washington, D.C., see Lou Frey Jr. and Michael T. Hayes, editors, *Inside the House: Former Members Reveal How Congress Really Works* (Lanham, MD: U.S. Association of Former Members of Congress and United Press of America, 2001).

Statistic on members carrying credit card debt: Josephine Hearn, "A Hill of Credit-Card Debt: Some Lawmakers Juggle Cards and Up to $250k Owed," *The Hill* (March 10, 2005), data from financial disclosures covering 2003.

Quote from Tim Bishop: J. Jioni Palmer, "Local Congressmen Reap Credit Card Debt," *Newsday* (March 14, 2005).

Quote on debt of Jan Schakowsky and Melissa Bean: Illinois Republican Party, "Reps. Bean, Schakowsky's Personal Spending Habits Should Worry Taxpayers," *US Fed News* (March 10, 2005).

Anecdote about a member's suitcase popping open at baggage claim: Frey and Hayes, *Inside the House*, 70–71.

Quote from Bill Pascrell: Ed Henry, "Sex in the City," *Roll Call* (November 8, 2001).

Chapter Five: Baby Boomers Beware

Statistics on rates of college attendance: "The Inheritor," *Time* (January 6, 1967). This was the cover story naming boomers "Man of the Year."

Quotes from Scott Wetzler: personal interview.

Quote about tyranny from member of Harvard Class of 1977: Bo Emerson, "The Burden of Expectations," *Atlanta Journal-Constitution* (July 8, 2002).

Quotes from Daphne Merkin: Daphne Merkin, *Dreaming of Hitler: Passions & Provocations* (New York: Crown, 1997).

Quotes from class notes: from recent issues of Ivy League alumni magazines.

For more on boomer earnings, wealth, inheritances, and inequality: Michael J. Weiss, "GREAT Expectations: Boomer Wealth Forecasts Wilt," *American Demographics* (May 1, 2003); Mary Elizabeth Hughes and Angela M. O'Rand, "The Lives and Times of the Baby Boomers," report published by the Russell Sage Foundation and the Population Reference Bureau (2004).

Quote from *American Demographics* on boomers not inheriting: Weiss, "GREAT Expectations."

Statistics about boomer spending: Bureau of Labor Statistics, 2003 Consumer Expenditure Survey.

Boomers having highest credit card balances: Federal Reserve, 2004 Survey of Consumer Finances.

Boomer vacations: Sally S. Stich, "Breaking Away: Holidaying Boomers Leave Rituals and Stress Behind," *Time* (September 4, 2005).

Boomers putting in pools and quote from pool industry report: Alan Naditz, "The Big Boom: For Baby Boomers, Buying a Pool or Spa Is a Case of Image," *Pool & Spa News* (November 21, 2001).

Boomers more likely to be taking on debt than paying it down, and quote from think tank about boomer expenditures: Tamara Draut and Heather C. McGhee, "Retiring in the Red," briefing paper published by Demos: A Network for Ideas & Action (February 2004).

Information on boomerangers and permaparenting: Kim Campbell, "More Graduates Opt to Live with Mom and Dad," *Christian Science Monitor* (July 9, 2001).

Quote from *Psychology Today* on permaparenting: Pamela Paul, "The Permaparent Trap: By Housing Their Twenty-Something Children and Financing Their Lives, Today's Parents May Be Compromising Their Own," *Psychology Today* (September/October 2003).

Indirect quote from president of a national credit counseling agency: Howard Dvorkin, Consolidated Credit Counseling Services, personal interview.

Work being the pension of the poor: Steve Lohr, "The Late, Great 'Golden Years,'" *New York Times* (March 6, 2005).

Survey about boomers working into retirement age because they need the money: press release from annual Del Webb survey, "Many Baby

Boomers Have New Homes, Money on Their Minds," *Business Wire* (June 7, 2005). This is also the survey showing healthcare a top financial concern.

Statistics on medical care expenditures: National Bureau of Economic Research.

Statistic on a third of large companies offering insurance: Kaiser Family Foundation and the Health Research and Educational Trust, "Employer Health Benefits 2005 Annual Survey."

Statistics on net worth, assets, retirement accounts and savings: Federal Reserve, 2004 Survey of Consumer Finances.

AARP survey of Americans over 45 and quotes: "Perspectives Past, Present and Future: Traditional and Alternative Financial Practices of the 45+ Community," AARP (2005).

Quotes from sociologist Erving Goffman: Erving Goffman, *Interaction Ritual* (Garden City, NY: Anchor Books, 1967).

Quote from psychologist Martin Seligman: Martin Seligman, "Boomer Blues: With Too Great Expectations, the Baby-Boomers Are Sliding into Individualistic Melancholy," *Psychology Today* (October 1988).

Statistic on suicide rates among the youth and elderly: National Center for Injury Prevention and Control at the Centers for Disease Control and Prevention.

Quotes from Bo Emerson: Emerson, "Burden of Expectations."

Median income statistic from Harvard Class of 1977: Jason Weeden, John Sabini, Melanie C. Green, et al., "The Harvard & Radcliffe Class of 1977 Longitudinal Study: 25th Reunion Report," Harvard-Radcliffe Class of 1977.

Information on retiring in Central and South America: Linda Stern, "Money: Running Away to Retire," *Newsweek* (March 14, 2005); Shabnam Mogharabi, "Latin Fever: Baby Boomers Are Retiring South of the Border," *Pool & Spa News* (November 1, 2004).

Chapter Six: Behind the Hedges

Statistic on number of New Yorkers making more than $500,000: Daniel Gross, "Don't Hate Them Because They're Rich," *New York Magazine* (April 18, 2005). The Census Bureau's American Community Survey 2004 estimates the number of Manhattan residents making more than $200,000 at 78,403.

Endnotes

New York Times article about making $200,000: Alex Williams, "Six Figures? Not Enough!" *New York Times* (February 27, 2005).

Quote on investment bankers making $600,000: Brooke Kroeger, "Feeling Poor on $600,000 a Year," *New York Times* (April 26, 1987).

Statistic of 1 in 100 Americans accumulating $1 million: Barry W. Johnson and Brian G. Raub, "Personal Wealth, 2001," Internal Revenue Service *SOI [Statistics of Income] Bulletin* (Winter 2005–2006).

Information on private banking categories: Robert Frank, "Rich, Richer, Richest: Private Banks' Class System," *Wall Street Journal* (September 8, 2004).

Quote from *Forbes* article: Joe Queenan, "Billionaire Blues," *Forbes* (October 6, 2003).

Wall Street Journal article on yacht competition: Robert Frank, "Making Waves: New Luxury Goods Set Super-Wealthy Apart from Pack," *Wall Street Journal* (December 14, 2004).

Journalist's mission to figure out the cafe crowd: Erika Kinetz, "Here's to the Loafers Who Lunch," *New York Times* (April 17, 2005).

Jamie Johnson's documentary on children of wealth: *Born Rich* (Shout Factory, 2004).

Quote from Margaret Mead: Margaret Mead, *And Keep Your Powder Dry: An Anthropologist Looks at America* (New York: W. Morrow and Co., 1942).

For more about the challenges of wealth and inheritances, see: Thayer Cheatham Willis, *Navigating the Dark Side of Wealth: A Life Guide for Inheritors* (Portland, OR: New Concord Press, 2003); Jessie O'Neill, *The Golden Ghetto: The Psychology of Affluence* (Milwaukee: The Affluenza Project, 1997); Eileen Gallo and Jon Gallo, *Silver Spoon Kids: How Successful Parents Raise Responsible Children* (Chicago: Contemporary Books, 2002).

Quotes from Jessie O'Neill: O'Neill, *Golden Ghetto*.

Anecdotes from therapist in Manhattan: Donna Laikind, personal interview.

Quote from anthology's footnote to the "Richard Cory" poem: William Harmon, *The Top 500 Poems* (New York: Columbia University Press, 1992), 887.

Line from Simon and Garfunkel song: "Richard Cory," *Sounds of Silence* (Columbia Records, 1966).

Discussion of equity theory: Robert A. Baron and Donn Erwin Byrne, *Social Psychology: Understanding Human Interaction* (Boston: Allyn and Bacon, 1991), 626.

Experiment with three sets of office workers: R.D. Pritchard, M.D., Dunnette and D.O. Jorgenson, "Effects of Perceptions of Equity and Inequality on Worker Performance and Satisfaction," *Journal of Applied Psychology* 56, no. 1 (1972): 75–94. Summarized in *Social Psychology*, cited above.

Definition of mammon by a scholar and quote from Ronald Nash on the camel and eye of the needle passage: Ronald Nash, "What Is Money?" published on the Internet, www.apuritansmind.com/Stewardship/Nash RonaldWhatIsMoney.htm (accessed March 28, 2005).

Quote from inheritor/social worker comparing welfare people and inheritors: Mark McDonough, quoted in Stephen Dubner, "Suddenly Popular," *New York Times Magazine* (June 8, 2003): 68.

Quotes from Thayer Willis about inheritors going out on their own: Willis, *Dark Side of Wealth*.

Examples of how to answer the question of "What do you do?": "What Do You Do?" *More than Money* (December 1993).

Anecdote and quote from the Portland money doctor about the inheritor in his thirties: Willis, *Dark Side of Wealth*.

Quote from Margaret Mead regarding ladder climbers: Mead, *Keep Your Powder Dry*.

Quotes from *Born Rich* and Johnson and the map dealer: the documentary *Born Rich* cited above.

Quote from social psychology textbook about working: Baron and Byrne, *Social Psychology*.

Quote from Jessie O'Neill on not having to work being terrifying: Michelle Goldberg, "Crying All the Way to the Bank: Trust-Fund Babies of the World Are Uniting to Share Their Secret Pain," Salon.com (October 29, 1997).

Chapter Seven: Conclusion

Information and quote from the book on marathon training: David A. Whitsett, Forrest A. Dolgener, and Tanjala Mabon Kole, *The Non-Runner's Marathon Trainer* (Chicago: Masters Press, 1998).

For more on the practice of using your mind to change reality, see Napoleon Hill's *Think and Grow Rich!* (San Diego, CA: Aventine Press, 2004).

Quote from Abraham Lincoln: www.quotationspage.com/quotes/Abraham_Lincoln.

New York Times Magazine article on Buddhist meditation: Stephen S. Hall, "Is Buddhism Good for Your Health?" *New York Times Magazine* (September 14, 2003): 46–49.

For more information on Jon Kabat-Zinn's meditation class (Mindfulness-Based Stress Reduction) and to find a local course, refer to the Center for Mindfulness at the University of Massachusetts Medical School, www.umassmed.edu/cfm/index.aspx.

Quote from Thoreau on the hurry and waste of life: Henry David Thoreau, *Walden* (1854).

Cadillac's "The Penalty of Leadership" ad: *Saturday Evening Post*, January 2, 1915. Full text accessible online at www.cadillacforums.com/cadillac/penalty1.html.

Quote from advertising professor James Twitchell: personal interview.

Quote from Rolex ad: Roy H. Williams, *The Wizard of Ads: Turning Words into Magic and Dreamers into Millionaires* (Austin, TX: Bard Press, 1998), 28–29.

Quote from social psychology textbook on downward comparison: Douglas T. Kenrick, Steven L. Neuberg, and Robert B. Cialdini, *Social Psychology: Unraveling the Mystery*, third edition (Boston: Allyn and Bacon, 2005), 83.

Discussion of exchange networks in poorer communities: Katherine Newman, *Falling from Grace: The Experience of Downward Mobility in the American Middle Class* (New York: Vintage Books, 1989).

Quote from the thesaurus, attributed to Samuel Miller: Marc McCutcheon, *Roget's Super Thesaurus*, second edition (Cincinnati, OH: Writer's Digest Books, 1998), 146.

Rabbi talking about loving yourself before your neighbor: Benjamin Blech, *Taking Stock: A Spiritual Guide to Rising above Life's Financial Ups and Downs* (New York: AMACOM, 2003), 28.

Quote from Jerrold Mundis's book based on Debtors Anonymous: *How to Get Out of Debt, Stay Out of Debt & Live Prosperously* (New York: Bantam Books, 1990), 58.

Quote from Cornelius Vanderbilt about having nothing to strive for: Williams, *Wizard of Ads*, 154.

Anecdote and quote about money coming from where it is right now: Deepak Chopra, *Creating Affluence: The A-to-Z Steps to a Richer Life* (San Rafael, CA: Amber-Allen Publishing and New World Library, 1993), 58.

Studies on the benefits of confession summarized and reported in James W. Pennebaker, Cheryl F. Hughes, and Robin C. O'Heeron, "The Psychophysiology of Confession: Linking Inhibitory and Psychosomatic Processes," *Journal of Personality and Social Psychology* 52, no. 4 (April 1987): 781–793.

Quote from anthropologist Margaret Mead: Margaret Mead, *And Keep Your Powder Dry: An Anthropologist Looks at America* (New York: W. Morrow and Co., 1942).

Suggested Resources

Personal Finance Books I Have Found Most Helpful

Financial Peace, by Dave Ramsey. An easy read, in the step-by-step guidebook style. It includes interesting and helpful sections about sales techniques and negotiation tactics among other tidbits to get your financial life in order.

How to Get Out of Debt, Stay Out of Debt & Live Prosperously, by Jerrold Mundis. To me, this book is a page-turner. It explains the steps and principles of the Debtors Anonymous program, but you don't have to be a big debtor to benefit from the storytelling and strategies given.

The 9 Steps to Financial Freedom, by Suze Orman. Along with nuts-and-bolts advice, Orman delves into financial psychology and the meaningfulness of money in life.

A Random Walk Down Wall Street, by Burton Malkiel. This is the book that stockbrokers don't want you to have. If you want to understand investing in the stock market, this is what you need to know. It shows why we should be broadly indexing rather than investing in a portfolio of individual stocks or managed mutual funds.

Smart Women Finish Rich, by David Bach. Even for couples, I always recommend this original volume. Although I don't agree with every bit of financial advice Bach puts forward, the book is a motivator and includes incredibly useful sections on setting and achieving goals (the techniques he uses are adapted from life coach Anthony Robbins).

Think and Grow Rich!, by Napoleon Hill. This self-help guide from the 1930s has a cult following among super-driven people. It's another endorsement of brain power and using perspective to your advantage.

Other Resources That Have Influenced *Green with Envy*

The Non-Runner's Marathon Trainer, by David Whitsett, Forrest Dolgener, and Tanjala Kole. Trains your mind to tackle any challenge and shows how to exert more control over your life.

The Seven Spiritual Laws of Success, by Deepak Chopra. A primer on how to consciously create your best life.

What the Bleep Do We Know!? An engrossing, truly mind-bending documentary that explores, among other topics, how we can consciously affect physical reality. If the principles of the marathon training program or of Chopra's book intrigue you, this serves as an advanced course that explains how they work on the level of quantum physics.

Index

NATURAL RESOURCES OF
THE SOVIET UNION

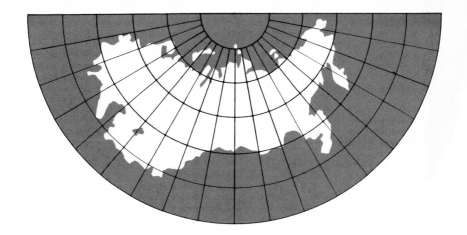

Natural Resources of the Soviet Union: Their Use and Renewal

$12.50

Edited by
I. P. GERASIMOV, D. L. ARMAND and
K. M. YEFRON

Translated from the Russian by
Jacek I. Romanowski

English Edition Edited by
W. A. DOUGLAS JACKSON,
University of Washington

"In the process of building communism, questions pertaining to the rational use and renewal of natural resources have occupied an important place among the problems facing the national economy of the USSR. . . .

"Today, within Soviet science, a new, wider conception of the term 'conservation of nature' has developed. . . . the term now means, above all, the organization of the proper utilization and renewal of natural resources in the national economy, occupancy of new areas, and enhancement of the natural endowment leading to an increase in productivity."

For many years, it was an accepted belief among Soviet officials and scientists that their planned society would automatically provide for more efficient use of natural resources than could be accomplished by non-Communist societies. During the past decade, this faith has been shaken. As the industrialization of the USSR has accelerated dramatically, the exploitation of natural resources in this nation of greatest land mass has become recognized as a serious problem. This report on natural resources prepared under the editorship of three members of the Academy of Sciences of the USSR reflects that concern.

Natural Resources of the Soviet Union: Their Use and Renewal, in the words of Professor Jackson, "marks a turning point in the official Soviet attitude toward resource use and the problems that have arisen as a result of nearly four decades of rapid Soviet economic development." Originally published in Moscow in 1963, it contains 15 articles, separated into six major areas. Considered in this volume are the economic significance of natural resources in the USSR, as well as problems that have developed in the use of water, climatic, land, vegetable, and animal resources. Since frequent reference is made in the text to the then-current Seven Year Plan of Development for 1957-65, Professor Jackson has compared the goals of that plan to its actual achievements as recorded in the official Soviet statistical handbook for 1965.

There are at present no comparable works in this area of study. This collection is certain to become a standard reference and source text for all studies concerned with geography and resource utilization in the Soviet Union—and elsewhere.

I. P. GERASIMOV, D. L. ARMAND, and K. M. YEFRON are members of the Institute of Geography, Academy of Sciences of the USSR.

W. A. DOUGLAS JACKSON is Professor of Russian Geography and Associate Director of the Far Eastern and Russian Institute, University of Washington.

W. H. FREEMAN AND COMPANY
660 Market Street, San Francisco, California 94104
58 Kings Road, Reading RG1 3AA, Berkshire, England

LOOK INTO THESE OTHER GOOD BOOKS FROM FREEMAN . . .

RESOURCES AND MAN
A Study and Recommendations
Committee on Resources and Man
of the Division of Earth Sciences,
NATIONAL ACADEMY OF SCIENCES—
NATIONAL RESEARCH COUNCIL

"An extraordinarily good book . . . as cool a collection of facts as is to be found within the covers of any one recent work . . ." *—Defenders of Wildlife News*

"Overwhelms the reader without scare language or excessive predictions . . ." *—Choice*

1969, 259 pages, 56 illustrations, 27 tables.
Clothbound $5.95, paperbound $2.95

POPULATION, RESOURCES, ENVIRONMENT
Issues in Human Ecology
PAUL R. EHRLICH and ANNE H. EHRLICH,
Stanford University

Here is the indispensable guide to the problems of humanity's relationship with the earth and to the possible solutions for those problems. The text warns and cautions, but it also encourages the reader. There are things to be done; the Ehrlichs are helping to get them done.

"The best single descriptive and analytic treatment."
—New York Review of Books

"The Ehrlichs will prevail because they are essentially right."
—New York Times Book Review

1970, 383 pages, 41 illustrations, 21 tables, 16 boxes. $8.95

MAN AND THE ECOSPHERE

Readings from SCIENTIFIC AMERICAN
With Commentaries by
PAUL R. EHRLICH, Stanford University
JOHN P. HOLDREN, Lawrence Radiation Laboratory
RICHARD W. HOLM, Stanford University

A new solution to the problem of suitable supplementary reading for courses in environmental studies. Twenty-seven articles from *Scientific American* organized into an integrated book that illuminates the history of man's relationship with his environment. Includes extensive commentaries on the articles.

1971, 307 pages, illustrated in color.
Cloth $11.00, paper $5.75

PHYSICAL GEOGRAPHY OF ASIATIC RUSSIA

S. P. SUSLOV, University of Leningrad
Translated from the Russian by Noah D. Gershevksy,
University of Washington, and edited by
Joseph E. Williams, formerly of Stanford University

A comprehensive geographical discussion of this very large but little known land area. Recommended to geographers, geologists, botanists, zoologists, and scientists in related fields.

1961, 594 pages, 168 illustrations, 50 maps, $16.00

First Class
Permit No. 7953
San Francisco
California

BUSINESS REPLY MAIL   No postage stamp necessary if mailed in the United States

Postage will be paid by

W. H. FREEMAN AND COMPANY
660 MARKET STREET
SAN FRANCISCO, CALIFORNIA 94104

Natural Resources of The Soviet Union: Their Use and Renewal

Edited by
I. P. Gerasimov, D. L. Armand, and K. M. Yefron

Translated from the Russian by
Jacek I. Romanowski

English Edition Edited by
W. A. Douglas Jackson, *University of Washington*

W. H. Freeman and Company

San Francisco

333.0947
N21
n9991
Sept 1972

Printed in the United States of America

Library of Congress Catalog Number: 74–138667

International Standard Book Number: 0–7167–0248–7

1 2 3 4 5 6 7 8 9

Contents

Part 6 FISH AND GAME

Foreword

Natural Resources of the Soviet Union: Their Use and Renewal (*Prirod-nyye resursy Sovetskogo Soyuza, ikh ispolzovaniye i vosproizvodstvo*) marks a turning point in the official Soviet attitude toward resource use and the problems that have arisen as a result of nearly four decades of rapid Soviet economic development. Prepared under the editorship of I. P. Gera-simov, D. L. Armand, and K. M. Yefron of the Institute of Geography, Academy of Sciences of the USSR, *Natural Resources* was published in limited edition (2,500 copies) in Moscow in 1963.

The volume, which consists of fifteen contributions, is divided into six major topics: the complex utilization of natural resources in the national economy; water; climate; land; the vegetative cover; and the animal world. Nothing is said of mineral resources, their study being regarded as the task of the geological and not the geographical sciences. Western and particularly North American readers may regret the restriction placed on the study as being too arbitrary, but discipline boundaries remain sharp in the Soviet Union. Despite the fact that the geographical discipline itself is substantially broader in scope in the Soviet Union than it is in the United States, a "complex" or an interdisciplinary approach to study and research is not common in the Soviet academic community. It will be seen, too, from comments in the following chapters, that resource use and planning in the Soviet Union have suffered severely from boundaries that divide, rather than being aided by the ultimate goals that should unite.

Soviet writers have long maintained that communism elevates man to a position of unprecedented supremacy over nature and permits more effective control of nature's basic forces, thus establishing the prerequisites for ra-tional planning of complex natural-resource utilization, conservation, and replenishment. The notion that the Soviet system, as "a higher order of society," can easily achieve a wise use of resources, may be traced back through Soviet official thinking to V. I. Lenin himself. In the past, Soviet writers have compared the exploitation of natural resources in the Union of Soviet Socialist Republics with that in the capitalist world, the latter being criticized for misuse and wastefulness. In the last decade, however, there has been sufficient evidence in the Soviet press, periodical, and monographic literature to reveal that Soviet performance—despite the emphasis on planning—has not shown more intelligence or wisdom than that of the West. Indeed, because of the forced tempo of Soviet economic development, especially under the Stalin five-year plans, the regime itself contributed substantially to the problems that have surfaced and are, for the first time, discussed generally and publicly in this book.

The U.S.S.R. occupies approximately one-sixth of the earth's surface; its resources, exclusive of the productive skills and capacities of its 240 million-or-more inhabitants, are enormous. Size, of course, creates problems of distribution, which strain the transportation facilities. A highly centralized administration and an enormous bureaucracy have not facilitated the implementation of decisions, even when they were wise. Some of the difficulties facing planners, scientists, and conscientious managers and workers may not be readily resolved, at least for some time to come. Still, the changing attitude toward resources, demonstrated above all in the Law Concerning the Conservation of Natural Resources in the RSFSR (adopted in 1960) and the publication of *Natural Resources of the Soviet Union,* represents a major step toward facing the realities of policies that were either unwisely made or hastily implemented.

Since the text contains references to the targets of the Seven-Year Plan of Development 1957–65, these have been compared wherever possible with the results obtained, as given in *Narodnoye khozyaystvo SSSR v 1965: Statisticheskiy yezhegodnik,* the official Soviet statistical handbook for 1965, published in Moscow in 1966 (identified as *Narkhoz SSSR, 1965* in the footnotes).

In order to help identify some of the species of land animals, birds, and fish described in Part 6, Latin equivalents are given. In transliterating Russian names, general adherence was made to the system proposed by the United States Board on Geographic Names.

I should like to acknowledge the assistance rendered by the Agnes H. Anderson Fund, which is administered by the Graduate School Research Committee, and by the Far Eastern and Russian Institute of the University of Washington, which made possible the translation of this text.

W. A. Douglas Jackson

Seattle, Washington

Preface

In the process of building communism, questions pertaining to the rational use and renewal of natural resources have occupied an important place among the problems facing the national economy of the USSR. During the last three years many books have been published devoted to these questions and the same questions have found their way into major government documents. In the Law Concerning the Conservation of Natural Resources in the RSFSR, approved by the Supreme Soviet of the RSFSR in October 1960,[1] the problem was raised to a new level of significance. The law lists the natural resources subject to conservation and then briefly defines the value of each. This law and others similar to it, which have been adopted in a majority of the union republics, together form the basis for a whole series of practical measures that have been undertaken by the state planning commissions, by the ministries, and by the organizations responsible for pertinent developmental projects.

The new Party Program adopted by the Twenty-second Congress of the CPSU, in October 1961,* devoted considerable attention to the conservation of natural resources, and listed those objectives upon which attention must be concentrated throughout the entire period of building a Communist society (in our country). The program emphasized that ". . . great attention will be devoted to the conservation, the rational use, renewal, and multiplication of forest, water, and other natural resources." The program discussed the importance of such improvements as the planting of shelter belts, the struggle with erosion, the planting and watering of green areas in cities, and the prevention of air, soil, and water pollution. All of this requires that the

---

[1] *Pravda,* October 28, 1960. [Footnotes that are reprinted from the original volume are numbered.]
* For the text of the 1961 program and its significance, see Jan F. Triska, ed., *Soviet Communism: Programs and Rules* (San Francisco: Chandler Publishing Co., 1962), 196 pp.

scientific-research organizations devote their efforts in every possible way to the questions raised in the program.

Today, within Soviet science, a new, wider conception of the term "conservation of nature" has developed. It is no longer interpreted as simply the establishment of natural preserves, where all activity that disturbs the uninterrupted course of natural processes is prohibited; or as the preservation of separate types of plant and animal life. Rather, the term now means, above all, the organization of the proper utilization and renewal of natural resources in the national economy, occupancy of new areas, and enhancement of the natural endowment leading to an increase in productivity.

This approach to the conservation of nature is complex geographically, requires an assessment of the natural conditions of every region, and can be successful only if geographical methods are employed. This latter requirement has not always been stressed sufficiently. Sometimes less consideration was given to statewide interests than was given to local interests or to the interests of the individual branches of the economy. The Institute of Geography of the Academy of Sciences of the USSR, having included the study and transformation of nature as a major topic in its research program and in order to achieve a multipurpose use of resources, has assumed the task of approaching and solving problems from the broad geographic as well as the national-economic point of view. *Natural Resources* contains the first results of such work.

In this collection of articles are proposals concerning possible steps that might be taken to achieve a greater use of natural resources, illustrations of both correct and incorrect exploitation, and ways to eliminate shortcomings. Land, water, climate, and biotic resources are analyzed. Traditional approaches to the study of biotic resources have pertained only to wild or semidomesticated plants and animals. On the other hand, this volume stresses the interdependency of the different elements of the natural environment and the impossibility of utilizing one resource without affecting the composition and value of the rest. Also emphasized is the importance of calculating the indirect consequences of human interference with the course of natural processes: consequences that are sometimes positive, sometimes negative.

A survey of mineral resources was not included because their utilization and conservation are studied primarily by geological (and not geographical) research establishments, within the context of other problems.

This collection is designed for workers in planning organizations, project institutes, specialists in the extractive industry, transport, agricultural and forest economy, and others. It will interest also students and teachers of geography and natural-science disciplines who are striving to relate their own theoretical concepts to practical applications in the national economy. The editors hope that it will aid managers to understand more clearly the problems connected with use of natural resources and in each case to find a solution satisfactory to the state's needs. The broad scientific and informational purpose of this collection, the limitations in its size, and the variety of questions touched upon have necessitated generalization. For a deeper understanding, the reader may refer to the bibliography found at the end of most chapters.

In addition to the chapters prepared by the staff of the Institute of Geography of the Academy of Sciences of the USSR, who formed the majority of contributors, the collection also includes chapters written collectively by the staff of the All-Union Scientific Research Institute of Fisheries and Oceanography, the Soil Institute (named after V. V. Dokuchayev), the Ministry of Agriculture of the USSR, the All-Union Scientific Research Institute of Water Melioration of the VASKhNIL,* the Council for the Study of the Productive Forces under the State Economic Council of the USSR, the Energy Institute of the Academy of Sciences of the USSR, and the Central Institute of Forecasting of the Hydrometeorological Service of the USSR.

---

* Vsesoyuznaya Akademiya Selskokhozyaystvennykh Nauk imeni V. I. Lenina: the All-Union Academy of Agricultural Sciences, named after V. I. Lenin.

NATURAL RESOURCES OF
THE SOVIET UNION

Part 1. THE COMPLEX USE OF
NATURAL RESOURCES IN
THE NATIONAL ECONOMY

1. Economic Significance and Basic Principles of Natural Resource Use

D. L. Armand and I. P. Gerasimov
(Institute of Geography, Academy of Sciences of the USSR)

Natural resources are those varied raw materials that man derives directly from nature and by means of which he sustains his livelihood. These resources are the natural vegetation and animal life that provide man with food and industrial raw materials; the air he breathes; the soil that nurtures his crops; the water he drinks and uses in agriculture, industry, and power production; the ores he smelts; the rocks with which he builds his houses; the coal and oil that serve as domestic fuel and provide energy for his machines; and much else. The material resources created by man are machinery, industrial and transportation facilities, clothing, and articles for the household—all of these, too, are made of natural raw materials. Energy is spent on their creation, energy derived from the combustion of mineral fuels or as a product of the transformation of hydroenergy. Thus, nature is the primary source of all the blessings at man's disposal. The correct use of this natural wealth is not simple, however.

Primitive man could utilize only an insignificant portion of his natural endowment, and the possibility of exhausting reserves was out of the question. With the growth of productive forces, however, there was a continued improvement in the techniques of resource use and, consequently, an absolute increase in consumption. Also raw materials previously either inaccessible or considered useless were introduced into the economy. Natural resources were thus spent at an ever-increasing rate, and shortages appeared in various regions of the world. In some places reserves of coal or ore were exhausted; overworked and eroded land lost its fertility. In other places, pasture lands were ruined or forests were depleted. Still elsewhere, the characteristics of river regimes were disrupted; floods were intensified in the spring, and in the summer the streams silted and dried up. Finally, as a result of overexploitation and merciless destruction, game, fish, and fur-bearing animals disappeared. In commenting on this waste, Karl Marx wrote: ". . . culture, when it develops spontaneously and is not consciously directed . . . creates a desert."

The depletion of some natural resources has prompted legitimate concern. Questions have arisen: will this process continue or can it be stopped? Is it necessarily tied to the continuous growth of demand or is it only caused by the faulty methods of exploiting natural resources? If in the capitalist world the shortage of natural resources is frequently artificially aggravated by an irrational distribution of uses, can this also occur in socialist countries, or in the future Communist society?

The Soviet reader, understandably, is interested first of all in the resource endowment of the Soviet Union, in its present status, in methods of rational exploitation, and in ways and means of enriching and renewing it. Obviously, different resources require different approaches.

Natural resources may be divided into three groups: (1) nonrenewable, (2) renewable, and (3) inexhaustible.

A large number of valuable minerals belong to the category of non-renewable resources (the exception being salt, which is precipitated in lakes and lagoons). Their use inevitably leads to exhaustion. Therefore, fresh deposits must be found and known reserves worked more efficiently. Maximum extraction from a given deposit should ensure protection of other natural resources affected by development. With wise use, mineral resources will suffice for a long time; by the time of their depletion, science will undoubtedly have found new deposits or substitutes. In many cases, metal will be replaced with plastics and concrete; for coal and oil will be substituted atomic, solar, tidal, and eolian energy, sources already initially tapped.

Among the renewable resources are soils, natural vegetation, and animal life. While they are being used, they are continuously replenished by nature. Their rate of natural reproduction—the restoration of soil fertility, forest or grass cover, the number of animals, and so forth—frequently does not correspond to the rate of utilization, however. Traditional practices associated with primitive economy have engendered the notion that these resources are inexhaustible. Under present conditions of intensive development, however, that concept increasingly conflicts with reality. The use of renewable resources (the cutting of the forests, widespread fishing, and so forth) is beginning to exceed the supply; the balance is tipping unfavorably. Nevertheless, there is a recognition that the proverb "as you sow, so shall you reap" applies to forestry, fishing, and hunting, as well as to agriculture;

but it has not yet been digested by the country's planning and economic organs.

During intensive use the renewable resources balance may be altered positively in various ways: (*a*) by more rational methods of extraction and use, partially through discarding methods that hinder the regenerative process; (*b*) by a timely introduction of untapped resources and termination of exploitation in exhausted regions; (*c*) by the artificial renewal of resources, which can greatly exceed natural renewal; (*d*) finally, through the search for substitutes.

With rational organization of national economic planning and renewable resource use, it should be possible to achieve a fuller productivity that would satisfy the growing needs of the state while maintaining a continuous quantitative and qualitative resource improvement. National planning can be considered rational only when the country possesses a stable, positive balance in all basic types of renewable resources; the achievement of such a balance is an important task of the planning organs of a socialist state and a prerequisite for transition to a Communist society.

Ampler productivity of renewable resources requires that measures for use and renewal be planned together as inseparable links of a single national-economic problem. It was not accidental that the Twenty-first Congress of the CPSU * gave its attention to the further utilization of natural resources, not simply in terms of using them but rather in terms of national economic accounting, that is, within the cycle of losses and gains. This formulation was reinforced by those sections (of the new Program of the CPSU) that dealt with the rational utilization and replenishment of our natural wealth.

Among the inexhaustible natural resources are water and climate. Water itself meets the needs of the population, of industry, and of agriculture; in rivers it serves as an energy source; finally, it facilitates transportation. Climatic resources consist of both solar radiation (a source of light, heat, and energy) and wind energy. Precipitation can be considered both a water and a climatic resource. While use of these resources does not lead to their depletion, unskillful or careless use may cause their pollution, the lowering of their quality, an undesirable change in their distribution, and, with respect to water, exhaustion, sometimes in regions of previous abundance. Ultimately, the poor condition of water and atmosphere can be a serious barrier to further development and sometimes results in the deterioration of the hygienic and cultural conditions of human life.

Such resources as these are inexhaustible only if their utility is maintained

---

* Which met in January 1959.

by preserving their purity and natural condition. Also, they must be developed so as to ensure their availability in places of greatest need.

Therefore, concern for the continuous expansion of the raw-material base of production and for the improvement in the working and living conditions of the population compels us to regard the rational use and renewal of natural resources as the broader problem of the active and directed transformation of nature, which is the highest form of the conscious influence of man on his natural environment. "Communism," it was stated in the program of the CPSU,* "elevates man to a tremendous level of supremacy over nature and makes possible a greater and fuller use of its inherent forces."

The USSR has the necessary political and economic prerequisites for planning the use and renewal of natural resources: national ownership of land, a planned economy, a unified economic policy, a just distribution of the products of labor, and, finally, a high level of productive capability, including to some extent the availability of an advanced technology in those branches of the economy that exploit resources.

Much has been done in the Soviet Union toward regulating use. Vast areas of virgin land that previously produced little have been brought into agricultural production; forests, recognized for their watershed significance, have been withdrawn from exploitation, and reforestation is being carried out; the beginnings of protective forest plantations have been made; and, through the regulation of the hunting industry, the population of many valuable animals (such as moose, antelope, beaver, and sable) has been restored and enlarged.

Party and governmental concern with the natural wealth of the Soviet Union is evidenced in the establishment of protective laws in most of the union republics. One example, the Law Concerning the Conservation of Natural Resources in the RSFSR, stresses rational use and expanded renewal of those resources being drawn into the national economy.

Despite this considerable success in rationalizing, the possibilities for state planning in this branch of the economy are inadequately realized in the USSR. Expanded reproduction of the greater part of our renewable resources has not always been attained, and even the need to strive toward this goal is not always recognized. In practice many planning and economic organizations do not take into account the need for a cautious and rational approach to natural resources. Nature is often regarded as an inexhaustible reserve, and the only concern is how fast the resource can be exploited.

We can observe results of prolonged, unwise, continuing exploitation in

---

* Published in Moscow in 1961.

many of the more densely populated regions of the Soviet Union. These include an irreversible destruction of crop and pasture lands, almost complete loss or qualitative degradation of forests, silting up of rivers, lowering of the water table, decline of fish catches, climatic deterioration, and a decrease of valuable animals.

Even significant reserves of virgin land, rich forests, water, and other resources in the less developed regions of the country do not justify an irrational approach, for exploitation of natural resources under unfavorable soil and climatic conditions requires a large investment. Moreover, development of new resources does not repair the damage already inflicted elsewhere, since each resource is not only a raw material but also a part of the composite geographic environment in which man lives and works. For example, a forest is not only a source of wood needed in the economy, it also is an important factor in moderating the climate, saving the soil, and protecting fields from dry winds and dust storms. More, it is a habitat for useful fauna, a collector of water that feeds the rivers, and, finally, a recreation spot for workers. Destruction of forests in any region of the European part of the USSR causes irreparable harm to the economy as well as to distant regions; this destruction is not compensated by exploiting unworked areas of the Siberian taiga, where virgin timber is still abundant.

The planned exploitation of the resources of unworked regions should continue at an increasing tempo. However, this development will depend on the growth of the productive forces of the country as a whole and not on the premature depletion of old regions.

Besides supplying an expanding industry with raw materials, there is the problem of the removal of the residue and everyday urban waste. Much fluid industrial waste poisons water and soil; gaseous wastes poison the atmosphere; solid waste impedes the work of enterprises and the life of the population. If this process continues, a serious threat to the health of the population and the normal functioning of the economy will arise. Many of these substances are actually valuable raw materials, and become harmful only when placed where they cannot or should not be used. Thus, because they are released into water and the atmosphere or dumped into heaps, the national economy sustains a twofold loss.

Further expansion of rational natural-resource use and the surmounting of existing inadequacies in renewal demand conceptually related nationwide measures. These are listed below:

1. The further study of natural resources, which is basically the function of scientific institutions.

2. A quantitative and qualitative assessment of these resources, including their typology, quality, and areal extent, to be carried out by specialized statistical and cartographic agencies in accordance with programs developed by planning and scientific organizations.

3. The planning for multiple use and expanded renewal of resources, implemented by the planning and project agencies, and including wide consultation with scientific institutions.

4. Their practical exploitation, to be carried out by national economic enterprises in accordance with approved technology.

5. Their renewal, to be essentially effected by the exploiting enterprises, including those especially created for that purpose.

6. Control over the observance of conservation laws and of rational use and renewal. This could be achieved by an inspection network, headed by a central authority created for this purpose.

These measures must be established for each natural resource, keeping in mind their close relationship. Undoubtedly, the specific characteristics of each will require a particularistic approach at each stage, but the approach should be based on major common goals.

In many stages of the introduction of resources into the national economy, a significant role must be played by the scientific institutions; this corresponds to the general law of development of the national economy in the epoch of Communist construction. To achieve most efficient exploitation, resource use should be closely associated with scientific research. Thus, both the planning of scientific work with reference to natural resources and the concrete assistance afforded by science to the planning and economic agencies in the effort to achieve rational use and renewal should steadily attain national significance and become an integral part of the plans of current national-economic construction.

Part 2. WATER

2. Multiple Use and Conservation of Water Resources

N. T. Kuznetsov and M. I. Lvovich

(Institute of Geography, Academy of Sciences of the USSR)

THEORETICAL PREMISES

One characteristic of water resources is their great mobility. They are in constant motion, and all their forms (rivers, lakes, ground water, and soil moisture) are linked by the hydrologic cycle. Use of one form of water affects the others. This means that a comprehensive approach to research, planning, and the actual use of water resources is required.

But water resources are also related to the other elements of the environment, including climate, soil, vegetation, and bedrock. Climate affects the state and volume of water, principally through such natural intermediaries as soil and vegetation. This brings us to the conclusion that (1) planning the use of water requires a consideration of other natural elements, and (2) these elements can be used to influence the condition and volume of water.

In agronomy and in forestry, changes in the local water balance are frequently achieved by means of increasing soil infiltration rates. Those working in the water economy sometimes underrate the role of soil moisture, even though it forms a principal source of water and is, to some extent, utilized by agriculture.

In view of this, the Law Concerning the Conservation of Natural Resources in the RSFSR, ratified by the Supreme Soviet of the RSFSR in October 1960, has exceptional significance, for it states that all sources of water, including soil moisture, are subject to conservation. This was an official recognition that the use of soil moisture in agriculture and silviculture must be planned in advance. The law also has a positive effect on other water resources, whether fluvial, lacustrine, or ground water.

A correct, thorough understanding of water resources can be obtained only by evaluating the structure and circulation of water, that is, on the basis of the water balance. Otherwise, only those reserves of water that are available at any given moment in the atmosphere, the soil, water bodies, and so forth can be appraised.

While the approximately 200–250 cubic kilometers of water * in the rivers of the USSR do not include all our water resources, their annual runoff represents a renewable supply. Similarly, reserves of ground water should not be considered at only one point in time, but in light of their supply. Their use in amounts exceeding their annual supply, therefore, leads to exhaustion of old reserves and threatens replenishment.

Presently, only in specific cases can the national economy afford to rely on those ground water resources that have been accumulated over the past. Usually such use has only a temporary benefit, and once past reserves begin to be depleted the whole regional water economy is upset. Hence, only ground water that is renewable within the water cycle represents a stable source for national economic use.

The concept of water resources is not limited to renewable and exhaustible supplies of water, but includes rivers and lakes that are used for navigation and rafting.

As with all other types of natural resources, the conservation of water resources should be based on preventing depletion. Conservation begins with the planning for use; implementation depends on correct accounting.

The development of water resources must take into account actual renewable supplies; this provides a basis for conserving water from exhaustion. If the demand for water exceeds renewable reserves and touches old reserves, such demand is usually piratical; it does not provide for renewal and results in exhaustion.

While the principle of expanded renewal is often concerned with biological resources, it may be applied to water as well, and water engineering has expanded, for example in Lake Sevan, the volume of both ground and lacustrine water. This expansion is achieved by diverting inaccessible or barely accessible water to usable water by means of change in the water balance or by increase or regulation of those elements that can be used.

One widely used method of increasing water availability is the regulation of river flow by means of reservoirs, which transform barely accessible,

---

* This figure represents the actual amount of water in the rivers (4,220 cubic kilometers) of the USSR at any one moment. The annual runoff, however, amounts to one-eighth of the entire runoff of the surface of the earth, which is 34,880 cubic kilometers (exclusive of 1,750 cubic kilometers, which represents the ice of Antarctica and Greenland). See p. 14.

unstable, and flood-prone runoff into stable, regulated flow—suitable for water and power supply, irrigation, water transport, and so forth. Other effective methods of regulating flow consist of the transfer of surface to subsurface flow or into soil moisture by improving water conditions in forested areas. Improving the quality of water is another method of expanding resources. Water pollution, increasing with the growing economy, has reached such proportions that even some naturally well-endowed regions have insufficient supplies. An improvement in water quality would increase the quantity suitable for use.

Summarizing, expanded renewal of water resources may be achieved by transforming the water regime and the water balance by one of two methods: (1) hydrotechnical, by means of which fluvial, lacustrine, and ground waters are modified; (2) forest hydromeliorative, which enables us to affect the water balance of a region before the water has run off into the drainage system or reached the ground water table.

THE WATER BALANCE AND WATER RESOURCES OF THE USSR

Until comparatively recently, the water balance of a territory and of river basins over prolonged periods was determined by the following equation:

$$P = R + E,$$

where P = atmospheric precipitation, R = river runoff, and E = evaporation.

The elements on the right side of the equation are dissimilar. River runoff consists both of subsurface water (U), which is the most stable component of the equation and has the greatest economic value, and of the unregulated surface flow (S). Evaporation is also composed of two parts: unproductive evaporation (N), evaporation directly from the soil, and productive evaporation or transpiration (T), necessary for the life of plants.

This yields a complex equation for the water balance:

$$P = U + S + N + T$$

The subsurface and surface components of river runoff are obtained through the approximate identification of the stable components of that runoff on graphs of daily discharge. Generalized data for nonproductive and productive evaporation are lacking and calculations are, therefore, made for total evaporation (E).

The most important element of the water balance is the volume of water absorbed annually by the soil, or the gross soil moisture receipt (W). This is equal to precipitation less surface runoff (or water that is irretrievably lost to the soil).

In accordance with the preceding equations, then:

$$W = P - S = E + U$$

Thus the gross soil moisture receipt is expended on evaporation and on the feeding of underground water.

The coefficient of river supply by subsurface water (K_U) and the evaporation coefficient (K_E) are correspondingly equal:

$$K_U = \frac{U}{W} \text{ and } K_E = \frac{E}{W}$$

Hence: $K_U + K_E = 1$

It has been established by experiments that the values of K_U and K_E, that is, of the proportion of the total moisture spent on subsurface flow and evaporation remain approximately constant despite significant variations in moisture supply. There is reason for assuming that most of the renewable reserves of subsurface water drain into rivers. The renewable reserves below the drainage horizon (that is, the volume of subsurface water that flows directly into the sea and is not intercepted by rivers) are, as a rule, not great. From this it may be deduced that the quantity of subsurface water that is intercepted by rivers is practically equal to the volume of water that supplies the underground reservoir.

Almost half of the precipitation in the USSR becomes part of the river runoff; the rest evaporates. River flow in the USSR barely exceeds one-eighth of the total river runoff of the earth, which is estimated at 34,880 cubic kilometers exclusive of 1,750 cubic kilometers in the form of ice from Antarctica and Greenland. The volume of water discharged from Soviet river basins (i.e., the annual amount of water draining through them) equals 195 millimeters; * this is below the world average of 263 millimeters.

A stable subsurface flow is of great value because its use does not require special management. This source of runoff comprises almost one-fifth of the total; the rest comes from surface (flood) flow, which is characterized

---

* This represents that portion of the annual precipitation, measured in millimeters, which drains through the river system.

by instability. Its use is, as a rule, impossible without regulation. The total moisture supply to the soil is very valuable because it provides water for plants and replenishes the subsurface reserves. Precipitation that supplies the soil with moisture does not therefore represent a "loss," as it is sometimes regarded. Of the total annual soil moisture supply, comprising 5,140 cubic kilometers, 17% replenishes subsurface reserves, which are than drained by rivers, and 83% evaporates. Thus, the coefficient for the supply of rivers with subsurface water (K_U) is, for the USSR as a whole, 0.17; and the coefficient of evaporation (K_E) is 0.83 (Table 1).

Since a large part of the subsurface water is drained by rivers, it is clear that renewable reserves comprise not less than 880 cubic kilometers annually. Further investigation will show what part of that renewable reserve is not intercepted by rivers but drains directly to the sea. In any case, in estimating the annual volume of subsurface water that can be used, one must consider a figure smaller than 880 cubic kilometers since that figure includes soil moisture located above the water table, dispersed and mineralized waters that do not have any practical significance.

As was stated above, the ratio of the productive and nonproductive parts of evaporation has yet to be determined for large areas. This has been established only for different types of specific sites. In the forest-steppe zone (Kamennaya Steppe) on grain fields, only one-third of the evaporating moisture comes from transpiration. On highly productive fields protected by shelter belts, transpiration increases to 50% of the total. The percentage of productive evaporation in forests is relatively high. The best calculations

Table 1
Annual Water Balance of the USSR
(After M. I. Lvovich and others, 1961)

Elements of the Balance	*Volume* (*In cubic kilometers*)	*Depth* [a] (*In millimeters*)
Precipitation	8480	390
Total river runoff	4220	195
Ground water (stable) runoff	880	40
Surface (flood) runoff	3340	154
Total soil moisture supply	5140	236
Evaporation	4260	196

[a] Depth refers to the average depth of water per year. Multiplied by area, it provides the volume figure. Thus 390 mm average depth represents 390 mm of precipitation.

Table 2
Examples of Water Balance in Regions of Different Geographical Zones (In millimeters)

Zone or Subzone	Basin	Precipitation P	Runoff			Evaporation E	Total Moisture Supply W	Coefficients		
			Total R	Subsurface U	Surface S			K_U	K_E	K_R*
Tundra	Shchuchya	450	340	34	306	110	144	0.24	0.76	0.76
	Amguyema	400	296	15	281	104	119	0.14	0.86	0.74
Taiga on permafrost	Vilyuy	300	117	13	104	183	196	0.07	0.93	0.39
	Olenek	350	177	14	163	173	187	0.08	0.82	0.50
Taiga outside permafrost	Pinega	490	302	106	196	188	294	0.36	0.64	0.62
	Vym	510	350	140	210	160	300	0.47	0.53	0.69
Mixed forest	Berezina	600	183	73	110	417	490	0.15	0.85	0.31
	Klyazma	500	158	63	95	342	405	0.16	0.84	0.32
Forest-steppe	Psel	500	82	16	66	418	434	0.04	0.96	0.16
	Oka	530	167	50	117	363	413	0.12	0.88	0.32
	Medveditsa	370	66	20	46	304	324	0.06	0.94	0.18
Steppe	Ingulets	435	28	3	25	407	410	0.01	0.99	0.06
	Sal	370	19	3	16	351	354	0.01	0.99	0.05
	Malyy Uzen	250	42	0.4	42	208	208	0.00	1.00	0.17
Semidesert	Turgay	175	10	0	10	165	165	0.00	1.00	0.06
	Sary-Su	175	5	0	5	170	170	0.00	1.00	0.03

* Runoff coefficient, i.e., the relationship of total runoff to precipitation.

indicate that of the 4,260 cubic kilometers of water that evaporates, 1,800–2,000 cubic kilometers is productive.

The elements of the water balance for the country as a whole are distributed unevenly and are subject to zonal regularities (Lvovich, 1957). The waters of the forest zone are particularly abundant and usable, except for regions of permafrost and the western part of the forest-steppe. In the forest zone, the greatest part of naturally regulated river runoff is of subsurface origin (U); surface flow (S) is relatively small. The total receipt of soil moisture (W), if not so abundant as to create excessively wet conditions, permits a rich vegetative growth. Least favorable is the water balance of the steppe and semidesert. Here, the very erratic surface flow is almost the sole source of water (Table 2).

When comparing reserves with water requirements, it should be noted that over 80% of the river runoff occurs in the economically underdeveloped basins of the Pacific and Arctic oceans. The inhabited regions within the Atlantic watershed and the region of internal drainage account for only 20%. The zone of low runoff, which occupies about 30% of Soviet territory, has only 2% of the total surface water resources. The result of this uneven distribution of river runoff is that the southern regions of the USSR, with their developed agriculture and industry, keenly feel a shortage of water.

In recent years, because of the rapid growth of industry, water shortages have appeared even in such comparatively well-supplied regions as the Donbass, the industrial Urals, the Bashkir and Tatar oil basins, and the Kuzbass. The number of such regions is constantly increasing.

The lack of correspondence between existing surface water and demand has necessitated interbasin transfers of river water from well-supplied to inadequately supplied regions. At first, such transfers took place on a comparatively small scale, as for example, the supply of water to Moscow by means of the Moskva-Volga Canal. In recent years, however, such transfers have increased in number and in distance. The Northern Donets-Donbass Canal, when completed, will supply the Donbass with water; the Kara-Kum Canal has been constructed; and work on the Irtysh-Karaganda and Dnieper-Crimea-Kerch canals is in progress. More and longer interbasin transfers can be expected: the transfer of water from the Pechora and the Vychegda into the Kama has already been planned.

The extremely unequal geographical distribution of river runoff is worsened by an unfavorable annual regime. Spring runoff prevails over the larger part of the USSR, and during spring floods, which last up to three months (on very large rivers as long as four), rivers carry from 50% to 100% of the volume of the annual flow. Runoff correspondingly diminishes rapidly during the low-water period. The rivers east of the lower Volga, of northern Kazakhstan, and of several other regions, dry up during the summer; many Eastern Siberian rivers freeze throughout the winter. But there are beneficial elements in this seasonal runoff, particularly considering the future use of water resources. Summer runoff prevails in most of the rivers of Eastern Siberia and of the Soviet Far East, while many rivers of Western Siberia and of European Russia have a small flow: these circumstances will undoubtedly be used as regulating factors when a unified power grid is built. Least adequate is winter runoff, because most of the rivers are located in the zone of severe winters and are fed during that season by subsurface water only.

Several mountainous regions, especially in the Caucasus and in Central Asia, have a favorable distribution of river runoff, both in time and space. Summer runoff, nourished by the melt of alpine glaciers, dominates in these areas and is used for irrigation on the piedmont, where heat and water allow for the development of intensive farming.

In addition to the irregularity of seasonal flow (particularly in the southern and central parts of the Soviet Union) there is an annual fluctuation, not uniform, but an alternation of cycles of high and low water years. These cycles are not the same throughout the Soviet Union, but an increase in river flow in the European part and in Western Siberia frequently coincides with a decrease of flow in Eastern Siberia. The sharp decrease in runoff in the 1930s encompassed particularly the eastern and central European parts of the USSR, Western Siberia, and the Kazakh steppe; in Eastern Siberia, river runoff was generally higher.

Almost all branches of the economy that use water require it in uniform annual amounts; large annual fluctuations, particularly those in the southern regions, therefore necessitate long-term regulation of runoff by the use of reservoirs to retain excess water in wet years for use in dry years. It is impossible to store the entire flow of the flood waters during wet cycles since part is released through the spillways of hydroelectric stations and, generally, the smaller the reservoir capacity the greater is the amount of water lost through the spillways. It is impossible, even on well-regulated rivers, to retain more than half of the mean annual flow: the entire cascade of the Volga reservoirs, for example, only can hold 70 to 80 cubic kilometers of water, about half of the average spring flood flow of the Lower Volga.

Ice formation on rivers has a considerable effect on the use of water resources, halting navigation for a period of from two to eight months. In ungraded sections and in mountain rivers, floating ice and ice jams impede both hydropower production and water supply.

Except for some rivers of the Caucasus and Central Asia, the amount of sediment transported by the rivers of the USSR is small, not exceeding a turbidity of 250 grams per cubic meter. Including the mountain rivers mentioned, where turbidity sometimes surpasses 4,000 grams per cubic meter, total discharge of suspended material amounts to about 580 million tons a year, almost half of which is carried by the rivers of the Caspian and of the Aral seas and other landlocked basins in Central Asia. The heavier, saline fraction of this load amounts to about one-tenth of the total (Lopatin *). Turbidity is a serious problem since it necessitates the purification of the water before use and causes silting of reservoirs and canals.

Approximately 84% of the territory of the USSR possesses, in a natural state, water of good quality; mineralization is low (less than 500–800 milligrams per liter) with a predominance of carbonaceous ions. In about 3% of the territory, located mainly in the southern and southeastern European parts of the USSR and in Central Asia, much of the water is sulfated; about half of the rivers in this area are fairly heavily mineralized (more than 1,000 milligrams per liter). Chlorinous rivers occupy about 7% of the USSR and are found north of the Caspian Sea, in northern Kazakhstan, and in the southern regions of Western Siberia. About two-thirds of the chlorinous rivers are highly mineralized (from 1,000 to 5,000 milligrams per liter). The total annual discharge of dissolved matter of all the rivers of the USSR is computed to be about 335 million tons (Alekin).

The economy uses not only river and lake water but also the rivers and lakes themselves. The combined length of those rivers of the USSR longer than 10 kilometers exceeds 3 million kilometers; combined area of lakes and reservoirs with an area greater than 10 hectares exceeds 330,000 hectares, of which 65,000 are in ponds and reservoirs.

At present, forty-three large reservoirs with hydroelectric installations have been established, with a total volume of 262 cubic kilometers, a useful volume of 162 cubic kilograms and a surface area of nearly 70,000 square kilometers. In addition, eighteen reservoirs with a total volume of 403 cubic kilometers, a useful volume of 148 cubic kilometers, and a surface area of 2,489 square kilometers, are being constructed. The existing reservoirs and those under construction will flood somewhat more than 40,000 square kilometers of territory (Avakyan, Sharapov).

---

* Sources are listed by authors' last names in the bibliographies at the end of articles.

THE USE OF RIVER RESOURCES

It is difficult to name an industry that does not use river water; it is used for the production of electric power, for irrigation, for the supplying of large cities and, finally, for the movement of passengers, freight, and timber (Table 3).

Approximate calculations show that the gross use of water by municipalities and industry amounts to almost 25 cubic kilometers annually, of which 3 to 4 are irretrievably lost and about 20 returned annually to the rivers. Irrigation uses about 120 cubic kilometers of river water a year, of which about 40 to 50 cubic kilometers are returned. At present, the combined uses of all branches of the economy approach 200 cubic kilometers a year, less than 6% of total river runoff, but from 18% to 20% of the reliable flow (subsurface supply to the rivers and runoff that is regulated by

Table 3
Water Resource Use in the USSR
(After S. L. Vendrov and G. P. Kalinin, 1959)

Use	1913	1940	1955	1958	1965 Planned	1965 Actual
Hydroelectric Power						
Output of hydroelectric plants (In billion kilowatt-hours)	0.04	5.1	23.1	46.5	100.0	81.4
Percentage of total electricity produced by hydroelectric projects	2.0	10.5	13.6	20.0	20.0	16.1
Navigation						
Length of internal waterways in use (In thousand kilometers)	64.6	107.3	132.0	133.4	152.0	142.7
Length of artificial water routes (In thousand kilometers)	3.1	4.6	5.6	9.7	15.1	16.5
Amelioration						
Land under irrigation (In million hectares)	3.5 [a]	6.1	7.0	8.0 [b]	10.6	9.9
Drained land (In million hectares)	2.8 [a]	5.9	8.2	8.4 [c]	12.4	10.6

NOTE: 1965 performance data were added for this edition from *Narodnoye khozyaystvo SSSR v. 1965 g. Statisticheskiy yezhegodnik* (Moscow, 1966), pp. 169, 363, 365, 479; V. Petrov and S. Ushakov, *Transport in the USSR.* (Moscow: Novosti Press, *ca.* 1966), p. 49.
   [a] Approximately.   [b] In 1959.   [c] In 1956.

lakes and reservoirs). By far the greatest part of the water is used, particularly by industry, in the European part of the Soviet Union, where river water resources are limited. Economic development of individual regions has reached such a level that local river flow in its natural state can no longer satisfy the needs.

The shortage of water, however, is attributable not only to unfavorable geographical distribution of the rivers, but to wastefulness, which is demonstrated particularly in the unreasonable rate of water consumption, the inadequate use of a circulatory water supply, the low efficiency of irrigation systems, and the excessive application of irrigation water.

Among the inadequacies of the water economy is the weak coordination by various branches of the economy and by enterprises in their use of water. The location of economic activities is frequently carried out without sufficient consideration for the adequacy of the water supply, especially in the light of the possibilities of continued economic growth, and further development of some has required expensive projects, which have greatly increased manufacturing costs.

The qualitative deterioration of water by pollution is even more harmful than quantitative exhaustion. Water pollution has become catastrophic in some regions and the problem is of increasing importance; the waters of the Volga, Kama, Oka, Belaya, Ural, Northern Donets and other rivers have lost or are losing their valuable natural properties. Industrial sewage causes odor, bad color, and hardness, and brings on a deterioration of chemical composition. This, of course, is not surprising: the discharge of polluted water into rivers has increased almost twenty times in the last forty years, and industrial waste contains such harmful elements as oil, oil products, sulfides, various acids, chlorides, alcohol, phenols, cyanides, and dyes. Added to this is the bacteriological pollution of rivers and other bodies of water by the discharge of domestic sewage.

The deterioration of river water is harmful to the entire national economy: when millions of cubic meters of industrial and domestic sewage are discharged into the upper reaches of rivers, the middle and lower areas become unfit for even technological use, much less for drinking. Polluted rivers have destroyed meadows, spoiled watering places, sickened or poisoned cattle and waterfowl, damaged some industrial production, and massively destroyed fish stocks.

In recent years, with the increased demand for water in the eastern regions of the USSR, there has been a basic change in the distribution of water consumption. This developing trend is reflected in the use of hydroelectricity, river transportation and, to some extent, industry.

Preliminary calculations indicate that with the existing rate of water consumption our country will require up to 650 to 700 cubic kilometers annually in twenty years; the greatest increase will occur in poorly endowed regions. Industrial needs alone in the more developed parts of the USSR will require no less than 300 to 320 cubic kilometers of water.

The growth in industrial demand is linked not only with the general increase in total production but also with greater water requirements, that is, the growth in water expenditure per unit of new products. Thus, for example, cotton textile factories use about 250 to 300 cubic meters of water per ton of fabric, but plants producing capron fibers require about 5,000 cubic meters. Even more water is expended on the production of other synthetic fabrics. In the production of synthetic rubber, each ton requires about 2,000 cubic meters of water. Some branches of light metallurgy, for example nickel plants, use 4,000 cubic meters of water per ton of production. For the refining of one ton of raw petroleum, up to 35 cubic meters of water is expended, and so on. The new, water-demanding branches of production tend to grow rapidly; therefore, the need for industrial water tends to grow faster than the total volume of industrial output. However, there are insufficiently utilized reserves: in most cases a circulatory water supply in industry enables a reduction in the demand and prevents the pollution of rivers by industrial sewage.

Taking into account the growth of the productive forces in the national economy, one may assume that the expenditure of water for the production of power in thermal electric stations will amount to roughly 400 cubic kilometers per year in fifteen to twenty years; that is, it will have exceeded the 1960 level by approximately eight times. But if all thermal electric stations were to operate on a recirculating water supply, the water loss would amount to only about 25 to 30 cubic kilometers annually. This, however, is not small, for it is the expenditure of water for only one branch of the national economy.

Speaking at a meeting of the Central Committee of the CPSU in January 1961, N. S. Khrushchev stressed:

We can obtain from irrigated lands an additional 1 to 1.5 billion poods * of grain, and if necessary, even more. This means that we will be able to satisfy 30% to 40% of the needs of the country with an assured supply of grain from irrigated lands, that is, we can obtain harvests independent of drought and other unfavorable natural phenomena.

---

* One pood is equal to 16.38 kilograms, or 39 pounds.

Posing the question: "Do we have such land?" and answering it affirmatively, Khrushchev noted that evidently

. . . it is most rational to invest in irrigation in those regions where the return is the highest. Such regions are Central Asia, including the area of the Golodnaya Steppe, the southern part of the Russian Federation, the southern Ukraine, Georgia, Azerbaydzhan, and Armenia.

The development of irrigation involves additional water, although the demand for water will increase at a slower rate than will the area of irrigated land. But the efficiency of existing irrigation systems is low and irrigation could be expanded by a more efficient use of the water currently applied: much is lost in irrigation canals, irrigation norms are too high, and considerable amounts are returned to rivers. The goal is to approach full (100%) use of irrigation water (including, on the positive side, water spent on flushing waterlogged soils). This would allow an increase in the irrigated area by at least two and one-half times with the quantity of water presently expended.

These examples demonstrate how necessary it is to adopt new methods of water use. Planning should be done with the future in mind, and should not be limited to immediate requirements. Planning should be multipurpose, that is, it should consider all types of water resources and all economic and social needs.

Difficulties caused by insufficient water can be overcome successfully in the future if all stages of water management are coordinated, from the distribution of water to the branches of the national economy to the utilization of the resources. By this means, protection and renewal should be secured. Economics is important in the solution of water problems, for modern technology makes it possible to have water of high quality at any place and in any volume, but in some instances the capital invested for such purposes may be a heavy burden on the cost of production. The important economic principle of a quick return on investment should be applied to water management and should not be disregarded.

THE TRANSFORMATION OF RIVER RUNOFF
AND THE WATER BALANCE OF THE REGION

The use of river water affects its runoff. The latter is regulated by reservoirs and reduced by consumption. However, as was pointed out earlier, such changes in river runoff occur even at the initial stage of its formation, on the slopes of the river basin under the influence of agriculture and of various ameliorative efforts that are constantly undergoing improvement and increasing in significance. Therefore, the structure of the water balance does not remain constant. It is possible to conclude, thus, that the dynamics of the water balance are conditioned not only by cyclical fluctuations of natural origin but also by changes linked with the economic activities of man.

Long-term fluctuations in runoff (that is, fluctuations occurring over centuries) are affected by cyclical variations of a few decades in length. Studies of the last few years indicate a tendency for the moisture supply of the Northern Hemisphere to decrease (Shnitnikov). If this tendency is confirmed by expanded investigation, it must be taken into account in water-management planning.

Late in the last century, V. V. Dokuchayev, A. A. Izmailskiy, and A. I. Voyeykov demonstrated that the water balance of the steppe had changed as a result of the overturning of the sod and of the use of primitive methods of agriculture. Although the scientists of that period could not evaluate the magnitude of the changes taking place, the changes were correctly defined (increased surface [flood] runoff, diminished supply to ground water [low dry-season runoff], with a general increase in annual runoff).

Investigations conducted within the last ten years have demonstrated that the general trend in the water balance and runoff has changed under the influence of modern, more productive agriculture, which decreases the surface [flood] runoff and slightly increases the subsurface [dry season] runoff, along with lowering the total annual runoff. Bringing about such changes are the perfection of agrotechnical methods, the mechanization of agriculture, and the raising of agricultural yields.

A very effective measure for transforming the water balance in a region, which began to be used in the thirties, is the widespread use of fall plowing, almost unknown prior to collectivized agriculture but now common in the steppe and forest-steppe zones. In the past, spring runoff from the fields formed on the stubble of a hardened soil, but it now forms on a surface with a higher absorption capacity, achieved through the coordination of proper cultivation, correct crop rotation, and fertilization. All of these measures increase the total soil moisture supply at the expense of surface runoff, and are applied in the development of virgin and fallow lands. The regulation of cattle grazing and the raising of the productivity of water meadows also are measures that substantially affect the water balance and runoff.

In zones of insufficient moisture supply, protective forest plantations play an important transforming role by promoting the accumulation of snow in the fields, intensifying the ground water supply, lessening evaporation and consequently lowering the coefficients of transpiration. The effect of the latter ensures that each unit of water produces more vegetation of economic value, raising the coefficient of soil-moisture use. The aggregate effect of tree belts leads to an increase in crop yields and slows down surface runoff, which lessens erosion. Such plantings also affect river runoff by decreasing the flood volume, increasing the low-season flow, and lowering the total flow.

Another significant factor in the transformation of the water balance is hydromelioration, that is, drainage and irrigation. Basic changes in the water balance take place on irrigated fields that are reflected even in such large rivers as the Syr-Darya.

The 1961 Program of the CPSU calls for an increase in shelter-belt planting. Through investigation and much experimental research, it was found that properly planned and carefully developed systems of shelter belts not only effectively alter the climate immediately above the ground but also change the water balance of the region. An increase of 20% to 30% in grain yields under the influence of mature shelter belts (in the steppe and forest-steppe zones) is quite realistic. It can be achieved by adapting the shelter-belt grid to climatic needs, increasing their incidence from every 100 to every 20 hectares, as the aridity of the area demands. The protective action of shelter belts is limited to a comparatively small radius, not more than 25 to 30 times the height of the trees in the belt. Consequently, there is no protective effect apparent in the middle of fields whose dimensions are 500 by 500 meters, if the neighboring shelter belts are not higher than 10 meters. Therefore, proposals for creating large fields between such belts cannot be taken seriously. As to the water-regulating action of the belts, it is limited to the downslope part of the field.

Experiments and calculations show that a rational distribution and proper spacing of shelter belts utilizing only 3% to 6% of the arable area can create an effective network of protection. This ratio necessarily increases in zones that are subject to drought, to frequent dry winds (*sukhovey*), and to dust storms, as well as in zones subject to severe erosion. Planning should take into account the need to extend the shelter belts beyond field boundaries, though this is not always possible. At any rate, a reduction in the arable area by 3% to 6% in favor of an increase of 20% to 30% in crop yields is quite rational. The loss of harvest from the land under shelter belts is compensated for five to tenfold by the increase in yields on the protected area.

For quickest results, the selection of trees should include a significant portion of rapidly growing species. Usually, the trees should be spaced in such a way as to allow the passage of air.

Shelter belts share with the forests of the forest zone the direct benefits of reducing surface runoff and, consequently, river floods, as well as increasing the supply of ground water. The water-regulating role of forests in general is considerable; every 10,000 square kilometers of taiga forest increases the annual supply of ground water to rivers by 0.7 to 0.8 cubic kilometers. In the deciduous forest subzone this quantity diminishes to 0.3 to 0.5 cubic kilometers.

The destruction of the forests and the transformation of the land into low-yielding farms lessens the natural water regulation of the region. Commercial timber cutting, with its use of heavy caterpillar-type tractors, and cattle grazing, which lowers the high water retention properties of the soil, bring about the same situation (Lvovich, 1958).

The present state of forestry, of forest protection, and of logging obviously reduces the water-regulative influence of the forests of the entire country. In this connection (some twenty-five years ago) urgent measures for perfecting a system of water-protective forests were adopted in the USSR and, in their time, played a valuable role. The scientific bases of this system originated in the assumption that the water-protective qualities of the forest are incompatible with exploitation; this idea evoked the prohibition of clear cutting in forest reserves along rivers and in other forests of the first category. In these areas cutting was allowed only to preserve the health and quality of the stand; it had no industrial significance. Such restricted forests comprise about 5% of the total forest area of the USSR. For example, in the Volga basin above Gorki, they occupy 6% of the region; above the city of Rybinsk, 10% to 12%; and the Moskva River basin, 20%. In forests of the second category, the usual commercial cutting is carried out with little or no restriction; the soil destruction by heavy tractors and the waste covering excessively large tracts of clear cutting prevent the natural renewal of the forest. Even where the forest does reestablish itself, its water retention properties are sharply reduced.

The reduction of the water-regulative role of the forests is avoidable. If the felling of trees is conducted rationally, that is, within the limits of the average yearly growth and with provision for renewal, the forests retain completely their positive role in the water cycle.

In forests adjacent to rivers the prohibition of commercial cutting is justified only in a narrow belt, within which the roots of trees protect the banks from channel erosion and wave action; it is also justified on slopes of ravines and creeks immediately tributary to the river. The principal river runoff forms over the entire area of the basin, and in this respect there is no difference between forests located near or far from the river. Both are significant for water retention, and both must be protected and exploited rationally.

Legislation designed to protect the water-retaining capacity of the forest should be directed not toward the prohibition of logging in relatively small sections and unlimited permission to log in the rest of the forest, but toward the establishment of a proper, enlightened forest management that would assure the renewal of high quality forests and the most uniform distribution of stands of older growth throughout the entire basin in any given period of cutting. It is also necessary to regulate the methods of logging, to prohibit the leaving of waste after cutting, and to prevent the use of heavy caterpillar tractors on slopes or on unfrozen soil in the summer. The removal of logs from the cutting area should be carried out by suspension cable or by other methods harmless to the soil; their further shipment should be achieved on ice roads, log roads, or by cable winch. In general, the technology of exploitation and forest renewal must be worked out in such a way that the water-regulative qualities of the forest are in no way reduced.

In this important matter no arbitrary standards are permissible; the rules for logging should be differentiated according to zonal and local conditions. For example, in the zones where less than half of the territory is forested, the destruction of the forests and their conversion into farmland should not be permitted. Exceptions can be made only when the cutover area, after suitable improvements have been carried out, is appropriate for agriculture of high productivity. The reduction of the forests in the taiga is permissible only if the total forested area is not allowed to fall below 50% and is not concentrated in excessively large stands. In the steppe and forest-steppe the percentage of forested land must be increased through shelter belts and plantings designed to prevent erosion. In forests where logging may cause erosion, it is necessary to limit the cutting to strips running parallel to the contours of the slope. In logging marshy areas, drainage must be provided. A strict regime of cutting should be introduced into the logging of mountain forests, particularly where the soils are thin. The prohibition of heavy logging must continue in the forests that afford rest and recreation around cities and in resort regions. The prohibition of cattle grazing should also be considered.

The organization of a new system of water-protective forests must be accomplished in the near future. The measures enumerated above will secure an increase in the productivity of forestry as well as the protection of the forest resources of the USSR and their protective influence. Limited, planned logging of overripe stands in those forests that until now have been classified in the first category will permit a slight increase in the output of lumber and will lead to forest renewal.

The transformation of the water balance of a region usually occurs as a result of measures concerned with other economic problems, especially those pertaining to agriculture and to forestry, whose influence on the water balance is positive.

Although the needs of agriculture for water are of primary significance, the task of controlling the water balance must be considered not only in the interests of agriculture and forestry but also in the interests of the water economy. In most cases these interests coincide; the water balance is more favorable in a highly productive region than in an unproductive one, because highly productive fields, meadows, and forests have a soil cover with high water-retention capacity. In regions of insufficient moisture supply, both agriculture and water management are interested in the over-all lowering of surface runoff and the transfer of water into the soil. Hence, by raising the productivity of fields, meadows, and forests, an improvement in the water balance and river runoff can be achieved.

An element in the water balance that is of greater concern to water management than to agriculture is the subsurface runoff, which flows at such depths that the capillary effect does not reach root level. Good water management uses this runoff to regulate the river regime, thereby supplementing the influence of reservoirs.

As was shown before, the naturally regulated river water of subsurface origin in the USSR amounts to about 880 cubic kilometers. To this must be added about 200 to 250 cubic kilometers of lake-regulated flow. Thus, 1,100 cubic kilometers of river flow require no regulation at all, but undoubtedly the remaining part of the surface runoff, amounting to 3,150 cubic kilometers, will require regulation in the future. If this were done with the aid of reservoirs, a prohibitively large area—perhaps 100 million hectares of useful land—would have to be inundated.

It is clear that along with reservoirs, it is necessary to make maximum use of the water-regulating properties of forests and cultivated lands. When the supply of underground water cannot be adequately increased by agrotechnical or forest-meliorative means, new answers (of a physical-chemical nature, for example) should be sought. These methods evidently will permit a great increase in the water penetration not only of the surface but also to a considerable depth of the soil.

As early as the 1930s, B. V. Polyakov, in his hydrological and water-management calculations pertaining to the Volga-Don canal project and to projects for Trans-Volga irrigation, assumed that the volume of runoff would be 10% to 15% less than given, considering the growth in agricultural productivity, which should lead to an increase in the expenditure of water and a decrease in flow at flood stages. Taking into account the measures then under consideration for the transformation of agriculture, M. I. Lvovich in 1952 estimated the expected decrease in river runoff, as compared to the runoff up to 1930, to average 14% for the entire Don basin, 6% to 20% for individual tributaries of the Don, 7% for the Dnieper, and 2% for the Volga. L. T. Fedorov, using the same criteria, evaluated the decrease in average volume of spring flow of the Oka at 23%, the Sviyaga at 37%, the Karpovka (Volgograd Oblast) at 40%, the Great Uzen at 44%, and the Tsimla at 60%. S. L. Vendrov conducted a large-scale investigation of the changes in Don River runoff and concluded that during the period from 1931 to 1957 the flow decreased by 10% compared with the period from 1881 to 1930. A. S. Shklyayev, using three different methods, determined that there was a decrease of 8% in the average runoff of the Oka in 1931 to 1941 compared with the runoff from 1885 to 1930. M. I. Lvovich (1960), comparing the runoff at the beginning of the 1960s with the period up to 1950, estimated that it had decreased by 9% to 12% for the Don, 9% for the Voronezh, 12% for the Khopr, 15% for the Medveditsa, 20% for the Chir, 8% for the Northern Donets, and 20% to 30% for the Sal. Using two independent methods, G. V. Nazarov calculated that the runoff of the Little and the Great Uzen for 1950 to 1956 was 20% to 22% lower than it had been in the period of precollectivized agriculture (1909 to 1932). It was 30% to 40% lower at the beginning of the 1960s, and as agriculture develops, the runoff of these rivers will probably decrease by 50%. I. A. Kuznik suggested the corrective coefficients for the volumes of earlier runoff of the rivers of the Volga Region: for the northern Trans-Volga, 0.85; for the southern Trans-Volga, 0.80; and, for the right bank of the Volga, 0.85.

With the growth of agricultural productivity, the change in runoff will become more significant. According to approximate calculations of the Institute of Geography of the Academy of Sciences of the USSR, the runoff of the rivers that form entirely in the steppe and forest-steppe regions will decrease by 35% to 50% by the second half of the 1970s.

Even in such a large river as the Don, one may anticipate a decrease of inflow from the 29 cubic kilometers per year (up to 1950) to 21 cubic kilometers, a reduction of almost 30%.

This survey of contemporary data relating to the changes in river discharges, even though incomplete, reveals the definite trend in the relationship in the elements of the water balance that must be considered in the planning of water-resource use and in hydrologic and water management accounts. It should not be regarded as correct procedure, therefore, to have designed and constructed almost all modern hydroelectric stations without considering the tendency of river levels to fall as a result of the growth of agricultural productivity. In planning such construction it was assumed that river volumes under identical climatic conditions were and would remain unchanged. It must be expected that the productivity of some hydroelectric stations, constructed on the basis of these incorrect premises, will prove to be lower than anticipated.

ON METHODS OF HYDROLOGICAL CALCULATION

The essential shortcoming in the planning of hydrotechnical facilities, especially dams and bridges, lies in the dependence upon formalistic statistical assumptions in hydrological calculations. In computing the maximum flow on which the choice of the size of dams and bridges depends, the usual basis for the computation is the volume of flood-flow maximum runoff, which is calculated by mathematical statistical methods, and which can recur once every 10,000 years (probability of 0.01%), once every 1,000 years (probability of 0.1%), or once every 100 years (probability of 1%), and so forth. The very selection of these probabilities is not substantiated, because the criteria used in determining probability and in selecting types of probability curves to compute the water discharge have no physical significance. Therefore, the dimensions of the facilities are selected with a wide margin of safety, unnecessarily increasing the cost of construction and requiring greater consumption of construction materials and metal.

In the Volgograd hydroelectric project, for example, the size of spillways was based on a statistically calculated maximum discharge of water equal to 76,000 cubic meters per second, but the observed maximum in the Volga for the last 250 years has never exceeded 60,000 cubic meters per second. Investigations show that under exceptionally favorable conditions of spring flood formation, the highest maximum discharge cannot be substantially greater than the observed magnitude. If one considers that eight large reservoirs with a total volume of 75 cubic kilometers (equal to 30% of the volume of the highest flood stage on the Lower Volga) are already constructed or are being constructed on the Volga, then it becomes clear that the ordinary discharge of water used in calculations does not need to be increased but may even be lowered. If, in the exploitation of hydroelectric stations, a flood forecast is utilized (which, particularly for large rivers, is fairly accurate), a significantly lower river discharge can be attained by adjusting the discharge of reservoirs.

There is reason, therefore, to believe that the calculated maximum discharge of water assumed in the planning of the Volgograd Hydroelectric Station was considerably inflated and the spillways of the dam are larger than necessary. The same overestimation occurred in other hydrostations: the Pirogovsk and Akulovsk dams on the Moskva-Volga Canal, calculated to allow the maximum discharge, which recurs once in 10,000 years, have not been opened in the more than twenty years of their existence; the gates of the Rybinsk hydroelectric dam, built in 1942, were opened only once, in 1955. Although the maximum in that year for the Upper Volga was the highest in seventy-five years, only one-fourth of the calculated maximum runoff was permitted through.

These examples demonstrate that, because of the use of formalistic statistical assumptions in calculations, current hydrotechnical construction allows considerable reserves to remain unused. There are newer, better substantiated methods of calculating runoff, methods based on physical analyses of possible maximum water discharge. Regrettably, this important problem has not been given sufficient attention in water management. Hydrological institutions concern themselves little with the question, and water technicians and economists do not offer science the necessary data nor do they apply the findings of up-to-date scientific research.

Our extensive use of ponds also shows a number of deficiencies, for hydrological and hydroeconomic calculations concerning them are often poorly founded. The formalistic application of a method of calculation that employs analogues often leads to the creation of ponds that have no water, or, conversely, the underestimation of maximum runoff leads to the destruction of the dams during flood stage. In addition to this, the quality of construction is inadequate: dams are often constructed without spillways, and rupture results; or the spillways, constructed without observing elementary technical rules, are washed out. In a number of cases, small reservoirs in the steppe and forest-steppe are subjected to intensive silting, reaching annually 4% to 5% and more of their original volume. Such ponds lose their value in as little as ten to fifteen years, yet the introduction of antierosion measures in spillways could increase their longevity as much or more than ten times. Fish breeding is inadequately developed, and where it is attempted the fish often barely survive because of the pollution of the waters by sewage. It is comforting to note that in the last four to five years, local water-management organizations have begun to devote more attention to the regulation of ponds.

One of the important problems in the further development of water economy consists in the evolution of new methods of hydrological calculation that would secure (*a*) the economic efficiency of hydrotechnical structures and of other water-management measures, and (*b*) quick return on capital investment along with complete guarantee of the durability of these structures and safety in their use (Lvovich, 1959b).

PROTECTION OF WATER RESOURCES

As the national economy develops, its various branches require even more water of higher quality. At the present time, the use of water in the USSR has reached such a level that conservation and renewal have become a critical problem, on the resolution of which depends the further growth of the entire economy.

The protection and renewal of water resources is regulated by pertinent directives: by resolutions of Party congresses and of higher state organs. At the basis of all these directives lie the instructions and thought of V. I. Lenin. Speaking on April 11, 1921, at a meeting of the Communist faction of the VTsSPS (All-Russian Central Council of Trade Unions), Lenin stated:

If we are to safeguard our national wealth, we must see that the scientific and technical regulations are observed. If we are to lease, say, a tract of forest we must see that the lumbering is done in a proper manner. If it should be an oil lease, we must stipulate measures to prevent flooding. In each case, there must be observance of scientific and technical regulations and rational exploitation.

Recalling Lenin's instruction that the protection of natural wealth must be part of the process of its exploitation, we are compelled to note that in recent times the protection of river water and ground water lags behind the scientific-technical rules that operate in production.

Until recently, the regulation of river runoff was restricted to the control of the water regime of reservoirs, but measures pertaining to the collecting basins received little attention. Certainly the problem of the differentiation of measures and scientific-technical rules for the protection and renewal of water resources in the various natural zones and regions was inadequately studied and poorly coordinated with measures for the protection of other natural resources.

A series of organizational and legislative measures to improve and develop water management have recently been introduced, one of which was the decree of the Council of Ministers of the USSR of April 22, 1960. Republic state committees for water management were set up, scientific institutes for the integrated study of water resources were planned, and a series of other improvements in their utilization were introduced.

The organization of the State Committee on Water Management under the Council of Ministers of the RSFSR, and of similar committees established in other union republics, is of great significance. Water management sections were opened in Gosplan (State Planning Commission) and in Gosekonomsovet (State Economic Council of the USSR). The decree of the RSFSR of October 28, 1960, is also of prime importance, because it governs the conservation of nature in that republic, providing protection for all surface and underground sources of water as well as soil moisture; similar decrees were issued in most of the union republics. The efforts begun in 1960 to create a general scheme for developing the water economy show considerable promise.

At present, therefore, we have the organizational basis for the improvement of water management that corresponds to the requirements of the program for building communism in our country.

It has been stated that there are two stages in the protection of water resources—the measures for the improvement of the water regime in collecting basins, and the preservation and renewal of river [channel] flow. Linked intrinsically, at the same time each has its own objectives and each is achieved by means of separate methods. The first stage is closely related to agriculture; the second, primarily to industry, to communal needs, and, to some degree, to irrigation. Measures regulating surface runoff lead to a change in the water balance of the earth's surface, while measures regulating river flow lead to a restructuring of the water supply to the economy. In both stages the goal is the correct use of water resources, based on the principles of careful use. Essential to achievement are—

1. Planning the use of water resources, taking their renewal into consideration.

2. Considering the effect of the exploitation of one source of water upon the other, which calls for a complex and integrated approach.

3. Assuring in the process of exploitation, the renewal and, if possible, the expanded renewal of water resources.

4. Achieving not only the primary use but also the widest use of water possible, for secondary but still important activities such as fishing in ponds and reservoirs established for purposes of energy production.

5. Carrying out the planning of water-resource use on a scientific basis over an extended period of time.

6. Basing the problem of providing economic enterprises with water on the principle of fastest return on investment.

The points enumerated above contain the principles for protecting water resources from quantitative exhaustion.

A second important problem pertains to the protection of the high quality of water. In the next twenty years, the quantity of water being discharged into rivers and water bodies will increase several times, even though a large segment of industry will transfer to systems of circulating water supply. The purification and neutralization of the discharge by means of sanitation plants demand a multimillion ruble outlay annually and, therefore, constitute a problem that is complex not only in a technical but also in an economic sense.

There are possible means of reducing the cost of sewage treatment. Urban sewage, even after the most advanced methods of purification, is not completely rid of all harmful substances; its use in irrigation deserves serious attention (Levitskiy; A. I. Lvovich, 1957). This solution is applicable to about half of all sewage water, including two-thirds of the communal and one-fifth of the industrial sewage. While it completely prevents a polluting discharge into rivers and reservoirs, this method increases agricultural production not less than 4 to 5 billion rubles per year by converting urban sewage into a source of crop irrigation and fertilization. Experiments of sections of several Moscow suburban state farms have demonstrated that crop yields on fields irrigated in this fashion are increased three to four times, that construction costs of such systems are recovered within three to four years, and that such fields are among the most profitable of all agricultural enterprises. In this way no less than 10 million tons of fertilizer contained in the annual volume of suitable urban sewage may be utilized. Fields irrigated by sewage water should stress crops that would allow the development of a dairy-meat economy, produce required by the cities that make such a method possible.

The use of sewage water for irrigating fields is linked with the development of sewage systems in cities, which must treat that part of industrial sewage water that is unfit for irrigation with prophylactic measures. All processes must be changed so that enterprises would not discharge sewage containing valuable substances that would at the same time contaminate water bodies. The complexity of the technical process in many cases will be repaid by savings on purification plants and by the recovery of extracted substances. The oil industry alone loses annually several hundred thousand tons of oil and oil products in its discharge water; pulp and paper combines suffer huge losses by discharging sulfate solutions from which may be obtained ethyl alcohol, albumin yeast, and pulp for wood alcohol. Many such examples may be cited. On the whole, the state economy, in not carrying out a rational utilization of sewage water, suffers losses amounting to hundreds of millions of rubles each year. Obviously, in the future many enterprises will have to be constructed as combines, making use of all elements that can be extracted in the course of the principal technical process.

At the present time, measures to prevent contamination of rivers and lakes are based on a passive principle of self-purification and on a gradual dilution of harmful substances. On the basis of this, limits of concentration of each element have been established for rivers. Self-purification of water obviously does occur; however, the permissible norms of concentration of harmful substances demand reexamination, since frequently they are formalistically applied. High norms, arrived at without consideration of the harm caused by the mixing and interacting of various poisonous substances, in many instances stimulated a concentration of plants and factories on large rivers. In such locations harmful substances are discharged in great quantities, and, even leaving out the question of use, little care is given to their purification. At present, the limits of permissible contamination for many rivers has been reached, and this slows down or even makes impossible the construction of new enterprises and the expansion of existing ones. Thus, the problem of a scientifically based and effective effort to counter the pollution of rivers and other water bodies must be given a significant role in the conservation of surface water.

Circulating systems of water, as yet not widely applied, offer great possibilities in the struggle against river and reservoir pollution. Only rarely do enterprises use the same water two and three times; one is the Saratov oil refinery, which repeatedly uses waste waters containing oil. The possibilities in the repeated use of water are quite significant: for each ton of extracted and concentrated copper ore, 8 cubic meters of water is expended, but a circulating water system would use only one-fourth as much; to produce one ton of pig iron and to transform it into rolled steel, the corresponding figures are respectively 170 to 200 cubic meters and about 20 cubic meters; for one ton of nickel, 4000 cubic meters and 600 cubic meters; and for rubber, 2,100 cubic meters and 165 cubic meters. The use of these hidden reserves can provide the economy cubic kilometers of "supplementary" water. Simultaneously, the reuse of waste water is one of the ways of fighting the pollution of rivers and reservoirs.

THE TASKS OF SCIENCE AND APPLICATION OF SCIENTIFIC KNOWLEDGE

The development of the water economy requires both a widening of creative scientific investigation and complex planning.

Among the primary tasks are: the study of the water balance and its transformation; the development of more effective methods of regulating the water balance of the earth's surface by agro-forest-hydro-melioration; a search for new ways of regulating the water balance by edaphic means; the creation of reliable means of protecting water resources from qualitative exhaustion; and the development of more economic norms and methods of hydrologic calculation. Also, it is necessary to develop experimental investigations of the water-regulative action of the soil under various physical-geographic and economic conditions.

Planning and economic organizations are too slow in the adoption of solutions to a number of problems already provided by science. Although methods for the differentiated study of the water balance, of forecasting changes in the water balance and river runoff due to the effects of economic activities, and of planting effective shelter belts have been already prepared and development of the essentials of a new, improved network of water-protective forests, methods for treating sewage through use in irrigation, and other measures have been developed, the results of this research are little used in the economy. Water management neither makes sufficient demands on science, nor does it fully use the possibilities that science opens up.

The most important organizational problem is the improvement of cooperation between scientific workers and those engaged in water management; experience shows that the more contact there is, the more progress there is.

We think that an essential improvement in water management may be accomplished through the organization of a project-planning bureau or institute for the solution of large, complex water-management problems, one which would put the interests of all branches of the economy in perspective. This organization should not work on the planning of concrete, individual, water-management measures; rather, it should concern itself with general problems, indicate the basic directions for water-resource utilization, and coordinate the interests of all branches of the national economy that are linked by their use of water. Finally, it should design plans for future water use. Together with scientific institutions, such an organization could undertake to resolve specific tasks, which would contribute to a more effective planning of various uses of water for irrigation, for hydro-power, for transportation, and for water supply. Such a new organization could play a leading role in the development of a general scheme of complex use of water resources in the future.

BIBLIOGRAPHY

Alekin, O. A. *Gidrokhimiya* [Hydro-Chemistry]. Leningrad: Gidrometeoizdat, 1952.

Armand, D. L. *Fiziko-geograficheskiye osnovy proyektirovaniya seti polezashchit-nykh lesnykh polos* [Physicogeographical Basis for Planning Shelter Belt Networks]. Moscow-Leningrad: Akademiya Nauk SSSR, 1961.

Avakyan, A. B. and Sharapov, V. A. "O klassifikatsii vodokhranilishch gidroelek-trostantsiy SSSR" [Concerning the Classification of Power Dam Reserves of the USSR]. In *Izvestiya Vsesoyuznogo geograficheskogo obshchestva* [Proceedings of the All-Union Geographical Society], vol. 92, no. 6 (1960).

Budyko, M. I. and Gerasimov, I. P. *Teplovoy i vodnyi balans zemnoy pover-khnosti, obshchaya teoriya fizicheskoy geografii i problema preobrazovaniya prirody* [Heat and Water Balance of the Earth's Surface, General Theory of Physical Geography and the Problem of the Transformation of Nature]. Leningrad, 1959. Materialy k III syezdu Geogr. ob-va SSSR. Doklady po probleme "Vodno-teplovoy rezhim zemnoy poverkhnosti" [Materials for the Third Congress of the Geographical Society of the USSR. Papers on the problem of "The Heat and Water Regime of the Earth's Surface"].

Dokuchayev, V. V. *Nashi stepi prezhde i teper* [Our Steppes, Before and Now]. St. Petersburg, 1892; also, *Izbr. soch.* [Collected Works], vol. 2. Moscow: Selkhozgiz, 1949.

Fedorov, L. T. "Issledovaniye i raschet maksimalnykh raskhodov snegovykh polovodiy rek Yevropeyskoy chasti SSSR" [Study and Calculation of Maximal Volumes of Snow Melt Floods of Rivers in the European Part of the USSR]. In *Problemy regulirovaniya rechnogo stoka* [Problems in the Regulation of River Runoff]. Bull. 5. AN SSSR, 1952.

Gerasimov, I. P. and Glazovskaya, M. A. *Osnovy pochvovedeniya i geografii pochv* [Principles of Pedology and Soil Geography]. Moscow: Geografgiz, 1960.

Glushkov, V. G. *Voprosy teorii i metody gidrologicheskikh issledovaniy* [Problems in the Theory and Methodology of Hydrological Research]. Moscow-Leningrad: AN SSSR, 1961.

Grigoryev, A. A. *Rezhim tepla i vlagi i geograficheskaya zonalnost* [The Heat and Moisture Regime and Geographical Zonality]. Leningrad, 1959. Materialy k III syezdu Geogr. ob-va SSSR. Doklady po probleme "Vodno-teplovoy rezhim zemnoy poverkhnosti." (See Budyko and Gerasimov.)

Izmailskiy, A. A. *Kak vysokhla nasha step* [How Our Steppe Has Dried Up]. Poltava, 1893; also, *Izbr. soch.* Moscow: Selkhozgiz, 1949.

Kuznik, I. A. *Obosnovaniye gidrologicheskikh raschetov pri proyektirovanii vodokhozyaystvennykh meropriyatiy v Povolzhye* [The Establishment of Hydrological Calculations for the Planning of Hydroeconomic Measures Along the Volga]. Saratov, 1958.

Levitskiy, A. M. "Ispolzovaniye stochnykh vod v selskom khozyaystve" [The Use of Runoff Water in Agriculture]. In *Soveshchaniye po ispolzovaniyu i obezvrezhivanniyu stochnykh vod na zemledelcheskikh polyakh orosheniya (Doklady)* [Conference on the Utilization and Purification of Runoff Water Through Irrigation (Papers)]. Moscow, 1957.

Lopatin, G. V. *Nanosy rek SSSR (Obrazovaniye i perenos)* [River Deposits of the USSR (Formation and Transportation)]. Moscow: Geografgiz, 1952.

Lvovich, A. I. "Osnovnye polozheniya ustroystva i proyektirovaniya zemledelcheskikh poley orosheniya" [Principal Considerations in the Formation and Planning of Irrigated Fields]. In *Soveshchaniye po ispolzovaniyu i obezvrezhivanniyu stochnykh vod na zemledelcheskikh polyakh orosheniya (Doklady)*. Moscow, 1957.

Lvovich, M. I. (a) "O metodike raschetov izmeneniy pitaniya rek podzemnymi vodami" [Concerning Methods of Calculating Changes in the Groundwater Supply to Rivers]. *Doklady AN SSSR,* vol. 75, no. 1 (1950).

Lvovich, M. I. (b) "Metodika raschetov ozhidaemykh izmeneniy rezhima rek pod vliyaniem osushchestvleniya plana lesonasazhdeniy" [Methods of Calculating Expected Changes in River Regimes Under the Influence of Implementing the Plan of Forest Plantings]. *Doklady AN SSSR,* vol. 75, no. 2 (1950).

Lvovich, M. I. "O preobrazovanii stoka rek stepnykh i lesostepnykh rayonov Yevropeyskoy chasti SSSR" [Concerning the Changing of the Runoff of the Rivers of the Steppe and Forest-steppe Regions of the European Part of the USSR]. In *Izvestiya AN SSSR, seriya geogr.* [Proceedings of the Academy of Sciences of the USSR, Geographical Series], no. 5 (1952).

Lvovich, M. I. "Effektivnost zapretnykh vodookhrannykh polos lesa vdol rek i problema ikh ekspluatatsii" [The Effectiveness of Protective Water-conserving Forest Belts Along Rivers and the Problem of Their Exploitation]. In *Izv. Vsesoyuzn. geogr. ob-va,* vol. 90, bull. 5 (1958).

Lvovich, M. I. (a) *Vodnyy balans sushi* [Water Balance of the Land]. Materialy k III syezdu Geogr. ob-va SSSR. Doklady po probleme "Vodno-teplovoy rezhim zemnoy poverkhnosti." Leningrad, 1959.

Lvovich, M. I. (b) "Kompleksnyy geograficheskiy metod v gidrologii i zadachi ego razvitiya" [The Complex Geographical Method in Hydrology and the Tasks of its Development]. In *Trudy III Vsesoyuzn. gidrol. syezda* [Transactions of the Third All-Union Hydrological Congress], vol. 7. Leningrad, 1959.

Lvovich, M. I. "Izmeneniya rechnogo stoka pod vliyaniem zemledeliya" [Changes in River Runoff Under the Influence of Crop Cultivation]. In *Kolebaniya i izmeneniya rechnogo stoka* [Variations and Changes in River Runoff]. Moscow-Leningrad: AN SSSR, 1960.

Lvovich, M. I., Bass, S. V., Grin, N. M., et al. "Vodnyy balans SSSR i perspektivy ego preobrazovaniya" [Water Balance of the USSR and the Perspectives of its Transformation]. *Izv. AN SSSR, seriya geogr.*, no. 6 (1961).

Molchanov, A. A. *Gidrologicheskaya rol lesa* [Hydrological Role of Forests]. Moscow-Leningrad: AN SSSR, 1960.

Nazarov, G. V. "Analiz yestyestvennykh i antropogennykh faktorov stoka v Yuzhnom Zavolzhye" [Analysis of the Natural and Anthropogenic Factors of Runoff in Southern Trans-Volga]. In *Kolebaniya i izmeneniya rechnogo stoka*. Moscow-Leningrad: AN SSSR, 1960.

Polyakov, B. V. "Vliyaniye agrotekhnicheskikh meropriyatiy na stok" [Influence of Agrotechnical Measures on Runoff]. *Meteorologiya i gidrologiya*, no. 4 (1939).

Shklyayev, A. S. "K voprosu o vliyanii khozyaystvennoy deyatelnosti cheloveka na stok basseyna r. Oki do g. Kalugi" [Toward the Question of the Influence of the Economic Activity of Man on the Runoff of the Basin of the Oka River Upstream to the City of Kaluga]. In *Ucheniye zapiski Permskogo gossudarstvennogo universiteta* [Scientific Reports of the Perm State University], vol. 9, bull. 1 (1955).

Shnitnikov, A. V. *Izmenchivost obshchey uvlazhennosti materikov Severnogo polushariya* [Changeability of the General Moisture Supply of the Continents of the Northern Hemisphere]. Zap. Geogr. ob-va SSSR, novaya seriya, t. 16 [Reports of the Geographical Society of the USSR, New Series, vol. 16]. Moscow-Leningrad: AN SSSR, 1957.

Vendrov, S. L. and Kalinin, G. P. *Resursy poverkhnostnykh vod SSSR, ikh ispolzovaniye i izucheniye* [Surface Water Resources of the USSR. Their Use and Study]. Materialy k III syezdu Geogr. ob-va SSSR. Doklady po probleme "Rol geografii v izuchenii, ispolzovanii, okhrane i vosstanovlenii prirodnykh resursov SSSR" [Papers on the Problem of "The Role of Geography in the Study, Utilization, Protection, and Reproduction of the Natural Resources of the USSR"]. Leningrad, 1959.

Voyeykov, A. I. *Vozdeystviye cheloveka na prirodu (Izbrannye stati)* [Influence of Man on Nature. (Collected Works)]. Moscow, 1894.

Vyzgo, G. S. "O kompleksnom ispolzovanii vodnykh resursov" [Concerning the Complex Utilization of Water Resources]. *Elektricheskiye stantsii*, no. 1 (1961).

3. Hydropower Resources and Their Use

N. A. Karaulov

(Institute of Energy, Academy of Sciences of the USSR)

The rivers of our country possess a huge power potential whose mean annual capacity is calculated at 434 million kilowatts, representing a potential output of 3,802 billion kilowatt-hours. This constitutes 11.4% of the world's hydroenergy resources. It is both technically and economically feasible to increase the present annual production fivefold, or up to 1,720 billion kilowatt-hours of hydroelectric power, 1,200 billion of which may be produced in large plants.

About 82% of the power potential lies in the Asian USSR; only 18% is in the European part. Of the total potential 54% is located in Siberia, where, in the near future, significant industrial expansion is to take place. Another 20% is found in Kazakhstan and the Central Asia republics, where such valuable irrigated crops as cotton, rice, grapes, and fruit may be expanded and animal husbandry may be developed by making water available in the desert. The mountainous Tadzhik, Kirgiz, and Georgian republics have the greatest concentration of hydro potential per unit area. Although somewhat less than half of the power potential of the Soviet Union as a whole can be developed, the ratio varies from region to region. The highest ratios of power potential that can be developed outside the Russian Federation are found in the Tadzhik, Kirgiz, Kazakh, and Georgian republics, which also have significant industrial resources (Table 1).

Data on the power potential of a number of large rivers, each of which could yield over 20 billion kilowatt-hours of electricity annually, are given in Table 2. About 80% of the energy of these rivers is concentrated in Siberia and the Soviet Far East, 15% in the republics of Central Asia, and the rest in European Russia.

Table 1
Hydroelectric Energy Potential of the USSR

Republic	Capacity[a] (In thousand kilowatts)	Possible Annual Production				Technically Feasible for Development (In billion kilowatt-hours)	Available in Industrial Volumes (In billion kilowatt-hours)
		Kilowatt-hours (In billions)	Percentage of Soviet Total	Kilowatt-hours (In thousands) per sq. km	per person[b]		
Russian Federation	320,859.7	2,810.7	74.0	164.6	23.9	1,343.0	953.0
Tadzhikistan	33,765.5	295.8	7.8	2,068.5	14.9	110.0	84.0
Kazakhstan	18,350.9	160.8	4.2	58.3	17.3	60.0	35.0
Georgia	18,169.8	159.2	4.2	2,274.3	39.3	46.0	33.0
Kirgizia	16,212.5	142.0	3.7	717.2	68.7	92.0	40.0
Uzbekistan	8,761.3	76.7	2.0	187.5	9.5	15.0	13.0
Ukraine	5,107.4	44.7	1.2	74.4	10.9	18.0	15.0
Azerbaydzhan	4,972.8	43.5	1.1	500.0	12.1	11.0	10.0
Turkmenia	2,644.9	23.2	0.6	47.5	1.5	8.0	8.0
Armenia	2,493.5	21.8	0.6	726.6	12.4	7.0	7.0
Belorussia	870.2	7.6	0.2	36.5	0.9	3.0	2.0
Latvia	827.2	7.2	0.2	112.5	3.4	3.9	3.0
Lithuania	622.5	5.5	0.1	84.6	2.0	2.5	2.0
Moldavia	230.8	2.1	0.05	61.8	0.7	1.0	1.0
Estonia	149.4	1.3	0.05	28.9	1.1	0.4	0.1
TOTAL USSR	434,038.5	3,802.1	100.0	170.5	18.3	1,720.8	1,206.1

[a] Data based on measurements of large and medium-sized rivers; estimated for small rivers.
[b] Calculations based on the official census of the population of the USSR of January 15, 1959, published in Moscow, 1960.

Table 2
Potential Hydroelectric Power Resources
of the Largest Rivers of the USSR

Principal Rivers and Their Tributaries	Potential [a] (In thousand kilowatts)	Potential Annual Output (In billion kilowatts)
Lena	18,358	161
Aldan	5,510	48
Vitim	5,425	48
Vilyuy	2,425	21
Olekma	4,007	35
Yenisey	18,213	160
Angara	9,879	86
Lower Tunguska	4,146	36
Amu-Darya	3,834	34
Pyandzh	5,822	51
Vakhsh	4,072	36
Bartang	2,429	21
Ob	5,735	50
Katun	3,753	33
Irtysh	3,177	28
Amur	6,432	56
Indigirka	6,199	54
Volga	6,196	54
Naryn	5,944	52
Kolyma	5,248	46
Khatanga	4,106	36

[a] Includes only the main stream.

From the above it is clear that our country will be assured of hydro-energy only if we continue to build efficient hydroelectric power stations (Voznesenskiy and Beschinskiy).

Huge potentials, together with the continually growing need for energy, flexibility in operation, and the ability to regulate quickly and economically energy output depending on load fluctuations, render large hydroelectric stations the most important component of our power grids. With the continuing unification of the latter, such large plants will become an important part of the unified energy system of the Soviet Union (Karaulov).

The output of hydroenergy will in future amount to 20% to 25% of the total output of electricity of the country. However, it is possible that in the very distant future this ratio will steadily decline. While the construction of thermal-electric plants is not yet limited by fuel reserves (already new types of fuel are being introduced), the sources of hydroenergy that are economically usable will be gradually exhausted. Nevertheless, hydroelectric power will always play a significant role in the total electrification of the country, because it is not only the least expensive but it also contributes to the reliability and flexibility of the power grid.

It might be recalled that in the solution of national economic problems, particularly with respect to water transportation and irrigation, river networks have to be regulated and deepened, which would be irrational without the simultaneous harnessing of their power. By providing the most desirable flow through the reservoir chains and by considering the diverse needs of the economy, we can assure the optimal use of the water and power resources of our rivers.

The production of hydroelectric power has an impact, either negative or positive, on many forms of river use; only a rational and multipurpose approach to the interests of the national economy will result in projects of favorable impact.

Outlined below, in a general way, is the nature of the impact of hydro-development on irrigation and water supply; on the possibilities of reducing the area and resultant losses caused by reservoir flooding; on flood prevention; on fisheries; on river navigation; on forestry and rafting; on water supply to various consumers; and on sanitation.

IRRIGATION AND WATER SUPPLY.   The usefulness of dams and reservoirs is demonstrated chiefly in the southern arid regions and, to some degree, in the zone of insecure water supply. The construction of hydroelectric stations permits a significant expansion in the irrigated area through the intensive and varied uses of river water; an improvement in irrigation by providing water to fields in the right amounts at the right time; an increase in the area of secondary irrigation; and, by raising water levels, a reduction in the costs of pumping water for irrigation and water supply to areas located at higher elevations.

Dams adversely affect flood-plain grazing areas. The periodic inundation that made the flood plains exceedingly fertile ceases and the pasture deteriorates (especially where the series of power stations remains unfinished). This loss may have a serious impact on the aimal husbandry of such regions where flood plains form the major fodder base. This impact has already been witnessed on the Volga-Akhtuba flood plain, in the valley of the Irtysh below the Ust-Kamenogorsk power dam, and elsewhere. The losses may be only partially reduced by occasionally opening the floodgates, since

Table 3
Areas of Potential Irrigation and Water Supply within the Sphere of
Influence of Selected Hydroelectric Stations

Station	River	Area, in million hectares	
		Irrigation	Water Supply
22nd Congress of the CPSU (Volgograd)	Volga	4	14
V. I. Lenin (Kuybyshev)	Volga	1	—
Kakhovka	Dnieper	3	—
Mingechaur	Kura	>1	—
Bukhtarma and Shulbinsk	Irtysh	2	—
Chardarinsk	Syr-Darya	0.6	4.2
Kayrakkum	Syr-Darya	0.6	—

the level of such flooding cannot equal that of the natural flood stage. The creation of flood meadows in these areas, to compensate for the losses in new areas, is of great importance. In the zone of insecure moisture supply, where meadow deterioration cannot be compensated for by irrigation, a regulated water regime should be established. All such meliorative measures must be planned concurrently with the hydroelectric power project and must be implemented as the reservoir is being filled.

The construction of large power plants, when rationally planned, makes it possible to substitute irrigated fields for those lost through inundation and even to increase agricultural output. Unfortunately, the planning of melioration has, up to now, seldom gone hand in hand with the planning and construction of power dams; where it has, delays have ensued. Worse yet, such measures are frequently not carried out at all. This situation must be fundamentally changed.

The potential areas of irrigation and watering associated with some schemes of hydroelectric power development are given in Table 3.

The feasibility of a common solution to the problems of hydroelectric power development and irrigation in the republics of Central Asia was pointed out by N. S. Khrushchev at the January Plenum of the Central Committee of the Communist Party of the Soviet Union. Calculations indicate that the Nurek power plant (under construction on the Vakhsh River) * with a capacity of 2.7 million kilowatts can provide for the irriga-

---

* To be completed in the Five-Year Plan, 1966–70.

tion of nearly 100,000 hectares in the Dangarinsk Steppe (southern Tadzhikistan). The inexpensive power of that station permits also the irrigation of some two million hectares in the Bukhara, Samarkand, and the Surkhan-Darinsk oblasts of the Uzbek Republic. The use of electric-pump irrigation to replace existing gravity flow on the best 500,000 to 700,000 hectares alone, will save about 400 million rubles. It must be stressed, though, that the savings can be achieved only by constructing a series of regulating dams downstream on the Amu-Darya. By relying on the Nurek plant alone, long-range regulation, despite the increase in water use, can lead during the period of irrigation to lower water levels in the middle and lower reaches of the Vakhsh and Amu-Darya.

RESERVOIR INUNDATION. The rapid tempo of hydroelectric development makes the loss of land to reservoirs a critical problem. The construction of dams destroys agricultural land, forests, populated areas, industrial enterprises, roads, mineral deposits, and other economic phenomena. Apart from direct inundation, much loss occurs around those reservoirs with gentle banks, for the raising of the water table results in waterlogging and bog formation.

At present the USSR has sixty large reservoirs in existence or under construction. They are used for power as well as for other purposes. The surface area of each of the nineteen largest reservoirs exceeds 100,000 hectares. According to tentative calculations, the total area of reservoirs that are to be completed by 1975 as well as those that are part of yet incomplete schemes amounts to about 30 million hectares (Vyzgo, 1960).

Now that the better virgin lands have already been cultivated and further expansion is possible only through extensive reclamation, a particularly cautious approach to hydroengineering projects (involving inundation) is required.

Methods of economically evaluating lands to be inundated remain poor. Hence, agriculture and other branches of the economy frequently are not adequately compensated for, while actual costs frequently exceed the original estimates of the power project. On lowland rivers in populated areas, compensation costs occasionally reach half the project cost.

The area of inundation can be decreased in a number of ways. In the future, the construction of power dams will tend to shift to upper reaches of rivers, which rise in those mountain areas where the inundation is less extensive. At the same time, an increasing amount of power will come from plants in the northern part of the USSR and Eastern Siberia, where the population is relatively small and the area flooded is of little use for agriculture. The introduction of high power-transmission lines permits the site of power generation to be located at a greater distance from centers of consumption. Such advantages should be realized as quickly as possible.

The shallow parts of reservoirs represent a particularly important loss. They lead to heavy evaporation and encourage the breeding of bloodsucking insects, including the malarial mosquito. The selection of a proper areal extent and pressure level for the reservoir can reduce the shallow water area to a minimum. These shoals, which are impossible to avoid under some conditions, can be used for the growing of wild rice and for the breeding of muskrat, nutria, and waterfowl.

The simplest way to decrease the area of inundation would be to lower the heads of the dams or, with the same effect, to increase the number of dams in the chain or cascade. However, this would lower their economic and technical efficiency by forcing the power plants to operate nearer capacity (and to be less capable of responding to variations in demand for power). This would also result in a greater seasonal range of production. An increase in the number of power stations in a completed chain would lead to a growth in investment and could even result in the abandonment, for economic reasons, of projected chains.

It should be stated, however, that present energy grids have a built-in regulative capacity whose significance will grow with the development of a unified grid and with the decrease in due time of the relative significance of hydroenergy. With this in mind it is possible in some cases to lower the normal pressure level at the dams. As for capital expenditures, the growing value of agricultural and other land will sooner or later lead to the recognition that the inundation of additional millions of hectares of land can sometimes be a greater loss than the small increase in the cost of construction and the consequent increase in cost of power.

In the process of planning power dams, all benefits and costs of every project variant should be carefully considered. The concept of regulation of runoff over a period of years, therefore, has been abandoned in some power projects in favor of annual regulation, which has led to a significant decrease in the area of inundation.

The diking of agricultural land and of other resources or installations that are in danger of being inundated is important. The improvement of excavation techniques can lower diking costs. If economical, diking can be done with floating excavators even in existing reservoirs. The planning of dikes should take into account the cost of the electrical energy used in pumping out the water that accumulates in the polders. Diking has already been employed in a number of cases (for instance, in the Kostroma lowland around the Gorki reservoir). The diking of the Sulinsk flood plains around the Kremenchug reservoir has been planned.*

The capacity of reservoirs can be cut by using pumping systems in power plants, which may in turn constitute a unique source of energy, one that can be utilized during peak hours. This is accomplished by constructing a smaller basin at higher levels, to which water is pumped during periods of low demand, using the energy of the power dams. Then, during peak hours, water is channeled through turbines to provide power for the grid. The high head of these installations, usually measured by hundreds of meters, can, by flooding small upland areas, provide the necessary regulatory capacity and reduce the control requirements of the lower dam. In this way the surface of reservoirs can be substantially reduced. Power stations relying on this type of pumping are being built in many countries of Europe and America.

One way of reducing the area of inundation is to use turbines that, under a significant decrease in pressure, can retain high efficiency without losing much of their capacity. One type of turbine has an adjustable speed of rotation that allows a uniform output of power. These machines permit a lowering of the normal pressure level of the power dam, decreasing the area of the reservoir.

Flood Prevention. The creation of large reservoirs on rivers that are periodically subjected to flooding (especially in the Soviet Far East) permits the production of power and provides for flood control.

Such multipurpose systems produce inexpensive power, permit, due to lower water levels, the partial or total elimination of disastrous floods, the agricultural use of some flood plains that are no longer subject to such destruction, and a decrease in capital investments in various structures built downstream (bridges, landing places, dikes, and so forth). A good example is the large, multipurpose, power complex planned for the Zeya River that, apart from producing 4.4 billion kilowatt-hours, will control floods and cut annual losses eightfold.

Fisheries. The effects of power dams and reservoirs on fisheries are diverse. The building of reservoirs significantly extends the water area and usually raises the volume of fish catch. Increases of up to twenty times or more are on record, as, for example, in the Tsimlyansk Reservoir. Fish growth is faster in reservoirs than in natural bodies of water because they

---

* Construction on the Kremenchug Hydroelectric Station was completed under the Seven-Year Plan, 1959–66.

have a greater food supply due to the flooding of fertile land and the accumulation from river inflow. Reservoir fisheries also allow a higher labor productivity than do river fisheries and require lower capital inputs.

By proper stocking, large lowland reservoirs can create ideal conditions for commercial fish breeding. Effective use of these fisheries, considering the fluctuations in the reservoir level, requires the provision of a stable water level for extended periods following the spawning season. This must be considered in planning the discharge of water through the generators and the spillways.

In some respects, however, the construction of dams and reservoirs can have a negative effect on fisheries: dams located on the lower or middle reaches of rivers present obstacles to fish migration; a change in riverine conditions may reduce spawning grounds; the feeding of commercial fish near estuaries is endangered by the decrease in the supply of river-borne nutrients. However, these losses may be compensated for by increased feeding in new reservoirs.

To counteract the negative effects of power dams and to increase reserves of migratory and semimigratory fish, such meliorative measures as the construction of fish ladders, elevators, fish farms, and hatcheries must be undertaken. The provision of water to the cascade, and the protection of the natural spawning grounds below it, are also important. Until recently, only salmon made regular use of ladders and elevators; however, the new fish elevator at the Volga power dam * has proven successful for sturgeon as well. Nevertheless, hatcheries are the best way to produce fry.

RIVER NAVIGATION. Dams substantially increase river depths and create favorable conditions for navigation (as for example on the Volga, Kama, Dnieper, and many others).

Canals are, as a rule, linked with hydroelectric production as, for instance, in the Volga-Don Ship Canal (named after V. I. Lenin) and the recently rebuilt Volga-Baltic Waterway. Hydroelectric dams not only increase depths but permit the straightening of channels and the decrease of flows to as little as 5% of their former rate. Power reservoirs have shortened shipping routes by up to 15% on the average.

These changes allow for an increase in freight capacity and shipping efficiency (assuming the reservoirs reach the upstream dams), which substantially lower and improve navigation in the low-water season and below the dam.

---

* The power dam at Volgograd was named after the Twenty-second Congress of the CPSU.

However, in some cases, these changes increase the incidence of freezing and shorten the navigable period. The movement of ships may be speeded up by the shortening of the channel but slowed by the presence of locks and waves on large reservoirs.

The reorganization of shipping on reservoirs requires a relatively large initial capital investment: locks must be installed, ship size must be increased, and finally, locking and navigation facilities must be provided. This investment simply reflects the progress in inland navigation.

FORESTRY AND RAFTING. The construction of power dams and reservoirs in the forest zone frequently improves the forest economy. It raises the flow capacity of the rivers, permits an increase in lumbering and an expansion into virgin forests that formerly lacked access. It also forces lumber-transport agencies to switch from the floating of logs with the aid of jetties—which lead to a loss of lumber and river obstruction—to the more economic towing of rafts or to the shipping of lumber by boat. These methods permit the exploitation of hardwoods (broad-leaved species, larch, and others). The shipment of lumber by boat shortens delivery by up to six times and prevents losses.

A good example of the beneficial influence of dams and reservoirs on forestry may be found in the Kama project, and also in the Vychegda-Pechora diversion project.

Reservoirs cause a deterioration in wind and wave conditions and reduce the speed of rafting, with concomitant difficulties for log transport; however, this difficulty could be easily counteracted.

In the construction of large reservoirs, especially on Siberian rivers, the costs of clearing timber from the sites are high. A floating timber combine is under construction to clear and partially process the timber as the reservoir fills, eliminating the need for temporary roads and the establishment of state lumber enterprises. Such combines will make lumbering profitable in regions where large power reservoirs are built and will also increase revenues by millions of rubles.

In a number of regions (Western Siberia and, to some extent, the European North), the better timber is found on river terraces, and the watersheds are covered by upland bogs and forests of low quality. For this reason, as the reservoir fills, the bulk of the timber (at the Bratsk site, about 30 million cubic meters) must be quickly removed from those lands that subsequently will be inundated. Consequently, the advantages of a deep waterway can be fully used.

WATER SUPPLY. Project estimates indicate that large reservoirs, with their low banks, make possible year-round supplies of drinkable water to centers of population and for industry. These reservoirs help to reduce the construction costs of water-supply systems and facilitate their regulation; they also improve the quality of the water that reaches the consumer.

One large water-supply system is the Ivankovo reservoir, which is a principal source of water to Moscow. Another is the Kakhovka reservoir, which supplies the Krivoy-Rog mining region. However, where reservoirs are adjacent to uplands (for instance, the west banks of the Middle and Lower Volga and of the Middle Dnieper); settlements that were well provided with water on low river terraces had to be removed to the high bank with dam construction. There water is sometimes obtained from deep wells, a development that is costly and difficult.

HYGIENIC MEASURES. Reservoirs, if they are maintained in a sufficiently hygienic condition, if their banks are properly developed, and if they have beaches and green areas, become recreational areas. Attractive sites on the banks of reservoirs are desirable for sanitaria, rest homes, and tourist facilities.

It is obvious from the above that we must not think in terms of a single use of water, even if it is for power. The goal is to provide a multipurpose use of the resource of any given river. This task should be solved by planning that takes into consideration development schemes for the regions adjacent to the reservoir.

THERMAL POWER STATIONS. Finally, the question of the influence of thermal power stations on river regimes must be considered. The operation of large steam plants requires large quantities of circulating water for the cooling of the condensers. Even if much of the system is air-cooled by means of a closed water system (evaporators and sprinkling basins), the balance still requires water cooling. A large volume of warm water returned to the river can cause significant damage to fisheries and to prevent this loss requires attention.

This indicates that the influence of power development on related branches of the economy is significant and complex. However, if solutions are found that optimize the benefits, the construction of dams will prove desirable not only as new sources of power but also in contributing to other branches of the economy.

BIBLIOGRAPHY

Avakyan, A. B. "Znacheniye vodokhranilishch gidroelektrostantsiy dlya razlichnykh otrasley narodnogo khozyaystva" [The Significance of Power Dam Reservoirs in Various Branches of the National Economy]. *Gidrotekhnicheskoye stroitelstvo*, no. 4 (1961).

Karaulov, N. A. "Problemy sovetskoy gidroenergetiki" [Problems of Soviet Hydroenergetics]. *Vestnik AN SSSR*, no. 7 (1958).

Magakyan, G. L. "Voprosy effektivnosti mnogootraslevogo ispolzovaniya vodo-energeticheskikh uzlov" [Problems of Effective Multipurpose Utilization of Hydropower Complexes]. *Geografiya i khozyaystvo*, vol. 8, Moscow, 1960.

Nesteruk, F. N. *Gidroenergeticheskiye resursy mira i osnovnye pokazateli oborudovaniya glavneyshikh zarubezhnykh gidroelektrostantsiy* [Hydropower Resources of the World and the Principle Indices of the Installations of the Most Important Foreign Power Stations]. Moscow-Leningrad: Gosenergoizdat, 1946.

Vozdvizhenskiy, V. I., Avakyan, A. B., and Sharapov, V. A. "Nekotoryye voprosy sozdaniya vodokhranilishch gidroelektrostantsiy v usloviyakh Vostochnoy Sibiri" [Some Questions on the Building of Power Dam Reservoirs Under the Conditions of Eastern Siberia]. In *Razvitiye proizvoditelnykh sil Vostochnoy Sibiri* [Development of the Productive Forces of Eastern Siberia]. Energetika, AN SSSR, 1960.

Voznesenskiy, A. N. and Beschinskiy, A. A. "Gidroenergeticheskiye resursy SSSR i narodnokhozyaystvennoye znacheniye ikh ispolzovaniya" [Hydropower Resources of the USSR and the National Economic Significance of Their Use]. *Gidrotekhnicheskoye stroitelstvo*, no. 11 (1957).

Voznesenskiy, A. N. and Terman, I. A. "Gidroenergeticheskiye resursy SSSR" [Hydropower Resources of the USSR]. *Gidrotechnicheskoye stroitelstvo*, no. 4 (1956).

Vyzgo, G. S. "O generalnom plane ispolzovaniya vodnykh, zemelnykh i energeticheskikh resursov" [Concerning the General Plan of Utilization of Water, Land and Energy Resources]. *Geografiya i khozyaystvo*, no. 6, Moscow, 1960.

Vyzgo, G. S. "O kompleksnom ispolzovanii vodnykh resursov" [Concerning the Complex Utilization of Water Resources]. *Elektricheskiye stantsii*, no. 1 (1961).

Part 3. CLIMATE

4. Agroclimatic Resources

F. F. Davitaya and G. A. Sapozhnikova
(*Central Institute of Forecasting of the GUGMS* *
under the Council of Ministers of the USSR)

The present distribution of agriculture in the USSR is the result of many centuries of rural land occupancy. Where that occupancy is of long standing, the more important climatic elements tend to be used effectively and agriculture seems to reflect the conditions of nature. This may be seen in the cultivation of grains in the Ukraine and the North Caucasus, viticulture in the Crimea and in Transcaucasia, cotton cultivation in Central Asia, and so forth. Correct distribution of production was aided by the proper planning of the sowing of the crops in the various pedoclimatic zones. Nevertheless, not all branches of agriculture are correctly distributed and, in some cases, vast climatic potentials remain unused.

Agroclimatic description and regionalization of the Soviet Union and the recognition of how the yields of various crops depend on weather and climate enable us to estimate the climatic resources of Soviet agriculture, which facilitates the planning of agricultural production.[1]

Of particular importance to agriculture is the accounting of heat and moisture supplies to plants. With a more secure heat supply, the proportion of late-maturing crops can be greater and, therefore, the yield can be higher. At the same time, the possibility of sowing a second crop increases, permitting two and even three harvests per field.

The temperature regime can be described by a number of indicators. The most widely accepted is the sum of the mean daily temperatures for the period when they exceed 10° C.

---

[1] *Atlas selskogo khozyaystva CCP* [Atlas of Agriculture of the USSR] Moscow: GUGK, 1960). See maps of Agroclimatic Resources, pp. 46–47, 48.

* Glavnoye upravleniye gidrometeorologicheskoy sluzhby (Central Office of the Hydrometeorological Service).

The temperature regime of the USSR may be divided into the following belts: arctic, subarctic, temperate, and subtropical.

The arctic belt, which includes the tundra, is almost entirely limited to the herding of reindeer; crop cultivation is possible only under cover.

The subarctic belt, located in the northern taiga, is characterized by oases of farming. The heat resources permit open-field cultivation of vegetables with a short growth cycle and low heat requirements, such as radishes, lettuce, spinach, green onions, turnips, cabbage, and potatoes. This belt also has reindeer herding, and animal husbandry based on stall feeding is becoming increasingly significant.

The temperate belt, where the four seasons of the year are sharply differentiated, encompasses the basic agricultural regions of our country. In winter, which varies in duration from one to eight months, the active growth of even the most frost-resistant plants ceases. Many types of crops, including grains, legumes, vegetables, fodder and industrial crops, and fruit are grown in this belt. Animal husbandry is based primarily on pasture-stall feeding, but seasonal grazing prevails in various dry regions.

The subtropical belt is found only on the southern margins of the country that are protected by the Greater Caucasus and the Kopet-Dag ranges. This belt has two vegetative seasons: the winter for frost-resistant crops (cereal grains and some vegetables for winter gardening) and the summer for heat-loving plants (for instance, cotton). Perennial subtropical crops (citrus, tea, olives, and others) also grow here.

The productivity of crops, given adequate heat and other growth requirements, depends primarily on moisture, the supply of which normally is measured by the amount of precipitation occurring throughout the year and during the vegetative period. The effectiveness of precipitation depends, however, on evaporation. It is, therefore, of more value to describe the moisture supply not simply by the amount of precipitation but by an index of moisture availability, which is usually presumed to equal the sum of the precipitation less potential evaporation—the maximum possible evaporation under conditions of plentiful soil moisture supply. According to this index, the USSR may be divided into three principal zones: humid, subhumid or semiarid, and arid.

In the humid zone, the amount of annual precipitation exceeds potential evaporation, the latter being an indication of how much moisture the plants require. In this zone a significant drop in yields because of insufficient moisture supply is unlikely; damage caused by an excess of moisture is more likely. In the subhumid or semiarid zone, annual precipitation is less than potential evaporation. Here, plants frequently suffer from moisture deficiency, which results in great variation in yield from year to year. In the arid zone, the amount of precipitation is so small that agriculture without irrigation is uneconomical.

A comparison of grain yields (of corn and of average and late-maturing varieties of oats and barley) with the availability of heat and moisture makes it possible to determine the level of yield obtainable per unit of heat (the sum of temperatures that equals 100) * under given moisture supply conditions.

On the basis of the relationship indicated, i.e., the sum of the temperatures and the amount of moisture available, the potential yield capacity of grains has been calculated. Actual yield would reach the potential if such grains are produced that fully utilize the entire vegetative period (that is, the period when the mean daily temperatures exceed 10°).

Used in the calculations were crop yields from the fields of the Gossortset [†] for the period up to 1960, yields that were almost twice those of state and collective farms. Such yields may be considered an objective toward which we must strive in the coming years. The potential yield of grains—our basic crop—can be used as a basis for evaluating the productivity of agriculture as well as of climate.

Knowledge of the agroclimatic potential can aid in solving some agricultural problems, particularly in the long-range planning of such large capital investments as the construction of irrigation systems and the establishment of differential norms of collective-farm revenue. Both tasks require a survey of natural resources, including climate.

The productivity of climate, arranged according to economic regions, is evaluated in Table 1. The productivity of the humid zone is estimated on the basis of the natural moisture supply; for the arid zone it is calculated from both the approximate natural moisture supply and optimal irrigation. In evaluating productivity, both the average yield and the stability of yield must be considered. Calculations of deviations from the mean (with 80% certainty) were made for the semiarid zone where yields are least stable.[2] Agroclimatic indices and data on average absolute minimum temperatures, which characterize winter severity, were also compiled. For regions of variable climate, data for oblasts having the most favorable conditions were added.

The European part of the Soviet Union, with two regions of optimal

---

[2] An 80% certainty means that greater deviations from average yield occur only in 20% of the years or less.

* That is, the sum of the excess of temperatures above the average daily temperature of 10°C.

† Gosudartsvennaya sortoispytatelnaya set (State Plant Variety Experimental Network).

Table 1
Agroclimatic Productivity (Grain Yield Potential) and Principal Agroclimatic Indices of the Economic Regions of the USSR (Regions of the Temperate Belt Plains)

Regions of the State Planning Commission (Gosplan), Union Republics[a] and Groups of (or Individual) Oblasts[b]	Climatic Productivity (In centners per hectare)			Agroclimatic Indices			Percentage of Area of Region in Subarctic Belt or in Arid Zone of Temperate Belt[c]
	Under Natural Moisture Supply	Under Optimal Irrigation	Fluctuations (with 80% certainty)	Sum of Temperatures (for the period with temperatures above 10°C.)	Moisture Supply Conditions	Average Annual Absolute Minimum Temperatures °C.	
				RSFSR			
Central Region (Moscow, Smolensk, Yaroslavl, Ivanovo, Vladimir, Ryazan,Tula, and Kaluga oblasts)	27	—	—	2,000	V	−30 to −35	—
Volga-Vyatka (Gorki, Kirov, and Kostroma oblasts; Mari, Mordvin, and Chuvash ASSR's)	24	—	4	1,900	V–Z$_s$	−30 to −40	—
Central Black Earth (Orel, Kursk, Belgorod, Voronezh, Lipetsk, and Tambov oblasts)	30	34	6	2,400	Z$_s$	−30	—
Northwest (Leningrad, Novgorod, Pskov, Murmansk, Vologda, Arkhangelsk, and Kaliningrad oblasts; Karelian and Komi ASSR's)	20	—	—	1,500	V$_o$	−30 to −45	35
Kaliningrad Oblast	32	—	—	2,300	V	−20 to −25	—

Volga (Povolzhye) (Tatar ASSR and Saratov, Volgograd, and Astrakhan oblasts)	30	43	14	2,800	N	−25 to −35	15
Astrakhan Oblast	—	56	—	3,400	S	−25 to −30	—
North Caucasus (Krasnodar and Stavropol krays; Rostov Oblast; Dagestan, Chechen-Ingush, North Osetin, Kabardino-Balkar, and Kalmyk ASSR's)	39	54	18	3,300	N	−15 to −30	15
Krasnodar Kray	45	58	13	3,500	Z_s	−15 to −25	—
Ural (Sverdlovsk, Perm, Chelyabinsk, Kurgan, and Orenburg oblasts; and Bashkir and Udmurt ASSR's)	22	—	—	1,850	$V–Z_s$	−35 to −45	—
Western Siberia (Altay Kray; Kemerovo, Novosibirsk, Omsk, Tyumen, and Tomsk oblasts)	20	—	4	1,600	$V–Z_s$	−40 to −45	30
Altay Kray	28	—	6	2,200	Z_s	−40 to −45	—
Eastern Siberia (Irkutsk and Chita oblasts; Krasnoyarsk Kray; Tuvinian, Buryat, and Yakut ASSR's)	15	—	—	1,400	N	−40 to −45	50
Krasnoyarsk Kray	20	—	—	1,600	V	−40 to −45	—
Far East (Maritime and Khabarovsk krays; Amur, Kamchatka, Magadan, and Sakhalin oblasts	24	—	—	1,800	$V–Z_s$	−25 to −45	60
Maritime Kray	39	—	—	2,600	V_s[1]	−25 to −35	—

Continued

Table 1 (cont.)

Regions of the State Planning Commission (Gosplan), Union Republics [a] and Groups of (or Individual) Oblasts [b]	Climatic Productivity (In centners per hectare)			Agroclimatic Indices			Percentage of Area of Region in Subarctic Belt or in Arid Zone of Temperate Belt [c]
	Under Natural Moisture Supply	Under Optimal Irrigation	Fluctuations (with 80% certainty)	Sum of Temperatures (for the period with temperatures above 10°C.)	Moisture Supply Conditions	Average Annual Absolute Minimum Temperatures °C.	
The West							
Latvian SSR	26	—	—	1,900	V_0	−25 to −30	—
Lithuanian SSR	29	—	—	2,100	V_0–V	−25	—
Estonian SSR	24	—	—	1,800	V_0	−25 to −30	—
Belorussian SSR	32	—	—	2,300	V–V_0	−25 to −30	—
Ukrainian and Moldavian SSR's							
Polesye (Volynian, Zhitomir, Kiev, Rovno, and Chernigov oblasts)	33	—	—	2,500	V	−25 to −30	—
Forest-steppe (Vinnitsa, Lvov, Poltava, Sumy, Ternopol, Kharkov, Cherkassy, Chernovtsy, Trans-carpathian, Stanislav, and Khmelnitskiy oblasts)	37	—	8	2,750	V–$Z_в$	−25	—
Transcarpathian Oblast	44	—	7	2,900	V	−20 to −25	—
Steppe (Lugansk, Dnepropetrovsk, Zaporozhye, Kirovograd, Crimean, Nikolayev, Odessa, Donetsk, and Kherson oblasts)	34	50	16	3,100	Z–$Z_в$	−15 to −25	—
Moldavian SSR	40	51	14	3,150	Z	−20 to −25	—

	Central Asia						
Turkmen SSR	—	85	—	S	5,000	−10 to −25	—
Uzbek SSR	—	72	—	S	4,300	−15 to −30	—
	Kazakh SSR						
Western Kazakhstan (Aktyubinsk, Guryev, and West Kazakhstan oblasts)	—	56	—	S	3,400	−20 to −35	ca 90
Aktyubinsk Oblast	24	41	14	Z_o	2,700	−35	—
Virgin Lands Kray	22	32	10	Z–Z_o	2,300	−35 to −40	ca 15
Central Kazakhstan (Karaganda Oblast) [d]	—	50	—	S	3,100	−35	60
Eastern Kazakhstan (East Kazakhstan and Semipalatinsk oblasts) [d]	16	32	11	Z_o	2,300	−40	15
Semipalatinsk Oblast	—	44	—	S	2,900	−35 to −40	—
Southeastern Kazakhstan (Alma-Ata and Dzhambul oblasts)	—	56	—	S	3,400	−30 to −35	—
Southern Kazakhstan (Kzyl-Orda and South Kazakhstan oblasts)	—	67	—	S	4,000	−25 to −30	—

NOTE: Data are from the economic division prior to January 1, 1961.

NOTE: The following abbreviations have been adopted for this table: V_o = very humid (*ochen vlazhno*); Z_s = subject to some drought, subhumid (*slabo zasushlivo*); Z = subject to drought, semiarid (*zasushlivo*); Z_o = subject to frequent drought, semiarid (*ochen zasushlivo*); S = arid (*sukho*).

[a] Agroclimatic indices were not established for the Armenian, Georgian, Kirgiz, and Tadzhik SSR's because of the predominance of mountains.

[b] Data for individual oblasts are provided when their agroclimatic characteristics differ appreciably from the averages of the Gosplan region or Union Republic of which they are a part.

[c] The percentage of territory in the arid zone is not shown when there is no arid land or when arid land extends over more than 90% of the region (southeastern and southern Kazakhstan, the Turkmen, and Uzbek SSR's, etc.).

[d] Data pertain only to areas outside the arid zone.

[1] V_s implies *slabo vlazhno*, or slightly humid, an abbreviation not listed above, and may be in error. Ed.

climatic conditions, occupies first place in agricultural productivity. They are the western piedmont of the North Caucasus, including in particular some districts in Krasnodar Kray, with plentiful heat and a good moisture supply, and the forest-steppe and the northern part of the steppe in the Ukraine.

Summer temperatures are fairly constant throughout the USSR. Hence, the northern thermal limits of various crops and of agriculture itself reach the same latitude in Western Siberia and northern Kazakhstan as in the eastern part of European Russia. In the former, however, the moisture supply is noticeably poorer.

While in the Ukraine drought coincides with a very warm vegetative period (the sum of the temperatures amounts to 2800° to 3400° and the frost-free period extends from five and one-half to six months), the drought-prone territories of Western Siberia (southern districts of Omsk and Novosibirsk oblasts) are cooler (the sum of the temperatures is only 2100° to 2200° with a frost-free period from three and one-half to four months). In other words, under almost the same relationships of precipitation to evaporation, the absolute magnitude of both indices is greater and the vegetative period is longer in the Ukraine than in Western Siberia. Thus, the general climatic productivity of agriculture in Siberia and in western Kazakhstan is lower than at the same latitude in the European part. The conditions of the latter are approximated in Asia only in some piedmont regions, as in the Altay, which has a better moisture supply. The similar soils of the Ukraine and of Western Siberia (excluding the Altay) have thus a different productivity (Table 2).

The lower productivity of Western Siberia (20 centners per hectare) compared with Belorussia (32 centners per hectare), other conditions being equal, suggests that meliorative measures would be less effective in Western Siberia than in the Belorussian Republic.

Table 2
Productivity of Regions with Chernozem Soils
(Centners of grain per hectare)

Soils	*Ukrainian SSSR*	*Central Black Earth Region*	*Trans-Volga*	*Western Siberia*
Degraded Chernozems	35–40	30–35	25–30	20–25
Ordinary Chernozems	30–35	25–30	25	20–25

Although climatic conditions in Western Siberia and northern Kazakhstan are less favorable for agriculture than in the European part of the USSR, full utilization of the former territories is of great value in regulating the grain supply of the country that, as is known, varies from year to year depending on the weather. As a rule, drought years in the Ukraine, Trans-Volga, Western Siberia, and northern Kazakhstan do not coincide. Thus, a poor harvest in the European part can be compensated for by high yields in the virgin lands, and vice versa.

The assessment of variations in productivity can be used to solve a number of problems, including the size of insurance funding. In the Middle Volga Region, which has the same productivity as the Central Black Earth Region (30 centners per hectare), the insurance reserves should be significantly greater since the variation amounts to approximately 14 centners per hectare, while at the same time in the Central Black Earth it is only approximately 6 centners.

The variation in grain yields in drought-prone regions affects production and export and requires that attention be given to raising yields of early grains in the humid non-chernozem oblasts. Grain yields in the latter oblasts do not reflect the climatic possibilities because of low soil fertility. This raises the question as to which is more economical: to struggle with drought in the semiarid zone (without entirely eliminating yield fluctuations) or to take measures to increase soil productivity in regions that are well watered and provide stable yields?

In resolving this question, one has to keep in mind that present methods of land improvement can change substantially the natural conditions of agricultural land (soil, relief, microclimate) and result in significant increases in fertility, provided the basic climatic factors are favorable. Semiarid zones, because of plentiful heat, have the advantage in that yield variations can be entirely eliminated through irrigation. However, irrigation is a costly measure justified only by the cultivation of high-value crops; for most of the grains it is not economical.

The eastward increase in the severity of the winters lowers the possibility of fruit production in Western Siberia and northern Kazakhstan, or at least necessitates special measures for protecting fruit trees from severe frost. The combination of low air temperatures and light snow cover in the territories extending from the Trans-Volga to the Altay piedmont creates unfavorable conditions for the survival of winter crops and requires the introduction of winter crops that are particularly frost resistant.

The climatic potential of Eastern Siberia is even poorer than that of Western Siberia. This is due not only to the extremely continental climate, the presence of permafrost and extended seasonal soil freezing, but also to the mountainous character of the terrain, which causes a general lowering of temperatures. Agriculture is possible there only in valleys and foothills. The continentality of climate, however, extends the thermal limits of a number of crops northward along the valleys in Eastern Siberia to the Arctic Circle, which is farther than they extend in either the European part of the USSR or in Western Siberia. This assures the northern industrial centers (Magadan, Aldan, Kolyma, and others) vegetables and feed for livestock. However, drought is possible, particularly when the permafrost table is lowered, requiring measures for moisture accumulation and even irrigation.

The agroclimatic conditions in the southern part of the Soviet Far East are quite different. Because of better precipitation, despite the very dry winter and spring, the conditions for agriculture are good.

The Lake Khanka lowland, in its intensity of heat and moisture, is similar to the southwestern districts of the Ukrainian forest-steppe. In agroclimatic regimes, the Blagoveshchensk and Khabarovsk regions are identical or somewhat better than Lithuania and Belorussia. This permits agricultural development in the southern part of the Soviet Far East. However, the climatic conditions, particularly the peculiarities of the annual moisture supply, can lower the yields of European varieties of crops. Therefore, it is necessary to draw extensivily here on the experience of the adjacent regions of China.

The agroclimatic resources of Central Asia, where there is much heat but little moisture, require particular consideration. It is here that irrigation is especially effective. Because of the length of the growing season, the irrigated fields of Central Asia yield not only bountiful harvests but also more than one crop per year. The abundance of solar heat permits the cultivation of such valuable crops as cotton, including the long-staple variety. Irrigation assures also the highest yield stability. The growing season lengthens toward the south, thus raising the yields of cotton and other crops. The efficiency of investment in irrigation systems also increases southward. The irrigated fields of Central Asia can produce the highest yields of all temperate zone crops provided their cultivation is properly timed. This region is, therefore, among the most promising in the growth of agricultural productivity.

The most productive regions of the USSR, both in yield and value of crops, have a humid subtropical climate (the Black Sea littoral of western Georgia and the district of Sochi in Krasnodar Kray). They produce tea, citrus, tung, and so forth. But the area of such favorable climate is limited, and only those crops that cannot be raised in other regions of the USSR should be grown here.

In a number of agricultural zones the reserves of unused heat and moisture reach tremendous proportions. Following the annual harvest of winter and early spring crops in regions of adequate moisture supply (the forest-steppe of the Ukraine, Belorussia, the Central Black Earth Region, and several districts of the Non-Chernozem Zone), sums of temperature of 1000° to 2000° and more (Transcarpathia) and a volume of water of from 1000 to 2000 cubic meters per hectare, remain unused. This amounts to 40% to 60% of the available resources of biologically useful heat and a somewhat lower ratio of water available for transpiration.[3] After the main harvest, the heat and moisture that remain to the end of the vegetative period can be used to raise a second crop. Leading farms in regions mentioned above are already taking advantage of these possibilities, obtaining after harvest about 200 to 300 centners per hectare of green corn fodder, leguminous hay, and other crops. According to preliminary estimates, it is possible to obtain two complete harvests annually from an area of several million hectares.

In regions of sufficient moisture, the substitution of clean fallow by fallow crops also can provide the country with hundreds of millions of poods of additional grain and concentrated feed. Second cropping can have considerable significance also in Georgia and on the irrigated lands of Armenia, Azerbaydzhan, Central Asia, and Kazakhstan. However, second cropping should be avoided where heat is abundant but moisture is inadequate and unreliable. Production of more than one harvest per year also depletes mineral and organic soil nutrients and, consequently, should be accompanied by increased use of fertilizers.

Three-fourths of Soviet sugar production is concentrated in the Ukraine, although a significant amount comes from the Central Back Earth. Agroclimatic analysis, confirmed by agricultural practice, reveals also the possibility of successful sugar-beet cultivation in large areas of the North Caucasus, in the southern half of Belorussia, in southern Lithuania, in Kaliningrad Oblast, in Transcaucasia, and in the Soviet Far East. In the last region, the area under sugar beets can be increased at least tenfold.

The soil and climatic potentials for the cultivation of wine grapes have not been reached either in the north or in mountain regions. By selecting

---

[3] One should keep in mind that the growing of wheat, oats, buckwheat, white mustard, rapeseed, peas, and leguminous crops requires an average 1600° of heat; barley, false flax (*ryzhik*-Camelina sativa), fiber flax, 1400°; potatoes and early cabbage, 1200°; vetch-oats mix for hay, 850°.

favorable sites, early varieties of grapes can be grown in Kiev, Chernigov, Orel, Kursk, Voronezh, Saratov, Kuybyshev, and Orenburg oblasts, as well as in the southern districts of Belorussia. Substantial potentials for viticulture and high quality fruit production remain unused in south-eastern European Russia, in the alpine regions of the Caucasus and Central Asia and also on the irrigated lands of the Trans-Volga. An important industrial region such as the Donbass could become self-sufficient in grapes and wine. The left [east] bank of the Lower Don, where grains were once the main crop, can in the coming years be covered with vineyards extending over thousands of hectares. All necessary climatic prerequisites for high yields of grapes exist here.

To extend the season of fresh fruit and grape consumption, not only very early but also very late varieties should be grown in the south.

Where the sum of the temperatures of the vegetative period exceeds 2800°, i.e., where average-maturing varieties of corn receive sufficient heat, corn should become the principal grain fodder crop. In these regions the productivity of corn, even in dry years, is one and one-half to two times higher than that of barley.

For more effective agroclimatic use and to serve the needs of the national economy, sorghum should be expanded in some semiarid regions of virgin and long-term fallow lands (particularly in western, southern, and eastern Kazakhstan); and, where fall-sown wheat has difficulty surviving the winter, higher yielding winter rye varieties should be introduced. In some very droughty regions of central and northern Kazakhstan, wheat should be replaced with millet, which gives higher and more stable yields.

On the flood plains of some districts of the Kuban, climatic conditions permit a great increase in the production of rice. For instance, in Rostov Oblast more than 35,000 hectares of flood-irrigated land can be planted to rice, not to mention 40,000 hectares in the Don River flood plain. Rice gives high returns here.

Flood plains with good hydrological conditions, among them the Volga-Akhtuba flood plain, form a large reserve for the expansion of vegetables, potatoes, and other crops. Flood-land meadows, which occupy millions of hectares, will increase their production immensely with two hay cuts a year.

An effective means of raising crop yields is *liman* * irrigation, which can be practiced on nearly seven million hectares of the semiarid regions of

---

* *Limannoye orosheniye;* essentially a form of paddy irrigation.

Kazakhstan, the RSFSR, and the Ukraine. Today less than two million hectares is irrigated in this fashion.

The extensive areas of wild fruit trees in the Caucasus, Central Asia, the Ukraine, in Kursk and Voronezh oblasts, and in the Soviet Far East, are of significant value. Their current use falls far short of their potential. By cultivating these wild fruit trees, exceptionally high yields and good quality fruit may be obtained.

The USSR has favorable climatic conditions for the development of mountain orchards. In the mountains of Alma-Ata and and in the southern Kazakhstan oblasts, more than 50,00 hectares can be put to such use. Many other regions have large areas of land where orchards can become an exceptionally important branch of the economy.

The forest and forest-steppe zones can in a short period provide our country with berries—strawberries, gooseberries, currants, and raspberries. Where soil-climatic conditions permit, around all the large cities, extensive green belts yielding berry crops, especially strawberries, currants, and gooseberries, should be established.

Yields of the steppe and forest-steppe depend on the spring reserves of productive moisture in the root layer of the soil and on moisture supply to the arable layer during the vegetative period. Progressive agrotechnology, forest melioration, and snow and water retention in the semiarid zone can raise the reserves of productive moisture in the upper layers of the soil by 60 millimeters (where the depth of spring runoff equals 10 to 20 millimeters) to 100 millimeters (where it approaches 40 millimeters).* The necessary level of agrotechnology has, however, not everywhere been reached. Until this is accomplished, proper crop rotations allow for the substitution of one crop for another, depending on the moisture reserves of a given crop season. Without such rotations in the southeasern semiarid regions, fall-sown crops in dry years germinate poorly and irregularly even if sown in clean fallow. In nonfallow land, sowings frequently are completely lost, secondary shoots generally do not form, and winter rye produces only a single stalk.

The average yield of winter rye in years following a dry autumn is about 70% of that of spring wheat; after humid summer and fall seasons the average yield of rye far exceeds that of spring wheat. For this reason, during a dry fall, fields scheduled for winter rye, even after clean fallow,

---

* This system of measurement involves the volume of productive soil moisture in millimeters found within a certain depth or layer of the soil.

should be left for spring crops. An indication of highly unfavorable conditions for winter crops is the complete desiccation of the upper 10 centimeters of the soil and a decrease in the reserves of productive moisture from a depth of 10 to 20 centimeters. On the other hand, if the autumn is humid, winter rye should be sown even in nonfallow land in place of a spring crop (oats, barley, millet).

In the spring, if there is an ample supply of soil moisture at the time of sowing, the proportion of early spring crops should be increased, since in the event of a dry summer, they would make better use of the moisture than would late crops. If soil moisture is low at sowing, the ratio of early spring crops should be reduced and the sowing of late crops expanded. Late crops, sown in soil with insufficient reserves of moisture, may use the higher precipitation of the second half of the growing season.

Norms of sowing should be established annually, depending upon the reserves of water in the soil, down to the depth of a meter. With a large amount of soil moisture, the density of sowing should be greater; with a low amount, it should be lower. In the steppe regions, including Kazakhstan and Siberia, when spring reserves of productive moisture in the upper meter of the soil are less than 60 millimeters (which usually means that not more than 30 centimeters of the soil is moist), late-maturing and drought-resistant crops (i.e., millet, sorghum), should be sown in place of early varieties.

In regions with irregular precipitation, therefore, the collective and state farms must have on hand a variety of seeds that will permit them to make a flexible adjustment to weather conditions.

BIBLIOGRAPHY

Davitaya, F. F., ed. *Agroklimaticheskiye i vodnyye resursy rayonov osvoyeniya tselinnykh i zalezhnykh zemel* [Agroclimatic and Water Resources of Regions of Virgin and Long-term Fallow Lands]. Leningrad: Gidrometeoizdat, 1955.

Davitaya, F. F. "Prirodno-klimaticheskiye usloviya i differentsirovannoye vedeniye selskogo khozyaystva" [Natural-climatic Conditions and Differentiated Agricultural Operations]. In *Materialy yubileynoy sessii posvyashchennoy 40-y godovshchinye Velikoy Oktyabrskoy sotsialisticheskoy revolyutsii. Vsesoyuznaya akademiya selskokhozyaystvennykh nauk imeni V. I. Lenina, 1957 g.* [Papers of the Jubilee Session Devoted to the 40th Anniversary of the Great October Socialist Revolution at the All-Union Academy of Agricultural Sciences, named after V. I. Lenin, in 1957]. Moscow: Ministerstvo selskogo khozyaystva SSSR, 1958.

Davitaya, F. F. and Shulgin, A. M., eds. *Voprosy agroklimatologicheskogo rayonirovaniya SSSR* [Problems of Agroclimatic Regionalization of the USSR]. Moscow: Ministerstvo selskogo khozyaystva SSSR, 1958.

Koloskov, P. I. *Agroklimaticheskoye rayonirovaniye Kazakhstana* [Agroclimatic Regionalization of Kazakhstan], pts 1, 2. Moscow-Leningrad: AN SSSR, 1947.

Sapozhnikova, S. A. and Shashko, D. I. *Agroklimaticheskiye usloviya razmeshcheniya i spetsializatsii selskokhozyaystvennogo proizvodstva* [Agroclimatic Conditions of the Distribution of and Specialization in Agricultural Production]. In *Materialy k III syezdu Geogr. ob-va. Doklady po probleme "Prirodnoye rayonirovaniye strany dlya tseley selskogo khozyaystva."* Leningrad, 1959.

5. Effects of Ground Cover and Surface on Climatic Conditions

Ya. I. Feldman

(Institute of Geography, Academy of Sciences of the USSR)

The usefulness of climate depends upon the amount, interrelationship, and distribution of heat and moisture in time and space. Climatic traits are conditioned by cosmic factors and the structure of the earth as well as by the nature of the earth's surface. Since man is significantly modifying that surface, his activity has a recognizable effect on climate. This effect can be either beneficial or harmful to the national economy. Man has also a direct influence on the physical composition of the atmosphere, polluting it with industrial waste products. As advantages are increased in the future, disadvantages can also multiply; it is necessary to plan for the prevention of the latter.

We are now able to influence local weather conditions, but any extensive climatic modification by means of changing the general circulation of the atmosphere and ocean currents is unlikely in the immediate future. The present, therefore, must be devoted to studying problems associated with directing climatic processes and in experimenting on an ever larger scale.

THE ZONALITY OF CLIMATIC RESOURCES

Changes in the ground cover, in its texture, in its radiational and heat and water properties, all influence the temperature and humidity of the air, the wind, and other features of the local climate. However, similar changes in ground cover may be beneficial in one climatic zone and harmful in another. Proper evaluation of the effects of economic activities on the ground cover and, consequently, on local climate, should be examined, therefore, in conjunction with the characteristics of each natural zone.

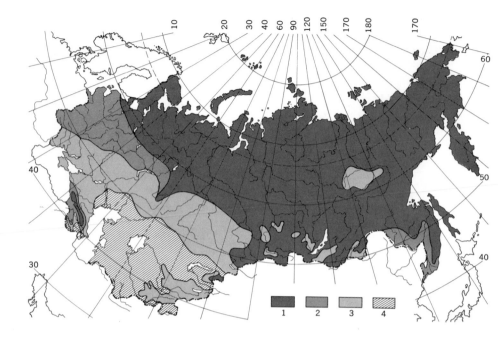

Figure 1

Schematic map of climatic types, determined on the basis of heat and moisture availability (compiled from maps of A. A. Grigoryev and M. I. Budyko; and from data of D. I. Shashko). Zones: (1) Sufficient or surplus moisture supply; aridity index up to 0.7 (for Siberia up to 1.0); sum of active temperatures (those above 10° C) up to 1800°. (2) Unstable moisture supply; aridity index 0.7–1.0; sum of active temperatures 1800–3000° (for Transcaucasia up to 4200°). (3) Insufficient moisture supply; aridity index 1.0–3.0; sum of active temperatures 3000–3600° (for Siberia 1200–2000°). (4) Extreme moisture deficiency; aridity index above 3.0; sum of active temperatures above 3600°.

The climatic classification of the USSR, which was devised by A. A. Grigoryev and M. I. Budyko,[1] is based on the following two criteria: (*a*) the sum of the temperatures of the earth's surface for the period when air temperatures exceed 10°C and (*b*) the aridity index (the relationship of the annual potential evaporation to annual precipitation). According to this classification, the USSR is composed of a series of large zones, which are given in Figure 1.

ZONE OF ADEQUATE OR SURPLUS MOISTURE WITH COOL, MODERATELY WARM, OR VERY WARM SUMMERS. This zone encompasses a large part of the coniferous forest region and some upland areas. Ordinarily these regions

---

[1] A. A. Grigoryev and M. I. Budyko. "Classification of Climates of the USSR," *Izvestiya Akademii Nauk SSSR, seriya geograficheskaya*, no. 3 (1959). ·

have a surplus of moisture and a deficit of heat. The problem is how to increase the sum of useful temperatures and lengthen the vegetative period by averting late spring and early autumn frosts.

ZONE OF HIGHLY VARIABLE MOISTURE SUPPLY WITH MODERATELY WARM OR WARM SUMMERS. This zone extends over the mixed and broad-leaved forests and the forest-steppe, of the western reaches of European Russia, the Soviet Far East, and the foothills of the western Caucasus (the latter having rather unique climatic conditions). The interior parts of the continent with this climate are poorly developed. The average conditions of heat and moisture are most favorable for cultivated crops and natural vegetation. However, the variations in those conditions from year to year are sharp, resulting in unstable yields. The task in this zone is to prevent drought on the one hand, and frost and excessive moisture on the other. Given technology this task can be attained only by means of land improvement.

ZONE OF INSUFFICIENT MOISTURE SUPPLY WITH WARM OR HOT SUMMERS. This zone encompasses predominantly the mountains and steppe of Central Asia and southern Central Siberia as well as the steppe and eastern forest-steppe of European Russia and Western Siberia. As a rule, summers are dry and moisture is seldom adequate. The lack of forests in the zone sharpens the moisture deficiency since it permits frequent, strong surface winds, which in turn increase evaporation. Land reclamation measures should strive to combat drought and dust storms.

ZONE OF EXTREME MOISTURE DEFICIENCY WITH VERY HOT SUMMERS. This zone is confined to the deserts of Central Asia. The moisture deficiency here is so great that crop cultivation without irrigation is impossible. With irrigation, the climatic resources of the zone, due to the abundance of solar radiation, are exceptionally favorable. This can be observed in the oases, whose local climates are markedly different from those of the surrounding desert. Irrigation and the provision of water are the most effective means of influencing the climate. This zone holds the greatest promise for direct use of solar energy.

MAN'S POTENTIAL INFLUENCE ON CLIMATE

Various surface features that have a clear influence on climate can be modified by man in the immediate future.

THE INFLUENCE OF FOREST COVER. Research on the climatic influence of the taiga on the European part of the USSR has shown that cloudy, rainy weather is more prevalent in summer in areas of dense forest than in neighboring, unforested, or sparsely forested areas. This may be explained chiefly by the fact that warm air masses, whose intrusions bring dense cloud cover, find a cooler surface over forested areas. Over forests, uniform condensation of water vapor takes place; over forest-free surfaces, on the other hand, there is a strong uplift of warm air that leads to the formation of daytime cumulus and thunderstorm clouds associated with rains of short duration. The character of the precipitation over forested and unforested land in the region differs, but its quantity remains the same.

The cloudy and rainy weather associated with dense forest cover is, under the conditions of the taiga zone, an unsatisfactory feature of the local climate. For this reason, logging that creates a differentiated landscape with timber of various ages alternating with small clearings actually has a favorable climatic effect.

THE INFLUENCE OF SHELTER BELTS. The climatic role of shelter belts consists chiefly in their effect on temperature, humidity, surface wind, and, as a result, on potential evaporation and snow distribution. The usefulness of shelter belts depends on their size and arrangement, tree height and density, local natural climatic conditions, and size of fields.

In winter, the distribution of snow is affected by shelter belts. In the open steppe, nearly 60%. of the snow is carried into depressions and ravines. If shelter belts are present, the snow accumulates primarily under their cover. Open (sparse) belts create wide snow trails across fields. Closed (thick) belts collect a large part of the snow immediately within the belt iself, or within its wind shadow.

As forest belts mature in height and cover more of the steppe and forest-steppe, the frequency of windstorms that sweep the snow from open fields and cause drifts in the roads diminishes. In the dry steppe, shelter belts can serve as protection for livestock.

The snow collected by shelter belts has an insulating effect. In the forest-steppe of Altay Kray the minimum soil temperature at a depth of three centimeters under a snow cover of thirty to fifty centimeters was ten to fifteen degrees higher than on bare lands. On the other hand, while snow protects the soil from freezing, due to its reflecting and isolating properties, it causes a cooling of the surface layer of air. This characteristic is never taken into account in snow-retention schemes; but while it causes an additional decrease in the air temperature of 5° to 10°C, it is not dangerous for most trees but can be destructive to fruit and to some other crops.

In the zone of sufficient moisture supply with unfavorable thermal conditions, the role of the shelter belt as a "storehouse of moisture" is undesirable. However, shelter belts protect the sown area from freezing in the wintertime, and protect fruit and berry crops from cold winds. Therefore, only open belts can be useful here because they do not permit the accumulation of snow in drifts. In regions with mild winters (for instance, in the Polesye), where sowings frequently suffer from heavy and excessive moisture, the creation of shelter belts is not recommended.

In the spring, shelter belts as well as other snow retention measures delay the melting of the snow and slow down the accumulation of heat. In areas that are deficient in heat, this trait should be considered in the selection of field crops. In the semiarid zone and in regions of appreciable erosion (in any zone), the utility of retaining additional spring moisture more than compensates for the reduction in the vegetative period.

In the summer, in the zone of insufficient moisture supply, the utility of protective tree planting lies mainly in the lowering of the rate of evaporation, in the weakening of the *sukhovey,* and in the prevention of dust storms. Tree belts lessen not only horizontal wind velocities but also the ability of the wind to carry moisture from the surface to higher altitudes. This reduces in turn the upward loss of heat, raising the temperature of protected areas by 1° or 2° over that of open fields. Although such a temperature increase is undesirable in the steppe, the damage from it is insignificant and is fully compensated for by the weakening of the winds. In the forest and forest-steppe zones, fields surrounded by trees also experience a temperature increase, which, according to the Main Geophysical Observatory, amounts to 15% to 20% of the total quantity of heat for the vegetative period. Here, however, the effect is very beneficial.

In the fall, shelter belts improve the heat and water regime during the germination period of fall crops (that is, when mean daily temperatures decrease from 15° to 0°) and enhance the retention of the first snow, which lessens the chance of a thaw and of resultant frost damage of the young shoots during the period when mean daily temperatures decrease from 0° to –5°.

THE INFLUENCE OF IRRIGATION. Irrigation sharply affects the local climate of the moisture-deficient zone. Particularly great is the difference in local climate between the irrigated and nonirrigated areas of the desert and (to a lesser degree) the semidesert where irrigation is a prerequisite for crop cultivation. Table 1 shows that the well-developed *sukhovey,* which are typical of the desert and which damage crops even when soil moisture is at its highest, are preventable in an extensive, well-watered oasis (as for

Table 1
The Frequency of *Sukhovey*, by Intensity
(In percentage of total number of days with *sukhovey*)

	Poorly Developed Sukhovey			Regular Sukhovey			Water Input for Irrigation (In cubic kilometers)
	Weak	Average	Total	Less Severe	Severe	Very Severe	
Oases							
Chirchik-Angren	41	59	100	0	0	0	4.2
Southern Khorezm	56	40	96	4	0	0	2.0
Middle Amu-Darya	50	46	96	4	0	0	1.5
Lower Zeravshan	27	60	87	12	1	0	1.6
Surkhan-Darya	13	69	82	14	4	0	0.8
Murgab	20	70	90	8	2	0	0.8
AVERAGE	35	57	92	7	1	0	—
Deserts							
Kyzyl-Kum	9	37	46	36	16	2	0
Kara-Kum	6	31	37	34	26	3	0
AVERAGE	7	34	31	35	21	3	—

example, the Chirchik-Angren oasis). The poorly developed *sukhovey,* which are observed mainly in the oases, are no threat to adequately irrigated crops.[2] Irrigation and shelter belts can thus eliminate, even in the desert, desiccation and *sukhovey* damage.

THE INFLUENCE OF LARGE RESERVOIRS. Reservoirs, like natural lakes, affect local weather. Shore winds are caused by the difference between the thermal conditions of a large reservoir and those of the surrounding land. These shore winds inhibit the vertical rise of air. For this reason, in the neighborhood of a large reservoir, insolation is prolonged (by about 10%) and precipitation is lessened (by about 50%). Rain and thunderstorms occur mainly at night and in the morning hours, before the appearance of cool onshore winds.

The impact of a reservoir on the temperature and humidity of the adjacent land depends on the time of day and on the season. In the central belt of the USSR, in the first half of the summer (May to July) large reservoirs are usually cooler than the land throughout the twenty-four hour period, but from August to September the heated reservoir exerts a warming influence on the land, particularly at night or during cloudy weather. Since formation of the Kuybyshev reservoir, the temperature of the air in its vicinity decreased in May to July by 0.4° to 0.6°, and rose in August to September by 1.7° to 2.2°. At the same time the relative humidity of the air increased in May to July by 4% to 8%, and in August to September by 2% to 3%. The vegetative season in the vicinity of a reservoir is thus shifted to a later date. In regions subject to drought a decrease in temperature and an increase in relative humidity during the first half of the summer, due to the presence of a reservoir, is very important; it is in the early summer that the danger of drought is especially great in drought-prone regions.

The moderating influence of reservoirs on the daily range of temperatures and the increase of insolation on their banks can be beneficial in regions of sharply continental climate with conifer and broad-leaved forests. But in the tundra and forest-tundra, the reservoirs that retain a low temperature for a long time have a negative effect on temperature and humidity conditions.

A slight increase in winds and windstorms can be expected on the banks of reservoirs. The climatic influence of even the largest reservoirs (of those already constructed) extends only a score of kilometers from the water.

---

[2] Weak or poorly developed *sukhovey* are dry winds whose moisture deficit is less than 20 millimeters. Regular *sukhovey* have a moisture deficit of more than 20 millimeters.

THE INFLUENCE OF SWAMP DRAINAGE.   The surface of a swamp is similar to a water surface and, to a greater or lesser degree, increases the relative humidity and lowers the temperature of surface air. In addition to this, swamps affect local climate in a unique way because of the low heat conductivity and low heat-retention capacity of their soils. In summer, swamps are sites of lowest temperature; daytime heating of the soil is limited to a thin surface layer that cools rapidly at night. Frosts occur over swamps in the fall and spring. In writer, due to their insulating characteristics, swamp soils freeze to a lesser degree than mineral soils; however, swamp soils retain a low temperature to the end of spring and even into the summer.

Improvement of the physical characteristics of swamp soils by drainage and the application of mineral matter, sand, lime, and so forth, reduces the danger of frost, speeds up and enhances spring heating, and consequently makes them suitable for agricultural use.

THE INFLUENCE OF COMPLEX TRANSFORMATION OF NATURE ON PRECIPITATION IN ZONES OF INSUFFICIENT AND IRREGULAR MOISTURE SUPPLY.   With the development of shelter belts, irrigation systems, reservoirs, and canals, the physical characteristics of adjacent areas become increasingly diverse, which intensifies the dynamic and thermal mixing of the air. Because of this and the additional evaporation from the retained runoff, air humidity will rise and the amount of precipitation will somewhat increase. The greatest increase in precipitation, on the order of 10%, can be expected in the northwestern regions of the forest-steppe. In the desert and semidesert zones, the water-vapor deficit of the air is so great that the expected increase in moisture under the influence of irrigation cannot possibly lead to the formation of cloud cover and to precipitation. At any rate, in these zones, where agriculture is based on irrigation, a small increase in precipitation would not play a noticeable role.

6. Protection of the Atmosphere From Pollution

M. E. Lyakhov

(*Institute of Aeroclimatology GUGMS* *
under the Council of Ministers of the USSR)

Protection of the atmosphere from pollution is one of the most important problems of our times. Where pollution is intensive, the population is more prone to disease. This is particularly true of children. In addition, some pollutants directly cause illness, plague among livestock, and damage and destruction to vegetation; there are industrial wastes that corrode metal structures, machines, and roofs, and damage wall surfaces. Soviet law contains decrees and regulations that obligate managers of enterprises to adopt measures preventing air pollution. However, the problem of protecting the atmosphere has not yet been solved. Air pollution in industrial areas continues to damage the health of the population and harms the national economy.

TYPES OF AIR POLLUTION

POLLUTION OF THE ATMOSPHERE BY INDUSTRY AND TRANSPORTATION. Industry pollutes the air with solid dust particles as well as with gaseous substances. The most widespread of industrial pollutants are soot, flying ash, sulfurous compounds (sulfurous gas, sulfur anhydride, and others), and carbon monoxide. Industrial plants, transportation facilities, and boiler and domestic furnaces where solid or liquid fuel is used are the sources of these pollutants.

The concentration of these pollutants is greater during the cold season than in summer. For example, the average concentration of carbon mon-

---

* Glavnoye upravleniye gidrometeorologicheskoy sluzhby (Central Office of the Hydrometeorological Service).

oxide (CO) in the air of large cities in the warm season of the year is 10 to 15 milligrams per cubic meter, but in the cold season it is 21 to 37 milligrams per cubic meter.[1] During the summer the content of other combustion products in the air also diminishes. Apparently, this is associated not only with the variation in the demand for fuel but also with meteorological factors. In summer, the vertical uplift and the mixing rate of the air increase, dispersing pollutants more than the more static air of winter.

In large cities and industrial areas the choice of fuel is important; coal and shale, for example, cause particularly intensive pollution. A thermal electric plant burning daily 1,500 tons of coal whose ash content of 25% is not caught by an ash-catcher discharges about 300 tons of flying ash. The Kashira GRES (regional thermal electric station) discharges daily up to 800 tons of ash. The actual ash content of the atmosphere of industrial regions and cities far exceeds maximum permissible norms. In the area of one of the Ural TETS (central thermal electric stations) the concentration of ash within a distance of 500 meters exceeds by 500 times the maximum permissible norm; and within 2 to 3 kilometers it exceeds the norm by a multiple of 300. In addition to ash, soot, and carbon monoxide, unburnt coal particles are liberated in combustion; the burning of coal also releases sulfur dioxide (SO_2), which has a toxic effect on the human organism. The greatest concentration of sulfur dioxide in smoke is observed in the burning of Kashpira shale (22 grams per cubic meter) and of Moscow lignite (10.4 grams per cubic meter); the smallest concentration, on the other hand, is found in burning Kemerovo coal (0.7 gram per cubic meter). Novomoskovsk GRES (average capacity), operating on Moscow lignite, discharges daily into the air 125 tons of sulfuric gas.

Industrial enterprises also pollute the air with their by-products, which vary with the industry. Gaseous sulfur compounds are discharged by the producers of sulfuric acid, synthetic ammonia, and cellulose, and by metallurgical plants, particularly those in light metallurgy that process sulfides. In the smelting of 100 tons of crude copper, 880 tons of sulfurous gas is discharged; in smelting 100 tons of tin, 120 tons. The concentration of sulfurous gas in the air in industrial centers, as a rule, exceeds the maximum permissible dose (0.75 milligram per cubic meter). In various districts of Moscow the maximum concentration has exceeded permissible norms by up to seventeen times.

In the vicinity of rayon and dye factories, of plants producing sulfurous

---

[1] Data on the amount of pollutants in the air that are cited in this chapter are taken from publications listed in the bibliography. Data on the maximum allowable content of pollutants are derived from norms accepted by the office of State Sanitary Inspection.

dyes, soda, chemical-pharmaceutical preparations, of coke-chemical, metallurgical, and oil industries (including oil fields), and of animal processing (tanning, glue, and gelatin plants), the air is polluted not only with sulfurous gas and products of combustion but also with hydrogen sulfide. The rayon and oil industries are particularly guilty of polluting the atmosphere with hydrogen sulfide. Measurements taken at a distance of one to two kilometers from a cracking plant have shown that the average concentration of hydrogen sulfide (H_2S) in the air is equal to 0.9 milligram per cubic meter while, according to sanitary norms, the maximum permissible daily concentration must not exceed 0.015 milligram per cubic meter. Rayon factories also discharge daily 1.6 to 2 tons of carbon bisulfide, contaminating the air within a radius of two kilometers.

Fluoride compounds and oxides of nitrogen and phosphorus are also widespread pollutants. In addition, some plants discharge into the atmosphere compounds of lead, chlorine, mercury, zinc, arsenic, and other substances. The air and surface of the earth are contaminated by fluoride compounds, chiefly in areas of aluminum and superphosphate production, and near plants producing fluorspar and fluoride salts.

Nitrate fertilizer plants, factories manufacturing dyes, sulfuric acid (tower process), and synthetic ammonia pollute the atmosphere with oxides of nitrogen. Synthetic ammonia plants, in the absence of gas-purifying devices, discharge daily up to one ton of nitrogen oxide into the air. The maximum concentration of nitrogen oxide in the air should not exceed 0.5 milligram per cubic meter. However, at a distance of 1 kilometer from some plants, concentrations of up to 70 milligrams per cubic meter, and a distance of 5 kilometers, concentrations of as much as 8 milligrams per cubic meter have been detected. Plants manufacturing phosphate fertilizers, yellow and red phosphorus, plastics, medical preparations, and matches pollute the air with phosphorus and its oxides.

The atmosphere is being polluted by natural and industrial dust. Industrial dust, which often includes such harmful products as lead, zinc, arsenic, and their compounds, can be poisonous. The most widespread and harmful dust is silicon dioxide (SiO_2). In the center of large cities the SiO_2 content in dust reaches 20% to 23%, that is, up to two and one-half times greater than the permissible maximum concentration. Cement and coal enterprises, metallurgical industries, gypsum works, plants producing abrasives, and large construction works are all great sources of air pollution. Large metallurgical combines, for example, discharge daily 1,200 tons of dust into the air.

Air pollution in populated places is caused by the rise of dust particles from the soil, roads, and streets, due to wind and traffic. On heavily traveled city streets that are not sufficiently sprinkled and lack asphalt or concrete surfaces, dust clouds, stirred up by wheels and carried by the wind, envelop houses and gardens, creating unbearable conditions in the life of the people.

AIR POLLUTION DUE TO NATURAL PROCESSES. Of the processes responsible for dust in the air, the most common is deflation, that is, the blowing of soil and sand and the eruption of volcanos. As a rule, however, the latter has only local significance and there are no active volcanos found in the Soviet Union except in Kamchatka and on the Kurile Islands. Only in such catastrophically strong eruptions as, for example, the eruption of Krakatoa (Indonesia) in 1883 and Katmai in Alaska in 1912 are ashes scattered in the atmosphere and spread throughout all of the Northern Hemisphere.

The principal areas of dust concentration are the deserts, semideserts, steppe, and forest-steppe, but dust-laden air frequently invades the forest zone. It is understandable that dust-saturated air masses occur most often in warm months, especially in dry years. In contrast to the industrial contamination of air with dust, which spreads within a radius of approximately 10 to 20 kilometers from the source, deflation pollutes hundreds, thousands, and even millions of square kilometers. Dust storms are particularly harmful to the economy, because they destroy the productive layers of soil, while the dust itself lowers the intensity of solar radiation.

Two basic conditions are necessary for the start of a dust storm: a strong wind (greater than twelve meters per second) and a dry, barren soil. These conditions occur most frequently in southeastern European Russia, in the North Caucasus, in Kazakhstan, and in the semidesert regions of Central Asia. Dust storms are often accompanied by *sukhovey;* however, dry winds are not always accompanied by dust storms. General measures are being rapidly applied to combat these destructive processes.

Pollution of the air with dust may occur even when there is no wind. Dust can be raised by convective air currents, which originate in the summer over intensely heated soil surfaces. Small dust devils form under such conditions, accelerating dust transfer into the higher layers of the atmosphere. Since barren soil becomes the most heated, it is the principal source of airborne dust.

Dust enters the atmosphere not only from the earth's surface and from volcanoes, but also from outer space. However, the amount of cosmic dust in the atmosphere is many times less than the amount of ordinary earth dust. The amount of cosmic dust falling over the entire surface of the earth during a twenty-four hour period is estimated to be 1,000 tons. By comparison, one dust storm in the Ukraine on April 26–27, 1928, raised over 15 million tons of black soil from an area of about 1 million cubic kilometers. Storms of similar magnitude occurred in March and April, 1960, in the North Caucasus and the Ukraine.

EFFECTS OF AIR POLLUTION

Let us now examine the effects of air pollution on the well-being of the population, the animal world, and the vegetation.

EFFECTS OF AIR POLLUTION ON THE POPULATION.   Air pollution can harm the human body either directly or indirectly by cutting the intensity of solar radiation.

Polluted air, particularly that containing soot and dust, lessens substantially the amount of solar radiation received by the earth, increases the number of foggy days and reduces visibility. Daylight in cities is sometimes cut in half; dusk begins earlier in the evening and dawn lasts later in the morning. A dust concentration of 0.2 to 0.3 milligram per cubic meter reduces radiation by 28%; a concentration of 0.7 to 0.8 milligram per cubic meter, by 49%; and one of 1.1 to 1.2 milligrams per cubic meter, by 57%. The maximum permissible average daily concentration is 0.15 milligram per cubic meter. At that level the loss of solar radiation amounts to 12%. With a concentration of soot and dust equal to 2 milligrams per cubic meter, the loss of daylight, as was shown in large industrial cities in England, may exceed 90%. According to observations conducted in Minsk (from March to the end of October 1956), the loss of ultraviolet radiation in residential blocks amounts to 16% and, on some days, up to 20%; in industrial quarters the loss is about 25% and, on some occasions, as much as 35%.

The reduction in ultraviolet radiation affects the phosphorus-calcium exchange in human organisms and enhances the spread of infection, particularly among children.

Air pollution harms health in many ways. Breathing becomes shallow, leading to various respiratory illnesses; dust, soot, and other materials in the air affect eyes, causing trauma, which is frequently accompanied by conjunctivitis and other eye diseases. Silicon dioxide (SiO_2) contained in dust and ash has a harmful effect on lung tissues, especially among children. Among people living near polluting industrial plants, the incidence of lung infection and tuberculosis is many times greater than among those living outside the polluted zone. Oxides of nitrogen cause irritation of mucous membranes of deeper respiratory channels, chronic bronchitis, intestinal sickness, decay of teeth, and so forth. Carbon monoxide causes headache, nausea, and dizziness. Its effects become serious at a concentration of about 120 milligrams per cubic meter. With a concentration of 20 to 30 milligrams per cubic meter, disturbances of the higher nervous system are observed. In places where automobile traffic is heavy, the concentration of carbon monoxide reaches 100 to 200 milligrams per cubic meter, with coincidental deleterious effects. Around metallurgical plants, air pollution causes the concentration of carbonylhemoglobin in the blood of children to rise.

After prolonged exposure, phosphorus and its compounds cause bronchitis, gastritis, emphysema, pneumoconiosis, disturbance in the mineral exchange in the organism, disease of the respiratory organs, and phosphorus necrosis of the jaws. Concentration of phosphorus oxides should not exceed 0.15 milligram per cubic meter.

Fluoride compounds cause osteosclerosis, the calcification of ligaments, tendons and so forth, chronic catarrh of the upper respiratory passages, and damage to tooth enamel. The permissible average daily concentration of fluoride and its compounds is 0.01 milligram per cubic meter, and momentary concentrations must not exceed 0.03 milligram per cubic meter. Around aluminum plants that lack pollution control, fluoride discharge has in some instances caused half the infants in the vicinity to become ill with rickets. Fluoride settles on soil and is assimilated by plants. The fluoride content in potatoes, vegetables, fruit, grass, and hay in areas of discharge is several times greater than its natural concentration. An increase in fluoride content in cow's milk results in fluorosis among children; adults in these regions suffer a sharp increase in catarrh of the upper respiratory passages, bronchitis, and chronic laryngitis.

Life is made difficult where industrial plants pollute the air with such foul-smelling gases as hydrogen sulfide, carbon sulfide, and sulfur dioxide.

These various harmful gases, smoke, and dust are so dangerous to the health of the population under certain meteorological conditions that, unless effective measures for prevention are taken, the pollution may result in mass poisoning. In London, in 1952, for example, a smoke-polluted fog with sulfurous gas of high concentration tripled the death rate. Consequences of a fog in Liège (Belgium) in 1943, and in Donora (Pa.) in 1948 are similar.

THE INFLUENCE OF AIR POLLUTION ON ANIMALS. Air pollution harmful to man also affects animals. Industrial pollution causes domestic animals to lose weight and, in some cases, may lead to widespread cattle plague. Areas of fluoride and arsenic pollution are particularly dangerous for cattle. In 1949, a heavy loss of livestock occurred during a discharge of a mixture of tar vapor and fluoride smoke from an aluminum plant in Fort Williams, Scotland. In the Soviet Union livestock and poultry deaths have been noted in regions of nonferrous metallurgy. Harmful substances (fluoride, lead, zinc, mercury, and others) accumulate in these organisms and cause serious illness. When such substances are present in meat, milk, and other livestock products, they enter the human organism in great quantities.

THE INFLUENCE OF AIR POLLUTION ON VEGETATION. Air pollution often results in the complete destruction of vegetation. In Novaya Gubakha (Perm Oblast), where the atmosphere is polluted by ash and hydrogen sulfide, plants perished not only inside the town but also in its environs, to a distance of ten kilometers. Birch groves were destroyed on the banks of the river Iset, near the city of Kamensk-Uralski. Hydrogen sulfide, hydrochloric acid, and nitrogen oxides have destroyed forests beyond ten kilometers of the Karabash, Krasnouralsk, and Kirovograd copper smelting plants and of the Kizel GRES.

Near central thermal stations as well as many other kinds of plants, green areas in cities either perish or survive only with great difficulty. Coniferous trees and alfalfa are especially sensitive to hydrogen sulfide. Even with a concentration of 2 to 6 milligrams per cubic meter, visible leaf damage occurs; they turn yellow and fall. The maximum safe concentration for plants is considered to be 0.75 milligram per cubic meter.

The vegetation suffers greatly, not only from pollutants of chemical compounds discharged from industrial plants but also from dust. During dust storms the leaves of plants are abraded, and the plant either perishes or remains for a long time in a weakened state. Young shoots in the fields and gardens are frequently covered by dust and sand, which clogs their pores, hampers gas exchange and transpiration, and increases surface temperature. Vegetation thus weakened is particularly noticeable along dusty roads.

Dust absorbs solar energy, and its rise in temperature warms the air. A. I. Voyeykov long ago noted that a large amount of dust in the air noticeably increases temperature and decreases relative humidity, thus contributing to the development of drought. Calculations show that the increase in air temperature caused by dust during a thick haze may reach as much as 3° or even more. Such an increase in temperature during hot, dry weather during the critical period of plant growth is sufficient to destroy the harvest. However, the ability of dust to absorb heat energy and the role of dust in the heat balance of the atmosphere and in the formation of droughts remain insufficiently studied.

MATERIAL LOSSES CAUSED BY DISCHARGES INTO THE ATMOSPHERE.   Losses to the state caused by air pollution cannot be fully calculated. In many cases it is impossible to separate the loss caused by pollution from the effect of other negative factors. For instance, a reduced harvest cannot be attributed to dust alone when drought, *sukhovey,* or soil deflation are present at the same time. The decline in worker productivity due to poor health and listlessness brought about by polluted air cannot be determined. From the above, however, we can state with confidence that the extent of the loss in both cases is enormous.

The urban economy also sustains large losses because of air pollution: corrosion and chemical weathering of roofs and wall coverings necessitate frequent repairs to and painting of houses; the development of green areas in cities is rendered more difficult and expensive. In London, for example, such losses amounted to 7 million pounds sterling before the war. The increase in smog requires greater expenditure on electricity for illumination; because of industrial and urban air pollution, fog is more frequent and denser than in rural areas. In Rostov-on-Don, for example, the number of days per year with fog is sixty-nine, but in nearby Persiyanovka it is thirty-four; in Taganrog, fifty-four; and in Azov, where there are fewer industrial plants, thirty-eight. Fog not only raises the consumption of electricity but increases traffic accidents and upsets the routine operation of airports.

Air pollution control will not only substantially reduce the amount of loss but will also enhance state income. After all, industrial pollutants are often valuable raw materials. Nonferrous metallurgy alone annually discharges into the air 800,000 tons of hydrogen sulfide worth 6 million rubles. One of our copper-smelting plants annually loses 1,200 tons of lead, 1,800 tons of zinc, and 300 tons of copper in its discharge.

The recovery of all waste would not only clean up the air but would be profitable for the enterprise. For example, an experimental device has been installed in the Dnepropetrovsk aluminum plant that recovers up to 98% of the fluoride that previously escaped, achieving a 300,000 ruble profit annually. Through the use of sulfur contained in discharge gases of zinc- and copper-smelting plants, it is possible to obtain up to 1.5 million tons of sulfuric acid annually, at a lower cost than by treating pyrites. Dust traps in nonferrous metallurgical plants provide the state with additional thousands of tons of light metals.

These examples of damage and financial loss and of the possible profits to be gained from the recovery of the various pollutants have convinced us of the necessity of preventing air pollution. Soviet law obliges directors of industrial plants to take steps to assure that air and water are not being polluted. A session of the Supreme Soviet of the RSFSR in 1960 was specifically devoted to the protection of nature, including the air.

CONTROLLING AIR POLLUTION

The struggle to protect the atmosphere from pollution, and to obtain clean, fresh air is carried on in three basic directions:

1. The installation of filters and other purifying devices to trap harmful admixtures.

2. The provision of electricity and gas as fuel for industry and housing.

3. The planting of green areas in cities and settlements, and the creation of parks and greenbelts.

Where directors have adopted effective measures to trap the harmful substances of industrial waste, and where extensive green areas have been established, the concentration of harmful pollutants in the air does not exceed permissible limits. The active participation of the inhabitants of cities and settlements in establishing green areas not only will ensure pure air, render life in industrial areas healthier, but will beautify our towns. A very important role in protecting the air from pollution and in recovering valuable by-products falls on engineers who are engaged in the development of new technology for new and reconstructed enterprises. Their efforts must be directed toward the discovery of processes and equipment by means of which harmful secondary substances will be converted into useful products. In a technological and economic sense, this is obviously the most promising way of dealing with harmful waste products. The protection of air against pollution must be subject not only to administrative supervision but also to social control.

BIBLIOGRAPHY

Goldberg, M. S. *Sanitarnaya okhrana atmosfernogo vozdukha* [Sanitary Protection of the Atmosphere]. Moscow, 1951.

Predelno dopustimye kontsentratsii atmosfernykh zagryazneniy. Pod red. prof. V. A. Ryazanova [Maximum Allowable Concentrations of Atmospheric Pollutants. Under the editorship of Prof. V. A. Ryazanov]. Vyp. 1–4. Moscow: Medgiz, 1952–60.

Ryazanov, V. A. *Sanitarnaya okhrana atmosfernogo vozdukha*. Moscow: Medgiz, 1954.

Tomson, N. M. *Sanitarnaya okhrana atmosfernogo vozdukha ot zagryazneniy* [Sanitary Protection of the Atmosphere from Pollutants]. Leningrad: Medgiz, 1959.

Voprosy gigieny atmosfernogo vozdukha (Sb. statey) [Hygienic Problems Pertaining to the Air. Collected Articles]. Leningrad: Medgiz, 1951.

7. Wind Energy and Its Use

E. M. Fateyev

(All-Union Institute of Agricultural Electrification)

The demand for mineral fuels in the Soviet Union increases daily, but reserves are limited. Scientists should search, therefore, for new sources of energy that will not be exhausted and, at the same time, not contribute to the pollution of water, soil, and air. Rivers, tides, winds, and the sun are potential sources of inexhaustible and "pure" energy. Of these, only the rivers are at present widely used, but man will soon be compelled to turn to other sources of energy. Only initial steps have been taken in the use of winds. Progress in aerodynamics has led to the construction of many wind turbines, but as yet these are little used.

The wind resources of the USSR are extremely large (Krasovskiy). Their distribution is shown in Figure 1, which illustrates wind zones of average annual wind velocities. The first zone—that of greatest velocity—embraces an area of 1.6 million square kilometers. Within its boundaries can be constructed power plants with a capacity of 1,000–2,500 kilowatts per square kilometer. The amount of electrical energy that may be obtained annually from this zone with currently available technology is 9,870 billion kilowatt-hours. The second zone—of medium wind velocity—has an area of about 8 million square kilometers. Here, power plants with a capacity of 500 to 1,000 kilowatts per square kilometer can be constructed, producing more than 10,000 billion kilowatt-hours of electrical power. The third zone—with a relatively low wind velocity—has an area of 12 million square kilometers, but it contributes little to the wind resources of the USSR. Only small windmills for various domestic needs should be constructed here. Thus, with reference to wind energy, only the first two zones (with a total area of about 10 million square kilometers and an electric-power potential of about 20,000 billion kilowatt-hours) are of significance. To obtain com-

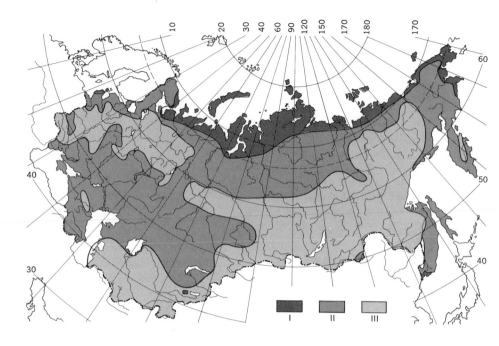

Figure 1
Zones of various average annual wind velocities. (I) 6–9 meters per second, (II) 4–6 meters per second, (III) 2.5–4 meters per second.

parable amounts of energy from thermal stations would require the expenditure of 10 billion tons of oil. The zonal and regional distribution of wind resources is given in Tables 1 and 2.

Wind technology in the USSR began to develop between 1918 and 1920, but as early as 1852, P. L. Chebyshev had raised the question of the most effective shape of blades on a windmill. The question was not solved until some time later. During 1918–20, N. E. Zhukovskiy determined theoretically the coefficient of wind-energy use and drafted a correct profile for the blades of a windmill. Subsequent work on the problem of wind use involved:

1. An evaluation of wind-energy resources.

2. The solution of theoretical problems in aerodynamics and the construction of windmills.

3. The application and use of windmills in agriculture.

The study of wind resources included the compilation of tables, graphs, and maps reflecting changes in wind velocity and direction for various

Table 1
Energy Potential of Regions of the Second Wind Zone

Region	Area (In thousand square kilometers)	Potential [a] (In million kilowatts)	Annual Output of Energy (In billion kilowatt-hours)
Komi ASSR	202.3	101.1	262.0
Mari ASSR	23.1	11.5	29.4
Udmurt ASSR	21.2	10.5	27.0
Mordvin ASSR	26.1	13.5	35.2
Chuvash ASSR	18.3	9.1	23.4
Tatar ASSR	67.6	33.8	87.5
Bashkir ASSR	143.5	72.0	188.0
Yakut ASSR	1,020.7	510.0	1,320.0
Estonian SSR	45.0	22.5	58.5
Latvian SSR	29.4	14.7	38.5
Lithuanian SSR	43.2	21.3	55.5
Belorussian SSR	15.0	7.5	19.5
Ukrainian SSR	401.8	200.0	520.2
Moldavian SSR	3.0	1.5	3.9
Kazakh SSR	2,296.5	1,140.0	3,000.0
Turkmen SSR	5.0	2.5	6.5
Uzbek SSR	10.0	5.0	13.0
Kirgiz SSR	10.0	5.0	13.0
TOTAL	4,381.6	2,181.5	5,701.1

[a] The minimal potential that can be developed in an area of one square kilometer of the second zone was assumed to be 500 kilowatts.

regions of the country. The data included summaries of the average wind velocities for ten-day and monthly periods. Also, records were made of the intensity and direction of wind at different hours of the day and night. Such records were kept for the eight principal compass points—these points are the so-called parameters of wind energy.

Considerable work on the determination of wind-energy parameters has been accomplished at the Institute of Energetics of the Academy of Sciences of the USSR, the Institute of Energetics of the Uzbek SSR (Grinevich), and other institutes. The nature of the distribution of velocities in the various wind zones has been determined. Charts of wind velocity for individual years have been related to data extending over many years in order to judge the economic utility of constructing wind-power stations in

Table 2
Energy Potential of Regions of the First Wind Zone

Region	Area (In thousand square kilometers)	Potential [a] (In million kilowatts)	Annual Output of Energy (In billion kilowatt-hours)
Arkhangelsk Oblast	200	200	1,210
Yamalo-Nenets National Okrug	340	340	2,040
Krasnoyarsk Kray	802	802	5,000
Chukchi National Okrug	240	240	1,450
Maritime Kray	16	16	100
Sakhalin Oblast	10	10	61
Azerbaydzhan-Apsheron Pen.	2	2	10
TOTAL	1,610	1,610	9,871

[a] The minimal potential that can be developed in an area of one square kilometer of the first zone was assumed to be 1,000 kilowatts.

any region of the country. For convenience, graphs of the distribution of the recurrence of wind velocities have been prepared through a series of formulae based on the law of distribution of recurrent wind velocities.

At the Institute of Energetics of the Academy of Sciences of the USSR, the curves of distribution of wind velocities derived from actual data have been compared with those based on theory. The comparison has shown that over the years the distribution of recurrent wind velocities varies within the same region. Obviously, this variation is linked not only to changes in weather conditions but also to changes on the surface of the earth that have been induced by man's economic activities.

On the basis of the study of curves of distribution of wind velocities, an important wind-energy formula has been devised that relates the performance of wind-powered motor of any given capacity to average wind velocity. This formula expresses the relationship between the energy actually produced by the motor and the energy that it could produce if it worked continuously at full capacity. Changes in this relationship, which depend on average daily and monthly wind velocities, are shown in Figure 2. To determine the economic effectiveness of wind-power stations, the recurrence and duration of periods of calm must be known.

Some methodological problems concerning the study of wind resources in the various zones of the USSR are being solved in the Institute of

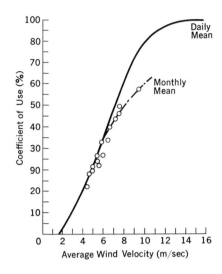

Figure 2
Change in the coefficient of use of wind energy by a windmill depending on wind velocity.

Energetics of the Academy of Sciences. At present the Institute is investigating the problem of changes in velocity and the energy characteristics of the wind within the confines of a small area. This important study should clarify the utility of wind-driven generators in the power system. The Institute has constructed a model wind-driven electric power station (VES) of ten units. The curves of capacity of individual units vary greatly, but the total capacity curve of all the units tends to be more uniform. The variation coefficient for an individual unit is 3.5, but it decreases for a group of units to 0.76. We may assume, therefore, that with the aid of a group of wind-driven generators it is possible to obtain an appreciably more uniform output of electrical energy.

Such a group of generators, spread over a large area and operating within the power grid, will enable us to reduce the fluctuations in wind-energy output over a twenty-four hour period and perhaps over even greater intervals of time (Baranova, 1948).

The work of scientific research organizations on wind-energy resources has yielded the following results:

1. A map of the distribution of wind-energy resources in several zones of the USSR has been compiled.

2. Some conclusions pertaining to the possibility of accumulating wind energy have been drawn.

3. Methods have been determined for (*a*) arriving at parameters of wind-energy computations, (*b*) estimating the size of wind-pump facilities for

providing water in steppe and semiarid regions, and (c) calculating wind-energy resources according to the zones of the USSR.

Before the war, Soviet theoretical aerodynamics and machine building permitted the construction and some use of power installations of considerable capacity. In 1931, for example, an experimental wind-driven electric power station (TsAGI D-30) with a capacity of one hundred kilowatts was built near Balaklava on the Karan Heights of the Crimea. It had a three-blade windwheel, thirty meters in diameter, which made thirty revolutions a minute. This power station functioned ten years, supplying current to the Sevastopol power system, and it provided data of value for the subsequent construction of more efficient installations that could be included in the power grid. The station was destroyed during the war. In 1938, on the top of Mount Ay-Petri, construction began on a 5,000-kilowatt wind-driven electric station with two three-bladed windwheels of eighty meters in diameter, but the war precluded its completion.

At present, several laboratories work on the theory of windmills and on experimental construction of new models of wind-driven generators (Sabinin; Fateyev, 1957a, b; Andrianov et al.). Theory and methods of aerodynamic calculation for windmills have been developed at the laboratory for the study of windmills in the Central Aerodynamics Institute (under the direction of G. Kh. Sabinin). These studies form the basis for the calculation and design of all contemporary Soviet windmills.

In the Central Scientific Research Laboratory on Windmills (TsNILV) new designs are being studied. There, the following types of windmills for supplying water to pastures and to arid steppe regions have been developed.

1. A type VP-3 wind pump of one horsepower, which lifts the water by means of a conveyor belt and supplies enough water for a herd of 1,000 sheep.

2. A type D-5 pneumatic water pump with a two-bladed, rapidly rotating windwheel, five meters in diameter. The windmill powers a compressor. From the compressor heated air moves through a pipe into a pneumatic pump that is set in a well and forces water upward into a reservoir.

3. A mechanically-operated wind pump with a rapidly rotating wheel, which lifts water vertically through a vibrating tube. Under the influence of inertia, the vibrating column of water rises until it spills from the upper end of the tube into the reservoir. At present, this unit is undergoing testing.

The Laboratory of Wind Utilization of the All-Union Institute of Rural Electrification (VIESKh) developed two wind-pump installations for water supply to dry pastures. Type TV-3, a multiblade windwheel of three meters in diameter, has a capacity of one horsepower at a wind speed of 8 meters per second. It is capable of lifting water from wells by means of suction pumps. The second installation (VPL-4) raises water by means of a conveyor belt, and has a six-bladed windwheel with a diameter of four meters. Its capacity, at a wind of eight meters per second, is two horsepower. The unit can provide power for a radio receiver and the illumination of a shepherd's home.

In the VIESKh laboratory a wind-powered electric pump (1D-12A) was developed for mechanizing the water supply and the lighting of a cattle farm. The windmill has a three-bladed windwheel with a diameter of twelve meters and a capacity of ten kilowatts. An inertia storage battery and a reducer permit the equalization of the power of the windmill. The unit is equipped with a device allowing it to operate in conjunction with a steam engine without the presence of an attendant; the windmill stops when the velocity of the wind falls, and at this point the load is transferred to the steam engine. This unit is currently being tested.

To electrify agriculture, mainly in regions far from industrial centers, but also in areas without thermal and hydroenergy sources, the laboratories of TsNILV and VIESKh have developed high-speed windmills.

A windmill (D-12) with a three-bladed windwheel of twelve meters in diameter and a capacity of ten kilowatts (with an average annual wind velocity of eight meters per second) can provide energy for the equipment on a cattle farm and also for lighting farms in regions having a mean annual wind velocity above five meters per second. A more powerful unit (D-18), having a three-bladed wheel with a diameter of eighteen meters and a capacity of twenty-five kilowatts (at a wind speed of 8 meters per second), has been developed for mechanizing large cattle farms.

At present, attempts to obtain greater power from one windmill with a wheel diameter of fifty meters or more are considered unrealistic. For technical reasons it is more convenient to obtain greater power not from one powerful unit with a large wheel diameter but from a number of units with wheels of smaller diameters. Different wind speeds that are found even in close vicinity also necessitate the construction of a wind-driven electric power station consisting of a number of small units.

The first experimental power station for the conversion of wind energy to electric power, consisting of twelve units (of the type D-18) with a total capacity of 400 kilowatts, was built at the Avangard collective farm near Tselinograd. Research on the construction of wind-driven generators is also conducted in foreign countries, in England for instance. One can assume that the future belongs to such generators. Once windmills are widely used, the atmosphere will be cleared of harmful gases and the exhausts of incomplete combustion of coal, oil, and peat, which in turn can be better utilized by the chemical industry for the manufacture of a wider variety of useful products.

In the immediate future the construction bureaus must develop reliable windmills to raise ground water to supply cattle in pastures lacking permanent surface water. In regions lacking thermal and hydropower resources, windmills may be successfully used for electrification. To electrify small rural points (field brigades, farms, radio centers), units of small capacity, 150–1,000 volts, have been produced.

Research on the rational exploitation of windmills is being conducted at the All-Union Institute of Rural Electrification (Fateyev, 1957b). The effectiveness of the windmill may be evaluated correctly only when operating conditions reflect motor design and if there is a constant load. It is also important that the curve of energy consumption coincide with the curve of energy produced. That part of energy that does not coincide with the curve of consumption is lost. Research has shown that such losses may reach 30% of the potential energy.

For successful exploitation of wind-power installations, wind motors must be correctly linked with various agricultural machines (Fateyev, 1949). This is easily achieved when a machines is connected with a wind motor of uniform power capacity, but inasmuch as wind velocity is not constant, the motor works at a changing rate, and only when wind power exceeds the capacity of the motor does the motor work at a constant velocity. Proper coordination of revolutions of the wind motor with the working machine is difficult but can be achieved through the installation of a power regulator.

Windmills are used primarily for water supply and for the grinding and preparation of feed, for which purposes 40,000 were manufactured in 1960. The demand for windmills is great, however. They are many times more economical than other types of motors, and 160,000 are needed for supplying water in the dry pastures of Kazakhstan, Uzbekistan, Turkmenistan, Kirgizia, and other arid regions alone.

In spite of the obvious advantages of using wind energy for water supply, the number of windmills remains very small. There are about 300 used for water supply in Kazakhstan, for example, but about 100,000 are needed.

Two factors hinder the development of the use of wind energy: first, industry and the construction bureaus have not at this point developed a windmill of the industrial type; secondly, the Ministry of Agriculture and the regional economical-administrative councils (*sovnarkhozy*) * have not arranged for their introduction on collectives. Nevertheless, some collective farms have correctly estimated the economic advantages of the application of windmills and have constructed several wind-power installations on their farms. For example, in the Tyukalinsk district of Omsk Oblast, the collective and state farms have from six to eighteen windmills each, which furnish all the water needed, making possible. considerable savings as well as reducing the work of the cattlemen.

The importance of windmills for water supply to pastures in steppe regions will not diminish even with complete electrification of collective farms. The supply of electric power to pastures in steppe areas is costly. Each kilometer of electric transmission costs 1,000 rubles, while wind-driven pumps that could supply enough water for 1,000 sheep cost only 250 rubles. Thus, windmills will remain for a long time the most convenient and economic sources of energy on pastures.

BIBLIOGRAPHY

Andreyev, I. D. "Poryvistost vetra vnutri chasovogo intervala" [The Gustiness of Wind Within the Period of an Hour]. In *Voprosy vetroenergetiki* [Problems of Wind Energy]. AN SSSR, 1959.

Andrianov, V. N., Byśtritskiy, D. N., Bashkevich, K. P., and Sektorov, V. R. *Vetroelektricheskiye stantsii* [Wind Electric Stations]. Moscow-Leningrad: Gosenergoizdat, 1960.

Baranova, 1948. [No further information given. Ed.]

Fateyev, E. M. "Osnovy agregatirovaniya vetrodvigateley s rabochimi mashinami" [The Basis of Linking Windmills with Machines]. In *Trudy Vsesoyuznogo nauchno-issledovatelskogo instituta mekhanizatsii selskogo khozyaystva* [Papers of the All-Union Scientific Research Institute of Agricultural·Mechanization], vol. 12. Moscow, 1949.

Fateyev, E. M. *Vetrodvigateli i vetroustanovki* [Windmills and Installations]. 2d ed. Moscow: Selkhozgiz, 1957. (a)

Fateyev, E. M. *Vetrodvigateli i ikh primeneniye v selskom khozyaystve* [Windmills and Their Application in Agriculture]. 2d ed. Mashgiz, 1957. (b)

Fateyev, E. M. *Metodika opredeleniya parametrov vetroenergeticheskikh raschetov*

---

* The *sovnarkhozy* were created in 1957 following the. Twentieth Party Congress and abolished after Nikita Khrushchev was removed from power in 1964. Initially there were more than one hundred economic-administrative regions, presided over by councils that directed industry and construction within their regional jurisdictions. In 1962, the number of councils was reduced to forty-seven.

vetrosilovykh ustanovok [Methodology of Determining the Parameters of Wind Energy Calculations of Wind Power Stations]. AN SSSR, 1957. (c)

Grinevich, G. A. *Opyt razrabotki elementov malogo vetroenergeticheskogo kadastra Sredney Azii i Kazakhstana* [An Attempt to Isolate the Elements of a Small Cadastre of Wind Energy in Central Asia and Kazakhstan]. Tashkent: Akademiya Nauk Uzbekskoy SSR, 1952.

Krasovskiy, N. V. "Vetroenergeticheskiye resursy SSSR i perspektivy ikh ispolzovaniya" [Wind Energy Potentials]. In *Atlas energeticheskikh resursov SSSR* [Atlas of Energy Resources of the USSR], vol. 1, pt. 3. Moscow-Leningrad, 1935.

Sabinin, G. Kh. *Teoriya i aerodinamicheskiy raschet vetryanykh dvigateley* [Theory and Aerodynamic Calculation of Windmills]. *Trudy Tsentralnogo aero-gidronamicheskogo instituta* [Papers of the Central Aero-Hydrodynamic Institute], no. 104. Moscow-Leningrad, 1931.

Shefter, Ya. I. "O ratsionalnykh skhemakh vetronasosnykh ustanovok dlya pastbishch" [Concerning Rational Systems of Wind Pump Installations for Pastures]. In *Vetroenergetika v selskom khozyaystve* [Wind Energy in Agriculture]. Moscow, 1960.

Part 4. LAND

8. Pedological Description of Land Resources

N. N. Rozov

(*V. V. Dokuchayev Soil Institute of the Ministry
of Agriculture of the USSR*)

DISTRIBUTION OF THE PRINCIPAL SOIL TYPES

The problem of estimating and evaluating the land resources of the USSR is of major significance for the state. Such data are important in planning an increase in the agricultural productivity of regions that have long been settled and in developing agriculture and forestry in new regions.

The solution to the problem is twofold. It must include: (1) quantitative and qualitative evaluation of the land of individual farms, which would be executed on large-scale maps of soils and of rural land organization (Cheremushkin; Panfilov); and (2) a national inventory of land resources based on agricultural statistics, and generalized land-use and soil maps. Only such a dual approach can assure a proper solution of the problem.

The first approach, though most precise, cannot be used in all regions of the Soviet Union because detailed soil maps are available for only about half the agricultural area. The second provides only approximate data, but it can encompass the whole territory.

The principles of and methods for a national land inventory have been developed by L. I. Prasolov (1932, 1933, 1941, 1945). Data based on new soil cartographic materials (Rozov, 1957, 1962) and prepared by the V. V. Dokuchayev Soil Institute using Prasolov's method are given below.

Three national inventories of soil areas have been compiled to date (in 1932, 1938, and 1946). In the past, only small-scale soil maps were used in computing the areas of various types of soils, but the most recent inventory is based on maps of various scales, the most important of which are state soil maps covering a significant part of the USSR. In order to combine all the inventory data and also to measure the areas of various soil types of northern European Russia, Eastern Siberia, and the Soviet Far East, a soil map of the USSR at a scale of 1:4,000,000 was used.[1] This map is not simply a generalization of soil-survey materials; rather, boundaries of soil types in regions little known to soil surveyors were determined by comparing the natural conditions with other known regions; it is for this reason that the data on soil areas for the country as a whole remain subject to revision.

Using three categories of soil texture, areal measurements were made of forty-two genetic soil subdivisions (Table 1).

Based on the present state of soil mapping in the agricultural regions of the USSR and on the accepted composition of the principal soil subtypes in these regions, we may assume that the data given in Table 1 are essentially correct in regard to areas of chernozem, chestnut, and gray forest soils. The data for the area of solonets, solonchak, and shifting sands most likely will not undergo significant change. The data on mountain-chernozem, chestnut, and meadow soils will possibly prove to be more or less accurate, but that for areas of taiga and tundra soils may be only approximate and subject to further refinement.

THE COMPOSITION OF THE SOIL COVER

Even in their first work on soil zonality, V. V. Dokuchayev and N. P. Sibirtsev turned their attention to the variation in the composition of the soil cover within individual zones. However, until recently, sufficiently detailed qualitative data on the soil cover of the principal soil-geographic zones and subzones of the USSR were unavailable. This is due to a lack: (a) of reliable schemes of soil regionalization of the USSR with realistic boundaries of soil-geographic zones and subzones, drawn on maps of sufficiently large scale; (b) of soil maps that encompass entire zones with adequate detail on intrazonal soils; and finally, (c) of a differentiated inventory of areas of intrazonal soils according to soil-geographic zones and subzones.

The coverage of such soil maps and the schemes of national soil-geographic regionalization (Rozov, 1954; Letunov; Ivanova et al.) permit such a differentiation of soils. Soil-geographic zones and subzones can be considered both as agricultural-geographical units forming a base for agricultural soil

---

[1] The map was compiled by N. N. Rozov, assisted by E. V. Lobova, under the general scientific editorship of I. P. Gerasimov, from data supplied by the V. V. Dokuchayev Soil Institute, and published by the Central Administration of Geodesy and Cartography [Glavnoye Upravleniye Geodezii i Kartografii] in 1954 and 1956.

regionalization and as inventory units. The results of a qualitative inventory of soil areas, according to the principal soil zones and subzones of the USSR, are given in Table 2 and Figure 1.

The soils of the polar-tundra zone, which occupies 8% of the USSR, are the least studied. Reindeer herding forms the principal agricultural use of the tundra. Extensive reindeer pastures are found on clay and loam soils, which cover about 100 million hectares. Scrub and forest are on such soils, as well as on alluvium. Near the southern boundary of the tundra, selected crops can be grown in the open but cultivation is confined to very small areas. An expansion of agriculture in the southern reaches of the tundra is possible only on soils of light texture and proper exposure and with specialized technology.

The taiga zone is the most extensive, covering one-third of the USSR. Cropland and pasture are found in limited areas. Much of the zone is forested, forming the basis for a forest and hunting economy. However, further expansion in the agricultural area is inevitable. The best agricultural soils are the turfy-podzolic clays and loams. In such soils cultivated crops can replace scrub and some forest. Of secondary importance are the podzolized clays and loams and, to some extent, soils overlying permafrost and subarctic sod. All of these soils require systematic applications of organic and mineral fertilizers and, in most cases, intensive liming.

Other taiga soils can also be assimilated for agriculture if necessary. In the southern part of the zone, half-bog and lowland bog soils rich in organic matter can be used to some extent, but would require extensive land improvement.

Only alluvial-meadow soils are sufficiently productive of natural hay, the output of which may be increased by clearing the scrub. Such soils serve also as a very valuable base for expanding gardening.

With respect to forest growth and exploitation, the soils of this zone can be grouped as follows: forests of spruce and of spruce and broad-leaved trees on carbonaceous and podzolic sod, clays, and loams; dark conifers, predominantly spruce and fir, on highly podzolized clays and loams; and pines on sandy podzolic sod and podzols. Soils formed on permafrost constitute a special group on which larch predominates while dark coniferous species are rare. Gley podzols, and especially those formed on permafrost, are not conducive to forest growth. Many of the half-bog soils and the decayed sod of Kamchatka are similar to gley podzols.

The quantitative survey of the soils of the forest-steppe and steppe, which comprise about 15% of the area of the Union and contribute substantially to the agriculture of the USSR, is of particular importance. An agricultural

Table 1
Soil Areas of the USSR
(1959 data in million hectares)

Soil Type	Total Area	Percentage of USSR Total	Clays and Loams	Sandy Soils	Stony Soils	Soils of Unknown Texture
		Lowland Territories				
Arctic and arctic tundra	51.7	2.3	—	—	—	51.7
Tundra gleys	100.1	4.5	—	—	—	100.1
Tundra-bog peat soils	11.6	0.5	—	—	—	11.6
Tundra-bog humic soils	8.3	0.2	—	—	—	8.3
Gleyey podzolic soils (including permafrost taiga gleys of Eastern Siberia)	127.6	5.8	48.0	17.9	—	61.7
Podzolic illuvial humic soils	14.8	0.7	—	14.6	0.2	—
Podzolic soils and podzols (including permafrost taiga and pale yellow solodic soils of Eastern Siberia)	183.7	8.3	132.0	30.9	0.8	20.0
Subarctic (turfy) sod and northern forest soils of Kamchatka	10.3	0.5	—	—	—	10.3
Turfy podzolic (including podzolized brown forest soils)	200.9	9.1	146.2	53.5	1.2	—
Turfy carbonaceous	4.2	0.2	2.9	—	1.3	—
Permafrost taiga carbonaceous	9.9	9.4	—	—	9.9	—
Podzolic swamp soils	85.3	3.9	42.2	36.4	—	6.7
Peat bogs (watershed)	62.8	2.8	—	—	—	62.8
Humic peat bogs (lowland and transitional)	18.9	0.9	—	—	—	18.9
Gray forest soils	51.1	2.3	48.0	1.2	1.9	—

Lowland Territories (cont.)

Solodized and gleyey gray forest soils	9.6	0.4	9.6	—	—
Solods	0.8	0.1	0.8	—	—
Meadow chernozems (partly solonized)	8.2	0.4	8.2	—	—
Solonized meadow chernozems with solonets	4.2	0.2	4.2	—	—
Leached and podzolized chernozems	45.8	2.1	44.7	0.9	0.2
Typical Ukrainian chernozems	8.2	0.4	8.2	—	—
Typical Central Russian chernozems	5.8	0.3	5.8	—	—
Typical Trans-Volga, Ural foreland and Altay foreland chernozems	2.5	0.1	2.5	—	—
Mycelial carbonaceous chernozems	9.4	0.4	9.4	—	—
Residual carbonaceous chernozems	5.0	0.2	3.2	—	1.8
Ordinary chernozems	44.2	2.0	41.3	0.6	2.3
Southern chernozems	32.9	1.5	28.7	1.0	3.2
Solonized chernozems	9.2	0.4	8.7	0.2	0.3
Chernozem solonets	5.7	0.3	5.7	—	—
Dark chestnut and chestnut soils	40.8	1.8	30.1	6.8	3.9
Dark chestnut and chestnut solonized soils with solonets	19.1	0.9	18.4	0.6	0.1
Light chestnut soils	25.1	1.1	13.4	5.2	6.5
Light chestnut solonized soils with solonets	18.2	0.8	15.2	2.6	0.4
Meadow chestnut (mostly solonized) soils	4.2	0.2	3.9	0.3	—
Chestnut solonets	16.2	0.7	15.9	0.3	—
Brown semidesert soils	19.8	0.9	11.2	7.0	1.6

Continued

Table 1 (cont.)

Soil Type	Total Area	Percentage of USSR Total	Clays and Loams	Sandy Soils	Stony Soils	Soils of Unknown Texture
Lowland Territories (cont.)						
Brown semidesert solonized soils with solonets	21.0	0.9	13.4	7.6	—	—
Brown solonets	13.8	0.6	8.4	5.4	—	—
Meadow brown semidesert (solonized) soils	1.0	0.1	1.0	—	—	—
Gray brown soils	40.8	1.8	29.3	6.3	5.2	—
Undeveloped (*takyr*) gray-brown soils	16.8	0.8	14.0	2.8	—	—
Takyr	1.7	0.1	1.7	—	—	—
Solonchak	16.6	0.8	—	—	—	16.6
Sand (shifting and partly overgrown)	61.5	2.8	—	61.5	—	—
Gray soils	32.8	1.5	23.8	4.3	4.7	—
Meadow gray soils	8.5	0.4	8.2	0.2	0.1	—
Gray dark-yellow-brown soils	1.4	0.1	1.4	—	—	—
Dark-yellow-brown soils	0.9	—	0.9	—	—	—
Red and yellow soils	0.6	—	0.6	—	—	—
Alluvial (flood plain) soils	56.5	2.6	—	—	—	56.5
Perennial snow and glaciers	9.0	0.4	—	—	—	9.8
Total area of soils of lowland territories	1,559.0	70.5	811.1	268.1	45.6	434.2

	Upland Territories					
Mountain tundra soils	167.5	7.6	—	—	167.5	—
Mountain meadow soils	15.3	0.7	—	—	15.3	—
Mountain meadow steppe soils	11.5	0.5	—	—	11.5	—
Mountain podzolic and permafrost taiga soils	338.5	15.3	5.8	—	332.7	—
Mountain turfy subarctic soils	9.3	0.4	—	—	9.3	—
Mountain gray forest soils	16.2	0.7	1.2	—	15.0	—
Mountain turfy carbonaceous soils	1.6	0.1	—	—	1.6	—
Mountain brown forest soils	18.7	0.9	0.2	—	18.5	—
Mountain yellow soils	0.1	—	0.1	—	—	—
Mountain dark-yellow-brown soils	7.6	0.3	0.7	—	6.9	—
Mountain chernozems	10.5	0.5	3.0	—	7.5	—
Mountain chestnut	12.7	0.6	1.4	—	11.3	—
Mountain gray soils	4.9	0.2	0.9	—	4.0	—
Alpine desert soils	5.1	0.2	0.8	—	4.3	—
Mountain bedrock outcrops	0.9	—	—	—	0.9	—
Total area of soils of upland territories	652.7	29.5	14.1	—	638.6	—
TOTAL AREA OF SOILS	2,211.7 *	100.0	825.2	268.1	684.2	434.2

* Including the area of inland water bodies (22 million hectares).

Table 2
Composition of Soil Area

Zones	Subzones (or Mountain Zones)	Total Area (In million hectares)	Zonal Soils							
			Clays and Loams		Sandy Soils		Stony Soils		Alluvial	
			m ha	%	m ha	%	m ha	%	m ha	%
Polar tundra	Arctic soils	60	51ᵃ	85.0	—	—	—	—	—	—
	Tundra soils	120	100ᵃ	83.3	—	—	—	—	2	1.7
	Total area	180	151ᵃ	83.4	—	—	—	—	2	1.1
Taiga	Gleyey podzolic soils (including permafrost taiga gleys)	240	40ᵃ	16.7	33	13.7	—	—	8	3.3
	Podzolic soils (including permafrost taiga soils)	255	44ᵃ	17.3	40	15.6	1	0.4	10	3.9
	Turfy podzolic soils	260	154ᵃ	59.2	54	20.8	1	0.3	15	5.8
	Total area	755	238	31.5	127	16.8	2	0.2	33	4.4
Forest-steppe and steppe	Gray forest soils	64	57	89.5	1	1.5	2	3.0	2	3.0
	Podzolized leached & typical chernozem	89	66	74.2	1	1.1	—	—	4	4.5
	Ordinary & southern chernozem	100	76	76.0	2	2.0	8	8.0	3	3.0
	Dark chestnut & chestnut soils	68	30	44.2	7	10.3	4	5.8	3	4.3
	Total area	321	229	71.4	11	3.4	14	4.5	12	3.7
Semi-desert and desert	Light chestnut and brown desert steppe soils	130	25	19.3	12	9.2	8	6.2	4	3.0
	Gray-brown desert soils	140	43	30.7	9	6.4	5	3.6	6	4.3
	Gray soils (sierozem)	33	23	69.7	4	12.2	5	15.1	—	—
	Total area	303	91	30.0	25	8.3	18	5.9	10	3.3
Mountain territories	Mountain tundra	165	—	—	—	—	165	100.0	—	—
	Mountain meadows	27	—	—	—	—	27	100.0	—	—
	Mountain podzolic, permafrost-taiga, and gray forest soils	400	7	1.8	—	—	393	98.2	—	—
	Mountain brown forests	18	—	—	—	—	18	100.0	—	—
	Mountain steppe and desert	42	7	16.6	—	—	35	83.4	—	—
	Total area	652	14	2.1	—	—	638	97.9	—	—
	TOTAL AREA OF USSR SOILS	2211	723	37.2	163	7.4	672	30.4	57	2.6

ᵃ Including sandy clays, sandy, and stony soils.
ᵇ Approximate data.

evaluation of the soils indicates that the gray forest clays and loams, the chernozems, and the chestnut soils do not need improvement other than erosion control; meadow-chernozems, a large part of the solonets and of solonetslike soils require both chemical and other improvement; sandy loams and sandy soils need special attention, including control of deflation; and marshy soils must be drained. Only selected alluvial soils are of agricultural use; stony alluvia are of little use and at times altogether useless.

Those soils that do not require improvement, that are best supplied with moisture, and that suffer least from drought are the gray forest soils and the podzolized, leached, and typical chernozems. In the typical and southern chernozems, the dark-chestnut and, particularly, the chestnut soils, the deficiency in natural moisture is greater and droughts occur more often. Here, measures to check surface drainage are of the greatest importance.

														Intrazonal Soils														
Half Bogs		Bogs		Meadow-steppe (Largely Solonized)		Solonized		Solonets		Solonchak and Takyr		Sands		Permafrost Taiga		Permanent Snow and Glaciers	
m ha	%	m ha	%	m ha	%	m ha	%	m ha	%	m ha	%	m ha	%	m ha	%	m ha	%
—	—	—	—	—	—	—	—	—	—	—	—	—	—	—	—	9	15.0
—	—	18	15.0	—	—	—	—	—	—	—	—	—	—	—	—	—	—
—	—	18	10.0	—	—	—	—	—	—	—	—	—	—	—	—	9	5.0
35[b]	14.6	34[b]	14.2	—	—	—	—	—	—	—	—	—	—	90[b]	37.5	—	—
30[b]	11.8	30[b]	11.8	—	—	—	—	—	—	—	—	—	—	100[b]	39.2	—	—
20[b]	7.7	16[b]	6.2	—	—	—	—	—	—	—	—	—	—	—	—	—	—
85	11.3	80	10.6	—	—	—	—	—	—	—	—	—	—	—	—	—	—
—	—	2	3.0	—	—	—	—	4[b]	4.5	—	—	—	—	—	—	—	—
—	—	2	2.3	12	13.4	9	9.0	2[b]	2.0	—	—	—	—	—	—	—	—
—	—	—	—	—	—	19	28.0	5[b]	7.4	—	—	—	—	—	—	—	—
—	—	4	1.2	12	3.7	28	8.7	11	3.4	—	—	—	—	—	—	—	—
—	—	—	—	5	3.8	40	30.8	25[b]	19.3	—	—	11[b]	8.4	—	—	—	—
—	—	—	—	8	5.7	—	—	—	—	18	12.9	51[b]	36.4	—	—	—	—
—	—	—	—	1	3.0	—	—	—	—	—	—	—	—	—	—	—	—
—	—	—	—	14	4.6	40	13.2	25	0.3	18	5.9	62	20.5	—	—	—	—
—	—	—	—	—	—	—	—	—	—	—	—	—	—	—	—	—	—
—	—	—	—	—	—	—	—	—	—	—	—	—	—	—	—	—	—
—	—	—	—	—	—	—	—	—	—	—	—	—	—	—	—	—	—
—	—	—	—	—	—	—	—	—	—	—	—	—	—	—	—	—	—
—	—	—	—	—	—	—	—	—	—	—	—	—	—	—	—	—	—
85	3.8	102	4.6	26	1.2	68	3.1	36	1.6	18	0.8	62	2.8	190	86	9	0.4

The most productive natural hay lands are found on meadow-chernozem and alluvial-meadow soils, which lie in flood plains. In the past, good harvests of hay were obtained on steppe watersheds, but at present such areas are under cultivation almost everywhere.

In the development of forestry and particularly in the development of shelter belts, the characteristics of forest-steppe and steppe soils are significant. Natural forests (in the European USSR consisting of broad-leaf species, and in the Asiatic part of small-leaf) grow well on gray forest soils and on podzolized and partly leached chernozems. Forest plantings and belts develop favorably also on typical and southern chernozems. Care and special selection of tree species are required, however, for dark chestnut and chestnut soils.

About one-seventh of the USSR lies within the semidesert and desert

ZONES	SUBZONES	(In millions of hectares)
Polar Tundra	Arctic Soils	60
	Tundra Soils	120

Taiga	Gleyey-Podzolic Soils (including Permafrost Taiga Gleys)	240
	Podzolic Soils (including Permafrost Taiga Soils)	255
	Turfy-Podzolic Soils	260

Forest Steppe and Steppe	Gray Forest Soils	64
	Leached and Typical Chernozems	89
	Ordinary and Southern Chernozems	100
	Dark Chestnut and Chestnut Soils	68

Semi-desert and Desert	Light Chestnut and Brown Desert-Steppe Soils	130
	Gray-Brown Desert Soils	140
	Gray Soils (Sierozems)	33

Mountain	Mountain Tundra Soils	165
	Mountain Meadow Soils	27
	Mountain Podzolic, Permafrost-Taiga, and Gray Forest Soils	400
	Mountain Brown Forest Soils	18
	Mountain, Steppe, and Desert Soils	42

Figure 1

Composition of the pedogeographic zones and subzones of the USSR (in percent of their areas). I. Zonal soils: (*a*) clays and loams, (*b*) sandy loams and other sandy soils, (*c*) stony soils. II. Intrazonal soils: (*d*) alluvial soils, (*e*) half-bogs, (*f*) bogs, (*g*)

[Composition of Soils, % of Subzone Area]

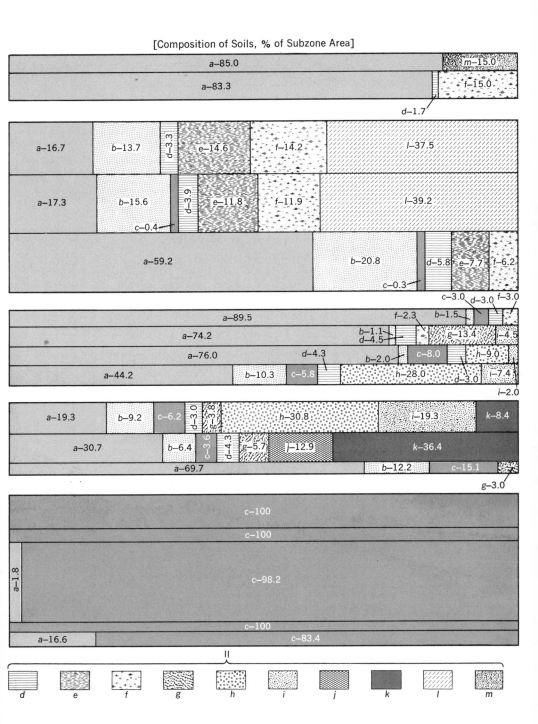

meadow-steppe (solonized), (*h*) solonized soils, (*i*) solonets, (*j*) solonchak, (*k*) fixed and shifting sands, (*l*) permafrost taiga soils, (*m*) permanent snow and glaciers.

zone. Intrazonal soils such as solonets, sand, solonchak, and *takyr* * cover over 55% of the area. Solonets-type soils are found mainly in the northern semidesert subzone, the remainder of which is covered by light chestnut and brown soils of various textures, by meadow-steppe, and alluvial soils and sand. In the subzone of gray-brown desert soils, much of the area consists of sand, both stable and shifting, solonchak and *takyr*. Meadow-steppe and alluvial soils are also found here. Zonal gray-brown soils occupy only 40% of this subzone. The area of gray soils is very small; over two-thirds of the subzone is covered by clay and loam.

Dry farming (*bogarnoye zemledeliye*) is possible only with a limited selection of crops and only on some gray desert (*sierozem*) soils. The greater part of the soils of the semidesert and desert zone may be effectively used for farming only if irrigation is practiced. The best for irrigated agriculture are the gray and meadow-gray loams and clays. In many cases, it is possible to obtain from them two harvests per year. Of lesser utility are the *takyr* and some varieties of gray-brown soils; while the non-solonets types of light chestnut and brown semidesert loams and clays are of little value.

Only an insignificant part of the above-mentioned soils is under irrigation. The use of these soils will expand at a more rapid tempo but will always be tied to the complex problem of developing irrigation and water supply. Pastoralism still prevails in the desert but the natural pastures vary with the soil. The best year-round and winter pastures are found on fixed sand; rich spring pastures on gray soils; and spring, summer, and fall pastures on light chestnut and brown semidesert soils.

Natural forests and scrub are encountered in the desert and semidesert only on sand (*saxsaul*) † and on alluvial-meadow soils (*tugay*).‡ Many valuable woody plants, including, in particular, fruit trees can be grown under irrigation.

Present information permits only a general assessment of vertical soil zonation in the mountain regions of the USSR. Areas of clay and loam soils, shown in Tables 1 and 2, are somewhat underestimated because of inadequate study. Their exact delimination would be useful in clarifying possibilities for developing agriculture in the mountains.

---

* A Turkic word denoting "smooth" or "even." The *takyr* is a depression in Soviet Central Asia and Kazakhstan, is occasionally inundated and, when dry, develops a smooth but strongly cracked surface. Soils formed in *takyr* have two well-developed horizons: the upper horizon is free of salts, poor in minerals, and of a clay texture and columnar structure.

† *Saxsaul* (Haloxylon) a plant of the goosefoot family, small in size (below 12 inches) found in semideserts and deserts of Central Asia, consisting of five types, three of which, black, white, and *zaysan,* grow in the USSR. They bear small leaflets or are entirely devoid of leaves. In this way transpiration is reduced to a minimum.

‡ Found in northern and Central Asia, under flood-plain forests.

The most suitable soils for agricultural purposes are mountain chernozem, chestnut, brown forest, and gray forest soils that are not excessively stony. Of importance also are the mountain gray soils of Central Asia on which nonirrigated (*bogar*) agriculture is possible. Of little value are the mountain podzols, and particularly, the taiga soils on permafrost. However, even these soils, if they are not too stony and possess good microclimatic conditions, are suitable for growing vegetables, berries, and even fodder and grain crops, all of which are important to some alpine industrial regions. Fodder for reindeer is found mainly on alpine tundra soils, and fodder for other livestock on alpine meadows.

Broad-leaf forests of the highest quality are found on mountain brown soils and to some extent on gray forest soils. Dark conifers cover the mountain podzols, while larch, frequently stunted and in open stands, prevails on alpine permafrost.

AGRICULTURAL USE OF SOILS

The first survey of the agricultural use of the soils of the USSR was made by L. I. Prasolov (1932). Subsequent studies were conducted by the Council for the Study of the Productive Forces within the Academy of Sciences of the USSR (see *Natural-Historical Regionalization of the USSR,* 1947), and by the V. V. Dokuchayev Soil Institute in 1950.[2] The latter made new computations during 1956–59. Agricultural areas of the administrative regions were summarized by soil provinces, subzones, and zones with corrections for divergent administrative boundaries (Figure 2 and Table 3).

To facilitate comparability, the Soil Institute data have retained the previous scheme of soil-geographic regionalization of the USSR (Rozov, 1956).

THE POLAR-TUNDRA ZONE. The agricultural land structure of the polar-tundra zone was not considered in the 1950 study. The new estimates yield only an approximate picture. New geobotanical and other data were used to determine the agricultural area. The distribution of land according to subzones shows that scrub and bog are limited to the southern subarctic subzone. Pastures occupy vast areas in the subarctic as well as in arctic subzones and encourage the development of large herds of reindeer. However, at present, they are used very little. Open field cultivation, found on tundra

---

[2] For a comparison of these definitions, see N. N. Rozov, 1957.

ZONES	SUBZONES	(In millions of hectares)
Polar Tundra	Arctic Soils	60
	Tundra Soils	120

Taiga	Gleyey-Podzolic Soils (including Permafrost Taiga Gleys)	240
	Podzolic Soils (including Permafrost Taiga Soils)	255
	Turfy-Podzolic Soils	260

Forest Steppe and Steppe	Gray Forest Soils	64
	Leached and Typical Chernozems	89
	Ordinary and Southern Chernozems	100
	Dark Chestnut and Chestnut Soils	68

Semi-desert and Desert	Light Chestnut and Brown Desert-Steppe Soils	130
	Gray-Brown Desert Soils	140
	Gray Soils (Sierozems)	33

Mountain	Mountain Tundra Soils	165
	Mountain Meadow Soils	27
	Mountain Podzolic, Permafrost-Taiga, and Gray Forest Soils	400
	Mountain Brown Forest Soils	18
	Mountain, Steppe, and Desert Soils	42

Figure 2

Agricultural use of the soils of the pedogeographic zones and subzones of the USSR (in percent of their areas). (*A*) arable, long-term fallow (*zalezh*), gardens and orchards; (*B*) hay lands; (*C*) pastures and grazing lands; (*D*) reindeer pasture; (*E*) forests and scrubland; (*F*) bogs, swamps, or marshes; (*G*) unusable or otherwise occupied.

[Agricultural Use, % of Subzone Area]

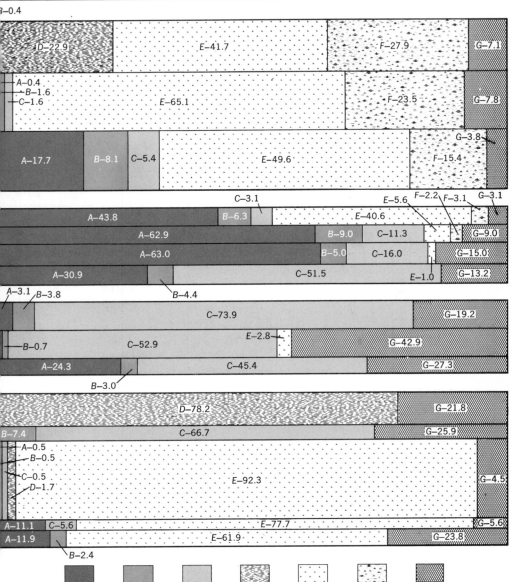

Table 3
Agricultural Use of the Soil Area (In million hectares)

Zones	Subzones (or Mountain Zones)	Total Area (In million hectares)	Arable, Zalezh, Gardens, Orchards		Hay Lands		Pastures and Grazing		Reindeer Pastures		Forests and Scrubland		Bogs, Swamps or Marshes		Unusable or Otherwise Occupied[a]	
			m ha	%	m ha	%	m ha	%	m ha	%	m ha	%	m ha	%	m ha	%
Polar tundra	Arctic soils	60	—	—	—	—	—	—	50	88.3	—	—	—	—	10	16.7
	Tundra soils	120	—	—	—	—	—	—	86	71.7	9	7.5	17	14.1	8	6.7
	Total area	180	—	—	—	—	—	—	136	75.6	9	5.0	17	9.4	18	10.0
Taiga	Gleyey podzolic soils (including permafrost taiga gleys)	240	—	—	1	0.4	—		55	22.9	100	41.7	67	27.9	17	7.1
	Podzolic soils (including permafrost taiga soils)	255	1	0.4	4	1.6	4	1.6	—	—	166	65.1	60	23.5	20	7.8
	Turfy podzolic soil	260	46	17.7	21	8.1	14	5.4	—	—	129	49.6	40	15.4	10	3.8
	Total area	755	47	6.2	26	3.4	18	2.4	55	7.3	395	52.3	167	22.1	47	6.3
Forest-steppe and steppe	Gray forest soils	64	28	43.8	4	6.3	2	3.1	—	—	26	40.6	2	3.1	2	3.1
	Podzolized, leached, & typical chernozems	89	56	62.9	8	9.0	10	11.3	—	—	5	5.6	2	2.2	8	9.0
	Ordinary & southern chernozems	100	63	63.0	5	5.0	16	16.0	—	—	1	1.0	—	—	15	15.0
	Dark chestnut & chestnut soils	68	21	30.9	3	4.4	35	51.5	—	—	—	—	—	—	9	13.2
	Total area	321	168	52.3	20	6.3	63	19.6	—	—	32	10.0	4	1.2	34	10.6
Semidesert and desert	Light chestnut & brown desert-steppe soils	130	4	3.1	5	3.8	96	73.9	—	—	—	—	—	—	25	19.2
	Gray-brown desert soils	140	1	0.7	1	0.7	74	52.9	—	—	4	2.8	—	—	60	42.9
	Gray soils (sierozem)	33	8	24.3	1	3.0	15	45.4	—	—	—	—	—	—	9	27.3
	Total area	303	13	4.3	7	2.3	185	61.1	—	—	4	1.3	—	—	94	31.0
Mountain territories	Tundra soils	165	—	—	—	—	—	—	129	78.2	—	—	—	—	36	21.8
	Meadow soils	27	—	—	2	7.4	18	66.7	—	—	—	—	—	—	7	25.9
	Podzolic, permafrost, taiga, & gray forest soils	400	2	0.5	2	0.5	2	0.5	7	1.7	369	92.3	—	—	18	4.5
	Brown forest soils	18	2	11.1	—	—	1	5.6	—	—	14	77.7	—	—	1	5.6
	Steppe & desert	42	5	11.9	1	2.4	26	61.9	—	—	—	—	—	—	10	23.8
	Total area	652	9	1.4	5	0.8	47	7.2	136	20.9	383	58.7	—	—	72	11.0
TOTAL AREA USSR SOILS		2211	237	10.7	58	2.6	313	14.2	327	14.8	823	37.2	188	8.5	265	12.0

[a] Otherwise occupied land includes land under buildings, roads, and other construction.

soils near the southern boundary of the zone, is very limited in area and cannot be precisely enumerated.

THE TAIGA ZONE. The new calculations permit the isolation of reindeer pastures of the taiga for the first time and show the distribution of the agricultural area by subzones. Croplands, hay lands, and pastures are—as might be expected—concentrated in the southern subzone on turfy-podzolic soils, but reindeer are concentrated in the northern subzone of gley-podzolic soils, where ordinary pastures cover less than one million hectares. These are not shown separately in Table 3.

In all of the taiga subzones, vast areas are covered by forests and brush. The central subzone (podzols) is the most heavily forested. In the southern subzone, considerable areas are used for agriculture, but about half is covered by forests and brush. In the northern subzone, forests and brush cover only 40% of the area while the rest of the territory is covered by open forests with reindeer pastures, swamps, and unusable land.

A comparison of agricultural land use with soil data reveals the potential of complex and thorough changes in land use as the population increases and the economy develops. In the southern part of the zone an expansion in the agricultural area and in the area of cultivated fodder crops is feasible. This would occur at the expense of a little productive pasture, brush, and some secondary forest growth found on turfy-podzol clays. This expansion will permit the linking of newly reclaimed land with existing pockets of arable land, thereby forming large agricultural tracts, interspersed by stands of forest that are important from the agricultural and hydroclimatic points of view. Natual fodder can be expanded on alluvial-meadow soils by clearing the brush. Turfy-gley, waterlogged podzols and lowland bog soils, all of which are rich in organic substance, can be effectively utilized if properly drained.

In the distant future, as the population of the taiga increases, an expansion in crop and in cultivated fodder production will take place on loamy and sandy turfy-podzols and, to some extent, on true podzols. This will cause a decline in forestry, requiring a more intensive management of the remaining forests, such as the stands in predominantly sandy and swampy areas, those of water-protective significance, the remnant woods between the fields, and above all, the stands on permafrost.

THE STEPPE AND FOREST-STEPPE ZONE. The greatest change that has occurred in recent years in the structure of the agricultural lands of the forest-steppe and steppe has been the opening up of virgin and long-term fallow lands, particularly after 1954. In the process, the area of arable land (including long-term fallow or *zalezh*) was increased by twenty-one million hectares through a reduction in the area of virgin, natural hay, and pasture lands.

An analysis of the distribution of the agricultural land according to sub-zones is of value. The subzone of gray forest soils is limited in area; 40% of it is covered by forest and scrub, which should be protected. The area of arable land is only a little larger but amounts to 74% of the unforested area. This is the highest arable ratio in the Union. About 63% of the subzone of degraded and typical chernozems has been plowed. Hay lands and pastures are more extensive here and the ratio amounts to only 68%. Hay lands are found extensively on meadow-chernozem and alluvial soils; pastures are located on the slopes of valleys and ravines or are confined to solonets and other soils unsuitable for cultivation without improvement.

Ordinary and southern chernozems constitute the largest subzone. The degree of cultivation is equal to the previous subzone, but the ratio of arable to total agricultural land is lower, or only 64%. This reduced ratio reflects the presence of solonets and stony soils, the development of intensive gully erosion, and a dense settlement pattern. About one-third of the subzone of dark chestnut and chestnut soils is under cultivation. Pastures are located principally on solonets, stony and sandy soils, with small areas on the chestnut soils of steeper slopes and gully-dissected relief. Further expansion of cultivation at the expense of pasture land in the subzone of dark chestnut and chestnut soils requires substantial soil improvement and irrigation.

Data on the agricultural use of the forest-steppe and steppe zone soils were compiled only in recent years. The cultivation of new land, excluding the plowing of *zalezh* but including former pasture, virgin, and hay land, amounts to 21 million hectares. Of these, nearly 10 million hectares are found on chernozem and to some extent on gray forest soils, and 11 million hectares on dark chestnut and chestnut soils. The chief area of the new lands in the chernozem zone is found in northern Kazakhstan and Western Siberia. Of 10 million hectares of new cropland in the chernozem zone, 7.5 million are located in Kustanay, North Kazakhstan, Kokchetav, Pavlodar, and Tselinograd oblasts and Altay Kray. There the areas of typical chernozem and of southern chernozem are, respectively, approximately 3 and 4.5 million (Rozov and Bazilevich, 1958; Rozov, 1960a, b, c; and Rozov and Doskach, 1960a, b).

The cultivation of virgin dark chestnut and chestnut soils developed more uniformly in all the subzones. In the regions mentioned above, nearly 4 million hectares of dark chestnut and chestnut soils have been plowed, amounting to over one-third of the expansion. The remaining two-thirds are located chiefly in central Kazakhstan and southeastern European Russia, including the lower Volga basin.

Inasmuch as the zone of forest-steppe and steppe soils is marked by a high degree of agricultural development, small-scale maps are inadequate for solving complicated questions pertaining to the transformation of land under varied local conditions. More accurate data on soil types are required and can in future be obtained from large-scale soils surveys, which so far do not cover the whole zone.

Particularly great difficulties arise in the assessment of soil areas located on erosion-prone slopes, which are unsuitable for traditional forms of agriculture. Estimates of such areas (Rozov, 1956) in the forest-steppe and steppe include 6 to 7 million hectares covered by gray forest soils, 19 to 23 million by chernozems, and about 6 to 7 million by dark chestnut and chestnut soils. The total area of soils on such slopes amounts to almost 35 million hectares.

What are the possibilities for the further development of land in the forest-steppe and steppe? Of 229 million hectares of clays and loams, 160 million are cultivated; 22 to 24 million are in forest and scrub (including shelter belts); and nearly 5 to 6 million are under various structures and roads. The remaining area, it would seem, is capable of agricultural use and amounts to 39 to 42 million hectares. However, as already shown, nearly 35 million hectares are unsuitable for normal cultivation because they consist of erosion-prone slopes, leaving an area of only 4 to 7 million hectares. The latter are located chiefly in the southern part of the zone, are subject to drought, and their agricultural use can be assured only after extensive research. Thus, the land fund in the forest-steppe and steppe, capable of agricultural development without fundamental improvement, may be considered exhausted or nearly so.

The land that can be developed only after costly improvement consists of (a) the erosion-prone slopes and of light sandy chernozem and chestnut soils, requiring protection from the wind; (b) solonets-type soils, usually requiring deep plowing, the application of gypsum, or supplementary or full irrigation (Antipov-Karatayev); and (c) marshy soils that need draining. The general areas of all these soils, including the land currently utilized, are shown in Table 2. With respect to those soils that can be utilized in future, a precise areal assessment can be made only on the basis of extensive soil, geomorphological, and other specialized studies.

Work on the development of shelter belts has yielded data on the tree-growth capacity of many steppe soils. In all regions of the steppe, soils and terrain characteristics have been identified that are conducive to the establishment of shelter belts, assuming the selection of proper tree species and the application of specialized technology. Apart from shelter belts, there is considerable value in the afforestation of steep slopes, of sandy and stony soils, and in the creation of orchards and berry plantations. Vineyards may be laid out in the southeastern part of this region.

Natural fodder areas in the wooded steppe and steppe, as evident in Table 3, are significant. However, their productivity is curtailed because of their location on slopes and on solonets, sandy, and stony soils. The afforestation of slopes and the cultivation of solonets soils will decrease the area of natural-fodder land. Consequently, the productivity of the remaining hay lands and pastures must be steadily increased through cultivation.

SEMIDESERT AND DESERT. The structure of land use in the semidesert and desert has changed little in recent years.

Most developed agriculturally are the gray soils on the southern foothills. Much less developed is the northern semidesert subzone of light chestnut and brown soils. The central subzone, the most extensive, is of desert character with gray-brown soils, but here cultivated and hay lands are insignificant.

Any substantial change in the structure of land use in the desert is possible only through a thoroughgoing transformation of its natural conditions. The most efficient means by which the region may be altered is through the provision of water and irrigation. On the light chestnut soils of the northern part of the zone, tree planting measures are also important, as shown by research at the Dzhanybek and Arshan-Zelmensk stations of the Dokuchayev Soil Institute. This has shown that crop cultivation is possible without irrigation, even on the solonets soils that are scattered within the light chestnut soil belt.

To determine the land reserves of the desert zone suitable for agricultural development, an inventory of the soils should be made only for those territories on which irrigation or shelter belts are feasible. Such an assessment is being made for only a few regions. To make the task possible, adequately detailed soil surveys with descriptions of hydrophysical and saline properties should be prepared and hydrogeomorphological and hydrogeological research should be carried out in order to find the potentials for obtaining water from open or subsurface reservoirs. The productivity and usefulness of pastures is also dependent on their water supply.

The planting of trees outside of irrigated areas is possible on some sands where *saxsaul* can be significantly expanded.

MOUNTAIN REGIONS. Agricultural land use in the mountains varies with latitude and altitude. An analysis of land use according to vertical soil zones, which reach different elevations depending on latitude but which always retain their specific pedogeographic characteristics, is of considerable value.

In the zone of mountain tundra soils, more than three-fourths of the area is covered by reindeer moss-and-lichen pastures; the rest of the area is unusable. However, these estimates are only crude. In the zone of mountain meadow soils, pastures, frequently highly productive, cover two-thirds of the area, hay lands an insignificant part, while the land in the rest of the zone is unusable.

Trees and scrub cover nine-tenths of the mountain podzols, permafrost, and gray forest soils. Reindeer pastures are very scarce; cropland, pastures, and hay lands, located in mountain valleys, constitute altogether not more than 1.5% of the zone.

The zone of mountain forest brown soils is agriculturally more developed. Over 10% of the area is occupied by cropland, half as much is in pastures, and the rest is mostly in forest. The zone of mountain steppe and desert soils is even more developed, mainly because pastures and not forests are found there.

The further expansion of the agricultural area on mountain chernozem, gray, brown, and chestnut soils is unwise without the implementation of antierosion measures. Soils already under cultivation are, moreover, also in need of protection. Clearly, terracing can expand the cropland, particularly by means of orchards and vineyards on the mountain brown-forest soils as well as on the red and yellow soils. On the remaining soils, as pointed out above, field cultivation and gardening are expedient only in regions of industrial development.

The afforestation of many mountain slopes that have lost their soil cover is essential to halt erosion due to extensive cutting and poor methods of lumber transportation, and to protect settlements. This is especially important in the Caucasus, in Central Asia, and in the Carpathians. Also important is an increase in the productivity of mountain pastures, which are associated with the correct utilization and the maintenance of proper livestock densities.

CHARACTERISTICS OF AGRICULTURAL LAND ACCORDING TO SOIL FACTORS

The new survey of the soils and their agricultural use makes it possible to determine the distribution of principal agricultural areas according to subzones and to define more precisely their qualitative soil and agroclimatic characteristics.

Here we refer primarily to the main changes that have occurred in the qualitative structure of land since 1950. They are expressed largely in terms of the changes in the qualitative composition of the fields. Due to the plowing up of virgin and *zalezh* lands, the share of arable land within the forest-steppe and steppe zone has risen from 68.7% to 70.9 %, correspondingly reducing the share of arable land located in the taiga and in mountain regions.

The distribution of arable land according to soil characteristics is given in Figure 3 and Table 4.

Of the total arable area of the USSR, that of the taiga today comprises only one-fifth, of the forest-steppe and steppe almost three-fourths, and, finally, of the semidesert only one-twentieth. Cropland within these soil groups varies sharply depending on their productivity (namely, on the heat and water regime, on the availability of minerals for plant life, on the need for fertilizer, on the agrotechnical properties, and on the requirements for land improvement. While the arable area of the first group (taiga zone)

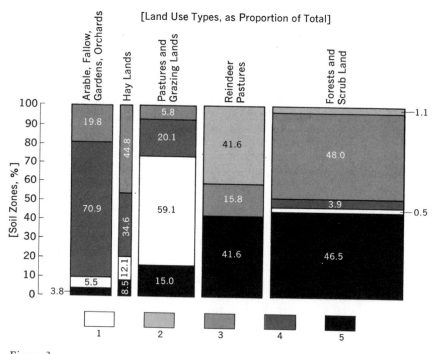

Figure 3

Zonal structure of principal types of land use in the USSR (in percent of land in soil zones). (1) Polar tundra zone, (2) taiga zone, (3) forest steppe and steppe zones, (4) semidesert and desert zones, (5) mountain zones.

Table 4
Distribution of Land Use

Land Use (In million hectares)	Total Area		Latitudinal Zones										Mountain Altitudinal Zones	
			Polar Tundra		Taiga		Forest-Steppe and Steppe		Semidesert and Desert					
	1950	1958	1950	1958	1950	1958	1950	1958	1950	1958			1950	1958
Arable, *perelog* (long-term fallow), orchards, and gardens	214	237	—	—	46	47	147	168	12	13			9	9
In percent	100.0	100.0	—	—	21.5	19.8	68.7	70.9	5.6	5.5			4.2	3.8
Hay lands and pastures	384	370	—	—	54	44	103	83	164	192			63	51
In percent	100.0	100.0	—	—	14.1	11.9	26.8	22.5	42.7	51.8			16.4	13.8
Reindeer pastures	16	327	16	136	—	55	—	—	—	—			—	136
In percent	100.0	100.0	100.0	41.6	—	16.8	—	—	—	—			—	41.6
Forests and scrubland	910	823	—	9.0	432	395	31	32	4	4			443	383
In percent	100.0	100.0	—	1.1	47.5	48.0	3.4	3.9	0.4	0.5			48.7	46.5

is situated in conditions of limited heat supply and a relatively short growing season, which reduces the productivity of crops, that of the second
group (wooded steppe and steppe zone) is adequately supplied with heat,
and parts of the third group (semidesert and desert zone) are capable of
producing such annual subtropical crops as cotton.

Differences exist in the supply of moisture. The arable area of the first
group seldom suffers from drought; more often it is a struggle with a
moisture surplus. On the arable area of the second group, measures for retaining and accumulating soil moisture, because of the frequent incidences
of drought, are important. Finally, the arable area of the third group is
almost entirely restricted to regions of irrigation.

With respect to the heat and water regime of the soil, the processes of
accumulation and decay of organic matter and the availability of minerals
for plant life vary, depending on the soil group. The differences in these
processes and ratios determine the agrotechnical measures required. Within
the limits of each of these soil groups, the arable land varies according to
the further differentiation of soils into subtypes and series and according to
the character of the soil material. This internal variation does not negate the
general characteristics of the soil groups.

The data in Table 5 permit an evaluation of the qualitative structure of
the land, and particularly of the arable area within soil zones.

Of the taiga zone, 19.8% is arable, mostly (19.4%) in the turfy-podzolic
subzone. Approximately 71% of the forest-steppe and steppe zone is arable,
the larger part of which (50.3%) is located in two chernozem subzones.
The arable area of the semidesert and desert is mainly located on meadow-
gray soils, and to a lesser degree on brown desert-steppe soils. Finally, the
arable land in the mountains, amounting to only 3.8% of the total area of
the USSR, is located principally on mountain steppe and desert soils, and
to a lesser extent on mountain podzols, gray forest, permafrost, brown
forest, yellow, and red soils.

The amount of natural hay and pasture land has also changed in recent
years as a result of the partial plowing up of the forest-steppe and steppe.
These lands, like croplands, are located primarily within four main soil
groups: taiga, steppe, desert, and the mountains (see Table 4).

Taiga hay lands and pastures comprise only 12% of the total grass fodder
of the USSR (exclusive of reindeer pasture); they have developed as a
result of forest clearing. They have little productivity, are adequately and
even superfluously wet, subject to bush growth, and respond effectively to
surface application of fertilizers.

Table 5
Distribution of Land Use
(Percentage of land by zones)

Land Use	Latitudinal Zones and Subzones												Mountain Altitudinal Zones				
	Polar Tundra		Taiga		Forest-steppe and Steppe				Semidesert and Desert								
	Arctic tundra soils	Tundra soils	Gleyey podzolic soils (including permafrost taiga gleys)	Podzolic soils (including permafrost taiga soils)	Turfy-podzolic soils	Gray forest soils	Bleached and typical chernozems	Ordinary and southern chernozems	Dark chestnut and chestnut soils	Light chestnut and brown desert-steppe soils	Gray-brown desert soils	Gray soils (sierozem)	Mountain tundra soils	Mountain meadow soils	Mountain podzolic, perma-frost taiga and gray forest soils.	Mountain brown forest soils	Mountain-steppe and desert soils.
Arable, *zalezh* (long-term fallow), gardens and orchards.	—	—	—	0.4	19.4	11.8	23.7	26.6	8.9	1.7	0.4	3.4	—	—	0.8	0.8	2.1
Hay lands	—	—	1.7	6.9	36.2	6.9	13.8	8.6	5.2	8.6	1.7	1.7	—	3.5	—	—	1.7
Pasture and grazing	—	—	—	1.2	4.4	0.6	3.1	5.1	11.1	30.6	23.5	4.7	—	5.6	0.6	1.2	8.3
Reindeer pastures	15.3	26.3	16.8	—	—	—	—	—	—	—	—	—	39.5	—	2.1	—	—
Forests and scrubland	—	1.1	12.2	20.0	15.7	3.2	0.6	0.1	—	—	0.5	—	—	—	44.8	1.8	—
Bogs, swamps, and marshes	—	9.0	35.6	31.9	21.3	1.1	1.1	—	—	—	—	—	13.6	2.6	6.8	—	—
Unusable or otherwise occupied	3.8	3.0	6.4	7.6	3.8	0.8	3.0	5.6	3.4	9.4	22.6	3.4	—	—	—	0.4	3.8

Steppe hay and pasture lands occupy approximately 22% of the total grass fodder area; for the most part they are remnants of steppe vegetation or old *zalezh* lands that have remained in places unsuitable for cultivation. The productivity of these lands increases significantly when measures are taken to enhance soil-moisture accumulation and to improve solonets soils. Desert pastures and some hay lands, comprising 52% of the total grass fodder area, have retained their natural vegetation. Mountain hay lands and pastures are diverse in composition and amount to about 14% of the grass fodder area.

There is for each of the listed zonal groups a specific relationship between hay lands and pastures. In the taiga zone, hay lands prevail over pastures and grazing lands; in the forest-steppe and steppe zone, on the other hand, they occupy only a fourth of the total natural fodder land; in the semidesert and desert zone, only one twenty-fifth; and in mountain regions about one-tenth.

The distribution of hay lands and pastures, according to subzones, is clearly evident in Table 5. The proportion of hay lands decreases almost continuously from north to south; the proportion of pastures, on the other hand, grows in the same direction.

An analysis of the distribution of forest and bush, according to zones and subzones, reveals their concentration on the podzolic, permafrost, and mountain soils; the gray forest soils and the podzolized and leached chernozems have only limited forest stands.

The results of this national inventory of land resources on the basis of small-scale soil studies are of twofold importance. On the one hand they provide, in spite of the tentative nature of some of the data, an indication of the location and size of areas capable of development with proper improvement. They are useful, therefore, in the planning of agriculture and forestry, and in the regulation of labor resources. On the other hand, the results of such an inventory permit the establishment of a schedule for republic and oblast work in the evaluation of land, which should be carried out on the basis of soil surveys of a larger scale.

At present, in a number of union republics, work is being carried out on a land inventory. In the Russian Federation, the Law Concerning the Conservation of Natural Resources in the RSFSR requires the Ministry of Agriculture of the RSFSR to conduct "an inventory of agricultural land on the basis of agricultural worth and soil quality, and to establish a land cadastre." This law also states that all departments that are concerned with the utilization of natural resources "are obligated to organize and conduct quantitative and qualitative inventories by means of cadastres, assessments, special maps, and so forth." [3]

In working out methods for cadastral studies, scientific organizations have based the qualitative evaluation of land on yield capacity, profitability, or other agricultural characteristics. However, these factors themselves depend on the natural conditions of each section of land and, above all, on the type and quality of the soil. The drawing up of complex cadastral maps must be based on specialized large-scale maps, the most important of which are soil maps. They are particularly necessary in those areas where land use is undergoing change, where land improvement is being carried out, or where natural conditions are being altered. It should be remembered that the genetic and lithologic subdivisions of soils reflect the principal bioclimatic regularities of the natural environment and should not be ignored to any degree in the development of agricultural land.

BIBLIOGRAPHY

Antipov-Karatayev, I. N. *O metodakh melioratsii solontsov v SSSR* [Concerning Measures for Solonets Melioration in the USSR]. Moscow, 1957. Soveshchaniye po voprosam naiboleye effektivnykh sposobov ispolzovaniya mineralnykh, organicheskikh i bakterialnykh udobreniy (Doklady) [Conference on the Problems of the Most Effective Methods of Use of Mineral, Organic, and Bacterial Fertilizers (Papers)].

Cheremushkin, S. D. "Kachestvennyy uchet i ekonomicheskaya otsenka zemel" [Qualitative Inventory and Economic Evaluation of Land]. *Ekonomika selskogo khozyaystva,* no. 6 (1957).

Ivanova, E. N., Letunov, P. A., Rozov, N. N., Fridland, V. M., and Shuvalov, S. A. "Pochvenno-geograficheskoye rayonirovaniye SSSR" [Pedogeographic Regionalization of the USSR]. *Pochvovedeniye,* no. 10 (1958).

Letunov, P. A. "Printsipy kompleksnogo prirodnogo rayonirovaniya v tselyakh razvitiya selskogo khozyaystva" [Principles of Complex Natural Regionalization for the Development of Agriculture]. *Pochvovedeniye,* no. 3 (1956).

Panfilov, A. T. "Gosudarstvennyy uchet zemel i ikh ispolzovaniye" [State Land Inventory and Land Utilization]. *Zemledeliye,* no. 2 (1959).

Prasolov, L. I. "Ploshchadi pochv i ugodiy SSSR" [Soil and Land Use Areas of the USSR]. *Priroda,* no. 4 (1932).

---

[3] Law Concerning the Conservation of Natural Resources in the RSFSR [Law of the Russian Soviet Federated Socialist Republic], *Pravda,* October 28, 1960, paragraphs 2, 13.

Prasolov, L. I. "Zemelnyy fond dlya rastenievodstva SSSR s tochki zreniya geografii pochv" [Land Fund for Plant Production in the USSR from the Pedogeographic Point of View]. In *Rastenievodstvo SSSR* [Plant Production in the USSR], vol. 1, pt. 1. Moscow-Leningrad: Selkhozgiz, 1933.

Prasolov, L. I. "Zemelnyye bogatstva SSSR" [Land Wealth of the USSR]. *Sovetskaya nauka,* no. 3 (1941).

Prasolov, L. I. "Geografiya i ploshchad rasprostraneniya tipov pochv" [The Geography and Area of Extent of Soil Types]. *Pochvovedeniye,* nos. 3–4 (1945).

Rozov, N. N. "Printsipy prirodnogo rayonirovaniya SSSR dlya tseley selskokhozyaystvennogo proizvodstva" [Principles of Natural Regionalization of the USSR for Agricultural Production]. *Pochvovedeniye,* no. 8 (1954).

Rozov, N. N. "Zemelnyye resursy SSSR i voprosy rasshireniya zemledeliya" [Land Resources of the USSR and the Question of Agricultural Expansion]. In *Osvoyeniye tselinnykh i zalezhnykh zemel v 1954 g.* [The Assimilation of Virgin and Long-term Fallow Land in 1954]. Moscow-Leningrad: AN SSSR, 1956.

Rozov, N. N. "Rezultaty i blizhayshiye zadachi rabot po uchetu zemelnykh resursov SSSR" [Results and Immediate Tasks of Efforts on the Land Resource Inventory of the USSR]. In *Voprosy genezisa i geografii pochv* [Questions Concerning the Genesis and Geography of Soils]. Moscow-Leningrad: AN SSSR, 1957.

Rozov, N. N. "Zemelnyye resursy Akmolinskoy oblasti i ispolzovaniye territorii" [Land Resources of Akmolinsk Oblast and the Utilization of the Territory]. In *Prirodnoye rayonirovaniye Severnogo Kazakhstana* [Natural Regionalization of Northern Kazakhstan]. Moscow-Leningrad: AN SSSR, 1960a.

Rozov, N. N. "Zemelnyye resursy Kokchetavskoy oblasti i ikh selskokhozyaystvennoye ispolzovaniye" [Land Resources of Kokchetav Oblast and Their Agricultural Utilization]. Ibid. (b)

Rozov, N. N. "Zemelnyye resursy Pavlodarskoy oblasti i ikh selskokhozyaystvennoye ispolzovaniye" [Land Resources of Pavlodar Oblast and Their Agricultural Utilization]. Ibid. (c)

Rozov, N. N. "Novye dannye o kachestvennoy strukture selskokhozyaystvennykh ugodiy SSSR po pochvennym priznakam" [New Data on the Qualitative Structure of the Agricultural Land of the USSR According to Soil Characteristics]. *Pochvovedeniye,* no. 9 (1961).

Rozov, N. N. "Obshchiy uchet i kolichestvennaya kharakteristika zemelnykh resursov SSSR" [General Inventory and the Quantitative Description of the Land Resources of the USSR]. In *Problemy pochvovedeniya* [Problems of Soil Science]. Moscow, 1962.

Rozov, N. N. and Bazilevich, N. I. "Zemelnyye resursy Altayskogo kraya i ikh ispolzovaniye v zemledelii (bez Gorno-Altayskoy A.O.)" [Land Resources of the Altay Kray and Their Utilization in Agriculture (Without the Gorno-Altay A.O.)]. In *Prirodnoye rayonirovaniye Altayskogo kraya* [Natural Regionalization of Altay Kray]. Moscow-Leningrad: AN SSSR, 1958.

Rozov, N. N. and Doskach, A. G. "Zemelnyye resursy Severo-Kazakhstanskoy oblasti i ispolzovaniye territorii" [Land Resources of North Kazakhstan Oblast and the Utilization of its Territory]. In *Prirodnoye rayonirovaniye Severnogo Kazakhstana* (see Rozov, 1960a). (a)

Rozov, N. N. and Doskach, A. G. "Zemelnyye resursy Kustanayskoy oblasti i ispolzovaniye territorii" [Land Resources of Kustanay Oblast and the Utilization of its Territory]. Ibid. (b)

Yestyestvenno-istoricheskoye rayonirovanniye SSSR [Natural-historical Regionalization of the USSR], ed., D. G. Vilenskiy. Moscow-Leningrad: AN SSSR, 1947. *Trudy Komissii po yestyestv.-istor. rayonirovanniyu SSSR*, t. 1 [Papers of the Commission for Natural-historical Regionalization of the USSR, vol. 1].

Zemskiy, P. M. *Razvitiye i razmeshcheniye zemledeliya po prirodnokhozyaystvennym rayonam SSSR* [The Development and Distribution of Agriculture by Natural-economic Regions of the USSR]. Moscow: AN SSSR, 1959.

9. Increasing Agricultural Productivity Through Irrigation and Drainage

S. F. Averyanov, E. N. Minayeva, and V. A. Timoshkina
(Institute of Geography, Academy of Sciences of the USSR)

The USSR leads the world in terms of land area suitable for agriculture. Because of its planned economy and the potential of its land resources, the USSR has great opportunities for expanding agricultural production.

Agricultural output can be raised by bringing new areas into production, by better land use, and finally, by an increase in land productivity. This can be accomplished by water reclamation, improved tillage, increased fertilization, and a shift to more productive crops.

This chapter is concerned principally with the hydrotechnical improvements of irrigation and drainage. These improvements affect the heat and water balance of the earth's surface by providing water where needed or by draining the land where moisture is excessive, permitting a fuller use of solar heat and an increase in the potential fertility of soils. The highest increases in productivity are achieved when there is a proper ratio of heat to moisture, a rational agricultural technology, proper use of chemical fertilizers, and mechanization of agriculture. Hydrotechnical improvement allows for the assimilation of new, potentially fertile lands that suffer either a shortage or surplus of water and for a substantial increase in the productivity of lands already in use.

The natural water supply in the soil is defined by means of the coefficient of moisture, which reflects the relationship between precipitation (either the total quantity or that less the runoff) and evaporation (or the maximum water requirements of the crops).[1] In areas with low coefficient values it is

---

[1] The literature contains a number of varying definitions of the physical significance of the moisture coefficient. (See, for instance, Budyko, 1956; Kostyakov, 1960).

necessary to use irrigation; in areas with high coefficient values, drainage is required.

Figure 1[2] shows the principal regions where land subject to irrigation and drainage is located. It is evident that the isolines of the moisture coefficient follow the boundaries of natural zones. In addition to possessing zonal characteristics, the distribution of these regions is significantly influenced by local conditions, mainly geomorphological, hydrological, and hydrogeological. Thus, when further runoff is hindered, excessive inflow of surface or ground water to lowlands leads to the formation of bogs or enhances the accumulation of salt in soil and ground water, causing salinity.

About 600 million hectares of land within the USSR suffer from a deficit of moisture; over 200 million hectares consist of bog and excessively wet land.* As a result, the water balance of about 40% of the arable area needs improvement. However, melioration of all lands that require improvement is unfeasible at the present time. If one takes into account the runoff of the rivers and the area of soils suitable for irrigation (without the transfer of water from arctic river basins to the south) it would be possible to irrigate up to 60 million hectares in Central Asia, Transcaucasia, and Kazakhstan, and in the semiarid regions of the North Caucasus and the Volga basin. About 80 million hectares of lowland swamp and about 20 million hectares of excessively wet land could be drained.

A project for expanding the areas of irrigation and drainage in the next ten to twelve years to satisfy the agricultural needs of the country has been prepared by the Council for the Study of the Productive Forces within the Academy of Sciences of the USSR.† The project foresees an increase in the drained area (with full agricultural use) of about 28 million hectares. In 1956 there were 7 million hectares of land with a drainage network; in 1961, 9 million, of which less than 6 million hectares were actually used.‡ The project also foresees a regular yearly increase in the area of land properly irrigated, reaching a total of 15 million hectares (in 1957 there were 7.2 million hectares),§ and an increase in the area of *liman* irrigation of up to 5 million hectares (in 1957 there were about one million). The project an-

---

[2] Figure 1 has been compiled from the map of moisture coefficients of D. I. Shashko and the map of hydromelioration of Zuzik (1959). (See Mirkin, 1960.)

* The author uses the Russian term *boloto;* depending on context, it may be translated as "swamp," "marsh," or "bog."

† Previously associated with the State Economic Council, under the Council of Ministers of the USSR.

‡ According to *Narodnoye khozyaystvo SSSR v 1965 godu. Statisticheskiy yezhegodnik* (Moscow, 1966), p. 365, there was a drainage network of 8.4 million hectares in 1956, of which 7 million were established on collective, state, and other farms. By 1965, these figures had reached 10.6 million and 8.9 million respectively, with 7.1 million in actual use.

§ By 1965, the area served by irrigation canals reached 9.8 million hectares, of which 9.3 million were actually irrigated, with 7.3 million in crops, the rest in orchards, vineyards, and pastures. *Narkhoz SSSR, 1965,* p. 363.

ticipates an increase in the drained area from 150 million hectares in 1959 to 235 million. Finally, the improvement of about 65 million hectares of land surrounding reservoirs is planned, to reestablish the agricultural productivity lost through waterlogging and the changing flood level (Mirkin).

To assess properly the scale of the task it should be remembered that the cost of intensive drainage is about 200 to 300 rubles per hectare; cost of irrigation, about 300 to 1,000 rubles per hectare. This means that in the next ten to twelve years about 10 billion rubles must be invested in hydromelioration. However, since land improvement raises yields up to four times, these investments can be redeemed within five years, approximately the same period as for the opening of the virgin lands.

It must be stated that, until recently, basic land improvement for raising agricultural productivity was not given much attention, largely because of the availability of virgin lands, which could be plowed without improvement.

In recent years, 40 million hectares of virgin land have been opened to agriculture. However, despite the vast extent of the country, the Soviet Union will not be able to increase the arable area in the future without extensive land improvement. Virgin land suitable for unimproved cultivation is almost exhausted and is found only in small, isolated parcels. Further development of agriculture is unquestionably linked with intensification.

Soviet and foreign experience have shown the profitability of hydrotechnical improvement of agricultural land. Crops produced on irrigated land, for example, cost half that of the world average. However, the irrigated area is only slightly more than 20% of the total arable area of the earth. In the United States, out of 130 million hectares of arable land, 12 million are irrigated and 60 million are drained, indicating that more than half of all the arable area is improved. The agricultural lands of England, the Netherlands, West Germany, East Germany, and of other European countries have been almost totally drained. In recent years sprinkling irrigation has been introduced as another method for regulating the water regime.

The high yields of cotton, vegetables, fruit, fodder, and other crops obtained on the irrigated lands of the Central Asian republics, Transcaucasia, and Moldavia are well known. Properly drained and intensively used lowland marshes in Belorussia, in the Ukraine, and in other regions afford yields of silage corn, vegetables, root crops, and perennial grasses that are two to three times higher than average. High yields on drained lowland marshes are due not only to improvements in the water and thermal balance but also to the use, after drainage, of reserves of colloidal fractions that for centuries have accumulated in the peat.

The program of the CPSU adopted at the Twenty-second Party Congress

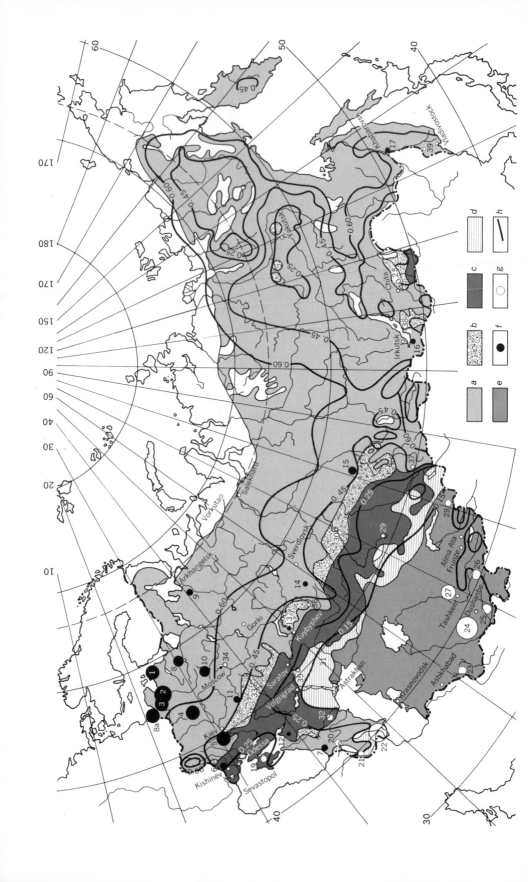

Figure 1

Natural zones of the USSR, zones of moisture availability, and the distribution of improved land (after D. T. Zuzik and D. I. Shashko).

Natural zones:

(*a*) forest zone, (*b*) forest-steppe zone, (*c*) steppe zone, (*d*) semidesert zone, (*e*) desert zone, (*f*) areas with a drainage network, (*g*) areas with an irrigation network, (*h*) isolines of indices of moisture supply (zones), according to D. I. Shashko: > 0.60 = excessively moist; 0.60–0.45 = moist; 0.45–0.25 = moderately moist; 0.25–0.15 = subject to drought; < 15 = dry.

For each geographical area, the extent of land (I) with a drainage network and (II) with an irrigation network is shown in thousands of hectares.

I. *Land with a drainage network:*

(1) Estonian SSR, 925.3; (2) Latvian SSR, 1,854.3; (3) Lithuanian SSR, 874.8; (4) Belorussian SSR, 1,021.1; (5) Ukrainian SSR, 1,031.2; (6) Moldavian SSR, 16.6; (7) Georgian SSR, 101.0;

RSFSR: (8) Northwest (without Kaliningrad Oblast) 744.9; (8a) Kaliningrad Oblast, 757.0; (9) North, 45.7; (10) Non-Chernozem Center, 544.3; (11) Central Chernozem, 6.6; (12) North Caucasus, 25.0; (13) Povolzhye, 0.2; (14) Urals, 6.3; (15) Western Siberia, 336.8; (16) Eastern Siberia, 49.4; (17) Soviet Far East, 47.6.

II. *Land with an irrigation network:*

(18) Moldavian SSR, 29.9; (19) Ukrainian SSR, 222.8; (20) Georgian SSR, 319.6; (21) Armenian SSR, 212.9; (22) Azerbaydzhanian SSR, 1,580.1; (23) Turkmen SSR, 720.6; (24) Uzbek SSR, 2,287.6; (25) Tadzhik SSR, 424.8; (26) Kirgiz SSR, 1,145.4; (27) Southern Kazakhstan, 1,666.1; (28) Eastern Kazakhstan, 280.9; (29) Central Kazakhstan, 50.0; (30) Northern Kazakhstan, 7.6; (31) Western Kazakhstan, 49.8;

RSFSR: (32) North Caucasus, 771.6; (33) Central Chernozem, 22.2; (34) Non-Chernozem Center, 16.5; (35) Povolzhye, 186.0; (36) Urals, 16.0; (37) Western Siberia, 30.7; (38) Eastern Siberia, 420.3; (39) Soviet Far East, 18.2. The size of the circles is proportional to the extent of irrigated or drained land.

stresses the need for agricultural intensification and points out the value of reclamation (irrigation and drainage) in agricultural development, which can guarantee high and stable yields in all natural zones and under any seasonal climatic condition. In fact, agricultural land reclamation must become (along with crop rotation, fertilization, tillage, and so on) an integral part of the zonal system of agriculture.

Land improvement, it should be kept in mind, also requires technological and organizational measures. If even one of these measures is ignored, the improvements made will fail and the considerable cost will have been expended fruitlessly.

Experience shows that the most effective and economically sound land-improvement systems are those made with advanced technology. Whatever the increased cost of these technologies may be, it is redeemed with interest through the reduction in losses, the increase in yields, reliability, and life expectancy of the system, whether the land is irrigated or drained. In those regions where economic considerations induced simplified methods of improvement (such as open drainage of swamps, a rather sparse network of drainage canals, irrigation without drainage, and so on), the projects quickly deteriorated or proved ineffective. Because of failure in a number of regions to prevent infiltration, about half of 65 billion cubic meters of irrigation water was lost before reaching the crops.

Rapid growth in the building-materials industry and in the production of electricity will, hopefully, permit a complete shift to the construction of modern, lasting, and economically profitable drainage and irrigation systems.

IRRIGATION

Of the natural zones that have substantial resources of heat, much is deficient in moisture, with the exception the small areas of western Georgia and the Talysh lowland. Territories whose coefficient of moisture is below 0.30 (Figure 1) suffer from a shortage of moisture. By way of comparison, a large part of the United States has annual precipitation in excess of 500 millimeters in association with substantial thermal resources.

A comparison of the water requirements of the principal crops with moisture reserves (precipitation during the vegetative period and usable reserves of soil moisture), shows that in the forest regions with a full use of precipitation during an average year, only land used for vegetables need be irrigated (Mirkin).

In the steppe, it is expedient to irrigate corn, root crops, and fruit as well as vegetables. In the lowlands of the desert, crops can be grown only with irrigation. One should also keep in mind that increased yields somewhat increase the demand for water. Consequently, irrigation will in time gradually shift to more northerly latitudes.

The reserves of agricultural land capable of irrigation but now used in unirrigated form are very large. Irrigation expansion is thus seldom limited by a shortage of suitable land but rather by the shortage of water. The water resources of the principal irrigated zone include the runoff of the Amu-Darya, Syr-Darya, Talas, and Chu in the Central Asian republics; the Ili and other rivers flowing into Lake Balkhash in southern Kazakhstan; and the Kura in eastern Azerbaydzhan. These rivers provide a total flow of 160 cubic kilometers per year (with a probability of 50%) or 120 cubic kilometers per year (with a probability of 75%).

According to N. A. Yanishevskiy, the total flow of the rivers of Central Asia (Amu-Darya, Syr-Darya) and of southern Kazakhstan (Chu, Ili), could irrigate 10.2 million hectares in these regions, and with regulated runoff, 12.6 million hectares. G. N. Manucharov indicates that the irrigated area in Transcaucasia can be increased to 1.83 million hectares (with 1.66 million hectares in the basin of the Kura, 0.10 in the rest of the Caspian basin, and 0.07 in the Black Sea basin).

A Giprovodkhoz * survey of water and land resources in the irrigation zones indicates the magnitude of the irrigation potential. According to the survey, it is possible to irrigate in the next few years an additional 7.4 million hectares of land in the principal irrigation zone, and 13.8 million in the semiarid zone. Multiannual regulation of rivers can provide irrigation for an additional 11.9 million hectares. With water transfer between the basins of the southern rivers, an additional 17.6 million hectares can be irrigated. The total area of irrigable land amounts to nearly 60 million hectares. According to Giprovodkhoz, the total area of potential irrigation is distributed as follows (in millions of hectares): Central Asia and southern Kazakhstan —21.5; northern, western, and central Kazakhstan—19.6; southeastern Russia—4.2; the North Caucasus—5.1; Transcaucasia—3.3; and the southern Ukraine and Moldavia—3.9. If 2 to 3 million hectares for secondary regions are added to the above, the total reaches 60 million hectares.

An additional reserve for expanding the irrigated area lies in reservoir regulation of runoff. A changeover from seasonal to multiannual control

---

* *Gosudarstvennyy institut po proyektirovaniyu vodnogo khozyaystva* [State Institute for the Planning of Water Economy].

will increase runoff utility. The efficiency of the irrigation systems and the use of ground water can be increased also. This would provide, for example, up to 500 cubic meters of water per second in Uzbekistan. Another important reserve of further irrigation is the transfer of northern river water to the steppe zone, and other interbasin transfers such as from the Lake Balkhash basin into the Chu Valley; or from the Volga into the semidesert Ural-Emba basin. Availability of water does not, for all practical purposes, therefore prove a hindrance to the expansion of irrigation in the immediate future.

Land is irrigated in all natural zones except the tundra, but most irrigated land is in the desert and semidesert (Table 1). The distribution of irrigated areas in 1951 by economic regions and Union republics are given in Table 2.

The irrigated lands of the desert and semidesert regions of Central Asia, southern Kazakhstan, Transcaucasia, and the southeastern part of the North Caucasus are concentrated in large tracts on broad plateaus, in river valleys, and in foothill regions. In the Central Asian republics and southern Kazakhstan, for example, 8.3% of the irrigated land lies in the mountains, 41% on the piedmont plains, 40.1% on the alluvial plains and ancient deltas, and 10.6% on coastal lowlands and river deltas. Irrigated land forms small islands within the agricultural area of other regions of the Soviet Union. All cotton and rice, one-third of the alfalfa, one-fourth of the vegetables, and one-fifth of the orchards and vineyards are irrigated. They comprise only 3.8% of the total sown area, but the value of their output amounts to 15% of all crop production.

The principal irrigated crops in regions of unreliable moisture supply—in the Central Black Earth, the Ukraine, Moldavia, and Western Siberia—are vegetables, potatoes, melons, and fruits. In drier regions—in southeastern European Russia, in the North Caucasus, as well as in Kazakhstan

Table 1
Distribution of Land with an Irrigation Network

Zone	Millions of Hectares	Percentage of Total Irrigated Area
Desert and Semidesert	9.60	87.4
Steppe	1.22	10.9
Forest-Steppe	0.15	1.4
Forest	0.03	0.3

Table 2
Distribution of Land with an Irrigation Network According
to Republics and Economic Regions
(After S. L. Mirkin, 1960)

Republic or Economic Region	Thousands of Hectares	Percentage of Total Area with an Irrigation Network
Russian Federation (RSFSR)	1,481.6	13.6
Non-Chernozem Center	16.5	0.1
Central Black Earth	22.0	0.2
European Southeast	186.0	1.6
North Caucasus	771.8	6.4
The Urals	16.0	0.1
Western Siberia	30.7	0.3
Eastern Siberia	420.3	3.7
Soviet Far East	18.2	0.2
Ukraine	222.8	2.0
Kazakhstan	2,054.4	18.9
Central Asia	5,178.4	46.2
Azerbaydzhan	1,580.1	14.4
Armenia	212.9	1.9
Georgia	319.6	2.8
Moldavia	29.9	0.2
TOTAL	11,079.6	100.0

NOTE: It should be kept in mind that the efficiency of existing irrigation systems is low in the Soviet Union, and that lands through which irrigation canals pass are not necessarily irrigated. (See Table 3.) Ed.

—they are grain, fodder, and technical crops; in Armenia and Georgia, grains, vegetables, and fruit; and in Uzbekistan, Turkmenia, and Tadzhikistan, cotton and subtropical crops are irrigated.

In 1922, the USSR had a total of 2.2 million hectares of irrigated land. In the thirty-five years following (to 1957), the actual area of irrigated land almost quadrupled, increasing 1.1 million hectares in the seven years from 1952 to 1958 (this figure includes an increase of 540,000 hectares in the cotton-growing regions). During this time the investment in water reclamation exceeded 900 million rubles (government and collective farm funds), of which nearly 700 million rubles were invested in irrigation. However, as already noted, the land that has an irrigation network may be far from fully utilized (Table 3).

In the RSFSR, the Kazakh, Azerbaydzhanian, and Armenian republics, only 80% of land with an irrigation network is actually irrigated. This in-

Table 3
Development and Use of Irrigation, 1945–1960
(In thousand hectares)
(After S. L. Mirkin, 1960)[a]

Indices	Year	Total	Distribution According to Republic										
			RSFSR	Kazakh-stan	Turk-menia	Uzbeki-stan	Tadzhi-kistan	Kirgi-ziya	Azer-baydzhan	Georgia	Armenia	Ukraine	Moldavia
Land with irrigation network, and used for agriculture	1945	6424	649	1027	397	1972	289	887	722	228	190	62	0.2
	1950	7387	1030	1195	385	2122	337	897	793	275	213	107	17
	1955	9248	1359	1585	397	2496	389	1112	1222	248	198	216	26
	1957	9326	1346	1457	408	2598	390	1128	1234	313	204	218	30
	1960	9893	1537	1479	480	2675	425	1146	1272	333	225	287	34
Actually irrigated	1945	5806	450	938	370	1918	283	756	712	170	182	26	0.2
	1950	6276	691	1000	352	2053	300	737	644	180	173	73	13
	1955	7046	749	1136	375	2261	335	812	832	181	175	144	20
	1957	7210	820	1054	398	2282	344	823	884	231	183	168	23
	1960	7936	966	1134	434	2389	394	889	1036	233	198	237	26
Growth of actually irrigated land between 1945 and 1960		2131	516	196	64	471	111	133	324	63	16	211	25.8
Irrigated land as a percentage of total land with an irrigation network		80	63	75	90	89	93	77	81	70	88	82	76

[a] In S. L. Mirkin's work, part of the data are given in graphic form. This table has been prepared by the authors. Data for 1960 are taken from the central Statistical Administration.

complete use of facilities is due to several factors: inadequate preparation for cultivation; withdrawal of previously irrigated land from agricultural use because of faulty irrigation networks; the lack of water in storage areas; and secondary salinization.

In the USSR, the highest percentage of unirrigated lands with an irrigation network is located in new regions of irrigation. In many cases irrigated lands are systematically used for nonirrigated crops; the network occupies useful land and hinders the operation of agricultural machines. This is especially true in regions where dry farming or animal husbandry had been the principal activities. In those areas irrigation is used to provide water for grains. In the development of new regions of irrigation it is obvious that not enough attention has been paid to the training of land-improvement workers and to the education of the population in new habits.

Irrigated land is not always used for valuable crops; in some regions, part of the area is irrigated for the production of low-value crops (grains and hay). The replacement of these crops is, in itself, a way to improve the use of irrigated lands.

Spring melt water is an important irrigation source; it may be used in flood (*liman*) irrigation, chiefly of hay land. Up to the present, such irrigation has been inadequately developed: only 1.4 million hectares are under *liman* irrigation, of which no more than 1.2 million hectares are used annually. Meanwhile, the total runoff in the steppe zone, even if an increase is allowed in the area of plowed land, equals 8.7 cubic kilometers (with a 75% certainty), 20.9 cubic kilometers (with a 50% certainty), or 40.4 cubic kilometers (with a 25% certainty). In view of the volume of flow, the only limitation on *liman* irrigation is the availability of suitable land with appropriate topography.

Irrigation can have a negative influence upon the soil cover and upon the quality of land if use is inadequate or careless. This may be expressed in the deterioration of the structure and mechanical composition of the soil, in soil leaching, in the formation of a soil mosaic, in the raising of the level of the ground water, in the development of marshiness and salinization, and sometimes even in the loss of some sections of land for agricultural use. At the present time, nearly 800,000 hectares in the cotton-growing regions are partly salinized, lowering yields to a level that is from five to seven centners per hectare less than from nonsalinized soils.

More than half of all the water conducted by the canals from its sources never reaches the fields but is lost in seepage, spillage, and evaporation; it incidentally produces salinization and waterlogging. Faulty installation of points of water distribution (from the trunk canals) is the main cause of spillage. To prevent salinization, drainage must be used when mineralized ground water lies close to the surface and runs off too slowly. The necessity for drainage as well as extent and time of its initiation are based on an analysis of the region's existing and prospective soil salt balances and on the benefit-cost considerations of the drainage project. If there is danger of salinization, there can be no doubt about the need; only economic considerations determine which system is to be built (i.e., lining the canals against seepage, and so forth).

Irrigation erosion usually takes place where the terrain is sloping, as in the piedmont, causing severe soil loss and a lowering of the yields of quality cotton fiber and seeds. When the slope exceeds 0.5° to 1°, furrow erosion develops if there is the slightest neglect of irrigation techniques.

The Council for the Study of the Productive Forces of the State Economic Council has computed the necessary extent of irrigated land for the next ten to twelve years. These data, which are based on the calculation of a full satisfaction of the country's needs for agricultural products, are presented in Table 4.

The table indicates that the total growth in actual irrigation should reach 8 million hectares, with the largest increase expected in the Central Asian republics, in Kazakhstan (mainly in the south), and in Azerbaydzhan (about 4.5 million hectares). This should ensure a further expansion in cotton cultivation; a substantial volume of corn, legumes, sugar beets, and alfalfa will be obtained in rotation with cotton. The semiarid zone (the North Caucasus, Ukraine, and other regions) should add 3.8 million hectares in irrigation, primarily to raise the production of vegetables, fodder, fruits, and grapes. A substantial development of *liman* irrigation is desirable in Kazakhstan. The production of corn for seed and silage, and of other fodder, should undergo significant expansion in the North Caucasus, Ukraine, southern Kakakhstan, and in the Kirgiz, Uzbek, and Azerbaydzhanian republics. The production of rice should be increased in the North Caucasus, the Soviet Far East, Kazakhstan, and Uzbekistan.

Despite the relatively small area involved, the role of irrigation in agriculture will become substantial because yields from irrigated lands are significantly higher than those obtained from dry farming. The gross output of raw cotton and rice produced on irrigated lands alone will reach about 10 and 1.6 million tons, respectively. Nearly 40% of the total output of fruit and grapes and 75% of all vegetable crops throughout the Soviet Union will also be obtained from irrigated lands, and it will provide a large part of the fodder for stock. In the future, agricultural production

Table 4
Irrigation, 1957, and Plan for Following Ten Years

Republic	Area of Irrigation Proper				Area of Liman Irrigation			
	Actually Irrigated in 1957		Planned for Eventual Irrigation		Actually Irrigated in 1957		Planned for Eventual Irrigation	
	Area (In thousand hectares)	Percentage of Sown Land	Area (In thousand hectares)	Percentage of Sown Land	Area (In thousand hectares)	Percentage of Sown Land	Area (In thousand hectares)	Percentage of Sown Land
RSFSR	819	0.7	2,970	2.0	82	0.7	2,108	4.3
Ukrainian SSR	168	0.5	1,017	2.8	2	0.2	246	12.0
Kazakh SSR	1,054	5.1	2,374	11.9	945	10.6	3,338	27.6
Kirgiz SSR	823	67.0	1,218	67.5	—	—	—	—
Tadzhik SSR	344	40.6	638	53.4	—	—	—	—
Turkmen SSR	398	100.0	946	100.0	—	—	—	—
Uzbek SSR	2,283	74.0	3,820	79.6	—	—	—	—
Azerbaydzhanian SSR	884	64.5	1,454	71.6	—	—	—	—
Armenian SSR	183	35.4	283	51.0	—	—	—	—
Georgian SSR	231	19.3	343	22.3	—	—	—	—
Moldavian SSR	23	1.1	141	6.1	—	—	—	—
TOTAL	7,210	3.8	15,204	6.5	1,029	1.8	5,692	8.6

from irrigated lands could reach 40% to 50% of the total output of the country.

At present, the State Economic Council is preparing a long-range plan for increasing the irrigated area to 28 million hectares during the next twenty years. In particular, a large base is to be constructed to include: (1) the basin of the Syr-Darya, where initial calculations indicate that 800,000 to 850,000 hectares of land in the Golodnaya Steppe (in the Uzbek, Kazakh, and Tadzhik republics) can be irrigated for cotton; (2) the Vakhsh River, where by means of the Nurek GES, about 1.2 million hectares (in the Uzbek and Tadzhik republics) are to be irrigated for rice, cotton, and other crops; (3) the Turkmen SSR where about 600,000 hectares of land are to be irrigated for cotton, using the Kara-Kum Canal; (4) the low-lands of the Amu-Darya, where 900,000 hectares of newly irrigated land are to be sown to rice. Also suggested is a full use of land and water resources in the Volga-Akhtuba flood plain and the Volga delta, in order to expand the irrigation of vegetables, rice, and corn, and improve fish and waterfowl breeding. Irrigation in the Volga region is to be increased on the basis of the energy of the Volga power stations at Volgograd and Kuybyshev. The water resources of the Don, Kuban', and other rivers in the southern European part of the RSFSR must be used for irrigating more than 1 million hectares of land and for increasing the production of rice, grapes, vegetables, and technical crops. Anticipated also is the expansion of irrigation in the Crimea and other southern reaches of the Ukraine and in Moldavia, relying on the waters of the Dnieper, Southern Bug, Dniester, and Danube. Approximately 4.5 million hectares of land will yield rice, corn, sugar beets, grapes, fruit, and vegetables, and develop animal husbandry. Large irrigation projects are planned for the regions of Transcaucasia, as well as a number of other regions.

A measure similar to irrigation but easier to implement is the provision of water to pastures. In the arid zone of the USSR, they occupy about 298 million hectares of which, in 1959, about 150 million hectares were fully or partly supplied with water for livestock. This included 83.5 million hectares in the Kazakh SSR, 44 million hectares in the Central Asian republics, and 19.9 million hectares in the southern and eastern regions of the RSFSR. The chief source of supply is ground water obtained by means of open wells, but over much of the region the number of wells is inadequate and the pastures are insufficiently exploited. To assure fuller use of those pastures now being opened up, it is possible and necessary to provide another 85 million hectares of land with water. More detailed data are available for 1955 only and are given in Table 5.

Table 5
Pastures Supplied with Water and Pastures Where Water Supply
Is Foreseen (In million hectares)
(After S. L. Mirkin, 1960)

Republic	Total	Used	Supplied with Water in 1955	Planned to be Supplied with Water	
				By 1965	After 1965
RSFSR	43.5	43.5	21.4	5.0	17.1
Ukrainian SSR	2.8	2.8	0.5	—	2.3
Kazakh SSR	173.4	115.0	44.0	55.0	16.0
Kirgiz SSR	8.6	8.5	6.6	0.9	1.0
Turkmen SSR	34.7	34.7	15.0	10.0	9.7
Tadzhik SSR	3.9	3.9	0.4	1.5	2.0
Uzbek SSR	27.1	23.4	8.9	5.0	9.0
Azerbaydzhanian SSR	2.0	2.0	0.6	0.7	0.7
Armenian SSR	0.8	0.8	0.3	—	0.5
Georgian SSR	1.3	1.3	0.6	—	0.7
TOTAL	298.1	235.9	98.3	78.1	59.6

Over half of all the sheep and about one-fourth of all the cattle and horses of the Soviet Union are kept on pastures that are supplied with water. Obviously, to increase the livestock population significantly, full water provision must be made to natural pastures in regions deficient or lacking in water.

Some conclusions and recommendations for further increases in the role, expansion, and improvement of the irrigation systems in the USSR are given below.

The plowing of most of the "virgin lands," which were suitable for cultivation without reclamation, requires the rejection of the limitation of irrigation to those crops grown under very unfavorable natural conditions and which cannot grow without it. Irrigation should be used wherever it can increase crop yields; in the next ten to fifteen years it will become the most important element in much of the zonal system of agriculture.

The economic effectiveness of new irrigation systems depends largely on the selection of those crops to which irrigation is necessary. Irrigation pays off when the effort devoted to it is small compared to the effort expended on plowing, cultivating, and harvesting, and when it produces significant results. Obviously, it is wise to irrigate fruit and vegetables that require eighty to ninety days work per hectare without irrigation; with irrigation only three to six days more are required but the yield increases from 100% to 300%. Substantial results are obtained from irrigating corn. On the other hand, the irrigation of grains increases labor expenditure by 60% to 80% but the increase in yields is not great enough to compensate for the additional labor cost.

In the USSR there are irrigation systems that were constructed in different years and consequently vary in quality. Some are antiquated and primitive, while some of the new ones have been poorly constructed or are of poor quality. In 1955 only one-fifth of all water storage construction was engineered; most canals were unlined, causing tremendous losses from seepage, which lead in turn to salinization and waterlogging. Only in recent years has drainage been introduced in the fight against salinization, but it is primarily of the simpler open type, often operating inadequately and hindering the mechanization of field work. The programing of land use is inadequate also, with consequent sporadic availability of water, occasional spotty salinization and, where there are significant slopes, soil erosion. Experience shows that in the final analysis the economies attained by simplified programing are not justified; irrigation systems lose their usefulness and the ensuing losses are not redeemed. Irrigation should be planned on a scale that would permit implementation at a high technical level.

However, serious deficiencies in the irrigation systems existed not only for these technical reasons, but also because there was inadequate consideration of natural processes, those that functioned prior to the establishment of the systems as well as those that developed as a result of changes in the water regime. In order to avoid such destructive developments in the future, it is necessary: (1) to assess the salt-water ratio of the irrigated area and adjacent territories in each existing project and on this basis to plan the use of the technology that would prevent secondary salinization and waterlogging; and (2) to use only those systems of irrigation (such as sprinkling) that prevent erosion on uneven terrain.

In both new construction and the reconstruction of old irrigation systems, reinforced concrete should be used; canals should be lined with cement, betonite, polyethylene, or plastic glass; and horizontal or vertical drainage as well as any secondary canals and drains should be covered. In each case irrigation should be planned with care; especially important are improvements that would induce increased productivity of work, such as portable and stationary pipelines, automated field dams with water flow through extended ditches, and so forth. Mechanical systems of water pumping should be used wherever feasible. To use these methods successfully under various conditions, extensive research and experimental and organizational work must be carried out, but no less important is the training of irrigation specialists in agricultural and hydrotechnical institutes; at present such training is inadequate.

As a result of widespread irrigation, a basic change in the water regime of sizable areas is to be anticipated, a change that can modify natural processes and may be reflected in both the national economy and the living conditions of the population. This problem must be understood in its broad regional aspect and has not yet been given adequate attention; its importance demands its inclusion in the plans of the leading research institutes.

DRAINAGE

As has been mentioned, the territory of the Soviet Union contains extensive marshes and excessively wet land that constitute a reserve of fertile soils. After drainage, such land could be used to produce high and stable yields of fodder, vegetables, grains, and technical crops. In addition, the Non-Chernozem Zone and other regions of the USSR have significant areas of agricultural land that suffer from periodic or permanent surplus of moisture, resulting in lower crop yields and more difficult agriculture. The experience of the Baltic republics and the northwestern regions of the RSFSR shows that drainage of such lands also brings positive results, increasing productivity by 50% or more. Finally, drainage is needed on the large and expanding area adjacent to reservoirs of hydroelectric stations. These areas, owing to a rise in the water level, are subject to shallow inundation and waterlogging.

Some drainage, however, does not yield substantial positive results because not only the initial investment for construction is required but also the implementation of a series of organizational, agrotechnical, phytological, and developmental measures. If these measures are not taken, the investment is not redeemed.

At present, the drainage and development of marshy land is deficient in a number of aspects; these deficiencies must be eliminated to increase agricultural production. Precipitation, ground water, spring melt, summer and fall flooding, and surface runoff all contribute to the formation of marshes and excessively wet land. Low drainage divides and other flat land that is covered by clays of low porosity tend to become marshy with precipitation. Excess precipitation either forms upland sphagnum bogs (the northern part of the European USSR, Siberia, and other areas) or, where the soils are clayey (the Ukrainian Polesye, the Soviet Far East, the Colchis low-land, the Baltic littoral, and the Non-Chernozem Zone of European Russia), the land becomes excessively moist. At the base of valley slopes and hills, where ground water comes to the surface, lowland swamps may develop, characterized by a stable water regime and a high reserve of mineral and or-ganic plant food that is of little use prior to drainage. Significant areas of marsh and bog form also in river flood plains. Their water regime is com-plex; they develop as a result of flooding and of runoff from hilly terrain.

The most promising agricultural use of lowland peat bogs comes from their high content of nutritional elements, particularly of nitrogen (bogs are usually poor in potash). Excessively moist soils have a lower supply of nutritional elements than peat bogs, but their drainage is less costly and so also represent a valuable reserve. Upland marshes, particularly of sphagnum, are poor in potash elements. Vegetative matter, as a rule, does not decay well in these areas and mineralization occurs only very slowly after drain-age. The water regime of these marshes depends to a large extent on varia-tion in annual precipitation. Although the drainage of upland marshes is difficult, such marshes have been drained and used in agriculture in Scandinavia and other countries where agricultural land is in short supply.

The total area of wet land suitable for drainage in the USSR amounts to about 98.5 million hectares. About 78.8% is located in Asian RSFSR, of which only about 0.5% is drained. The remaining wet land is found in the European part and in Transcaucasia, where there are extensive areas of high population density (Tables 6 and 7).

Drainage is especially important in the Baltic republics, Belorussia, the northwestern part of the Ukraine, and the Russian Non-Chernozem Zone. In some of these regions excessively wet land comprises 25% of the terri-tory. Of the land used for agriculture in the northern regions of the Soviet Union, the ratio of excessively wet land is 30% to 50% and in some places reaches even 100%.

Table 8, which illustrates the development of land drainage from 1917 to 1960, shows clearly what has been accomplished during the Soviet period.

In spite of the great progress, it must be concluded from data of the land fund (*The Economic Effectiveness of Land Reclamation,* 1960) that even in industrial, densely populated regions that have great need of livestock and garden produce, unused reserves of excessively wet land remain (Table 9).

The change in the Union's land fund, caused by the creation of hydro-electric reservoirs with the resultant inundation of flood plains, has become a serious problem in recent years. Such land is frequently very valuable

Table 6
Humid Land with Drainage, Distribution and Use, 1956 (In thousand hectares)
(After S. L. Mirkin, 1960)

Republic	Excessively Humid [a]				With Drainage Network [b]					
	Total Area	Marshes	Excessively Wet Mineral Soils	Capable of Development	Total Area	Usable	With Covered Drainage	In Need of Additional Drainage	Requiring Agrotechnical Improvement	Unused for Technical and Organizational Reasons
RSFSR	192,363	181,056	11,307	90,398	2,178	1,032	465	1,146	585	416
Europe	23,250	18,226	5,024	12,919	1,819	942	465	877	479	183
Asia	169,113	162,830	6,283	77,479	359	90	—	269	106	233
Belorussian SSR	2,824	1,246	1,578	1,922	876	291	3	585	172	169
Latvian SSR	886	410	476	699	1,480	466	26	1,014	218	51
Lithuanian SSR	1,403	202	1,201	1,233	751	286	32	465	122	38
Estonian SSR	907	490	417	729	626	228	30	398	198	77
Ukrainian SSR	2,099	925	1,174	1,509	962	348	19	614	151	74
Central Asian Republics, Kazakhstan, Trans-caucasia and Moldavia [c]	1,984	1,351	633	1,984	112	97	—	15	12	10
TOTAL	202,466	185,680	16,786	98,474	6,985	2,748	575	4,237	1,458	835

[a] Incomplete data
[b] Without land of the State Forest Fund and of the State Land Fund
[c] Data for 1955

Table 7
Humid Land with Drainage, Distribution and Use, 1960
(In thousand hectares)

Republic	Total Area with Drainage Network	New Construction 1956–1960	Reconstructed and Altered 1956–1960	Area with Drainage [a]	
				Total	Built in 1956–1960
RSFSR	2,440.3	373.5	307.1	519.2	54.2
Europe	1,874.79	318.42	298.85	518.6	53.6
Asia	565.51	55.08	8.25	0.6	0.6
Belorussian SSR	970.7	149.3	72.3	15.3	12.6
Latvian SSR	1,598.4	82.3	177.3	154.6	116.3
Lithuanian SSR	921.9	211.5	80.4	156.7	123.5
Estonian SSR	660.2	18.4	49.9	59.4	20.1
Ukrainian SSR	1,056.2	88.1	178.6	38.3	10.9
Central Asian, Kazakh, Transcaucasian and Moldavian SSR's	134.1	17.6	5.5	0.2	—
TOTAL	7,781.8	940.7	871.1	943.7	337.6

[a] Data of the Central Statistical Office. The difference between areas with a drainage network in 1960 and the area of land drained between 1956 and 1960 does not correspond with the data for 1956 given for some republics in Table 6. This is explained by a change in the method of calculation. The more recent data are more accurate.

Table 8
Distribution of Land with a Drainage Network (In thousand hectares)
(After S. L. Mirkin, 1960)

Republic	Prior to 1917	1928	1940	1945	1950	1956	1960 [a]
RSFSR [b]	906	1029	1201	1129	1747	2178	2440
Belorussian SSR	499	551	1204	665	810	876	971
Latvian SSR	1267	1503	1775	1619	1752	1480	1598
Lithuanian SSR	15	93	594	498	616	751	922
Estonian SSR	50	267	463	265	668	626	660
Ukrainian SSR	73	73	644	707	853	962	1056
Moldavian SSR	—	—	—	—	13	17	31
Georgian SSR	—	2	20	20	43	95	103
TOTAL	2810	3518	5901	4903	6502	6985	7781

[a] 1960 data obtained from the Central Statistical Office
[b] Together with the previous Karelo-Finnish SSR

for agriculture and, prior to flooding, was used for gardens and grazing meadows. Inundation has had a negative influence on the fodder balance and upon the development of animal husbandry, especially in the Non-Chernozem Zone of European Russia. In 1958 an area of about 2 million hectares was submerged in reservoirs. With the completion of all hydro-electric projects planned to 1965, this figure will exceed 5 million hectares (Zuzik), and in the future (according to some project variants) will reach 30 million hectares, of which 47% will have been forest, 30% hay lands and pastures, 5% cropland, and 18% scrub land (Vyzgo).

The creation of reservoirs not only causes waterlogging and a consequent decrease in soil quality but forms marshes, and changes the function of the river, affecting the water regime of the flood plain. Desiccation and steppe formation occur on the higher meadows that were previously subject to flooding, and there is an increased discharge of water from dams during the low-water period that causes extended flooding of the lower meadows hitherto inundated only at high-water periods. Land adjacent to reservoirs should therefore be also considered for melioration.

These data reveal that proper drainage could not only expand the agricultural area, it could also increase the yields of much agricultural land now in use by as much as 50%.

The data in Table 10 clearly show that most of the collection pools, canals, and regulatory network of drainage systems are in an unsatisfactory

Table 9
European RSFSR: Non-Chernozem Requiring Drainage

Oblasts and Autonomous Republics	Total Area		Of Which, in Thousand Hectares		
	In thousand hectares	Percentage	Arable	Meadows and Zalezh	Marshes
Kalinin	760.3	19.5	152.4	404.7	203.2
Pskov	558.0	22.4	55.2	344.3	158.5
Vologda	381.3	15.4	129.2	247.7	4.4
Smolensk	335.2	10.7	17.3	214.5	103.4
Novgorod	326.5	19.4	86.0	109.5	131.0
Moscow	263.4	14.9	88.4	153.3	21.7
Yaroslavl	232.3	13.6	51.7	162.5	18.1
Kirov	199.2	4.5	81.1	109.6	8.5
Leningrad	185.5	24.6	45.7	45.4	94.4
Kostroma	172.7	10.7	79.0	78.7	15.0
Bryansk	153.4	7.6	6.8	118.8	27.8
Ryazan	136.8	5.5	25.2	87.7	23.9
Gorki	103.5	3.4	27.7	59.3	16.5
Ivanovo	90.7	9.2	14.0	60.3	16.4
Kaliningrad	84.1	11.9	31.1	38.0	15.0
Vladimir	75.7	6.7	5.1	58.2	12.4
Kaluga	66.1	4.3	12.0	39.3	14.8
Udmurt ASSR	37.3	2.1	2.8	7.8	26.7
Mari ASSR	14.6	1.9	1.4	7.9	5.3
Tula	12.3	0.6	3.8	7.6	0.9

condition. In many republics the land area on which the system needs remodeling and restoration exceeds the drained agricultural land where the system is in satisfactory condition.

In the last decade the rate of growth of the area with a drainage network has decreased, since part of the land that was previously drained has, because of the inadequate drainage network, again become wet.

The deficiencies in the development and use of land with drainage systems are the result of several factors. Included in the inventory of land drainage is all land located within 100 meters (or sometimes more) of the drainage ditches, without consideration of their quality. A large part of such land is equipped only with a network of open, shallow canals, fre-

Table 10
Technical Composition of the Drainage Network
(After S. L. Mirkin, 1960)

Components	Length (In thousand kilometers)	Operative	Needing Reconstruction	Needing Capital Repairs	Needing Minor Repairs
			(In percentages)		
Water Intakes	7.2	22.5	15.7	34.9	26.9
Feeder Canals	190.3	10.9	22.8	41.5	24.8
Regulatory Network	449.0	6.1	34.3	38.2	21.4

quently sparsely distributed. The technical features of existing drainage systems are given in Table 11.

The data in the table show how imperfect much of the drainage network built prior to 1956 is. They indicate the low ratio of covered to uncovered ditches and the sparse network of open canals (excluding those in the Latvian and Estonian SSR's).

There is no basic change in the water regime on extensively drained lands because the network of shallow canals and collection pools removes only a part of the excessive water. Until recently, drainage systems were planned for the improvement of natural meadows, except in the Baltic republics, the northwestern regions of the RSFSR, and in Georgia, where they were specifically intended to improve arable land. Even in these areas, the canals were still shallow and few; acceptable only under conditions of individual farming where mechanization was lacking. Such drainage was inexpensive and quickly redeemable, but now, with the general intensification of agriculture, the mechanization of field work, and the use of drained land for a variety of crops (including those that require soil aeration), older primitive methods of drainage have proven unacceptable.

Some drainage systems have been designed without adequate consideration of the natural conditions, especially hydrogeology, and they could not, therefore, operate efficiently even if the project had been completed properly. Examples of inadequate design may be found in the original drainage systems (prior to reconstruction) of the Colchis lowland, in the river flood plains of the Yakhroma, Pekhorka [near Moscow], and Kudma [near Gorki], and the Nerussa [in Bryansk and Orel oblasts].

Until recently, little attention has been given to the construction of road networks to accompany drainage systems. Without roads, however, it is impossible to transport agricultural produce from the fields; and the labor

Table 11
Technical Characteristics of the Drainage Network
(After S. L. Mirkin, 1960)

Republic	Drained Land (Percentage of available marsh land)	With Covered Drains, (Percentage of total drained land)	Average Density of Network of Open Drainage Canals (In meters per hectare)	Average Distance between Canals (In meters [a])
Russian Federation	1	19 [b]	56	179
Belorussia	15	3	33	303
Latvia	48	3	122	82
Lithuania	33	5	46	218
Estonia	46	4	128	78
Ukraine	39	2	33	303
Georgia	36	2	21	477
TOTAL	4	8	72	139

[a] Data by the author
[b] This ratio is due mainly to the high percentage of covered drainage in Kaliningrad Oblast.

and other costs expended on drainage and crop cultivation are not justified. Thus, for instance, the bountiful harvests of vegetables and potatoes of the Kirov Collective Farm, Rostov District, Yaroslavl Oblast (in 1950 and 1953) suffered an 80% loss because of the lack of roads. Often the financial setback from the loss of one season may exceed many times the cost of construction of the best of field roads.

The development, repair, maintenance, and reconstruction of drainage systems are for the most part unsatisfactory due to limited staff, means, and machinery available for such tasks. As a result, many systems fall into disuse prematurely. The Baltic republics, and especially Lithuania where the use of drainage systems is at the proper level, are the exception.

The existing gap between the development of drainage systems and the subsequent development of the land is also attributable to inappropriate use of land. Particularly unsatisfactory is the agricultural technology employed on peat-bog soils, where such measures should be substantially different from those applied to dry lands. However, the collective and state farms, lacking in experience and without proper instruction, work these lands as if they were dry. The results are predictably unsatisfactory; the farmers soon lose faith in the possibility of profitable exploitation of the drained lands, abandoning them to revert quickly to their former condition. The application of fertilizers, particularly of potassium, is unsatisfactory on the drained peat lands of collective and state farms.

At present, the RSFSR has only six experimental stations, four supporting stations, and one experimental field engaged in studying questions of drainage, a program not commensurate with the needs. Prior to 1917 there were ninety-five stations where research on drainage and marsh cultivation was carried out. These stations could not be compared to present experimental stations but work significant for that time was accomplished by all of them. We also have an insufficient number of stations working on crop selection for peat bogs, where natural conditions are highly variable and where the sowing of common seed leads to losses while special types of seed produce high yields.

Finally, the inadequate mechanization of construction, land improvement, and cultivation should be mentioned. The RSFSR had only 100 stations concerned with meadow improvement and 71 stations concerned with mechanized land improvement in 1959, which is clearly not enough, especially when neither type had sufficient machinery and equipment. What machinery is available is too often used for general construction and agriculture instead of land improvement; and because of the inadequate number of stations, too wide an area is dependent on the few machines available. Meadow-meliorative and machine-meliorative stations work most successfully in regions where drained lands compose a large part of the total agricultural area as, for example, in the Baltic littoral.

The elimination of these inadequacies in the development and use of drained lands is a difficult and labor-consuming task, though absolutely necessary if high and stable yields are to be obtained. Experience shows that if the drainage systems are planned properly, well constructed, and maintained in operational condition, and if drained lands are used intensively with specialized technology, the results can be economically significant.

There are many examples of efficient drainage effected by means of clay pipes. In Latvia, where the land is drained in this way, potatoes yield 200 to 300 centners per hectare; grains, 20 to 30 centners per hectare; oat-vetch hay, 40 to 50 centners per hectare; and fodder cabbage, 550 to 700 centners per hectare. The labor outlay for the production of 1,000 fodder units, which until drainage was 34.4 man days, was reduced to 4.3 to 1.1 man days, with a simultaneous lowering of the cost of a fodder unit from six kopeks to one kopeck. In comparison with an open network, covered drainage raised corn yields by 75% and wheat and sugar beet yields by 25% to 30%. Such construction is relatively costly (from 200 to 400 rubles¹ per hectare), but because of the increase in crop yields the cost can be redeemed within three to five years (*The Economic Effectiveness of Land Reclamation*).

To measure the impact of reclamation, yields of an area of 80,000 hectares that were drained in Lithuania in 1959 may be compared with average yields for that republic. Such a comparison shows clearly the effectiveness of intensive drainage on mineral-rich, but excessively moist land, where a large part of the drainage is of the covered type (Table 12).

Table 12
Average Crop Yields and Yields in Drained Lands in
the Lithuanian SSR (Materials on the Technology of Irrigation
and Land Improvement, 1961)

Crop	Yield in Centners per Hectare		Yield Increase, (In percentage)
	Average	On Drained Land	
Rye	8.8	12.2	37
Potatoes	79.0	104.0	32
Fodder Roots	115.0	167.0	45
Silage Corn	333.0	371.0	11
Perennial Grasses	17.4	21.2	22

Analogous data on the increase in yields are available for Belorussia in 1959, where drainage on lowland bogs was principally of the deep, open-ditch type. These data confirm the effectiveness of draining agricultural land (Table 13).

For effective reclamation of land, the program of drainage must involve the following:

1. Existing systems must be reconstructed, and complex measures for the full development of land equipped with a drainage network must be undertaken. This requires the implementation of hydrotechnical and agrotechnical work over an area of 4.2 and 1.5 million hectares, respectively.

2. Marshy and seasonally wet land used in agriculture without being drained must be reclaimed. The USSR contains about 9.3 million hectares of such land: the RSFSR, 5.3 million; Belorussia, 1.8 million; the northern Ukraine, 0.9 million; Lithuania, 0.7 million; and Latvia and Estonia, 0.7 million (Mirkin).

3. Marshes and marshy lands with no seasonal fluctuation must be drained and brought into agriculture. The future development of agricul-

Table 13
Crop Yields on Drained and Dry Lands in the Belorussian SSR
(Materials on the Technology of Irrigation and Land Improvement, 1961)

Crop	Yield in Centners per Hectare		Yield Increase (in percent)
	Dry Lands	Drained Lands	
Grains	5.0	15.1	202
Potatoes	56.0	147.0	163
Fodder Roots	54.0	277.0	413
Silage Corn	220.0	550.0	150
Perennial Grasses	11.0	35.6	224

ture in the USSR requires the reclamation of 13.2 million hectares of now unusable marshes and marshy meadows.

4. Solutions to the problems of inundation and waterlogging caused by the construction of reservoirs must be sought. That is, the negative effects of such large projects carried out in the interests of other branches of the economy must be anticipated and dealt with.

The total territory of drained land used in agriculture in 1956 amounted to 5.66 million hectares; after the completion of the program mentioned above, it will reach 28.2 million and amount to 15% of the present total area of cultivated land. Taking into consideration the yield increase on drained land (and especially on lowland swamps), it will be possible to produce approximately 68 million tons of hay and 55 million tons of potatoes (Mirkin). In a number of republics, agricultural output will be derived principally from drained land (Table 14).

A summary of factors that must be considered in the carrying out of extensive drainage projects follows.

In the planning and construction of drainage systems, natural conditions should be analyzed in order to select both the proper drainage method and the layout of canals. The sources of excessive land moisture and the types of water supply of the region must be considered if land is to be changed in the desired direction. Extensive low-quality forms of drainage and subsequent land use should be discouraged and the land should be brought to the most productive uses: arable land, cultivated meadows, and pastures. It is unwise to regard drainage as inexpensive, simple, and appropriate only for the limited improvement of natural meadows.

The most desirable drainage is both deep and covered, assuring intensive use of the reclaimed land with the aid of modern agricultural machinery.

Table 14
Area of Drained Land and Anticipated Yield
(In relation to total agricultural area and total output)

Republics and Economic Regions	*Ratio of Drained to Total Agricultural Area*	*Ratio of Output from Drained to Total Agricultural Area*
Russian Federation	120.0	139.7
European North	22.0	23.7
Northwest	36.0	41.3
Non-Chernozem Center	10.1	12.4
Northeast	9.4	11.3
Mid-Urals	11.4	13.8
Western Siberia	8.7	10.7
Soviet Far East	22.4	26.5
Ukrainian SSR (Polesye and Carpathians)	38.5	44.9
Belorussian SSR	36.3	41.2
Latvian SSR	58.9	64.0
Lithuanian SSR	42.2	47.5
Estonian SSR	48.7	54.3

A few open but sufficiently deep drainage canals may be built as a temporary measure, permitting future conversion to covered drainage.

In the zone of inadequate precipitation, it is necessary to create drainage-irrigation systems that would permit a complete regulation of the water regime in any year, regardless of conditions.

The methods used to change water and air conditions of drained lands should reflect the economic peculiarities of the region. In regions with a denser population, developed industry, and good communications, it is expedient to drain more intensively than in sparsely settled regions of low industrial development.

Drainage should also be based on new technology, both in the construction of the system (new types of materials for the construction of covered drains, efficient equipment, mechanical water pumping, and systems of reversible control, and so forth), and in the method of carrying out the drainage (fully integrated mechanization of the drainage operation).

Primarily, it is necessary to increase the number of meadow-meliorative and machine-meliorative stations, to provide them with machinery for drainage and agrotechnical work, and to construct enterprises for the production of clay pipes in regions of intensive drainage. It is also very important to develop a network of good roads and bridges while planning and constructing drainage systems.

The servicing of the drainage systems must be improved so that they are not only kept in good repair but that they are also adjustable to annual moisture conditions.

Technical indices of operation should be recorded in maintenance ledgers and provided to the administration of each system to insure the proper utilization of improvements. Also, a survey of available potential collection pools necessary for future drainage efforts and the establishment of local hydrological stations should be implemented. (The existing network of hydrological stations of the Hydrometeorological Service does not satisfy the needs of drainage reclamation since it has been organized mainly for the needs of hydropower and river transport.)

In addition to the above, it is also necessary to expand the network of experimental stations: (*a*) for study and research in agrotechnology suitable to the various natural zones and the various types of drained land, and (*b*) for the selection of crops suitable for different types of peat and different water and climatic conditions. The supply of mineral fertilizers (especially potash) to collective and state farms that are reclaiming peat lands should also be improved substantially.

Everything that has been said about the inadequacy of scientific work and research and of the preparation of specialists in the field of irrigation, is equally true of drainage. It is necessary in all agricultural institutes to introduce courses on meliorative agriculture on drained lands. Without that it is impossible to raise the efficiency of their use.

BIBLIOGRAPHY

Budyko, M. I. *Teplovoy balans zemnoy poverkhnosti* [Heat Balance of the Earth's Surface]. Leningrad: Gidrometeoizdat, 1956. Also available in English as *The Heat Balance of the Earth's Surface*. Department of Commerce, Weather Bureau. Washington, D.C.: U.S. Government Printing Office, 1958.

Ekonomicheskaya effektivnost melioratsii zemel [Economic Effectiveness of Land Melioration]. Moscow: Selkhozgiz, 1960.

Kostyakov, A. N. *Osnovy melioratsii* [Principles of Melioration]. 6th ed. Moscow: Selkhozgiz, 1960.

Materialy po tekhnologii irrigatsionnykh i meliorativnykh rabot [Materials on the Technology of Irrigation and Meliorative Work]. Moscow: Selkhozgiz, 1961.

Mirkin, S. L. *Vodnye melioratsii v SSSR i puti ikh razvitiya* [Water Melioration in the USSR and Methods of its Development]. Moscow-Leningrad: AN SSSR, 1960.

Narodnoye khozyaystvo SSSR v 1958 g. Statisticheskiy yezhegodnik [National Economy of the USSR in 1958. Statistical Annual]. Moscow: Gosstatizdat, 1959.

Smirnov, A. V. and Nefedov, V. D. *Pereustroystvo osushitelnykh sistem* [Reconstruction of Drainage Systems]. Moscow: Selkhozgiz, 1957.

Stankevich, V. S. and Rubin, P. R. *Osusheniye i osvoyeniye bolot i zabolochennykh zemel* [Drainage and Development of Marshes and Marshy Lands]. Moscow: Selkhozgiz, 1956.

Vovchenko, I. T. "Vodokhozyaystvennoye stroitelstvo v semiletii 1959–1965 gg." [Hydroeconomic Construction in the 1959–1965 Seven-Year Plan]. *Gidrotechnika i melioratsiya,* no. 2 (1959).

Vyzgo, G. S. "O kompleksnom ispolzovanii vodnykh resursov" [Concerning the Complex Utilization of Water Resources]. *Elektricheskiye stantsii,* no. 1 (1961).

Yestyestvenno-istoricheskoye rayonirovaniye SSSR [Natural-historical Regionalization of the USSR]. Ed., D. G. Vilenskiy. *Trudy Komissii po yestyestv. -istor. rayonirovaniyu SSSR,* t. 1 [Papers of the Commission for Natural-Historical Regionalization of the USSR, vol. 1]. Moscow-Leningrad: AN SSSR, 1947.

Zemskiy, P. M., Ivanchenko, A. A., Letunov, P. A. et al. *Opyt opredeleniya obyemov selskokhozyaystvennogo proizvodstva SSSR na perspektivu* [An Effort to Assess the Volume of Future Agricultural Production in the USSR]. Moscow, 1957.

Zuzik, D. T. *Ekonomika vodnogo khozyaystva* [Economics of Water Economy]. Moscow: Selkhozgiz, 1959.

10. Efforts to Combat the Processes of Erosion and Deflation of Agricultural Land *

S. I. Silvestrov

(Institute of Geography, Academy of Sciences of the USSR)

THE DEVELOPMENT OF EROSION AND DEFLATION AND THE DAMAGE CAUSED TO THE NATIONAL ECONOMY

The origin and development of soil erosion and deflation are due to the faulty use of land under particular natural conditions.

Mountain and upland areas that have undergone economic development are most subject to erosion by water; they are greatly dissected by strong and irregular annual surface runoff of snow melt or rain. By contrast, there is little erosion on plains, no matter what the degree of their development, nor in underdeveloped regions even if the terrain is in high relief. Most subject to deflation are the highly developed, droughty steppe, semidesert, and desert regions of sands, sandy loams, and carbonaceous soils. Deflation in such regions develops on any type of relief, but most frequently in open plains where the wind is not impeded. Deflation is practically absent in little-developed areas and also under conditions of excessive or sufficient moisture, no matter how hilly the terrain. The incidence of erosion and deflation reflect varied geographical conditions.

Historically, extensive erosion and deflation in the USSR reflected the faulty use of agricultural lands prior to the October Revolution, but such use has not been completely eliminated even today. Agriculture is both the chief cause and the principal victim of erosion and deflation, and the damage to its economy is both great and varied. It occurs in the following forms: (1) the removal of top soil on slopes, affecting soil fertility, lowering

---

* The author distinguishes between erosion by wind (deflation) and erosion by other forces of nature (erosion).

yields, and resulting ultimately in strongly denuded wastelands; (2) the washing out of soil material and the formation of ravines and hollows, resulting in the destruction of useful lands and the prevention of productive use of adjacent areas; (3) the transportation of the destructive sediments (silt, sand, and rubble) to cultivated areas (pastures, meadows, gardens, populated places) in river valleys, in the bottom of ravines, and in intermontane basins; (4) the loss of water in tremendous amounts, intensifying soil drought and lowering yields.

The damage to agriculture caused by deflation is primarily in areas of light or dusty soils (mainly light sandy loams, humic sands, and carbonaceous soils); their dry and exposed state allows strong winds to carry off the upper layer of the soil, affecting their fertility and ultimately transforming them into wastelands.

If the areas subject to deflation are under crops (particularly young crops), the latter are destroyed or harmed; in places, dust accumulates on fields, shelter belts, and so on. Barren sands are carried to neighboring cultivated areas, destroying crops and covering roads, sources of water, and communities.

Apart from their chief victim—agriculture—erosion and deflation injure other branches of the national economy. Their disturbance of the water regime, causing erosion and the washing away of agricultural land in small basins, is transformed into disaster in large river basins. In the spring and after extensive rains, floods in eroded regions drown river valleys, along with their cities, settlements, industries, roads, and bridges. Not only are various structures affected, but damage is done to river transport, the water supply, and the hydroelectric economy because of the alluviation of river channels and reservoirs.

In developed but arid mountain areas much damage is incurred when flood-level mountain streams carry substantial amounts of alluvium down the valleys and harm settlements, power dams, and irrigation systems. Railroad and road transport suffers from erosion and deflation because of inadequate repairs to roads and road equipment and lack of protection from floods and drifting sands. Gullies in cities and settlements that are not adequately provided with runoff facilities are also a constant threat.

Deflation in its extreme form—dust storms—leads to the transfer of huge amounts of dust far beyond their origin to cover roads, to muddy water supplies, and to pollute the air of cities, affecting the health of the population.

Because of the lack of widespread information pertaining to the development of erosion and deflation, there are no precise quantitative data on either the processes or the damage that results to the entire country. Attempts to secure approximate quantitative data on the development of erosion, based on research in key regions, were made by the All-Union Scientific Research Institute of Agro-Forest-Reclamation (VASKhNIL) (Silvestrov, 1949; Kozmenko, 1957; Braude), by the V. V. Dokuchayev Soil Institute (Sobolev, 1948), and by the Institute of Geography, Academy of Sciences of the USSR (*Agricultural Erosion and the Struggle with It,* 1956). These data concerned only the plains of European Russia and the central part of the forest-steppe zone, but similar data were obtained by local scientific organizations in the Ukraine, Moldavia, Bashkiria, Azerbaydzhan, and some other regions (Skorodumov; Turovtzev; and others). It was established, very roughly, that in the USSR the total area subject to erosion amounts to about 50 million hectares, of which 30 million are arable. The area of gullies was found to be from 4 to 5 million hectares.

Under the direction of the present author, the Institute of Geography, Academy of Sciences of the USSR, attempted in recent years to ascertain the geographic distribution of land subject to erosion. The country was regionalized according to the basic factors of erosion, and seven zones, of varying broad types of heat and water regimes, were defined.

I. Excessively moist and cold.

II. Continuous surplus of moisture and moderately cold.

III. Adequate (periodically excessive) moisture supply, temperate.

IV. Unstable (periodically insufficient) moisture supply, moderately warm.

V. Subject to drought, moderately hot.

VI. Dry and hot.

VII. Humid, warm, and hot.

The zones then were divided according to relief conditions into mountain and plain subzones. The subzones were subdivided into areas of predominant agricultural specialization, which in turn were broken down into provinces according to those natural and economic conditions significant to agriculture and the struggle with erosion. Thus, each province has its special combination of climate, relief, and agricultural traits, permitting the development of differential systems of countererosion measures and the compilation and evaluation of data pertaining to the geographical distribution and development of erosive processes.

The influence of individual factors of erosion and of their regional composites was evaluated by means of specially prepared methodology, resulting in eight categories within the USSR. The sequence of enumerated categories increases with the greater degree that climate, relief, and agricultural use contribute to erosion. If for any particular area within a category there are factual data pertaining to current erosion processes, such data may be, with a high degree of accuracy, applied to the entire category.

Land use was determined for each category and available data on the actual distribution of current erosion phenomena were generalized. The distribution of the categories over the USSR is shown in Figure 1.

The wide extent of the categories shown on the map reflects only the predominant character of distribution of current erosion phenomena. Therefore, the degree of intensity of erosion should be considered only as average —that is, typical for much of the area within the category. It should also be noted that in mountain regions the delineated categories and their characteristics pertain only to lower elevations.

A description of territories corresponding to the different categories, the character of their agricultural use, and the degree of distribution of current erosion phenomena, are discussed below.

The most level regions of the country are in the first category, where regardless of climate and the degree of agricultural use of the territory, erosion cannot develop widely. These regions are virtually free of erosion processes and will remain so. The general character of agriculture there may be grouped into three large but sharply distinguished divisions: (a) northern regions (within boundaries of Zones I and II)—almost undeveloped, heavily forested, and swampy; (b) desert regions (Zone VI)—little used, with a dominance of natural grazing lands and virtual absence of forest and swamps; and (c) the other regions (Zones III, IV, V, and VII), considerably and intensively utilized, moderately supplied with natural fodder lands, and with few forests and swamps.

In the second category are regions in which erosion at the present time is hardly noticeable, but where there is a potential danger. Included here are northern regions of mountains or upland, with little agriculture, where the topography and climate create conditions for erosion but the almost undisturbed natural vegetation retains its effective protective function. In areas belonging to this category that are undergoing development, it is necessary to employ a series of antierosion measures. These regions are characterized by extensive forest cover, swampiness, and readily available pasture lands.

The first two categories cover almost two-thirds of the collective and state-farm land of the country; because they include the northern regions they are predominantly swamps, forests, and natural pasture. Arable land occupies only a little more than one-third and fruit and other perennial crops about one-fourth of the total area of collective and state-farm land. Thus, about two-thirds of the area of kolkhoz-sovkhoz plowland and three-fourths of the perennial plantings are located in regions of the remaining six categories, which suffer to some extent from erosion.

The third category includes regions with mild erosion. These are some upland areas of droughty zones of low agricultural development where climatic factors have little influence on the development of erosion. Here, among collective and state-farm lands, natural pastures predominate (74%); there is a small amount of arable land (7%); forests and scrub land amount to only 4%. There are no specific data on the distribution of current erosion in these regions; our estimate is that 1% to 5% of the total agricultural area is affected by erosion. Here, erosion is completely linked with pastoral use of the land.

The fourth category includes regions with mild current erosion, of upland and mountain character, of Zones III, V, and VI and with moderate to heavy agricultural use. Natural pastures dominate the collective and state farm lands (average 57%); the ratio of plowland is moderate to significant (average 20%); where moisture supply is adequate, forests exist, but in droughty regions the tree cover is sparse. For some regions in this category there are data relative to the spread of current erosion processes; for instance 5% to 10% of the land is affected in the Baltic hills and identical figures are given for some parts of the lower Trans-Volga and the southern part of Western Siberia. Figures of this order (6 to 10%) have been used in evaluating the spread of erosion on collective and state-farm lands. In regions with adequate moisture, erosion associated with tillage prevails; in droughty regions, erosion is linked with pastoralism.

The fifth category embraces regions of moderately developed erosion, including upland and mountain regions of Zones III, IV, V, and VI. The land use on state and collective farms is very diverse, depending both on the zone and on the topography, but the average pattern for the entire territory is 42% arable, 0.4% orchards, 36% natural fodder, and 13% forest and scrub. Regions of this category are already agriculturally significant.

The extent of erosion may be judged by various disparate data pertaining to some regions of the European part of the USSR. Comparing the map (Figure 1) of current erosion intensity with that of eroded soils, compiled by S. S. Sobolev in 1948, it is evident that less than 10% of its surface is eroded in part of the area, and 10% to 20% is eroded in the rest. The data of several investigators of different areas reveal that soil erosion reaches

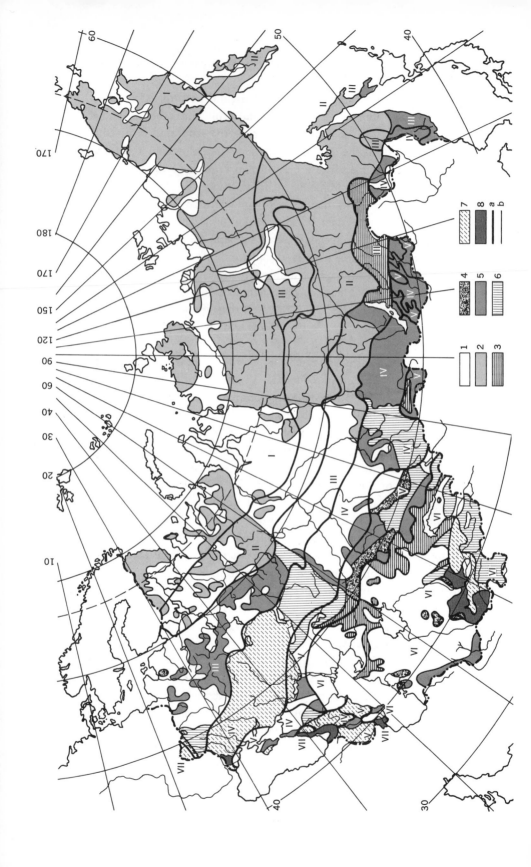

Figure 1

Distribution of contemporary erosion processes over the USSR. Map compiled on the basis of evaluating the effect of principal erosion factors: climate, relief, and type of agricultural use.

A. Natural zones:

(I) Excessively moist and cold (arctic deserts, tundra, northern taiga); (II) Continuous surplus of moisture and moderately cold (central taiga); (III) Adequate (periodically excessive) moisture supply, temperate (southern taiga and deciduous forests); (IV) Unstable, periodically insufficient moisture supply, moderately warm; (V) Subject to drought, moderately hot (dry steppe and northern semidesert); (VI) Dry and hot (southern semidesert and desert); (VII) Humid, warm and hot (deciduous forests of the humid subtropics and regions transitional to them).

B. Categories of erosion development:

Virtual absence of current erosion processes: (1) Will remain virtually free of erosion; (2) Potentially endangered by erosion; Subjected to current erosion processes; (3) Very limited erosion; (4) Limited erosion; (5) Moderate erosion; (6) Appreciable erosion; (7) Severe erosion; (8) Very severe erosion. (*a*) Boundaries of natural zones. (*b*) Boundaries of various intensities of erosion processes.

20% to 35% of the arable land under specific crops (in Moscow and Kirov oblasts, in Belorussia, in eastern districts of Lithuania, and in other places). The average distribution of erosion processes in this category amounts to about 11% to 15% of the agricultural area of state and collective farms. In the regions of the fifth category where moisture is adequate but unreliable, erosion is linked with tillage; in the droughty regions it is associated with pastoral use.

The sixth category includes regions of Zones III, IV, and VI, of plains and mountains where erosion processes are widely distributed. The upland plains in this category are agriculturally well developed, have an average supply of fodder land, and very few forests. The mountain areas are in moderate agricultural use, are well provided with natural fodder lands, and are lightly forested under conditions of adequate but unreliable moisture supply, but sparsely forested where moisture is inadequate. On the average, land is used on collective and state farms as follows: 40% arable; 0.5% orchards; 39% natural fodder; and 5% for forest and scrub. According to Sobolev's map and the selected data of some investigators (Turovtsev; Pastushenko; and others), the average degree of erosion of agricultural land for the sixth category is 16% to 20%. On the upland plains, erosion connected with tillage predominates; in the mountain regions it is linked with pastoralism.

The seventh category consists of regions of widespread or severe erosion, including a number of upland plains and mountain regions of Zones III, IV, V, and VI. The upland plains are characterized by intensive agricultural development with little existing natural fodder land or forest. The greater part of the mountain regions is considerably developed, with adequate fodder land and few forests. The state and collective farms average 61% arable, 3% in perennial crops, 23% in natural fodder lands, and 4% in forest and scrub. Regions of this category are agriculturally important in the USSR.

For this territory there are relatively abundant data on the extent of erosion. On some collective farms and regions, according to several authors, 30% to 60% of the agricultural area is subject to erosion (Shaposhnikova; Sobolev, 1948; Silvestrov, 1949; Kholupyak; Skorodumov; Alekperov; Kozmenko, 1957; Zaslavskiy and Gorbunov; Pastushenko). In the large area of the central forest-steppe, according to our generalized calculations (Silvestrov, 1949), one-third to one-fourth of the land of state and collective farms has been subjected to erosion. Taking all data into account, the average erosion of agricultural lands of state and collective farms for all areas in this category is estimated at 21% to 30%. In upland plains the prevailing

Table 1
Distribution of Lands According to the Development of Erosion
(In percentage of total area of each classification)

Category	Total Area of Collective and State Farm Land	Arable Land *	Orchards, Vineyards and other Cultivated Perennial Plantations	Natural Fodder Land	Forests and Scrub	Swamps
1	38.0	35.0	27.2	42.0	31.2	42.4
2	27.0	1.5	—	27.0	53.0	52.1
3	2.2	0.6	0.3	4.0	0.5	0.1
4	2.2	1.8	—	3.0	1.6	0.5
5	11.3	20.0	8.0	9.8	8.5	4.0
6	8.0	13.5	7.0	7.5	2.6	0.4
7	10.0	25.8	44.5	5.4	2.2	0.5
8	1.3	1.8	13.0	1.3	0.4	—

* It should be noted that the arable-land category is a broad one and includes all the land considered fit for cultivation, whether in crop, short-term fallow (*par*) or long-term fallow (*zalezh*).

erosion is linked with tillage; in the mountain regions it develops both on tilled and pasture lands; and in some regions, erosion processes are associated with floods.

The eighth category includes regions of very severe erosion: the foothills of the humid subtropics (Black Sea Coast of the Caucasus and the Talysh Mountains); the most developed regions of Central Asia, southern Crimea, and the Moldavian Kodra. The area is very diverse agriculturally. The piedmont is highly developed for pastures, orchards, and vineyards; natural fodder lands are extensive only in the mountains of Central Asia; forests only in the Caucasus. The land-use structure in this category includes 32% arable, 6% orchards and other perennial plants, 43% natural fodder lands, and 5% forest and scrub.

With their specialized agricultural output, the regions of this category are important to the economy. According to some authors, the percentage of eroded agricultural land for parts of the region and for some collective farms reaches 40% to 70% of the total area (Gussak; Skorodumov; Alekperov; Kocherga; and others). The average degree of erosion of agricultural land in this category equals 31% to 40%.

In addition to the description of the categories in Table 1, data show the

Table 2
Approximate Area of Eroded Land
(In millions of hectares)

Category	Total Eroded Area	Arable Land, Orchards, and Vineyards	Pastures	Ravines
1	—	—	—	—
2	—	—	—	—
3	0.6	0.1	0.4	0.1
4	1.3	0.5	0.7	0.1
5	11.0	6.3	4.1	0.6
6	12.0	6.0	4.4	1.6
7	23.0	16.6	4.8	1.6
8	4.1	2.0	1.6	0.5
TOTAL	52.0	31.5	16.0	4.5

ratios of total state and collective farmland and of different land uses to the degree of erosion.

The table reveals that about 61% of the arable area and nearly 73% of the orchards and vineyards are located in categories five to eight, that is, in regions where the incidence of erosion is moderate to very severe. Indeed, nearly 28% of all the arable area and nearly 58% of orchards and vineyards are found in regions of severe and very severe erosion.

In Table 2 are presented the approximate areas that actually suffer from erosion, summarized according to category and type of land use.

From Table 2 it is apparent that categories six, seven, and eight contain more than three-fourths of the eroded arable land, two-thirds of all the eroded pastures, and five-sixths of the total area of gullies. The struggle with erosion should thus be directed toward these regions.

Our data are not analogous to the distribution of deflation, and for that reason it is possible to provide only a general calculation of the pertinent areas. For this purpose only approximate areas of state and collective farms that are located in regions subject to the danger of deflation can be established; they are divided into the groups and subgroups following.

The first group includes regions where deflation occurs but erosion is absent. Here one need only be concerned about deflation:

A. Regions of continuous or periodic deflation, predominantly in the form of soil blowing or extensively plowed land.

B. Regions of continuous deflation in specific areas, chiefly the blowing and shifting of sands of little tilled territories with a pastoral economy.

The second group includes regions where deflation occurs with erosion, and where deflation-control measures should be considered supplementary to erosion control:

C. Regions where the processes of soil blowing predominate.

D. Regions where sand blowing predominates.

The first group contains the most level areas of the droughty zones (V and VI) and the southern half of the zone of unstable moisture supply (IV). On state and collective farms that are located in regions of subgroup A, arable lands occupy 53%, orchards 6%, natural fodder lands 36%, forest and scrub lands about 3%. In regions of subgroup B, 5% of the land is arable, 75% is in natural fodder, and about 3% is forest and scrub.

The second group is comprised of the upland regions of Zones IV, V, and VI, and the mountain regions of Zones V and VI. In subgroup C, arable lands occupy 51%, orchards 1%, natural fodder lands 37%, and forest and scrub about 3%. In subgroup D, arable lands occupy 12%, orchards 0.7%, natural fodder 61%, and forest and scrub 2%.

Table 3 illustrates the ratio of state and collective farm land as well as that of arable and natural fodder land lying within the groups and subgroups of the regions where deflation is possible.

It is obvious that not all the arable land and pasture in regions subjected

Table 3
Distribution of Principal Agricultural Land According to Groups
and Subgroups of Regions of Potential Occurrence of Deflation
(In percentage of total area of each classification)

Group	Subgroup	Total Area of Land of Collective and State Farms	Arable Land	Natural Fodder Land
1	A	7	16	6
	B	10	2	17
2	C	14	30	12
	D	7	3	11
Not Subject to Deflation		62	49	54

to the danger of deflation actually experience soil blowing. Territories that are potentially endangered by deflation, that is, those that have dusty or light soils and are poorly located with respect to prevailing wind (wind corridors, windward slopes, and so on), must be, therefore, distinguished from those actually subjected to wind erosion. The total area of land in the Soviet Union that is potentially endangered by deflation is unknown. An attempt to reach an estimate for the southern and southeastern districts of the Ukraine has been made by G. M. Karasev,[1] who states it to be 3.5 million hectares, which, according to our calculation, represents 20% of the arable and pasture land of those districts. Assuming that this figure is typical, the total arable area potentially endangered by deflation amounts to 20 to 25 million hectares; and in the case of pastures, 30 to 35 million hectares. Thus, the extent of deflation is not less than that of erosion. The area of arable land subjected to deflation is approximately 1.2 times less than that subjected to erosion, but the relationship is reversed in the case of pastures.

Somewhat more reliable data can be provided for land areas where deflation occurred in specific years. Such areas are significantly less than potentially endangered areas since meteorological conditions causing deflation in any particular year do not form identically in all regions at the same time. Data relative to land areas that suffer from deflation in some geographic regions in different years are given below.

In 1952 dust storms destroyed several tens of thousands of hectares of crops in the Kuban and about 18% of the agricultural area of Bashkiriya. In Pavlodar Oblast in 1955 nearly 170,000 hectares of crop land were damaged and about 127,000 hectares of crops were destroyed; in 1956 much the same occurred. In eastern Georgia in 1953 deflation caused the loss of 145,000 hectares of crops. In the Naurskaya District in the Chechen-Ingush ASSR in 1954, about 60,000 hectares of crop land were blown away, and in 1955 a similar area was also affected. In 1955, in Russkaya Polyana District in Omsk Oblast, deflation destroyed 20% to 58% of the sown grain.

An attempt to generalize the average extent of the crop area annually suffering from deflation has been undertaken by A. G. Gayel.[2] He has found that in the steppe an average of 5 to 6 million hectares of sown land is subjected annually to deflation, of which up to 1.5 million hectares is completely destroyed. Dust storms, which in the spring of 1960 enveloped

---

[1] Paper delivered at the All-Union Conference on the Struggle with Erosion, held in Moscow in 1960.

[2] Paper delivered at the session of the Subcommission on the Struggle with Soil Erosion, of the Sixth Commission of the All-Union Society of Pedologists, held in Moscow in 1960.

the southern and southwestern regions of European Russia, according to a report of A. G. Gayel, A. G. Doskach, and A. A. Trushkovskiy, damaged more than 4 million hectares of sowings.

Thus the struggle with deflation, as with erosion, is of vital significance for very wide regions and requires massive protective measures in the principal agricultural regions of the country.

THE CONTEMPORARY STATUS OF RESEARCH ON SOIL EROSION AND DEFLATION

Large-scale socialist agriculture has all the necessary preconditions for the realization of an effective system of antierosion and antideflation measures; however, these possibilities are as yet scarcely realized. Since their creation, collective farms have significantly increased their managerial, economic, and technical levels of agricultural production with, undoubtedly, a positive effect on the regulation of runoff and soil protection in regions of long-established agriculture. Factors having a positive influence on the control of erosion and deflation are: (*a*) the liquidation of small peasant strips and the boundary furrows that served as water collectors and caused soil erosion and gulley formation; (*b*) the exclusion from tillage of some steep and badly eroded slopes and land endangered by gully formation, which in the past had been cultivated by peasants who had too little land; (*c*) the increase (in conjunction with mechanization) in the depth of plowing from 10 to 12 centimeters to 20 to 25 centimeters, and, finally, (*d*) the establishment of local protective forest plantings.

With these positive developments there were others that intensified the potential threat of erosion and deflation. (*a*) Massive assimilation of virgin and long-fallow lands in steppe regions are the shining victory of our agriculture,* but these extensive areas require a dependable system of antierosion and antideflation measures, which, at the moment, are absolutely inadequate. (*b*) At the same time, the most important indicator of the technical and economic growth of collective and state farms is reflected in the unswerving increase in the ratio of those crops that are of great value to the economy but, if lacking special precautionary measures, can under certain conditions cause an increase in erosion and deflation. (*c*) Finally, the basis of large-scale mechanized agriculture and highly productive land

---

* The statement seems totally out of context and may have been inserted by the Soviet publishing house for obvious reasons.

are the large fields and the great extent of monoculture. However, without careful protection, these massive fields can be subjected to erosion and deflation under certain conditions. (*d*) It is also important to mention that the rapid development of animal husbandry requires proper organization of the fodder base and of summer feeding, to assure the prevention of pasture-land erosion and deflation.

Thus, the liquidation of the small private farm and the increase in the technical level of the state and collective farms do not mean that erosion and deflation will cease. That can only be attained by means of a widespread application of measures that have both a protective significance and an ability to raise the economy to a higher technical and cultural level. It is necessary that the whole economic life of a region suffering erosion and deflation be closely associated with the struggle to eliminate destructive processes.

A leading element in developing the rural economy is the formation of a proper system of farm management on all state and collective farms—one that would reflect local natural and economic conditions and that would secure the most effective use of the productive forces of the land. This is essential if the proper measures of combating erosion and deflation are to be implemented from the initial stages of farm organization; further losses of soil and water would seriously reduce economic effectiveness and ultimately inhibit development.

It is not by accident that in the last few years the struggle with erosion and deflation has been given much attention, not only by scientific and communal organizations but also by the leading agencies of the country. The majority of the union republics have passed laws for the protection of nature, laws emphasizing the requirements for the protection of agricultural land against water and wind erosion, the protection and rational use of forests, the conservation of water, and the active management of the water regime. One example is the Law Concerning the Conservation of Natural Resources in the RSFSR,[3] in which all users of land are obligated to undertake measures to combat water and wind erosion, and which also prohibits the use of methods of development that would promote these destructive processes.

In addition to these laws, special resolutions concerning water and wind erosion have been passed to aid in the development of organizational and technical measures essential to erosion control and in the development of rational land use to ensure the protection and improvement of the produc-

---

[3] *Pravda*, October 28, 1960.

tive forces. In governmental decisions, the control of water and wind erosion is considered an integral part of all economic activities that involve the use of land.

Thus, we have the legal prerequisites for combating erosion and deflation on a comprehensive scale; needed now is the practical application of measures that have already been defined by science.

Above all, the state and collective farms must be provided with large-scale land-use maps that contain relief and soil data as well as the areal extent of land that is to some degree subject to erosion or deflation. Soil surveys, including qualitative evaluations, have been greatly expanded in recent years; soon all state and collective farms will have soil maps describing the potential for rational use of their land. Unfortunately, soil maps as a rule are based on (cadastral) land-use maps that do not show topography and hence are inadequate for erosion control (as well as for many other needs). This weakness must be corrected in the immediate future by the agricultural agencies.

The territorial arrangement of the collective and state farms should allow for the determination of the proper location and effective application of erosion- and deflation-control measures.

In areas suffering from erosion and deflation this organization is still inadequate and frequently fails to protect the land from these harmful processes. Shortcomings relate primarily to the structure of land use and the system of crop rotation, for fields in use on the state and collective farms must each be considered independently, in terms of their potential for rational and erosion-free utilization.

Specialized and field-rotation systems concerned primarily with technical and row crops should occupy areas that are free of erosion and deflation or only mildly subjected to it; on arable, but appreciably eroded lands, soil protection rotation systems of different types should be used; strongly eroded and deflated areas should be planted to grasses or forested. As elementary and obligatory as these demands are, they often are not obeyed. Different demands should be made of the internal organization of crop land, for the existing practice of dividing rotation areas into blocs of different crops is inadequate on lands endangered by erosion or deflation. Rotation fields have become so large that in regions subject to erosion it is practically impossible to operate along the contours, and the sparse network of borders between fields is inadequate for protection by shelter belt or grass strip. The notions of those specialists who will not concede the need of further subdividing the fields of rotated crops should be categorically rejected: it is necessary to plan within the fields a network that is designed (*a*) to distribute tree and grass belts, and (*b*) to fragment the fields into units that can be tilled, sowed, and harvested along contours.

Particularly careful measures must be taken against erosion within the fields of mountainous and strongly dissected regions, where the problem tends to be more complex. They should include strip plowing, contour and lenticular cultivation, and specially adapted forms of sowing and planting.

Basic measures in the struggle with erosion and deflation include the proper distribution of hay and pasture lands and controlled grazing. These are frequently implemented in regions of animal husbandry; however, they are equally important in regions where crop cultivation predominates and where grazing ordinarily takes place in ravines and where the density of livestock and the degree of erosion are particularly high. Here, the system of controlling grazing should be uniform for both the natural and cultivated fodder areas, and the livestock density should not be excessive. Since pastures are limited in some regions of intensive agriculture, it is important to introduce partial summer stall feeding or even complete barn maintenance of cattle.

Agrotechnical, phytomeliorative, and hydrotechnical measures of erosion and deflation control, which at present are inadequate, should be implemented on state and collective farms in a massive and stable way. Among these measures, the most widely used is contour plowing and sowing, which is conducive to water retention and which reduces soil erosion. However, even these elementary methods are not always used though they are prescribed in agricultural handbooks because of the lack of properly delimited units of cultivation within the fields and the lack of concern of the tractor operators for contour plowing, which is necessarily linked with shorter furrows.

The various specialized methods of tillage conducive to water retention (i.e., broken furrowing, walling, deep plowing, and so forth) are applied only on a few state and collective farms and on small areas largely because of a lack of specialized equipment. It should be stressed that agricultural regions subject to erosion and deflation can no longer be reconciled to the absence of the technology essential to the struggle with these processes. It is necessary to lend to all forms of agrotechnical measures a water-retentive and soil-protective character. Success will be attained only (*a*) with conditions of differentiated methods of erosion and deflation control, depending on regional agrotechnical needs; (*b*) by a corresponding territorial organization; and finally, (*c*) by assuring the collective and state farms of the proper machines and implements.

It is useful to recall that the catastrophic spread of erosion and deflation in the U.S.A. that began in the 1930s, forced the farmers to give serious attention to measures of soil protection, leading to their widespread application. Contour plowing is widely used in the United States (13.3 million hectares in 1949) as well as basin listering (vesicular plowing), deep ripping of the subsoil with mulching of the surface (13 million hectares), basin sowing of crops, and a series of other protective measures whose use has been widespread owing to the availability of specialized equipment (Bennett).

Perennial grasses remain significantly protective when they are used for permanent meadows on strongly eroded land unsuitable for cultivation. Those eroded lands that technically can still be cultivated but have lost so much of their productivity that their yields are extremely low should be put under protective rotation, which would include many grass crops. With sophisticated agricultural technology, and with the aid of shelter belts, these lands can produce sufficiently high yields, and erosion can be halted. This is confirmed by numerous data from experimental stations and farms (Bronzova). Only in the most drought-prone regions, where moisture is inadequate for grasses, does their protective significance diminish, requiring a more intensive reliance on agrotechnical and hydrotechnical methods, and on forest-reclamation.

In semiarid regions subject to erosion, perennial grasses should be accompanied by nitrogenous crops, since they are most effective in replenishing the soil within a rotation cycle. In drought-prone regions, particularly in areas of deflation, long-stemmed plants (sunflowers, corn, sorghum, mustard, and others) should be widely grown to aid snow retention and to protect the fields from the wind.

It must be emphasized that the use of protective crops is the most profitable way of combating erosion and deflation and should be carried out in a diversified manner, depending on local, natural, and economic conditions. In this respect, the twenty-five year experiment of the U.S.A. is instructive. At first there was overwhelming enthusiasm for hydro- and agrotechnical methods of combating erosion and deflation (terracing, basin listering, contour plowing, and so forth), but after the 1940s a multifaceted approach to the problem was adopted, consisting in most regions of the use of protective cultivated plants that also could be used as feed. Grasses and other soil-protective crops are employed in rotation, in strip plowing, and in erosion prevention through the establishment of meadows on steep slopes of ravines and along gullies (Bennett).

Particular attention in erosion and deflation-prone regions should be given to protective forest plantings. Inequities arising from the 1948–53 period have caused a sharp decrease in such reclamation work. Up to 1956, of three million hectares of previously planted shelter belts, only about one million have survived and there has been little change to date.

Since shelter belts form only a small part of the total area of land used on collective and state farms of the steppe and forest-steppe, they cannot effectively regulate the water and wind regime nor provide soil protection in most of the regions subject to erosion and deflation.

The natural forest and scrub lands of the state and collective farms in the level regions of the steppe and forest-steppe do not exceed 4%, and even the state forest fund covers less than 10% of the total territory. Clearly, most of the state and collective farms are in need of shelter-belt protection, which can provide an effective means of regulating the water and wind regime and the means of retaining snow, reducing evaporation, and generally improving the moisture conditions to support and increase the agrotechnical and hydrotechnical measures that are taken. The current necessity to combat erosion and deflation requires a rapid expansion of forest reclamation efforts. Even for minimal shelter-belt protection, forests should cover on the average 4% to 5% of the total arable land suffering from erosion, deflation, and *sukhovey*. Obviously, under some conditions, significant deviations from the ratio are possible; this ratio does not include, either, the forestation of ravines and gullies, which could be quite numerous. It is particularly important to expand shelter-belt plantations in the virgin and idle lands, where such measures have not been employed to date.

Hydrotechnical efforts to combat soil erosion (the fixing of gullies, the dispersal of concentrated runoff on arable land, terracing, the construction of a water-regulative network, and territorial planning) also have not received significant attention in the agriculture of our country. They have been implemented on a limited scale in some regions of the Caucasus, in the Crimea, and Central Asia (on lands under orchards, tea, citrus, other subtropical crops), and in Moldavia (with the great expansion of viticulture). In other erosion-prone regions the control and improvement of gullies that endanger roads or settlements is carried out, but also on a limited scale.

The most expensive hydrotechnical construction obviously must be carried out in mountainous regions and on lands producing valuable crops, where returns quickly justify the investment. However, in some regions that are subject to erosion, where there is a significant development of fruit production and vineyards on level areas, it would be expedient to terrace the steep slopes of gullies and valleys suitable for these crops. Among such regions are all of Moldavia, the southern districts of the Ukraine, the piedmont of Krasnodar and Stavropol krays, the coastal stretches of the Lower Don and on the Lower Volga.

In all level regions subject to erosion, small-scale antierosion hydrotechnical measures should be widely applied. Primarily, these would be runoff and dispersal levees of earth, boulders, or wood placed along hillside ravines (particularly in places where they are crossed by shelter belts and roads), at the foot, sides, and heads of such ravines, along roads, field boundaries, and other similar elements of microrelief that concentrate runoff and promote washouts and gullies. Such effort will be a significant supplement to the phytomeliorative and agrotechnical erosion-control measures, provided proper territorial organization is carried out.

As noted, the absence of adequate machinery and implements seriously inhibits the successful realization of erosion-control measures. Many widely used agricultural machines in our country are designed for level areas and very large fields and are of little value for serious erosion control under conditions of complex relief. In addition, a series of control measures for erosion require specialized equipment.

Needed are: stable and maneuverable tractors for working with equipment on steep slopes and along short furrows; shuttle tractors and reversible plows for contour tillage; implements for water retentive (vesicular) tillage, for broken furrowing, cultivation, agrotechnical walling; implements for basin sowing and planting; specialized sowing combines for seeding grasses into stubble concurrently with loosening soil along furrows and applying fertilizers; terracing equipment; dibbing machines for local preparation of soil for tree planting on very steep slopes; maneuverable bulldozers, and scrapers, graders, and so forth. Such machines and implements are already available in some foreign countries.

The specialized network of experimental institutions concerned with erosion and deflation control is inadequate. The Novosilsk Agro-forest-reclamation Experimental Station of VNIALMI * (Orel Oblast), the Kletsk Agro-forest-reclamation Experimental Station of VNIALMI (Volgograd Oblast), the Desna Experimental Ravine Station of the Ukrainian Scientific Research Institute of Forestry and of Agro-forest-reclamation (Chernigov Oblast), the Moldavian Soil Erosion Station, the Soil Erosion Station of Azerbaydzhan, the Chatkalsk Mountain Reclamation Experimental Station, the Shakhimardan and Amankutan experimental stations of the Central Asion NIILKh,† the experimental stations of the former Bashkir

---

* Vsesoyuznyy nauchno-issledovatelskiy institut agrolesomelioratsii (All-Union Research Institute of Agro-Forest Reclamation).

† Nauchno-issledovatelskiy institut lesnogo khozyaystva (Scientific Research Institute of Forestry).

Experimental Station (formerly the Bashkir Scientific Research and Agricultural Institute), and also the Kiev Scientific Research Institute of Agriculture have all directed prolonged and complex work pertaining to erosion control. Some experimental points of VNIALMI, the Ukrainian NIILKh, and the Central Asian NIILKh carry out work on the control, improvement and agricultural utilization of sands. We have no special experimental station and field stations dealing with the struggle with deflation of light and dusty soils.

In spite of the scarcity of specialized research institutions, some research on various problems of erosion and deflation control is being carried out by agricultural and forest experimental stations. Such research has also been undertaken by various agricultural colleges and soil institutes (for instance, the Kharkov, Poltava, Gorki, Cheboksary agricultural institutes and the Kharkov, Tbilisi, and Tashkent soil institutes).

In spite of the number of institutions taking part in research on erosion and deflation control, a rapid and specialized solution to the problem of working out regional programs of erosion and deflation control measures for all areas subject to these harmful processes is not assured. Many of these units concern themselves only with isolated protective measures, and most of the regions suffering from erosion and deflation in an unusual form have no specialized research stations.

A network of properly distributed experimental stations and field stations designed for further research on erosion and deflation should be established and those that exist should be reorganized to encompass more facets of the problem. Considering only the large geographical regions, which have significant natural and economic differences, the total number of stations concerned with erosion and deflation and with mountain-reclamation in the Soviet Union should number at least thirty to thirty-five (keeping in mind that in the smaller regions there should be experimental field stations of these main stations). For comparison we can point out that in China in recent years three to five complex experimental stations concerned with erosion and deflation were set up in every province suffering from these processes. A dense network of erosion-preventive stations exists in the United States.

One of the most important and significant tasks in the struggle with erosion and deflation is the creation of a network of model demonstration state and collective farms. For the present, there are no farms that could serve as examples of full and effective application of erosion and deflation control systems, or that could serve as a base for the establishment of such a regional program.

At present, there is much expansion in the organization of model collective and state farms of the general type, some of which should be transformed into model farms of erosion and deflation control. If such farms were created in each administrative region, then the problems could be focused on two to three farms of each oblast suffering from such destructive processes.

Some deficiencies in this struggle are associated with the lack of a single administrative center to direct the over-all solution to the problem. The leading role in this respect is played by the agricultural institutions, which cannot assure any fundamental solution in all parts of the country without the participation of the personnel of the water and hydropower branches of the economy, of the river and surface transport, and a series of other branches. There is no single scientific center for dealing with this problem.

The institutes of the academies of science of the USSR and of the union republics, the universities, a series of scientific-research and scholarly institutes of agriculture, water and forest economy, of water and land transport, and others are all preoccupied with various theoretical and practical aspects of erosion and deflation and of their control. All of this effort requires planned direction, methodical coordination and control, and rapid organization of a special and active series of soil conservation forces throughout the agricultural administration; it also requires a single scientific-methodological center.

BIBLIOGRAPHY

Alekperov, K. A. "Rasprostraneniye erozii pochv v Azerbaydzhane" [Distribution of Soil Erosion in Azerbaydzhan]. *Pochvovedeniye,* no. 1 (1957).

Armand, D. L. "Osobennosti selskokhozyaystvennogo ispolzovaniya erozionnykh zemel v stepnoy i lesostepnoy zonakh SSSR" [Characteristics of Agricultural Use of Soils Subjected to Erosion in the Steppe and Forest-steppe Zones of the USSR]. *Voprosy geografii* [Problems of Geography]. Sbornik statey dlya XVIII Mezhdunar. geogr. kongressa [Collection of papers for the XVIII International Geographical Congress]. Moscow-Leningrad, 1956.

Armand, D. L. *Fiziko-geograficheskiye osnovy proyektirovaniya seti zashchitnykh lesnykh polos* [Physico-geographical Bases of Planning of Shelter Belt Networks]. Moscow-Leningrad: AN SSSR, 1961.

Bennett, Hugh Hammond, *Elements of Soil Conservation.* New York and London: McGraw-Hill Book Company, Inc., 1947, 406 pp. (Russian language edition, Moscow, 1958, cited by author.)

Braude, I. D. *Zakrepleniye i osvoyeniye ovragov, balok i krupnykh sklonov*

[Fixing and Utilization of Ravines, Gullies, and Steep Slopes]. Moscow: Selkhozgiz, 1959.

Bronzova, G. Ya. *Sozdaniye kormovykh ugodiy na smytykh pochvakh (v tsentralnoy lesostepi i sukhoy stepi)* [The Establishment of Fodder Land on Eroded Soils (In the Central Forest Steppe and the Dry Steppe)]. Moscow: Selkhozgiz, 1955.

Dyachenko, A. E., Zemlyanitskiy, L. T. "Deflyatsiya pochv Bashkirii i mery borby s ney" [Soil Deflation in Bashkiria and Measures of Combating It]. *Pochvovedeniye*, no. 8 (1946).

"Eroziya pochv" [Soil Erosion]. Materialy Vsesoyuzn. soveshchaniya po borbe s eroziyey pochv 12–16 dekabrya 1955 g. [Papers of the All-Union Conference on the Struggle With Soil Erosion Held on December 12–16, 1955]. Edited by S. S. Sobolev. Moscow: Selkhozgiz, 1957.

Gayel, A. G., Doskach, A. G., Trushkovskiy, A. A. "O pylnykh buryakh v marte-aprele 1960" [On the Dust Storms of March–April, 1960]. *Isvestiya AN SSSR, seriya geogr.*, no. 1 (1961).

Gussak, V. B. *Borba s poverkhnostnymi smyvami pochvy na kulturnykh zemlyakh* [Struggle With Surface Soil Erosion on Cultivated Land]. Tiflis: Zakgiz, 1934.

Kholupyak, K. L. "Erozinni protsesy i borotba z nymy [Erosional Processes and the Struggle With Them]. In *Polezakhysni lisonasadzhenyya* [Shelter-belt Plantations]. Kharkiv, 1949.

Kocherga, F. K. *Izyskaniya, proyektirovaniye i proizvodstvo gornomeliorativnykh rabot v Sredney Azii* [Research, Planning and Execution of Meliorative Work in the Mountain Terrain of Central Asia]. Tashkent, 1959. *Trudy Sredneaz. n. -i. in-ta lesnogo khozyaystva, vyp.* 7 [Papers of the Central Asian Scientific Research Institute of Forestry, Issue 7].

Kozmenko, A. S. *Osnovy protivoerozionnoy melioratsii* [Principles of Erosion Preventive Land Melioration]. Moscow: Selkhozgiz, 1954.

Kozmenko, A. S. *Borba s eroziey pochvy* [The Struggle with Soil Erosion]. 2d ed. Moscow: Selkhozgiz, 1957.

Pastushenko, V. O. *Sivozminy v kolhospakh Ukrainy* [Crop Rotations in the Collective Farms of the Ukraine]. Kiyiv, Ukr. akad. k.-g. nauk [Ukrainian Academy of Agricultural Sciences]. 1959.

Selskokhozyaystvennaya eroziya i borba s ney [Agricultural Erosion and the Struggle With It]. Sb. statey [Collection of Papers]. Moscow-Leningrad: AN SSSR, 1956.

Selskokhozyaystvennaya eroziya i novye metody yeye izucheniya [Agricultural Erosion and New Methods of Studying It]. Sb. statey. Moscow-Leningrad: AN SSSR, 1958.

Shaposhnikova, A. P. *Eroziya i lesomelioratsiya v borbe s neyu* [Erosion and the Use of Forest Melioration in Combating It]. 1947.

Silvestrov, S. I. *Voprosy organizatsii territorii kolkhozov v rayonakh erozii* [Problems of Organizing the Collective Farm Territory in Areas Subject to Erosion]. Moscow, 1938.

Silvestrov, S. I. *Eroziya i sevooboroty v tsentralnoy lesostepnoy zone* [Erosion and Crop Rotation in the Central Forest-Steppe Zone]. Moscow: Selkhozgiz, 1949.

Silvestrov, S. I. *Relef i zemledeliye (v erozionnykh rayonakh)* [Relief and Agriculture (in Regions Subject to Erosion)]. Moscow: Selkhozgiz, 1955.

Skorodumov, A. S. *Eroziya pochv i borba s ney* [Soil Erosion and the Struggle With It]. Kiev: AN Uk. SSR, 1955.

Sobolev, S. S. *Razvitiye erozionnykh protsessov na territorii Yevropeyskoy chasti SSSR i borba s nimi* [The Development of Erosion Processes in the European Part of the USSR and the Struggle With Them], vols. 1, 2. Moscow: AN SSSR, 1948, 1960.

Sobolev, S. S. *Eroziya pochv i borba s neyu* [Soil Erosion and the Struggle With It]. Moscow: Geografgiz, 1950.

Turovtsev, M. M. *Vodnaya eroziya pochv Bashkirii* [Water Erosion of Soil in Bashkiriya]. Ufa: Bashknigoizdat, 1958.

Zaslavskiy, M. N. and Gorbunov, I. F. "Narodnokhozyaystvennoye znacheniye borby s eroziey pochv Moldavii" [National Economic Significance of the Struggle with Soil Erosion in Moldavia]. In *Mery borby s eroziey pochv Moldavii* [Measures of the Struggle with Soil Erosion in Moldavia]. Kishinev, 1959.

Part 5. VEGETATION

11. Forest Resources and Forest Economy

P. V. Vasilyev

(Council for the Study of the Productive Forces
of the State Economic Council,
under the Council of Ministers of the USSR)

FOREST RESOURCES

The Soviet Union exceeds all other nations in its vast forest reserves. This position was clearly revealed in the statistical summary of the Forest Section of the United Nations Food and Agricultural Organization, where data pertaining to the USSR are listed alongside those for entire continents (World Forestry Inventory, 1960). These data are presented with some corrections in Table 1.

Of a total forest area (comprising 2,438 million hectares) that is accessible for exploitation, more than one-third lies within the USSR,[1] giving the Soviet Union the largest forest reserves in the world. The total area of forests under exploitation is 1,900 million hectares, of which 460 million hectares are found in the USSR. The division into exploited and non-exploited forests is, however, artificial inasmuch as the degree of use varies rapidly in time. A number of countries do not make such a subdivision of the forest area at all.

The world reserves of timber in forests under exploitation is 128.6 billion cubic meters. The timber reserves in all forested areas is approximately 160 to 180 billion cubic meters. The distribution of timber reserves under exploitation is given in Table 2.

---

[1] The survey of forest resources of the USSR carried out in 1961 does not indicate any sharp deviations from the data given here. Forestry statistics of the USSR consider and evaluate the forest area according to three different categories: (1) the forested area, equaling 722,300,000 hectares; (2) the forested area including pockets without forest (burned-over, cut-over areas, and so forth), equaling 836,000,000 hectares; and (3) the total area of the forest land fund managed by forestry organizations, equaling 1,131,000,000 hectares. In comparing these data with those of foreign countries, the second category should be used as it is most similar to foreign statistical data.

Table 1
Area in Forests, 1958

Region	(In million hectares)			Percent-age of Area in Forest	Per Capita Forested Area (Hectares)
	Territory	Total Forested Area	Area of Forests Accessible for Exploitation		
Europe (without USSR)	473	141	138	30	0.24
North America	1,874	733	400	39	3.7
Central & South America	2,047	1,031	332	51	5.4
Africa	2,978	753	380	25	3.3
Asia (without USSR)	2,718	520	326	19	0.32
Australia and Oceania	854	96	26	11	6.0
Subtotal	10,944	3,274	1,602	30	1.15
USSR	2,234	836	836	37	4.2
TOTAL WORLD	13,178	4,110 [a]	2,438	31	1.34

[a] The FAO Summary gives a total forested area of 4,405 million hectares, which includes the total area of the Soviet forest land fund (1,131 million hectares). The latter includes 295 million hectares of unforested land.

Characteristically, almost half the total world reserves of exploited coniferous forests are found in the USSR. The timber reserves of the USSR exceed 75 billion cubic meters, of which coniferous varieties account for 64.4 billion. Annual growth amounts to almost 860 million cubic meters, over 600 million cubic meters of which occurs in exploited forests. With such extensive timber reserves, the USSR naturally has a very high per capita endowment of forests (4.2 hectares of forested area). Of the industrially developed countries only Canada (24.5 hectares) and Finland (5.3 hectares) have higher per capita reserves; the United States has only 1.8 hectares; Sweden, 3.2 hectares; Norway, 2.3 hectares; and in most of the other countries of Europe, between 0.1 and 0.4 hectares.

The Soviet Union leads the world in the volume of timber cut. The annual average for the period from 1953 to 1958 was 335 million cubic meters for the U.S.A., 95 for Canada, 65 for Japan, 61 for Sweden, 39.5 for Finland, 35.5 for France, 23.5 for West Germany, while in the USSR the average for the same period was 356. In 1958 it was 375 million cubic meters; in 1959 it was 398 million. By the end of the Seven-Year Plan, despite measures adopted for improving the use of timber, the total volume

Table 2
Exploitation of World Timber Reserves, 1958

Region	Percentage of Total Forest Area Surveyed	Timber Reserves (In million cubic meters)			Average Reserves (In million cubic meters per hectare)		
		Total	Coniferous	Nonconiferous	Total	Coniferous	Nonconiferous
Europe (without USSR)	96	10,780	7,120	3,660	80	90	65
North America	100	36,640	27,140	9,500	100	135	60
Central America	24	1,080	330	750	80	85	80
South America	20	8,300	1,060	7,240	115	135	110
Africa	71	5,620	70	5,550	45	30	45
Asia (without USSR)	96	22,020	4,620	17,400	100	120	95
Australia & Oceania	97	1,320	220	1,100	65	50	70
Subtotal	—	85,760	40,560	45,200	—	—	—
USSR [a]	100	42,813	34,610	8,203	94	108	59
TOTAL WORLD	—	128,573	75,170	53,403	91	107	79

[a] For comparability, the timber reserves were calculated in the same manner as those of other world regions in per hectare of forest area, whereas usually in the USSR they are calculated per hectare of forest-covered area.

Table 3
The Area of Forest Cover of the State Forest Fund
(Exclusive of Collective Farm Forests) and the
Dominance of Various Species (January 1, 1956)

	Forest Cover	
Dominant Species	*Million Hectares*	*Percentage of Total*
Needle Leaf		
Larch	274.3	40.2
Pine	109.5	16.1
Spruce	72.1	10.6
Cedar	32.1	4.7
Fir	23.1	3.4
Others	20.3	3.0
TOTAL	531.4	78.0
Broad Leaf		
Birch	91.8	13.5
Saxsaul	19.8	2.9
Aspen	14.5	2.1
Oak, Beech, Ash	11.5	1.7
Alder, Poplar, Linden	5.3	0.8
Others	6.6	1.0
TOTAL	149.5	22.0

of timber cut in the country probably will approach 400 million cubic meters.* In the more distant future it should reach nearly 550 million cubic meters.

It is necessary to dwell at some length on the composition of Soviet forests. Areas occupied by the basic species (or rather, forests with certain predominant species) are shown in Table 3.

The fact that four-fifths of the forested area of the Soviet Union consists of coniferous species is significant inasmuch as the conifers possess a number of advantages for extensive utilization.

Soviet coniferous forests occur mainly in the taiga, which stretches across the northern part of the country from the international boundary in the west to the shores of the Pacific Ocean in the east. Among the coniferous

*In 1965, it amounted to 378.1 million cubic meters. See *Narodnoye khozyaystvo SSR, v 1965 godu Statisticheskiy yezhegodnik* (Moscow, 1966), p. 207.

species, pine, as is generally known, provides the timber that is most widely used for commercial purposes and that dominates the forests of Karelia, of Leningrad, Novgorod, and Arkhangelsk oblasts, the Komi ASSR, and also of the Urals. The amount of pine in the forests of Siberia is also considerable, comprising 20% to 30% of the entire forested area. In the Soviet Far East, however, its proportion drops to 4%.

Spruce, also of high industrial value, grows with pine in most parts of the forest; sometimes groves of spruce alternate with groves of pine. Spruce groves are most extensive in the Ural foreland. Although the pulp and paper industry has recently begun to make use of many varieties of timber, the manufacture of high quality paper nevertheless will apparently continue to rely on spruce for some time.

Larch dominates the forests of Eastern Siberia and the Soviet Far East; it possesses exceptionally high physical-mechanical properties and although it is well suited to the manufacture of cardboard, paper, and the like, it is still little used in industry.

Large tracts of the taiga are covered by deciduous species—birch, aspen, alder, and others. In severely logged areas, with lack of proper care, they have succeeded the previous stands of coniferous forest. This circumstance (together with better determination of the reserves) was undoubtedly one of the reasons why coniferous forests in the state forest reserves, according to data for January 1, 1961, covered only 500 million hectares, as against 531.4 million in 1956.

To the south of the taiga extend the mixed and deciduous forests. Oak is the most valuable of the economically useful deciduous species. The total area of oak-dominated forests amounts to 8.5 million hectares, but much of this, unfortunately, is composed of young second-growth trees that have lost their former value. A wide variety of valuable deciduous species are found in the Caucasus and in the Soviet Far East.

In the future, the national economy will require both a large volume of mature timber and some reduction in the forested area. However valuable the forest resources and significant the hydroclimatic role of forests, the development of the economy often requires the utilization of forest lands for other purposes—for agriculture, industry, settlements, and so forth. Particularly large areas of forest are lost due to hydropower development, which in the USSR has assumed huge dimensions.

The press has published summary data concerning the forest area already flooded and that scheduled to be flooded by the construction of hydroelectric stations (Vyzgo; Fogel and Shiglovskiy). Table 4 provides such data, supplemented with tentative figures regarding the reserves of timber

Table 4
Potential Decrease in the Forest Area and Timber Reserves
Due to the Construction of Hydroelectric Power Stations

Region or River Basin	Inundated Area (Millions of hectares)		Timber Loss (Millions of cubic meters)	
	Total	Forested	Total	Exploitable
Western Siberia	15.0	8.6	770	460
Eastern Siberia	4.0	3.7	370	260
Volga	4.2	1.7	160	80
Dnieper, Dniester, Don	2.1	0.5	60	30
Pechora-Vychegda-Kama	1.6	1.4	110	80
Other Regions	3.7	1.7	170	100
All Regions and River Basins	30.6	17.6	1,640	1,010

lost, calculated at minimal norms of forest reserve per hectare of the major forest areas and according to minimal yield from recoverable timber.

The forests that have been inundated or waterlogged following the construction of hydroelectric stations are equal in extent to the entire forested area of Arkhangelsk Oblast. In Siberia and the North European part of the USSR, inundation destroys many riverbank forests of high productivity. In the basins of southern rivers inundation frequently destroys the only forests extant. Because of this and because of the flooding of other valuable lands, the need to build hydroelectric stations with smaller reservoirs or to find alternate solutions to the power problem is being increasingly voiced in the Soviet press and at scientific conferences.

Ten to twelve million hectares of forested land can be shifted to agricultural use in the immediate future. It is desirable to transfer such territory that meets the following conditions: (1) suitability for agriculture with minimum expenditures on land reclamation; (2) the presence of unforested lands within the forest reserves, or of open forests, or of forests of low quality and scrublands; and (3) the retention of forests within this territory in small pockets so that they might alternate with arable land.

In the next few decades the agricultural area can be expanded without any serious infringement upon the timber supply if the forest resources are handled with care. However, in a number of regions we are already experiencing difficulties in the supply of timber, difficulties associated with the extremely irregular distribution of the forests—with the existence of regional disproportions between size of forest reserves, size of population, and industrial consumption of timber. The degree of forestation of the economic-administrative regions of the USSR varies from 75% of Irkutsk Oblast to 0.2% of Rostov Oblast. Over 80% of the forests lie in the thinly populated regions of Siberia and the Soviet Far East. In the densely populated and industrially developed areas of the European part of the Union the forests were already drastically reduced in the last century, and still did not satisfy local needs.

Under the conditions of a rapidly developing Soviet national economy it was inevitable that the scale of timber exploitation in the industrially developed central and southern regions of the country be restricted, that increased productivity of forest resources in those regions be assured, and that the unexploited sections of the forests of the European North, the Urals, Western and Eastern Siberia, and the Soviet Far East be brought into economic use. This resulted in the need to change decisively the geography of the entire timber industry, with the goal of locating production as near as possible to the sources of raw material.

DISTRIBUTION OF THE INDUSTRY

The shift of the forest industry to the sources of raw material and the more heavily forested regions had begun before World War II. The share of the northern regions of European Russia in lumbering increased from 5.3% in 1913 to 12.9% in 1940; and in Western and Eastern Siberia and the Soviet Far East, from 8% to 22%. At the same time the regions of the center, the northwest, the Volga, and the west declined to only 42.5% of the total volume as against 67.8% in 1913. In the regions of the European North and the Urals, as well as in the new industrial centers of Siberia and the Soviet Far East, a sizeable development of milling and wood processing has occurred. The absolute volume of cut and sawn timber in the heavily forested areas has shown a particularly sharp increase in postwar years (Table 5).

Over the twenty-year period (1940–59), the volume of logging in the heavily forested zone increased by almost 80%, the volume of sawn timber nearly tripled, and the production of paper quadrupled. However, a substantial expansion took place in the moderately and sparsely forested zones as well, so that the share of production in the heavily forested zone in comparison with the other zones changed little. The present distribution of the forest industry still does not correspond to the distribution of forest resources. As in previous years, a considerable part of the industry is still concentrated in timber-poor regions, and there is still a lack of balance

Table 5
Zonal Distribution of Principal Branches of the Forest Industry

Item	Densely Forested (North, Urals, Western & Eastern Siberia, Soviet Far East)	Moderately Forested (Northwest, Center, West)	Sparsely Forested, Arid Unforested (Remaining Regions)	Total USSR
Timber reserves in the state forest fund				
Billion cubic meters	67.8	5.3	2.5	75.6
Percentage	90	7	3	100
Logging				
1940				
Million cubic meters	126.7	94.1	25.3	246.1
Percentage	51	38	11	100
1959				
Million cubic meters	228.5	130.5	39.0	398.0
Percentage	58	33	9	100
Milling				
1940				
Million cubic meters	16.4	11.0	7.4	34.8
Percentage	47	31	22	100
1959				
Million cubic meters	45.9	30.7	27.4	104.0
Percentage	48	29	23	100
Paper Production				
1940				
Thousand tons	209.4	522.8	80.2	812.4
Percentage	26	64	10	100
1959				
Thousand tons	816.9	1,266.9	242.7	2,326.5
Percentage	35	54	11	100

between the supply of raw materials, the location of processing plants, and the consuming centers (Table 6).

As may be seen from Table 6, 90% of all the forest resources are concentrated in the heavily forested zone, but it produces only 58% of all lumber and consumes only 22%. Therefore, the sparsely and nonwooded regions, whose forest resources make up only 3% of the total reserves of the Union, account for 9% of timber cutting and 46% of consumption. In this

Table 6
Relation of Zonal Timber Resources and Supply to Demand (1959)

Zone	Reserves in State Forest Fund		Supply		Distribution of Population		Approximate Demand	
	Billion Cubic Meters	%	Million Cubic Meters	%	In Millions	%	Million Cubic Meters	%
Heavily forested	67.8	90	228.5	58	43.5	21	90	22
Moderately forested	5.3	7	130.5	33	59.6	29	130	32
Sparsely forested and nonforested	2.5	3	39.0	9	105.7	50	178	46
Total USSR	75.6	100	398.0	100	208.8	100	398	100

way, the shifting of the lumbering and processing base into the heavily forested regions still lags behind the over-all pace of the development of the productive forces of the country. Moreover, in recent years there has been almost no improvement in distribution of the timber industry, and in some respects it has even become worse. Thus, in the heavily forested regions, despite a comparatively rapid development of timber cutting, the preparation and processing have developed very slowly. At the same time, in the sparsely forested regions there was an unjustifiable increase in the volume of timber cutting and a very intensive increase of milling based on raw materials brought from the other regions. As shown in Table 5, from 1940 to 1959, in the regions lacking forest resources, the volume of lumber increased almost four times. More detailed data are provided in Table 7.

Among the oblasts rich in forest resources, milling fell substantially behind logging over the twenty years from 1940 to 1959. In individual heavily forested oblasts, the production of lumber fell behind, although a number of favorable measures were implemented. Thus, in Perm Oblast, the economic administrative council obtained a significant expansion in milling capacity, but in 1959 the oblast's mills, the total capacity of which was 5,745 cubic meters, produced only 3,130 cubic meters of sawn timber. At the same time, many oblasts lacking adequate forest resources increased milling nine to seventeen times over the twenty years. All other branches of the timber industry, as well, have been concentrated in regions lacking adequate resources. According to 1959 data, such regions contain 74.3% of the output of the plywood industry; 71.3% of the production of paper; and 33% of cardboard production. Because of this, the

Table 7
Imbalance Between Logging and Milling Increases
in Regions of High and Low Forestry

Oblast or Kray	Percentage of Area Forested	Extraction 1940	Extraction 1959	Milling 1940	Milling 1959	Increase Factor Extraction	Increase Factor Milling
		(In thousand cubic meters)					
Irkutsk Oblast	75.3	2,304	16,524	983	4,984	7.1	5.1
Tomsk	58.1	1,875	5,211	739	1,217	2.8	5.1
Perm	56.1	5,305	13,193	748	3,130	3.6	4.1
Sverdlovsk	53.2	8,235	16,180	2,393	5,904	1.9	2.5
Krasnoyarsk Kray	45.7	4,168	13,320	1,374	4,420	3.2	3.2
Tyumen Oblast	31.2	1,010	4,416	479	1,042	4.4	2.2
Penza	18.7	439	892	55	484	2.0	8.8
Kuybyshev	11.0	370	522	300	1,059	1.4	3.5
Tula	13.5	74	202	57	949	2.7	16.7
Voronezh	9.0	112	232	47	408	2.1	8.7
Kursk	6.0	32	36	8	117	1.1	14.6
Stavropol Kray	3.7	249	306	64	398	1.2	6.2
Rostov Oblast	0.2	15	62	79	740	4.0	9.4
Astrakhan	0.9	12	56	132	685	4.7	5.2

average distance of rail shipments of unprocessed timber increased excessively: from 1,019 kilometers in 1940 to 1,660 kilometers in 1959.*

In the Seven-Year Plan, measures were stipulated that would secure a significant increase in the share of the forest-rich area in the output of lumber and forest products. However, in practice, little was done in this direction in 1959–60. The plan envisioned a reduction in the volume of timber cutting in Group II forests [2] of the timber-poor regions by 24 million cubic meters (from 117 to 93 million cubic meters), so as to prevent the exhaustion of the forests in those regions. However, these measures will be carried out only with some delay, and not in all oblasts.

In 1958–59, as in the preceding decade, cutting, particularly in coniferous forests, exceeded substantially the planned volume in many timber-poor oblasts and republics. For example, in Bryansk Oblast, which possesses 14.5 million cubic meters of exploitable timber of Group II forests, the

---

[2] The forests of Group II are those of timber-poor regions that have a water-protective and climate-regulative function and, therefore, represent a purely local supply of lumber.

* By 1965, the end of the Seven-Year Plan, the average length of haul had declined to 1,616 kilometers. See *Narkhoz SSSR, 1965*, p. 462.

Table 8
New, Mature, and Overripe Stands in all Types of Forests
of the State Forest Fund

Republic or Oblast	Percentage of Area Forested	Age Groups of Total Forested Area (In percent)	
		New (Under 40 years)	Mature and Overripe (Over 80 years)
Mari ASSR	53.2	40.0	35.3
Vladimir	42.1	51.8	6.1
Moscow Oblast	37.2	45.3	13.0
Chuvash ASSR	31.8	48.9	35.0
Kalinin Oblast	27.1	41.7	15.2
Mordvin ASSR	23.6	56.0	11.0
Belorussian SSR	22.5	60.0	5.5
Smolensk Oblast	21.5	45.2	13.3
Ryazan Oblast	20.9	60.0	4.0
Tatar ASSR	15.7	52.8	22.3
Tula Oblast	13.5	69.0	6.2
Ukrainian SSR	11.3	60.0	9.0
Voronezh Oblast	9.0	78.5	4.0
Kursk Oblast	6.0	81.7	—

NOTE: The percentage of trees of average growth and trees reaching maturity are not included.

allowed cutting for principal use is 1,290 cubic meters. However, the actual volume cut amounts to about 2,000 cubic meters annually. The same can be said for Moscow, Ryazan, Kursk, Penza, Tambov, and other oblasts.

In these oblasts there has been no outright decrease in the forested area as was the case before the Revolution. Forested areas are not decreasing, but reserves of mature stands of timber are being reduced and this will result inevitably in an interruption in forest use in the very near future. The characteristic results of overcutting that impinge upon the growth structure of coniferous forests are given in Table 8.

Under conditions of proper forest management, the ratio of young trees in coniferous forests should be about 40%, and 20% in mature and overmature stands. Table 8 shows that in all timber-poor oblasts the percentage of mature forest is lower and young stands exceed the norm, the result of continuous overcutting. In oblasts with exhausted reserves of mature timber, the time will soon arrive when cutting will have to cease for ten to twenty years to allow for new stands to develop; it would be intolerable for the oblasts to revert to the cutting of immature stands.

The data in Table 8 are more or less characteristic for all oblasts of the European Russian zone of average and poor timber resources. Because of inadequate regulation in the deliveries of timber and of insufficient forest restoration in exploited forests, the stands of forests have deteriorated in a number of regions in European Russia. The cut of deciduous varieties (birch, aspen, hornbeam, alder, and so forth), even in the forest-poor regions, falls short of the available volumes. Here, consequently, is a considerable reserve of forest raw materials. At the same time, in recent years large areas formerly covered with pine and spruce have become overgrown after cutting with birch, aspen, and alder. Data for several republics (whose boundaries have remained relatively constant) are presented in Table 9.

It should be mentioned that some foresters do not consider the replacement of coniferous with small-leaved deciduous species a negative development since the latter grow faster and the change in vegetation in the long run has just as much utility as crop rotation. However, the present needs of the national economy are much larger for coniferous species than for deciduous.

In order to maintain volume, voluntary selective logging and the use of leftover cuttings have been expanded in recent years. By these means, additional amounts of timber have been made available; simultaneously, the forest has been improved and without endangering future supply. Unfortunately, selective cutting is frequently misused, and stands are cut by 50% or more instead of by the permissible 30% to 40%.

In the adoption of new plans and in newly created projects, methods were stipulated for alleviating the irrational distribution of the timber industry. The most important of these pertain to the creation of large timber-industry complexes in the Komi ASSR, in Western and Eastern Siberia, and in the Soviet Far East. They are designed to exploit and to use fully the large quantity of raw materials, and to produce lumber, veneer, paper, cardboard, plywood, furniture, and products of chemical processing. Many of these industrial complexes will call for the formation of whole forest-industrial regions and centers, exceeding in size the Arkhangelsk complex.

Table 10 shows how fully forest raw materials can be used in industrial complexes to provide for the planned manufacture of products; the figures accord with the leading foreign norms of output per hundred cubic meters of timber.

The industrial complexes will depend on the exploitation and use of the

Table 9
The Replacement of Spruce by Birch Groves

Republic	Forests Dominated by Spruce			Forests Dominated by Birch		
	1937 (In thousand hectares)	*1958*	*Decrease* (%)	*1937* (In thousand hectares)	*1958*	*Increase* (%)
Karelian ASSR	2,047	1,823	11	339	695	105
Mari	257	231	10	191	272	42
Chuvash	32	17	47	92	114	24
Udmurt	790	701	11	146	278	90
Tatar	39	26	33	111	142	28
Bashkir	310	305	2	1,023	1,335	31

Table 10

Scheme of Multipurpose Use of Forest Raw Materials in Large Processing Combines

	Number of Enterprises	Consumption (In thousand cubic meters)		Production		Waste and Waste Use		
		Fresh Raw Material	Waste	Gross	Per Hundred Cubic Meters of Supplied Lumber	Total Waste from Primary Production (In thousand cubic meters)	Volume Reused in Secondary Production (In thousand cubic meters)	% of Initial Waste
Timber Supply (including possible imports)[b]	15–20	5,000	—	—	—	1,000 in logging process	250	25
Production of timbers for fuel or in raw state	—	600	—	—	—	—	—	—
Production of smoked logs	—	400	—	—	—	—	—	—
Processed products		4,000	—	—	—	—	—	—
Sawmill products	4–5	1,600	—	1 million m³	22 m³	550	330	60
Plywood	2–3	240	—	100,000 m³	2 m³	130	80	62
Wood products[a]	3–4	160	—	—	—	300	180	60
Marketable cellulose for export[b]	1	400	40	90,000 tons	1.8 tons	—	—	—
Paper	1	1,000	80	220,000 tons	4.4 tons	—	—	—
Cardboard	1	400	300	160,000 tons	3.2 tons	—	—	—
Plates made of wood shavings	3–4	80	100	120,000 m³	2.4 m³	—	—	—
Plates made of wood fibre	2–3	80	200	90,000 tons	1.8 tons	—	—	—
Hydrolysis and production of sulfite alcohol	1	20	80	200,000 hectolitres of alcohol and other products	—	—	—	—
Forest chemical and other products	—	20	40	—	—	—	—	—

[a] In producing wood products, the use of a combination of 400,000 m³ of sawmill materials and 100–150 thousand m³ of plywood and plates is foreseen.
[b] Imports and exports refer to shipments to or from the combine.

resources of all the main tree species. One important feature of the complexes will be the technological demand for a large volume of low-quality timber. Another important feature will be the full use of all waste from the initial processing and of a large part of the slash left by forest cutting.

For the regions mentioned, the characteristic complexes will be the Krasnoyarsk, Yenisey-Maklakovsk, and Bratsk enterprise groups, and the Dobryansk combine of the Perm Economic Administrative Council. These combines need not always have all branches in one locality, they may be comprised of a wide network of individual, technically well-equipped enterprises: for the production of lumber, for the production of materials for house construction, and for the production of furniture. The capacity of the new combines must be related to a continuous exploitation and hence coordinated with the annual volume of the forests that are assigned to them. It is necessary also to organize a "continuous economy" in the forests (that is, uninterrupted use and regeneration). The former clean-cutting system, which called for continually shifting the location of lumber enterprises, should be replaced by a system of continuously operating enterprises, including, as was envisioned in its new structure, all processes of forest economy and production.

The development of the timber industry in the heavily forested regions, together with the relative stabilization (even reduction) of production in the less well endowed regions, will lead eventually to a more uniform distribution of these branches of the national economy and to more rational management of forestry throughout the country. Anything less than this reconstruction of the forest economy, no matter how well conceived and carried out, may lead only to partial and temporary success.

THE DISTRIBUTION OF FORESTRY MEASURES

In the first years of economic construction the Soviet state had to face the problem of a rational distribution of activities associated with forestry. As early as 1918, in an address to the Council of People's Commissars on April 5, V. I. Lenin stated:

The Council of People's Commissars considers it necessary to report . . . that the legacy of the unfortunate war has left enormous areas of denudation, which it is necessary in the interests of the people to immediately plant and sow with trees.[3]

---

[3] *Sbornik uzakoneniy RSFSR* [Collection of Laws of the RSFSR] no. 42 (1918), p. 522.

Since then, the question was dealt with mainly by dividing the forested areas into zones of forests of various uses and characteristics, and by determining specific methods and regulations for each zone. In 1930, the forests were divided into zones of silviculture and industrial significance, with basic forestry concentrated in the first zone; in 1936, the water-protective forests were recognized as a separate zone. In 1943, all forests of the USSR were divided into three groups: Group I was comprised of forests in parks, and forests of protective significance (coastal forests, green belts, forest parks, and so forth); in Group II, forests of the sparsely forested zone of exploitable significance; and in Group III, other forests of essential economic significance. The system of basic forestry (silvicultural work, the use of slashings, and so forth) was concerned with the maintenance of Group I and II forests. In Group III forests, concern was largely for fire protection and the production of timber. For Groups I and II, cutting and use were restricted but all forms of cutting and use were permitted in forests of Group III, depending on the needs of the national economy.

About the end of 1959, at the time of the amalgamation of forestry (*leskhoz*) and the lumber industry (*lespromkhoz*), the system of subdividing the forests into three groups was supplemented by the introduction of two zones of forest management. Much of Group III and part of Group II fell under the jurisdiction of the economic administrative councils; forests of Group I, along with those remaining in Groups II and III, situated in the sparsely forested regions, were controlled by the newly created Central Administration of Forest Economy and Forest Protection, under the Council of Ministers of the RSFSR and of analogous organs in the union republics. These zones and the division of control were introduced: (*a*) to create a unified system of integrated enterprises for forestry and forest exploitation, completing the cycle of protection and use, and (*b*) to permit a broad development of forest renewal in the forest-rich areas, using the methods previously employed by forest industrial enterprises.

With the division of the forests into zones and categories, the implementation of forestry measures became diversified. In the heavily forested regions, the main problem was protection from fires and pests as well as the rational use of accumulated reserves of mature and overmature timber under conditions of mandatory renewal of logged-over areas. In moderately forested regions, represented mainly in Group II, the approach was one of restricted use of renewable reserves, i.e., of logging within the limits of replenishment. In these forests basic silviculture was practiced. In the lightly forested, and especially in the unforested, steppe regions, the most important problem was to increase the stand by means of new plantations and the development of protective forest belts.

Considerable success was attained in carrying out these measures, an achievement evidenced in the sharp increase in forest renewal and expansion efforts.

From the end of the seventeenth century to 1914, in the fifty *guberniyas* of tsarist Russia, according to data of M. A. Tsvetkov, 67 million hectares of forests were cut and only 1.3 million hectares were reforested. The average annual area of timber planting from 1905 to 1911 did not exceed 60,000 to 65,000 hectares. During the Soviet period, 10 million hectares of forests have been established and the rate of afforestation has increased annually. Thus, in 1958, 1,283,400 hectares were planted, which somewhat exceeded the area cut in 1957 (Kovalin). It should be noted that the correlation between cutting and planting of forests in different republics varies greatly. The Ukraine now plants more than it cuts, but there are oblasts where reforestation still falls far short of the area of annual cut.

The control figures for the national economy of the USSR from 1959 to 1965, adopted at the Twenty-first Congress of the CPSU, foresaw ". . . the utilization of forest resources, not only for full satisfaction of current needs but also for their preservation and replenishment as well." [4] The improvement in their qualitative composition and an increase in their productivity would be achieved.

In the Law Concerning the Conservation of Natural Resources in the RSFSR, it is emphasized that the planning of forestry and supply should consider not only the timber requirements of the national economy and the population, but also the necessity of preserving and replenishing the forests. "All forest users are obliged to carry out complex forestry measures in order to assure the quick replenishment of the logged-over areas with valuable timber species and the protection of the forests." The law further enumerated agencies that ". . . are obliged to take measures towards improving and increasing forest resources, creating forests in the sparsely forested regions, creating shelter belts, and other protective plantation." [5]

The documents mentioned above represent a further development in Soviet forestry. They envision the necessity of fulfilling three basic tasks: (1) mandatory reforestation in all logged-over areas to ensure expanded

---

[4] *Materialy vneocherednogo XXI syezda KPSS* [Materials of the Special Twenty-first Congress of the CPSU]. 1959, p. 207.

[5] *Ob okhrane prirody v RSFSR (Zakon Rossiyskoy Sovetskoy Federativnoy Sotsialisticheskoy Respubliki)* [Law Concerning the Conservation of Natural Resources in the RSFSR (Law of the RSFSR)], *Pravda,* October 28, 1960.

reproduction of forests; (2) a sharp expansion in the artificial renewal of forests, since in many cases only in this way can the logged-over areas be renewed with the required species; and (3) wide-scale mechanization of forestry, particularly of silvicultural efforts, inasmuch as the task of the current plan can be attained only by mechanized work.

The organizational base for the solution to these problems is a new system of unified, complex enterprises engaged both in exploitation and forestry management. This offers highly favorable conditions for reforestation. However, it is to be regretted that local forestry agencies fail to utilize fully the possibilities built into the new system and often permit gross deviations from requirements.

According to data of the Central Administration of Forestry and Protection of RSFSR, the timber-cutting organizations and enterprises in Krasnoyarsk Kray, Irkutsk, Kostroma and several other oblasts assume only nominal responsibility for replenishing and managing; the timber industry in these locations violates the rules of forest utilization, negligently abandons logged-over areas, decreases the size of appropriations for forestry, and the technical means that were formerly utilized in silviculture are diverted to lumbering. In the struggle against such excesses much depends on forest inspection—established at the end of 1959—to regulate the activities of forest enterprises to ensure adherence to the laws.

A mandatory prerequisite for the successful implementation of forestry measures is a proper knowledge of the existing forests in each of the various regions. The usual index is simply the percentage of the total area in forest, but such an index does not reflect exact reserves, since within the same area there may be great differences in density, quality, and maturity of the forest. Therefore, for economic purposes, the usual description of the forest (in terms of percentage of forest cover) needs to be supplemented by data on reserves of timber per hundred hectares of forested area (Table 11).

As shown in the table, more accurate representation of the forest wealth or a region can be obtained from data concerning timber reserves than from ordinary ratios of forest cover. Thus, for example, the forested area of Kalinin Oblast is significantly larger than that of Krasnodar Kray, but in terms of volume of timber the latter greatly exceeds the former. Moreover, data on the average reserves of timber do not reflect the manner in which the forests are distributed over the area under consideration. With respect to economy and hydrology, it is relevant how the forests are distributed, whether uniformly or in clusters. However, it is important to find indicators that would define the absolute area of forests, the percentage of

Table 11
Comparative Indices of Forest Cover and Timber Reserves,
According to Oblasts and Republics

Oblast or Republic	Percentage of Area Forested	Reserves (Cubic meters per 100 hectares)
Heavily Forested		
Irkutsk Oblast	75.3	114.4
Komi ASSR	67.0	63.4
Maritime Kray	68.4	97.5
Tomsk Oblast	58.1	84.6
Perm Oblast	56.1	88.2
Vologda Oblast	53.8	53.6
Mari ASSR	53.2	59.4
Kemerovo Oblast	49.3	64.6
Leningrad Oblast	48.4	54.9
Moderately and Sparsely Forested		
Moscow Oblast	37.5	35.0
Kalinin Oblast	27.1	26.0
Pskov Oblast	23.9	22.0
Krasnodar Kray	21.2	46.7
Tatar ASSR	18.1	18.7
Voronezh Oblast	9.0	7.6
Kursk Oblast	6.0	3.2
Chechen-Ingush ASSR	5.9	9.0
Orel Oblast	5.0	3.7

the territory occupied, and the degree of uniformity of distribution. At the present time, investigations in this direction are being conducted by the present author, in the Council for the Study of the Productive Forces, under the State Economic Council.

It should be noted that a relatively uniform distribution of forests among other land uses is always a positive factor. The belief of the distinguished forester, A. F. Rudzskiy, that in the future all arable land should be alternated with forests was undoubtedly progressive. The realization of this goal would require a tremendous and prolonged effort, but it is worth striving for since it creates the most advantageous conditions not only for forests but also for land, water, and climatic as well as wildlife resources.

In practicing forestry one should know not only the existing but also the desired amount of forestation. For the most efficient implementation of such measures over large areas, a method was put forward in the first years of Soviet power for estimating the forested area and for determining its optimum size. It was mentioned for the first time in 1918 in the decree "On Forests" signed by V. I. Lenin and Ya. M. Sverdlov.[6] By touching on a number of fundamental questions on forest utilization and renewal, this decree has retained even to the present day its significance as an important scientific-economic and legal document. According to the decree, the Central Ministry of Forests was charged with the duty of determining a forested area norm for each part of the Russian Republic, and with proposing instructive directions for each region, giving the required extent of forested area, which would serve as a basis for determining the maximum limits of timber use. The decree obligated each local forest organization to take any necessary measures to increase the forested area within its territory in order to attain the norm.

Unfortunately, the implementation of the measures envisioned in this historic decree encountered difficulties in the very first years of Soviet power, and later these measures no longer attracted the proper attention. Therefore, they have never attracted sufficient scientific study, and meanwhile, as a result of the discovery and exploitation of mineral wealth, the formation of new industrial regions, the development of virgin lands, the bringing into use of remote forest resources, and the creation of large man-made plantations, the question of determining a norm for forested areas has become all the more urgent. The present level of scientific development in the fields of economics, geography, forestry, and other disciplines will permit the development of means for solving the problem under consideration.

Under current conditions the question of establishing norms of forest cover is, from an economic point of view, primarily the problem of how each economic region should arrange its forests, depending on their economic, protective, or other significance. It is a question of how this is to be attained in light of the demands of a planned, proportional development of the national economy and a rational distribution of the productive forces.

From geographic and silvicultural points of view, the degree of cover should be extended in such a way as to play the most effective role in those natural processes that are helpful to the region's economy. As was pointed

---

[6] *Sobraniye uzakoneniy RSFSR* [Collection of Laws of the RSFSR], no. 42 (1918), p. 552.

out by forest hydrologists (A. A. Molchanov and others), the composition, age, density, and other qualitative elements of forests are significant in this regard.

Both domestic and foreign literature frequently refers to an average optimum forest cover. Of course, the figure can serve only as a very general reference and is bound to change, depending on historical, economic, and geographic factors, and on the quality of the forest itself.

Among the basic factors that must be considered in any determination of an optimum norm of forest cover are the following: (1) the geographic features of the region, beginning with its zonal characteristics and relief; (2) the population and general economic development, including in particular the level of development of industry, agriculture, and transport; (3) the region's specialization and its interregional links; (4) the economic usefulness of the forest and the demand, determined on an all-union basis, for import or export of forest materials to or from the given region; (5) the features of the hydrographic network, the status of water management, and the need for water-protective forests; (6) the condition of the agricultural land and the need for, and research on, shelter belts; and (7) the nature of the distribution and characteristics of cities and other settlements, particularly health resorts as well as tourist and vacation areas, which require plantings for recreational and landscaping purposes.

Local sources of raw materials no doubt play a large role, particularly in satisfying the needs of collective farms, local industry, and the population. However, the increasing need for these resources makes it necessary to find ways to expand the commercial forests in those regions where natural conditions favor their growth and where the nature of the timber industry has already been determined, i.e., primarily in the taiga zone. The use of historic or new timber industry regions may be particularly effective if they manufacture locally such transportable products as paper, cardboard, plywood, and so forth.

The industrial use of the forests of these regions should be multipurpose. In addition to logging, the collection of cedar nuts, mushrooms, berries, and medicinal plants should be developed; and it should be kept in mind that these forests are important to the climate in a significant part of the Soviet Union. However, a large part of the taiga is of little use for agriculture so the density of its forest will continue, perhaps forever, to be greater than in regions to the south. An increase in forest reserves of economic significance in the south will occur mainly on the basis of a rise in the productivity of the available forest lands; only a relatively small expansion in the forest cover is possible, by the forestation of land unsuited to agriculture, and by the establishment of special plantations of quick-maturing species. The planting of such forests was undertaken in recent years in a number of republics and oblasts (the Ukraine, Saratov Oblast, and others). More substantial changes in the sparsely forested regions will be achieved by creating protective forests that incidentally satisfy part of the local needs for timber.

Considering only the demand for timber, some generalizations may be made about optimum forest cover. The USSR currently consumes 400 million cubic meters of timber annually. Specialists consider that although the demand will grow it may stabilize in the foreseeable future at a level of 500 to 550 million cubic meters, provided that there is a rational, multipurpose use of raw materials. What extent of forest area is necessary for this? The average annual growth of timber in all forested areas of the USSR is 1.2 cubic meters per hectare; in developed forests it is 1.7 cubic meters per hectare. In forests of commercial significance it reaches 2 to 3 cubic meters per hectare, but ordinarily does not exceed 1.5. Although the forests of Group I have a higher productivity, the fact that, by necessity, logging is of a restricted nature there precludes any expectations of high quotas. An annual growth of 1.5 cubic meters per hectare is the practical norm for all of the forested area on which it is possible to rely during subsequent decades, since measures for increasing forest productivity have not had time to affect the yield of mature timber.

For the delivery to the national economy of the more than 500 million cubic meters of timber mentioned above, it will be necessary to conduct continuous forest operations on an area of as much as 400 million hectares. If this area should be distributed over the whole economically developed territory of the USSR, then the average forest cover would have to reach 25% to 30% of the total area. The actual forest cover of the entire USSR exceeds that ratio only slightly (32.4%). The USSR has tremendous possibilities for increasing forest productivity: over sizeable areas, selective logging will enhance the annual effective growth and prevent natural decay of overripe stands; a large increase in growth can be obtained eventually by drainage, improvement in the variety of species, and so on. Such intensification and rational use of the timber potential of 400 million hectares will make it possible to produce annually sufficient timber to supply surplus for export. The development of new forests will still further augment these possibilities.

Assessments of timber requirements of oblasts of varying levels of economic development permit us to make the following preliminary quantitative predictions.

A forest cover of 5% to 6%, under conditions of proper distribution, is usually sufficient to protect fields from *sukhovey,* dust storms, and erosion (in regions where desiccation is not a severe problem), but such cover does not provide a significant local source of timber. A forest cover of 8% to 10%, under correct management, assures not only field protection but the possibility of a timber supply for the nearby settlements and farms. A forest cover of 10% to 15% is sufficient to satisfy regional needs and some construction materials. Areas with a 20% to 25% forest cover can have the foregoing as well as a forest processing industry. Finally, with a cover of more than 25%, export in raw or processed forest products is possible.

The above indicators, of course, both depend on and vary with natural conditions, the productivity and quality of the forests, the specialization of the economy, and the local availability of various types of fuels.

In the distribution of forestry measures, evaluation of the protective watershed of the forests requires the most serious attention.

Highly interesting data on the role of forests in the replenishment of rivers have been published in the U.S.A. (Worell). According to the research that has been done in a territory that is 20% forested, forest cover provides 40% to 45% of the stable runoff supply and, with a 40% forest cover, it provides 80% to 95%. In other words, 1% of the forested area provided 2% to 2.5% of the stable runoff supply of the river basin. According to O. A. Drozdov, every 10% of additional forested area in the windward portion of a region causes an increase in summer precipitation of 4%. These are highly significant indices of the great water-protective value of forests. A comparison of two interdependent processes, the deforestation of the basin and the runoff of the river, can serve as a useful illustration of the above (Tables 12 and 13).

Until recently it was widely held that the only forests of water-protective significance were those located along rivers. In reality, this is not so. The runoff develops from the entire basin; it can be regulated only by forests that are relatively uniformly distributed throughout, most significantly by forests that cover the watersheds. If the surface of the basin is bare, the runoff, together with the sediments, proceeds without difficulty into gullies and from there through larger ravines and small streams into large rivers. In this case the forests located along rivers can have little influence on the volume and annual regime of the flow. This, however, should not lead us to the conclusion that all riparian forest areas and belts should be exploited in the same way as nonriparian forests. In many places, riparian forests play a particular role: they control part of the flow, small in volume but heavy in sediments, which enter the river from the gully and ravine systems that drain into it. On the portions of the river with sloping banks they

Table 12
The Decline in the Forest Area in the Basin (115,870 km²)
of the Upper Oka River
(After V. F. Kharitonova)

Period and Year	Forest Area	
	km²	*% of Basin*
Period of the General Survey (end of 18th century to beginning of 19th)	18,200	18.8
1860	7,820	6.7
1894	4,180	3.6
1950	3,580	3.1

NOTE: The calculation of the forest area was carried out under the author's direction.

Table 13
The Decline in Runoff and the
Modular Coefficient of the Oka
(After P. S. Kuzin, 1947)

Year	Average Annual Runoff (m³/sec.)	Modular Coefficient
1881–1890	1,505	1.21
1891–1900	1,244	1.00
1901–1910	1,228	0.99
1911–1920	1,118	0.96
1921–1930	1,227	0.99
1931–1940	1,136	0.92
1941–1945	1,035	0.84

NOTE: The modular coefficient is the relationship of the runoff for a given period to the average runoff over the total measured period.

anchor the riverbed, preventing its meandering. These forests restrain the wind, lessen the turbulence of streams and the loss from evaporation. And, finally, along navigable rivers and near river settlements they are of recreational and cultural significance.

Our own published data show that the riparian zones of almost all rivers of the Black and Caspian Sea basins have at present less forest cover than exists in adjacent regions (Vasilyev). Large-scale measures for creating protective forest plantations along the Dnieper are already being implemented in the Ukraine, and similar work is projected around the Volgo-grad, Tsimlyansk, Kremenchug, Kakhovka, Dneprodzerzhinsk, and other reservoirs.

Some comment should be made concerning the required and possible scale of reforestation and silvicultural effort on the lands of the State Forest Reserve, which will play a great role in changing the forest cover of various regions of the country. Of the three million hectares of annual cut, only 30% to 35% is currently restored with economically valuable species; half of the areas become overgrown with deciduous varieties; and 10% to 15% is not reforested at all. There are also large barren areas from previous years of logging. Because of this, reforestation should become primarily the planting and sowing of trees. Measures to assist the natural renewal of forests, usually ineffective, should be considered adequate only in locations with the most favorable conditions for the growth of needed species. In order to bring the total area of certain reforestation to the size of the current "exploitation area" and to begin the reforestation of areas previously logged but still unforested, it is necessary for the area of annual sowing to increase in the next fifteen to twenty years from 750,000 hectares (1960) to 2 to 2.5 million hectares. With the possible high level of forest technology this goal is quite practicable.

The character and direction of reforestation should vary with the region. In the sparsely forested regions of European Russia the objective should be to increase forest productivity and to ensure the fullest introduction of fast-growing, economically valuable species. This will enable those republics, krays, and oblasts that now import timber to cease such import altogether, or to sharply curtail it. The Ukraine has been successful in this endeavor, creating in recent years large poplar plantations on forest reserves and un-productive lands. By 1965, 750,000 hectares of poplar plantations are to be established (Skorodumov et al.). Because of their rapid rate of growth, poplars produce as much as four yields per century while pine is capable of only one. Consequently, these plantations will be equivalent in value, if not in quality, to two million hectares of pine forest.

The growing of quickly maturing tree species is also given much attention in foreign countries, i.e., in Czechoslovakia, the German Democratic Republic, and others. This experimental work should be expanded to a number of sparsely forested oblasts in the RSFSR and to other union republics. Such expansion should be envisaged in conjunction with the shipment of the most transportable wood products, processed in the mills and combines of the densely forested northern and Siberian regions.

The protective role of forests reflects, to the highest degree, on the condition of agricultural land and even on land use. The protection of agricultural land from harmful natural processes—erosion, deflation, and waterlogging—and the improvement of poor land, have been considered important goals for the national economy since the first years of Soviet power, and much has already been done. Specifically, in the USSR, and mainly in its European part, there are about 750,000 hectares of shelter belts on state and collective farms; the Kamyshin–Volgograd, Belgorod–Don, Voronezh–Rostov-on-the-Don, and other state forest belts have been established. Plantations, mainly pine, have also been established on 370,000 hectares of sand; about 30,000 hectares of protective plantings cover gullies and ravines.

Although the achievements have been significant, a comparison of the area under forest-reclamation plantations with the area that requires such improvement reveals that the tasks that remain are still exceptionally great. The determination of the requirements of land for forest protection, on the basis of regional plans and detailed projects of territorial organization, may lead to the establishment of optimal forest cover of sparsely forested regions that exceeds the indices given on the basis of timber needs alone.

Our possibilities and experience in forest protective work are such that, given the necessary technical and financial support, we could cover the agricultural land of the steppe and forest-steppe regions in the course of two decades with a network of shelter belts of adequate density (in the case of the Ukraine, Armenia, and a number of oblasts of the Russian Republic, this would take only five to ten years). The same time would also suffice to fix all of the ravines and gullies (starting with those that enter large reservoirs), and to complete work on stabilizing and afforesting sands that lie within state and collective farms of European Russia and the developed territories of Central Asia and Kazakhstan. The realization of this program would ensure fundamental and long-term improvement of state and collective farm lands in the zone of variable and inadequate moisture supply (an area of about 150 million hectares), and to obtain ultimately additional products from crop cultivation and livestock raising in volumes not inferior to the average gross yield from the virgin lands during 1956–61.

The area under shelter belts, encompassing 750,000 hectares, should be expanded to about 3.5 million hectares. For this, it is necessary to provide for the protection of 150 to 170 thousand hectares of state and collective farm fields annually. Plantings·in gullies and ravines should be made on not less than 1.5 million hectares, and up to 1.8 million on sands. Protective forest plantings should be carried out not only in the steppe and forest-steppe regions of European Russia but also in those regions of Siberia, the Soviet Far East, and Central Asia where the need is obvious. In the Asian part of the USSR, however, the need for protective plantings is not encompassed by the indices above. Here, apparently, fundamental forest reclamation work will continue beyond the fifteen or thirty-year period.

The total area of all types of protective plantations will ultimately exceed 6 million hectares. Apart from their direct protective significance, these plantations, by producing 3 cubic meters per hectare of timber annually, will yield about 18 million cubic meters of timber, i.e., somewhat more than the annual requirements of the Ukraine.

The creation of parks and green belts around cities and workers' settlements should be expanded. Calculations show that about 1.2 million hectares of such green areas should be established, including more than 700,000 hectares in the RSFSR. Parks should serve as places of rest for the workers and at the same time reflect the achievements of the science and practice of forestry. As one illustration of the above, the schematic project that we proposed in 1956 for the creation of a national park, Russkiy Les, in the vicinity of Moscow may be cited. It was to be composed of three parts, each containing several thousand hectares. The first section, which would connect with one of the existing parks on the outskirts of the city, would serve as a place of rest; here there would be groves of various forest plantings and a forest museum. In the second, Soviet and foreign foresters would have the opportunity of establishing plantings reflecting their own original schemes. At the same time, groves of all species of the temperate zone should be established. The third section would demonstrate proper organization of forest economy.

The achievement of all forms of forest renewal and development on the suggested scale will lead to a significant increase in the forest cover of individual oblasts and regions. According to available estimates, therefore, the forest cover of the Povolzhye (within the boundaries of the Gosplan region prior to 1960) * will increase from 7.7% to at least 10.3%; of the Ukrainian SSR, from 10.3% to 14.5%; and of the Uzbek SSR, from 11.5% to 14.2%.

In order to satisfy fully needs for timber and forest-chemical products, both internal and for export, as well as to strengthen the protective, hydrologic, climatic, and recreational role of forests; in order to optimize the forest cover and at the same time to raise the productivity of forests of all

---

* The pre-1960 Gosplan Volga (Povolzhye) Region included those provinces on either side of the river from the Volga-Kama confluence to its mouth in the Caspian Sea. (The thirteen-region Gosplan scheme that had existed since the early part of World War II was modified in 1956–57 when the number of regions was raised to sixteen. In May, 1961, a new scheme, consisting essentially of nineteen regions, was introduced only to be modified again in 1962.)

groups, it is necessary to utilize carefully the forest wealth, to ensure expanded renewal, and to intensify the training of cadres in forest work and scientific research in the fields of forestry and forest reclamation.

BIBLIOGRAPHY

Drozdov, O. A. *Krugovorot vlagi i ego rol v prirodnykh protsessakh* [Moisture Circulation and its Role in Natural Processes]. Leningrad, 1960. Materialy k III syezdu Geogr. ob-va SSSR. Doklady po probleme "Vodno-teplovoy rezhim zemnoy poverkhnosti" [Materials of the III Session of the Geographical Society of the USSR. Papers concerning the problem "The Heat and Water Regime of the Earth's Surface"].

Fogel, D. and Shiglovskiy, B. "Perebros stoka severnykh rek" [Transfer of Run-off of the Northern Rivers] *Lesnaya promyshlennost,* no. 5 (1961).

Kovalin, D. T. *Lesnoye khozyaystvo SSSR v 1959–1965 gg.* [Forest Economy of the USSR in 1959–1965]. Moscow-Leningrad: Goslesbumizdat, 1959.

Kuzin, P. S. "O vliyanii vyrubki lesa na stok r. Volgi" [Concerning the Influence of Deforestation on the Run-off of the River Volga]. In *Trudy Gos. gidrol. in-ta* [Works of the State Hydrological Institute], vol. 1, no. 55. Leningrad, 1947.

Lesnoye khozyaystvo SSSR 1917–1957 [Forest Economy of the USSR 1917–1957]. Moscow-Leningrad: Goslesbumizdat, 1958.

Lesnoy fond RSFSR (Statisticheskiy sbornik) [Forest Fund of the RSFSR (Statistical Handbook)]. Moscow-Leningrad: Goslesbumizdat, 1958.

Molchanov, A. A. *Gidrologicheskaya rol lesa* [The Hydrologic Role of the Forest]. Moscow: AN SSR, 1960.

Rudzskiy, A. F. *Lektsii gosudarstvennogo lesnogo khozyaystva, chitannye v 1885–1886 gg.* [Lectures on the National Forest Economy, read in 1885–1886]. Petrograd, 1917.

Skorodumov, O. S., Pastushenko, V. O., Dunayevskiy, V. N. *Eroziya hruntiv i borotba z neyu* [Soil Erosion and the Struggle With It]. Kiyiv: Ukraynska akademiya silskohospodarskikh nauk, 1961.

Spravochnik po uchetu lesnogo fonda SSSR (na 1 yanvarya 1956 g.) [Handbook for Calculating the Forest Fund of the USSR, as of January 1, 1956]. Moscow: Min-vo selsk. khozyaystva, 1957.

Tseplyayev, V. P. *Lesa SSSR. Khozyaystvennaya kharakterestika* [The Forests of the USSR. Economic Characteristics]. Moscow: Selkhozgiz, 1961.

Tsvetkov, M. A. *Izmeneniye lesistosti Yevropeyskoy Rossii s kontsa XVII stoletiya po 1914 g.* [The Change in Forest Cover of European Russia from the End of the 17th Century to 1914]. Moscow-Leningrad: AN SSSR, 1957.

Vasilyev, P. V. *Voprosy geograficheskogo izucheniya i khozyaystvennogo ispolzovaniya lesov* [Problems of Geographical Study and Economic Use of Forests]. Leningrad, 1959. Materialy k III syezdu Geogr. ob-va SSSR. Doklady po probleme "Rol geografii v izuchenii, ispolzovanii, okhrane i vosstanovlenii prirodnykh resursov SSSR" [Materials of the III Session of the Geographical Society of the USSR. Papers concerning the problem "The Role of Geography in the Study, Utilization, Protection and Renewal of Natural Resources of the USSR"].

Vasilyev, P. V. et al. *Ekonomika lesnogo khozyaystva SSSR* [Economics of Forestry of the USSR]. Moscow-Leningrad: Goslesbumizdat, 1959.

Voprosy lesovedeniya i lesovodstva (Doklady na V Vsemirnom lesnom kongresse) [Problems of Forestry (Papers of the Vth World Forest Congress)]. Moscow: AN SSSR, 1960.

Vyzgo, G. S. "O generalnom plane ispolzovaniya vodnykh zemelnykh i energeticheskikh resursov" [Concerning a General Plan of Utilization of Water, Land, and Energy Resources]. *Geografiya i khozyaystvo*, no. 6. Moscow, 1960.

World Forestry Inventory, 1958. Rome: United Nations FAO, 1960.

Worrell, A. C. *Economics of American Forestry*. New York: Wiley, 1959.

A World Geography of Forest Resources. Edited for the American Geographical Society by Stephen Haden-Guest, John K. Wright, and Eileen M. Teclaff. New York: Ronald, 1956.

12. Natural Fodder Lands: Their Use and Improvement

L. N. Sobelev

(*Institute of Geography, Academy of Sciences of the USSR*)

The national economic plan of the USSR foresees the complete satisfaction of the growing needs of the population in livestock products. This achievement, as is known, rests primarily upon an increase in the production of feed. In comparison with 1958, the latter must be increased by more than three times. In order to reach this goal much will have to be done.

There are two ways of producing fodder: by field cultivation and through the use of natural pastures and hay lands. According to the Twenty-second Congress of the CPSU, attention should be directed mainly toward the development of cultivated fodder production.[1] However, the challenge of increasing the use of natural-fodder lands cannot be ignored.

The area of natural fodder lands in primary use in 1958 was 726 million hectares, i.e., one-third of the total area of the country. Of this, 354 million hectares consisted of reindeer pastures in the tundra, 317 million hectares of other pastures, and 55 million hectares of hay lands.[2]

The average productivity of our natural fodder lands is low. Exclusive of the tundra, hay yields average less than 13 centners per hectare, and pastures produce less than 4 centners of fodder (translated into hay units). By comparison, the average productivity of natural fodder lands in the United States is 20 centners per hectare. This discrepancy can be explained by the fact that the area of improved fodder lands is relatively low in the Soviet Union (somewhat more than one million hectares) and that natural pastures have been neglected.

---

[1] See N. S. Khrushchev, Speech on behalf of the Central Committee of the CPSU to the Twenty-second Congress of the CPSU and the consequent resolution of the congress, in *Materialy XXII syezda KPSS* [Materials of the Twenty-second Congress of the CPSU]. Moscow, 1961.

[2] Pasturing and hay production are practiced not only on lands designated for such use, but also secondarily on forest lands, long-term fallow lands, and so forth.

Seeding increases significantly natural hay production. One hectare of good natural flood-plain meadowland can yield about 25 centners of hay; however, one hectare sown to a mixture of clover and timothy yields 80 to 120 centners. This difference is especially important in places where the area used for fodder production is small. However, not only the sowing of perennial grasses but also the maintenance of their productivity requires appreciable expenditures, including those for fertilizer. Sown grasses require a labor input of as much as twice that required for natural hay lands. Cultivated fodder crops require even higher labor inputs (Table 1).

Mountain hay lands require six times the effort of those in lowland or level regions. The difference in labor, and consequently in production costs, is even greater between cultivated and natural pastures; the cost of use of the latter in some regions represents no more than the payments to the herder.

Intensive methods of cultivated fodder production are economic wherever natural pasture lands are limited and when low-cost natural fodder is insufficient. In those regions, however, where there is little cultivated or arable land, or where the labor force is limited, natural fodder production remains significant. Thus, a full and proper use of natural hay lands and pastures, together with maintenance and improvement, are important in the development of animal husbandry. Such natural hay lands, however, are far from being fully and rationally used, largely owing to deficiencies in organization. Many agricultural workers consider that natural hay lands and pastures need no production inputs, but these areas actually require attentive, rational, and cautious care, varying according to their different natural conditions. The volume of feed obtained from unimproved lands can be raised by increasing yields as well as by expanding the area of use.

Table 1
Gross Labor (in man-days) Expended Annually on Various Fodder Crops and Natural Hay (USSR averages per hectare)

	Degree of Mechanization	
	Low	High
Root crops	98.2	48.2
Silage crops	19.2	5.0
Perennial grasses	8.8	2.5
Annual grasses	6.0	1.6
Natural hay (on plains)	4.0	1.1

The fodder base and feed requirements differ greatly in the different parts of the Soviet Union, so an increase in feed production cannot be achieved by applying standard methods everywhere.

In regions of intensive land use, a further expansion in animal husbandry can be achieved by stall feeding cattle and by assuring a supply of concentrated and succulent fodder, which entails replacing crops of low productivity with crops of high productivity. Special attention should be given to producing grain (particularly corn) and legumes (mainly peas and beans, and also chickpea and soybeans) to provide the stock with needed albumen. To accomplish this, special crop rotations should be established in areas already under cultivation, and lands of little productivity, which are in the process of being improved (for example, marsh lands) should also be used. Their development requires a heavy labor input and in many regions of intensive agriculture labor reserves must be adequate to the task.

In those regions where the labor force is inadequate for intensification or where natural conditions are unfavorable, attention should be given primarily to the improvement of natural hay lands and pastures. Much of these lands where the production of cultivated crops is impossible could be successfully sown to perennial grasses. A uniform, thoughtless application of grass seeding within a crop rotation system will lead to a reduction in output, although if carried out in proper proportion it may not only increase production but also improve the soil (through the development of drained marshes, of leached solonets and sandy soils, and the protection of slopes from erosion).*

An appraisal of the potentials of fodder production in the various regions of the Soviet Union is a geographical task that requires an evaluation of physical and economic data.

The USSR is divided into several natural zones, each of which is characterized by a specific combination of natural pastures and hay lands (Table 2).

In the tundra and forest-tundra zones, the pastures consist of berries, lichens, and mosses, yielding up to 5 centners of dry fodder per hectare.

---

* It seems likely that the reference to "uniform, thoughtless application of grass seeding" pertains to the *travopol* system that was expanded during the 1930s. This entailed the indiscriminate sowing of grasses throughout the USSR under natural conditions that led to unsatisfactory results: In many regions, the widespread application of the system led to a reduction in livestock fodder. In the Non-Chernozem Zone, for example, clover, the most important element in the grass mixture, did not survive. In the Ukraine, the sowing of grasses led to a reduction in the valuable winter wheat crop. Finally, in 1954, Khrushchev criticized the indiscriminate sowing of grasses, after which there was a decrease in grass fodder production. Grasses were further downgraded in 1962 as the regime sought other solutions to the livestock feed problem.

Table 2
Distribution of Hay Lands and Pastures Within Each Natural Zone of the USSR (In percentages)

Types of Natural Fodder Lands	Tundra	Forest		Forest Steppe and Steppe		Semidesert and Desert		Mountain Areas of the South and Southeast		Total USSR	
	Pastures	Hay Lands	Pastures	Hay Lands	Pastures	Hay Lands	Pastures	Hay Lands	Pastures	Hay Lands	Pastures
Dry meadow	—	15.7	29.4	0.7	0.3	—	—	6.5	0.9	8.6	1.1
Meadow steppe	—	—	1.2	15.3	14.4	—	—	7.8	1.0	5.0	1.6
Steppe on loam soils	—	—	—	14.1	60.4	3.5	12.3	12.0	6.7	5.8	10.8
Sandy steppe	—	—	—	3.3	10.5	—	—	—	0.1	0.9	0.9
Semidesert and desert on loam soils	—	—	—	—	—	10.8	41.5	2.1	10.2	1.7	16.0
Sandy semidesert and desert	—	—	—	—	—	13.1	36.0	0.2	1.5	1.7	12.9
Lowland and coastal meadows	—	29.3	34.3	4.7	1.6	2.3	—	2.3	0.2	15.9	1.3
Liman	—	—	—	18.3	7.1	27.6	3.3	5.0	1.5	9.0	2.0
Solonchak	—	—	—	—	—	1.4	5.2	0.1	0.8	0.2	2.0
Subject to short-term flooding	—	18.0	7.4	21.4	4.3	19.6	1.3	10.0	2.2	18.3	1.6
Subject to long-term flooding	3.3	11.7	2.6	16.9	0.7	14.3	0.1	11.6	—	13.5	1.5
Mountain meadow	—	—	7.9	—	—	—	—	11.3	6.5	1.2	1.0
Mountain steppe	—	—	—	—	—	—	—	18.0	25.7	2.1	3.1
Mountain semidesert and desert	—	—	—	—	—	—	—	1.9	17.8	0.2	2.1
Alpine meadow	—	—	—	—	—	—	—	5.6	19.0	0.6	2.3
Alpine semidesert and desert	—	—	—	—	—	—	—	—	5.0	—	0.6
Mountain tundra	—	—	2.3	—	—	—	—	—	—	—	0.1
Tundra	96.7	—	—	—	—	—	—	—	—	—	38.3
Other	—	25.3	14.9	5.3	0.7	7.4	0.3	5.6	0.9	15.3	0.8

Meadows are concentrated here only in the flood plains of large rivers and, as in other zones, they are highly productive, yielding up to 25 centners of hay per hectare.

In the forest zone, especially in the European part of the USSR, most of the cleared land was converted into plowland but meadows remain on some dry and low-lying watersheds and flood plains. Watershed meadows, particularly those that are dry, are less productive than flood plains; they are, moreover, frequently interspersed with bogs. With proper use, dry meadows can yield up to 15 centners of dry fodder per hectare while flood plains could yield up to 30.

The same types of natural fodder land also characterize the forest-steppe zone. Watershed meadow and, to some extent, steppe fodder lands are concentrated here in ravines and depressions. In the southern part of the zone they are found in solonchak flats as well as in flood plains. The rest of the area, with the exception of the forests, is under cultivation.

The steppe zone has still more land unsuitable for cultivation, particularly in Siberia and Kazakhstan. Here the soils are salty, sandy, and gravelly. They are used for pasture and yield only from 3 to 5 centners of hay per hectare, but can be improved through seeding. In addition, there are hay lands along the flood plains of the rivers. The arable land in the steppe is almost completely cultivated.

In the semiarid and arid zones, there are large expanses of grass and sagebrush steppe and of sagebrush and thistle desert. Without irrigation, these lands are of little use for agriculture, especially where brown, gray-brown, and gray soils are widespread and where the soils are intensively solonized and gravelly. Desert sands also occupy large areas here. These lands are used for grazing but yield no more than 3 centners of dry fodder per hectare. Finally, in the semidesert and desert zones are a series of valleys, lacustrine lowlands and basins in the sands, covered by meadows of the flood plain and *liman* type. They can provide up to 30 centners of hay per hectare and are an important fodder reserve for grazing.

The natural fodder areas of northern mountain regions differ little from the meadows of the plains. On the other hand, the fodder lands of the southern mountains—the Caucasus, Pamir, Tyan-Shan, and Altay—differ from the neighboring level areas. Here mountain meadow, mountain steppe, and even mountain desert lands are used for grazing and in part for haying, in conjunction with the pastures of the piedmont. The mountain meadows of the Altay are especially productive.

A summary of the conditions of the fodder base of the USSR, according to Gosplan economic regions (within the boundaries of 1961), is given below. Ways in which this base can be improved, taking into consideration the decisions of the Twenty-second Congress of the CPSU, are also indicated. Each region is described according to the present composition of its fodder base, the future development of fodder production, and the measures necessary for the improvement of natural hay lands and pastures. Problems associated with the organization of cultivated fodder production are not discussed since they are linked with crop cultivation.

1. *The Northwest Region* (total area 1,678,000 square kilometers) includes Murmansk, Arkhangelsk, Vologda, Leningrad, Novgorod, Pskov, and Kaliningrad oblasts, and the Komi and Karelian ASSR's. The region can be divided according to the nature of its pastures into three parts: the northern (tundra and forest-tundra), the southeastern, and the southwestern, the latter two of which are of a forest type.

Natural fodder lands predominate in northern Murmansk and Arkhangelsk oblasts. Coniferous pastures (up to 25% of the territory), which suffer severely from trampling and overgrazing, replenish their fodder stocks very slowly. Grass-scrub pastures occupy up to 40% of the territory; meadows are located only along the southern boundary. They require some clearing, do not exceed 5%, but are rarely cut for hay. The largest area is occupied by bogs (which in the north constitute as much as 70% of the territory). In the south about 30% of the land is covered by sparse forests.

Reindeer herding is the principal form of husbandry in the northern part of the region, but dairying is practiced near large mining settlements.

Improvement and proper utilization of the fodder base require the following: drainage of marshes, expansion of meadows (by clearing brush and boulders), introduction of haying, control of grazing with a more uniform use of the grazing area, and provision of stall-feeding supplies for cattle.

The southeastern part of the region includes southern Murmansk and Arkhangelsk oblasts, Vologda Oblast, and the Komi and Karelian ASSR's. Here, forests predominate and there is relatively little crop land; there are many bogs, with large areas of flood-plain meadows along the rivers. Animal husbandry is largely confined to dairying, and the feed supply should consist of natural hay and cultivated fodder grains, legumes, and root crops.

Large areas of natural hay lands and pastures require drainage and clearing of brush and boulders. In Karelia, where the average productivity of hay lands is less than 10 centners per hectare, the drained meadows on the Polar Pioneer State Farm produce 60 centners. Fertilization of meadows is also effective here.

The southwestern part of the region includes Leningrad, Novgorod,

Pskov, and Kaliningrad oblasts. Forests have been cleared over large areas and the ratio of land under cultivation is higher than in the southeast. However, there are also many swamps and meadows that need to be cleared of brush and boulders. Livestock raising in this region is largely for dairying and hog breeding, to meet the needs of the population of several industrial cities. Potatoes, root crops, grains, and legumes, as well as hay from improved and cultivated hay lands, should be widely used for fodder. Meadow fertilization is effective, and the successful experience of Kaliningrad Oblast in the cultivation of grasses is well known.

2. *The Central (Moscow) Region* has a total territory of 460,000 square kilometers and includes Kalinin, Yaroslavl, Kostroma, Moscow, Ivanovo, Vladimir, Smolensk, Bryansk, Ryazan, Kaluga, and Tula oblasts. Its northern part belongs to the forest zone; its southern to the forest-steppe. Agricultural lands in different oblasts vary between 30% and 80% of the territory, with more than one-half the agricultural land arable. There is a shortage of pastures; as a result, the livestock graze on stubble, postharvest cultivated grasses, and in forests in the north (grazing in forests is harmful). Ravine slopes are used for grazing in the southern part of the region. Stall feed consists primarily of silage, natural hay, and concentrates.

To satisfy the growing food requirements of this important region, with its rapidly developing industry, the production of fodder crops such as grains, corn for silage (which yields up to 800 centners of green silage per hectare), legumes (peas and beans), and root crops must be increased appreciably. The area of fodder land can be expanded by means of developing new fields from logged-over, brush-covered, or marshy lands.

It should be mentioned that some of the flood-plain hay lands that are potentially highly productive should not be put to cultivated fodder, because a small additional investment could realize their natural productivity. Moreover, cultivated land is subject to erosion or alluviation.

3. *The Volga-Vyatka Region,* with a territory of 263,000 square kilometers, includes Gorki and Kirov oblasts, and the Chuvash, Mari, and Mordvin ASSR's. As in the Central Region, the northern part belongs to the forest and the southern part to the forest-steppe. The right bank of the Volga is agriculturally more developed than the left. Agricultural land occupies from 25% to 60% of the territory; the ratio of arable land is lower than in the Central Region, but on the other hand, there are more forests and marshes.

Fodder crops should be developed in the same manner as in the Central Region. Since agriculture is less developed and there is a lack of labor in the region, much attention should be given to the improvement and expansion of the natural fodder area. Fundamental improvement of flood plains of low productivity has produced excellent results. The Agitator Collective Farm in the Dalne-Konstantinov District of Gorki Oblast, for example, which improved flood plains of low productivity for cultivated pasture rotation, has obtained 230 centners of hay per hectare from two cuttings. Significant areas can be drained and cleared of brush and stumps.

4. *The Central Black Earth Region,* with a territory of 192,000 square kilometers located in the forest-steppe zone, includes Voronezh, Lipetsk, Kursk, Belgorod, Orel, and Tambov oblasts. Its black soils are highly productive, and agriculture is intensively practiced, with 80% to 85% of the territory in farmland, much of which is arable. Livestock graze on slopes of ravines and in the flood plains of small streams. Pastures are badly trampled and weed-infested and eroded on slopes, although the erosion is not as severe as on cultivated slopes. Livestock are turned loose on stubble and in fields sown to grass after harvest. Fodder-crop production is well developed and stall feeding is supplemented by straw.

To expand livestock production it is necessary to increase the share of fodder crops in rotation (corn for grain and green silage, Sudan grass, grain-legumes, fodder melons, and root crops), and to increase their yields. In areas where erosion is a danger, systems of crop rotation should be established to protect the soil, and the area under perennial grasses should be increased. Furthermore, hay lands and pastures must be used wisely to control livestock densities and to prevent overgrazing and trampling, and the proper time for harvesting hay must be observed.

5. *The Volga Region,* with a territory of 461,000 square kilometers, can be divided according to natural conditions into three parts:

(*a*) The northern, or the forest-steppe zone, including the Tatar ASSR, Penza, Ulyanovsk, and Kuybyshev oblasts, and the northern part of Saratov Oblast.

(*b*) The central or steppe zone, which includes the southern part of Saratov and the northern part of Volgograd oblasts.

(*c*) The southern, or semidesert zone, containing the southern part of Volgograd Oblast and Astrakhan Oblast.

The northern region is partly forested and is dominated by gray forest loams and leached chernozems. Here, crop cultivation, dairying, and hog raising are developed. The central part is almost free of forests, is dominated by ordinary and southern chernozems, and is widely cultivated. The south is also without forests, and typically has chestnut and brown soils. Only small areas are cultivated, principally under irrigation. In the Caspian Sea lowland, sheep raising predominates. The area of pastures and hay lands in the region varies from 20% in the north to 75% in the south.

The changes that have occurred since the construction of the power dams on the Volga have been of great significance; the meadow land in the Volga valley has disappeared, but at the same time great potentials for irrigation have been opened, which is essential for the production of fodder.

The expected expansion in livestock requires a threefold increase in fodder production, which means the development, in the northern and central parts of the region, of such crops as corn for grain and silage, Sudan grass, sunflowers, sugar beets, melons, peas, and beans; chickpea must be developed in the most southerly districts. In the semiarid lands of the south, which are unsuited to cultivation, pastures must be improved by crop rotation, creating hay reserves for dry years, and by introducing snow-retention schemes. The organization of *liman* irrigation as well as regular irrigation is of special significance here since great possibilities exist.

Areas suitable for *liman* irrigation, according to SOPS * data for 1958, were calculated at 88,000 hectares for Kuybyshev; 84,000 for Saratov; 183,000 for Volgograd; and 43,000 in the former Kamensk Oblast (Ostrovnaya). *Liman* irrigation permits, in places where hay and pasture lands yielded only 3 to 5 centners of dry fodder, an increase in output of an average of up to 50 centners of couch-grass hay, and with the sowing of a grass mixture (alfalfa, sainfoin, broom, and meadow fescue grass) up to 100 centners per hectare. On some of these lands it is possible, through *liman* irrigation, to produce field fodder crops. Therefore, such irrigation is especially important for animal husbandry in the southern part of the region. The sowing of grass (wheat grass, alfalfa, lady fern) is advisable here, even on unirrigated and uncultivable land.

6. *The North Caucasus Region,* with a territory of 431,000 square kilometers, contains Rostov Oblast, Krasnodar and Stavropol krays, and the Kabardino-Balkar, North Osetin, Chechen-Ingush, Dagestan, and Kalmyk ASSR's.

The Azov Sea littoral, in the northwest, has fertile black soils under intensive use, including the production of fodder crops. In the northeast lie the semidesert pastures of Kalmykia and the Nogay steppe. In the south are the foothills and the northern slopes of the Great Caucasus Range, with its natural hay lands and pastures. The southwest is part of the Black Sea

---

* Sovet po Izucheniyu Proizvoditelnykh Sil [The Council for the Study of the Productive Forces].

littoral, an area whose natural conditions are very similar to those of the humid subtropics.

Natural fodder lands cover about 35% of the entire territory. The ratio between hay lands and pastures varies from region to region: in the mountains, hay lands occupy up to 10%, pastures as much as 40%; in Kalmykia there are only pastures; while in the Azov Sea lowlands, the pastures occupy up to 40% and hay lands up to 8%.

The mountains and semidesert areas are most suited for sheep and cattle grazing, but where crops are cultivated, hog raising should be expanded. The volume of fodder production per hectare of agricultural land should be tripled.

In the northwestern and southwestern parts of the region and in the Caucasus piedmont, the cultivation of fodder crops should be increased. Corn is of special value here because it can produce over 1,000 centners of green fodder per hectare (the average is 600 centners) and 35 centners of grain per hectare. In the "Memory of Ilych" Collective Farm in Novo-Titarov District in Krasnodar Kray, Sudan grass has produced up to 127 centners of hay per hectare. Melons, root fodder crops such as potatoes, together with pulses, should be considered important. Good results have been obtained by keeping sheep in feed-lot corrals; experiments with complete feed-lot maintenance have been carried out in Stavropol and Krasnodar krays.

The semidesert part of the northeast is in need of those measures that were recommended for the semidesert part of the Volga region, if the pastoral economy is to be improved. The proper use of the Terek-Kuma sand expanses (the Nogay steppe) is of great importance, but a sod must be established on the sands.

In the southern, mountainous part of the region, the natural pastures must be subjected to controlled grazing and improved, i.e., scrub cleared, grass seeded, and so forth. Grazing in mountain forests, particularly in forest reserves and areas of reforestation, must not be tolerated. Cattle can be kept on the plateaus of highland Dagestan even in the winter.

7. *The Ural Region,* with an area of 2.3 million square kilometers, includes Sverdlovsk, Perm, Chelyabinsk, Tyumen, Kurgan, and Orenburg oblasts, and the Udmurt and Bashkir ASSR's. This region contains the Ural Mountains and adjacent plains. The territory extends along a north-south axis and can be divided into four zones: tundra and forest-tundra, forest, forest-steppe, and steppe. The fodder base and the resources of the northernmost zone of this region are analogous to those of the tundra of the Northwestern Region. The forest zone is predominantly taiga; agri-

cultural land occupies about 20%. The West Siberian Lowland, situated to the east of the Ural Mountains, is very swampy, with few pastures; grazing often occurs on postharvest growth, on stubble, and in forests. Natural hay and silage are used for stall feeding.

Crop cultivation is not as well developed as in the forest regions further to the west, leading to a shortage of cultivated fodder crops. Livestock raising should serve the population of the industrial centers and should be directed toward meat and dairy cattle and hog raising. Thus, cultivated fodder production must be expanded in order to double the quantity of concentrated and succulent feed (potatoes, corn for silage, root crops, grains and pulses). However, since the amount of arable land is low, and the population is employed mainly in industry, considerable attention should also be paid to the expansion and improvement of the fodder area, through draining the marshes, clearing burned and cutover areas and scrub land, and by improving the meadows through effective grass seeding.

The forest-steppe and the steppe zones of the Ural Region include principally Bashkiria, and Kurgan and Orenburg oblasts. Tillage and cultivated fodder production are appreciably more developed here than in the forest zone. Livestock raising is fairly well developed and considerable areas of virgin land have been recently opened up.

More grain corn, pulses, corn and sunflowers for silage, root plants, and melons should be grown. Natural fodder lands consist of nonarable solonets and sandy steppe soils and, in the southern Urals, of mountain meadow lands. They require improvement, clearing, snow retention, and proper timing of haying. Part of the land in the steppe zone could be successfully reclaimed through the sowing of grasses (brome grass, wheat grass, sainfoin, and alfalfa). The organization of *liman* irrigation is important in the steppe. Thus, with an annual volume of runoff that is guaranteed available 50% of the time, 15,000 hectares of land can be irrigated in Bashkiria; 72,000 in Chelyabinsk Oblast; 43,000 in Kurgan Oblast; and 194,000 in Orenburg Oblast.

8. *The Western Siberian Region* includes Tomsk, Novosibirsk, Omsk, and Kemerovo oblasts, as well as Altay Kray, occupying about one million square kilometers. According to its natural conditions, the region may be divided into three zones: the northern (taiga), the central (forest-steppe and steppe), and the southern (mountains).

The northern zone is relatively undeveloped, with little arable land and the fodder base consisting of natural pastures and hay lands. The extent of the latter is inadequate and, as a result, forest grazing occurs.

In the center of the region, crop cultivation is important, particularly on the chernozems (about 20 million hectares). The cultivation of virgin land continues here, with great possibilities for the expansion of fodder crop cultivation, using crops similar to the corresponding zone of the Ural Region. Lands unsuited to tillage, such as solonets and sandy soils, should be used as natural fodder land, partially under sown grasses, which are essential to the building of turf. The forest-steppe, and especially the steppe, have great possibilities for *liman* irrigation, which can raise the productivity of natural fodder lands from 5 to 40 centners per hectare. Part of the lands under *liman* irrigation should be used for the production of cultivated fodder crops. Potential areas of *liman* irrigation, using local runoff with a 50% certainty, amount to 147,000 hectares in Novosibirsk Oblast, 50,000 in Omsk Oblast, and 148,000 in Altay Kray (Ostrovnaya).

The southern region belongs to the Altay Mountains, and crop cultivation is confined to fodder crops in valleys. Much of the territory is covered by mountain forests, meadows, and steppes. Meadows and steppes reach 2,800 meters above sea level, and in alpine reaches are replaced by tundra. Part of the mountains can be used for winter grazing if adequate supplementary fodder is stored. Hay cutting in the mountains should be developed and fodder crop production should be expanded in the valleys.

9. *The Eastern Siberian Region,* covering 7.2 million square kilometers, includes Krasnoyarsk Kray, Irkutsk and Chita oblasts, and the Yakut, Buryat, and Tuvinian ASSR's. It can be divided into the tundra and forest-tundra in the north, the taiga in the center, and the steppe in the south. The last occupies a rather small area, including parts of Chita Oblast and the Tuvinian and Buryat ASSR's.

The northern part of the region is similar to the tundra and forest-tundra of the Northwestern and Ural regions. The central part, forested and mountainous, is little developed. Meadow and steppelike areas are found only in the central Yakut lowland. There is little crop cultivation, the arable area amounting to less than 1%, while the total agricultural area comprises only about 4%. The southern part of the region, which includes the larch forest-steppe and the steppe, is more developed. Somewhat more arable land is found here although pastoral activities dominate the southern margins of the region.

The expanding industrial centers of Eastern Siberia should be surrounded by an agriculture that is equally dynamic, particularly an animal husbandry that would obviously necessitate an increase in the production of cultivated fodder and an expansion and improvement in the natural hay lands and pastures. Irrigation from water springs and snow retention, both practical in the Eastern Siberian steppe, permit an increase in the productivity of meadows from 4 to 30 centners of hay per hectare, particularly when these measures are combined with the application of fertilizer.

10. *The Soviet Far Eastern Region* includes Kamchatka, Magadan, Amur, and Sakhalin oblasts, and Maritime and Khabarovsk krays, with a territory exceeding three million square kilometers.

The northern part lies in the tundra and forest-tundra, with a fodder base analogous to that of similar territories in the other regions. The rest of the Soviet Far Eastern Region is forested. Agriculture is very little developed, not exceeding 3% of the territory.

Waterlogging and the lack of nitrogen, calcium, and phosphorus in the soils have a negative influence on the quality of fodder and the condition of the livestock. Hay yields up to eleven centners and pastures up to six centners of dry fodder per hectare. Hay and pasture lands require drainage, fertilization, and liming. Experience on the "Road to Communism" Collective Farm in Khabarovsk Kray shows that discing (loosening and combing) of the turf is an effective land improvement measure.

Suitable for the production of field fodder are soybeans, Sudan grass, and silage corn. Fallow lands under couch grass create valuable pastures, requiring no additional labor inputs. In the development of land it is, therefore, expedient to retain part of them for hay.

11. *The Western Region,* covering 174,000 square kilometers, includes the Estonian, Latvian, and Lithuanian SSR's. The region is similar in its fodder base to the Belorussian SSR, which contains 194,000 square kilometers, and which is also included here.

The region is forested, has many marshes, poor soils, and extensive sands. Agricultural lands comprise no more than one-half the territory of the area. Frequently these lands must be cleared of boulders (especially in the Baltic republics) and of scrub.

In the Estonian SSR, the arable area comprises 45% of all the agricultural land; in Latvia it is 65%; in Lithuania, 75%; in Belorussia, 62%. Everywhere hay lands exceed the area of pastures. The leading forms of animal husbandry are dairying and hog raising, with cultivated crops as the principal sources of fodder, although the Baltic republics also lead in the organization and use of cultivated hay lands and pastures, particularly those that have been drained. Corn is sown successfully for silage. In the "Tyotus" Collective Farm in the Keylas District of Estonia, 1,000 centners of green fodder per hectare have been obtained; average yields of silage crops range from 400 to 600 centners per hectare.

New lands can be developed through drainage and the clearing of scrub, logged, and burned-over areas. Belorussia contains the greatest potential.

Various perennial grasses (clover and timothy) should be used for land improvement.

12. *The Southwestern Region* includes Chernigov, Volyn, Rovno, Zhitomyr, Kiev, Trans-Carpathia, Lvov, Stanislav, Khmelnitskiy, Ternopol, Chernovtsy, Cherkassy, Vinnitsa, and Kirovograd oblasts, totaling 293,000 square kilometers. The Moldavian SSR possesses a similar fodder base (its territory is 33,700 square kilometers).

The region is a black-earth plain, with about 85% of the agricultural land arable. Only in the west is the plain disrupted by the Carpathian Mountains, containing rich pastures. In the remaining parts of the region there is little pasture and hay land. Large areas of flooded meadows have disappeared as a result of the construction of dams and reservoirs on the Dnieper River; their loss should be compensated for by the development of fodder crops in irrigated areas.

Cattle breeding and hog raising predominate, with up to 85% of all feed currently consisting of fodder crops, of which a considerable amount is straw. Grazing on stubble and in fields after harvest is widespread.

A further increase in the output of feed should come from increased use of rotation fodder crops and an increase in yields (of grains; particularly of the pulses; of silage crops; and, in the north, of potatoes). A postharvest corn crop can be obtained in the southern part of the region and in Moldavia. Pastures should be expanded and improved through the clearing of lands covered by scrub, by draining marshes, and by pasture control on the slopes of ravines accompanied by measures for erosion prevention.

Careful attention should be paid to the production of fodder in the Carpathian Mountains where grazing control, the clearing of pastures and, in some places, the additional seeding of grasses and fertilization (for instance, on the mountain mat-grass regions) should be practiced.

13. *The Southern Region,* a territory of 111,000 square kilometers that includes Odessa, Nikolayev, Kherson, and Crimean oblasts, is well developed. About 85% of all agricultural land is arable. Cattle breeding and sheep raising are the predominant branches of animal husbandry but there is little pasture, and hay lands and field crops provide the bulk of the feed. The pastures along the Black Sea are partly sandy, saline, and of low productivity. Cattle are also grazed in the Crimean Mountains.

There is a shortage of fodder, and further development of livestock raising demands a substantial increase in the production of cultivated fodder crops, especially of corn (both for grain and for green fodder), of root crops, and melons. *Liman* irrigation is inadequately developed, although the territory is suitable for it, especially in northern Crimea. The sandy alluvial flats should produce hay. Proper irrigation in the Dnieper Valley can also increase the production of field-grown fodder and of cultivated hay lands and pastures.

Grazing in the Crimean Mountains should be strictly regulated everywhere, and in some places it should be completely prohibited because the vegetation of the mountain slopes is essential to erosion control.

14. *The Donetsk-Dnieper Region* is one of the most populated and industrially developed regions of our country. It includes Dnepropetrovsk, Zaporozhye, Sumy, Kharkov, Poltava, Lugansk, and Donetsk oblasts in the Ukrainian SSR, with a territory about 197,000 square kilometers.

This steppe (and, to some extent, forest-steppe with black earth) is agriculturally well developed. About 85% of the agricultural land is arable; 2% is in hay lands and 10% in pastures. More than 85% of all the feed is field produced. Cattle graze on the slopes of ravines and in flood plains, and because of overgrazing, the pastures are weed infested and trampled; the slopes are sources of erosion; and the soils of flood plains are frequently salinized. Widespread grazing on stubble and in postharvest fields also occurs.

To speed up the development of animal husbandry, the volume of fodder produced per hectare of agricultural land must be significantly raised. This can be achieved by expanding the share of fodder crops in rotation (corn, Sudan grass, fodder melons, root crops, potatoes, and pulses), together with an increase in yields. Furthermore, hay lands and pastures must be improved wherever field cultivation is not suited. Finally, these hay and pasture lands must be carefully used, hay harvesting must be properly timed, grazing must be regulated, and overgrazing prohibited.

The improvement of the natural terrain can raise the productivity of hay harvests up to 40 centners and more per hectare; surface fertilization of erosion-prone meadows unsuited for tilling has raised yields to 50 on a number of collective farms in Kharkov Oblast, and the formation of meadows in ravines has enabled the collectives of the Reshetilov District in Poltava Oblast to increase yields up to 50 from a previous 6 to 10 centners per hectare.

15. *The Transcaucasian Region* includes the Georgian, Azerbaydzhanian, and Armenian SSR's with a territory totaling 186,000 square kilometers.

The region is dominated by mountain slopes covered with forests, hay lands, pastures, and wasteland. Limited areas in mountain valleys and on coastal plains are suited to crop cultivation.

Agricultural lands occupy about half of the territory of each republic, but a little less than half is arable. Hay lands comprise only a small percentage while the rest is in pasture. Consequently, there are three sources of feed in Transcaucasia: (1) field-grown fodder crops, (2) alpine natural summer hay lands and pastures, and (3) steppe and semidesert pastures on plains where some sheep are wintered. However, there is a shortage of such pastures in Georgia and Armenia, and part of the wintering takes place outside the republics on the black soils of the North Caucasus Region. In Azerbaydzhan, on the other hand, there is a shortage of summer pastures.

In Georgia and Armenia, the production of winter stall feed, using cultivated fodder, must be increased and the area and yields of alpine hay lands must be enlarged in order to eliminate long drives to winter pastures. Once these measures are carried out the composition of herds may be changed by increasing the number of dairy cattle and hogs; but until then, and as long as it is necessary to use winter pastures, secure reserves of fodder must be established and water supplies and sheep corrals must be maintained.

In Azerbaydzhan, where there is not enough summer fodder, a part of the livestock should be transferred to year-round feed lots. However, the principal means of expanding the summer fodder base should be through an increase in the productive capacity of alpine summer pastures. For this purpose, additional seeding, together with fertilization, irrigation, and a properly controlled fenced pasturing, will improve the natural pastures. Pastures may also be expanded by providing access to isolated mountain meadows and by clearing the land.

According to approximate calculations, 700,000 hectares of cultivated hay lands and pastures in Azerbaydzhan, about 550,000 hectares in Georgia, and about 350,000 hectares in Armenia must be created. The area that is partly suitable for the development of pastures in 1955 amounted to 2,688,000 hectares in Azerbaydzhan, 1,400,000 in Georgia, and 773,000 in Armenia (Pelt).

To increase the production of cultivated fodder crops, the sown area of grains, especially of corn and pulses, as well as of root crops, melons, Sudan grass, sorghum, and green bristle grass, should be expanded. In Georgia, corn can yield two crops annually.

16. *The Kazakhstan Region,* 2,750,000 square kilometers, embraces the Kazakh SSR. This vast territory includes steppe, semidesert and desert plains, bounded by the Tyan-Shan in the south and the Altay Mountains in the east and may be divided into three parts according to the nature of the fodder base: steppe, semidesert plains, and desert mountains.

The plains that are used for crop cultivation are located in the north, including the northern parts of West Kazakhstan and Aktyubinsk oblasts, almost all of the Virgin Land Kray except for the southern part of Kustanay Oblast, and the northern part of Semipalatinsk and Karaganda oblasts. The proportion of arable land varies from 30% to 70%. At the present time, about half of the region consists of lands that are unsuited to cultivation since they contain solonets, stony, and sandy soils. These areas are used for grazing, although part could be sown to perennial grasses (wheat grass, awnless brome grass, sainfoin, alfalfa, and so forth).

To develop an intensive animal husbandry (cattle and goats) in this part of Kazakhstan, the production of fodder crops must be greatly expanded by alternating fodder grains and row crops; corn and pulses with grain, corn, sorghum, and sunflowers used for silage; and fodder root crops and melons. Grazing on virgin lands unsuitable for tillage should be controlled.

To the south lies the semidesert and desert plain of Kazakhstan, including a large part of West Kazakhstan and Aktyubinsk oblasts, the southern part of Kustanay Oblast, the larger part of Karaganda, Semipalatinsk, Alma-Ata, Dzhambul, and South Kazakhstan oblasts, and all of Kzyl-Orda and Guryev oblasts. The arable area is very limited and can be utilized effectively only with irrigation. Pastures of low productivity predominate, and grazing is possible only by providing water. Since the number of watering places is far from adequate, large pasture areas are little used or completely unused.

In Aktyubinsk Oblast alone, the inadequacy of water supply and poor planning of grazing have affected about five million hectares of pasture. However, the proper organization of seasonal grazing of livestock,* this part of Kazakhstan could become a major source of inexpensive animal products, such as meat and wool.

To utilize fully the grazing potentials of semidesert and desert pastures, the following measures should be carried out. An extensive water supply by means of artesian and other wells equipped to regulate the supply should be provided; ponds should be established; water holes should be cleared; and winter or summer fodder reserves should be provided when there is a natural feed deficiency, which until recently caused periodic mass starvation. Year-round supplementary feeding with stall fodder in order to improve the feed balance, the construction of cattle sheds and quarters for attending personnel on more distant pastures, and the planning of cattle-drive routes are also necessary.

---

* *Otgonnoye zhivotnovodstvo*, a seasonal movement of livestock between pastures, accompanied by supplementary provision of feed and veterinarian services.

The regulation of grazing in the above oblasts is of exceptional importance. The trampling of pastures affects the composition of the grasses and decreases their productivity (sometimes to as little as one-third), turns sandy pasture lands into shifting sands and meadows into solonchak areas.

The development of *liman* irrigation is very important for the plains of Kazakhstan. There are 3,338,000 hectares that are suitable for this purpose (with a 50% guarantee of runoff), but they have not yet been used. *Liman* irrigation can increase the productivity of grasslands by four to five times, even without supplementary seeding (Ostrovnaya). The area of inundation and the security of runoff can in time be increased by means of organized snow retention. The principal seeding in the flooded areas is in wheat grass, alfalfa, and awnless brome grass, but sweet clover, alkali grass, and slough grass are also useful. Seeding is of great importance with ordinary irrigation as well.

The production of hay for a fodder reserve on distant pastures opens up the possibility of the most efficient use of land by means of seasonal livestock grazing. Such grazing involves livestock drives within the desert zone of Kazakhstan or, during the summer, into the northern steppe and southern mountains of the republic.

The mountainous part of the region includes East Kazakhstan Oblast, part of Semipalatinsk Oblast, and the southern part of Alma-Ata, Dzhambul, and South Kazakhstan oblast. This area is characterized by a combination of crop cultivation in the piedmont and livestock grazing, with the latter depending upon cultivated fodder crops and natural mountain-fodder lands as well as on desert winter pastures.

Field-grown fodder crops (made possible by irrigation in the south) are used primarily for dairy cattle, which are kept in barns or feed lots in the piedmont. The leading fodder crops are: grain corn and corn, sorghum, and sunflowers for silage. The expansion of the sown area in pulses (peas, beans, chickpea), in melons, and in root plants (especially sugar beets) is necessary. This should be associated with the seeding of alfalfa in rotation with wheat and other grasses on those lands that are not irrigated. Under irrigation, the grasses sown should be brome, cultivated rye, orchard, and others. Such seeding produces an inexpensive and valuable feed along the margins of the fields.

17. *The Central Asian Region,* an area of 1,238,000 square kilometers, consists of the Turkmen, Uzbek, Tadzhik, and Kirgiz SSR's, and is largely desert plains and high mountains.

Desert plains predominate in the Turkmen and Uzbek republics, but in Kirgizia and Tadzhikistan they occupy rather limited areas in valleys.

Crop cultivation, predominantly under irrigation, is developed at the base of the mountains and to some extent in the piedmont and low mountain regions. Cotton in rotation with alfalfa, or with alfalfa and grains, is especially significant.

Arable land and orchards occupy about 30% of all agricultural land in the Tadzhik SSR; in the Uzbek SSR about 20%; in the Kirgiz SSR about 15%; and in the Turkmen SSR less than 5%. Pastures occupy over 80% of the agricultural land in the Uzbek and Kirgiz SSR's; more than 90% in the Turkmen SSR; and about 70% in the Tadzhik SSR.

Some cattle, particularly of the dairy type, are fed on field-grown fodder and cultivated grass crops produced in the piedmont agricultural belt. Other livestock, mainly sheep and horses, are pastured in the mountains in summer, advancing gradually into higher elevations with the season and returning to the plains in the autumn. Here cattle are kept in feed-lot corrals in winter or are driven to pastures in the desert. Such a drive (*otgon*) is widely practiced in the Uzbek and Turkman SSR's where there are large areas of sandy deserts especially suitable for winter grazing. These two republics also maintain sheep and camels throughout the year in the sandy deserts.

In the Tadzhik and Kirgiz SSR's, on the other hand, a part of the herd is kept the whole year in the mountains and cattle are grazed on high plateaus even in the winter.

To provide a better supply of stall feed for cattle, cultivated fodder-crop production must be expanded in the piedmont belt, along the rivers, and on irrigated lands along the new canals in the desert. Leading fodder crops in these areas could be corn for grain and silage, different types of sorghum for silage, legumes (chickpea) for grain, and alfalfa or alfalfa-grain mixes, melons, and root crops.

In the piedmont, other feed crops can also be produced in the field on unirrigated land. The cultivation of grasses provides a cheap and nourishing fodder; grasses could also be sown beyond the cultivated fields.

The establishment of year-round maintenance of cattle in the mountains, where they are grazed even in winter, creates problems of ensuring the cattle with stall feed as well as producing cultivated fodder crops under alpine conditions.

Irrigation and dry-land farming in the mountains, carried out by institutes and collective farms in the Tadzhik and Kirgiz SSR's, have yielded good results. Their experience is being ever more widely utilized.

Measures for a wider and fuller use of natural mountain pastures and hay lands include construction of new roads in the mountains, purification of watering places, clearance of pastures, elimination of weeds from hay lands, and, finally, proper grazing control.

On waterless desert plains, artesian and shaft wells as well as reservoirs must be dug to retain spring runoff on the *takyrs*. Also necessary are the creation of artificial reservoirs and the purification of salty water.

It is equally important to ensure reliable feed reserves in the desert to handle feed deficiencies—in summer but more particularly in winter. Areas suitable for harvesting wild grasses in the desert are very small; the best harvests are obtained near the Amu-Darya and Syr-Darya, and along irrigation canals. Increased productivity of desert pastures should be accomplished through grazing control, supplementary seeding of some desert plants, and the planting of *saksaul* on the sands.

This brief geographic survey of the fodder resources of the USSR by economic regions reveals how greatly that base varies; moreover, developmental possibilities for the near future are not uniform across the country.

In a number of regions, development is directed toward the dominance of cultivated fodder crops. However, apart from such regions, the USSR has many other regions where extensive areas are either untillable or where cultivation would require large capital and labor inputs. In such regions, natural pastures will continue to play a significant role in feed production.

Data on the extent and yield capacity of natural hay lands and pastures permit us to calculate the total harvest of natural feed available in the Soviet Union (Table 3). One kilogram of hay or of dry pasture feed is taken to equal half a fodder unit, that is, half a kilogram of oats in feed value.

The value of natural hay and pasture feed within the total feed base, including cultivated fodder crops, varies from region to region. This value depends upon the possibilities of cultivating fodder crops, on the composition of the livestock herds, and on the extent and yield capacity of natural hay lands and pastures. The growing of fodder crops can play a dominant role in the southern part of the Northwestern Region, in the northern part of the Povolzhye in the Ukraine, in the Central, and Central Black Earth Regions, in the southern part of the Western Siberian Region, in the Virgin Land Kray, and in the irrigated and piedmont districts of Kazakhstan and Central Asia. However, even where cultivated fodder-crop production is predominant, natural fodder lands obviously retain their importance for short-term feeding.

In less populated regions with little crop cultivation, the role of natural pastures remains very important. Where it is necessary to supply several industrial centers with livestock, and especially with dairy products, the

Table 3
Gross Harvest of Fodder from Natural Hay Lands and Pastures
of the Soviet Union (In millions of fodder units)

Republic and Economic Region	Hay Lands	Pastures [a]
RSFSR	25,563	20,865
Northwestern	2,306	834
Central	3,273	1,278
Volga-Vyatka	1,089	470
Central Black Earth	683	664
Povolzhye (Volga)	1,344	2,871
North Caucasian	1,807	5,070
Ural	4,814	3,642
Western Siberian	4,648	1,539
Eastern Siberian	3,652	3,860
Soviet Far Eastern	1,947	637
Estonian SSR	451	205
Latvian SSR	558	166
Lithuanian SSR	484	178
Belorussian SSR	1,854	459
Ukrainian SSR	2,208	2,014
Moldavian SSR	21	122
Georgian SSR	106	855
Armenian SSR	84	350
Azerbaydzhanian SSR	89	776
Kazakh SSR	3,297	32,985
Turkmen SSR	7	2,675
Uzbek SSR	139	3,924
Tadzhik SSR	36	892
Kirgiz SSR	235	2,676
TOTAL USSR	35,132	69,142

[a] Gross harvest of fodder from reindeer pastures not included.

production of cultivated fodder should be concentrated around such centers.

To increase their productivity many natural pastures require various types of improvement. One type entails the slow transformation of the natural terrain into fields; another, the significant alteration of its character without tillage; a third through minor modifications. The following improvement measures are basic:

1. Draining, liming, fertilizing, and grass seeding of swamp lands, particularly in the northern regions, permitting some land to be put into cultivation.

2. Clearance in burned-over, logged, scrub, and rocky areas, largely in the northern regions.

3. Reclamation of a significant part of eroded, deflated, and overgrazed lands for hay production and controlled grazing once the soil is anchored and water retention and wind protection measures have been implemented. Tillage, however, can be expected on only very small segments of land.

4. Irrigation (either normal or *liman*), particularly in the southern regions. Part of the irrigated land could be cultivated.

5. Desalinization of unirrigated lands in salinized areas (solonets and solonchak) in the southern regions, by means of gypsum and phytomelioration (the cultivation of perennial grass mixtures) where the soils cannot be flushed out. Part of these lands in future can be cultivated.

6. The provision of water for winter pastures and the accumulation of fodder reserves in deserts and semideserts, where land reclamation is impossible.

7. The strengthening of riverbanks and straightening of courses in extensive flood plains, and the clearing, draining, and irrigation of portions of flood plains. After such measures have been implemented, the flood plains can be used either for cultivated fodder crops or as natural hay lands, which, with the improved grass composition, can yield much hay. In deciding on the nature of flood-plain use, it should be remembered that tillage frequently disrupts the structure of the soils.

8. Clearance, road and bridge construction, and water provision in alpine natural hay lands and pastures.

9. The regulation of grazing on the pastures in the tundra and forest-tundra lands. Small pockets can be cut for hay.

Table 4 shows what measures are of most importance in any particular economic region of the Soviet Union. From this point of view, the Union may be divided into four groups.

The first includes the steppe and forest-steppe; the Central Black Earth, Povolzhye, North Caucasus, Donetsk-Dnieper, Southwestern, and Southern regions. This, the most cultivated part of the Soviet Union, includes some mountains and is characterized by black and gray forest soils. Major pasture-land improvement measures are associated with erosion and deflation control, and irrigation. The second group includes the forest zone: the Northwestern, Central, Volga-Vyatka, and Western regions, which are agricultural but have poor podzolic soils. Here, the most important meas-

Table 4
Regions Where Measures are Needed for the Expansion and Improvement of Natural Fodder Lands in the Various Economic Regions of the USSR (According to 1961 Regionalization)

Economic Region	Places Where Measures Are Needed								
	On Swampy or Marshy Ground	On Land in Need of Clearance	On Eroded or Erosion-Subject Land	On Land Requiring Irrigation	On Salinized, Non-irrigated Land	On Desert Land	In Flood Plains	In Mountains	In the Tundra
Northwestern	+	+					+		+
Central	+	+					+		
Volga-Vyatka	+	+					+		
Central Black Earth			+				+		
Povolzhye (Volga)			+		+	+	+		
North Caucasus			+		+	+	+	+	
Urals	+	+	+	+	+		+	+	+
Western Siberian	+	+	+	+	+		+		
Eastern Siberian	+	+		+			+		+
Soviet Far Eastern	+	+					+		+
Western	+	+					+		
Southwestern			+	+			+	+	
Southern			+	+			+	+	
Donetsk-Dnieper			+	+			+		
Transcaucasian				+	+	+	+	+	
Kazakhstan			+	+	+	+	+	+	
Central Asian			+	+	+	+	+	+	

ures include drainage, clearance of meadow hay lands and pastures, liming, and fertilization. The third group includes the desert and mountain areas of Transcaucasia, Central Asia, and Kazakhstan, as well as the southern piedmont plains, which to some extent are being assimilated for cultivation, and mountain hay lands and pastures. Principal improvement measures include irrigation, desalinization of soil, erosion control, and the improvement of mountain hay lands and pastures. The fourth group, with vast regions of varying conditions of fodder production, are predominantly forested and little settled. Included are the Urals, Western Siberia, Eastern Siberia, and the Soviet Far East. The measures vary from region to region but include clearance, drainage, irrigation, erosion control, desalinization, and others.

The regions of the first and second groups have the most favorable conditions for the development of the cultivation of fodder crops and for the full transition to stall raising of livestock. In the large areas of the third and fourth groups, natural pastures will retain their importance.

The above survey of the characteristics of the natural fodder lands of the USSR illustrates the reasons for their low productivity. Widespread incorrect use of pastures and hay lands together with a lack of improvement are the chief causes of low productivity.

Essential deficiencies in the use of pastures are: (1) excessive grazing; (2) unequal use of existing grazing lands; (3) poor timing of grassland use; and (4) the lack of the necessary equipment and improvements.

Overgrazing results from excessive livestock densities in one area for too long a time. In such a situation, the herds eat down to the roots, weakening the most valuable fodder plants, lowering their regenerative potential, and disrupting the soil. As a result, the productivity of pastures decreases and indigestible and poisonous plants take over. The average decrease in pasture productivity caused by trampling reaches 50%.

While the cause of overgrazing in a number of western regions of the USSR (for instance, the Ukraine), is due to the scarcity of pastures, the grazing capacity of the latter can be increased by cultivation. In the east, vast semidesert and desert areas are overgrazed because of faulty management. Many farms restrict grazing to only a part of their land; cattle are herded close to the base where trampling and overgrazing occur, while remote pastures remain unused. Consequently, the grass cover contains remnants of the vegetation of previous years and the quality of the pastures declines. The irregularity of grazing, particularly in the deserts, is caused to some extent by an insufficient network of watering places, and the cattle are confined to small areas provided with water. Therefore, desert grasslands suffer from wind erosion that originates around the watering places and even when the network is expanded, the deflated areas are lost. Unequal livestock densities are also a chief shortcoming in the use of reindeer pastures in the tundra and forest-tundra.

Pastures also suffer greatly from poor timing of use. Grazing should take place at the time of vegetation growth, after which the grasses could regenerate their loss and regain their nutrients. If the timing of grazing is consistently faulty the grass cover weakens and degenerates; annuals of little value take over, and productivity declines.

Proper use of pastures is possible only with the right equipment and, in some locations, after improvement of the land. Vast areas of pastures in the forest zone are not cleared of brush and tufts and remain undrained. Thus, in the North European part of the USSR the marshy lowland pastures amount to 24% of the total area; in Leningrad Oblast, to 28%; and in Belorussia, to 48%. Only in the transition to steppe does the marshiness decline to 4%; however, erosion gains in significance, with the result that water measures (intricate agro- and hydrotechnical measures and forest improvement) together with a transformation of the microrelief must be carried out.

In Central Asia and Kazakhstan, the total area of pastures amounts to some 240 million hectares. Because about 130 million hectares lack a water supply the national economy loses more than 2.5 million tons of pasture feed (dry mass) every year that could be used for grazing. The lack of roads, particularly in the mountains, also has a negative effect.

The principal handicaps in the use of hay lands are the following: (1) areas suitable for haying are used for pasturing, or they remain totally unused; (2) haying is carried out at the wrong time of the year; and (3) the hay lands remain in a neglected and unmanaged condition.

Grazing in areas suitable for haying is very widespread, especially in the forest zone, where a shortage of pastures exists. Here, pasturing on hay lands is frequently practiced in the fall after the harvest, in the spring "until prohibited," after which grazing is stopped and the grasses are allowed to grow. As a result, the exposed soil surface is disrupted, tufts develop, and weeds spread. Grazing in forests is both very widespread and very damaging. In the steppes and deserts of the Asiatic part of the USSR where there are extensive pastures, the meadows are often used for pasturing, which is usually justified by the poor condition of their surface, although the cleaning of these meadows and the removal of tufts would not be difficult. Many hay meadows are used as pastures in the mountains, especially where the terrain makes it difficult to ship hay, or where mechanization is impossible.

Thus, beautiful grass stands yielding twenty to thirty centners of hay per hectare are not only unconsumed but are trampled, and only about 40% of the grasses is used. At the same time, the sod on the slopes is disrupted and a thick, high-growing, indigestible grass mosaic develops. This deficiency can be removed by building proper roads to mountain pastures.

In the flood plains of large rivers, valuable meadows are sometimes unused because they are separated from the settlements by streams, old meanders, marshes, and brush, or because they are silted, covered with debris, or are subject to washing out as a result of a lack of proper management. Inadequate use of hay lands is especially frequent in the flood plains of the rivers of the desert zone: the Amu-Darya, Syr-Darya, Ili, and others. Despite a sharp deficit in hay reserves, over half of the potential hay land remains unused.

Delays in harvests, or excessive periods of harvesting, extending frequently into late fall, are still common, negatively affecting both the nutritive quality and the digestibility of the hay. Even if the harvest is timed properly, some farms delay the gathering of the cut grasses, which leads to their degradation. There is another phenomenon: sometimes local organizations demand delivery of all hay and punish those farms that fail to comply; the climate, however, requires the creation of hay reserves for two to three years, and farms should be encouraged to establish them.

Hay lands are frequently neglected. The curse of the northern hay harvester is overgrowth of scrub. In many places the hay lands are covered with boulders that prohibit mechanized or even manual haying. Good roads to the hay lands are rare, or nonexistent, leading sometimes to the placement of hay stacks at some distance from winter pastures. In West Kazakhstan Oblast there were cases of state-farm sheep being driven from remote pastures to hay stacks only to collapse and die of exhaustion.

An appreciable loss is caused to the fodder areas of riverbank hay lands in regions of hydropower construction, not only because of the inundation of the meadows close to dams but also because of the desiccation of the meadows below the dams, which no longer have seasonal flooding. In the future, reservoir construction plans must include measures to hold at a minimum the loss of highly productive hay lands. Meadows should be surrounded by protective dikes and, where their loss is unavoidable, they should be compensated for by the creation of irrigated hay lands and by an increase in cultivated fodder-crop production.

Many of the inadequacies in the fodder areas could be easily prevented by means of better organization and by simple improvements. As indicated, improper use is one of the chief offenses. Meanwhile, Soviet scientists concerned with pastures and the development of husbandry have made field studies of proper pasture organization ("regulated grazing"). The main elements include the establishment of enclosed pastures, a green-feed conveyor, and proper rotation of pasture land. Enclosed pasturage, their studies show, is very effective; for example, used on the collective farm "New Path" in Perm Oblast it doubled milk production per cow. A herd of 146 animals placed for fattening on the collective "12 years of October" in Orenburg Oblast increased its live weight from 213 to 385 centners.

The importance of supplying water to pasture lands, which permits the use of additional millions of hectares of land in the desert zone, was mentioned previously. But even in areas provided with water, livestock suffer occasionally from the irregular distribution of watering places and feed-lot corrals. Overcoming these deficiencies invariably leads to an increase in milk and meat production.

The simplest measures for improving hay harvests are clearance of scrub, tufts, and stones; weed prevention; additional seeding; fertilization; proper timing of hay harvesting; and proper methods of harvesting and hay storage.

Clearing pastures of scrub, tufts, and stones can increase their productivity anywhere from 20% to 70%, and grass seeding can increase it by two to three times, or even more. Fertilizing natural pastures can bring about an even greater improvement, especially when it is associated with other measures such as clearance, weed removal and supplementary seeding; these measures should not be undertaken individually but should be combined into an efficient system. Some of these measures are very effective if used in combination, but may prove useless or even harmful if used in isolation or in an incorrect sequence.

Basic measures for improving pastures and hay lands are drainage, irrigation, the establishment of turf on unproductive land, and the improvement of solonets soils. Such measures are usually accompanied by the seeding of specially selected plants. They can be significantly beneficial: with fertilization, nonproductive lands can become meadows with an output of as much as twenty centners per hectare. The draining of marshy sedge meadows does not increase the yield so much as it improves the quality of the fodder. The institution of *liman* irrigation transforms desert steppe lands of less than three centners per hectare productivity into couch-grass meadows yielding up to thirty centners per hectare. On desert-steppe sands subject to deflation due to trampling and overgrazing, up to ten centners per hectare of wheat-grass hay can be produced. The seeding of *saksaul* from the air in regions of deflated sands transforms extensive areas of useless land into pastures for karakul sheep, yielding two to three centners of dry mass per hectare. The last measure is very inexpensive but its results are just as important as other basic means of improvement.

Fundamental improvements are costly but they are fully economic if the improved pastures are kept in good condition after treatment. A very important means of improving desert steppe soils lies in the improvement of solonets soils, which occupy very large areas but are of low productivity, yielding only two to four centners of dry matter per hectare. Plowing and the seeding of yellow alfalfa, wheat, and other grasses along with a steady increase in the depth of tillage, followed by additional seeding and, even better, the application of gypsum, will progressively weaken the structure of solonets soils. This method can transform very large areas (in the opinion of I. V. Larin, 35 million hectares in Kazakhstan alone) of little-productive land, mainly desert-steppe pastures, into arable land, suitable for grass mixtures for pasturing and haying. However, such measures require constant care of the improved land and very strict accounting of the natural conditions; if not, they can result in damage.

It should be noted that the effectiveness of these improvements depends as much on sustaining the achievements as on the technical realization of the improvement itself, which is, in fact, only the beginning. Often after basic improvements have been made, however, the need for maintaining the lands in proper condition as well as fully using the advantages is forgotten.

Considering the future development of animal husbandry and, consequently, the increase in the volume of fodder production, we must plan to increase the area of cultivated fodder-crop production. In 1958, 23% of the sown area of the USSR was in fodder crops; in the future this rate should grow to as much as 30%.* In a number of West European countries where animal husbandry is well developed, the share of fodder crops in rotation is even higher.

The enrichment of feed rations with protein is very important. Most of the grain fodder (but not pulses) as well as overripe hay from natural hay lands are deficient in protein, and to assure livestock of the necessary protein, fodder rations have to be excessive. Consequently, an increase in the protein content of the fodder will lead to savings. This may be accomplished by the production of grain pulses (peas, beans, chickpea, and soybeans) and by their inclusion in silage and fodder mixtures (as a valuable fodder flour) and in grass mixtures. Early timing of hay cutting and pasture grazing while the grasses are still rich in protein, as well as the introduction of

---

* By 1965, it had reached 24.4%. *Narkhoz SSSR, 1965,* pp. 278, 285.

nitrogenous fertilizers in the fodder-crop lands, are necessary. It is also desirable to include industrial protein wastes and fodder of animal origin in the livestock feed base.

Possibly the most important element in the strengthening of the fodder base is the organized accounting, study, planning, and controlled use of the fodder resources. Work on the strengthening and expansion of the feed base cannot be properly organized until it becomes very clear what kind of measures should be implemented, and where. It seems clear that the regulation of fodder production must begin with the organization of a broad, geographic, scientifically based evaluation of the feed base, singling out both the natural conditions of the land and the character of its use. A survey will serve as a stable basis for implementing scientific recommendations leading to the improvement of fodder production.

Such an accounting is not new to Soviet science. As early as 1931–33, the All-Union Institute of Feed, under the leadership of L. G. Ramenskiy and I. V. Larin, was given the task of an all-union inventory of fodder areas by the Narkomzem SSSR * Unfortunately, the results of that work have remained unpublished. Later, various institutions conducted research on the fodder base, but that research had one basic handicap: different methods were used in different regions in different years, and the maps were prepared on different scales—all of which greatly decreased their comparability and value.

At the present time, a more detailed inventory of pasture lands, "a census of hay lands and pastures," is being conducted. After completion, every institution that uses land will receive materials on land evaluation. The work on the geographical description and evaluation of the fodder lands should be continued and its methodology should be assured. Several stationary points should be organized to permit the study of the seasonal sequence of grass growth, yields, and methods of use.

Experimental stations have developed many valuable varieties of fodder plants and have worked on a number of systems for pasture and fodder-crop rotation and measures for land improvement. This research work should be continued; equally important is a study of methods of feeding animals and the determination of proper rations. As well as continuation of research, the achievements of several research stations on leading collective and state farms should be applied. In regions of livestock pasturing, the research should be facilitated by a special pasture service that would oversee the proper use of fodder land on the basis of a land quality account,

---

* Narodnyy komissariat zemledeliya [People's Commissariat of Agriculture].

stressing proper livestock densities on the pastures, and proper timing of grazing and of haying. This same service could prescribe measures for improving pasture lands, make an account of feed stocks and, especially for winter stall feeding, regulate stocks according to weather forecasts. Such a pasture-land service could be united with agencies in the republics concerned with the protection and improvement of soils, land use, and land-fund evaluation.

In order to conduct a qualitative evaluation of fodder areas and the organization of a pasture service, specialists must be trained. Young specialists graduating from the biology departments of universities are generally not familiar with the research concerned with productivity, lack interest in it and, if ending up in such work, are compelled to make decisions beyond their competence. Agricultural institutes often give insufficient preparation in meadow management and turn out too few specialists in this area. The curricula must be reconstructed to produce a greater number of specialists knowledgeable in meadow management and land evaluation. This kind of preparation must be provided by the biopedological and geographical departments of the universities and by the agricultural institutes.

A network of botanical, pedological, and geographical institutes and institutes of animal husbandry and fodder should direct the work on fodder areas.

BIBLIOGRAPHY

Alampiyev, P. M. *Ekonomicheskiye rayony nashey strany* [Economic Regions of Our Country]. Moscow: Geografgiz, 1961.

Larin, V. I. *Lugovodstvo i pastbishchnoye khozyaystvo* [Meadow Management and Pasture Economy]. Moscow-Leningrad: Selkhozgiz, 1956.

Materially 2–g0 soveshchaniya po yestyestvenno-istoricheskomu i ekonomiko-geograficheskomu rayonirovaniyu SSSR dlya tseley selskogo khozyaystva 1–5 fevralya 1958 g. [Materials of the 2nd Meeting on Natural-Historical and Economic-Geographic Regionalization of the USSR for Agricultural Purposes, February 1–5, 1958]. Moscow: Izd-vo MGU, 1959.

"O vypolnenii gosudarstvennogo plana i sotsialisticheskikh obyazatelstv po proizvodstvu i prodazhe gosudarstvu produktov zemledeliya i zhivotnovodstva v 1960 godu i o meropriyatiyakh po dalneyshemu razvitiyu selskogo khozyaystva" [Concerning the Fulfillment of the State Plan and Socialist Commitments on the Production and Sales to the State of Agricultural and Livestock Products in 1960 and Concerning the Measures for the Further Development of Agriculture]. In *Postanovleniya yanvarskogo plenuma Tsk KPSS ot 18 yanvariya 1961 goda* [Resolutions of the January Plenum of the Central Committee of the CPSU of January 18, 1961]. Moscow: Gospolitizdat, 1961.

Opyt opredeleniya obyemov selskokhozyaystvennogo proizvodstva SSSR na perspektivu [An Attempt to Establish the Volumes of Agricultural Production of the USSR in the Future]. Moscow and Leningrad: AN SSSR 1957.

Ostrovnaya, N. N. "Vozmozhnosti razvitiya limannogo orosheniya v SSSR" [Possibilities of Developing *Liman* Irrigation in the USSR]. In *Kormovaya baza zhivotnovodstva SSSR i puti yeye razvitiya* [The Fodder Base of Animal Husbandry in the USSR and the Means of its Development]. Moscow and Leningrad: AN SSSR, 1959.

Pelt, N. N. *Kormovaya baza zhivotnovodstva SSSR i puti yeye razvitiya.* Ibid.

"Prirodnaya kormovaya ploshchad SSSR i osnovnye puti yeye rekonstrukstii" [The Natural Fodder Area of the USSR and the Principal Means of its Reconstruction] (Lecture Notes). Botan. in-t im. V. L. Komarova. Leningrad, 1960.

SSSR v tsifrakh v 1960 godu. Kratkiy statisticheskiy sbornik [USSR in Figures in 1960. Short Statistical Handbook]. Moscow: Gosstatizdat, 1961.

Udachin, S. A. *Zemelnyy fond SSSR i yego ispolzovaniye* [The Land Fund of the USSR and its Utilization]. Moscow: Selkhozgiz, 1960.

Zemskiy, P. M. *Razvitive i razmeshcheniye zemledeliya po prirodnokhozyaystvennym rayonam SSSR* [The Development and Distribution of Agriculture According to Natural-economic Regions of the USSR]. Moscow-Leningrad: AN SSSR, 1959.

Part 6. FISH AND GAME

13. Land Game

Yu. A. Osakov, S. V. Kirikov, and A. N. Formozov

(Institute of Geography, Academy of Sciences of the USSR)

THE ECONOMIC SIGNIFICANCE
OF THE HUNTING INDUSTRY

The commercial resources of our terrestrial fauna, possessing substantial and irreplaceable material wealth, are gigantic. Over the last forty years some species (for instance, waterfowl) have become noticeably depleted; others have increased. Sable, marten, elk, and antelope have been restored to their former large numbers. During the same period, such fur-bearing animals new to our country as the muskrat and American mink have been successfully acclimatized. Also, a group of secondary species (mole, hamster, marmot, chipmunk, and others) that formerly were barely exploited have become valuable now that there is an improvement in the technique for dressing small pelts.

The hunting of wild animals, which developed in our country many thousands of years before animal husbandry and crop cultivation, continues to be important in some sparsely populated regions of the USSR. For example, during the summer the reindeer breeders of northern Siberia obtain meat by hunting, avoiding the need to slaughter domesticated reindeer when hides are poor. In winter, in addition to herding reindeer, they hunt the polar fox, whose fur is highly valued. A large catch of the latter is assured, moreover, by the very presence of reindeer, since they are used for travel to the wooden traps scattered widely about the tundra and in organized collective hunts. In addition, hunting in the regions of northern reindeer herding is the only means of combating the wolf, a great threat to domesticated herds. The importance of commercial hunting in the greater part of the densely populated regions of the USSR, which has a highly developed agriculture and industry, has markedly decreased in recent decades. On the other hand, sport hunting has steadily grown. Our sportsmen combat the wolves successfully, extract and deliver thousands of game hides of other animals annually, and implement measures for enriching the land with valuable game species.

The decrease in the importance of commercial hunting, noted above, has caused some economists to conclude mistakenly that the disappearance of hunting as an industry is imminent. In reality, this conclusion cannot be substantiated. In the Khanty-Mansi National Okrug, for example, furs valued at about six million rubles are processed annually. How profitable this is for the collective farmers is obvious from the fact that during the 1950s the income from a day of hunting was twice that from fishing. Nonetheless, the planning of the economy and the distribution of the labor force are carried out in such a way that they contribute to the decline in hunting (during the decade from 1946 to 1956, the number of hunters decreased threefold; Trofimov).

Along with the view that the hunting industry is dying out, there is a rather widespread belief that valuable beasts and birds "retreat from civilization" to remote uninhabited areas. This notion is also entirely erroneous, for many species are forced out not by civilization but by the uncivilized, clumsy use of the land and by the predatory treatment of its vegetative and animal life. Observations show that with adequate protection and standardized procurement of animals, based on scientific data, elk, marten, mink, otter, squirrel, ermine, and polecat can live in the environs of such large and busy cities as Moscow. The experiences of Czechoslovakia, Hungary, Bulgaria, the German Democratic Republic, and a number of other countries prove that from arable land and small forest tracts it is possible to obtain annually a large amount of first-class game: partridge, pheasant, hare, and roe and European deer. Our statistics also show that in terms of the value of commodity yield, the furs from a unit area in the densely populated central oblasts of the European part of the USSR (Kalinin, Moscow, Vladimir, and others) surpass Central Siberia and Yakutia where the extremely valuable sable, squirrel, and other fur-bearing animals live. This is due to the higher aggregate density of fur-bearing animals in the central oblasts than in Yakutia with its severe climate, and the hunting of game is better organized, thanks primarily to the greater number of hunters.

The economic importance of game birds and beasts lies in the fact that their forage is of little economic value and is scattered throughout the tundra and taiga, in the mountains and steppe. The sable, with its valuable pelt, lives primarily on useless and often destructive small forest rodents, and eats berries and nuts from fallen cedar cones. The gray partridge, whose meat is exceptionally fine in quality and who promises to be a good prospective game animal, produces from 16 to 24 chicks, which in turn eat blades of grass, weed seeds, and wheat chaff in the fields; they meanwhile destroy masses of insects harmful to the economy. Marshy, nearly impenetrable reed thickets, considered "wretched" places, yield millions of quality furs annually after they are populated with muskrat. These are in great demand in domestic markets and abroad. The muskrat feeds on the leaves and roots of hygrophites or submerged plants, which for the most part are not utilized in agriculture.

The hunting industry, when affecting regions in which the primary economic role is played by some branch of agriculture, yields valuable supplementary products for local consumption in remote settlements. It does not damage the primary branches of the economy and, on occasion, even makes a substantial contribution (such as the destruction of harmful rodents, wolves, and so forth).

In every region, it is possible to create a hunting industry that functions harmoniously with other branches of the economy. This may be accomplished by conservation, enrichment, and skillful use of the wildlife in order to achieve the greatest possible additional production from the largest area of forests, arable lands, and water bodies.

But in spite of the extremely favorable natural conditions of the country and the presence of rich fauna, the huge potentials of the hunting industry are not being adequately exploited. In most of the union there is a hunting industry for sport only, but not a game economy, since the lands allotted to the collectives, the state hunting enterprises, and the sporting associations are not being managed. Under these conditions, measures for regeneration of game and improvement in the habitat of commercial wildlife (biotechnical measures) are poorly implemented or are nonexistent. In the taiga as well as the tundra, vast areas, even those with possible productive hunting, are completely undeveloped, and such areas continue to increase. The number of hunters in these regions, compared with the decade from 1925 to 1935, has sharply declined. The youth try to find better paying positions in forest industry, prospecting, or construction; therefore, conditions that will raise the material incentives for the hunter must be created. Only after resolving the organizational-economic aspect of the problem will it be possible to develop the large reserves of game and wildlife and to create proper conditions for the protection and propagation of waterfowl.

COMMERCIAL HUNTING SPECIES

In the Soviet Union there are more than forty species of commercial land game (including those newly acclimatized). These animals are by no means of equal value to the economy of the country and judgment concerning the significance of any one species should involve appraisal of the conditions of exploitation, of its total numbers, and of the character of its fecundity. Among the major natural conditions that determine the number of animals are the feed reserves available and accessible in any one locality and the protection that the locality provides. But of particular significance is the anthropogenetic factor, that is, the influence of man, who harvests the animals or changes their environment.

A change in the native habitat, by the plowing of the steppe, the cutting of the forests, and the drainage of marshes has brought about the complete disappearance of some species and a reduction in others, accompanied by a corresponding decrease in areal extent. An excessive use or harvest of a valuable species whose numbers are limited and whose fecundity is low can lead rapidly to a reduction in females, to the detriment of the entire commercial stock. Such situations have been repeatedly observed in our hunting as well as in that of foreign countries; history records dozens of examples of the complete extinction of very valuable species from predatory exploitation. Therefore, rational utilization of useful commercial game presupposes a study of numbers and distribution, the environmental conditions in which they live, and their past numbers and areal extent. Particular care should be given to the endemic fauna and to the most valuable of the fur-bearing animals.

Experience has shown that proper management can replenish the populations of even decimated species, but protection is not the only factor necessary. The tempo with which the former extent and number of animals can be restored depends on the extent of the territory in which they can find food and shelter. These principles have been graphically corroborated in the USSR in the restoration of both sable and elk.

Together with those animals that have an obvious commercial value, there are species that produce valuable fur but at the same time destroy cultivated crops or other commercial animals. Sometimes the value of the pelt fails to compensate for the harm that they do. For example, the *kharza* or Nepalese marten and the lynx and wolverine are all fur-bearing predators that destroy many valuable commercial animals. These three species are recognized as harmful and are subject to elimination, with hunting permitted without restriction. Also unrestricted is the harvesting of some species that provide "summer pelts" (prepared in the warm half of the year), such as the hamster, little marmot, water rat, chipmunk, and other animals that are harmful to field and forest or which carry tularemia, plague, encephalitis, and other infections.

The distribution of commercial land animals throughout the USSR is irregular. In the tundra zone only the polar fox and wild northern reindeer are of major economic significance; the other species (the fox, white hare, ermine, wolverine, wolf) play only negligible roles. The killing of polar bears is forbidden, but their numbers continue to fall and decisive measures are required to preserve this very valuable animal.

The forest zone is very rich in commercial species. Besides marten, sable, squirrel, lynx, and wolverine, there are also the northern reindeer, roe deer, Siberian stag, elk, wild boar, fox, ermine, Siberian ferret, mole, white hare and, of the water-dwellers, otter, muskrat, and beaver. In the northern taiga there are, some years, many polar foxes. The quality of fur of most of the forest species living in northern European Russian and east of the Urals is high. Great changes in the natural conditions of the forest zone, associated with intense logging and forest fires, unfavorably affect the lives of several valuable species (squirrel, sable, marten). This is especially critical because the forest zone is not only the most productive in furs but it also has the greatest number of commercial hunters.

The forest-steppe is considerably poorer in terms of variety, but the populations of some species are very large. Among them are the fox, wolf, muskrat, the white and common hare, squirrel, ermine, forest and light polecat, roe deer, and wild boar. The reserves of commercial animals in the forest-steppe of Western Siberia, northern Kazakhstan, and Transbaykalia are still so large that individual inhabitants of these regions subsist by hunting alone, although the relative number of professional hunters is smaller than in the tundra and taiga.

As one moves southward from the steppe zone to the semidesert and desert, the number of species of commercial game decreases and the quality of the fur sharply deteriorates. Here the fur trade is largely dependent on the fox, wolf, Corsak fox [*Vulpes corsac*], light polecat, hare, little marmot, and the marmot badger. In some places many hoofed animals remain: wild boar, Central Asian gazelle, and antelope [*Saiga tatarica*]. But in this entire vast belt, hunting is a secondary occupation, with the exception of regions abounding in muskrat, where there are specialized enterprises.

The development of the virgin lands in the steppe and forest-steppe has brought about profound changes in the natural conditions that have transformed the animal world. Plowing destroys the marmot badgers, particularly evident in the Virgin Land Kray, reduces the number of Corsak foxes and jerboa [*Dipodidae*], but raises the hamster population. The clearance of birch groves and the destruction of reed thickets in lake basins leads to the expulsion of roe deer and wild boars, but the number of foxes, common hare, and light polecat remains at a sufficiently high level. Thus, despite the transformation of the virgin lands into a continuous belt of cultivated land, a number of game animals have survived. Conditions for commercial hunting have also been preserved, but in a somewhat altered form.

As has been shown, each of the natural zones of the Soviet Union has its own assortment of commercial game, among which five or six species constitute the basis for hunting. For example, in the northern forest of European Russia, the value of the furs of commercial animals comprises from 40% to 75% of the total value of the furs procured in the European part. Of greatest importance here are the squirrel, white hare, marten, ermine, and black polecat; of secondary importance is a group of widely distributed species, the fox and mole, the value of whose furs in some years reaches 43% of the value of all furs. The share of the polar fox fluctuates from 5% to 25%, while that of the commercial water species, mink, muskrat, and water rat, amounts to only 5%. On the other hand, in the southern forest zone of European Russia, the principal commercial value lies in such widely distributed species as the mole, fox, and wolf (up to 61% of the value of delivered furs) and, secondarily, by the squirrel, white hare, marten, ermine, black polecat, and the acclimatized raccoonlike Ussuri dog. Species inhabiting the open spaces, the common hare, light polecat, and fur-bearing water animals, contribute in total about 12% of the fur value (Danilov, 1950). In Yakutia, the value of the fur of commercial forest species, squirrel, sable, white hare, and ermine, averages 70% of the value of all delivered furs. Of secondary importance is the polar fox (about 25%). Of some value also are the fox, muskrat, and water rat.

The productivity of hunting areas is usually evaluated according to the value of the fur obtained from one hectare. The water areas in the central and southern regions, densely inhabited by muskrat, have the greatest productivity; the tundra has the lowest (roughly one-half that of the fields and meadows in the forest zone and one-third that of the forest areas). Data for the period from 1937 to 1947 and for a number of earlier years have shown that the greatest productivity is in the southern part of European Russia, Western Siberia, and the Altay (Danilov, 1950), and is the result of the saturation of the land with fur-bearing animals and the important level of hunting. The density of hunters varies sharply from region to region. For example, according to data for 1937 to 1947, there were 13,-300 hectares per hunter in Yakutia; 9,500 in Eastern Siberia; 7,600 in Transbaykalia; 3,800 in Western Siberia; and 900 in the southern part of the European USSR. Since the number of hunters in some oblasts has sharply declined in the last decade, as has already been noted, the area per hunter has become even greater, indicating a decline in the use of the land and the volume of procurements per unit area. Of the wild animals, the fur-bearing ones are the most significant.[1]

For a very long time, furs were the principal source of foreign exchange for the Russian state and they played an important role in the internal market. Exports included the skins of the sable, fox, squirrel, beaver, marten, and desman [*Desmana moschata*]. Subsequent excessive exploitation (which often assumed manifestly rapacious forms), lack of caution in stock reproduction, forest fires that enveloped huge areas, forest reduction, epidemics, and other unfavorable circumstances depleted the stocks of some of the most valuable species. This depletion was particularly pronounced at the turn of the century.

The Soviet government took urgent steps to preserve a number of species (first of all the beaver, which was threatened with complete annihilation), and it strove to restore the commercial reserves of sable, desman, pine marten, and several other species. Now their numbers throughout the greater part of the regions of exploitation have been restored and the significance of their fur in the economy of the country remains high. The aggregate value of fur procured annually in the USSR has reached (in recent years) approximately fifty million rubles (Kolosov, Lavrov, and Naumov), and its share in exports is about 1.5% (Klyatis).

Fur farms now seriously compete with fur obtained by hunting. In the United States, for example, the value of mink pelts, almost all produced in captivity, in recent years comprised about three-fourths of the value of all fur sold. In 1959, there were more than nine million pelts of farm-bred mink on the international market (Kaplin). Nevertheless, the "wild" pelt has not lost its economic importance, since only a very few species whose furs are fashionable at a particular time and enjoy special demand are raised on farms.

A group of hoofed animals that were killed primarily for their meat and hides has lost its former national significance to a much greater degree than have the fur-bearing animals, and their numbers are declining. This is

---

[1] This division in reference to fur-bearing animals is arbitrary. The hare, for instance, may be considered fur-bearing, but it is also a meat animal. The value of the skin of the badger is significantly lower than that of its fat, which is used for medical purposes, and so forth.

related first of all to the expansion of cultivation: the steppe has been almost entirely transformed into fields, and the forest-steppe and southern limits of the forest zone have become densely populated rural parklands. These changes have caused either complete disappearance of large ungulates from the steppe, or of their concentration in relatively small spaces where the steppe has survived. In 1869, A. F. Middendorf (p. 93) was correct in asserting that such wild ungulates as the aurochs [*Bos primigenius*], wild horse, and the antelope could live and find safety not in secluded corners but in "the boundless expanses of their habitats."

The forests, deserts, semideserts, and mountains have been much less transformed by human occupancy than the steppe and forest-steppe, and here the wild ungulates fare better; restoration and an increase in their numbers in these areas is more promising. This is also true of species dependent on a high density of forest meadows; during the last thirty years, considerable success has been achieved in the restoration of two wild hoofed species, elk and antelope.

The following is a description of the status of the stocks of the most important species that live in the forest, steppe, tundra, and water bodies. Among the animals of the forest, the fur-bearing, in particular the squirrel, sable, and pine marten, are the most significant.

SQUIRREL. In the last century the squirrel was very important in the fur trade of our country: up to 12 million were procured [killed and obtained by the government] in a good year in the middle of the nineteenth century, and up to 6 million in a poor one (Silantyev, 1898). In the first decade of the twentieth century, the ouput reached 15.5 million per year (Silantyev, 1914), and in the thirties it fluctuated between 14 and 17 million (Kaplin).

Squirrel is procured mainly in Siberia where it is most abundant, the output being several times that of the European part of the USSR. In addition, Siberian squirrel is more valuable than European. In 1956, 1957, and 1958 the largest number of pelts was procured in Yakutia (1,003,-000; 911,000; and 979,000, respectively), in Krasnoyarsk Kray (882,000; 1,085,000; 519,000), and in Irkutsk and Tyumen oblasts. In the European part of the USSR in the same years, much of the squirrel came from Arkhangelsk Oblast (473,000; 155,000; 92,000), and the Komi ASSR. Small numbers were obtained even in the Ukraine. In recent years procurement of squirrel has begun also in the Crimea and the Caucasus, where it was introduced between 1937 and 1940 and where it has been successfully acclimatized. This introduction has not had any real economic benefit because the fur has rapidly lost its valuable qualities (this is especially true of a type of the common squirrel [*Sciurus vulgaris exalbidus*] that was settled in the Crimea). Also in some areas the squirrel has proven harmful to gardens and vineyards.

The squirrel population, like that of other rodents, often undergoes sharp fluctuations, depending on the availability of coniferous seeds in fall and winter. In the broad-leaved and mixed forests, acorns and linden nuts are also of great importance. In the European part of the USSR, because of the cutting of the forests and the replacement of mature coniferous stands and oak groves by birches, aspens, open forest, and scrub, the squirrel's habitat has deteriorated and correspondingly the catch has decreased. In Siberia, where logging is less extensive, the decline is due to the reduction in the number of commercial hunters, with the remaining hunters preferring the convenience of hunting sable. A large increase in the number of sable and pine marten may also lead to a decrease in the squirrel population since they feed on the latter.

The decline in the squirrel catch, however, is undoubtedly temporary and in regions where forests are not subjected to continuous cutting the previous high output may again be reached.

Quality pelts enjoy a steady demand and they are exported in great quantities, as for example in 1939 (13,377), in 1947 (12,582), and in 1957 (5,648) (Kaplin). In the forties and fifties squirrel pelts composed from 17% to 30% of Soviet fur exports.

SABLE. The sable had a much wider range in the past. In the seventeenth and eighteenth centuries it was still found far to the west of its present limits—in the Kola Peninsula, in the Pechora taiga, sometimes in Lithuania, Belorussia, the Smolensk area, and in Bryansk Oblast (Kirikov). At present, the sable is found nowhere in European Russia save in the taiga of the Urals piedmont; its main reserves are concentrated in Siberia and the Soviet Far East.

Sable fur, like the squirrel, is exported abroad in large and steadily increasing quantities. For example, in 1933, 14,000 pelts were exported; in 1943, 18,100; in 1945, 40,400; in 1955, 67,500; and in 1956, 68,500. In recent years, sable has composed about 6% of the fur export (Kaplin). Much of the procurement comes from Krasnoyarsk Kray, where 32,000 skins were obtained in 1956; 32,600 in 1957; and 36,700 in 1958. Considerably more sable is taken now than at the turn of the century, but this amount is still far below that of the first half of the seventeenth century, when reserves in Siberia (with the exception of the western districts) had not yet been touched.

A question that has arisen pertains to the scope of the plan of state purchases of sable in the next few years. The opinion is sometimes expressed that, for example, in Krasnoyarsk Kray over twice as much sable could be procured as in 1958. In this connection, it is wise to remember that Siberia's vast sable stocks were exhausted in the seventeenth century in a matter of a few decades. This was clearly demonstrated in the Mangazeya District, which occupied part of the territory of the present-day kray. In the years from 1630 to 1639, soon after the sable trade began there, annual procurements fluctuated from 30,000 to 67,000 pelts. But such exploitation obviously did not provide for renewal, and the stock declined catastrophically. Thus by 1668 only 6,896 sable were taken and the total in 1699 was 563, less than 1% the number of sable obtained in 1636. The same thing occurred in other Siberian regions, and must not be repeated. Also, it must not be forgotten that in order to attain the present favorable situation, years of hunting restriction were necessary and great effort was required to restock sable in Siberia and the Urals, which between 1927 and 1957 amounted to about 12,500 animals (Kolosov, Lavrov, Naumov). In addition, there was neglect, caused both by a governmental ban on sable procurement and by lack of management in those years when hunting was allowed (in the thirties, when collectivization of peasant farms occurred in the Siberian taiga, and also during the Second World War).

Plans for the procurement of sable pelts in the coming years must take the following factors into consideration: (a) excessive densities of sable must not be allowed since this could lead both to a wide transmission of disease should infection arise and to a shortage of feed; (b) overexploitation must not be allowed either because it could, in only two or three decades, result in the reduction of stocks that would annul previous conservation measures.

PINE MARTEN. At present, as in the past, the bulk of the marten population is concentrated in the European part of the USSR. The marten is now largely confined to some of the southern oblasts of the forest zone and in the Caucasus. Although its range is considerably less than that of the sable, its exploitation in the past was similar. At the turn of the century, marten extraction was only 10,000 to 20,000 pelts less than that of sable (Turkin and Satunin). Now, this difference has increased and in 1956–58 reached 30,000 to 40,000. The greatest number of marten pelts was procured in 1956–58 in the Ukraine (respectively 7,970, 7,700, and 7,820); in Bashkiria (5,200, 4,600, and 4,536); in Perm Oblast (5,160, 4,330, and 7,219); and in Krasnoyarsk Kray (3,850, 3,350 and 2,710).

A mature or medium-growth forest is required for the existence of the pine marten, since the latter avoids immature stands. In those southern oblasts of the forest zone and the forest-steppe where extensive cutting has occurred, the marten has become scarce, a fact reflected in state procurements. For example, in Kuybyshev Oblast in 1956–58 only 120, 130, and 95 marten pelts respectively were obtained; in Penza, 60, 130, and 226; in Tambov, 180, 140, and 70; and in Tula, 190, 150, and 201. Although the favorable habitat for the pine marten continues to shrink as a result of the clearing of the forests, many forested regions remain where the marten is systematically underexploited, and in all probability the number of marten procured will remain stable in the next few years. In fur exports, marten has a lesser importance than sable, amounting to 1% in 1933 and to 4% of the total fur export in 1951 (Kaplin).

SIBERIAN POLECAT. The present habitat of the Siberian polecat partially overlaps the habitat of the sable, but in the European areas the latter has retreated far to the east during the last two or three centuries, while the polecat has moved somewhat to the west.

According to state procurements for past years, it is obvious that the distribution of the polecat differs from that of the sable. The former is obtained primarily in the Soviet Far East and in Eastern Siberia (99,200 in 1956; 130,700 in 1957; and 97,400 in 1958). About 10,000 pelts are procured annually in Krasnoyarsk Kray, which is approximately one-third of the number of sable pelts; in Western Siberia and in the Altay Kray about 30,000, or up to four times the number of the sable pelts, are procured. In the Urals and the Ural piedmont the numbers of sable and polecat procured have not differed significantly in the same years; in 1956, 870 polecat and 910 sable; in 1957, 970 and 1,500, respectively; and in 1958, 2,343 and 1,799.

After the Second World War, polecat pelts were exported abroad in great quantities (from 200,000 to 275,000 annually). In total Soviet fur exports, the pelt of the polecat varied from about 2% to 4.5% during that period (Kaplin).

LYNX. In recent years, lynx pelts have proven highly valuable on the international market (up to thirty-five dollars and more). But the reserves of lynx are not large and not many are procured (in 1956, 5,200 were obtained; in 1957, 4,500; and in 1958, 4,700). Most of the lynx are from mountain taiga habitats: the Urals, the Altay, Transbaykalia, and Tuva. Transbaykalia in the past was relatively rich in lynx.

WHITE HARE. The extent and stocks of the white hare are closely associated with the extent of forests and scrub (among the latter, the most favorable are willow thickets). The reduction of the forests in the forest-steppe zone of the European part of the USSR moved the southern boundary of the white hare's habitat northward (in the 1760s, for example, the white hare still populated the forests of the Belgorod District in Kursk Province). In the forest-steppe areas where the white hare remained, its numbers declined significantly, while the common hare increased in number, an occurrence similar to that which transpired in the southern forest zone that was transformed into rural parkland. Where cutover areas had a renewal of forest growth, such renewal was in open deciduous forest, and conditions for the white hare improved rather than worsened.

The white-hare population and therefore the procurement of pelts vary sharply from year to year. In 1956, 1,605,000 furs were procured; in 1957, 1,063,000; and in 1958, 833,000. Most of the pelts were obtained in Yakutia (in 1956, 885,000; in 1957, 459,000; and in 1958, 315,000), but fluctuations in procurements are especially great there. During the period from 1924 through 1957, three massive slumps in the number of hare occurred, in 1924, 1936, and 1947 (declines probably attributable to epidemics and insufficient winter forage). In the same period there were comparably larger increases: in 1929, 1942, and 1953 (Naumov). During the first of these great increases, procurements increased 242-fold over the previous minimum. Other areas of procurement are Krasnoyarsk Kray, with 70,000 in 1956; and 48,000 in 1958; Irkutsk Oblast, with 43,000, 51,000, and 44,000, respectively; and Tyumen, with 50,000, 66,000, and 66,000. In the years of its increasing numbers in Siberia, the white hare was obviously underexploited (Naumov). There are no white hare in the European Russian steppe, and they are scarce in the forest-steppe and along the southern edge of the forest zone.

In the regions where the white hare is hunted for sport rather than for commerce, few pelts are turned in to the processing agencies and it is difficult, therefore, to estimate the actual number caught.

After the Second World War, the value of hare fur dropped severely on the international fur market and, since 1951, export from the Soviet Union has been discontinued (Kaplin).

ELK. Of the ungulates whose distribution and life are closely associated with the forest, the elk is of greatest importance.

Within the European part of the USSR during the last two and one-half centuries, there twice occurred such severe reductions in the number of elk that they became a great rarity in some regions and disappeared entirely in others. The first reduction occurred between the 1740s and the 1770s. At that time elk became scarce in the northwestern and central regions of European Russia and Bashkiria, and the last elk was killed in 1760 in the Carpathian foreland in the Ukraine (Galicia).

The decline in the elk population was so serious that an imperial ukase was promulgated in 1740 forbidding hunting for ten years in the Russian and Livland provinces. The sharp drop in elk numbers was due apparently not so much to overexploitation as to disease. It is theorized that the elk were infected by Siberian plague and by cattle plague, infected from domestic cattle driven along the stockyard routes. The restoration of the elk population and their reappearance in regions where they had long been absent occurred during the two decades following 1850, but they again sharply declined in European USSR in the first quarter of the twentieth century, this time because of reckless, predatory exploitation. Elk hunting, therefore, was forbidden in those years. From the thirties on, their number and extent increased until they were distributed over a huge area—from Belorussia to Kazakhstan, spreading both northward and southward. In places, in the forests along rivers and ravines, the elk penetrated the steppe zone, and through river reed thickets into the tundra.

According to a 1954 estimate, the RSFSR contained about 300,000 elk (Isayev). The lowest densities were in Yakutia and Krasnoyarsk Kray (about one elk per 5,000 hectares). This may be explained in all probability by the fact that the larch taiga of Eastern Siberia is less favorable for elk than the mixed coniferous-deciduous taiga and swampy coniferous forests of Western Siberia.

The greatest density of elk is found in populous oblasts located on the southern rim of the forest zone or in the forest-steppe, such as Tula, Moscow, Kuybyshev, and Tambov. Here there is more or less satisfactory protection for elk, and poaching does not reach the intensity that it has in such other regions as Western Siberia, the Komi ASSR, and the Urals. For example, in a stretch of six kilometers near the town of Iremel the carcasses of eight elk that had fallen into wire traps placed around water holes during the previous winter were found in the summer of 1952 (Tsvetayev). In the winter of 1959–60, poachers caught more than fifty elk in similar traps near the settlement of Yag-el (Inta District, Komi ASSR).

In some localities with many elk, there is inadequate winter forage, and elk have begun to damage young pine plantations and natural saplings. Means for winter feeding in order to divert them from the pine plantations must be devised, such as the cutting of aspen at the beginning of winter, and, when the bark and branches have been cleared by the elk in the spring the logs could be converted into lumber and firewood. In places where forests are cut in the winter, twigs and branches of birch and aspen could be piled up and what the elk leave could be burned the following spring. It is known that elk seldom eat hay, but experimentally, it would be useful to set out stacks of "elk hay," that is, hay mowed in the damp forest clearings and along riverbanks, where there is a great deal of spirea, bogbean, and other grasses readily eaten by the animal. At the same time, the permissible density of elk should be ascertained and when the limit is exceeded, licensed hunting of the surplus could be initiated. The norms will differ from place to place but they must be determined on the basis of available winter forage.

ROE DEER. In the recent past, the roe deer was one of our country's most numerous animals. At the end of the nineteenth century, about 500,000 head were procured annually. They were found in greatest densities in the forest-steppe of the western Ukraine, Belorussia, Volyn, the eastern slopes of the southern and central Urals, the forest-steppe beyond the Urals, the Western Siberian forest-steppe, the southern part of Eastern Siberia, and the Soviet Far East. The abundance of roe in the southern part of Eastern Siberia is shown by the fact that in the 1840s about 60,000 were procured annually in Verkhneudinsk Okrug alone. At the turn of the century, roe stocks severely declined, but beginning in the thirties they began to renew themselves in a number of regions. In Kazakhstan it is now possible to procure about 24,000 head per year (Sludskiy and Shubin). In Bashkiria the population rose significantly between 1930 and 1940, but during the deep snow of the winter of 1940–41 and in the years of the Second World War, roe suffered tremendously from poachers and wolves, and to this day remain scarce. According to an approximate census in 1954, there were about 150,000 roe in the RSFSR, of which 25,000 were in Amur Oblast; 15,000 in Khabarovsk Kray; 41,000 in Irkutsk Oblast; 45,000 in Krasnoyarsk Kray; 10,000 in Kurgan Oblast; and 9,000 in Novosibirsk Oblast.

The experiences of Czechoslovakia, Poland, and several other European countries suggest that stocks of roe can be greatly multiplied in the USSR.

Until the First World War, Germany, for example, had no less than 40 roe per 1,000 hectares of forest area (Fedyushin).

In order to increase their number, poachers and wolves must be dealt with more resolutely, and supplementary winter feeding must be supplied when the snow is deep. This is especially important in those places where the depth of the snow cover exceeds 50 centimeters.

NOBLE DEER. From the fifteenth through the eighteenth centuries, the noble deer was found between Belorussia, the Ukraine and the Pacific Coast and between the southern edge of the steppe zone, the mountains of the Caucasus and Central Asia and the mixed-forest zone. By the turn of the present century, its areal extent had become fragmented and the deer disappeared from many places of its previous habitat. In European Russia, it remained only in parts of the Baltic, the Crimea, and the Caucasus foreland, and then only in isolated districts. Though common in the Caucasus, the noble deer became a rarity in the Tyan-Shan, Urals, and Ural foreland, while in Kazakhstan and the West Siberian lowland it was almost annihilated. Most noble deer now remaining are in the Caucasus, where a preserve has a population of about 4,000 (Aleksandrov).

In the thirties and forties, successful resettlement of the Siberian sub-species, the maral [*Cervus elaphus sibircus*], were undertaken in Mordvin, Khoper, and Bashkiria preserves. Such resettlement should be expanded, particularly in the southern and, to some extent, central Urals, the southern foothills of the Urals, and the central Kazakh upland. All that is required is to safeguard the maral from wolves and poachers and to ensure feeding in winters of heavy snowfall. In the greater part of the European USSR, hunting the noble deer is forbidden, but in some parts of the Crimea and the Caucasus, sport hunting is permitted. In Siberia, young deer are procured primarily for their unossified antlers, from which a medicinal preparation is made.

Of all the natural habitats, the steppe has been the most transformed by man, resulting in a sharp change in the extent and number of commercial game. These changes lead in different directions for different species. Those whose existence depends on virgin steppe or long-term fallow land (for instance, the steppe marmot and tarbagan [*Marmota sibirca*]), have been reduced in both the area of distribution and in number.

STEPPE MARMOT. The steppe marmot remains in very few places in the European part of the USSR; their numbers are probably not over one thousand. However, eighteenth-century travelers referred to the "innumerable" and "extremely great" quantity of steppe marmots on the western bank of the Dnieper and in the Don Basin. They were even more numerous in the Volga upland, the Trans-Volga, as well as in the Orenburg and Kazakh steppes. Now steppe marmots are hunted commercially only in Kazakhstan, where 42,000 were obtained in 1956; 55,700 in 1957; and 60,800 in 1958. Before long the steppe marmot will remain in very few places, as "relics of nature" only.

Of the other indigenous marmots, tarbagan are procured in Chita Oblast (in 1956, 75,000 pelts; in 1957, 66,600; and in 1958, 42,600). Most gray marmots are procured in the Kirgiz SSR (in 1956, 117, 900; in 1957, 118,-100; and in 1958, 102,000).

About half the marmot pelts are exported (in 1956, 107,000 and in 1958, 76,000). Marmot furs are comparatively high in value—in 1951, a top-quality pelt of the gray Altay marmot brought nearly $3.50, and the pelt of a Transbaykal tarbagan about $2.50 (Kaplin).

Among the small marmots, the yellow (the sand marmot) found in the southern Trans-Volga, in Kazakhstan, and in Central Asia is the most important. Until 1955, these animals were fairly significant commercially and in some years as many as 6.6 million pelts were obtained (over half of which were exported, yielding up to $1.10 per pelt). In recent years the stocks of yellow marmot have been greatly reduced and at present only about one million pelts are obtained (Kaplin).

Pelts of the other little marmots are of small value. These rodents are more properly looked upon as harmful agricultural pests.

Formerly there were few small marmots in the virgin steppe. But with excessive grazing, the vegetation was eaten away and trampled down and a change occurred in the relationships between the species of steppe plants. In the last century, the southern Ukrainian feather-grass-steppe was transformed into sheep pastures. The tuberous mint plant multiplied greatly and its bulbs were readily eaten by the small marmot. In the second half of the nineteenth century, reports were prevalent that "small marmots were breeding by the millions." This was particularly so in Tavrida, Kherson, and Yekaterinoslav provinces. Simultaneously, the small marmot began to spread northward.

Cattle grazing and the consequent transformation of the steppe and dry-valley meadows into pastures of low, drought-resistant vegetation proved favorable for the small, big, and dotted marmots, and their increased numbers have led to grain losses during harvesting and shipment. Great quantities of marmots are killed: 75 million in 1956 and 90 million in 1957.

In 1958, 7.9 million small marmot pelts were procured in Saratov Oblast alone, and 22.3 million and 13.3 million respectively in Volgograd and Rostov oblasts. The great number of small marmots caught in recent years cannot be considered an achievement: it suggests instead a lack of success in the fight against this pest.

STEPPE POLECAT. The light or steppe polecat is an eager predator of the small marmot and its destruction by hunting is obviously harmful to the grain economy of the steppe. It should be protected but instead continues to be hunted, especially where small marmots are numerous. In Volgograd Oblast in 1956, 1957, and 1958, 10,100, 1,500, 1,200 pelts, respectively, were extracted; in Saratov, 3,800, 5,300, and 6,100; in Orenburg, 7,600, 15,600, and 22,500; and in Kazakhstan, 49,900, 34,100, and 25,500.

GRAY HARE. The gray hare is now not so much a steppe as a field animal. Its numbers fluctuate but not as greatly as those of the white hare. The greatest number of pelts within the last twenty-five years were obtained in 1935 (4.9 million); and from 1957 through 1959 about 1,600,000 annually were procured. Up to 1956 a large percentage of the pelts were exported, since in 1955 a first-class pelt was worth as much as ninety cents. After 1956 nearly all of the pelts were utilized by our own industry (Kaplin). The greatest quantity of pelts between 1956 and 1958 came from the Ukraine (827,100, 770,800, and 633,700, respectively), from Krasnodar Kray (64,000, 115,000, and 96,200), and from Stavropol Kray (40,300, 39,400, and 32,500). In the steppe and forest-steppe zones of the Trans-Volga and Ural piedmont, few gray hare were obtained in those years. How well the gray hare has adapted to rural parkland is demonstrated by the sizable state procurements of pelts in such regions as Belorussia, Smolensk, and Kaliningrad oblasts. In Belorussia in the same years 131,300, 109,400, and 128,400 pelts were obtained; in Smolensk Oblast, 12,400, 9,200, and 9,900; and in Kaliningrad Oblast, 18,700, 12,800, and 20,600.

Without doubt, the gray hare population can be multiplied. This is shown by the example of Czechoslovakia where, under conditions of intensive agricultural development and a highly productive rural economy, the density of gray hare is much higher than in our country. The possibilities for increasing stocks improve because Kazakhstan and Siberia have been recently invaded by the gray hare.

ANTELOPE [SAIGA TATARICA]. Of the hoofed animals living in the steppe and semidesert, the antelope is of the greatest economic importance. However, the extent of its distribution has significantly diminished during the last three centuries. It has disappeared from the steppe of the Ukraine, along the Don and the Volga (except the Lower Volga), and of Orenburg. In the Kalmyk, Astrakhan, Stavropol, and Kazakh dry steppes and semideserts, the antelope population periodically decreased greatly (mainly during the cattle famine and as a result of predatory hunting), but their numbers have again increased. Since the thirties, the antelope has multiplied to become the most numerous of the ungulates in our country, thanks both to the ban on hunting that was in effect for several years and also to the decline of nomadism in the dry Kazakh and Kalmyk steppe. In Kazakhstan alone the number of antelope was estimated to be between 1.2 million and 1.3 million (Sludskiy and Shubin). Large herds are also found in Stavropol Kray, in Astrakhan Oblast, in the southern part of Volgograd Oblast, and in the Kalmyk Republic. In 1958 there were about 540,000 head along the western littoral of the Caspian Sea. During the cattle famine in the winter of 1953–54, antelope died en masse (Zhirnov), and only in the spring of 1960 did their number here recover the 1952 level (180,000).

According to A. A. Sludskiy, commercial antelope hunting at the present time could be carried out in nine Kazakh oblasts, with a procurement of no less than 280,000 head annually. At the same time, Sludskiy raises the problem of regulating hunting. In Kazakhstan, hunting licenses were given to all who wanted them and, as a result, antelope hunting took on a predatory character.

CENTRAL ASIAN GAZELLE [GAZELLA SUBGUTTUROSA]. The gazelle is found in the plains and foothills of Central Asia (except for the Fergana Valley), in the deserts of Kazakhstan (except in the Zaysan Basin), and in the plains and foothills of southeastern Transcaucasia. It has been mercilessly decimated in recent years (Kolosov, Lavrov, Naumov). Effective protection for the gazelle and strict regulation of hunting are essential.

MONGOLIAN GAZELLE [GAZELLA GUTTUROSA]. Found in the southeastern and steppe regions of Transbaykalia, the Mongolian gazelle is also encountered in low density in the Chu steppe.

The tundra zone ranks third in reserves of useful game. Of the fur-bearing animals, the arctic fox is most important. Its pelts are sold on both the domestic and the export markets. In 1955, 31,000 were exported; in 1956, 32,000; and in 1957, 40,000. In 1955, 1% of fur exports was arctic fox. In 1958 and 1959, exports increased and a top-quality pelt sold for thirty dollars. In total, 107,000 arctic foxes were procured in 1955; 77,000 in 1956;

and 102,000 in 1958 (Kaplin). About four-fifths of the entire number came from the Siberian and Soviet Far Eastern tundra.

According to observations made in the Yamal Peninsula, there are in the arctic tundra subzone about five fox burrows per thousand hectares and only one and one-half in the southern tundra (Skrobov, 1961). The fluctuations in their population depends largely on the fluctuations in the population of the lemming and the other small rodents upon which the fox feeds. When lemmings are abundant in the tundra of the western piedmont of the Urals, the number of whelps in an arctic fox's litter reaches an average of eight; but in years of few lemmings a litter averages only from three to four (Skrobov, 1958). In general there is a decline in the arctic fox population. How this decline can be slowed is yet not clear. Supplementary feeding of foxes in lean years may have some value. In such years, too, it is important to hunt those areas where feed for arctic foxes is inadequate, thus reducing densities in order to avert a rise in epidemics (Kolosov, Lavrov, Naumov).

WILD NORTHERN REINDEER. Among the tundra animals other than the arctic fox, the wild reindeer has vital economic significance. Its extent, like that of most other wild ungulates, has contracted greatly during the last two or three centuries. Its total numbers have declined, due to overexploitation, the burning of reindeer (needle-leaf) pastures, and the development of domestic reindeer herding. In the last twenty to thirty years, an increase in the number and extent of wild reindeer has become noticeable in the Asiatic part of the USSR. At present, most are concentrated in the Taimyr Peninsula and the northern part of the Central Siberian taiga (Andreyev). At the end of the 1940s, the number of reindeer in this territory was estimated at nearly 350,000. In the summer of 1959, utilizing more exact methods of calculation, the number of reindeer in Taimyr was estimated at between 100,000 and 110,000 (Andreyev).

Along with those animals that live in a specific zone, there are species that are spread throughout the forest as well as in the steppe and tundra, and sometimes even in the desert. Among such fur-bearing animals are the fox, ermine, and wolf.

Fox. The fox is obtained in great quantities in our country. For example, in 1952, 706,000 pelts were procured; in 1954, 648,000; in 1956, 675,000; and in 1958, 620,000 (Kaplin). It is widely but very unevenly distributed. Most favorable habitats are the mixed-grass steppe and the sandy semidesert with well-developed brush vegetation. In parts of Stavropol Kray, burrows number from 120 to 250 per 100 square kilometers (Kolosov, Lavrov, Naumov), but in the Eastern Siberian taiga there is only 1 burrow per 200 to 400 square kilometers. Foxes are also scarce in flat clay semideserts; for example between the Emba and Ural rivers there are only 7 to 8 burrows per 100 square kilometers. There are few in the tundra. Other habitats are intermediate in density.

Up to 1950, a great many furs were exported: in 1946, 348,000; and in 1948, 487,000. In 1948, fox fur composed 1.6% of fur exports (Kaplin). However, fox furs have gone out of style abroad and they are used only in the domestic market. The pelt of the Kamchatka "fiery fox," the most expensive of the foxes, was valued on the external market at $12.50 in 1959; the Bashkir fox at nearly $6.00; and the Don [steppe] fox at $3.33.

The low value of fox fur and the harm inflicted by the fox, who destroys wild as well as domestic birds in some places, was the basis for declaring the animal an "outlaw" and for permitting year-round hunting. In a number of regions in the last few decades the fox has begun to suffer seriously from mange. This thinning out of the foxes may prove beneficial since contact between healthy and infected foxes will decrease. When disease has been brought under control it will be necessary to restrict fox hunting. In steppe and desert localities, where he feeds primarily on mice, the fox should not be exterminated at any time of the year by any of the methods available, for in those areas the fox can accomplish more good than harm.

ERMINE.   The ermine plays a very substantial role in state fur procurement. From 1957 through 1959, about 200,000 pelts were obtained annually. The main reserves are concentrated in Siberia where the ermine has long been procured in great quantity. In 1752, for example, 156,500 ermine pelts were shipped from Siberia to European Russia through the Verkhoturye customs alone. The bulk of ermine are prepared in Yakutia (about 150,000). In postwar years, ermine furs have comprised from 2% to 4% of the fur export (Kaplin).

Among fur-bearing animals there is quite a sizable group of species that live in and around water bodies and in embankment thickets of scrub, reeds, and cane.

BEAVER.   For a number of centuries the beaver has had special significance. Beaver pelts, and later the castoreum as well, were valued very highly and beaver hunting has contributed substantially to the national economy.

Thoughtless exploitation led to the virtual extinction of the animal at the beginning of this century. In our whole country fewer than 900 survived. In the 1930s, therefore, decisive steps were taken to restore the population. Hunting was strictly forbidden everywhere and several preserves were established (at Berezina, Voronezh, and Kondo-Sosva), whose primary task was the preservation and improvement of beaver stocks. Great efforts were made to distribute the beaver more widely; 2,800 were stocked between 1930 and 1958 (according to I. B. Kiris and I. G. Safonova). At present there are many times more beavers than there were at the beginning of the century, and they inhabit again many of the places in which they were found in the past. But many more of the areas in which they dwelt in the sixteenth to eighteenth centuries still remain uninhabited.

Part of their water habitat has changed significantly: surrounding forests and scrub have been logged or cleared; the water bodies themselves have shrunken; the riverbank marshes have disappeared. The introduction of the beaver into such transformed water bodies would be senseless, but many rivers, streams, and marshy lakes are still completely suitable for them. In every case the reservoir should be inspected beforehand and information about the former distribution of the beaver can facilitate the search for places suitable for stocking.

There are no beaver in the tundra. In the forest-tundra they are trapped on the Kola Peninsula, and in rather small quantities in the Ob and Yenisey forest-tundra. In the more easterly portions of the forest-tundra there are no data pertaining to their existence. There were few beaver on the northern edge of the taiga; though more common and numerous in the central and southern taiga, their distribution was very uneven. Much historical data concerning beaver runs relates to the basins of the Northern Dvina, Vychegda, Upper Mezen, Vashka, Middle Vyatka, Cheptsa, and Upper Vetluga. In the Western and Central Siberian taiga, the beaver were more common in the marshy sections of river basins. They were extremely scarce in Eastern Siberia due to the very severe winters and lack of snow, which results in solid freezing of the streams. The southern part of the forest zone of European Russia was the richest in beaver, found mostly in Belorussia, the Ukrainian Polesye and in the territories of what are now Smolensk, Bryansk, and Gorki oblasts and the Mari Autonomous Republic. Beaver were also common in many places in the forest-steppe, particularly in Podolia, along the Dnieper, on the Voronezh-Khopr interfluve, in the western piedmont of the Urals, and in the forest-steppe of Western Siberia. Beaver were rare along steppe rivers.

Obviously, the bulk of the beaver population today remains in European

Russia. The animal should be stocked in all appropriate habitats, including the eastern part of Smolensk Oblast in the future, and at a faster pace in the Komi ASSR. The beaver population in Western Siberia can and must be increased.

DESMAN.   The areal extent of the desman, like that of the beaver, has been severely curtailed and its numbers have sharply declined. In 1836, the Nizhegorod * Fair alone marketed 100,000 desman pelts, but by the end of the nineteenth century only 20,000 to 30,000 were procured per year. In 1920, with the aim of preserving the species, which is encountered only in European Russia, desman hunting was forbidden. The prohibition continued until 1933, when licensed desman hunting was permitted. In that year about 19,000 pelts were obtained. After that, extraction was once again forbidden until 1946. In 1949, 22,300 pelts were procured, but output began to fall again, and in 1958 the total catch was only 2,600. At that time the largest supply of desman was obtained in Vladimir (1,300) and Ryazan (537) oblasts.

What are the causes of the unsuccessful attempt to restore the desman? First of all, its primary habitat, the flood-plain lakes and small rivers, was flooded in many places in the Volga and Don basins as a result of the creation of reservoirs. The discharge of industrial wastes into the rivers has also had a destructive effect. Of the natural processes, winter flooding is harmful. For example, in Tambov Oblast the number of desman decreased by 80% after the high floods of the winter of 1954–55. In the reservoirs where American mink were stocked, the desman fell prey to the mink and their population declined. Quite a few desman perish when they fall into gill and set nets. It is necessary, thus, to prevent poachers from using illegal methods to catch fish.

OTTER.   In the last two to three decades, after some years of protection, otter stocks have largely been restored. An increase in numbers has been noted, for example, in Belorussia, the Ukraine, and in Smolensk and Sverdlovsk oblasts. Nevertheless, extraction is small, amounting to about 10,000 pelts per year (Kaplin), and its catch should be permitted only under license. In some areas, in Sverdlovsk Oblast for example, it is possible to increase procurement considerably (Bakeyev and Koryakov).

AMERICAN MINK.   This animal, transplanted from North America, was stocked in various regions, with quite variable results. It should not have been stocked in desman regions, but in some of the many other areas

---

* Or Nizhnyy Novgorod, now Gorki.

available. This valuable fur animal can be bred suitably on mink farms. The American-mink trade almost entirely replaced the trade in European mink, whose number dropped considerably (Kaplin).

MUSKRAT. The first muskrats were brought to the USSR in 1927 and settled in the European North, in Siberia, in the Soviet Far East, and in Central Asia. The greatest success in stocking was achieved in the deltas of the Amu-Darya and the Ili, where 40% of the muskrat are now procured (Kolosov, Lavrov, Naumov). The procurement in Kazakhstan and Uzbekistan was 310,000 in 1956, 3.6 million in 1957, and 212 million in 1958. Second in importance is Western Siberia, where in the same years procurements were respectively 1.6, 1.4, and 1.4 million pelts. Eastern Siberia and the Soviet Far East delivered 944,000, 814,000, and 820,000 pelts, respectively. The rest of our country produced about 500,000 pelts. In recent years, the muskrat has occupied third place in fur export value, nearly 9% (Kaplin). In 1952, a first-class muskrat fur was worth $1.80.

The future of the muskrat will depend primarily (*a*) upon the water level of the lakes of Western Siberia and Kazakhstan, and the quality of their shoreline vegetation and (*b*) upon the state of the reed thickets in the deltas of the Amu-Darya and Syr-Darya.*

In the USSR the stocking of alien animals as well as the redistribution of some of our own species throughout the country where they had not previously been found have occurred. One of these species is the Japanese dog [*Nyctereutes procyonoides*]. Opinions concerning the results of transporting the dog from the Soviet Far East to European Russia conflict. Some indicate that it has had favorable results; others note that in the places where the animal has multiplied, game birds, especially grouse, are being destroyed. The Japanese dog also is susceptible to rabies; it has been connected with the outbreaks of the disease that occurred in the forties and fifties in the central and western oblasts of the USSR, and along the lower Volga. That is why broader and more substantial research into the animal's biology is necessary.

COMMERCIAL GAME BIRDS

In terms of stocks and variety of valuable, commercially hunted birds, the USSR occupies a primary position in the world. Unfortunately, calculations of total numbers have been poor and commercial hunting does not

---

* The Tyuyamuyun reservoir project on the lower Amu-Darya may severely restrict the muskrat habitat in the delta.

extend throughout the entire country; additionally, the game obtained by hunters is unaccounted for. It is very difficult, therefore, to obtain a clear-cut appraisal of the present state of commercial reserves for it would necessarily be based on incomplete, heterogeneous data.

In the years of the greatest development (1931–32), centralized procurement contributed up to 11 million forest and water game. In terms of weight, this represents at least 8,000 tons of meat, extremely palatable and of high nutritional quality. However, even in those years, the state procurement system embraced no more than half the territory of the main commercial-hunting regions, and only a small part of the catch of the hunters was received at collection depots. Among all the species peculiar to the coniferous forests, the hazel grouse (according to 1927–28 data) has the greatest commodity yield (12%). That of waterfowl is much less; in many oblasts nearly all the output is locally consumed. In the noncommercial, thickly populated oblasts, where amateur sportsmen comprise the main contingent of hunters, all birds shot are consumed locally. It may be assumed, therefore, that the number of commercial birds obtained in the USSR exceeds the production figure quoted by up to ten times and approaches 100 million per year, equal to 50,000 to 80,000 tons of high-quality meat. The great economic value of birds and the importance attached to sport hunting compel us to give attention to questions of preservation and restoration.

Commercial birds may be divided into four categories: forest (gallinae); steppe (bustard [*Otis tarda*] and strepet [*Otis tetrax*]); water (duck, goose, swan, and coot); and marine (guillemot and eider). In procurements, forest birds occupy first place, because the hunting season falls in the cold season, when the flesh of some birds is particularly tasty and demand from foreign markets is high. Before the First World War, an average of about 6,473,000 birds of this group were killed annually; in 1931, 4,755,000 birds were received at the depots; but later the size of the output decreased by 90% and in 1955–56 amounted to only 458,000.

HAZEL GROUSE.   In commercial importance, the hazel grouse is first among the gallinae. Before the October Revolution, it provided 82.6% of the total volume of game export and game sent to large city markets; an average of over 5 million birds were taken annually. From 1928 through 1932, from 400,000 to 700,000 were received annually at the Leningrad export depot, but in the 1954–55 season only about 123,000 were taken in the entire country.

In the USSR the hazel grouse dwells in the subzone of coniferous and mixed forests, from its western to its eastern boundaries. The cutting of the forests has had an adverse effect on its numbers and in the central oblasts of European Russia it no longer has commercial value. At the turn of the century, the hazel grouse was procured on a commercial scale in the provinces of Vologda (458,000), Vyatka (336,000), Kostroma (88,000), and Kazan (35,000), as well as in Simbirsk, Yaroslavl, and other provinces (Silantyev, 1898). At present, in northern European Russia, the hazel grouse is procured only in Arkhangelsk Oblast and the Komi ASSR and only in insignificant quantities—in all, less than 45,000. The smaller procurements can be explained only partially by the decline in the number of grouse along the southern edge of the forest zone. Hazel grouse are abundant in many regions of Vologda, Arkhangelsk, and other northern oblasts (up to 55 mature birds per 1,000 hectares [Karpovich]), and in the Urals and Western Siberia they are also sufficiently numerous to permit commercial hunting. With correct organization of hunting and the training of hunters, the size of state procurements can be raised to several million without damage to reserves.

WOOD GROUSE. This bird has always been relatively low in procurements. The quantity obtained in 1928–32 at the Leningrad export depot did not exceed 31,000 per year. Since meat of the wood grouse is quite tough, it has never enjoyed great demand on international markets, and, consequently, it has been principally an object of sport hunting.

Wood grouse are distributed throughout the subzone of coniferous and mixed forests and in the recent past have been found in the larger woods of the forest-steppe. At the beginning of the nineteenth century, for example, they were found in the forests of Kharkov Province and as far south as Voronezh and the Pre-Volga Heights almost down to Kamyshin (Kirikov). During the last hundred years, as a result of intensive logging, the range of the wood grouse has moved considerably northward in European Russia and they have become rare in the central oblasts. In the winter of 1956–57, the population of wood grouse in Belorussia was estimated at 3,200, with an average of 0.6 birds per 1,000 hectares of forest area (Dolbik).

Lithuania has only from 600 to 700 birds, or 3.2 mature cocks per 1,000 hectares where they are found (Logminas, 1960). The density of the wood-grouse population in the Lapland Preserve fluctuates from 20 to 290 birds per 1,000 hectares, and in the pine forests of the Pechora taiga, between 70 to 200 (Semenov-Tyan-Shanskiy, 1960). In Arkhangelsk, Vologda, and Leningrad oblasts and the Karelian and Komi ASSR's are found from 1.9 to 9.5 wood grouse per 1,000 hectares of forested area (Karpovich); in the

Mordvin and Tatar ASSR's and in Kuybyshev and Tambov oblasts, not more than one; and in Yaroslavl and Vladimir oblasts, 3.1 to 3.3. According to data obtained by V. I. Osmolovska, based on a survey of males, the number in the northern European part of the USSR does not reach commercial densities, and continues to fall catastrophically. In the Central Urals, as well as on the flanks of the Urals, their numbers are somewhat higher and amount to from 4.3 to 6 birds per 1,000 hectares. The wood grouse reaches truly commercial density in the less populated regions of the Northern Urals. In Sverdlovsk Oblast they total about 50,000; by mid-August this number grows, due to the appearance of the chicks, to 140,000 (Danilov, 1961). There are many wood grouse in the Irtysh taiga north of Tobolsk (an average of 6 per 1,000 hectares), along the lower course of the Ob, and in Krasnoyarsk Kray. The stony wood grouse, which populates the taiga in Eastern Siberia, Transbaykalia, and the Amur region, is quite plentiful: according to 1958 data, it averaged from 4.5 to 6.5 birds per 1,000 hectares (data of Osmolovska).

The primary reason for the sharp reduction in the number of wood grouse throughout European Russia is the continuous cutting of the forests that goes on over large areas and leads to the destruction of the mating places. By selective logging, which is more expedient for other reasons as well, the destruction of mating places could be avoided. The number of wood grouse also are severely reduced in those forest areas where pines are tapped for their sap and where cattle graze. Collectors of resin and herdsmen frighten off the sitting hens and often ruin their nests. The tapping of the forests of Vologda and Kostroma oblasts (Osmolovska) is especially harmful. Finally, a third important reason for their decline is excessive hunting in several of the central oblasts.

BLACK GROUSE. At present, as was true in the past, the black grouse is important in game procurements. From 1904 through 1913, commercial depots averaged 511,000 per year. From 1928 through 1932, the Leningrad export depot received from 260,000 to 412,000 per year, but in 1954–55 only 62,000 were procured. The very sharp decline in procurements does not correspond to the number of birds, for the black grouse is widely distributed over the USSR. It populates the entire forest zone as far as its northern limits, while in the south it is common in the forest-steppe. The continuous plowing of virgin lands and the cutting of forests in the forest-steppe regions of the European USSR have considerably reduced its total number, but the intensive cutting of the forests in the taiga, for example in northern Kostroma Oblast, has had the opposite effect. It has led to the overgrowth of large areas by aspen and birch, simultaneously improving the living conditions of the black grouse and promoting its increase.

In the western part of the country, in Lithuania in 1956, 10,700 black grouse nests were accounted for (Logminas, 1959). In the northern European part of the USSR, from Murmansk Oblast and the Komi ASSR to Novgorod and Vologda oblasts, the number of black grouse per 1,000 hectares fluctuates from 9.8 to 44.4 (Karpovich). In Sverdlovsk Oblast, in the most favorable regions, densities reach 12 to 15 grouse, and the total number of mature birds amounts to 90,000 (Danilov, 1961). Black grouse are especially plentiful in Bashkiria, the Central Urals, and to the east of the Urals. There they average 30 to 40 birds per 1,000 hectares, while as many as 100 cocks may be in the mating congregations. In winter they gather in large flocks, facilitating commercial hunting. Their numbers are even higher in southern Tuymen Oblast, in Omsk, the central districts of Tomsk Oblast, in the foothills of the Altay, in the Kazakh forest-steppe, and in southern Buryatia. The severe decline in the number of black grouse in the central part of the European USSR and in parts of southern Siberia was caused not so much by changes in natural conditions as by excessive hunting (Osmolovska).

WILLOW PTARMIGAN. Very significant commercially, this bird is in greatest number in the southern tundra and near the northern boundaries of the taiga, where islands of forests alternate with mossy swamps. In the taiga itself ptarmigan are rather rare, while in the forest-steppe of Siberia and Kazkhstan they are very abundant. In many regions hunting is carried out on a large scale; in some years, for example, the Ust-Usinsk cannery used the meat of the willow ptarmigan as its basic raw material, processing 60,000 birds annually. The total output in those same years in the former Pechora Kray reached about seven hundred thousand.

At the beginning of the eighteenth century the willow ptarmigan was widely distributed in the European USSR (Kirikov), but it has now disappeared. In August, the number of willow ptarmigan in the Lapland Preserve averages 390 per 1,000 hectares; in September and October, an average of 80 along the middle course of the Pechora River (Semenov-Tyan-Shanskiy, 1959). In the northern oblasts of European Russia, the quantity of mature birds per 1,000 hectares of forest area fluctuates from 4.9 to 38.1 (Karpovich). Beyond the Urals there are still many willow ptarmigan. However, even there commercial quantities of this species remain only in isolated spots within the forest-tundra, the forest-steppe, and along the southern border of the forest zone. The number of ptarmigan in the south is being reduced due to the cutting of the forests, drainage of the swamps, and excessive hunting.

PARTRIDGE. The conditions for survival of the partridge are unfavorable. This valuable commercial bird is peculiar to the steppe and forest-steppe zones; unlike most of the other gallinae, its extent has not been reduced by logging and plowing but rather is extending further toward the north. At the end of the nineteenth century the number of partridge increased in Yaroslavl and Novgorod provinces, and in the twentieth they advanced into the southern regions of Arkhangelsk Oblast and into the Karelian and Komi ASSR's. But their number was simultaneously reduced in its principal range—the forest-steppe south of the forest zone in European Russia, and in Western Siberia. Until recently the partridge was procured in these areas by the tens of thousands. In former Perm Province alone, and in the North Caucasus, partridges were the principal game for sport hunters, while on the eastern slope of the Urals and in Western Siberia they were procured commercially.

At present, in Lithuania for example, the average density of the partridge is nearly 5.5 per 1,000 hectares (Logminas, 1959); in Tula and adjacent oblasts (including designated hunting preserves) it is 6 to 8 per 1,000 hectares; and even in Rostov Oblast it does not exceed 10 (Osmolovska). The partridge has commercial density only in selected places in Western Siberia.

How low the stocks of the common partridge are can be judged by comparing them with the densities in foreign countries. In densely populated Czechoslovakia the number of partridges is 200 to 400 per 1,000 hectares on nearly 30% of its territory, and 800 per 1,000 hectares in some places. Without harming the basic stock, the shooting of 208 birds per 1,000 hectares annually can be permitted, procuring about 2.5 million partridges or 768,000 kilograms of valuable meat, for domestic use and export. In money, this procurement is worth 15 million korunas. In Great Britain these birds average 312 per 1,000 hectares, and in the better habitats as much as 1,250.

It is obvious from these examples that the partridge can exist very successfully under agricultural conditions. Its catastrophic decline in number in the USSR was caused, first of all, by the continuous plowing of huge steppe areas with complete destruction of all islands of forests and shrubs. Equally detrimental (just as for the black grouse, woodcock, and other birds) is the grazing of cattle in the few remaining steppe groves, and the clearing of bushes from natural pastures and hay lands. The destruction of the bushes deprives the birds of their nesting places and cover for the chicks. In the interests of game and the need for the clearing of agricultural tracts, we recommend that forest-bush belts be left or planted around sufficiently large fields and natural fodder lands. Simultaneously, such plantings can have importance in field protection. Osier beds on riverbanks in flood lands aid in the deposition of alluvia and in the protection of the flood plains from erosion. Experience has shown that near the forest strips the number of partridge is always higher.

In agricultural areas, partridge settle readily and with greatest density in potato and beet fields, where they find good cover from the sun and predators, and also plentiful forage. It has been noted in Czechoslovakia that the partridge, by destroying beetroot weevils and other vermin, increases beet yields by 50%. Under our conditions the partridges also destroy many harmful insects and snails.

Reports have been received recently from many points concerning the death of partridge, black grouse, and pheasant from poisoning by grain treated with granozan (a weed killer) and also by mineral fertilizers. Frequently the partridge perishes in great numbers after severe winters. In its northern habitat this occurs when there is a deep snow cover of long duration, and in its southern habitat, when the ground is covered with ice. In these periods, the partridge is in need of supplementary feeding and artificial cover.

The following steps are necessary for the preservation and restoration of the partridge population: a temporary cessation of all partridge hunting, a resolute campaign against poaching, and artificial breeding in the European part of the habitat.

The reserves of two other species of valuable hunting birds are also declining sharply—pheasant and quail.

The decline of the pheasant is connected with the cutting of the taiga and the clearing of thickets in the foothill and semidesert regions in the southern part of the country, and with the spring burning of dry grasses, a practice in a number of regions. In order to increase the number of pheasants, it is necessary to preserve the existing thickets and to create new ones of corresponding density and area.

The decrease in quail in the steppe of European Russia is due primarily to their mass destruction in the Mediterranean countries where they winter. Quail procurements in Italy, Algiers, and Egypt are of a commercial character: not long ago, from 400,000 to 800,000 European quail were exported from Alexandria to Europe. The restoration of this species may be furthered by implementation of an international convention regarding the limitation of procurement in winter.

STREPET AND BUSTARD. Even less favorable than the state of birds in other regions is that of steppe birds, particularly the strepet and the bustard. This is at least partially understandable since the habitat of both species has been reduced by the plowing of virgin steppes. Economic development in the steppe has contributed particularly to the decline of the strepet, which was, at the end of the eighteenth century, still nesting in southeastern Belorussia and in the forest-steppe regions of Orel, Kursk, and Tambov provinces (Kirikov). About 1,850,000 strepet were estimated in Voronezh Province (Severtsev), but from 1920 to 1930 the edge of its habitat in European USSR ran along the southern edge of the forest-steppe; at present, strepet nesting occurs in only a few isolated regions. Its number in Kazakhstan also declined catastrophically following the plowing of virgin and long-fallow lands. As yet there is no basis for anticipating the restoration of the habitat of this valuable species, but if its stock is to be preserved and increased it is necessary to prohibit hunting, to intensify the struggle against poachers, and to create a network of long-term preserves.

The bustard, unlike the strepet, reacts less to the plowing of the steppe; it does not avoid cultivated lands and readily nests among winter field crops. Nevertheless, it has been reduced in number almost as significantly, owing to man. In the last few years destruction has been extraordinarily hastened by the rapid development of auto transport: the number of bustard in the steppe of the European USSR has declined to a minimum; in Siberia and Kazakhstan its stocks are threatened with annihilation. With a complete cessation of hunting and the eradication of poaching, stocks of this exceptionally valuable bird can be restored, and it may appear again in places where it has entirely disappeared.

WATERFOWL. It is most difficult to establish and subsequently eliminate the causes leading to the sharp reduction in waterfowl reserves. The birds of this group are migratory: Gumenniki geese [*Anser fabalis*] nest in the tundra of Central Siberia and spend the winter in northern Europe; white geese fly from Wrangel Island to the Pacific Coast of the United States; ducks from the lower stretches of the Ob and Irtysh moult in the Volga delta and then migrate in winter to Transcaucasia, the Balkans, and Egypt. Therefore, the effect of natural geographical conditions, of man's economic activities, or of the destruction of the birds in any region, is often reflected in their number in quite distant localities.

It is even more difficult to enumerate the reserves of waterfowl than to appraise forest birds. Organized procurement of waterfowl was practiced for only a few years in a very limited territory, and even then only an insignificant portion of the total take of hunters actually reached procurement points. In 1931 a total of 5.5 million ducks, geese, swans, and coots were procured, nearly one-half of which (2,264,000) was obtained in Western Siberia, primarily in the lake country of the forest-steppe. In that same natural region east of the Urals, 1,240,000 birds were procured, and in Kazakhstan, 285,000. The Ukraine totaled 203,000 birds; Karelia, 37,000; and the former Northern Kray, 23,000. The remaining regions, rich in waterfowl, produced almost nothing.

However, one cannot evaluate the quality of waterfowl harvested annually on the basis of available data, for in the years preceding the Second World War, hunters in Azerbaydzhan alone procured between 700,000 and 750,000 birds annually. More than 200,000 birds were obtained in a single season in the Volga delta; hundreds of thousands in northern Asia [*sic*] and the Soviet Far East; and even more in northern Siberia. It is well known that sportsmen frequently hunt ducks, and it is probable that throughout the USSR more waterfowl than forest birds are procured.

Waterfowl reserves are obviously and steadily declining in most regions, the decline being particularly rapid during the last twenty-five to thirty years. Among the general causes are the continually growing number of hunters, the increasing intensity of hunting (mainly for sport), the still persistent poaching, and the gathering of eggs. According to observations in the Oka flood plain, 42% of mallard fledglings and 76% of teal die before the development of feathers. About 60% of the fledglings are taken by hunters in the hatching area. In the Oka flood plain, 93 ducks (counting the slightly wounded) are destroyed for every thousand hectares. The average number of ducks taken by one hunter in a season in the best hunting areas of the central oblasts of the RSFSR is nearly 10 (the local averages range from 2.3 in Yaroslavl Oblast to 14.3 in Tambov). The overall number of birds obtained does not change from year to year, although the number of hunters undoubtedly varies. Hence, the hunters here annually procure all the waterfowl available. The intensity of hunting in the central oblasts is growing constantly, as indicated by the rising percentage of the return of bands from ducks that were tagged in the central course of the Oka (Sapetin).

During the last thirty years the wintering conditions of the birds have deteriorated sharply. Even at the beginning of the twentieth century, the Azerbaydzhanian wintering areas alone extended over about one million hectares and provided normal living conditions for a gigantic number of birds. Now the vast swampy lowlands where the ducks and geese previously found refuge in winter are gradually being drained and are used for agriculture. These changes have occurred in the Colchis and the Kura-Araks lowlands where millions of ducks, geese, and coots gather in winter. The fall in the level of the Caspian Sea, the reclamation of the Mugan steppe, the drainage of the Lenkoran Lowland, and the change from rice cultivation to tea growing—all have reduced the territory suitable for wintering to one-tenth of its former size. The second most important wintering place is the shallow Bay of Gasan-Kul. Its area decreased from 1,030 hectares in 1888 to 20,000 in 1932, and at present the bay is almost completely dry.

This reduction in areas serving as wintering places for our migratory birds is also occurring abroad. The swampy lowlands of Lincolnshire in Great Britain have long been covered with orchards and gardens; the Zuider Zee in the Netherlands is being drained, as well as the Venetian lagoon in Italy; and irrigation works are being carried out in the Enzeli Lowland (Iran), in the valley of the Euphrates (Iraq), in the Nile delta, and in other regions. As a result, migratory birds are compelled to concentrate during the winter on a few small reservoirs where they are hunted intensively. In the Bay of Kyzylagach near the Lenkoran, up to five million ducks, excluding coots, gather in winter. There, in the shallow waters of the bay, up to 850 river ducks or 50 to 90 coots per hectare feed simultaneously. This area cannot provide for such large numbers, and the forage is being quickly exhausted, forcing the fowl to fly farther south in search of adequate bodies of water. Many leave the USSR.

The banding of ducks moulting in the Volga delta showed that only 73% of the mallards winter in the USSR, and the remainder fly outside our borders. Even more of the other species leave our country: 60% of the shoveler duck, 82% of the widgeon, and 84% of the garganey (Sapetin and Shevareva).

The deterioration of the wintering areas, with its extremely pernicious effect upon the number of ducks and geese, requires the immediate implementation of primary biotechnical works; international agreements concerning the preservation of wintering places for birds abroad must also be made.

During the nesting period, waterfowl populate the entire USSR, but habitat conditions and, accordingly, the status of the stocks, varies from zone to zone (Isakov). In the deserts and semideserts, the nesting places of the ducks and geese are in the valleys of large rivers and are noticeably dispersed. While the number of nesting places is still large (the flood plains of the Sary-Su, the lower stretches of the Syr-Darya), they have greatly diminished in recent years due to the settlement of these areas by man, the development of fishing, and the burning of the reeds. It is possible to eliminate some of the causes for the decline in bird numbers through simple administrative measures. On the positive side, several new bodies of water, including large reservoirs on the Zeravshan River and the expanded Kelif lakes, are being created in the deserts; they are used for nesting wintering places by a considerable number of birds.

In the steppe and forest-steppe, waterfowl populate the river flood plains, but their reserves are especially great on the broad, lake-country plains. Not too long ago there were quite a few ducks and geese in the European USSR, and commercial hunting of birds was widespread on many steppe rivers (the Don, Psyol, Dyoma, and others). The valleys of steppe rivers were rich in reed thickets and flood-plain oak groves. But the river valleys were brought under cultivation as the population grew, and there are now few remaining places suitable for ducks. The stocks of birds in this area are paltry and can be restored only through the creation of a network of long-term preserves that should, beyond conservation, develop a program to bring reservoirs up to a standard suitable for the settlement of ducks and geese.

In the Asiatic USSR, the main concentrations of waterfowl occur in the lake regions of Kazakhstan, east of the Urals, and in the Baraba steppe. Some idea of the abundance of game in the Kazakh steppe may be gained from the following figures: During the nesting period in 1959, about 14,000 waterfowl were counted on Lake Kurgaldzhin; during the moulting period, about 147,000 ducks and geese; in the same year, about 400,000 ducks, coots, and flamingos were registered at Lake Tengiz (Gavrin). This vast territory yields the greatest volume of ducks, geese, and coots, but the size of the state purchases changes severely from year to year, reflecting sharp fluctuations in lake levels due to climatic conditions. The present state of this nesting region is favorable enough, but planned vast land-reclamation projects in the northern part of Baraba may considerably reduce its productivity.

It is very difficult to evaluate the waterfowl reserves in the forest belt since the ducks nesting there are scattered, forming significant concentrations only in the valleys of large rivers. Their stocks at present in European Russia are not great and reach commercial density only in selected areas of the north. The flood plains of the large rivers in this area have been settled and developed and very few places suitable for waterfowl nesting remain.

The construction of large reservoirs brings about fundamental changes in the entire natural complex. In the first stages of their existence, the reservoirs promote growth in the number of some waterfowl species (mallard), while at the same time they cause a sharp decline in others (teal, quacker, shoveler, coot). Soon, some river valleys (the Volga, Dnieper, Kama, and others) will become unbroken chains of reservoirs and for this reason it is necessary to use them properly in the hunting economy. To accomplish this, each should have a permanent preserve where a cycle of biotechnical measures would be assured, the most important of which would be the maintenance of a constant level in the reservoirs chosen for the introduction of a hunting industry.

In the taiga of Siberia the waterfowl reserves are much greater than in Europe and are not threatened to the same degree; however, here too, both local and transient game is constantly declining in number. The reasons for this include the rapid settlement of the taiga, especially the river valleys; the increase in the number of sport hunters; and the worsening of the moulting and wintering conditions for local birds.

The tundra and forest-tundra possess gigantic stocks of waterfowl. It is probable that in terms of local production these territories are even richer than the lake country of the forest-steppe. Besides the very large quantity of ducks, more than six species of geese nest here. Their abundance is characterized by the fact that fairly recently on Kolguyev Island alone there were nearly 20,000 geese taken. However, even in the tundra that has been least affected by man's economic activities, the game stocks are notably decreasing—in places, almost catastrophically. For example, brant have been reduced to one-tenth of their previous number during the last fifty years, while the white goose, formerly numerous, remains only in a few isolated colonies. This phenomenon is explained by the immoderate hunting of moulting geese in the north and the overexploitation of waterfowl in the West European and North American wintering areas. This overexploitation is corroborated by the huge figures on brant output in Jutland and by the hunting of ducks with the use of snares of the "decoy" type. The destruction of the primary feed of the brant, common eel grass, over vast areas is also significant. Finally, in recent years, the pollution of the sea by oil has caused the death of large numbers of birds. Many of the pochard ducks [*Aythya ferina*] that inhabit the tundra spend their winters in the Baltic and North seas, vast sections of which are regularly polluted by petroleum products. In January, 1957, for example, near Gotland Island more than 30,000 polar ducks [*Clangula hyemalis*] perished from pollution. Following this incident, these ducks disappeared almost entirely from their nesting places in the huge territory of Swedish Lapland. Similar destruction of waterfowl has also occurred along the Murman Coast and on Kamchatka Peninsula, while in Azerbaydzhan oil pollution causes an annual destruction of up to 25,000 birds. Legal measures are necessary to prevent further water pollution.

Among the birds of the northern maritime coasts, the eider has great importance, its down exceeding 20 rubles per kilogram in value. In its time, the gathering of eiderdown was one of the lucrative enterprises of the local population, but the hunting of eider and gathering of its eggs has much reduced its number. The stocks of eider in some places, for example on the Karelian Coast of the White Sea, have been diminished severely. In 1960, only 1,094 pair of eider were counted on the Murman Coast (Gerasimova). The renewal of eider stocks calls for strict protection and the implementation of a series of relatively simple biotechnical measures.

The birds that nest in large seaside colonies, especially the guillemot, play a large role in the lives of the population of the Far North. The reserves of guillemot are considerable and yield a large output of eggs, which in terms of fat content and vitamins exceed that of the gallinae. Under the difficult conditions of arctic life, the importance of guillemot eggs as a food source is very great (Uspenskiy).

MEASURES FOR THE RENEWAL AND EXPANSION OF STOCKS OF COMMERCIAL GAME

This survey of commercial animals and birds indicates that each species reacts differently to the steadily accelerating process of economic development. If the reserves of one are sharply reduced, other species retain their numbers and even increase. In conjunction with this survey, it is possible to subdivide all commercial game into several groups according to their current population and the possibilities for their expanded reproduction in future. Different situations and different natural conditions alter the grouping of species in each area. The assignment of an animal or bird to a group must be determined by the basic means necessary in a given area to preserve and expand its population.

One group is composed of the beasts and birds whose lives are highly dependent on specific natural habitats with characteristic fauna and flora. Such game never attains significant numbers outside its specific native habitat. Any encroachments on this habitat by the economic activities of man unfavorably affects the status of such game.

This group can be subdivided into two subgroups: (*a*) the inhabitants of the tundra, taiga, desert, water-divide swamps, and northern seacoasts; (*b*) the inhabitants of the steppe, forest-steppe, the broad-leaved and mixed forests, river flood plains, and steppe lakes.

In the first subgroup are: the northern reindeer, the polar fox, the sable, the squirrel, onager, the wood and hazel grouse, tundra geese and ducks, the inhabitants of the bird bazaars, flamingo, and mountain goose. The zones inhabited by these species within the USSR still retain the basic profiles of their inherent natural conditions. Under these circumstances, the resources for large-scale reproduction of each of the species in this subgroup can be assured for the present with proper organization of the hunting economy. However, conditions for survival are not uniform for each of the species. In some regions a number of species are being sharply reduced with unrestricted hunting and poaching, while overpopulation occurs with others due to insufficient extraction. These basic measures for expanding stocks and output must be undertaken: organized extraction, census of reserves, regular procurement, and strict control in observance of hunting laws.

Among the species of the second subgroup are the steppe marmot, strepet, desman, and ducks that inhabit the steppe and river flood plains (gray duck, teal, quacker, and others), also the species that moult on steppe lakes and winter on inland water bodies. Parts of the area that they populate are being catastrophically reduced and some are completely disappearing. It is impossible to count upon an increase in the number of such species as the steppe marmot, strepet, and desman unless preserves are immediately created for their conservation and propagation. Restoration and a further increase in the stocks of waterfowl are entirely possible, principally by creating a broad network of permanent preserves at the most important gathering points for birds: for nesting or moulting; during migration; and for wintering. Such preserves require complex improvement measures.

The next group is composed of those species that are less sensitive to deforestation, agricultural development, and other forms of economic development, if such development is planned correctly. To this group belong elk, roe and noble deer, beaver, forest marten, white hare, antelope, bustard, black grouse, eider, and several other species. Large-scale reproduction of all these species is entirely possible with an approach to the use of natural resources that considers equally the requirements of agriculture, forestry, and hunting.

Members of this group react favorably to the areal expansion of economic development. The replacement of forests by fields promotes the growth in number and an expansion of the habitat of the gray common hare, partridge, and quail. Irrigation of desert pastures increases the number of ducks and snipe; and the creation of reservoirs in Central Asia and Transcaucasia establishes new wintering areas for waterfowl. This group appears to be a particularly good prospect for the highly developed territories of the European USSR and of Western Siberia. The interests of game reproduction, procurement regulation, and the implementation of a simple range of biotechnical measures must be taken into consideration when planning shelter belts and meadow-improvement projects, permitting considerable production returns from hunting, even in the most populous regions.

Finally, several measures necessary for the restoration and expansion of industrial game preserves should be mentioned.

1. No enterprise, not even hunting, can exist without an assessment of reserves and productivity. It is necessary, therefore, to make new estimates of the number of the most valuable species of game and the distribution of their reserves. This could be done, for example, by an agency similar to the Biological Survey, established in the Main Administration of Hunting and Preserves of the RSFSR. At the same time it is necessary to reappraise the total extraction possible, relating it to the needs of commercial and sport hunting enterprises, hunters, and foresters. On the basis of such data it will then be possible to assess the over-all status of the animal population as well as the degree of commercialization desirable in the various regions. Methodological guidance for the inventory of useful fauna should be entrusted to the Academy of Sciences of the USSR.

2. In the past, in places where hunting was one of the main means of subsistence of the population, the hunting terrain was divided and assigned to specific groups of people. The need for such division is even more important now, but the assignment of the terrain should assume different forms and should depend upon the natural characteristics of the region and upon the commercial or sporting character of the hunting.

3. Current extraction of the various animals and of the hunting territories is uneven. Therefore, it is necessary to establish the industry in remote areas in presently unused taiga and tundra territories, simultaneously limiting hunting in the densely populated regions; also, zones must be created around large cities where hunting should be prohibited except for licensed hunting for species threatened by overpopulation, such as elk.

4. The preservation and increase of some species of game, particularly waterfowl, can be accomplished only through the creation of a network of

large government preserves. The experience of the United States, where about ten million hectares were set aside as national preserves (data from 1949) has indicated the high profitability of such a measure. Governmental preserves, in addition to wildlife conservation, must also strive for the improvement of game habitats and of animal redistribution.

5. Considerable increases in the population of such commercial game may be attained by integrating the interests of agriculture, forestry, and hunting in the process of developing the economy of each individually. For example, overlogging is unfavorable for the renewal of game stocks. Such logging leads to the rise of nonrenewable cuttings or to the creation of uniform forest growth of single species (principally pine). It would be desirable to change to the cutting of selected pockets that would promote the formation of variegated and multigrowth plantings. In the improvement of meadows, protection must be provided for nesting birds by leaving hedgerows. The protective forest plantings in regions with much cultivated land serve this same purpose. Grazing in forest glades and protective plantings must be halted; it is also necessary to forbid the burning of reed thickets and, during reed harvest, to leave belts of reeds adequate for game refuges.

Since forests of our country provide hunting areas as well as wood, it is necessary to plan uses that unify both economies. Forestry workers should be responsible for the conservation of hunted fauna and the implementation of very simple biotechnical measures.

6. Particular attention must be given to the struggle against poaching. In this important matter we must involve the regional soviets, agricultural soviets, the worker's militia, social organizations, and, most importantly, the hunting groups themselves.

7. It is necessary to regulate the number of ungulates procured and to prohibit hunting of partridge, bustard, strepet, and swan in the European USSR. The hunting of the gray goose should be restricted as should the hunting of the wood grouse in the central oblasts.

8. In the planning of scientific research, primary as well as secondary tasks should be considered. The existing All-Union Scientific Research Institute of Animal Raw Materials and Pelts (in Kirov) is occupied principally with questions of biology, distribution, and rationalization of the hunting of fur-bearing animals. Its program should include a second research center for detailed study of hoofed animals and feathered game. At the same time, the renewal and expansion of commercial fauna resources should be included in the plans of other kindred scientific research institutes:

the institutes of the Academies of Sciences of the USSR and the Union Republics, the zoological faculties of the universities, and the agricultural institutes.

BIBLIOGRAPHY

Aleksandrov, V. N. "Metody ucheta i dinamika chislennosti oleney v Kavkazskom zapovednike" [Methods of Calculation and the Variance in Population of the Deer in the Caucasus Preserve]. In *Soveshchaniye po voprosam organizatsii i metodam ucheta resursov fauny nazemnykh posvonochnykh* [Meeting on the Questions of Organization and Methods of Assessing the Resources of the Land Vertebrate Fauna]. Papers. Moscow, 1961.

Andreyev, V. N. "Izucheniye chislennosti severnykh oleney i putey ikh migratsii s pomoshchyu aerometodov" [The Study of the Population of Northern Deer and of their Migration Routes from the Air], *Zoologicheskiy zhurnal* [Zoological Journal], vol. 40, no. 1 (1961).

Bakeyev, N. and Koryakov, B. "Polneye i pravilneye ispolzovat okhotnichye-promyslovuyu faunu" [To Use More Fully and Correctly Industrial Fauna], *Okhota i okhotnichye khozyaystvo* [Hunting and Hunting Economy], no. 1 (1960).

Danilov, D. N. "Vliyaniye urozhayev lesnykh semyav na produktivnost okhotnichikh ugodiy" [Influence of Forest Seed Yields on the Productivity of Hunting Terrain]. In *Trudy in-ta okhotnichyego promysla* [Papers of the Institute of Hunting Industry], no. 9. Moscow, 1950.

Danilov, D. N. *Okhotnichi ugodya SSSR. Promyslovaya otsenka i ustroystvo ugodiy* [The Hunting Lands of the USSR. An Economic Evaluation and Organization of the Terrain]. Moscow: Izd-vo Tsentrosoyuza, 1960.

Danilov, N. N. "Uchet zapasov promyslovykh kurinykh ptits Sverdlovsky oblasti" [Survey of Reserves of the Industrial Gallinae of Sverdlovsk Oblast]. In *Soveshchaniye . . .* (See Aleksandrov.)

Dolbik, M. S. "Zapasy glukharya i tetereva v BSSR i faktory, opredelyayushchiye osobennosti ikh razmeshcheniya" [Wood and Red Grouse Reserves in the Belorussian SSR and Factors Affecting Their Distribution Characteristics]. In *Vtoraya Vsesoyuznaya ornitologicheskaya konferentsiya* [Second All-Union Ornithological Conference]. Papers, no. 3. Moscow, 1959.

Fedyushin, A. V. "Opyt biosyemki i kartirovaniya poseleniy nazemnykh pozvonochnykh v lesnichestvakh Rechitskogo Polesya" [Experience of Biological Survey and Mapping of the Settlement of Land Vertebrates in the Forestries of the Rechitsa Polesye]. In *Geografiya naseleniya nazemnykh zhitvotnykh i metody yego izucheniya* [Geography of the Settlement of Land Animals and Methods of Study]. AN SSR, 1959.

Gavrin, V. F. "K voprosu o metodakh kolichestvennogo ucheta vodoplavayushchikh ptits v Kazakhstane" [Concerning Methods for a Quantitative Survey of Waterfowl in Kazakhstan]. In *Soveshchaniye* . . . (See Aleksandrov.)

Gerasimova, T. D. "Resultaty ucheta morskikh kolonialnykh ptits i gagi na Murmanskom poberezhye" [Results of the Survey of Marine Bazaar Birds and Eiders on the Murman Coast]. In ibid.

Isakov, Yu. A. "Razmeshcheniye i sovremennoye sostoyaniye zapasov promyslovykh vodo-plavayushchikh ptits v SSSR" [Distribution and Present State of Reserves of Industrial Waterfowl in the USSR]. In *Texisy dokladov vtorogo soveshchaniya po voprosam zoogeografii sushi* [Papers of the Second Conference on the Problems of the Zoogeography of Land]. Alma-Ata, 1960.

Isayev, E. M. "O sostoyanii pogolovya dikikh kopytnykh zhivotnykh na territorii RSFSR" [Concerning the State of the Population of Wild Ungulates in the RSFSR]. In *Soobshcheniya in-ta lesa* [Scientific Information of the Forest Institute], no. 13. Moscow: AN SSSR, 1959.

Kaplin, A. A. *Pushnina SSSR* [Furs of the USSR]. Moscow: Vneshtorgizdat, 1960.

Karpovich, V. N. "Uchet chislennosti borovoy dichi marshrutnym metodam na bolshikh ploshchadyakh silami lesnoy okhrany leskhozov i lespromkhozov" [Calculation of the Number of Forest Wildlife by Means of the Traverse Method over Large Areas Using the Labor Force of the Forest Service of the Forestry and Forest Industry Enterprises]. In *Soveshchaniye* . . . (See Aleksandrov.)

Kirikov, S. V. *Izmeneniya zhivotnogo mira v prirodnykh zonakh SSSR (XIII–XIX vv.). Stepnaya zona i lesostep* [Changes in the Animal World in the Natural Zones of the USSR (XIII–XIX Centuries). Steppe and Forest-steppe]. AN SSSR, 1959. *Lesnaya zona i lesotundra* [Forest and Forest Tundra]. AN SSSR, 1960.

Klyatis, B. D. "Sotsialisticheskoye okhotnichye khozyaystvo—na uroven sovremennykh zadach" [Socialist Hunting Economy—to the Level of Present Tasks]. In *Izvestiya Irkutskogo selskokhozyaystvennogo instituta* [Proceedings of the Irkutsk Agricultural Institute], no. 18. Irkutsk, 1960.

Kolosov, A. M., Lavrov, N. P., and Naumov, S. P. *Biologiya promyslovykh zverey SSSR* [Biology of Industrial Animals of the USSR]. Moscow: Vysshaya shkola, 1961.

Logminas, V. V. "Materialy po ekologii kurinykh ptits Litovskoy SSSR" [Materials on the Ecology of Gallinae in the Lithuanian SSSR]. In *Trudy 3-y Pribaltiyskoy ornitologicheskoy konferentsii* [Papers of the Third Baltic Ornithological Conference]. Vilnyus, 1959.

Logminas, V. V. "Izmeneniye chislennosti i rasprostraneniya kurinykh ptits v Litve" [Changes in Population and Distribution of Gallinae in Latvia]. In *Tezisy dokladov 4-y Pribaltiyskoy ornitologicheskoy konferentsii* [Papers of the Fourth Baltic Ornithological Conference]. Riga, 1960.

Middendorf, A. F. *Puteshestviye na sever i vostok Sibiri. Otd. V. Sibirskaya fauna* [Journey to the North and East of Siberia. Part V. Siberian Fauna]. St. Petersburg, 1869.

Naumov, S. P. "Obshchiye zakonomernosti chislennosti vida i yeye dinamika" [General Laws of the Population of a Species and Its Dynamics]. In *Issledovaniya prichin i zakonomernostey dinamiki chislennosti zaytsa-belyaka v Yakutii* [Studies on the Causes and Laws of Population Dynamics of the White Hare in Yakutia]. AN SSSR, 1960.

Sapetin, Ya. V. "Biologicheskiye obosnovaniya uporyadocheniya okhrany i dobychi vodoplavayushchikh ptits v tsentralnykh oblastyakh Yevropeyskoy chasti RSFSR" [Biological Bases of Regularizing the Protection and Extraction of Waterfowl in the Central Oblasts of the European Part of the RSFSR]. In *Vtoraya Vsesoyuznaya ornitologicheskaya konferentsiya.* (See Dolbik.)

Sapetin, Ya. V. and Shevareva, P. P. "Raspredeleniye na zimovkakh utok i lysukh, gnezdyashchikhsya v SSSR" (The Distribution on Wintering Places of Ducks and Coots, Which Nest in the USSR). *Ornitologiya* [Ornithology], no. 2. Moscow, 1959.

Semenov-Tyan-Shanskiy, O. I. "Uchet vozrastnogo sostava populyatsii teterevinykh ptits i yego prakticheskoye primeneniye" [Calculation of Age Composition of the Grouse Population and Its Practical Application]. In *Vtoraya Vsesoyuznaya ornitologicheskaya konferentsiya.* (See Dolbik.)

Semenov-Tyan-Shanskiy, O. I. "Ekologiya teterevinykh ptits" [Grouse Ecology]. In *Trudy Laplandskogo gos. zapovednika* [Papers of the Lapland State Preserve], no. 5. Moscow, 1960.

Severtsev, N. A. *Periodicheskiye yavleniya v zhizni zverey, ptits i gad Voronezhskoy gub.* [Periodical Occurrences in the Life of Beasts, Birds and Reptiles of Voronezh Guberniya]. Moscow, 1855.

Silantyev, A. A. *Obzor promyslovykh okhot v Rossii* [Survey of Industrial Hunting in Russia]. St. Petersburg, 1898.

Silantyev, A. A. "Ikhota" [Hunting]. In *Aziatskaya Rossiya* [Asiatic Russia], vol. 2. St. Petersburg, 1914.

Skrobov, V. D. *O nekotorykh voprosakh biologii i ekologii pestsa Bolshezemelskoy i Malozemelskoy tundr.* [Concerning Some Problems of Biology and Ecology of the Arctic Fox in the Bolshezemelskaya and Malozemelskaya Tundra]. Naryan-Mar, 1958.

Skrobov, V. D. "Uchet zapasov pestsa i yego razmeshcheniye po tundram Yamala" [Calculation of Arctic Fox Reserves and Their Distribution in the Yamal Tundra]. In *Soveshchaniye* . . . (See Aleksandrov.)

Sludskiy, A. A. and Shubin, I. G. "Aviavizualnyy uchet okhotnichye-promyslovykh zverey v zone pustyn Kazakhstana" [Air Survey of Game Animals in the Desert Zone of Kazakhstan]. In ibid.

Trofimov, G. A. "Kustovye soveshchaniya, posvyashchennye razvitiyu okhotnichyego promysla" [Meetings Devoted to the Development of the Hunting Industry]. In *Ratsionalizatsiya okhotnichyego promysla* [Rationalization of the Hunting Industry], vol. 6. Moscow, 1957.

Tsvetayev, A A. *Gory Iremel (Yuzhnyy Ural). Fiz.-geogr. ocherk* [The Iremel Mountains (Southern Urals). Physical-geographical Description]. Ufa, 1960.

Turkin, N. V. and Satunin, K. V. *Zveri Rossii* [Animals of Russia], vol. 1, no. 1. Moscow, 1900.

Uspenskiy, S. M. *Ptitsy Sovetskoy Arktiki* [Birds of the Soviet Arctic]. AN SSSR. 1958.

Zhirnov, L. V. "Kolichestvennyy uchet saygakov v Zapadnom Prikaspii" [A Quantitative Survey of the Antelope in the Western Caspian Littoral]. In *Soveshchaniye* . . . (See Aleksandrov.)

14. Problems Associated with the Development of Commercial Game Resources

E. E. Syroyechkovskiy

(Institute of Geography, Academy of Sciences of the USSR)

The problem of wise use, reproduction, and protection of the game resources in the USSR is associated with the nature of development of individual regions. Much of the USSR is being intensively developed through industrialization, the exploitation of mineral wealth, the creation of an energy base, and the expansion of agriculture and forestry.

Such regions include the larger part of European Russia, Central Asia, Kazakhstan, the Caucasus, and Siberia mainly to the south of 56° north latitude. In these regions the natural environment is undergoing fundamental transformation. By contrast, the tundra is still sparsely inhabited; what development exists is due primarily to the exploitation of its wild animal resources. A similar situation prevails throughout the larger part of the taiga, though forestry is the leading economy here and game resources are of secondary significance. Together, the tundra and taiga provide about 80% of all the furs and almost 90% of the forest game. These regions produce almost all the pelts of such valuable species as squirrel, sable, polar fox, ermine, Siberian ferret, and mink.

The rest of the USSR could also be fairly productive in game, but at present the catch is insignificant only because insufficient attention is given to the reproduction and effective protection of useful animals, and because the large army of sportsmen, still inadequately organized, destroys animals in huge quantities.

We shall touch briefly on the recent history of the primary commercial game regions.

The interior of Siberia, which today is considered "godforsaken" and "remote," was exploited in a commercial sense far more fully a century or more ago. Even in the seventeenth century, according to the historians, there were, for example, in the basin of the Stony Tunguska, nearly as many Russian hunters as now. In addition, the Russians, through economic and administrative means, forced the local inhabitants to procure furs in large quantities. They hunted as a rule not only with guns but with traps (Middendorf; Skalon, 1950; Timofeyev and Nadeyev; Syroyechkovskiy and Rossolimo).

Uncontrolled hunting continued until the beginning of the present century, with a large number of hunters throughout the taiga and tundra. At the same time, the number of native hunters gradually declined since, under conditions created by the tsarist regime, the native peoples quickly died out.

In the two or three decades that followed, the situation changed. The size of the population in remote Siberian regions and in the northern European part of the USSR grew. However, for a number of reasons a sharp redistribution of population took place. The number of taiga inhabitants decreased and many small taiga settlements declined or completely ceased to exist. Simultaneously, the population concentrated in large settlements, leading to a depopulation of the hunting areas. In many regions formerly overrun with hunters there were far fewer than were required for rational exploitation. For example, in 1940 there were 1,300 hunters in the Turukhansk region but only 366 in 1957 (Yakushkin). In the Evenki country, in the basin of the Stony Tunguska, in the years when hunters gathered in large numbers (during the "sable rush" a century or more ago), there were about 2,000 hunters (according to estimates). In 1931 there were still over 1,000 hunters there (Kurilovich and Naumov), but in 1956 only 413 (Syroyechkovskiy and Rossolimo). In Krasnoyarsk Kray, in a twenty-five to thirty-year period (up to 1956–58), the number of hunters in the southern regions decreased by as much as 90% and in the northern regions as much as 80% (Numerov). In the Khanty-Mansi National Okrug during the same period the number of hunters was halved, while in Narym Kray it declined more than 80% (Zhdanov; Potapov). Now approximately the same situation may be observed in the "nonindustrialized" regions of Siberia (Shergin).

According to V. N. and N. N. Skalon (1958), in most of Siberia somewhat less than half the total hunting lands are being exploited. This estimate may possibly be optimistic since the hunting agencies and land users often count as exploited tracts all areas visited by hunters. This, however, does not signify that hunting in adequate intensity is taking place.

The situation is further complicated by the fact that hunting techniques are not given adequate consideration. Little attention is given to hunting with dogs and to trapping. According to 1952 registration data, taiga commercial hunters had only 38,000 dogs whereas in 1938 their number approached 70,000. During the last twenty-five to thirty years the number of steel traps used for squirrel in the main hunting regions of the USSR decreased to 10% of the previous number (Shergin; Potapov).

Both underexploitation and conservation measures have in recent decades led generally to a sharp growth in the number of commercial game in remote and little developed regions. At present, extensive and valuable hunting tracts abound in beasts and birds, raising questions about the need for rational exploitation of this "virgin taiga."

The sable merits considerable attention in this respect. About one-third of the area in which the sable lives remains unexploited (Zaleker and Kondratov). Meanwhile, the sable, due to extended protection from hunting and other measures designed to secure an expansion in numbers, now inhabits almost the entire Siberian forest. In places the density is very great—anywhere from 5 to 10 per 1,000 hectares. Undoubtedly, in those regions where sable abound, hunting could and should be expanded considerably.

The otter, whose numbers have grown notably, too, is also underexploited in the same regions.

The number of elk in the taiga to the east of the Urals in Western Siberia is high. Zoologists who have examined the Pelym hunting enterprise have noticed the exhaustion of the feed base of the elk–the willow, mountain ash, and other broad-leaved species (Bakeyev and Koryakov).

The density of commercial game is large in many parts of the Siberian forest, particularly in Western Siberia. There are places where hunters could procure from 300 to 500 wood grouse in an autumn season. For instance, in 1956, in Tomsk Oblast, 194,000 forest game animals were obtained. According to A. P. Zhdanov, this could be increased up to three times if hunting encompassed the remote regions of the oblast.

Many similar examples could be given. They should not, however, create the impression that there is a general abundance of all types of game in the taiga and tundra. In reality this is not so: the number of commercial animals is large but they are underhunted only in specific, though sometimes vast, regions.

The taiga and tundra have also regions that are very poor in game; this is particularly true in northern and eastern Siberia where larch forests predominate, and in the West Siberian lowland where there are interfluvial swamps. Many areas, especially in the European part of the USSR and in southern Siberia near the centers of population, are impoverished as a result of excessive hunting and require game protection, not greater exploitation. In principle, however, this does not alter the basic situation: reserves for expanding commercial hunting are very great. The need for rational exploitation should not create any doubts; the important thing is that the approach should be adapted for each locality so that procurement regions are established on the basis of a knowledge of the animal balance. This would lead not only to protection but also to the further enrichment of the number of valuable animals.

Correct and adequate development of hunting areas should be based on the following principles: (1) the achievement of a balance between exploitation and renewal; (2) a proper coordination of the various branches of activity in taiga collective farms; (3) a speed-up in the organization of commercial hunting enterprises (perhaps in the form of specialized state and collective farms); (4) an improvement in the training of hunters and clarification of their legal position and rights; (5) the establishment of bases for sport hunting.

We shall examine these recommendations in more detail.

Legal responsibility for hunting tracts must be assigned if effective use of the area and its resources is to be achieved. This will entail: first of all, a survey of the use of hunting areas; secondly, a determination of the needs of the population; finally, the demarcation of the boundaries of future hunting bases (Skalon and Skalon, 1960). The above will reveal the productivity and use of the land. The legal assignment of the land to users (collectives, cooperatives, government and sport hunting groups), establish who is responsible for the hunting tracts and who should carry out measures for wise use of the commercial resources.

Within the near future, projects for the expansion of hunting in the densely populated regions of the European USSR will be, for the most part, completed. Particularly successful in this development are the regions along the Baltic and in the Ukraine. In Kazakhstan, Central Asia, and the Caucasus the development is slower.

Many taiga collectives are oriented toward crop cultivation and animal husbandry, neither of which is very profitable (Skalon, 1956; Kopylov; Krasnyy and Shunkov; Skalon and Skalon, 1960; and others). Even in the southern and central taiga, such an economy cannot be highly productive. It contributes to the state almost no commercial output, monetary profits grow very slowly, and the investments hardly change. Therefore, wages paid in such kolkhozy are low (Krasnyy and Shunkov).

On the other hand, taiga collectives have the means to organize highly profitable enterprises for hunting, fishing, and nut- and berry-gathering.

However, due to inadequate planning, the collective farmers are unable to spend more than 20 days a year at hunting instead of the approximately 130 (in the autumn and winter seasons) required by the specific nature of the industry. As a rule, almost the entire output on the hunting industry, except for fur, goes for personal consumption. It must be stated that since the October Revolution the organization of the hunting economy has changed much less than has industry or agriculture.

Research shows that wise use of this commercial resource could greatly improve the economic position of many of the taiga collectives within one or two years (Krasnyy and Shunkov).

First of all, where necessary, hunting should be collectivized. V. N. and N. N. Skalon (1960) distinguish two groups of collectives: (1) where hunting is the basic branch of production (in accordance with the plan), and (2) where hunting is important but a mixed economy is foreseen. Many Siberian collectives have already taken this path and have achieved considerable success (Krasnyy and Shunkov). The profits from hunting in such collectives have multiplied within a short period, and many remote areas have begun to be opened up.

The successful development of a collective-hunting economy requires the establishment of legal responsibility (and a proper organization) in the hunting areas, which entails the assignment of hunting areas to brigades or individuals. Only this can bring remote taiga regions to a level of use equal that of settled regions and eliminate overhunting in sectors near populated points.

To achieve proper bookkeeping, hunting in the collectives must be regulated and valid economic and technical output norms must be established for the hunters. An incentive payment system should be worked out. In many collectives where hunting and reindeer herding have long been the principal sectors of the economy, definite success has been had in that respect, as for example, several collectives in the Baykit region of the Evenki National Okrug.

In the development of remote and sparsely populated hunting areas, mixed commercial hunting enterprises should be organized. Such large enterprises, whose purpose is a wise and comprehensive use of the raw material base of the remote taiga, are being established as self-supporting units in the system of the Tsentrosoyuz (Centrosoyuz) * of the USSR and in the Glavokhota.† Hunting in these enterprises is carried on by state

---

* The Central Union of Cooperatives.
† Chief Administration of Hunting.

hunters to whom specific areas have been assigned. They also prepare other taiga products such as cedar nuts, berries, mushrooms, medicinal and technical raw materials, and fish.

The Seven-Year Plan, by a resolution of the Rospotrebsoyuz * of the RSFSR, anticipated the creation of more than one-hundred hunting enterprises, nearly all to be located in Siberia in Krasnoyarsk Kray, in Irkutsk, Tyumen, Tomsk, and other oblasts, with a few in the northern European part of the USSR. Many of these will manage territories of up to five million hectares. Eighty enterprises have already been established. The significance of this undertaking is exceptionally great. It is particularly important that the enterprise not only exploit the taiga, but also deal with the reproduction of stocks of commercially important species and with surveys of their populations.

Many enterprises have in a short period made definite progress. In the Sayans, for example, eight enterprises were formed in two years, to which were assigned over one-half the territory of this mountain region. In January 1960, they already had 510 hunters and the fur output of the Sayans increased by 30% over 1952–54. In a single season, some hunters took as many as sixty sable alone. However, here too, due to the shortage of labor and poor organization, some of the enterprises cover only up to 30% of their territory. In many other Siberian enterprises, especially those far from industrial regions, the hunting tracts are even less exploited. In all these enterprises, entirely too little attention is devoted to the reproduction of animals.

Not more than 20% of the area suitable for development is now encompassed by a network of hunting enterprises. With the aim of further developing remote hunting lands, the organization of enterprises where there are now none must be speeded up: in the tundra and in the northern and central taiga. The performance of the few hunting enterprises that exist there (Omulyov hunting enterprises on the Taimyr) has shown that they can be as profitable as those in the southern taiga.

Organizational measures must be preceded by a scientifically based plan for the development of the enterprises, which would consider the geographical and economic peculiarities of individual natural zones. A specific type of hunting enterprise should be organized for each natural zone or subzone. The creation of a system of enterprises—the leading forms of production—will enable us not only to develop the resources of the tundra and taiga more fully but also to create the best conditions for socialist

---

* The Union of Consumer Cooperatives of the Russian Federation.

construction and for the material and cultural development of the minorities of the north.

Simultaneously, the work of the hunting enterprises already in existence must be improved. Scientific studies of raw-material resources carried out jointly by biologists, geographers, and economists can render great assistance in this respect.

The organization of hunting enterprises in the sparsely forested and un-forested regions of the south must pursue a somewhat different goal. Areas suitable for the establishment of such enterprises are much more limited here, and where located are in regions more suited to the organization of sport hunting or unsuited for hunting altogether. At present, in the southern part of the country, enterprises use the semidesert areas (antelope) and the marshy stretches of lake shores and river estuaries (muskrat). Although prospects for the development of such enterprises are great, they cannot be compared with those in the north.

A. Sludskiy and E. Strautman were entirely correct in considering the creation in Kazakhstan of hunting enterprises that would use all the game resources (antelope, muskrat, roe deer, wild boar, feathered game). Such enterprises would have the greatest economic effect, and their workers would be concerned with production throughout the entire year.

In considering the proper development of game resources, one must take into account the difficulty in the near future of obtaining adequate labor in these sparsely populated regions. The training of workers is a time-consuming process; the forms of production and even the technical equipment for the industry can be reconstructed much more rapidly. The new hunting enterprises and other organizations are already experiencing an acute lack of qualified workers; even among the indigenous population of Siberia it is a haphazard matter. The basic hunter contingent is composed of old men whose number is rapidly waning and for whom there are al-most no replacements. For example, according to Rospotrebsoyuz data, in 1957 the Nanay District in Khabarovsk Kray had only 293 hunters (in 1930 there were 768), and 81% of them were over thirty-five years old.[1]

Secondary schools can assist greatly in the training of hunters. Polytechni-cal institutes in the hunting regions of the north must be reorganized so as to take into consideration the local peculiarities of production. Planned pro-

---

[1] One of the basic causes of the reduction in the number of hunters is their vague legal situation. For example, the hunter who loses his ability to work receives a pension that is not commensurate with his actual labor wage. The hunters have no paid holidays, no travel passes, and so forth. All this leads to the loss of qualified workers. The legal position of state hunters belonging to consumer cooperative hunting enterprises has improved in recent years.

grams regarding hunting, reindeer herding, fishing, and animal breeding should be introduced into the schools. Practical work in the taiga and tundra must also be implemented. This is entirely feasible, all the more so since a significant portion of the children of the native population study in governmental boarding schools.

In 1961, the Institutes of Geography and Ethnography of the Academy of Sciences of the USSR handed the Ministry of Education of the RSFSR a precise proposal entitled "On Specialized Labor Education in the Rural Schools of the Northern Regions of the RSFSR." The Ministry approved the proposal and new educational plans and programs, as well as systematic textbooks, are being prepared.

In the densely populated regions there are few professional hunters; the hunting contingent is made up of amateurs who are united in voluntary hunting societies. In the RSFSR alone in 1959 there were more than 750,000 hunters in such societies. The organization of a network of sport-hunting groups must also secure the elimination of irresponsible overexploitation. All lands of sport-hunting importance should be allotted to specific sporting societies, entrusting to them the care of the land and the reproduction and conservation of game. This would likewise facilitate the control of hunting by governmental and social organs.

Where necessary, it would be preferable to assign separate districts of the hunting enterprises to local hunting collectives. This would to an even greater extent increase the responsibility of the individual members of the collectives for the conservation and reproduction of animals. Strengthened as well would be the personal interest in the proper management of the enterprise. In this respect the role of the local hunting collective would be analogous to that of the hunting brigade in a commercial hunting enterprise. The activities of both the collectives and the individual societies must be centralized. Large hunting unions, acting according to a uniform plan, play a very positive role. The Rosokhotsoyuz * created in 1959, has an extensive and useful program. In 1959 alone, the number of local participating collectives grew from 8,158 to 19,992. The education of the hunters as well as the exposure and punishment of lawbreakers is thus made considerably easier.

Organized amateurs also participate in the procurement of fur and game. In 1959, the hunters of the Russian Federation, under contract, turned in more than 4.7 million rubles worth of fur. The quantity of furs procured by hunting societies in the densely populated oblasts is very large. For example, in Smolensk Oblast they procured 81% of all furs turned in; in Yaroslavl, 71% : and in Pskov, 82%.

---

* The Union of Hunting Enterprises of the Russian Federation.

At present, the assignment of land to sport societies is being carried out intensively in the European part of the USSR. As was previously mentioned, considerable progress in this respect has been achieved along the Baltic littoral and in the Ukraine. In 1959 only 205 groups were registered, while in 1961 there were already 700. In the densely populated regions of Siberia such work is only beginning to develop and must necessarily be hastened, since in regions of new development these measures have perhaps an even more urgent character than in the European part of the country. According to Rosokhotsoyuz, in the near future the hunting system must be completed in ten oblasts of the central part of European Russia; Siberian lands have been given a lower priority. The Rosokhotsoyuz should approach the Siberian hunting lands differently and should remember that, in addition to the underdeveloped hunting regions, Siberia also has regions of intensive economic development.

In conclusion, it must be once again emphasized that the organization of a proper hunting economy is, in itself, the fastest and most effective way to resolve the problem of rational use and reproduction of commercial game resources.

BIBLIOGRAPHY

Bakeyev, N. and Koryakov, B. "Polneye i pravilneye ispolzovat okhotnichye-promyslovuyu faunu" [To Use More Fully and Properly the Hunting-Industry Animal Life]. *Okhota i okhotnichye khozyaystvo* [Hunting and Hunting Economy], no. 1 (1960).

Kopylov, I. P. "Pravilno sochetat otrasli v tayezhnykh kolkhozakh Sibiri" [To Integrate Correctly the Branches in the Taiga Collectives of Siberia]. In *Trudy vsesoyuzn. n.-i. in-ta zhivotnogo Syrya i pushniny* [All-Union Scientific Information Institute of Animal Raw Material and Fur], no. 17. Moscow, 1958.

Krasnyy, N. M. and Shunkov, V. M. *Puti podyema ekonomiki tayezhnykh kolkhozov* [Methods of Raising the Economy of the Taiga Collectives]. Irkutsk, 1959.

Kurilovich, A. P. and Naumov, N. P. *Sovetskaya Tungusiya* [Soviet Tungusiya]. Moscow-Leningrad, 1934.

Middendorf, A. F. *Putishestviye na sever i vostok Sibiri* [Journey to the North and East of Siberia]. *Siberskaya fauna* [Siberian Fauna], vol. 2, issues 5 and 6, pt. 5. St. Petersburg, 1869, 1877.

Numerov, K. D. "Rasprostraneniye i reakklimatizatsiya sobolya v Krasnoyar-skom Kraye" [The Distribution and Reacclimatization of the Sable in Krasnoyarsk Kray]. (See Kopylov.)

Potapov, S. "Potrebitelskaya kooperatsiya i okhotnichiy promysel" [Consumer

Cooperation in the Hunting Industry]. In *Okhota i okhotnichye khozyaystvo,* no. 6 (1959).

Shergin, I. A. "O rabote Vostochno-Sibirskoy nauchnoy kompleksnoy ekspeditsii VNIIZhP, 1957 g." [Concerning the Work of the East Siberian Scientific Complex Expedition of the All-Union Research Institute of Animal Raw Materials and Furs in 1957]. In *Byull. nauchno-tekhn. informatsii Vsesoyuzn.* [Bulletin of Scientific-Technical Information of the All-Union Scientific Research Institute of Animal Raw Material and Fur], no. 3 (1958).

Skalon, V. N. "Problema sobolya na sovremennom etape" [The Problem of the Sable at the Present Stage]. *Okhrana prirody* [Protection of Nature], vol. 11. Moscow, 1950.

Skalon, V. N. *Tezisy po voprosu o putyakh khozyaystvennogo stroitelstva v rayonakh Severa RSFSR* [Themes on the Problem of Economic Development in the Regions of the North of the RSFSR]. Irkutsk, 1956.

Skalon, V. N. and Skalon, N. N. *Prakticheskiye rekomendatsii po organizatsii okhotnichego khozyaystva v Sibiri* [Practical Recommendations Pertaining to the Organization of the Hunting Economy in Siberia]. Irkutsk, 1958.

Skalon, V. N. and Skalon, N. N. *Rekomendatsii po sozdaniyu i razvitiyu kolkhoznogo okhotnichego khozyaystva* [Recommendations for the Establishment and Development of a Collective Hunting Economy]. Irkutsk, 1960.

Sludskiy, A. and Strautman, E. "Kompleksno ispolzovat khozyaystva" [To Utilize the Enterprise More Comprehensively]. *Okhota i okhotnichye khozyaystvo,* no. 11 (1960).

Syroyechkovskiy, E. E. and Rossolimo, O. L. "Sobol v basseyne Podkamennoy Tunguski" [The Sable in the Basin of the Stony Tunguska]. *Zool. zhurnal* [Zoological Journal], no. 11 (1960).

Tavrovskiy, V. A. "Sobol severo-zapadnoy Yakutii i puti vosstanovleniya yego promysla" [The Sable of North-Western Yakutiya and Methods for Reestablishing Its Industry]. In *Trudy in-ta biologii Yakutsk. filiala AN SSSR,* no. 4. (See Kopylov.)

Timofeyev, V. V. and Nadeyev, V. N. *Sobol* [The Sable]. Moscow: Zagotizdat, 1955.

Yakushkin, G. D. "O sostoyanii pogolovya i promysel ondatry na severe Krasnoyarskogo kraya" [Concerning the Muskrat Population and Industry in the Northern Part of Krasnoyarsk Kray]. In *Byull, nauchno-tekn. . . .* (See Shergin.)

Zaleker, V. L. and Kondratov, A. V. "Sovremennoye sostoyaniye sobolinogo promysla i perspektivy ego razvitiya" [The Current State of the Sable Industry and Perspectives of Its Development]. In *Byull. nauchno-tekn. . . .* (See Shergin.)

Zhdanov, A. P. "Pushnoy promysel Tomskoy oblasti i puti yego uluchsheniya" [The Fur Industry of Tomsk Oblast and Methods of Its Improvement]. In *Byull. nauchno-tekhn. . . .* (See Shergin.)

15. Fisheries Resources [1]

L. G. Vinogradov, L. M. Gordon, G. F. Dementyeva,
S. V. Dorofeyev, L. A. Zenkevich, M. S. Kireyev,
N. I. Kozhin, Yu. Yu. Marti, and P. A. Moiseyev
(*The All-Union Scientific Research Institute of Fisheries and Oceanography*)

SIGNIFICANCE AND IMMEDIATE TASKS OF SOVIET FISHERIES

The commercial fish found in inland waters and surrounding seas are quite diverse. Our southern seas abound in species of sturgeon [*Acipenseridae*] (sturgeon proper [*Acipenser*], the stellate sturgeon [*A. stellatus*], and the white or great sturgeon [*Huso huso*]), and of carp [*Cyprinidae*] (bream [*Abramis brama*], wild carp [*C. carpio*], Caspian roach [*Rutilus rutilus caspicus*], and others). Our lakes and rivers abound in pike perch [*Lucioperca lucioperca*], perch [*Perca fluviatilis*], and pike [*Esox lucius*]. Whitefish [*Korigonae*] are widely found in the rivers of Siberia and of northwestern European Russia. Of great importance, too, are salmon [*Salmonidae*]. Atlantic salmon [*Salmo salar*] are found in northern rivers; the rivers of the Soviet Far East contain the pink, chum, red, coho, king, and cherry. The Barents Sea contains cod, haddock, herring, ocean perch, halibut, several species of flounder, and wolffish. Herring, flounder, cod, Siberian cod, mackerel, and Pacific saury are found in the Far Eastern seas and tuna in the open waters of the Pacific.

The surrounding seas of the Soviet Union also contain many edible invertebrates, such as mussels, scallops, shrimps, and oysters; there are also water plants that are suitable for a variety of uses.

Sea mammals are also well represented in our seas. Annually, a large school of Greenland seals enters the neck of the White Sea, and *pinnipedia,* including harbor seal, fur seal, and walrus are common in Far Eastern seas,

---

[1] The concept of fisheries includes, in addition to the extraction and breeding of fish, the harvesting of marine mammals, invertebrates, and sea flora.

where large dolphin and white whale are also found. Schools of baleen whales [*Cetacea Mysticeti*] such as the fin, blue, and sei, as well as the sperm, one of the toothed whales [*Cetacea Odontoceti*], enter the Bering, Okhotsk, and Chukchi seas for feeding. Dolphins are also numerous there. In the Caspian Sea are found significant reserves of harbor seals and in the Black Sea, dolphins. Table 1 and the accompanying figure show the principal commercial fishing regions and their yield.

The USSR has many ponds, the total area of which reaches some hundred thousand hectares. A fishing industry based here can provide the country with a large amount of high-quality fish. Artificially created reservoirs can become a source of substantial fish reserves, if they are used for fish breeding as well as for energy, transport, and irrigation purposes.

In prerevolutionary Russia only migratory and fresh-water fish were commercially produced, and then only at spawning time. A limited coastal catch of marine fish was carried on only in isolated areas. The country had too few fishermen and, consequently, every year several million centners of herring were imported from abroad. The total annual catch of fish in Russia on the eve of the First World War was 10.5 million centners.

Because of the predominant development of heavy industry, which is the basis of socialist economy, the fish industry, during the first two five-year plans, was given a solid material and technological base that ensured substantial growth. The technical reconstruction of the fishing industry, which entailed the introduction of efficient methods of production in different regions of the world's oceans, utilizing the latest radio-navigation

Table 1
Fish Catch According to Principal Fishing Regions
(In million centners)

Region	1940	1950	1958	1960
North Atlantic	2.18	2.90	9.27	12.80
South Atlantic	—	—	0.04	0.44
Far East	3.22	4.84	8.48	8.61
Caspian Sea	3.51	3.19	4.18	3.85
Baltic Sea	0.25	1.13	1.53	1.55
Azov and Black seas	2.38	2.34	1.95	1.80
Aral Sea	0.38	0.35	0.46	0.44
Other inland water bodies	2.12	2.21	1.37	1.37
TOTAL	14.04	16.96	27.28	30.86

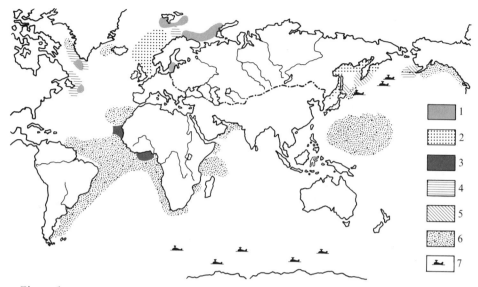

Figure 1
Regions of Soviet high sea fisheries: (1) cod, (2) herring, (3) sardines, (4) flounder, (5) bass, (6) potential areas of fishing, (7) whales.

and detection equipment and other efficient gear, aided the rapid development of fishing industry on the high seas.

Today, Soviet vessels operate hundreds and thousands of miles beyond our coasts. The Soviet flag may be encountered near the shores of Spitsbergen, in the Bering and Norwegian seas, on the Grand Banks of Newfoundland, near the coast of Western Greenland, in the Gulf of Guinea, near the southwestern coasts of Africa, and in the waters of Antarctica. Table 2 demonstrates the increasing proportion of the sea catch in the total fishing economy during the Soviet period. The organization of a vast sea industry has required not only a new fleet, new techniques of detection and processing, and qualified personnel, but also the implementation of comprehensive scientific fisheries research.

The discovery of "fish routes" in the seas and, even more important, in the open ocean, required numerous expeditions, ocean bottom research, the study of currents, of the distribution of fish food, and of paths of migration. Soviet scientists have not only assured the development of Soviet ocean fishing but have also contributed to the world's knowledge of the wealth of the ocean. Contemporary sea fisheries developed only half a century ago, but since then their extent has grown many times. At present, the world seas yield annually about 360 million centners of fish and non-fish products. Though the Soviet Union began to develop its sea fisheries

Table 2
Extraction of Fish, Sea Mammals, and Other Products from the Open Seas and Inland Waters of the U.S.S.R. (In million centners)

Types of Water Bodies	1913	1922	1930	1940	1946	1950	1960
A. From all water bodies	10.51	4.83	12.83	14.04	12.08	16.96	35.04
B. From open seas and oceans	2.08	0.97	3.80	5.65	5.48	7.80	26.02
As a percentage of A	19.1	20.0	29.6	40.2	45.3	46.1	74.3
C. From inland seas, lakes, and rivers	8.43	3.86	9.03	8.39	6.60	9.16	7.65
As a percentage of A	80.9	80.0	70.4	59.8	54.7	53.9	25.7
D. Catch of the commercial fishing fleet	0.16	0.22	1.10	3.75	2.45	5.92	26.0
As a percentage of A	1.5	4.5	9.4	26.9	20.0	33.8	75.0

much later than a number of other countries, it has rapidly overcome the lag. Indeed, the expansion in the decade following 1950 alone raised our catch almost three times, amounting in 1960 to more than 30 million centners.

Notwithstanding the short history of our sea fisheries, there are already signs of yield stabilization as well as losses in productivity in many of those oceans that have been extensively exploited. This indicates that a further increase in yield in such areas is possible only with rational management, constant supervision, and the initiation of international regulatory measures. We must proceed from an unregulated exploitation to an organized industry. For internal waters these are immediate problems; for the seas and oceans they are problems of the near future. It is easier to manage internal fisheries resources than those of the oceans since we are the sole masters of the former and can readily implement new forms of control. On the other hand, rational management of high seas fisheries calls for international agreement.

Proper use of fisheries resources, if optimal yields over the long run are to be maintained with minimum input, demands a deep understanding of fish biology.

Slow growth and advance to full maturity are characteristic of the vast majority of fish. Most are fully mature after three to six years of growth, but a few (cod, flounder, and sea perch) require ten years or more. Especially late maturing are the sturgeon and its most numerous representative, the white sturgeon, which reproduces only after reaching the age of between sixteen and eighteen. Late maturity results in slow regeneration of fish stocks and requires a careful organization of their extraction.

A second characteristic of fish is a sharp fluctuation in fertility. The number of offspring in many species varies tremendously, with the margins of variance at between one and five and occasionally as much as one and twenty-five. Fish generations born in low fertility years contribute little to the economy, while those of fertile years determine (in the long run) the success of the fishing industry. This important feature of fish biology requires that careful attention be given to replenishment (*Variations in the Population and Conditions* . . .).

Fish grow during their entire lifetime, and maximal weight increases frequently occur after maturity. The largest catch from any given water body can be obtained only when most of the fish have obtained their maximal weight increment. Premature harvesting leads to huge commercial losses in subsequent years. The extraction of 100,000 to 200,000 centners of immature fish can result in losses of 500,000 to 1,000,000 centners of full-value commercial fish.

For a long time it was believed that fishery reserves in water bodies were limited by the amount of feed and that fishing, by reducing the number of fish, would aid in the growth of feed. Such a view led to the notion that a universal intensification of fishing, ignoring reproduction, was expedient. This idea greatly harmed the fishing industry in a number of areas.

Detailed research into trophic (feed) interrelationships of sea life have indicated that fish productivity is limited not by the abundance of feed but by the degree and intensity of use of that feed by the fish. Hence, an effective method of regulating biological processes is a proper extraction of fish, designed to assure the greatest efficiency of feed use. Full utilization of the feed resources of any water body can be achieved only when the fish population is varied and extensive. Recent research has shown that older fish, thought earlier to be competitors of younger fish and therefore subject to extraction, actually feed on different organisms than do young fish. Thus older fish participate just as effectively as younger fish in the creation of a fishery.

Excessive extraction always leads to a reduction in catch since less feed is converted to fish. Moreover, the sharp decrease in unit labor productivity leads, initially, to higher costs and therefore to a lower profitability. The most important aspect of fisheries is, therefore, the determination of a rational volume of extraction.[2]

The recent establishment of large-scale marine fisheries will enable us to solve the problem of utilizing this resource of our internal water bodies

---

[2] By volume of catch we mean the quantity and type of vessels and equipment as well as the intensity of fishing, which fully guarantees the greatest possible catch in any given water body.

more efficiently. In the latter, in a number of cases, the industry is carried on without the necessary attention being given to the peculiarities of fish reproduction and growth.

Many complex questions remain to be solved with respect to inland fisheries, especially in relation to the construction of large hydroelectric power stations. Many fish, including sturgeon, salmon, and even migrating herring, have been cut off by the dams from their spawning grounds. This has required the building of fish ladders and the establishment of hatcheries. In some cases, year-round operation of the power dams on the lower reaches of rivers require a curtailment of spring floods, vital to the reproduction of many species in the delta regions.

The fishing industry has been greatly harmed by the discharge of industrial wastes into rivers and lakes; by logging and the floating of timber; by explosions carried out in connection with seismic surveys; and by other factors associated with economic development. Nevertheless, it is not in these activities alone that we should search for the causes of the decline in our inland fishery reserves. Far greater harm is achieved by unwise extraction.

Despite the conditions created by the newly constructed Volga Cascade,* the reserves of sturgeon in the Caspian Sea can both be preserved and significantly increased. This is possible if, for instance, spawning grounds below the Volgograd Dam are maintained, and if a series of fish-breeding stations are constructed in the Volga delta. Of course, these measures can be effective only in conjunction with a proper extraction of the sturgeon. The future diversion of the waters of the northern rivers into the Caspian Sea could, while preserving the interests of the fishing industry, lead to a complete recovery of reserves, which not long ago were the richest in the world.

The limited catch through the use of seine nets has produced very hopeful results in the Azov Sea. The proportion of pike perch and bream has grown, productivity has increased, and the cost of fishing has decreased. The simultaneous implementation of a number of fish breeding measures (up to now on an inadequate scale) allows us to anticipate a further improvement in Azov Sea reserves, which in turn will permit the magnitude of the catch to increase further over the years (*The Reconstruction of the Fishing Economy of the Azov Sea*).

Of considerable value is the biological improvement of water bodies and, above all, the elimination of fish of little commercial value, which in many

---

* A series of hydroelectric stations on the Volga begun in the late 1930s.

cases have quickly multiplied due to overexploitation of commercial species.

The wise management of inland fisheries with the reestablishment of output, is of great importance. The highly valuable inland fisheries cannot be fully replaced by ocean fisheries. We must, therefore, in the immediate future rationalize the use of these fisheries, establish proper controls, create an effective system of hatcheries of a variety of valuable species for inland water bodies, and organize a carp economy, which can yield many millions of centners of fresh fish (*Papers of the Conference on Fisheries in 1954*).

The development of marine as well as proper use of inland fisheries, together with a continuous effort to expand existing reserves, will assure our population a wide array of fish products.

THE POLAR SEAS AND THE NORTH ATLANTIC

The open expanses of the North Atlantic and the Barents, Norwegian, and Greenland seas constitute one of the world's most productive fishing grounds. Here, where the warm waters of the Atlantic meet the cold waters of the polar seas, are the conditions for the rapid growth of water organisms and, consequently, of fish. From an area amounting to roughly one-sixth of the world's oceans (including inland water bodies), 120 million centners of fish, or more than one-third of the world's catch, are obtained.

The fish species of this area are numerous, but they belong to a few related families. Three of these—codfish, herring, and sea perch—constitute about 75% of all the catch of the temperate and subpolar zones.

While commercial fisheries have existed in this region as far back as the seventeenth and eighteenth centuries, additional fishing grounds have been opened in recent years. Attaching great significance to the development of the North, V. I. Lenin, through a decision of the Sovnarkom,* created several large expeditions to study the Barents Sea and the adjacent regions of the Arctic Ocean, research that promoted the development of fishing in the Barents Sea.[3] Subsequently, the study of the fishery resources of this region was entrusted to the Polar Scientific Research Institute of Fisheries and Oceanography, which carried out numerous studies in an attempt to assess the raw-material base of Arctic fisheries.

The world catch of the most important fish in this zone, the cod, amounts to nearly 25 million centners annually. Cod is found within the coastal shoals and the continental shelf of the temperate and subpolar regions of

---

[3] Decree of the Sovnarkom of the RSFSR of March 10, 1931. *Izvestiya,* March 16, 1931.
* Sovet Narodnykh Komissarov (The Council of People's Commissars).

the Northern Hemisphere, in the Atlantic Ocean both from Cape Cod (in North America) to Labrador and western Greenland and from the Bay of Biscay to Spitsbergen and Novaya Zemlya.

Within this area, cod forms three largely separate schools: the Arctic, the Iceland-Greenland, and the Newfoundland. The first breeds along the northwestern coast of Norway and develops in the Barents Sea and near the Medvezhyy and Spitsbergen islands; the second fluctuates widely, reaching western Greenland where in the warm season proper conditions for reproduction exist, leading to the development of a separate school; the last occupies the shoals off Newfoundland and the nearby continental shelf of North America.

The cod can feed on deep-water organisms, large cancroid planktons, krill, and many species of small fish like the capelin, polar cod, and herring. It migrates long distances in search of food, which it usually finds, if only of one type. Cod grow fast but mature relatively late, in the eighth to tenth year. Cod meat contains much protein, and oil rich in vitamins A and D is recovered from the liver.

The recent cod catch is distributed by regions: the Barents Sea and adjacent areas, nearly 6.5 million centners (in the best years the catch has reached 12.5 million); the Iceland area, nearly 4.5 million; off western Greenland, 3 million; in the waters of North America, about 5 million; and in the North and Baltic Seas, about 1.5 million. In many regions, recent cod catches were close to the limit and an increase could be achieved only through efficient exploitation. This implies essentially an increase in the ratio of mature fish caught, since now the largest part of the catch is made up of immature fish (*Papers of the All-Union Conference on Biological Foundations, 1958*).

At present, the most promising region of cod exploitation is the western [*sic*] sector of the Atlantic. The Soviet fleet takes cod from all parts of this sector, but particularly from the southern part of the Barents Sea, near Spitsbergen off the Medvezhyy Islands, and on the Newfoundland Banks. Our total catch of cod in polar waters and in the North Atlantic amounts to nearly 6 million centners per year.

Similar to cod are green cod and haddock. The green cod is especially numerous in the Norwegian Sea. Haddock abound in the North Sea in the coastal waters near Murmansk and in the waters adjacent to the Pechora Sea, as well as in the western sector of the Atlantic along the coast of Nova Scotia and in the southern part of the Newfoundland shoals. Both species are biologically like the cod, but the green cod inhabits predominantly upper waters while the haddock, on the other hand, dwells close to the ocean floor. The green cod is a predator, and the haddock a consumer of sea-floor organisms. Haddock is more tasty and more highly valued than cod. Our commercial data do not distinguish between haddock and cod catches, but the total catch of the former is about one million centners in all regions.

The sea perch is another deep-sea fish, which is related to the scorpion-fish [*Scorpaenidae*]. Relatively new commercially, exploitation developed only after the Second World War. This deep-sea fish lives on the edge of the continental shelf and on the continental slope. Where the cod seldom remains beneath 350 to 400 meters, the sea perch lives at depths of from 300 to 600 meters and more. The deep-sea perch, recently discovered and described by the Polar Scientific Research Institute of Fisheries, is found at particularly great depths.

Usually the commercial perch is about 50 centimeters in length. Characteristically, it grows slowly, reaching sexual maturity at fifteen to sixteen years, when it is about 35 to 40 centimeters in length. In the last decade many areas of sea-perch concentration have been discovered. These are found along the Barents Sea shelf, along a series of banks in the Danish Straits, and on the banks of the western Atlantic. In each of these regions, after three or four years of intensive exploitation, the productivity of the industry dropped sharply and the catch per hour of trawling was reduced by half.

In recent years the world catch of sea perch has reached five million centners, of which the Soviet portion was nearly two million. Lately, in response to decreasing productivity, the Soviet fleet has tended to change over to cod fishing. However, if caught in proper quantities, the productivity of sea perch remains profitable. The most promising region for the industry is the western sector of the Atlantic where reserves of ocean perch are significantly larger than in the north.

Trawler fishing, in the regions under consideration here, is turning somewhat to wolffish, several species of flounder, as well as white and pink haddock. However, these species do not constitute more than a small percentage of the trawler catch. The importance of herring in the North Atlantic fishing industry is extremely great but it is difficult to say whether cod or herring plays the major role in the region's fisheries. They are equally important in size of catch, but cod is sought after by more countries than is herring.

Herring, under the influence of the warm North Atlantic Drift, is found throughout the whole northern part of the Atlantic and adjacent regions of the Arctic Ocean. Living in regions of varied conditions, the herring is represented by a significant number of varieties distinguished by the tempo of their growth, by the time needed to reach sexual maturity, and by the conditions of propagation.

Among the herring should be mentioned the Atlantic-Scandinavian herring, which inhabits the Norwegian, Greenland, and Barents seas; the bank herring of the North Sea and adjacent straits; the Baltic herring [salakia]; the summer-spawning herring of Iceland and Greenland; and the herring inhabiting the waters adjacent to North America.

The main commercial goal of our herring industry is the ocean type, which is the most numerous and least attached to coastal waters. Occupying a vast and productive zone, this herring is distinguished by its large size, rapid growth, and very long life. It matures at five to six years and lives for fifteen to eighteen years or more. A mature school has about ten or twelve growth categories, which contribute to its well-known reserve stability.

At present, there is intensive extraction of herring, and the replenishment of reserves is not given adequate attention. For a long time, our catches of Atlantic-Scandinavian herring were maintained at a level of 5 to 6 million centners. Moreover, only large, mature herring, migrating to spawning places on the Norwegian coast, were caught. Over the last ten years, Norway has sharply increased the intensity of its fishing (in 1956, the catch reached more than 15 million centners), and along with the increased catch of large herring, it has begun to catch the young. In ten years, Norway caught more than 17 million small herring, averaging from 12 to 15 grams weight, inflicting great damage to herring reserves and, most of all, to the principal fishery, the winter-mature herring industry. From 1957 on, the catch of large herring in Norway dropped annually and in 1961 amounted to only 800,000 centners.

Our industry, utilizing only the grown schools of herring fattened in open waters, has developed successfully; but in the last few years the catch has grown only in proportion to increased fleet size. The catch per vessel has remained at the level of previous years and apparently will drop in the near future, since schools of mature fish will substantially increase only after the abundant 1959–60 generation reaches commercial size.

The Soviet fleet has begun in recent years to develop trawler catching of sardines and yellowtail along the west coast of Africa. This region is undoubtedly promising with regard to the expansion of our fisheries. Tuna reserves in the subtropical waters of the Atlantic have scarcely been touched. Thus, the Atlantic fishing industry is tending toward an intensification in the western sector of the Atlantic and in subtropical waters.

THE SEAS OF THE FAR EAST
AND OF THE NORTH PACIFIC

The wealth of the Far Eastern and of the North Pacific waters enables the Soviet fishing industry to increase significantly the catch of fish and other marine life both through expansion into new areas and through efficient operation.

This basin and its fauna possess a number of peculiarities that must be considered in an evaluation and use of resources, and in the planning of the expansion of the fishing industry. The extensive island arcs, stretching from the Aleutian chain to Indonesia, a distance of more than 3,000 miles, separates the waters of the open Pacific from the large Far Eastern boundary seas. The total area of the Bering, the Okhotsk, the Japanese, the Yellow, the East China, and the South China seas is almost 10 million square kilometers.

The Far Eastern boundary seas, united by straits with the Pacific Ocean, have a characteristic physical-chemical regime that depends on the general Pacific Ocean system and especially on the powerful ocean currents of the Kuroshio and Oyashio. But at the same time, each of these seas has its own specific features, associated with its latitudinal position, the depth and width of the straits, the relief of the floor, the degree of contiguity with the continent or with the mass of semi-islands or islands, and the nature of local atmospheric processes.

The Bering, Okhotsk, and Japanese seas are characterized by broad, deep trenches that occupy a large part of their area, and by a small continental shelf, the ocean side of which drops sharply to a depth of 3,000 meters or more. In the Yellow, East China, and South China seas there are many continental shallows, with far fewer deep trenches.

The Pacific Coast of North America is somewhat different since the area of shallow water is less extensive, but the region has a broad archipelago of islands in the Gulf of Alaska and along the coast of British Columbia, associated with oceanographic conditions favorable to a large number of several species of marine animals. Hence, bottom feeders (black sea perch, halibut, and so forth) and pelagic fish (herring and others) are found in abundance.

The huge extent of the northern Pacific Ocean—from the subarctic to the tropics—causes truly substantial differences among the hydrological regimes of its several parts.

Because of the severe climate of adjacent continental regions, the directions of winter monsoons that blow from the cool continent seaward, and because of the separation of the Far Eastern seas from the Pacific Ocean by the island chains, the surface waters of the Bering, Okhotsk, Japanese, and Yellow seas, parts of the East China Sea, and the Alaskan Straits, are intensively cooled in winter. Moreover, in a number of cases the strongly cooled areas are unable to regain temperature in the warm season. In more southerly regions, especially south of the Canton–San Francisco Great Circle, the degree of winter cooling is really not great, and the temperature of the water rarely is lowered to less than 15°C. The strong warm current, the Kuroshio, frequently contains layers of cold water, and forms a broad front of conflict between subtropical waters (of the Kuroshio, or Japan Current) and subarctic waters (the Oyashio, or Okhotsk Current). The boundary of this front can fluctuate from year to year, deviating by hundreds of miles from the long-term average position.

Peculiar to frontal zones are sharp horizontal changes in temperature and a high concentration of oxygen, as well as significant and constant pockets of rising cold water, with large-scale vertical temperature changes and a high concentration of salts—phosphates, nitrates, and other mineral foods. The presence of the latter is the principal condition for the creation of sea organisms.

The peculiar regime and geological history of the North Pacific Ocean cause exceptionally varied fauna and flora and a high population of a number of commercial species. Here live more than 2,000 species of fish and many thousands of species of invertebrates.

About 300 of these species of fish have commercial importance; but of those with a large population that may yield an annual harvest of not less than 100,000 tons, only about 15 species stand out. More than 80% of the catch is comprised of cod, Alaska pollack, herring, sardines, anchovy, Pacific saury, tuna, flounder, large or small yellow perch, and salmon. These fish will undoubtedly play an important role in the future of the industry and must attract the attention of scientists and other personnel engaged in fish production. But, at the same time, researchers have the task of studying intensively and preparing for the commercial extraction of other fish of this region.

Most of the commercial fish in the Far Eastern boundary seas have developed unique peculiarities that distinguish them from similar fish dwelling in other basins and that enable them to adapt to the local water regime. These peculiarities are revealed in the localization of the feeding grounds of the separate schools, in seasonal migrations from deep to shallow water, in the relatively short distance of migration for most species living in the coastal zones, and in the deposition of eggs in the sea floor layer or in quiet, coastal open sea regions. These adaptations have allowed Far

Eastern species of fish, notwithstanding some truly unfavorable conditions of habitation, to reach relatively high numbers (Moiseyev).

Many countries carry out extensive fishing in the North Pacific Ocean. By 1953, the prewar level of extraction of fish and other products had already been reached and in recent years the total catch has begun to grow substantially. In the northwestern part of the Pacific Ocean in 1960, catches of fish had increased more than 50% over 1953 catches. Significant increases in catch have occurred also in other parts of the North Pacific, increases chiefly involving tuna.

The Soviet share in the North Pacific fishery is still relatively small (only 5%, excluding whales). The scale of the Soviet fishery in the Pacific Ocean does not correspond to either the material possibilities or to our interests. Even so, Soviet catches have significantly increased since the war. The 1940 catch amounted to 3.2 million centners, growing to 6 million by 1953, and to 8.2 million in 1957. Such an increase was reached as a result of the commercial development of the Japanese and Okhotsk seas, and also the coastal waters off Kamchatka's east coast. The principal species in the catch is herring of the Okhotsk, Gizhiginsk, Sakhalin-Hokkaido, Primorye, Korfokaraginsk, and other local schools of the Peter the Great Bay, the Aleksandrovsk Banks, the gulfs of Terpeniya and Aniva, of the West Kamchatka Banks, of the Olyutorsk Gulf, and other regions.

Quite a serious situation has developed in recent years with respect to the most valuable commercial fish, which is the Far Eastern salmon [the Siberian, hump-backed, red, and others]. In the prewar period the total catch in the northwestern Pacific reached 4 million centners (Pravdin). At present the catch amounts to 2.5 million centners and the trend continues downward. This is due, in addition to some natural causes, to excessive and irrational Japanese extraction in the open seas, which includes immature fish. To prevent a further decline in catch and to reestablish reserves, the Japanese industry must be restricted. Of importance also is the prevention of log drowning and of pollution of our Far Eastern rivers where the salmon spawn.

The intensity of fishing reached its maximum in 1956-58 and in many instances the catch was unusual. At the same time the resources of many fish, either those of less value (*mintae*,* dorse) or those that require specialized fishing technology (cod, *terpug* * and others), remain inadequately exploited.

Thus, in contrast to the prewar period when the Far Eastern industry relied exclusively on coastal equipment catching the fish in migration to

---

* English equivalent cannot be identified.

spawning grounds, in the postwar period, thanks to the expansion of scientific and prospecting efforts and the introduction of many small and medium tonnage ships, there has developed the extraction of salmon, herring, flounder, and crab, which are found in Far Eastern coastal waters. However, it is the ocean fisheries, in particular the resources of the far reaches of the Pacific Ocean (*sayra*,* perch, black sea perch, tuna, anchovy, halibut, black cod), that have begun to develop only in recent years and have produced significant results. It is clear that the further development of our fisheries in the Far East is possible only with the expansion of the ocean catch and of the extraction in new, unexploited regions.

To increase total catches it is necessary to develop the fisheries of the northeastern Pacific and the southern seas, as well as of a number of new regions in the Bering Sea. Moreover, we must extract new species that are already important in Japanese fisheries. We are primarily concerned with such species as tuna, Pacific saury, swordfish, and sardines. The world catch of these fish today amounts to only 15 million centners. It is possible, therefore, to increase this significantly, a development that is facilitated by the wide distribution of these fish, their long migration routes, large numbers, and spawning in the open seas.

The Bering Sea has large concentrations of bottom fish (cod, flounder, perch, halibut, black cod, and others), some of which the fishing industry has recently begun to exploit. The joint expedition of the Pacific and All-Union Scientific Research Institute of Fisheries and Oceanography has discovered a large concentration of flounder in the eastern part of the Bering Sea, the extraction of which has already produced several million centners.

The limited scale today of research on the discovery of concentrations and ways of catching tuna, sardines, cod, black cod, halibut, and other fish, still does not permit with sufficient detail the preparing of long-range plans for the expansion of Soviet fisheries in the North Pacific. In the meantime, data show that with the exploitation of tuna, Pacific saury, and other fisheries in the open waters of the Pacific, of the bottom fisheries of the Bering and other seas, and also with the proper use of the resource base, the total catch can be significantly increased (*Papers of the All-Union Conference on Biological Foundations, 1958*).

INLAND SEAS

Our inland seas, Azov, Caspian, Black, and Aral, are particularly significant. Low salinity permits the adaptation of a great number of fresh-water

---

* English equivalent cannot be identified.

fish, pike, perch, bream, carp, roach, Azov roach [*Vimba vimba certa*], shemaya [*Chalcalburnus chalcoides*], and many others. These fish propagate in the rivers, but fatten in the fresh-water regions of inland seas. Gradually they have been transformed into anadromous or semianadromous species, utilizing the great amount of food available in the seas and favorable conditions for multiplication. These factors determine their large numbers, rapid growth, and long life.

In the Caspian Sea there are several species of shad and sea herring, distinguished by their great size and quality of taste. But the most valuable fish of our southern seas is the sturgeon. The Caspian and Azov seas have significant schools of stellate, common, and white sturgeon. At present they are not caught in great quantity, but at the beginning of the century they were important in the fish supply.

The importance of the southern seas in providing the population of the country with fish is determined by their proximity to industrial centers and by the possibility of quick transport to the consumer.

We conclude that the inland waters have all the prerequisites for a fisheries economy and guarantee a high output of the most valuable commercial species of fish.

Therefore, in spite of the very complex nature of the resource base, we have at the present time every possibility of preserving and expanding stocks, provided the problem is properly approached.

THE CASPIAN SEA. In spite of the inefficiency of the Caspian fish industries, past catches have been quite significant: up to 500,000 centners of sturgeon, 1 million centners of pike, 1.5 million centners of Caspian roach, 1.5 million centners of herring, a few hundred thousand centners of bream, carp, catfish, and other valuable fish.

The decline in the valuable fish stocks of the Caspian Sea began around 1933, when, following a period of drought, the discharge of the Volga was sharply reduced and the level of the sea lowered, resulting in an increase in the area of shallow water in the northern Caspian that critically affected the fattening of anadromous and semianadromous fish. The conditions of spring flooding were also changed, which influenced the effectiveness of propagation. This period of deteriorating fish reproduction in the Caspian Sea coincided with a sharply increasing rate of extraction.

Between 1929 and 1932, the catches of valuable commercial fish in the Caspian amounted to nearly 6 million centners per year. The superior condition of the stocks at the beginning of the 1930s and the noticeable increase kept the catch at a high level throughout the decade. From 1933 to 1940, catches were not less than 3.5 million centners. Later, when reproduction dropped but exploitation continued at an intensive and irrational level, the catch began to diminish. It continued to drop and by 1960 amounted to about 2 million centners.[4] In recent years, additional factors such as the regulation of Volga River flow following the construction of the Volga-Kama Cascade, have begun to affect the situation. The dams on the Volga have obstructed the migration of sturgeon, whitefish, and some herring to spawning grounds, have sharply changed the reproduction conditions of pike, bream, carp, and roach. Moreover, with regulation of runoff, the cessation of flooding had negative effects on the breeding grounds. This has resulted in a very serious situation with respect to the stocks of valuable commercial Caspian Sea fish.

In recent years, although discharges from reservoirs have been regulated, timing has not coincided properly with the spawning period. Enrichment of reserves has been unsatisfactory also, but fishing in the northern Caspian has nevertheless continued at an intensive rate, with the consequence of strongly diminishing fish reserves.

Up to the present, problems associated with the creation of proper water regimes (even if only in part of the delta), improvement of natural spawning grounds, and the building of fish ladders, have not been resolved. The projected construction of fish factories and hatcheries to replace natural spawning is proceeding very slowly. Work on the preservation of the sturgeon, which has a long life cycle, and whose renewal must begin now, is especially important; a delay would greatly complicate future resolution of the problem.

Is it possible to renew the fish wealth of the Caspian? This question can be answered in the affirmative.

To achieve this goal it will be necessary to create conditions along the whole length of the Volga below the Volgograd GES that are most favorable to the increase of valuable commercial fish (above all, to the sturgeon). Very decisive measures for purifying the Volga must be taken. Old spawning grounds must be improved and new ones created for sturgeon in the river channel, even if only in part of the delta, by assuring a regulated flooding of the spawning grounds. Sturgeon hatcheries must be constructed that will provide not only for preservation but also for renewal of sturgeon stocks at the highest level commensurate with the feed base of the Caspian.

The projected diversion of water from north-flowing rivers * into the Caspian Sea will provide for the renewal of the level and future stabiliza-

---

[4] The data shown in Table 2 are higher than given here because they include species of little value, such as the *tyulka*, Crimean anchovy, etc.

* That is, of the Pechora and Vychegda, which flow northward toward the Arctic.

tion of the Caspian, which will favorably affect the feed base. Water should be diverted into the Volga as well as into the Ural River, a measure that would sharply improve the conditions of breeding and fattening of many commercial fish in the northeastern sector of the sea.

The measures enumerated above, however, will be of benefit only if the Caspian fishery is exploited at a level corresponding to the sea's biological potential. Planned catches must reflect stocks; the fish should be extracted at that stage in growth at which they have gained sufficient weight. In the reservoirs a quantity of breeding stock to provide sufficient offspring must be retained. The industry should be greatly concentrated so as to allow for the freeing of many fishermen and for reducing the amount of fishing gear. All these measures will lead to an increase in catch, a rise in the magnitude of the resource base, an increase in the productivity of labor, and a decline in cost.

THE AZOV SEA. The changes in the regime of the Azov Sea, which were brought about first of all by an extended dry period and later by the regulation of runoff of the Don, have led to a substantial deterioration in the conditions of reproduction of anadromous and semianadromous fish. Due to this, the number of such fish in the postwar period has diminished (*The Reconstruction of the Fish Economy of the Azov Sea*). This decline was caused also by the intensive development of a trap-net industry catching *tyulka* and Crimean anchovy. In some years these nets caught more than one million centners of *tyulka* [*Clupeonella delicatula cultriventris*], taking at the same time a great quantity of valuable young fish. In 1956, however, strict measures for the regulation of the fishing industry of the Azov Sea were introduced. One of these was a complete prohibition of *tyulka* and anchovy [*Engraulis encrasicholus*] fishing, and a limitation on the catch of sturgeon, herring, pike, bream, and roach. Such measures have led to a lowering of the intensity of fishing and to some increase in fish reserves, in particular of pike and roach. In recent years the take of valuable fish has been held at about 300,000 centners but, in addition, 650,000 to 700,000 centners of goby [*Neogobius fluviatilis*] have been caught. Apart from measures for the regulation of the Azov fishery, there has been extensive fish hatching directed toward increasing reserves of pike, bream, roach, and sturgeon.

THE BLACK SEA. The reserves of commercial fish in the Black Sea constantly undergo sharp fluctuations. The greatest fluctuations are observed in pelagic fish, both those that inhabit the Black Sea permanently and those that enter it temporarily. Pelagic fish are the main fish resource of the Black Sea, and include the Black Sea and Azov anchovy, the pelamid, the horse mackerel, and the Atlantic mackerel.

The change in the number of Black Sea fish is connected with generally unstable conditions of reproduction, the unregulated entry of some species of fish from the Marmora and Aegean seas, and a number of other causes (*Papers of the Conference on the Dynamics of the Fish Population*).

In 1949 the fish reserves of the Black Sea were augmented by a new commercial species, the great horse mackerel, which up to this time had been encountered only occasionally. The increase in the great horse mackerel is connected with the occurrence of some very productive generations, predominantly those of 1948 and 1949. Consequently, from 1954 to 1959 a high level of catch was maintained, but its present reserves have significantly diminished. The role of new generations in adding to the schools is as yet not sufficiently understood.

Especially sharp fluctuations of catch are seen in the pelamids. In some years the catch does not reach 10,000 centners, but sometimes, with a well-organized fleet, it may reach 250,000. These fluctuations are connected with the periodicity of pelamid breeding and with entry into the Black Sea from the Sea of Marmora. In the last fifty years the passage of pelamids into the Black Sea has been noted in the years 1910 to 1913, 1921 to 1923, and to a much greater extent in 1934, 1943, and in 1954 to 1956.

The total catch of fish in the Black Sea, including the anchovy that enters from the Azov, is maintained at a level of nearly 700,000 centners per year.

THE ARAL SEA. The total catch of fish in the Aral Sea for the last ten years has increased from year to year and in 1959 reached 461,000 centners. The growth in yield was brought about by a good condition of fish stocks, which in turn was caused by an improvement in reproduction, connected with increased runoff from rivers and the rising level of the sea. But in 1959 and 1960 a slight deterioration in fish reserves began, as a result of a decline in river runoff, much of which was due to irrigation. To compensate for losses, the following measures for the artificial expansion of commercial fish must be carried out: (1) the construction of hatcheries for the breeding of stellate sturgeon, spring sturgeon, and barbel; (2) the construction of hatching-raising enterprises for the production of carp species (bream and carp); (3) improvement of the natural spawning grounds of semianadromous fish (roach, bream, and carp); and (4) the acclimatization of new species that can live in brackish waters and do not require fresh water for breeding (the experiment in transferring Baltic herring from the Gulf of Riga to the Aral Sea has already yielded positive results).

INLAND FRESH-WATER BODIES

The Soviet Union has a large number of inland fresh-water bodies, including the following: (1) Forty-six river systems, the total extent of which exceeds three million kilometers. (2) Nearly one hundred reservoirs, formed by the dams of hydroelectric stations, the total area of which amounts to approximately four million hectares, the largest of which are the Kuybyshev (645,000 hectares), the Rybinsk (445,000 hectares), the Volgograd (347,000 hectares), the Tsimlyansk (217,000 hectares), the Kakhovka (216,000 hectares), and the Perm (185,000 hectares). (3) Numerous lakes, whose area exceeds twenty-five million hectares, including such large lakes as Ladoga, Onega, Baykal, Balkhash, and Ilmen, favorable to the habitation of valuable commercial fish (salmon, whitefish, carp, and others). In addition, many small lakes in the Northwest, the Urals, Siberia, the Soviet Far East, Belorussia, Latvia, Lithuania, and other regions, are capable of fisheries development and may become valuable fishing grounds. (4) Finally, ponds, with a total area (according to approximate data) of more than 350,000 to 400,000 hectares.

The exploitation of fresh-water bodies by the fishing industry is economically important because they are located relatively close to centers of consumption; by contrast, ocean fisheries are exceptionally distant and becoming increasingly remote. The use of fresh-water fish products will permit us to satisfy the population with live and fresh fish.

Many species of fresh-water fish have significantly better nutrition and taste than most sea fish. In developing an efficient inland fishing industry it is necessary to intensify and, consequently, to increase the catch of fish per man-hour and to regulate the assortment and age of fish.

The scale and form of activity with regard to fish, and the conditions of the environment of inland fresh-water bodies are completely dependent upon the level of development of fisheries science, the level of capital investment, the growth rate of extraction, and the working out of biological and economic bases for an increase in the raw-material base. In addition, the total economic effect of these measures to increase the importance of inland fisheries may be of benefit to the entire domestic fishing industry over a long period of time.

Despite the large number of fresh inland bodies of water in the USSR.

they have not become substantial sources of food for the country. On the contrary, the absolute growth of the catch in these inland waters and their importance compared with marine fisheries has in recent decades decreased many times. The quantity of fish extracted in fresh water fluctuates from 1.8 to 2 million centners, and over the last fifteen years there has been a sharp deterioration in quality. Low-value fish (roach, perch, ruff, bleak, and others) make up approximately 45% to 55% of the total catch.

The state of the present fresh-water fishing industry is due to many factors. In particular it is connected with the disturbance of the reproductive conditions, irrational extraction, inadequate exploitation of many inland waters by the fishing industry, and the pollution of water bodies by industry and forestry.

Thus, in Lakes Ladoga and Onega the improper organization of fishing is reflected in the sharp lowering of stocks of whitefish, salmon, and pike. An analagous situation has occurred in Lakes Pskov, Chudskoye, and Ilmen with reserves of bream and pike, and in Lake Baykal with reserves of omul [*Coregonus autumnalis*].

The pollution of inland water bodies fatally affects the quantity and quality of the fish. Many rivers (the Tom, Ufa, Belaya, Kama, and others) in which fishing was formerly prosperous have now completely or partially lost their commercial significance. They cannot even be used for the re-production of reserves of valuable anadromous fish. Even in the new large reservoirs we find massive destruction of commercial fish and of their young due to pollution. According to data of the State Scientific Research Institute of Lake and River Fisheries of the RSFSR, the annual loss incurred by the fishing industry from pollution is assessed at several hundred million rubles (1961).

The potentialities of inland waters are not realized because only 10% of the existing eleven million hectares of small lakes are exploited commercially. The catch in these lakes does not exceed 350,000 centners. The quantity of fish from one hectare of lake area does not exceed six kilograms, although with an intensive and knowledgeable economy it is possible to extract ten to fifteen times more. The seven-year plan of development of the fishing industry indicated that rational exploitation of lakes was necessary to assure a sharp rise in their productivity.[5]

The creation of a rational, highly productive fishing economy in inland waters would achieve an increase in the catch of fish from 2 to 4 or 4.5

---

[5] The Seven-Year Plan for the Development of the Fishing Industry of the USSR.

million centners at the end of the seven-year plan. *The Proceedings of the 1961 Conference on the Biological Bases of the Fishing Industry in the Inland Waters of the USSR* recommended that such a volume of catch could be reached if the following measures were undertaken:

1. To organize on specially prepared small lakes in the central and southern parts of the USSR a fishing economy whose production in individual water bodies could reach as much as 150 kilograms per hectare. If the area exploited could reach 2 million hectares, then up to 1 million centners of valuable fish could be harvested in a year.

2. To construct fish hatcheries for the breeding of high-value fish, such as the salmon, in Lakes Onega and Issyk-Kul and in other lakes; for the sturgeon in the Ob, Irtysh, Yenisey, and in Lakes Baykal and Balkhash; for whitefish in Lakes Pskov, Chudskoye and Seliger, and in the Ob and Yenisey rivers.

3. To remove the debris (of old, flood-plain lakes) on the Ob River in Tyumen, Tomsk, and Novosibirsk oblasts, covering an area of 600,000 hectares.

4. To divide the Yudinskiy Basin in Lake Chany in order to increase and improve the level of catch.

5. To divide the shallow parts of the Volga, Don, and Dnieper reservoirs, using them for raising fish in an area of not less than 20,000 hectares.

6. To plant fish feed, first of all, in the Kuybyshev, Gorki, Volgograd, Bukhtarma, Perm, and Katta-Kurgan reservoirs; in Lakes Ladoga, Ilmen, Pskov, and Chudskoye; in the small lakes of Leningrad, Novogorod, and Pskov oblasts; and in the Lena River. This action could produce, according to approximate calculations, an additional fish production of up to 200,000 centners a year.

7. To introduce mechanical and electrical fish protective systems in order to prevent massive loss of valuable young fish in irrigation systems and in the lower tail waters of reservoirs.

8. To introduce methods of fish catching in small rivers and in overgrown and debris-filled lakes with the aid of electrical equipment.

For reservoirs and lakes located south of 55° north, massive stocking with young silver and grass carp may have great significance in increasing productivity. After some time, the catch of these species may reach 300,000 centners per year.

FISH FARMING

The problem of fish breeding, successfully resolved by Soviet fishery science, foresees the realization of a series of measures directed toward the protection and increase of fish stocks.

The primary objective is the preservation of natural fish reproduction, which is being accomplished on the basis of the study of the breeding habits of various species. Other measures include artificial fish breeding, the acclimatization of fish and of palatable invertebrates, and the rearing and creation of new fish species.

Great attention is given by Soviet fishery science and industry to the artificial reproduction of sturgeon (white, common, stellate, spring, and sterlet). This is accomplished now not by the release of fingerlings but of hatchery-reared young, who are stronger and more lively. Sturgeon fish-breeding plants are being planned in the basins of the Volga, Kura, and Don rivers. By now, all stages in the process for the rearing of salmon have been worked out.

In order to raise young semianadromous fish on a massive commercial scale, and to maintain and increase stocks, especially in southern rivers with regulated flow, hatcheries are being created upon the recommendation and under the guidance of scientists. Such hatcheries have been constructed and are in operation in the deltas of the Volga and the Don, in the lower Kura, and in Kuban coastal lagoons (*Papers of the Conference on Fisheries in 1954*).

The rearing of young semianadromous fish in hatcheries is a new form of massive fish breeding, applied only in the USSR. In these hatcheries carp (wild carp and bream) and perch (pike perch) are being raised. Recently, these hatcheries have also begun to rear Azov roach (in the Kuban lagoons), *kutum* (Caspian), and Azov roach and *shemaya* (in the Kuban Basin). This form of artificial fish rearing is beginning to be used in reservoirs for the raising of the fingerlings of wild carp, bream, pike perch, sturgeon, sterlet sturgeon, and other fish intended for future annual release; reservoirs are used for fattening fish as well.

The problem of maintaining natural spawning and artificial fish hatching is closely linked with measures for the improvement of natural breeding places. In the USSR the means of improvement are extremely varied: In the lower reaches of rivers, efforts are being made to save valuable young commercial fish that are caught in spring floods and are unable to return to the river and the sea for fattening. Hydrotechnical improvement of conditions includes provision of spawning grounds (for instance, in the Kuban lagoons), and establishment of spawning-fattening bodies of water (the Gulf of Kirov and in the southern part of the Caspian). The greatest improvements are being made in the Soviet Far East, in the breeding grounds of Far Eastern salmon; for example, fish ladders are being constructed to permit spawning fish to get around dams from the lower to the upper reaches of rivers. The effectiveness of fish ladders depends both on the biological characteristics of those species supposed to pass through the fishways and on the construction of the fishways themselves.

In order to enrich fish life and to obtain the greatest utility from the natural productivity of the water bodies, the scientific fishery organizations of the Soviet Union are carrying out an extensive amount of work on the acclimatization of marine, and particularly of fresh-water fish, and of invertebrate food animals (*Acclimatization of Fish*). As early as 1930 to 1934, for example, the successful stocking of the Caspian with the gray mullet [*Mugil*] from the Black Sea was carried out. Under the new conditions, the mullet quickly multiplied. Today, the Caspian mullet is well known to the Soviet consumer. The transplanting of the Caspian mullet to the Aral Sea has been attempted in recent years, and beginning in 1948, stellate sturgeon from the Caspian have been transplanted to the Aral. The first mature sturgeon were recovered from the Aral in 1956. From 1956 to 1960, Pacific salmon were introduced into the basins of the Barents and White seas, and it is generally expected that the project will be successful. In 1960 pink salmon were taken for the first time. More than 50,000 pink salmon were caught (in the Barents and White Sea basins), each weighing nearly two kilograms. Similar catches were recorded in Norway and Finland.

The inland-water bodies of the country must play a great role in supplying the population with a variety of valuable fish. To accomplish this, a broad segment of our scientists and technical personnel must undertake measures for restoring the former fish productivity of the inland seas, above all of the Caspian and Azov seas. To realize this goal during the Seven-Year Plan, extensive measures have been specified in order to improve and expand the stocks of inland waters. Forty-four fish-breeding hatcheries must be constructed with an annual output of more than 400 million young salmon, whitefish, and sturgeon. At the same time 55,000 hectares should be provided for spawning and raising farms, for a yearly output of 6.2 billion young bream, pike, sturgeon, and several other species. For the improvement of conditions of natural breeding on a large scale, an area of 537,000 hectares of spawning grounds must be improved.

The most practical and really profitable branch of fish breeding is the raising of fish in ponds, where the hydrological regime and much of the life processes are controlled and directed by man. Consequently, they are the most valuable fish in terms of nutrition and economics, and include carp, pike, goldfish [*Carassius carassius*], peled carp [*C. peled*], and some other species. Pond-fish breeding allows also for an improved structure in fish production, including increased output of live and fresh fish, and the possibility of locating production near centers of consumption.

Fish with different biological characteristics, of course, require different environmental conditions. (Thus, carp are best raised in water with a temperature from 14°C to 20°C; trout prefer a temperature significantly lower.) This variation permits the selection of fish for rearing in the ponds of different natural zones, allowing the distribution of fish breeding over a wide territory. Ponds make it possible to raise an extremely large quantity of fish per unit area; the more progressive hatcheries now raise about 20 centners of fish per hectare and more, although the average yield for the USSR before 1959 was barely 4.4 centners per hectare. With a growth in pond fishing, capital expenditures will be lowered, and the unit cost of production will also be reduced. The unique technology of the pond fish-rearing industry excludes the necessity of capital investment in supply, ship-building, ship repairs, and fish processing.

Pond fisheries permit a more intensive use of land that otherwise would be inefficiently used for agriculture or not even used at all. This new land use raises the level of utility of neighboring land under rice, of irrigation systems, and irrigation reservoirs.

The feed base for fish raised in ponds is provided within the pond itself. The quantity of fish produced per hectare of pond (from the natural feed base) averages from 150 to 200 kilograms in the USSR. The improvement of the natural feed base through fertilization, melioration, and supple-mentary supplies permits a substantial increase in output of fish per hectare.

Table 3 shows a comparison of the economic effectiveness of feeding cattle as opposed to rearing pond fish. It is evident from the table that carp raised in ponds provide a return approximately three times higher than cattle in terms of edible matter and two and one-half times higher in terms of protein. The actual cost of the edible portion of the carp is 41% lower per centner than for cattle; protein is 32% lower. The labor cost of pond fish-ing is also lower than that of cattle raising.

In spite of the exceptionally favorable conditions for the development of pond fishing, only 220,000 centners of pond fish are procured in the USSR, less than 11% of the total volume of fish production.

The implementation of measures for the improvement of inland waters

Table 3
Economic Indices of Raising Cattle and Pond Fish

		Pond Fish (Carp)	
Indices	Cattle	Scattered Feed	Granulated Feed
Production from 8 centners of feed (in kilograms)			
Live weight	100	200	270
Consumable weight	34.0	94.0	127.0
Protein	6.7	15.0	20.3
Cost of production, 1961 (in rubles per kilogram)			
Live weight	88	60	—
Consumable weight	259	124	—
Protein	1314	764	—
Labor cost (in man-days per centner)			
Live weight	7.8	2.8	
Consumable weight	22.8	6.0	
Protein	116.2	37.2	

will ensure that N. S. Khrushchev's instruction will be fulfilled. At the Twenty-first Congress of the Communist Party of the Soviet Union, he said, "Along with the further development of the fisheries in the open seas and oceans, it is necessary to utilize the inland reservoirs, from which it is possible to receive annually not less than 6 to 8 million centners of fish." [6]

As we have seen, pond-fish rearing will permit a significant overfulfillment of this task.

SEA MAMMALS

The seas of the Soviet Union offer many representatives of both the *Pinnipedia* and the whale family [*Cetacea*], from the whales to the dolphins. In addition, whales are extracted from the North Pacific and the Antarctic oceans. The Soviet whaling industry began in 1932 with the first whale flotilla, the *Aleut*. In the postwar period the whale industry in the Pacific Ocean expanded because of the creation of whale-processing combines in the Kurile Islands.

In the waters of the North Pacific, our Far Eastern whalers procure all

[6] Materials of the Extraordinary Twenty-first Session of the CPSU, p. 22.

the species of whale found in the world's oceans, with the exception of those that by international law are preserved (Zenkovich; *The Whale Industry of the Soviet Union*).

All whalers hunt principally in the waters of the Okhotsk and Bering seas. The basis of our Far Eastern fishery is the toothed or sperm whale, the largest of which reaches a length of 20 meters. Of the baleen whales in the Far East, we catch the blue, which sometimes reaches a length of 27 meters; the finback or herring whale, up to 23 meters; the humpback, 18 meters; and the sei, 17 meters. The inhabitants of the Chukchi Peninsula, joined in hunting collectives, annually take several dozen whales of each species.

From 1932 to 1960, all Soviet Far Eastern whalers caught more than 22,000 whales, of which 19,000 were sperm whales. From this whale resource was obtained a great quantity of fat products, meat-bone flour, fertilizer, liver, frozen and cold meat, as well as canned goods.

The Soviet whale industry began in the Southern Hemisphere in the waters of the Antarctic in the 1946–47 season. It was directed by the whaling flotilla *Slava*, which was composed of a floating base and eight whaling vessels. The basic object of our industry in the Antarctic is the baleen whale: the blue, the finback, and to some extent the humpback and sei. The whales of the Antarctic are generally larger than those of the Far East. The blue whales here reach a length of more than 33 meters, while the finback reaches 27 meters. The humpback and sei whales are, by comparison, nearer to Far Eastern whales in size. The Soviet whaling industry extracts sperm whales in the Antarctic only until the baleen whale season begins, and then only in a relatively small quantity. From 1946 to 1960, nearly 45,000 whales were caught of which no more than 4,000 were sperm whales.

In 1960 our whaling fleet consisted of four mother ships, the *Aleut, Slava, Soviet Ukraine,* and *Yury Dolgorukiy*. In 1961, construction on a new large-tonnage mother ship, the *Soviet Russia,* began.

From 1946 on, the USSR participated in the international convention for the regulation of the whaling industry, and our representatives took part in different committees of the International Whaling Commission. In accordance with the rules of the international convention, substantiated by our directives, the Far Eastern industry of baleen whales extends for a season of six months, and of sperm whales for eight months. In the waters of the Antarctic, the pelagic whale industry is regulated by special agreements of the International Whaling Commission, which annually defines the beginning and the end of the season, the periods of exploitation of individual species, as well as the limit of the catch of baleen whales.

For a number of years the season began on December 28 or on January 7, and continued through April 7; the sum total of catch for all countries was fixed at 15,000 standard units of blue whales (one standard whale equals one blue whale, or two finbacks, or two and one-half humpbacks, or six seis).

For the 1959–60 and the 1960–61 seasons, the quota of whales, determined by the Commission, was cancelled. Because of this, in the 1960–61 season, the open-seas fleets of all countries that hunted in the Antarctic (twenty-one floating mother ships and two hundred forty-eight whaling vessels), caught 38,812 baleen whales, equal to 16,386 standard units. Our three flotillas caught 2,782 standard units, that is, 16.3% of the total take of all the fleets.

Measured by the catch of whales and whale products, and also by the size and tonnage of the whaling fleet, we are third in the world (after Japan and Norway).

After considering the sad experience of the almost total destruction of white whales in all the oceans of the world, and of blues and humpbacks in the North Atlantic, our representatives urged the International Commission to regulate the whaling industry in the waters of the Antarctic. An over-all quota should be established for all whales, subdivided into national limits. By preliminary agreement, the national quota of the USSR must consist of not less than 20% of the total quota of the pelagic fleet of the Antarctic. The introduction of a limitation on the whaling industry will permit the preservation of a great nutritional resource over the long run.

The basis of the sea-mammal industry in the north is the Greenland seal. Because of intensive exploitation, conducted for a long time by Soviet hunters and by Norwegian concessionnaires, seal reserves have greatly diminished, and at present the yearly catch in the neck of the White Sea is limited to 100,000 head, which should be lowered to 45,000 to 50,000 head.

In the Caspian Sea, the average yearly take of seals for the last ten years was nearly 40,000 head per year. However, the possibility exists that no less than 100,000 seals a year could be taken, and in future the catch may reach 150,000 head, if one considers the small scale of extraction in the past decade. Other than the Caspian, seals live in two very large fresh-water lakes in our country, Ladoga and Baykal. Before World War I, in Lake Baykal about 10,000 ringed seals were caught annually, and prior to World War II, about 8,000. The skins of the Baykal seal are used in the internal market.

Nearly 37,000 dolphins are caught in the Black Sea (the average figure for the past fifty years). In the Far East, the maritime seal industry operates mainly in the Sea of Okhotsk, where already 80,000 head are taken annually. A further increase in catch is of no avail since the reserves of the stock may be sharply reduced. There do remain unutilized stocks in the Bering Sea. However, because of the lack of adequate data for this region, the industrial potential cannot now be determined.

In the seas of the Far East, in the Bering and Chukchi Seas, apart from the seals and dolphins are schools of walrus. Because of their peculiar biology, ease of exploitation and significantly diminishing reserves, the state hunting of walrus is totally prohibited. This prohibition is extended also to the European North. Walrus can be harvested only by the local inhabitants of the Chukchi Peninsula, who are allowed to procure 2,000 of these animals a year.

Sea lions are another species of *Pinnipedia* whose hunting is prohibited commercially. The resting places of these seals are preserved only in some places in the Far East, as on Iona Island, Cape Shipunsk, and on the Commander and Kurile Islands. Only the inhabitants of Commander (Komandorskiy) Island and the Aleuts are allowed to harvest these animals and then only for subsistence.

Thanks to the agreement for the protection of fur seals, renewal of the stocks of these valuable animals is possible. Fur seals, which inhabit the northern part of the Pacific Ocean, are subdivided into three subspecies: the Commander, the Kurile, and the Alaskan. Each of these subspecies comprises a special school, the magnitude of which does not depend on the condition of the reserves of the fur seals of other subspecies. The Soviet school of fur seals breeds on Seal and Commander Islands and lately has noticeably increased to a population of nearly 215,000 head. Research has shown that on Seal Island the fur-seal birth rate has risen 28% from 1957 to 1960. Our schools may increase even more. This is particularly true for the Commander school, the population of which has risen to one million head in the last century. The number of animals in the Kurile school has not been calculated, but it is noteworthy that in addition to Seal Island, the school has a series of resting places on the Kurile Ridge. There is evidence that these schools, with suitable protection, can be restored to former size. This is suggested by the American experience with the Pribilof school, which in 1911 consisted of only 123,000 head but now has reached nearly two million.

Apart from the above sea mammals, there is wide interest in the sea otter or *kalan*, which inhabits the coasts of the Kurile and Commander Islands. Sea otters have a pelt more valuable than any land animal. The introduction of a complete ban on the hunting of these fur animals has allowed the school to reach more than 1,000 head on the coast of Commander Island and nearly that number on the coasts of the Kuriles.

A great role in sustaining the schools of commercial sea animals is played by protecting and preparing resting places, eliminating poachers, and preventing senseless killing of animals for noncommercial purposes.

INVERTEBRATES AND WATER PLANTS

Of the many extensive species of invertebrates and plants in our waters, some twenty have primary economic significance. Some of these are fully utilized by our industries, others are being adapted. The Seven-Year Plan and plans for long-range economic development foresee a maximal use of a number of sea products, which require that much attention be given to these resources, that reserves be used rationally, that technology of extraction and processing be improved, and that a clear understanding of biological traits and their commercial value be determined.

The Soviet Union possesses the world's largest fleet of floating crab canneries and is the chief exporter of canned crab goods. These process the meat of the Kamchatka crab, whose stocks inhabit mainly the coast of Kamchatka. Here, on the western coast of the peninsula, six Soviet and four Japanese floating factories produce more than 300,000 standard boxes of canned goods in one year, which is approximately 375,000 standard boxes of raw products.[7]

From the postwar period until 1954 only the Soviet fleet worked this region. In 1954, 250,000 standard boxes of canned crab were produced. In 1955 the Japanese fleet arrived off the coast of Kamchatka and reserves began to diminish quickly. In 1959 our production shrank to 160,000 boxes. As a result of urgent requests by the Soviet Union, the Soviet-Japanese Fisheries Commission adopted important measures for the preservation of crabs: production quotas for canned goods for the USSR and Japan were established, zones where young crabs lived were taken out of production, laws for net setting were worked out, and regions of exploitation for both countries were delimited. Both countries are conducting coordinated biological research, which is resulting in a yearly consideration and specification of measures for the improvement of the state of the reserves and for the establishment of the potential size of the total production of canned crab. Apart from bilateral measures, the Soviet Union has initiated some on its own. For several years we have reduced our quota to 75% or 80% and we have abstained from switching from cotton nets to the more effective synthetic

---

[7] A standard box contains 96 cans of 227 grams each, with a guaranteed weight of 184.3 grams of pure meat.

nets, which catch more young crabs. Synthetic nets are used by the Japanese fishery.

As a result of these measures, a turning point in the state of reserves of the Kamchatka crab has been successfully reached, and our output is increasing. However, it is only the beginning of the renewal of stocks. The basic problem lies in the total preservation of the young, the largest number of which perishes in the nets. The most effective way in which to preserve the young, and this is being considered in fisheries regulations, is to prohibit harvesting in places where they are concentrated. Of great value would be a fundamental change in gear so that the young with a shell width of less than 13 centimeters would be excluded from the catch; however, to this day no such gear has been invented.

The observance of fisheries regulations will lead to a significant improvement in the material reserves of the crab, which—with the opening up of secondary fishing regions in the Maritime Kray, on Sakhalin and the Kurile Islands, and in the Bering Sea—will double the extraction. Further increases are possible with the development of secondary species of crab such as the spiny, strigun, and hairy crabs, the meat of which is estimated to be 30% to 50% cheaper than the meat of the Kamchatka crab. These species also live in the Far East. They are similar in size to the Kamchatka crab, and their canning can be undertaken without a fundamental change in the technological process. The extraction of these secondary species amounts to no less than 50% of the contemporary extraction of Kamchatka crab.

There is great demand in our country for shrimp and river crayfish. However, in recent years the quantity of shrimp produced in the Black and Azov seas and in the Far East has not exceeded 1,000 centners. They are brought to market in fresh, cooked, or dried form. In 1960, the Glavdalvostokrybprom * rapidly sold the first consignments of frozen shrimp. This organization and some administrative councils in European Russia began catching shrimp with trawlers in northern and tropical waters. Also, experiments in shrimp canning have been carried out on a commercial scale. The large Far Eastern shrimp has been resettled in the Black Sea. Shrimp extraction should be developed further. The countries that extract shrimp in tropical waters catch significantly more than we (Japan—565,000 centners, USA—949,000 centners, per year).

The maximum volume of extraction of crayfish in the inland waters of the USSR and in the Caspian Sea has reached 15,000 centners. With a well-organized industry this figure can be exceeded.

---

* Glavnoye upravleniye po dalnevostochnoy rybnoy promyshlennosti [The Chief Administration of the Far Eastern Fish Industry].

The feed meal and mineral fertilizer from the by-products of sea crustacea processing are highly valued. All new floating factories plan the full use of crustacea.

The production of sea cucumber and greben [*grebeshok*], has substantial significance in the Far East. They form quality products highly valued in the Eastern markets. The sea cucumber, thus named because of its shape, belongs to the *Echinodermatae* [the family of star fish and sea urchins]. The volume of catch of the sea cucumber is determined by fluctuations in consumer demand. Frozen greben is enjoyed in the USSR with well-deserved success.

The oyster is the predominate mollusk on the domestic market, and is sold either live or canned. They are procured by divers in the Far East and by small trawlers that drag the bottom of the Black Sea. There are also large reserves of oysters in the White Sea and along the Murman coast. The extraction of these mollusks, the main reserves of which are in the Black Sea, can amount throughout the USSR to many hundreds of thousands of centners. The production of feed meal from oysters was recently initiated, and expansion of the process is planned, but they are a valuable food product, and feed meal should be processed only from low-quality products.

Feed meal from mollusks should be developed with those too small and unsuitable for eating and with those which inhabit regions where they are not used by commercial fish for food. Such reserves are calculated in many millions of centners, In the Black Sea are found phaseolin [*sic*]; in the North and Far East are the *makoma*,* led, and other species living near the bottom of the sea, where temperatures are constantly low. There are wide areas of concentration of these mollusks in the Barents Sea, along the southwestern coast of Novaya Zemlya, and in the Far East in the Gulfs of Terpeniya and Anadyr. At the same time caution should be taken to avoid the harvesting of the masses of small mollusks that inhabit the feeding areas of fish. Thus, for instance, one should not plan to use for feed meal the Caspian mitilaster, which the unique school of sturgeon feed upon. It would be better to construct at first a small experimental coastal factory for the preparation of feed meal on the Black Sea and thereafter a larger one. Apparently it is more profitable, in the North and Far East, to use floating processing factories. In order to develop the procurement of food mollusks, we must organize the breeding of mussels and oysters.

Good results can be expected also from harvesting squid. This mollusk

---

* In the context given here, *makoma* is a mollusk; however, *makoma* is translatable as water poppy, which is not a mollusk.

can be produced in great quantities (not less than one million centners) with the same boats and implements used for catching Pacific saury.

We can obtain a variety of food products and raw materials from water plants. The potential of this industry is not significantly utilized at present in the USSR.

We are undertaking the development of agar production, utilizing the red water plant, agar, to produce a fluid forming a gel used by the confectionary industry, for medicine, and for other purposes. At the present time, we get agar from the water plant *anfeltsiya,* produced in the White Sea, in the Gulf of Peter the Great, in Buss Bay on Sakhalin Island, and in the Izmeniya Straits of Kunashir Island. Recently, in the Baltic, a new water plant, *furtselliariya,* was discovered and tentatively determined as a significant reserve. From this species agar may also be produced. In the Black Sea there are large reserves of *fillofora,* from which is obtained agaroid, a substance used in food processing and for technical purposes.

Common eel grass has a stable demand because of its value as a stuffing material used in the production of seating for various transport machines. Its procurement is now limited by the amount cast on shore and by hand mowing. Mechanical mowing is only the beginning and its further development will allow us to increase production in the White Sea, the Far East, the Black and Azov seas and, in small volume, in the Caspian.

Not completely satisfied is the demand for sea kale, out of which is made medicinal seaweed flour and dietetic confectionary products. There is also an insignificant output of technical products from sea kale: seaweed meal (a starch substitute in the textile industry), *alginat* (a gel-like substance used in the food industry, technology, and medicine), and *manit* (used in the production of paper, textile products, and in pharmacology).

The reserves of sea kale in our seas are huge, for thermal conditions in Soviet seas are most favorable. Countries south of the USSR are forced to cultivate it artificially. Our procurement is now limited only by the lack of mechanical mowing machines. The utilization of models proposed by our engineers will allow a significant rise in the production of sea kale in the Far East and in the North.

Another important seaweed raw material is rockweed, used locally as a stabilizer in clay solutions used in drilling, and as a substitute for agar or sea kale, both of which have a high food value.

The realization of the measures enumerated above, in combination with measures for strict regulation of the industry, the normalization of catch by quantity and species of fish and nonfish products, the unremitting struggle with poaching, and the elimination of water pollution, will lead to the renewal and future increase in fish reserves in inland waters. It is projected in the Seven-Year Plan to increase the procurement of fish, sea animals, and nonfish products by 60%. To achieve this, the rate of growth of production for the period from 1959 to 1965 must exceed the rate of development of the fishery by one and one-half times (Shparlinskiy).

In light of the Seven-Year Plan and the prospective program of development of the fisheries, the role of fishery science will grow immensely. The task entails the transition from a simple fishing industry, limited only by the size of the fishing fleet and gear, to a planned economy including both procurement and the wide reproduction of fish, sea animals, invertebrates, and water plants through the opening up of heretofore unexploited regions, the preservation and regulation of the industry in exhausted waters, and the artificial breeding of useful water fauna.

Practical research on the raw-material base of the world's oceans, the development of which interests many countries, demonstrates that the scientific and practical value of these investigations increases with closer collaboration of the scholars of these countries and with more concerted work, subordinated to a single coordinated plan.

BIBLIOGRAPHY

Akklimatizatsiya ryb i kormovykh organizmov v moryakh SSSR. Sb. statey [Acclimatization of Fish and Food. Organisms in the Seas of the USSR. Collected Works]. Edited by A. F. Karnevich and E. A. Yablonskiy. No. 1. Moscow: Pishchepromizdat, 1960. In *Trudy Vsesoyuz. n.-i in-ta morskogo rybnogo khozyaystva i okeanografii,* t. 43 [Papers of the All-Union Research Institute of Marine Fisheries and Oceanography, vol. 43].

Berg, L. S. *Ryby presnykh vod SSSR i sopredelnykh stran* [The Fresh-Water Fish of the USSR and of Adjacent Countries], pt. 1. Moscow-Leningrad: AN SSSR, 1948.

Biologiya i promysel morskikh mlekopitayushchikh. Sb. statey [The Biology and Extraction of Sea Mammals. Collected Works]. Edited by B. A. Zenkovich. Moscow: Pishchepromizdat, 1958. In *Trudy Vsesoyuz. . . ,* vol. 33. (See *Akklimatizatsiya. . .*)

Derzhavin, A. N. *Vosproizvodstvo zapasov osetrovykh ryb* [The Reproduction of Sturgeon]. Baku, 1947.

Issledovaniya kitov Antarktiki. Sb. statey [Study of the Whales of the Antarctic. Collected Works]. Edited by S. V. Dorofeyev and V. V. Kolchev. Moscow: Pishchepromizdat, 1953. In *Trudy Vsesoyuz. . . ,* vol. 25. (See *Akklimatizatsiya . . .*)

Kitoboynyy promysel Sovetskogo Soyuza. Sb. statey [The Whale Industry of the Soviet Union. Collected Works]. Edited by S. E. Kleynenberg and T. I. Makarova. Moscow: Rybnoye khozyaystvo, 1955.

Kolebaniya chislennosti i usloviya promysla donnykh ryb v Barentsovom more. Sb. statey [Variations in the Population and Conditions of Extraction of the Bottom Fish of the Barents Sea. Collected Works]. Moscow: Pishchepromizdat, 1957. *Trudy Polyarnogo n.-i. in-ta morskogo rybnogo khozyaystva i okeanografii, t.* 10 [Papers of the Polar Scientific Research Institute of Marine Fisheries and Oceanography, vol. 10].

Moiseyev, P. A. "Treska i kambala dalnevostochnykh morey" [Cod and Flounder in Far Eastern Seas]. *Izv. Tikookeansk. n.-i. in-ta rybnogo khozyaystva i okeanografii* [Journal of the Pacific Scientific Research Institute of Fisheries and Oceanography], vol. 40. Vladivostok, 1953.

Pravdin, I. F. "Obzor issledovaniy dalnevostochnykh lososey" [Survey of Research on Far Eastern Salmon]. Ibid., vol. 18. Vladivostok, 1940.

Promyslovye ryby SSSR [Commercial Fish of the USSR]. Moscow: Pishchepromizdat, 1949.

Rekonstruktsiya ikhtiofauny Kaspiyskogo morya. Sb. statey [Reconstruction of the Fish Life of the Caspian Sea. Collected Works]. Edited by L. G. Vinogradov and M. V. Fedosov. No. 1. Moscow: Pishchepromizdat, 1959. In *Trudy Vsesoyuz . . .*, vol. 38. (See *Akklimatizatsiya . . .*)

Rekonstruktsiya rybnogo khozyaystva Azovskogo morya. Sb. statey [Reconstruction of the Fish Economy of the Azov Sea. Collected Works]. Edited by A. F. Karpevich. Nos. 1, 2. Moscow: Pishchepromizdat, 1957. In *Trudy Vsesoyuz. . .*, vol. 31. (See *Akklimatizatsiya. . .*)

Shparlinskiy, V. M. *Rybnaya promyshlennost SSSR* [The Fish Industry of the USSR]. Moscow: Rybnoye khozyaystvo, 1959.

Sovetskiye rybokhozyaystvennyye issledovaniya v moryakh Yevropeyskogo Severa. Sb. statey [Soviet Fisheries Research in the Seas of the European North. Collected Works]. Moscow: Rybnoye khozyaystvo, 1960.

Trudy Soveshchaniya po dinamike chislennosti ryb [Papers of the Conference on the Dynamics of the Fish Population]. Moscow: AN SSSR, 1961. In *Ikhtiol komissiya. Trudy soveshchaniy,* vyp. 4 [Ichthyological Commission. Papers of the Conference], no. 13.

Trudy Soveshchaniya po voprosam lososevogo khozyaystva Dalnego Vostoka [Papers of the Conference on Questions Concerning the Salmon Economy of the Far East]. AN SSSR, 1954. In *Ikhtiol. . .*, no. 4. (Ibid.)

Trudy Soveshchaniya po voprosam povedeniya i razvedki ryb 1953 g. [Papers of the Conference on the Problems of the Behavior and Breeding of Fish in 1953]. Moscow: AN SSSR, 1955. In *Ikhtiol. . .*, no. 5.

Trudy Soveshchaniya po rybovodstvu 1954 g. [Papers of the Conference on Fisheries in 1954]. AN SSSR, 1957. In *Ikhtiol. . .*, no. 7.

Trudy Vsesosoyuznogo soveshchaniya po biologicheskim osnovam okeanicheskogo rybolovstva 1958 g. [Papers of the All-Union Conference on the Biological Foundations of the Ocean Fisheries in 1958]. AN SSSR, 1960.

Zenkovich, B. A. *Kity i kitoboynyy promysel* [Whales and the Whale Industry]. Moscow: Pishchepromizdat, 1953.

Index